# Fodor's

# HOLLAND

3rd Edition

---

**Where to Stay and Eat
for All Budgets**

---

**Must-See Sights
and Local Secrets**

---

**Ratings You Can Trust**

---

Fodor's Travel Publications   New York, Toronto, London, Sydney, Auckland
**www.fodors.com**

## FODOR'S HOLLAND

**Editors:** Emmanuelle Alspaugh and Sarah Gold

**Editorial Production:** Tom Holton
**Editorial Contributors:** Shirley J. S. Agudo, Becky Baker, Nicole Chabot, Margaret Kelly, Steve Korver, Anna Lambert, Kim Renfrew, Tim Skelton, Jonette Stabbert, Charlotte A. R. Vaudrey
**Maps:** David Lindroth, *cartographer*; Rebecca Baer and Bob Blake, *map editors*
**Design:** Fabrizio La Rocca, *creative director*; Guido Caroti, *art director*; Moon Sun Kim, *cover designer*; Melanie Marin, *senior picture editor*
**Production/Manufacturing:** Angela L. McLean
**Cover Photo** (tulip fields, Vagelenzang) Mark Tomalty/Masterfile

Third Edition

ISBN: 1–4000–1644–4

ISBN-13: 978–1–4000–1644–0

ISSN: 1537–5617

## SPECIAL SALES

This book is available for special discounts for bulk purchases for sales promotions or premiums. Special editions, including personalized covers, excerpts of existing books, and corporate imprints, can be created in large quantities for special needs. For more information, write to Special Markets/ Premium Sales, 1745 Broadway, MD 6-2, New York, New York 10019 or e-mail specialmarkets@ randomhouse.com.

## AN IMPORTANT TIP & AN INVITATION

Although all prices, opening times, and other details in this book are based on information supplied to us at press time, changes occur all the time in the travel world, and Fodor's cannot accept responsibility for facts that become outdated or for inadvertent errors or omissions. So **always confirm information when it matters,** especially if you're making a detour to visit a specific place. Your experiences—positive and negative—matter to us. If we have missed or misstated something, **please write to us.** We follow up on all suggestions. Contact the Holland editor at editors@fodors. com or c/o Fodor's at 1745 Broadway, New York, New York 10019.

PRINTED IN THE UNITED STATES OF AMERICA

10 9 8 7 6 5 4 3 2

# Be a Fodor's Correspondent

Your opinion matters. It matters to us. It matters to your fellow Fodor's travelers, too. And we'd like to hear it. In fact, we *need* to hear it.

When you share your experiences and opinions, you become an active member of the Fodor's community. That means we'll not only use your feedback to make our books better, but we'll publish your names and comments whenever possible. Throughout our guides, look for "Word of Mouth," excerpts of your unvarnished feedback.

Here's how you can help improve Fodor's for all of us.

**Tell us when we're right.** We rely on local writers to give you an insider's perspective. But our writers and staff editors—who are the best in the business—depend on you. Your positive feedback is a vote to renew our recommendations for the next edition.

**Tell us when we're wrong.** We're proud that we update most of our guides every year. But we're not perfect. Things change. Hotels cut services. Museums change hours. Charming cafés lose charm. If our writer didn't quite capture the essence of a place, tell us how you'd do it differently. If any of our descriptions are inaccurate or inadequate, we'll incorporate your changes in the next edition and will correct factual errors at fodors.com immediately.

**Tell us what to include.** You probably have had fantastic travel experiences that aren't yet in Fodor's. Why not share them with a community of like-minded travelers? Maybe you chanced upon a beach or bistro or B&B that you don't want to keep to yourself. Tell us why we should include it. And share your discoveries and experiences with everyone directly at fodors.com. Your input may lead us to add a new listing or highlight a place we cover with a "Highly Recommended" star or with our highest rating, "Fodor's Choice."

Give us your opinion instantly at our feedback center at www.fodors.com/feedback. You may also e-mail editors@fodors.com with the subject line "Holland Editor." Or send your nominations, comments, and complaints by mail to the Holland Editor, Fodor's, 1745 Broadway, New York, NY 10019.

You and travelers like you are the heart of the Fodor's community. Make our community richer by sharing your experiences. Be a Fodor's correspondent.

*"Goede reis!"* (Happy traveling!)

**Tim Jarrell, Publisher**

# CONTENTS

## CLOSEUPS

# ABOUT THIS BOOK

## Our Ratings

Sometimes you find terrific travel experiences and sometimes they just find you. But usually the burden is on you to select the right combination of experiences. That's where our ratings come in.

As travelers we've all discovered a place so wonderful that its worthiness is obvious. And sometimes that place is so unique that superlatives don't do it justice: you just have to be there to know. These sights, properties, and experiences get our highest rating, **Fodor's Choice,** indicated by orange stars throughout this book.

Black stars highlight sights and properties we deem **Highly Recommended,** places that our writers, editors, and readers praise again and again for consistency and excellence.

By default, there's another category: any place we include in this book is by definition worth your time, unless we say otherwise. And we will.

Disagree with any of our choices? Care to nominate a place or suggest that we rate one more highly? Visit our feedback center at www.fodors.com/feedback.

## Budget Well

Hotel and restaurant price categories from ¢ to $$$$ are defined in the opening pages of each chapter. For attractions, we always give standard adult admission fees; reductions are usually available for children, students, and senior citizens. Want to pay with plastic? **AE, D, DC, MC, V** following restaurant and hotel listings indicate whether American Express, Discover, Diner's Clb, MasterCard, and Visa are accepted.

## Restaurants

Unless we state otherwise, restaurants are open for lunch and dinner daily. We mention dress only when there's a specific requirement and reservations only when they're essential or not accepted—it's always best to book ahead.

## Hotels

Hotels have private bath, phone, TV, and air-conditioning and operate on the European Plan (aka EP, meaning without meals), unless we specify that they use the Continental Plan (CP, with a Continental breakfast), Breakfast Plan (BP, with a full breakfast), or Modified American Plan (MAP, with breakfast and dinner) or are all-inclusive (including all meals and most activities). We always

list facilities but not whether you'll be charged an extra fee to use them, so when pricing accommodations, find out what's included.

## Many Listings

| | |
|---|---|
| ★ | Fodor's Choice |
| ★ | Highly recommended |
| ⊠ | Physical address |
| ✛ | Directions |
| ⌂ | Mailing address |
| ☎ | Telephone |
| 🖷 | Fax |
| ⊕ | On the Web |
| ✉ | E-mail |
| 🎫 | Admission fee |
| ☉ | Open/closed times |
| ► | Start of walk/itinerary |
| Ⓜ | Metro stations |
| ▭ | Credit cards |

## Hotels & Restaurants

| | |
|---|---|
| 🏨 | Hotel |
| ⌯ | Number of rooms |
| ⌂ | Facilities |
| ❍⦿❍ | Meal plans |
| ✕ | Restaurant |
| ⌯ | Reservations |
| 🏠 | Dress code |
| ⤮ | Smoking |
| ⎙℗ | BYOB |
| ✕🏨 | Hotel with restaurant that warrants a visit |

## Outdoors

| | |
|---|---|
| 🏌 | Golf |
| ⛺ | Camping |

## Other

| | |
|---|---|
| ℃ | Family-friendly |
| 🔟 | Contact information |
| ⇨ | See also |
| ⊠ | Branch address |
| ☞ | Take note |

# WHAT'S
# WHERE

**AMSTERDAM**

Built on rings of concentric canals bordered by time-burnished, step-gabled houses, Amsterdam is custom made for sightseeing. You almost have to get to know the city from the water to be properly introduced and glass-roof canal boats make that possible. Helpfully, the city is held together by the linchpins of its great public squares: the Dam, the Rembrandtplein, the Munt, and the Leidseplein.

The sector you first see upon leaving the storybook gates of Amsterdam's Centraal Station, the eastern half of the Centrum (or city center) literally drips with history—a history where sex and religion come equally represented. But the **Red Light District,** or Rosse Buurt, remains reined in—and surprisingly safe. The district is part and parcel of the city region known as the **Oude Zijde,** or Old Side.

To the west of the Old Side is the area known as the New Side, or the **Nieuwe Zijde.** This is really just as ancient—relatively speaking—as the Old Side, from which it is separated by the Oudezijds Voorburgwal street. The center spotlight of the Nieuwe Zijde is always shining upon the city's focal square, the bustling **Dam,** with its opulent **Koninklijk palace** and **Nieuwe Kerk.**

Set to the west and south of the city center is the famous Grachtengordel. Call it a "belt" or a "girdle," but the Golden Age product that consists of the three main encircling canals—Prinsengracht (Princes' Canal), Keizersgracht (Emperors' Canal), and Herengracht (Gentlemen's Canal)—form a ring of unparalleled historical beauty. The point where these canals intersected with Nieuwe Spiegelstraat became known as the Golden Bend—the *Gouden Bocht*—since houses here were occupied by the richest families of Amsterdam. Heading a few blocks over to what is called the **Eastern Canal Ring** you'll find assorted treasures, including Baroque-era interiors on view at the magnificent 17th-century Willet-Holthuysen Museum. The northern sectors of the Grachtengordel center around Amsterdam's beloved Jordaan (probably derived from the French for "garden," *jardin*). Although this cozy, scenic, and singular neighborhood's working-class roots have long sprouted branches of gentrification, it remains a wanderers' paradise where you can take in leafy canals, hidden courtyards *(hofjes),* and funky shops and restaurants.

# WHAT'S WHERE

Near the southern end of the city, the **Museum District**—centered around the Museumplein square—gives you, in short, the history of art at your fingertips as Rembrandts, Van Goghs, and Bill Violas are all on evocative display in the city's three main art museums: the Rijksmuseum, the Van Gogh Museum, and the Stedelijk Museum of Modern Art. Set to the south of the Museum District is **Amsterdam Zuid,** or South Amsterdam, a neighborhood which harbors many posh residences, not to mention the most elitist shopping options along the country's most famous fashion strip, PC Hooftstraat. To the east of the center and the Amstel River lies the extension of the Old Jewish neighborhood known as the stately and serene **Plantage** (plantation).

**METROPOLITAN HOLLAND: ROTTERDAM & RANDSTAD**

Like filings around the end of a magnet, four major urban centers cluster in a heart-of-Holland arc, commonly known as the Randstad, just to the south of Amsterdam. West of the city the **Bloemen Route** (Flower Road) leads from Aalsmeer—one of the greatest floral villages in Europe—to the famed Keukenhof gardens and the town of **Lisse.** This is the Holland of tulips, hyacinths, and narcissi, aglow with the colors of Easter in spring and generally a rainbow of color year-round. It is a short step from this ocean of seasonal color to a haven of perennial color—the city of **Haarlem,** the earliest center of Dutch art, which gave rise to one of the most important schools of landscape painting in the 17th century. **Leiden,** the birthplace of Rembrandt and site of a great university, remains a charming town where windmills rise over the cityscape. The tree-lined canals, humpbacked bridges, and step-gabled houses of **Delft** preserve the atmosphere of the 16th and 17th centuries better than any other city in the country, captured unforgettably in the canvases of Vermeer and Pieter de Hoogh.

**Rotterdam,** a true phoenix of a city, rose from the ashes of World War II to become one of the busiest ports in Europe. In **Utrecht**'s history-soaked town center, not far from the Oude Gracht (Old Canal), stands the 338-foot tower of "the Cathedral That Is Missing." This city is the centerpiece of a region that is considered by many Dutch to be the most beautiful in the country: the landscape fairly bursts with lovely old trees (a rarity in the polders, or countryside reclaimed from the sea) and storybook castle-châteaux. Other destinations include **Brielle**—the redoubt of the legendary Sea Beggars; the famous 19 windmills of **Kinderdijk; Dordrecht,** whose historic town center is replete with delightful and typical Dutch canal vistas; **Gouda,** whose name brings to mind a weekly cheese market, the manufacture of clay pipes, and the priceless stained glass in the Sint Janskerk; and the **Kasteel de Haar,** Holland's most opulent, fairytale castle.

**THE HAGUE**

Called 's-Gravenhage or Den Haag by the Dutch (and "the Largest Village in Europe" by residents), **The Hague** is a royal and regal city—filled with patrician mansions and gracious parks and home to Queen Beatrix and the International Court of Justice. Its downtown is stuffed with fine restaurants and posh antiques shops. Although Amsterdam is the nation's constitutional capital, The Hague is the seat of the Dutch government and the International Court of Justice. If the city center near Centraal Station is dominated by postmodern high-rise towers, the ritzy dwellings of the rich and famous of centuries gone by are still here to enchant. At the heart of the Centrum— the historic city center—is the **Ridderzaal,** or Knights' Hall, which stands alone in the middle of the Binnenhof, or Inner Court, its 13th-century towers recalling an era when architects were as much concerned with defense as shelter. On the far side of the Binnenhof is the fabled **Mauritshuis** (much more intimate than the Rijksmuseum), where the canvases on display are world famous—Vermeer's *View of Delft* and *Girl with a Pearl Earring* are just two. At the **Museum Mesdag,** period rooms are lined with 19th-century daubs and paintings of The Hague School, and the **Haags Gemeentemuseum** contains the world's largest collection of Piet Mondriaan paintings.

**THE BORDER PROVINCES & MAASTRICHT**

In most Dutch provinces the sea presses in to the land, constantly striving to win a foothold; Zeeland, to the contrary, pushes out into the water, invading the invader's territory and looking for trouble. On strips of land, like thumbs of a right hand, pointing westward toward the North Sea, Zeeland remains an ancient and romantic place. **Zierikzee** is a yachting port, and **Veere** is relentlessly picturesque; **Middelburg, Breda,** and **'s-Hertogenbosch** all have historic significance, the latter as the hometown of that 16th-century surrealist Hieronymus Bosch. The southernmost province of the Netherlands, Limburg differs from the rest of the country in many ways, most especially in its rolling hills and dense forests. Here lies **Maastricht,** the oldest city in the Netherlands. Wedged somewhat hes-

# WHAT'S
# WHERE

itatingly between Belgium and Germany, the town remains an intoxicating mixture of three languages, times, currencies, and customs. The milder southern climate in this region contributes its share to the city's exuberant and sophisticated street life. Each March, the European Fine Art Fair—some say this is the best art fair in Europe—draws Prince Bernhard, high rollers, and the richest collectors of old-master paintings in the world.

| | |
|---|---|
| **THE GREEN HEART**<br /> | Although as steeped in history as any other Dutch region, Gelderland seems to put the emphasis on the beauties of outdoor life, for it is a province studded with national parks and Edenic forests. Glorying in the title "The Largest Garden City in the Netherlands," **Apeldoorn** is so lavishly endowed with trees, natives challenge visitors to find the place. Thousands do every year, mostly to visit the incomparably charming yet superbly elegant 17th-century **Palace Het Loo**—the Dutch Baroque castle and hunting lodge that was home to William and Mary (who went on to become king and queen of England). Set within **De Hoge Veluwe**, the nation's largest natural preserve, is the celebrated **Kröller-Müller Museum**, which has extraordinary paintings of the postimpressionists as well as a multitude of works by Van Gogh, including his *Sunflowers* and *Potato Eaters*. This region is, above all, a walking and bicycling paradise, and hikes through lush woods and moors can often end delightfully at grand country mansions, such as Het Wezenveld, Bruggenbosch, and Hunderen, outside Apeldoorn. The major towns of the region—**Zwolle**, **Deventer**, **Zutphen**—all have historic churches or town squares. The capital of the region is **Arnhem**, best known for "the bridge too far" of World War II. Its chief attractions are the battlefields, memorials, and war cemeteries that have become sacred places of pilgrimages, set in a region rich in scenic beauty. |
| **THE NORTH & THE WADDEN SEA ISLANDS**<br /> | **Leeuwarden** is the capital of Friesland and birthplace of Saskia, Rembrandt's wife, and of the mysterious Mata Hari. Crafts are a highlight here: the fine Netherlands Ceramic Museum and the Fries Museum are a great introduction to the cultural heritage of the province. Out on a promontory, the former port of **Hindeloopen** seems to have been lost in time. In nearby **Makkum** is Tichelaar's Royal Makkum Pottery and Tile Factory. Flotillas of yachts tack across the myriad interconnected lakes around **Sloten** and **Sneek**, where the province's connec- |

tion with the sea and water is most evident. The **Wadden Sea Islands,** just a short ferry ride from the Mainland, are also home to seafarers. The largest of these five islands, **Texel,** is easy to reach from Amsterdam to the port of Den Helder. The other islands are more remote, though the roadway across the **Afsluitdijk** (Enclosing Dike) at the northern end of the IJsselmeer reduces journey times considerably. **Terschelling** is the most popular island, with bustling terraces during the high season and the extraordinary theatrical events of the Oerol Festival in June. The more exclusive, secluded, car-free island of **Schiermonnikoog,** an oasis of unspoiled nature on bird migration routes, is a favorite weekend getaway for the Dutch. Farther east is **Groningen,** a sophisticated university town, filled with architectural delights, pretty canals, and the magnificent gardens of the Prinsenhoftuin, where 250 years of topiary, lawn making, and hedge growing have produced a masterpiece on nature's canvas. Here and there, distinctive storks' nests mounted atop wheels perch high upon poles—a fitting icon for this lovely, verdant agricultural region.

# GREAT
# ITINERARIES

## If You Have 3 Days

After arriving in Amsterdam and viewing the famous gables from the comfort of a canal boat (tours take one to two hours), feast your eyes on Rembrandts and Van Goghs in the city's museums. Your first night is spent in Amsterdam, so there's plenty of time to explore the backstreets of the Jordaan (Amsterdam's version of Greenwich Village) and to find a cozy restaurant. Next morning, check out some of Amsterdam's quirkier shops—or visit a diamond-cutting factory if that's more your style. Then set off along the A4 for The Hague to visit a palace or two and the Madurodam miniature village in Scheveningen. End the day with a rijsttafel in one of The Hague's excellent Indonesian restaurants. In the morning, take a tram (20 minutes) to nearby Delft and visit its renowned porcelain factory; then set off back along the A4 to Leiden. If it's springtime, take the N206 out of town and through the bulb fields to the spectacular Keukenhof gardens. Otherwise, spend the afternoon exploring this attractive old university town, for many years home to the Pilgrim Fathers. Leiden is just half an hour from Schiphol Airport, along the A4.

## If You Have 5 Days

Your first night is in Amsterdam. This gives you a day on either side for exploring canals, museums, bustling markets, and the Jordaan district. In the afternoon of your second day, head off along the A4 to Leiden. If it's springtime, follow instead the A9 and the N208 through the bulb fields, allowing an hour for visiting the Keukenhof gardens on the way. After a morning spent seeing Leiden's 15th-century church and beautifully restored windmill, continue along the A4 to The Hague, seat of the government and home to some ex-

cellent art collections. Next day, take a tram to Delft, one of the most beautifully preserved historic towns in the country, conveniently situated on the outskirts of The Hague. Then take the A12 to Utrecht, where you can climb the Gothic Dom-toren, the highest church tower in the Netherlands, for a panoramic view of the countryside. Back on ground level, you can visit a delightful museum of music boxes, player pianos, and barrel organs. On the fifth day take the A28, then the A1, out to the Hoge Veluwe national park, near Apeldoorn, where you can spend time walking in the forest or visiting the Kröller-Müller Museum with its extraordinary collection of Van Goghs and modern art. From Apeldoorn, you can continue your journey into Germany or take the A1 back to Amsterdam.

## If You Have 9 Days

Two days and two nights in Amsterdam give you time for a leisurely exploration of the city. On the third day, follow the A4 to Leiden (or take the N208 bulb route if it's springtime), and then travel on to The Hague. Visit the historic center and porcelain factory of Delft on the morning of the fourth day; then head across to Utrecht on the A12. On the way, stop off in Gouda, famed not only for its cheeses but also for its medieval city hall and the magnificent stained glass in the Sint Janskerk. From Utrecht take the A2 south, stopping for the night in an ancient Limburg manor house or castle, such as the medieval Kasteel Wittem near Heerlen. Spend Day 6 in Maastricht (just a short drive from Wittem on the N278), which has an abundance of sidewalk cafés and a carefree French air. Maastricht also boasts the Bonnefanten-museum, which is well stocked with superb religious carvings and intriguing contem-

village of Hindeloopen with its painted traditional furniture, and the port of Harlingen along the way. If you have additional time, you can take the ferry from here to the island of Terschelling. Option two: On Day 8 travel north to Groningen (follow A50 to Zwolle, then A28 to Meppel, and turn finally onto A32). If time allows, spend a night on the restful island of Schiermonnikoog (take N361 northbound to the Lauwersoog ferry terminal).

In both cases, return to Amsterdam on the A7, which takes you over the Afsluitdijk, the long dike that closes off the IJsselmeer from the North Sea. If you are heading straight back to Amsterdam, stay on the A7. The island of Texel is only a small detour (take N99 and N250 to the ferry terminal at Den Helder). Return to the A7. The picturesque towns of Enkhuizen and Hoorn (take the N302 turnoff from the A7) are typical of the former fishing ports of West Friesland and merit an overnight stay or a short visit to their museums.

porary art. Then travel along the German border to the Hoge Veluwe national park near Apeldoorn (take the A2 out of Maastricht, turn off onto the N271, and follow it up to Nijmegen, from which the A325 and the A50 take you into the park). The pretty little town of Zutphen, which has a library of rare and beautiful early manuscripts, makes a good overnight stop (follow the N345 out of Apeldoorn). There are now two possibilities in the northern provinces. Option one: On Day 8 travel north to Leeuwarden (follow the A50 to Zwolle, then the A28 to Meppel, and turn finally onto the A32). After visiting the National Ceramics Museum and viewing some of Leeuwarden's elegant 18th-century facades, you can take the A31 to the IJsselmeer coastline. Take the dike road (N31), exploring coastal towns such as the pottery town of Makkum, the former fishing

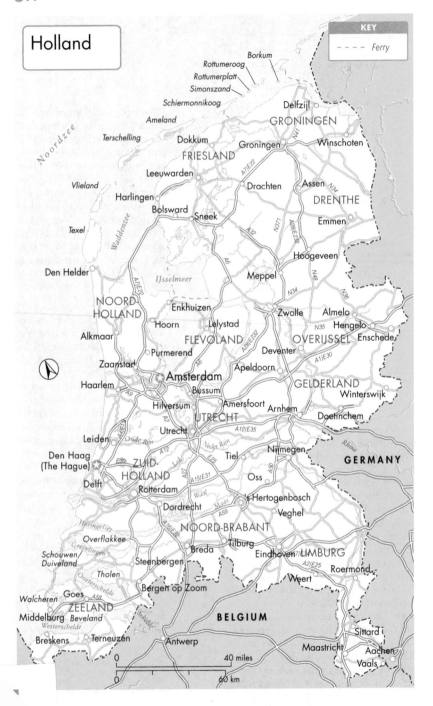

Holland

# WHEN TO GO

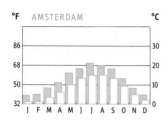

Because the famous tulip fields bloom during April and May, this is perhaps the best time to visit Holland. Spring is also the driest time of the year. Rain, however, can arrive year-round, so, like the locals, always have an umbrella at the ready, as sunny afternoons are often preceded by stormy mornings.

From tulip time (mid-April to mid-May) onward, it becomes increasingly difficult to obtain hotel reservations. If you are making an extended tour of Europe, consider scheduling Holland for the beginning or end of your itinerary, saving July and August for exploring less crowded countries.

But if you have to visit in high summer, be sure to take a vacation from your Amsterdam vacation and discover the cities that have that quaint Dutch beauty (not to mention cultural and social happenings plus historical interest), all without the crush. Optimum times to visit are May through June and September through October. Swimming is possible from May or June onward but is reserved for the hardy.

## Climate

Weather-wise, the best months for sightseeing are April, May, June, September, and October, when the days are long and the summer crowds have not yet filled the beaches and the museums to capacity. The maritime climate of the Netherlands is very changeable, though, and during these months expect weather ranging from cool to pleasant to wet and windy to hot and surprisingly humid. Eastern and southeastern provinces edge toward a more Continental climate, with warmer summers and colder winters than along the North Sea coast, which can itself be very cold from December through February and March.

🔲 Forecasts **Weather Channel Connection** ☎ 900/932-8437 95¢ per min from a Touch-Tone phone ⊕ www.weather.com.

# ON THE CALENDAR

The top seasonal events in Amsterdam are listed below, and any one of them could provide the stuff of lasting memories. The Netherlands are at their most beautiful in spring, when the bulb fields southwest of Amsterdam burst out in vast blocks of bright color. Summertime in the Netherlands is festival time. The Holland Festival in Amsterdam in June attracts a glittering array of international stars in the fields of music, opera, theater, and dance. The North Sea Jazz Festival in The Hague in July is one of the premier jazz events in the world. Utrecht hosts the Holland Festival of Early Music, and pop festivals sprout up in country areas throughout the season. In early September there is a massive Flower Parade from Aalsmeer to Amsterdam.

| | |
|---|---|
| **WINTER** <br><br> January– <br> February | The widely acclaimed International Film Festival Rotterdam (☎ 0900/403–4065) celebrates international avant-garde cinema. More than 300 noncommercial films are screened in the Pathé on the Stadschouwburgplein, the IMAX Waterstad Theater, Lantaren/Venster, and the Luxor (and others), and run over 10 days from the last week of January to the first week of February. <br><br> If it is cold enough—sometimes 20 years go by before the weather is deemed frigid enough—Friesland hosts its famous Elfstedentocht, a one-day, 11-city ice-skating race through some of Holland's prettiest medieval towns. There is no set day, but it usually happens sometime in January or February. Thousands of participants don garb to honor the glowing hues of the House of Orange and set out to Hans Brinker their way from Leeuwarden, capital of Friesland, through the circuit towns of Sneek, IJlst, Sloten, Stavoren, Hindeloopen, Workum, Bolsward, Harlingen, Franeker, and Dokkum. All of Holland watches the race on TV. |
| February | Toward the end of February, just before Lent, the festivities of Carnival are kicked off in Limburg province, the most Catholic part of the country. The city of Maastricht is particularly famed for its merrymaking parades and events, although even Amsterdam up in Noord-Holland sports a Carnival parade. |
| March | The Stille Omgang (Silent Procession) (☎ 023/524–6229) has local Amsterdam Catholics processing through the streets on the Saturday night after March 10 to commemorate the 1345 Miracle of the Host, which has traditionally been regarded as a founding date for the city proper. <br><br> Held at Maastricht's MECC Congress and Exhibition Hall, the European Fine Art Fair (✉ European Fine Art Foundation, Box 1035, 5200 BA 's-Hertogenbosch ☎ 073/614–5165 ⊕ www.tefaf.com) |

presents a panoply of old-master paintings that attracts one of the fanciest crowds of collectors from around the world for 10 glamorous days beginning every mid-March. A fabled team of experts examines items to weed out any pieces of dubious authenticity—of those items that pass the test, the best known and most sought after are probably the paintings of the Renaissance to Baroque eras.

## SPRING

### April

During the last Saturday in April, the *Bloemen Corso,* or Bulb District Flower Parade (☎ 0252/434710) passes through Lisse to open the National Flower Exhibition.

At Keukenhof Gardens, the National Floral Exhibition (☎ 0252/465555) heralds the peak days for visiting the famous tulip fields. The 32-km (20-mi) route runs from Noordwijk to Haarlem.

National Museum Weekend (⊕ www.museumweekend.nl), usually the third weekend in April, opens 450 museums across the country to visitors free or at a discount.

April 30 is the unforgettable Queen's Day, the Dutch monarch's official birthday, when Amsterdam erupts with a citywide, all-day street party and the queen makes a more sedate official visit to a selected town in the provinces. This is actually the birth date of Queen Juliana, but her daughter Queen Beatrix now celebrates her B-day all the same. Because of a one-day, "free-license" law, thousands of Amsterdammers mount a gigantic "yard sale" by lining the streets with stalls filled with their attic bric-a-brac. April 29 sees an all-night party in some cities, with Utrecht being a center for the party-hearty crowd.

### May

May 4 and 5 are Remembrance and Liberation Day respectively and are marked by solemnity on the former and huge frolicsome music festivals throughout the country on the latter.

Every imaginable art form is represented at the annual arts fair, KunstRAI (☎ 020/549–1212), in Amsterdam's southern suburb RAI convention center, usually beginning near the end of the month. National Bicycle Day (May 8) has both professionals and novices racing through the Netherlands.

An international modern dance festival, Spring Dance (☎ 030/232–4125), bounds into Utrecht.

Usually the second Saturday in May, Nationale Molendag is Holland's National Windmill Day, when more than half of the nation's 1,000 windmills are in action and open for visits by the public.

# ON THE
# CALENDAR

| | |
|---|---|
| | Also in May, the Asparagus Season is upon kitchens across the land as chefs make hay to create concoctions with Holland's fabled bumper crop of "white gold." |
| **SUMMER** June | Usually around June 3, the famed herring fleets of Scheveningen unfurl festive banners, decorate ships, and hold crafts markets to ceremoniously celebrate Vlaggetjesdag (or Flag Day), the traditional start of the herring season, by racing out to haul in the first barrel of *groene* (fresh) herring to grace the table of Queen Beatrix. |
| | Green thumbers and lovers of luxury will love the Open Garden Days (☎ 020/320–3660), sponsored by Stichting de Amsterdamse Grachtentuin, when private houses along the posh Herengracht, Keizersgracht, and Prinsengracht open their private gardens and salons for several days in mid-June. |
| | Over a period of 10 days, the Amsterdam Roots Festival (☎ 0900/0191) brings together the best global acts in the city's best venues. |
| | Holland Festival of the Performing Arts (☎ 020/530–7110) captures Amsterdam, spilling over to The Hague, Rotterdam, and Utrecht, making this the biggest national fête for the performing arts. Most opera, dance, theater, and concert presentations are held in Amsterdam, and tickets usually go on sale May 1. |
| | Parkpop (☎ 070/361–8888), a pop music festival, livens up The Hague. |
| | To enjoy open-air concerts and theater, check out the Vondelpark Theater (☎ 020/673–1499) and its summer calendar, running from June through August. |
| July | Rotterdam's Metropolis Pop Festival hosts national and international performances on three stages in the Zuiderpark on the first Sunday of July. |
| | The Hague hosts the North Sea Jazz Festival (☎ 015/214–8900) with live performances by top international artists. |
| | The International Organ Competition (☎ 023/511–5733) brings musicians to Haarlem in even-number years. |
| August | The Amsterdam Canal Festival brings flotillas of boats for classical music performances on a floating stage on the canal. |
| | For two weeks Parade (☎ 033/465–4577) re-creates and updates a Breughel painting by bringing together absurd theatrics in Martin Luther Park. |

| | |
|---|---|
| | The Gay Pride Boat Parade (☎ 020/620–8807) fills Amsterdam's canals with over-the-top spectacle and the canal sides with as many as a quarter million spectators on the first Saturday in August. |
| | Rotterdam mounts a Heineken Jazz and Blues Festival in various locations during August. |
| | Around August 20, Scheveningen Pier and Boulevard, not far from The Hague, hosts a three-day Fireworks Festival. |
| **FALL**<br><br>September | The Bloemen Corso Floral Parade (☎ 0297/325100) makes a day-long procession of floats from Aalsmeer to Amsterdam in early September. |
| | Gaudeamus International Music Week (☎ 020/694–7349) honors contemporary classical music and its young composers in Amsterdam. |
| | The Opening of Parliament (☎ 070/356–4000) takes place in The Hague on the third Tuesday—the queen arrives in her golden coach in a ceremonial promenade that heads out from the "office palace" of Noordeinde to the famed medieval complex at the Binnenhof. |
| | During the first Saturday in September, Open Monumentendag means that you can enter many historic buildings normally closed to the public. |
| | The famous collection of historic windmills in Zaandam takes center stage every September 30 during Zaanse Windmill Day in the Zaanse Schans area, just to the north of Amsterdam. |
| October | The Holland Dance Festival (☎ 0900/340–3505) brings ballet and other dance companies to The Hague. |
| | After a few years in Amsterdam, Crossing Border (⊕ www.crossingborder.nl) has returned to The Hague to continue its good work as a "literary festival that rocks." |
| November–December | With the St. Nicolaas Parade (☎ 0900/400–4040) in Amsterdam on November 18 and in cities throughout the country, the arrival of Sinter Klaas launches the Christmas season. Indeed, the American Santa Claus is a holiday descendant of the Dutch saint, who, with little padding (wouldn't you know, the jolly fat Santa is an American invention) arrives then to dispense ginger cookies. The biggest day is Sinterklaasvond, December 5. People offer poems heralding their friends, and many towns host St. Nicholas, who gallops from house to house, leaving gag presents behind. In Amsterdam, Santa arrives by barge near Sint Nicholasskerk, along with his "Moor- |

ish" helper, Zwarte Piet (Black Peter). Real presents are often saved for the more commercial festivities on December 25. Amsterdam's Christmas Market in the Museumplein square is held December 7–24. Unfortunately, because of global warming, the canals of Amsterdam freeze up more and more infrequently, but when a frigid cold wave moves in from the North Sea, the locals hope the city will permit skating on the canals, often under the stars.

Of a much more adult nature, High Times Cannabis Cup (☎ 020/624–1777) employs the Melkweg avenue to celebrate harvest season with five days of wastedness punctuated with bands, banquets, and much-coveted awards for farming abilities.

Around December 19, Gouda hosts a beautiful Gouda by Candlelight festival.

The globally prestigious International Documentary Film Festival (☎ 020/626–1939) is centered around Leidseplein and attracts tens of thousands to its hundreds of screenings.

# PLEASURES & PASTIMES

## DIAMONDS & DELFT

As old as Amsterdam is, some things never seem to change. The bustle and noise of crowds of shoppers in the area surrounding its Dam Square is reminiscent of the cattle drives that only a few centuries ago thundered to market through the Kalverstraat (Calf's Street), now one of the major shopping streets. The city's mercantile roots go as far back as Rembrandt's day, when the maritime Dutch West India and East India companies were busy colonizing a trading empire so far-flung the sun never set on it entirely. The resulting plunder—spices from Java, porcelains from China, furs from Russia, rugs from Turkey—made Amsterdammers into the very first shop-till-you-droppers. Today, Holland shines with equal radiance for shoppers. Hunting in Holland for that special purchase is akin to grand entertainment. Clothing, cosmetics, food, household items, furniture, gifts, and toys from every corner of the globe are on offer. Of course you'll particularly want to shop for Dutch specialties.

Diamonds have always been an Amsterdammer's best friend. Starting with the Spanish conquest of 1576, many diamond experts fled north, from Antwerp to the Netherlandish capital. Shiploads of raw diamonds from India or Brazil led to a spate of feverish activity, lasting until the cargo was cut and the finished stone sent off, usually to Paris. This stream became a flood when the children of a Dutch farmer living near Hopetown, South Africa, discovered that pebbles in a nearby stream made marvelous toys. Soon, the diamond rush was on and Amsterdam became famed as the home of diamond cutters. A visit to one

of the city's modern diamond centers (there are several around the Rokin) offers the visitor a brief education in this fascinating business.

What other gifts "say" Holland? Holland is a chocoholic's mecca, and everyone knows the mmmm-boy flavors crafted by Droste and Van Houten. Those good Dutch chocolates are available in prepackaged bars, but head to a shop such as Amsterdam's Puccini Bomboni, centrally located on the Singel canal, to stock up on large slabs or handmade bonbons with exotic fillings. Many travelers wind up delving into Delft. If you want to serve your choice Gouda in the proper manner back home, you may want to purchase a piece of authentic Delftware. The key word is "authentic." A variety of blue and white "delft" is available in a range of brands and prices, and you can pick up attractive souvenir-quality "delft" pieces at any giftware shop. But the real McCoy is known as Royal Delft, and it can be found in the better giftware shops, such as those on Amsterdam's Rokin and the PC Hooftstraat.

# PLEASURES & PASTIMES

## REMBRANDT & COMPANY

During Holland's Golden Age of the 17th century, an estimated 20 million paintings were executed and every native seemed to have an oil painting tacked on the wall. But before the great age of Rembrandt and Vermeer, the Netherlands already had a rich and varied artistic history.

To begin, it is important to make the distinction between Flemish and Dutch painting. In the late 16th century, the Netherlands were divided into a Flemish, predominantly Roman Catholic south, still under Spanish rule, and an independent alliance of seven Dutch Protestant northern provinces. Until then, most of the painters hailed from the southern cities of Ghent, Antwerp, and Bruges, and their subject matter was mostly biblical and allegorical. A few of the most influential include Jan van Eyck (1385–1441), who founded the Flemish School and perfected the technique of oil painting, and Rogier van der Weyden (1399–1464), who swept the canvas clean and focused on the personalities of his subjects, injecting an emotional intensity into his work and straying from the typical devotional pictures that were crammed with detail and symbolism and showed static groups of bodies. Two other notables were Hieronymus Bosch (1450–1516), whose meticulously detailed, macabre allegorical paintings can take hours to decipher, and Pieter Bruegel the Elder (1525–69), whose scenes depicting peasant life in Flemish landscapes are an amalgam of color and texture.

In the northern provinces, around Haarlem, a different style of painting began to surface. Jan Mostaert (1475–1555) and Lucas van der Leyden (1489–1553) were on the cusp of this new movement, which brought a kind of realism into previously static and religious paintings. In Utrecht, meanwhile, followers of the Italian master Caravaggio made a complete break with mannerist painting. The chiaroscuro technique used light and shadow to play out dramatic contrasts and created realism as had never been seen on canvas before. Gerrit van Honthorst (1590–1656) is probably the most well-known Dutch representative of this particular style.

Out of these two disparate schools flowed the Golden Age of Dutch painting. Hals, Rembrandt, and Vermeer were all influenced by such diversity of technique. During the height of the Golden Age, paintings were mass produced and artists specialized in different genre paintings to keep up with the demands of the market. Religious paintings and portraits remained highly popular, but maritime, city, landscapes, and other genre paintings found an outlet as well.

Frans Hals (1581–1666) has been called the first modern painter. A fantastically adept and naturally gifted man, he could turn out a portrait in an hour. He delighted in capturing the emotions of a moment—a smile or a grimace—in an early manifestation of the same impressionist preferences that were to capture art in the 19th century. In his works he breaks with the static tradition, and his naturalistic portraits capture the emotional expression of his subjects while also giving the impression of an informal, relaxed scene. His psychological portraits, however, are not generally considered as perceptive as those of his most famous contemporary. Rembrandt van Rijn (1606–69) is regarded as the most versatile artist of the 17th century, and his fame is uncontested. Born in Leiden, the fifth child of a miller, he grew rich from painting and tuition paid by his pupils (two of whom, Govert Flinck and Ferdinand Bol, are now considered to be the authors of many a masterwork previously thought to have been painted by Rembrandt); for a while his wealth was such that he became a noted collector of art. When his whole material world crashed about him, though he was blackmailed and ruined, he unaccountably continued to turn out art that grew greater and greater. His marvelously skilled use of light and shadow is a text and source of wonder. He began his career painting commissioned portraits for wealthy merchants but soon grew bored of pleasing the increasingly political and fickle rich. His quick temper and his interest in darker subjects made him unpopular in those more elite circles. The *Night Watch* (1642), his major group portrait, was considered artistically innovative but failed to please his audience, and he soon found himself at the margins of "good" society; still, he continued to work. Some of his most impressive work dates from that later period in his life.

Jan Vermeer (1632–72) is the third in this triumvirate of artists and is a different case altogether. He produced only 35 known paintings during his career, but these exquisite portraits of simple domestic life make him the most precious genre painter of his time. He brought genre art to its peak; in small canvases of a sometimes overwhelming realism, he painted the soft calm and everyday sameness of scenes from middle-class life, with the subjects caught and held fast in the net of their normal surroundings. A rather reticent man, he lived his whole life in Delft and died poor.

Around the middle of the century, Baroque influences began to permeate Dutch painting, bringing with it a trend for both the picturesque and the utterly natural. As for the latter, artists such as Jacob van Ruysdael, Salomon van Ruysdael, Albert Cuyp, and Meindert Hobbema started producing landscape painting, making landscape—once relegated to the background of most canvases—the primary subject. Their tranquil scenes of polder lanes, rustic hillocks, grazing cows, and windswept canals were coveted by 17th- and 18th-century collectors stuck in noisy cities and obviously offered a sort of "visual Valium" to them. Other masters were more playful in tone. Probably the most famous recorder of riotous scenes was the tavern keeper Jan Steen (1625–79). His lively, bitingly satiric, sometimes lewd domestic scenes are imbued with humor; a "Jan Steen household" suggests a scene of disorder. He was the painter par excellence of the Dutch shopkeeper and his family—the lower middle class. He had trouble finding a market for his art; when he died, he supposedly had 500 unsold canvases. Steen's works are still a joy to see today, even if some of the nuances are lost on us.

# PLEASURES & PASTIMES

Gerard Terborch (1617–81) developed a mastery of painting textile texture and served up a series of thoughtful "conversation pieces" posing his subject talking. Pieter de Hooch (1629–after 1688) excelled in painting the haute bourgeois interior, often populated by elegant matrons and burgher masters—he remains a connoisseur's favorite. Leiden's Gerard Dou (1613–75) also is famous for his interior domestic scenes, often with stunning light by candlelight. His paintings became highly fashionable in the 19th century and were collected by the dozen by the Rothschilds.

With the deaths of Hals, Rembrandt, and Vermeer and the French invasion, the Golden Age was gone for good. Following French models, painting became overrefined and stylized, falling away from its earlier innovations. Even in landscape painting, formulaic daubs in the Classical style were created by such masters as Jan Both (1618–52) and Nicolaes Berchem (1620–83). Fortunately not everyone followed that school, and some painters used this period to inject more humor into established styles; Cornelis Troost (1697–1750) became famous for his delicately composed satires. It is interesting that painters such as Gerard de Lairesse (1640–1711) and Jacob de Wit (1695–1754) were masters at painting and decorating not only grand new canal mansions but public buildings as well. With the resurgence of the Catholic churches, De Wit also made a fortune painting lavish interiors.

The 19th century moved toward a more documentary style of painting. The use of allegories disappeared, and landscapists such as A. G. Bilders (1838–65) and Johan Barthold Jongkind (1819–91) became popular. George Breitner's (1857–1923) almost photographic renditions of Amsterdam were a welcome exception and became a precursor to French impressionism and The Hague School. The greatest Dutch painter of the 19th century is undoubtedly Vincent van Gogh (1853–90). During his short but troubled life, he produced an array of masterworks. He did not begin painting until 1881, and his first paintings often depicted dark peasant scenes (the most famous being the *Potato Eaters,* 1885) and many self-portraits. Because he never received much recognition during his lifetime, Van Gogh supported himself by painting copies of famous paintings. During the last four years of his life, which he spent in France, he produced his most colorful and arresting works. In 1890, however, he committed suicide after having struggled with depression and mental health problems for years (he had cut off part of an ear earlier in life). To this day, his powerful legacy continues to move art lovers around the world.

The 20th century brought new confusions to the art scene. Unsure what style to adopt, many artists attempted to reinvent themselves. Piet Mondriaan (1872–1944) is a beautiful example of someone who evolved with his century. Early in his career Mondriaan painted in the tradition of The Hague School. Bucolic landscapes, cows, and windmills belonged to his repertoire. Then, in 1909, at the age of 41, he painted the *Red Tree,* noted for its explosion of expressionism. Mondriaan once said, or so the story goes, that when he found his true personality, he would drop the second "a" in his name. The *Red Tree* must have been a step in this direction, because he signed the canvas "Mondrian." (Dutch museums do not acknowledge that name change, preferring the original.) After flirting with cubism, he developed a style of his own called neo-plasticism. Using only the primary colors of yellow, red, and blue set against neutral white, gray, and black, he created stylized studies in form and color. In 1917, together with his friend Theo van Doesberg (1883–1931), he published an arts magazine called *De Stijl* (*The Style*) as a forum for a design movement attempting to harmonize all the arts through purified abstraction. Although the movement lasted only 15 years, its effect was felt around the world and across the arts. In 1940, Mondriaan moved to New York City to escape the war.

The most vibrant movement that emerged after World War II was the experimental CoBrA (made up of artists from Copenhagen, Brussels, and Amsterdam), which was cofounded by Karel Appel (1921–) and Constant (nee Constant Nieuwenhuis, 1920–). With bright colors and abstract shapes, their paintings had a childlike quality. They searched for what they called a *volwassen kinderstijl* (grown-up child style), and their canvases often provoked the rote exclamation: "My child could do that!" It was an extremely vital movement, and the artists involved continue to have influence in their respective countries.

If CoBrA art remains an acquired taste for many, the greatest Golden Age canvases are adored by all visitors who discover, even in the largest cities, corners where the real world appears to dissolve and, just for a moment, they have the sensation of stepping into a 17th-century painting. Browse through a book of Dutch art before you come to Holland, and have a look at paintings of church interiors by Saenredam and De Witte, and views of Delft, of Utrecht, or of Haarlem's St. Bavokerk. Store them away in your mind's eye and, sure enough, as you look across a market square from a certain angle, turn a corner of a canal, or wander through a church, you'll feel as if you've stepped into a Hobbema or Vermeer.

# PLEASURES & PASTIMES

## WHEEL ESTATE

Cycling's not merely a pastime in Holland, it's a way of life, providing a convenient means of transport for kids going to school, shoppers to market, and workers to the office. In this country of 15 million people there are 12 million bikes, making bike theft a major problem in the bigger towns. A lighthearted Dutch legend predicts that if you holler "That's my bike!" when a crowd of cyclists is whizzing past, at least three of them will pull over, abandon their saddles, and head off to the nearest side street.

The flatness of the Netherlands makes it ideal cycling terrain, and throughout the country some 17,000 km (10,000 mi) of special lanes and pathways ensure that it's also very safe, which explains why only speed cyclists tend to wear any form of protective gear, such as helmets. That said, amateur cyclists engage in enough precarious riding styles to leave visitors wondering if helmets wouldn't be a good idea for everyone. There's the delicately balanced "side-saddle" passenger technique (a friend hops on to the bar at the back), for example, not to mention the pull-along wooden boxes that are attached to the bicycle and are sometimes seen holding as many as three small children, plus a dog and the week's groceries. In the bigger cities, watch out for all the special bike lanes. Even though the traffic may be flowing in one direction, bikers are allowed to head in both, and just because the light is red doesn't mean you might not be overtaken by a slew of bikers heading your way.

If you want to try it, bike rentals are nearly always available at train stations, and many of the larger hotels will have them, too. You'll probably need to have your passport at hand. Give your *fiets,* or bicycle, a short test ride before you going off with it, to be sure you haven't rented a *rammelkast,* or "bone shaker." Another thing to be aware of is the unusual factory-installed protective chain beneath the saddle that's then passed through the wheels. If you get one of these, make sure the bike shop shows you how it operates before you cycle off; the same applies to the lights, which sometimes have the switches in the most unexpected places. Many bikes in Holland use the back-pedal brake system. If you're not used to it, practice for awhile before going out into traffic. If you're planning on doing a lot of cycling, you may want to invest in a set of *panniers,* special canvas saddlebags that will easily hold the necessary essentials: picnic, map, water bottle, and sweater. You can pick these up cheaply from Hema stores (found in almost every larger town), and they simply strap onto your bicycle.

Once on the road, the signs to look for consist of direction pointers with red letters on a white background. A special lane or *fietspad* is indicated by a round blue sign with a white bike in the middle. Elsewhere, ultraclear signage allows you to cycle from one spot to another using numbers as your guide; maps of such cycle routes are available from any VVV and most railway stations. When it comes to an environmentally friendly and healthful mode of travel that will allow you to see everything at your own pace, the Dutch will assure you: a bike can't be beat.

# THE GREAT OUTDOORS

The development of the Netherlands offers insight into countryside as a man-made landscape in flux. For centuries, the low-lying land has been pumped dry, reclaimed from the sea to make it cultivable. However, nowadays many people complain about the recent ribbonlike business developments along highways, akin to the strip malls that have sprung up in the United States. The Dutch government enforces stricter planning laws for the construction of new homes outside already-developed areas, but the need for housing results in dense developments between and on the outskirts of cities, encroaching on agricultural land and leading to ever more intensive farming methods.

Tactics to combat this rampant urban spread include wildlife corridors of untouched nature under railways and highways, so that wild animals can still wander or migrate safely, and compensatory greenery exchanged for ground consumed by development. Infrastructure is hidden to stop it from polluting the view: Railways are dug under meadowlands, and highways are screened behind landscaped hills and sound mufflers.

Although almost no land is untouched by man, the protection and preservation of natural areas have created and preserved places of outstanding beauty and protected indigenous wildlife. Wild boar and roe deer roam protected woodland areas, and mushrooms and toadstools abound in this damp climate. Reed warblers nest in the reed beds on the banks of freshwater lakes, gray herons stand tall and proud, and harriers hover as they hunt the resident voles and harvest mice. One of the reasons for the ardent nature preservation here is the importance of the country for migratory birds. Eider ducks, barnacle geese, and wigeons pass through on their way to breeding grounds in the north, while golden plovers and curlews spend their winters here, grazing the grasslands. No fewer than 850 species of bird have been spotted in the Dutch countryside.

# FODOR'S
# CHOICE

The sights, restaurants, hotels, and other travel experiences listed below are our editors' top picks—the crème de la crème chosen from the lists of Fodor's Choices found on the opening pages of the chapters in this book. They're the best of their type in the area covered by the book. In addition, the list incorporates many of the highly recommended restaurants and hotels our reviewers have come to treasure. In the chapters that follow, you will find all the details.

| | |
|---|---|
| **LODGING** | **Grand Sofitel Demeure, Amsterdam.** Once a *Prinsenhof* (Prince's Courtyard) that welcomed such illustrious guests as William of Orange and Maria de Medici, this grandly renovated hostelry now has a guest book littered with names such as Mick Jagger and President Chirac of France. Café Roux opens out onto a glorious courtyard for the enjoyment of afternoon tea. |
| $$$$ | |
| $$$$ | **Inter-Continental Amstel Amsterdam.** Elegant enough to please Audrey Hepburn, extroverted enough to welcome Madonna, this grand dowager has wowed all onlookers since it opened its doors in 1867. You'll feel like a visiting VIP yourself when entering the magnificent lobby, a soaring salon covered with wedding-cake stucco trim and replete with a grand double staircase that demands you glide, not walk, up it. |
| $$$–$$$$ | **Dikker and Thijs Fenice, Amsterdam.** "Lavish," "classical," and "cozy" are some of the adjectives typically used to describe this hotel, which has a regal address on the Prinsengracht canal. |
| $$–$$$ | **Ambassade, Amsterdam.** Ten 17th- and 18th-century houses have been folded into this hotel on the Herengracht, now home-away-from-home for such literati as Lessing, Le Carré, Eco, and Rushdie. |
| $$–$$$ | **Het Canal House, Amstersam** The owners have put a lot of love and style into this 17th-century (1640) canal-house hotel. It's a beautiful old home with high plaster ceilings, antique furniture, old paintings, and a backyard garden bursting with plants and flowers. |
| $$–$$$ | **Seven Bridges, Amsterdam.** Set in an 18th-century house in the heart of "Golden Bend" country, this hotel offers uniquely stylish guest rooms and one of the more famous canal sights in Amsterdam, the lineup of seven consecutive bridges that can be seen gracing Reguliersgracht. |
| $–$$ | **Washington, Amsterdam.** A discreet stone's throw from the Museumplein, this meticulously polished, sparkling clean property often attracts international musicians who perform at the nearby Concertgebouw. |

| | |
|---|---|
| **BUDGET LODGING**<br><br>¢–$ | **Museumzicht, Amsterdam.** Directly across the street from the Rijksmuseum, this guest house is filled with wonderful objects like the Murano glass chandelier in the breakfast room–lounge and Art Deco pottery on the chimney walls. |
| $ | **Quentin England, Amsterdam.** Both a budgeteer's and a connoisseur's delight, this place is set in a series of adjoining buildings dating from 1884, each built in an architectural style of the country whose name it bears. Adorned with a Tudor gable and five-step gable, the Quentin delightfully occupies the England and Netherlands buildings. |
| **DINING**<br><br>$$$$ | **De Librije, Zwolle.** Housed in the stunning, beamed, former library of a 15th-century monastery, owner-chef Jonnie Boer's restaurant walls are lined with accolades, searing his reputation as Holland's *crème de la crème*. His "Cuisine Pure" is a dazzler, based on local ingredients such as nettles, water mint, berries, rose hips, wild mushrooms, mustard, and even cat's tails (the plant version, of course). |
| $$$$ | **Supper Club, Amsterdam.** Simple, artful, white, and sleek, this spot offers up endless courses of food (and drink . . . ) marked by irreverent flavor combinations. DJs, VJs, and live performances enhance the clublike, relentlessly hip vibe. |
| $$–$$$ | **Blue Pepper, Amsterdam.** One of the more widely acclaimed of recent newcomers in town, this blue-toned Indonesian spot features the inspired cooking of an award-winning chef. Bliss may be your dessert. |
| $$$—$$$$ | **D' Vijff Vlieghen, Amsterdam.** The "Five Flies" is a rambling dining institution that takes up five adjoining Golden Age houses, all giving off a densely evocative Golden Age vibe, complete with bona fide Rembrandt etchings, wooden *jenever* (Dutch gin) barrels, crystal and armor collections, and an endless array of old-school bric-a-brac. The ambience is probably more delicious than the food. |
| **BUDGET DINING**<br><br>$ | **Café Bern, Amsterdam.** This dark and woody café, as evocative as a Jan Steen 17th-century interior, has been serving the same cheese fondue for decades and for good reason: it's just about perfect. |
| ¢ | **Bakkerswinkel, Amsterdam.** This genteel yet unpretentious bakery/tearoom evokes an English country kitchen, where breakfasts, high tea, hearty-breaded sandwiches, soups, and divine (almost manly) slabs of quiche are served. |

| | |
|---|---|
| **QUINTESSENTIAL HOLLAND** | **Anne Frank House, Amsterdam.** The swinging bookcase that hid the door is still here, as well as the magazine pictures that young Anne pasted on the walls for decoration. It is impossible not to be moved as you wander through the secret apartment where the Frank family hid from the Nazis, and where the young girl wrote her famous *Diary of Anne Frank*, thereby giving a face to the Holocaust for millions of readers. |
| | **Begijnhof, Amsterdam.** Feel the gentle breeze of history in the solitude of a serene courtyard that has hardly changed since the Pilgrim Fathers worshipped here centuries ago. |
| | **Amsterdam canals at night.** Walking along the canals of Amsterdam after dark is one of the simplest, cheapest, and most memorable experiences that Holland has to offer. Pedestrians (and cyclists) rule over traffic, the most beautiful gables are subtly lighted up, and the pretty humpbacked bridges are festooned with lights. Alternatively, get up early and stroll out before the city is awake as the mist gently rises off the water. |
| | **Bikes on dikes (most anywhere).** Trundling along the top of a dike on a Dutch bicycle, with the sea to one side of you, wetlands (alive with bird life) on the other, and the wind in your hair, is transporting in more ways than one. Enhance the delight by stopping over at one of myriad waterside cafés or charming villages along the way. |
| | **Lisse & the Bulb Fields.** How could you visit Holland and not tiptoe through the tulips? If you are in Amsterdam in April, it's easy to sample one of the best-known aspects of quintessential Holland—the bulb fields, in an area around the town of Lisse. |
| **CASTLES & PALACES** | **Binnenhof and the Ridderzaal, The Hague.** The Inner Court and Knights' Hall are the Netherlands' tranquil and majestic seat of government. |
| | **Kasteel de Haar, near Utrecht.** The largest and most sumptuously furnished castle in the Netherlands is a Neo-Gothic extravaganza replete with moat, spires, and machicolated towers. |
| | **Paleis Het Loo, Apeldoorn.** Stroll through the elegant formal gardens, view the sumptuous Dutch Baroque palace that was home to the Dutch royal family until the 1960s, then pop inside to feast your eyes on the rich furnishings. |
| **MUSEUMS** | **Escher in Het Paleis Museum, The Hague.** Devoted to the Dutch graphic artist M. C. Escher, this museum is replete with his perspective-altering prints and engravings. |

**Gemeentemuseum, The Hague.** This architectural masterpiece houses sumptuous period rooms full of Golden Age silver, Greek and Chinese pottery, historic musical instruments, and paintings by Monet, Van Gogh, and Mondriaan.

**Mauritshuis, The Hague.** One of the greatest art museums in Europe, the Mauritshuis has 14 Rembrandts, 10 Jan Steens, and 3 Vermeers, including the *View of Delft* and *Girl with a Pearl Earring.*

**Museum Amstelkring, Amsterdam.** Steal into a nondescript canal house to visit this singular mysterious chapel from the Reformation, when Catholics were not permitted to worship openly.

**Museum Boijmans van Beuningen, Rotterdam.** This museum ranks as one of the greatest painting collections in Europe, along with Amsterdam's Rijksmuseum and The Hague's Mauritshuis.

**Museum het Rembrandthuis, Amsterdam.** Once fitted out with the ultimate in fashionable 17th-century furnishings, this former home of the great Rembrandt today casts but a dim shadow of its glory days. However, the many engravings and prints on view by the master are spectacular enough.

**Museum Mesdag, The Hague.** This oft-overlooked treasure-house is nearly wallpapered with grand paintings, glittering frames, delicate ceramics, and exquisite period fabrics and tapestries.

**Rijksmuseum, Amsterdam.** "The Rijks" is one of the world's most famous museums, with the best collection of Dutch Golden Age art, plus a cornucopia of other works, from early Oriental Buddhas to 17th-century four-poster beds.

**Vincent Van Gogh Museum, Amsterdam.** None of the reproductions you may have seen can match the luster of Van Gogh's original paintings, where brilliant blues appear unexpectedly between the bright yellows and greens. More than 200 Van Gogh paintings, including *Sunflowers,* are on view here.

**Willet-Holthuysen Museum, Amsterdam.** Amsterdam's 17th-century Golden Age comes to life at this elegant Neoclassical mansion, brimming with sumptuous damasks, Old Master paintings, and French chandeliers.

**TOWNS & VILAGES**

**Bronkhorst, Gelderland Province.** It's as though Dickens's Tiny Tim has left his thumbprint on Bronkhorst, the tiniest official town in the Netherlands. Wander along its cobblestone streets paved with nostalgia and punctuated with a Charles Dickens Museum and a lot of curiosity shops.

# FODOR'S
# CHOICE

**Alkmaar, Noord-Holland.** As one of the "cheese towns," Alkmaar may be most noted for its traditional cheese market, but it is also worth visiting for its several hundred historical monuments, many windmills, and beautiful medieval courtyards—a concentration of all things Holland.

**Amersfoort, Utrecht Province.** Poised for battle with its fortress gates and double-ringed canal—the only such vein in all of Europe—this is a highly walkable town with winding, cobblestone streets, parts of which are closed to traffic, where you can almost hear the clack of hooves of jousting horses.

**Delft.** Imagine a tiny Amsterdam, canals reduced to dollhouse proportions, narrower bridges, merchants' houses less grand, and you have the essence of Old Delft. For many travelers, few spots in Holland are as intimate and attractive as this town.

**Giethoorn, Overijssel Province.** Vying for first-place prize in photogenicity (some cynics might say photo infamy), Giethoorn is a verdant, miniature version of Venice—an irresistible punter's paradise flanked by a profusion of thatched-roof cottages. Are you in Hansel and Gretel's garden or Alice in Wonderland's fantasy?

**Heusden, Noord Brabant.** Fronting the River Maas, this little town is a must-visit stop—there are no specific buildings or museums to see, but the entire town radiates a very special atmosphere, composed as it is of a windmill, a harbor, little cobbled streets, perfectly restored buildings, and history—and no less than 11 centuries of it.

**Sloten, Friesland.** As the elf of the 11-city Elfstedentocht ice-race towns, Sloten seems to have been frozen in time. Once a fortress at the southwestern gate to Friesland and settled around 1063, it can probably all be seen in about three hours, but there's not a drop in its bucket to be missed. The epitome of charming towns, Sloten has a sleepiness that is to be savored.

**Veere, Zeeland.** This famously pretty 16th-century town is crowned with a Gothic Town Hall, whose fairy-tale facade is decorated with statues commemorating Veere's former lords and ladies.

# SMART TRAVEL TIPS

## ADDRESSES

Fittingly, for a country with a history as venerable as Holland's, the country's *straats,* or streets (and other places) are often named after its famous sons and daughters. In Delft, for one example, Hugo de Grootstraat is named in honor of the city's lawyer-philosopher. In a bigger city, you get all the variations: Jacob Catsstraat, Jacob Catskade, Jacob Catsplein, ad infinitum. Of course, kings and queens feature: Wilhelminastraat is named after Queen Wilhelmina, the grandmother of the current queen, Beatrix. In Amsterdam, Vondelpark is named after Holland's most celebrated poet, Joost van den Vondel. A *plein* is a square; a *grote markt* is a market square, usually an old town's historic center, such as the one you find in Haarlem.

Other geographical terms to keep in mind are a *dwarsstraat,* or street that runs perpendicular to a street or canal, such as the Leidsestraat and the Leidsedwarsstraat. A *straatje* is a small street; a *weg* is a road; a *gracht* is a canal; a *steeg* is a very small street; a *laan* is a lane. *Baan* is another name for a road, not quite a highway, but busier than an average street. Note that in Holland, the house number always comes after the street name on addresses.

The Dutch have an infinite range of names for bodies of water, from *gracht* to *singel* to *kanaal* (all roughly equating to "canal"). A singel is a major canal within a city. The difference between a singel and a gracht is hard to define, even for a Dutch person. In fact, the names can be confusing because sometimes there is *no* water at all—many grachten have been filled in by developers to make room for houses, roads, and so on. Near harbor areas you'll notice *havens* (harbors), named after the goods that ships used to bring in, like in Rotterdam, *Wijnhaven* (Wine Harbor) and *Vishaven* (Fish Harbor).

Don't let common address abbreviations confuse you. BG stands for *Begane Grond* (ground floor); SOUT for *Souterrain* (sublevel/basement apartment); HS for *Huis* (a ground-floor apartment or main entry). Some common geographical abbreviations are *str.* for *straat* (street); *gr.* for *gracht* (canal); and *pl.* for *plein* (square). For example: Leidsestr., Herengr., or Koningspl.

Finally, first things last. Every guidebook on Holland is titled . . . Holland. In fact, Holland is a term that, legally, refers to only 2 out of the country's 12 provinces (i.e., Noord-Holland). But, as the term "Holland" has been generally favored for millennia, so this book, as common usage has it, uses it interchangeably with the Netherlands.

## AIR TRAVEL

### CARRIERS

When flying internationally to Holland, you usually choose between a domestic carrier, the national flag carrier of the country, and a foreign carrier from a third country. You may, for example, choose to fly KLM Royal Dutch Airlines to Holland for the basic reason that, as the national flag carrier, it has the greatest number of nonstop flights. Domestic carriers offer connections to smaller destinations. Third-party carriers may have a price advantage.

KLM and its global alliance partner Northwest—together with their regional partner airlines—fly from Amsterdam's Schiphol Airport to more than 400 destinations in more than 80 countries worldwide. Nearly 100 of those are European destinations, with 3 or 4 daily flights to most airports and up to 17 flights a day to London alone. Northwest Airlines now handles all reservations and ticket office activities on behalf of KLM in the United States and Canada, with KLM's biggest North American hubs in Detroit and Minneapolis, as well as Memphis, New York, and Washington among its gateways. KLM's direct flights connect Amsterdam to Atlanta, Los Angeles, and Miami, and numerous other cities. Including connections via KLM's hubs, the airline flies to more than 100 destinations in the United States from Amsterdam. In Canada, KLM/Northwest serves Montreal, Toronto, and Vancouver. For more information, contact the airline at one of the reservation numbers below or go to KLM/Northwest's Web site.

MartinAir Holland makes transatlantic flights to some of the regional terminals in

Holland. If your carrier offers Rotterdam as a final destination, you fly into Amsterdam then transfer. KLM Cityhopper and KLM Excel offer a varied schedule of flights connecting Amsterdam with the smaller regional airports, and British Airways provides a number of domestic flights; between them, the whole country is covered. Transavia Airlines flies from Amsterdam and Rotterdam to a number of European destinations, and many other carriers link European capitals with Amsterdam; for instance, Air France offers a direct route between Amsterdam and Paris. Check with your travel agent for details.

🛪 **KLM Royal Dutch Airlines** ☎ 300/303747 in Australia, 020/474-7747 in Holland, 09/309-1782 in New Zealand, 0870/507-4074 in U.K. ☎ 800/447-4747 for Northwest/KLM sales office in U.S. and Canada ⊕ www.klm.com. **Air Canada** ☎ 888/247-2262 in U.S. and Canada, 020/346-9539 in Holland ⊕ www.aircanada.com. **Air France** ☎ 800/237-2747 in the U.S., 020/654-5720 ⊕ www.airfrance.com. **American Airlines** ☎ 800/433-7300 ⊕ www.aa.com. **British Airways** ☎ 0870/850-9850 in U.K., 020/346-9559 in Holland ⊕ www.britishairways.com. **British Midland/BMI Baby** ☎ 0870/607-0555 ⊕ www.flybml.com. **Continental Airlines** ☎ 800/523-3273 in U.S., 020/346-9381 in Holland ⊕ www.continental.com. **Delta Air Lines** ☎ 800/241-4141 in U.S. and Canada, 020/201-3536 in Holland ⊕ www.delta.com. **Lufthansa** ☎ 800/645-3880 in the U.S., 0900/123-4777 in Holland ⊕ www.lufthansa.com. **MartinAir Holland** ☎ 800/627-8462 in U.S., 020/601-1767 in Holland ⊕ www.martinair.com. **Scandinavian Airlines** ☎ 800/221-2350 in the U.S., 0900/7466-3727 in Holland ⊕ www.scandinavian.net. **Transavia Airlines** ☎ 020/406-0406 in Holland ⊕ www.transavia.nl/home. **United Airlines** ☎ 800/538-2929 in U.S., 020/201-3708 in Holland ⊕ www.united.com. **US Airways** ☎ 800/428-4322 in U.S., 020/201-3550 in Holland ⊕ www.usairways.com.

### CHECK-IN & BOARDING

Always **find out your carrier's check-in policy.** Plan to arrive at the airport about 2 hours before your scheduled departure time for domestic flights and 2½ to 3 hours before international flights. You may need to arrive earlier if you're flying from one of the busier airports or during peak air-traffic times. To avoid delays at airport-security checkpoints, try not to wear any metal. Jewelry, belt and other buckles, steel-toe shoes, barrettes, and underwire bras are among the items that can set off detectors.

Assuming that not everyone with a ticket will show up, airlines routinely overbook planes. When everyone does, airlines ask for volunteers to give up their seats. In return, these volunteers usually get a several-hundred-dollar flight voucher, which can be used toward the purchase of another ticket, and are rebooked on the next available flight out. If there are not enough volunteers, the airline must choose who will be denied boarding. The first to get bumped are passengers who checked in late and those flying on discounted tickets, so get to the gate and check in as early as possible, especially during peak periods.

Always **bring a government-issued photo ID** to the airport; even when it's not required, a passport is best.

### CUTTING COSTS

The least-expensive airfares to Holland are often priced for round-trip travel and must usually be purchased in advance. Airlines generally allow you to change your return date for a fee; most low-fare tickets, however, are nonrefundable. It's smart to call a number of airlines and check the Internet; when you are quoted a good price, book it on the spot—the same fare may not be available the next day, or even the next hour. Always check different routings and look into using alternate airports. Also, price off-peak flights and red-eye, which may be significantly less expensive than others. Travel agents, especially low-fare specialists (⇨ Discounts & Deals), are helpful.

Consolidators are another good source. They buy tickets for scheduled flights at reduced rates from the airlines, then sell them at prices that beat the best fare available directly from the airlines. (Many also offer reduced car-rental and hotel rates.) Sometimes you can even get your money back if you need to return the ticket. Carefully read the fine print detailing penalties for changes and cancellations, purchase the

ticket with a credit card, and confirm your consolidator reservation with the airline.

When you fly as a courier, you trade your checked-luggage space for a ticket deeply subsidized by a courier service. There are restrictions on when you can book and how long you can stay. Some courier companies list with membership organizations, such as the Air Courier Association and the International Association of Air Travel Couriers; these require you to become a member before you can book a flight.

Many airlines, singly or in collaboration, offer discount air passes that allow foreigners to travel economically in a particular country or region. These visitor passes usually must be reserved and purchased before you leave home. Information about passes often can be found on most airlines' international Web pages, which tend to be aimed at travelers from outside the carrier's home country. Also, try typing the name of the pass into a search engine, or search for "pass" within the carrier's Web site.

EasyJet has low fares to Amsterdam flying in from Barcelona, Belfast, Edinburgh, Geneva, Glasgow, Liverpool, London (Gatwick and Luton), and Nice. BasiqAir flies to Amsterdam and Rotterdam from Barcelona and Nice. BMIBaby flies to Amsterdam from its hub in Nottingham.

🛪 Consolidators & Low-Cost Airlines **AirlineConsolidator.com** ☎ 888/468-5385 ⊕ www. airlineconsolidator.com; for international tickets. **BasiqAir** ☎ 0900/0737 in Holland. **Best Fares** ☎ 800/880-1234 ⊕ www.bestfares.com; $59.90 annual membership. **Cheap Tickets** ☎ 888/922-8849 ⊕ www.cheaptickets.com. **EasyJet** ☎ 023/568-4880 in Holland ⊕ www.easyjet.com. **Expedia** ☎ 800/397-3342 or 404/728-8787 ⊕ www.expedia.com. **Global Travel** ☎ 416/516-1113 in Canada. **Hotwire** ☎ 866/468-9473 or 920/330-9418 ⊕ www.hotwire.com. **Now Voyager Travel** ☎ 212/459-1616 ⊕ www.nowvoyagertravel.com. **Onetravel.com** ⊕ www.onetravel.com. **Orbitz** ☎ 888/656-4546 ⊕ www.orbitz.com. **Priceline.com** ⊕ www. priceline.com. **Travelocity** ☎ 888/709-5983, 877/282-2925 in Canada, 0870/111-7061 in U.K. ⊕ www. travelocity.com. **Up & Away Travel** ☎ 212/889-2345. **World Courier of Canada** ☎ 905/678-6007. 🛪 Courier Resources **Air Courier Association/ Cheaptrips.com** ☎ 800/211-5119 ⊕ www.aircourier.

org or www.cheaptrips.com; $20 annual membership. **Courier Travel** ☎ 303/570-7586 🖷 313/625-6106 ⊕ www.couriertravel.org; $50 annual membership. **International Association of Air Travel Couriers** ☎ 308/632-3273 🖷 308/632-8267 ⊕ www.courier.org; $45 annual membership. **▯ Discount Passes All Europe Airpass** ☎ 800/639-3590 ⊕ www.allairpass.com. **Discover Europe Airpass** ☎ 800/788-0555 ⊕ www.flybmi-canada.com. **FlightPass,** EuropebyAir, ☎ 888/387-2479 ⊕ www.europebyair.com. **oneworld visitor pass** ⊕ www.oneworld.com. **Passport to Europe** ☎ 800/447-4747 ⊕ www.nwa.com. **SkyTeam European Airpass** ☎ 800/223-5730 ⊕ www.alitalia-specials.com. **Star Alliance European Airpass** ☎ 800/864-8331 ⊕ www.staralliance.com.

## ENJOYING THE FLIGHT

State your seat preference when purchasing your ticket, and then repeat it when you confirm and when you check in. For more legroom, you can request one of the few emergency-aisle seats at check-in, if you're capable of moving obstacles comparable in weight to an airplane exit door (usually between 35 pounds and 60 pounds). Seats behind a bulkhead also offer more legroom, but they don't have under-seat storage. Don't sit in the row in front of the emergency aisle or in front of a bulkhead, where seats may not recline. SeatGuru.com has more information about specific seat configurations, which vary by aircraft.

## FLYING TIMES

Flying time to Amsterdam is 21½ hours from Auckland; 1 hour from London; 10½ hours from Los Angeles; 7 hours from New York; 29 minutes from Amsterdam to Rotterdam; 20 hours from Sydney; and 8 hours from Toronto.

## HOW TO COMPLAIN

If your baggage goes astray or your flight goes awry, complain right away. Most carriers require that you **file a claim immediately.** The Aviation Consumer Protection Division of the Department of Transportation publishes *Fly-Rights,* which discusses airlines and consumer issues and is available online. You can also find articles and information on mytravelrights.com, the

Web site of the nonprofit Consumer Travel Rights Center.
**▯ Airline Complaints Aviation Consumer Protection Division** ✉ U.S. Department of Transportation, Office of Aviation Enforcement and Proceedings, C-75, Room 4107, 400 7th St. SW, Washington, DC 20590 ☎ 202/366-2220 ⊕ airconsumer.ost.dot.gov. **Federal Aviation Administration Consumer Hotline** ✉ For inquiries: FAA, 800 Independence Ave. SW, Washington, DC 20591 ☎ 800/322-7873 ⊕ www.faa.gov.

## RECONFIRMING

Check the status of your flight before you leave for the airport. You can do this on your carrier's Web site, by linking to a flight-status checker (many Web booking services offer these), or by calling your carrier or travel agent. Always confirm international flights at least 72 hours ahead of the scheduled departure time.

## AIRPORTS

Located just outside Amsterdam, **Luchthaven Schiphol** is the main passenger airport for Holland. With the annual number of passengers using Schiphol approaching 40 million, it is ranked among the world's top five best-connected airports. At Schiphol, transfers to and from intercountry flights are quick and easy, as both international and country services have been integrated into one terminal. If you plan to fly via Schiphol from a regional airport, transfer times are minimal, and the connection fares tend to be very reasonable.

**Rotterdam** is the biggest of the regional airport options and provides daily service to many European cities; other regional airports include Eindhoven, Groningen, and Maastricht. An increasing number of international charter flights choose these airports, as benefits include shorter check-in times and ample parking. However, there are no rail links that connect such regional airports with nearby cities, so passengers must resort to taking buses or taxis.
**▯ Airport Information Aachen Luchthaven (Airport)** ✛ 15 km [8 mi]north of Maastricht ☎ 043/358-9898. **Amsterdam Luchthaven (Airport) Schiphol** ✛ 17 km [11 mi] southwest of Amsterdam

☎ 0900/0141. **Eindhoven Luchthaven (Airport)** ✈ 12 km [8 mi] northwest of Eindhoven ☎ 040/ 291-9818. **Groningen Luchthaven (Airport) Eelde** ✈ 5 km [3 mi] west of Groningen ☎ 050/308-1300 or 050/309-7070. **Rotterdam Luchthaven (Airport)** ✈ 17 km [11 mi] northwest of Rotterdam ☎ 010/ 446-3444.

## AIRPORT TRANSFERS

Once you disembark from your plane at Amsterdam Luchthaven (Airport) at Schiphol, you can travel to and from the city center in several ways. The Schiphol Rail Link operates between the airport and the city 24 hours a day, with service to Centraal Station—Amsterdam's central railway station—or to stations in the south of the city. From 6:30 AM to 12:30 AM, a train departs from or arrives at Schiphol every 15 minutes; other hours, there is one train every hour. The trip takes about 15 minutes and costs €3. Trains leave from the platforms of Schiphol Station, found beneath Schiphol Plaza. They head into the city using one of three routes. The most popular is the NS Schiphollijn, which runs to Centraal Station (with two stops in west Amsterdam). Another route heads to the Amsterdam Zuid/WTC (South/World Trade Center) station in south Amsterdam, and another line heads to the RAI section, near the big convention center. From these south Amsterdam stations, Tram No. 5 goes to Leidseplein and the Museum Quarter; from RAI, Tram 4 goes to Rembrandtplein. Keep in mind that Schiphol Station is one of Holland's busiest—make sure you catch the shuttle to Amsterdam and not a train heading to The Hague! As always, when arriving at Amsterdam's Centraal Station, keep an eye out for any stray pickpockets. Other than taxis, you may wish to hop aboard a tram or bus to get to your hotel, so go to one of the **Gemeentevervoerbedrijf (GVB) Amsterdam Municipal Transport** booths found in front of the Centraal Station. Here you can find directions, fare information, and schedules.

KLM Shuttle operates a shuttle bus service between Amsterdam Schiphol Airport and 16 of the city's major hotels (among them, the Krasnapolsky and the Toren), along with stops that are convenient to many other hotels in the city. The trip takes about half an hour and costs €10.50 one-way. Hours for this bus shuttle are 7 AM to 6 PM, every half hour; between 6 PM and 9 PM, departures are every hour.

Finally, there is a taxi stand directly in front of the arrival hall at Amsterdam Schiphol Airport. A service charge is included, but small additional tips are not unwelcome. New laws determine that taxi fares are now fixed from Schiphol to Amsterdam; depending on the neighborhood, a trip will cost between €25 and €30. When you're returning home, a ride to Schiphol from Amsterdam center city area, the Centrum, will cost €22. A new service that might be convenient for budget travelers who count every euro is the Schiphol Travel Taxi. The taxi needs to be booked at least 48 hours in advance and rides are shared, so the trip will take a bit longer, as the taxi stops to pick up passengers.

🚡 **Taxis & Shuttles KLM Shuttle** ☎ 020/653-4975. **Schiphol Rail Link** ☎ 0900/9292. **Schiphol Travel Taxi** ☎ 020/0900-8876.

## DUTY-FREE SHOPPING

Although the European Union eliminated duty-free shopping in airports in Holland and in Europe, Schiphol's tax-free shopping center, See-Buy-Fly, maintains its ability to sell cheaper goods thanks to a subsidy from the airport; you can also make in-flight duty-free purchases.

## BIKE TRAVEL

Holland is truly geared for bicycles, with one of the most comprehensive and well-maintained networks of bicycle paths in the world. Many Dutch people spend at least a few weekend hours biking, and some 30% commute to work by bike.

Most train stations have shops that rent bicycles and even provide repair services. The normal rental bike is a three-speed *fiets* (bike) with handlebar brakes, but racing and mountain bikes can also be found. Average rental costs are €5–€10 per day, plus a deposit of about €50 per bike. You'll need a passport or other identification. The more days you rent, the cheaper the price, and rates by the week are even more competitive.

## GETTING AROUND BY BICYCLE

In this flat country, with its 19,000 km (10,000 mi) of *fietspaden* (cycle paths) in and between cities, a bicycle is an ideal means of getting around. Many hotels, cafés, and restaurants are located along the most popular bike routes, so finding places to stop and take a break is easy. Always lock up your bike when you make a stop. There is a rapid turnover of stolen bikes no matter what quality or condition. Use a "D" lock, which can't be cut with the average thieves' tools, and lock your bike's frame to something that can't be shifted, such as a railing. Bicycle stands are located outside most cafés, restaurants, museums, and train stations.

You can purchase *fietsroute* (bike route) maps for €1–€2 at the tourist offices or VVVs, although most are printed only in Dutch. Major cities will have English versions so be sure to ask for them. Bike routes between towns are so well signposted, however, that you do not have to rely on a map. The best fietspaden are paved lanes that run parallel to most secondary roads and are separated by concrete curbs. Note that a fietspad might easily be mistaken for a pedestrian path. If you see a circular sign, with a bicycle ringed in blue, then only bikes can use the fietspad. If, however, there is also a *bromfiets* (moped) on the sign, then mopeds can use the path. The youngsters riding them tend to drive exceptionally fast, so beware of the potential hazards of meandering across a seemingly quiet fietspad.

As a cyclist, you'll notice that most fellow cyclers don't really observe the traffic signs and rules, nor do they stay in the bicycle lanes marked out for them, unless the road has particularly heavy traffic. However, as a result of accidents caused by aggressive cyclists, fines and other penalties are being rigorously imposed (you can also be fined for riding at night with no lights, and for drunken cycling). Cars that are turning across your path are supposed to stop for you, but it is wise to watch out.

🚲 **Bike Transport Information** ⊕ www.bikeaccess.net

## BOAT & FERRY TRAVEL

### FROM ENGLAND

Traveling from the United Kingdom, there are two daily Stena line crossings between the **Hoek van Holland** (Corner of Holland, an industrial shipping area west of Rotterdam) to Harwich, on the fast car ferry, taking approximately 3 hours. The overnight crossing takes about 7 hours. These are the only ferry crossings that can be booked at the international travel window in large railway stations. There is one PO North Sea overnight crossing between the Europoort in Rotterdam and Hull, which takes about 14 hours, and one DFDS Seaways overnight crossing from Newcastle to IJmuiden, in Amsterdam, taking 15 hours.

Ferries and superfast hydrofoils are run between Harwich and Hook of Holland twice daily by Stena Line. In England, ferries to Holland are run daily from Harwich International Port in Harwich and also overnight between Hull and Rotterdam by PO North Sea Ferries. The trip takes 3 to 11 hours, depending on the route.

🚢 **From the U.K. DFDS Seaways** ☎ 0255/546666 🖷 0255/546655 ⊕ www.dfdsseaways.com. **Harwich International Port** ⊠ Harwich International Port, Parkeston Quay, Harwich, Essex CO12 4SR England ☎ 01255/242000. **PO North Sea Ferries** In Holland ⊠ Beneluxhaven, Havennummer 5805, Rotterdam/Europoort ☎ 020/201-3333 ⊕ www.ponsf.com/index ⊠ King George Dock, Hedon Rd., Hull HU9 5QA England ☎ 08705/202020. **Stena Line** In Holland ⊠ Hoek van Holland Terminal, Stationsweg 10, 3151 HS Hoek van Holland ☎ 0174/315800, 0900/8123 booking [€0.10 per min] 🖷 0174/389389 ⊕ www.stenaline.nl.

### WITHIN HOLLAND

An extensive ferry system serves Holland. DFDS Seaways is a leading carrier. Ferries run from several locations in Friesland, including Lauwersoog, Harlingen, and Holwerd, to the Frisian Islands. Ferries cross the IJsselmeer from Enkhuizen to Stavoren (no cars) and to Urk. Ferries connect Den Helder to the island of Texel in Noord-Holland. Ferries in Zeeland have ports in Breskens and Vlissingen.

🚢 **Boat & Ferry Information Den Helder Ferries to Texel** ☎ 0222/369600. **DFDS Seaways** ⊠ Sluis-

plein 33, 1975 AG IJmuiden ☎ 0255/546666
📠 0255/546655 🌐 www.dfdsseaways.com.com.
**Enkhuizen Ferries** ☎ 0228/326-6667 to Stavoren
[no cars] ☎ 0527/683407 to Urk. **Friesland Ferries**
☎ 0519/349050 Lauwersoog ☎ 0900/363-5736
Harlingen ☎ 0900/363-5736 Holwerd. **Zeeland
Ferries** ☎ 0117/381663 Breskens ☎ 0118/465905
Vlissingen.

## GETTING AROUND BY BOAT

**Hire your own boat** or take a guided city
canal tour of Amsterdam, Leiden, or Delft;
alternatively, take a harbor tour to **check
out Rotterdam's extensive Europoort,** the
world's biggest harbor, and the flood barrier. There are pedestrian ferries behind
Amsterdam's Centraal Station across the
IJ. For more specific information about
guided tours, small-boat rental, and details
about passenger and car ferries to the islands in the north of the country, including
Texel, Terschelling, and Schiermonikoog,
*see* individual regional chapters.

## BUSINESS HOURS

### BANKS & OFFICES

Banks are open weekdays 9:30 to 4 or 5,
with some extending their business hours
to coordinate with late-night shopping.
Some banks are closed Monday mornings.

The main post office in each town is open
weekdays 9 to 5 or 6, Saturday 10 to 1:30.
In every post office you'll also find the
Postbank, a money-changing facility,
which has the same opening hours.

### BARS & RESTAURANTS

As a general guide, bars in the larger cities
open at various times during the day and
close at 1 AM throughout the week, at 2 or
3 AM on Friday and Saturday. Restaurants
are open evenings 5–11, although some
kitchens close as early as 9, and many are
closed Sunday and Monday.

### MUSEUMS & SIGHTS

Major sights, such as Amsterdam's Koninklijk Paleis, have summer opening hours;
churches and cathedrals are open daily
9–3; parks are open dawn to dusk; *hofjes*
(almshouses) open at the discretion of
their inhabitants. Museum hours vary; to
give some Amsterdam instances, the city's
famous Rijksmuseum is open 10–5, the

Van Gogh museum is open 10–6, and the
Anne Frank House is open 9–7 and until 9
in summer.

Note that when this book refers to summer hours, it means approximately Easter
to October; winter hours run from
November to Easter. The Keukenhof floral
displays are open only in spring and late
summer; VVV (tourist information centers) also have extended summer hours.
Always check locally.

## PHARMACIES

*Apotheken* (pharmacies) are open weekdays from 8 or 9 to 5:30 or 6. There are
always pharmacies on-call during the
weekend. The after-hours emergency pharmacy telephone number is ☎ 70/310–
9499. Operators always speak English.

## SHOPS

Most shops are open from noon to 6 on
Monday, 9 to 6 Tuesday through Saturday.
In smaller towns and villages, shops often
close for lunch. Hairdressers are generally
closed Sunday and Monday. In recreation
and resort areas most shops are open from
early morning until late at night and on
weekends. In the centers of Amsterdam,
Rotterdam, and Scheveningen, the coastal
resort of The Hague, shops are open on
Saturday and sometimes on Sunday from
noon to 6. Thursday or Friday is a designated late-night shopping night in the
larger towns. *Markts* (markets) selling
fruit, flowers, and other wares run from
10 to 4 or sometimes 5. Larger settlements
have bakeries open seven days a week in
addition to small *avondwinkels* (late-night
shops) selling food, wine, and toiletries,
which are open from afternoon until midnight or later. Supermarkets are open
weekdays until 8 or 10 PM and Saturday
until 5 or 7 PM.

## BUS TRAVEL

The bus and tram systems within Holland
provide excellent transport links within
cities. Frequent bus services are available
in all cities in the Randstad (the provinces
of North and South Holland, and Utrecht)
and most larger settlements throughout
the rest of Holland; trams run in Amsterdam, The Hague, between Delft and The

Hague, and in Rotterdam. Amsterdam and Rotterdam also have subways, referred to as the metro. Amsterdam's metro system has lines running southeast and southwest; Rotterdam's metro system also has only two lines (east to west and north to south), which extend into the suburbs and cross in the city center for easy transfers. The newer metro trains are cleaner and more agreeable to use, but old and new operate on all lines, so you can't predict what you'll get.

Connexxion is one of the larger companies providing bus and tram services, and it operates across the country. Other companies include BBA and Arriva, in addition to the extra services provided in each larger urban settlement, where, for example, GVB provides additional services in Amsterdam; HTM in The Hague; GVU in Utrecht; and RET in Rotterdam. There are usually maps of each city's network in individual shelters, and diagrams of routes are found on board. Between stops, trams brake only when absolutely necessary, so listen for warning bells if you are walking or cycling near tram lines. Taxis use tram lines, but other cars are allowed to venture onto them only when turning right.

The newer fleets of buses are cleaner, therefore nicer to use, and bus lanes (shared only with taxis) remain uncongested, ensuring that you travel more swiftly than the rest of the traffic in rush hour. If the bus is very crowded, you may have to stand, so hold on to a handrail, as the buses can travel quite fast; to avoid rush hour, don't travel between 7 and 9 in the morning or between 4 and 6:30 in the afternoon.

🚍 Bus Information/Europe-Wide Travel **Arriva** ☎ 0900/9292 [€0.70 per min] ⊕ www.arriva.nl. **BBA** ☎ 0900/9292 [€0.70 per min] ⊕ www.bba.nl. **Connexxion** ☎ 0900/9292 [€0.70 per min] ⊕ www.connexxion.nl.

## TO & FROM HOLLAND BY COACH

Eurolines runs a coach service, which is essentially a well-equipped bus, to transfer passengers between countries but not between cities in the same country. You can travel from London, crossing via the Channel Tunnel or by ferry, or from Brussels to Rotterdam or Amsterdam, but the journeys are exhaustively long. With the advent of EasyJet, it is worth looking into noncommuter-time flights that beat the price of even a Euroline ticket.

🚍 Bus Information/Europe-Wide Travel **Eurolines** In Holland ✉ Rokin 10, Amsterdam ☎ 020/421-7951 or 020/560-8788 ⊕ www.eurolines.nl ✉ In England ✉ 4 Cardiff Rd., Luton, Bedfordshire, LU1 1PP England ☎ 0870/514-3219 in U.K., 845/228-0145 in U.S.

## TICKETS

The same ticket can be used in buses, trams, and metros throughout Holland. Called a *strippenkaart* (strip ticket), a 2- or 3-strip ticket can be bought directly from the bus driver. If you buy a ticket in advance, this works out much cheaper per journey: a 15-strip ticket is €6.50 and a 45-strip ticket costs €19.20. You can buy these at railway stations, post offices, and many bookshops and cigarette kiosks, and they remain valid until there are no further strips left, or for one year from the first stamp.

Each city is divided into zones, and the fare you pay depends on the number of zones you travel through. A small city is one zone (two strips), but to travel across The Hague takes you through four (five strips) zones. These zones are displayed on transport maps. Each journey you make costs one strip plus the number of zones you travel through. When you get on a bus, you show the driver your strippenkaart and simply say where your final destination is, or the number of zones you plan to travel through, and let him or her stamp the strips.

In a metro you have to stamp your ticket yourself in the small yellow machines found near the doors, and you can often do this in a tram. Count the number of strips you need (note that most tourists will be traveling within a one-zone area and therefore the tickets they buy directly from the driver only contain two or three strips), fold your ticket at the bottom of the last strip required, and stamp the final strip in the machine. A stamp on a strip uses that, and the strips above it. Two or more people can travel on the same strippenkaart, but the appropriate number of units must be stamped for each person. The newest trams in Amsterdam (recognizable by their large windows) have ticket control booths in the center of the tram. You may only board the tram there, unless you already have a valid stamp on your ticket, in which case you may board at the front and show your ticket to the driver. On older trams, you can usually board only at the rear, where you will encounter either a ticket controller (*conducteur*) or a stamping machine. This makes for a lot of confusion, as you need to be in the right place when the tram arrives. Follow the lead of other passengers to be sure you don't miss getting on.

The maps at the tram and bus stops show the zonal regions, and there are also map diagrams inside the trams. The stamp indicates the zone where the journey started, and the time, and remains valid for one hour, so you can travel within the zones you have stamped until the hour is up. If you make a mistake and stamp too many strips, tell the driver and he or she will put a sticker over the incorrect stamp.

Teams of ticket inspectors occasionally make spot checks. This doesn't happen often, but if you are checked and you don't have a stamped strippenkaart, you face a €27 fine.

**🚌 Bus Information** Information on public transportation, including schedules, fares for **trains, buses, trams, and ferries** ☎ 0900/9292. **Lost and found** ☎ 020/460-5858.

## CUTTING COSTS

Paying the full travel fare, without using a pass or reduction card, means that toddlers under 3 travel for free; children from 4 to 11 have an automatic 40% reduction, and those over 12 are charged the full fare. If you plan to use buses, trams, and metros more often than four days a week, it is more economical for you to buy a weekly pass. Each different company offers slightly different reductions, so it depends on which cities you want to travel in, the extent of your travel, and the length of time you want the pass to remain valid. Ask a transport information officer which pass suits your plans best.

Ask about all reduction cards and passes by calling the public transport information line, asking at the local transport window in large railway stations, or dropping in to the nearest VVV (tourist office).

### CAR RENTAL

*Auto-verhuur* (car rental) in Holland is best for exploring the center, north, or east of the country, but is to be avoided in the heavily urbanized northwest, known as the Randstad, where the public transport infrastructure is excellent. Signage on country roads is usually pretty good, but be prepared to patiently trail behind cyclists blithely riding two abreast (which is illegal), even when the road is not wide enough for you to pass. Major car-rental companies have boxy Renault cars and Peugeots in various sizes that are always in good condition.

**🚗 Major Agencies Alamo** ☎ 800/522-9696 ⊕ www.alamo.com. **Avis** ☎ 800/331-1084, 800/879-2847 in Canada, 0870/606-0100 in U.K., 02/9353-9000 in Australia, 09/526-2847 in New Zealand ⊕ www.avis.com. **Budget** ☎ 800/527-0700 ⊕ www.budget.com. **Dollar** ☎ 800/800-6000, 0800/085-4578 in U.K. ⊕ www.dollar.com. **Hertz** ☎ 800/654-3001, 800/263-0600 in Canada, 0870/844-8844 in U.K., 02/9669-2444 in Australia, 09/256-8690 in New Zealand ⊕ www.hertz.com. **National Car Rental** ☎ 800/227-7368 ⊕ www.nationalcar.com.

## CUTTING COSTS

Most major American rental-car companies have offices or affiliates in Holland, but the rates are generally better if you make a reservation from abroad rather than from within Holland.

For a good deal, book through a travel agent who will shop around. Do look into wholesalers, companies that do not own fleets but rent in bulk from those that do and often offer better rates than traditional car-rental operations. Prices are best during off-peak periods. Rentals booked through wholesalers often must be paid for before you leave home.

**🚗 Wholesalers Auto Europe** ☎ 800/223-5555 or 207/842-2000 📠 207/842-2222 ⊕ www.autoeurope.com. **Destination Europe Resources** (DER) ✉ 9501 W. Devon Ave., Rosemont, IL 60018

☏ 800/782-2424 🖷 800/282-7474. **Europe by Car**
☏ 800/223-1516 or 212/581-3040 🖷 212/246-1458
⊕ www.europebycar.com. **Kemwel** ☏ 877/820-
0668 or 800/678-0678 🖷 207/842-2124 or 866/726-
6726 ⊕ www.kemwel.com.

## INSURANCE

When driving a rented car you are generally responsible for any damage to or loss of the vehicle. Collision policies that car-rental companies sell for European rentals typically do not cover stolen vehicles. Before you rent—and purchase collision or theft coverage—see what coverage you already have under the terms of your personal auto-insurance policy and credit cards.

## SURCHARGES

Before you pick up a car in one city and leave it in another, ask about drop-off charges or one-way service fees, which can be substantial. Also inquire about early-return policies; some rental agencies charge extra if you return the car before the time specified in your contract while others give you a refund for the days not used. Most agencies note the tank's fuel level on your contract; to avoid a hefty refueling fee, return the car with the same tank level. If the tank was full, refill it just before you turn in the car, but be aware that gas stations near the rental outlet may overcharge. It's almost never a deal to buy a tank of gas with the car when you rent it; the understanding is that you'll return it empty, but some fuel usually remains.

## CAR TRAVEL

A network of well-maintained superhighways and secondary roads makes car travel convenient, but traffic is exceptionally heavy around the bigger cities, especially on the roads in the Randstad, and those approaching the North Sea beaches on summer weekends. There are no tolls on roads or highways, and only one tunnel has a toll: Kiltunnel, near Dordrecht, which costs €3.40 round-trip.

Your driver's license may not be recognized outside your home country. International driving permits (IDPs) are available from the American and Canadian automobile associations and, in the United

Kingdom, from the Automobile Association and Royal Automobile Club. These international permits, valid only in conjunction with your regular driver's license, are universally recognized; having one may save you a problem with local authorities.

## FROM THE U.K.

Take the train or drive through the Chunnel to the north coast of France. From Calais, you can drive along the coast in the direction of Ghent, Antwerp (both in Belgium) to Breda, Rotterdam, and Amsterdam.

## EMERGENCY SERVICES

If you haven't joined a motoring organization, the **ANWB** (Royal Dutch Touring Club) charges €100 for 24-hour road assistance. If you aren't a member, you can call the ANWB after breaking down, but you must pay a €78 on-the-spot membership charge. Emergency crews may not accept credit cards or checks when they pick you up. If your automobile association is affiliated with the **Alliance International du Tourisme** (AIT), and you have proof of membership, you are entitled to free help.

To call for assistance push the help button on any yellow ANWB phone located every kilometer (½ mi) on highways, and a dispatch operator immediately finds you. Alternatively, phone their 24-hour emergency line or their information number for details about their road rescue service.

🚩 **ANWB (Royal Dutch Touring Club)** ☏ 0800/0888 emergency number, 0800/0503 office number ⊕ www.anwb.nl.

## GASOLINE

Gas stations are generally open Monday–Saturday 6 or 7 AM–8 PM or later, with longer opening times on Sunday. But note that in some towns, gas stations can be closed Sunday. All stations have self-service pumps. Gas stations on the motorways are open 24 hours. Unleaded four-star costs about €1.30 per liter.

## PARKING

Parking space is at a premium in Amsterdam as in most towns, but especially in the *centrum* (historic town centers), which have narrow, one-way streets with large areas given over to pedestrians. Most towns are metered from 9 AM to 7 PM, so it is a good idea (if not the only option) to **leave your car only in designated parking areas.** *Parkeren* (parking lots) are indicated by a white "P" in a blue square. Illegally parked cars get clamped and, after 24 hours, if you haven't paid for the clamp to be removed, towed. If you get clamped, a sticker on the windshield indicates where you should go to pay the fine (from €63 to more than €100).

### ROAD CONDITIONS

Holland has an excellent road network, but there is a great deal of traffic using it every day, as you might expect from a country with a very high population density. In cities, you will usually be driving on narrow one-way streets and sharing the road with other cars, buses, trams, and bicyclists, so remain alert at all times. When driving on smaller roads in cities, you must yield to traffic coming from the right. Traffic lights are located before intersections, rather than after intersections as in the United States. Traffic circles are very popular and come in all sizes. Driving outside of cities is very easy; roads are very smooth and clearly marked with signs. Traffic during peak hours (7–9 and 4–7) is constantly plagued with *files* (traffic jams), especially in the western part of the country. If you are going to drive here, you must be assertive. Drivers are very aggressive; they tailgate and change lanes at very high speeds. All road signs use the international driving symbols. Electronic message boards are used on some freeways to warn of traffic jams and to slow traffic down to 90, 70, or 50 km per hour.

### ROAD MAPS

Michelin maps are regularly updated and are the best countrywide maps; they offer the advantage of being consistent with Michelin maps of other countries you may visit. They are available at newsagents and bookshops across the country. Free city maps are generally available at VVV (tourist offices), and more detailed city maps can be bought at bookshops or large gas stations.

### RULES OF THE ROAD

Driving is on the right, and regulations are largely as in Britain and the United States. Speed limits are 120 kph (75 mph) on superhighways, 100 kph (62 mph) on urban-area highways, and 50 kph (30 mph) on suburban roads.

For safe driving, go with the flow, stay in the slow lane unless you want to pass, and make way for faster cars wanting to pass you. In cities and towns, approach crossings with care; local drivers may exercise the principle of priority for traffic from the right with some abandon. Although the majority of cyclists observe the stoplights and general road signs, many do not expect you, even as a driver, to give way. The latest ruling states that unless otherwise marked, all traffic coming from the right has priority, even bicycles.

The driver and front-seat passenger are required to wear seat belts, and backseat passengers are also required to wear available seat belts. Fines for driving after drinking are heavy, including the suspension of license and the additional possibility of six months' imprisonment.

### CHILDREN IN HOLLAND

Be sure to plan ahead and involve your youngsters as you outline your trip. When packing, include things to keep them busy en route. On sightseeing days, try to schedule activities of special interest to your children. If you are renting a car, don't forget to **arrange for a car seat** when you reserve.

Discounts are prevalent, so always ask about a child's discount before purchasing tickets. Children under a certain age ride free on buses and trams. Children under 18 are sometimes admitted free or have a lowered rate on entry to museums and galleries. If you are renting a car, don't forget to arrange for a car seat when you reserve. For general advice about traveling with children, consult *Fodor's FYI: Travel with Your Baby* (available in bookstores everywhere).

### FLYING

If your children are two or older, ask about children's airfares. As a general rule, infants under two not occupying a seat fly at greatly reduced fares or even for free. But if you want to guarantee a seat for an infant, you have to pay full fare. Consider flying during off-peak days and times; most airlines will grant an infant a seat without a ticket if there are available seats. When booking, confirm carry-on allowances if you're traveling with infants. In general, for babies charged 10% to 50% of the adult fare you are allowed one carry-on bag and a collapsible stroller; if the flight is full, the stroller may have to be checked or you may be limited to less.

Experts agree that it's a good idea to use safety seats aloft for children weighing less than 40 pounds. Airlines set their own policies: if you use a safety seat, U.S. carriers usually require that the child be ticketed, even if he or she is young enough to ride free, because the seats must be strapped into regular seats. And even if you pay the full adult fare for the seat, it may be worth it, especially on longer trips. Do **check your airline's policy about using safety seats during takeoff and landing.** Safety seats are not allowed everywhere in the plane, so get your seat assignments as early as possible.

When reserving, request children's meals or a freestanding bassinet (not available at all airlines) if you need them. But note that bulkhead seats, where you must sit to use the bassinet, may lack an overhead bin or storage space on the floor.

Most hotels in Holland allow children under a certain age to stay in their parents' room at no extra charge, but others charge for them as extra adults; be sure to find out the cutoff age for children's discounts.

### SIGHTS & ATTRACTIONS
Places that are especially appealing to children are indicated by a rubber-duckie icon (🐥) in the margin.

### CUSTOMS & DUTIES
When shopping abroad, keep receipts for all purchases. Upon reentering the country, **be ready to show customs officials what you've bought.** Pack purchases together in an easily accessible place. If you think a duty is incorrect, appeal the assessment. If you object to the way your clearance was handled, note the inspector's badge number. In either case, first ask to see a supervisor. If the problem isn't resolved, write to the appropriate authorities, beginning with the port director at your point of entry.

You are allowed to bring no more than 5 kilos of flowers, bulbs, plants, and fruit into Holland. Animal products and illegal drugs, including marijuana, may not be imported. If you need to bring in prescription drugs, bring your prescription as well.

### IN CANADA
Canadian residents who have been out of Canada for at least seven days may bring in C$750 worth of goods duty-free. If you've been away fewer than seven days but more than 48 hours, the duty-free allowance drops to C$200. If your trip lasts 24 to 48 hours, the allowance is C$50; if the goods are worth more than C$50, you must pay full duty on all of the goods. You may not pool allowances with family members. Goods claimed under the C$750 exemption may follow you by mail; those claimed under the lesser exemptions must accompany you. Alcohol and tobacco products may be included in the seven-day and 48-hour exemptions but not in the 24-hour exemption. If you meet the age requirements of the province or territory through which you reenter Canada, you may bring in, duty-free, 1.5 liters of wine *or* 1.14 liters (40 imperial ounces) of liquor *or* 24 12-ounce cans or bottles of beer or ale. Also, if you meet the local age requirement for tobacco products, you may bring in, duty-free, 200 cigarettes, 50 cigars or cigarillos, and 200 grams of tobacco. You may have to pay a minimum duty on tobacco products, regardless of whether or not you exceed your personal exemption. Check ahead of time with the Canada Border Services Agency or the Department of Agriculture for policies regarding meat products, seeds, plants, and fruits.

You may send an unlimited number of gifts (only one gift per recipient, however) worth up to C$60 each duty-free to Canada. Label the package UNSOLICITED

GIFT—VALUE UNDER $60. Alcohol and tobacco are excluded.

**⑦ Canada Border Services Agency** ✉ Customs Information Services, 191 Laurier Ave. W, 15th fl., Ottawa, Ontario K1A 0L5 ☎ 800/461-9999 in Canada, 204/983-3500, 506/636-5064 ⊕ www.cbsa.gc.ca.

## IN THE U.S.

U.S. residents who have been out of the country for at least 48 hours may bring home, for personal use, $800 worth of foreign goods duty-free, as long as they haven't used the $800 allowance or any part of it in the past 30 days. This exemption may include 1 liter of alcohol (for travelers 21 and older), 200 cigarettes, and 100 non-Cuban cigars. Family members from the same household who are traveling together may pool their $800 personal exemptions. For fewer than 48 hours, the duty-free allowance drops to $200, which may include 50 cigarettes, 10 non-Cuban cigars, and 150 ml of alcohol (or 150 ml of perfume containing alcohol). The $200 allowance cannot be combined with other individuals' exemptions, and if you exceed it, the full value of all the goods will be taxed. Antiques, which U.S. Customs and Border Protection defines as objects more than 100 years old, enter duty-free, as do original works of art done entirely by hand, including paintings, drawings, and sculptures. This doesn't apply to folk art or handicrafts, which are in general dutiable.

You may also send packages home duty-free, with a limit of one parcel per addressee per day (except alcohol or tobacco products or perfume worth more than $5). You can mail up to $200 worth of goods for personal use; label the package PERSONAL USE and attach a list of its contents and their retail value. If the package contains your used personal belongings, mark it AMERICAN GOODS RETURNED to avoid paying duties. You may send up to $100 worth of goods as a gift; mark the package UNSOLICITED GIFT. Mailed items do not affect your duty-free allowance on your return.

To avoid paying duty on foreign-made high-ticket items you already own and will take on your trip, register them with a local customs office before you leave the country. Consider filing a Certificate of Registration for laptops, cameras, watches, and other digital devices identified with serial numbers or other permanent markings; you can keep the certificate for other trips. Otherwise, bring a sales receipt or insurance form to show that you owned the item before you left the United States.

For more about duties, restricted items, and other information about international travel, check out U.S. Customs and Border Protection's online brochure, *Know Before You Go.* You can also file complaints on the U.S. Customs and Border Protection Web site.

**⑦ U.S. Customs and Border Protection** ✉ For inquiries and complaints: 1300 Pennsylvania Ave. NW, Washington, DC 20229 ☎ 877/227-5551 or 202/354-1000 ⊕ www.cbp.gov.

## DISABILITIES & ACCESSIBILITY

Although it is said that Holland is a world leader in providing facilities for people with disabilities, the most obvious difficulty that people with disabilities face in Holland is negotiating the cobbled streets of the older town centers. Businesses in the tourism and leisure industry are, however, making their premises more easily accessible, and when they are found to be independently accessible for wheelchair users, the International Accessibility Symbol (IAS) is awarded. For information on accessibility nationwide, relevant to travelers with disabilities, contact Access Wise (whose official title is the Vakantie Informatie Punt, or Holiday Information Center) or the NIZW (Nederlands Instituut voor Zorg en Welzijn, or National Institute for Care and Welfare).

Some cinemas and theaters have a forward-looking approach and are accessible. Train and bus stations are equipped with special telephones, elevators, and toilets in larger stations, and the metro is accessible to users of specific wheelchairs. Most trams, however, have high steps, making them inaccessible to wheelchair users, although the newer trams have low-mount doors. Visitors can obtain special passes to **ensure free escort travel on Dutch trains—** for general assistance contact the Nederlandse Spoorwegen (or NS, the

Netherlands Railways) before 2 PM at least one day in advance, or by 2 PM Friday for travel on Saturday, Sunday, or Monday, or public holidays, using the number below. For information on tours and exchanges for travelers with disabilities, contact Access Wise (Vakantie Informatie Punt), whose bank of information is partly sourced from Mobility International.

🚹 **Local Resources Access Wise** ☎ 026/370-6161 🖷 026/377-6420. **Nederlandse Spoorwegen** (Netherlands Railways) ☎ 030/230-5566. **NIZW** (National Institute of Care and Welfare) ✒ Postbus 19152, 3501 DD Utrecht ☎ 030/230-6311. **Wheelchair Hire** ✉ Haarlemmermeerstraat 49-53, 1058 JP Amsterdam ☎ 020/615-7188, €20 per wk, with a security deposit of €200.

## TRAVEL AGENCIES

In the United States, the Americans with Disabilities Act requires that travel firms serve the needs of all travelers. Some agencies specialize in working with people with disabilities.

🚹 **Travelers with Mobility Problems Access Adventures/B. Roberts Travel** ✉ 206 Chestnutt Ridge Rd., Rochester, NY 14610 ☎ 800/444-6540 ⊕ www.brobertstravel.com, run by a former physical-rehabilitation counselor. **CareVacations** ✉ No. 5, 5110-50 Ave., Leduc, Alberta T9E 6V4 Canada ☎ 877/478-7827 or 780/986-6404 🖷 780/986-8332 ⊕ www.carevacations.com, for group tours and cruise vacations. **Flying Wheels Travel** ✉ 143 W. Bridge St., Box 382, Owatonna, MN 55060 ☎ 507/451-5005 🖷 507/451-1685 ⊕ www.flyingwheelstravel.com.

🚹 **Travelers with Developmental Disabilities Sprout** ✉ 893 Amsterdam Ave., New York, NY 10025 ☎ 888/222-9575 or 212/222-9575 🖷 212/222-9768 ⊕ www.gosprout.org.

## EATING & DRINKING

The restaurants we list are the cream of the crop in each price category. Properties indicated by a ✕☐ are lodging establishments whose restaurant warrants a special trip. For price categories, *see* the price charts found under the Where to Eat and Where to Stay sections in Chapter 1 (Amsterdam) and under the About the Restaurants & Hotels sections in the regional Chapters 2, 3, 4, 5, and 6.

## MEALS & SPECIALTIES

Dutch cuisine is very simple and filling. A typical Dutch *ontbijt* (breakfast) consists of *brood* (bread), *kaas* (cheese), *hard gekookte ei* (hard-boiled eggs), ham, yogurt, and fruit.

Lunch is usually a *boterham* (sandwich) on a soft roll or a baguette. Salads and warm dishes are also popular for lunch. One specialty is an *uitsmijter*: two pieces of bread with fried eggs, ham, and cheese, garnished with pickles and onions. *Pannenkoeken* (pancakes) are a favorite lunch treat topped with ham and cheese or fruit and a thick *stroop* (syrup).

A popular afternoon snack is *frites* (french fries); try them with curry ketchup and onions, called *frite speciaal*, with a *kroket* (a fried, breaded meat roll) on the side. Another snack is whole *haring* (herring) served with raw onions. Stay away from *frikandel*, a long hot dog that can contain anything.

*Diner* (dinner) usually consists of three courses: an appetizer, main course, and dessert, and many restaurants have special prix-fixe deals. Beverages are always charged separately. Dutch specialties include *erwtensoep* (a thick pea soup with sausage), *zalm* (salmon), *gerookte paling* (smoked eel), *hutspot* (beef stew), *aardappel au gratin* (potato au gratin), and *lamsvlees* (lamb). Beef should be avoided; it is usually tough and stringy. An oft-seen dessert is *Dame Blanche,* meaning White Lady and made of vanilla ice cream with hot fudge and whipped cream. Holland is famous for its cheeses, including Gouda, Edam, and Limburger. Indonesian cuisine is also very popular here, and a favorite lunch or dinner is *rijsttafel,* which literally means "rice table" and refers to a prix-fixe meal that includes a feast of 10–20 small spicy dishes.

## MEALTIMES

Restaurants open for lunch start at 11 AM, while restaurants opening for dinner will accept guests as early as 5 or 6 PM, closing at midnight. Most restaurants are closed Monday. Unless otherwise noted, the restaurants listed in this guide are open daily for lunch and dinner.

## RESERVATIONS & DRESS
Reservations are always a good idea; we mention them only when they're essential or not accepted. Book as far ahead as you can, and reconfirm as soon as you arrive. (Large parties should always call ahead to check the reservations policy.) We mention dress only when men are required to wear a jacket or a jacket and tie.

## ELECTRICITY
To use electric-powered equipment purchased in the United States or Canada, **bring a converter and adapter.** The electrical current in Holland is 220 volts, 50 cycles alternating current (AC); wall outlets take Continental-type plugs, with two round prongs.

If your appliances are dual-voltage, you'll need only an adapter. Don't use 110-volt outlets marked FOR SHAVERS ONLY for high-wattage appliances such as blow-dryers. Most laptops operate equally well on 110 and 220 volts and so require only an adapter.

## EMBASSIES
🏚 Australia **Australian Embassy** ✉ Carnegielaan 4, The Hague ☎ 070/310–8200.
🏚 Canada **Canadian Embassy** ✉ Sophialaan 7, The Hague ☎ 070/311–1600.
🏚 New Zealand **New Zealand Embassy** ✉ Carnegielaan 10/ET4, The Hague ☎ 070/346–9324.
🏚 U.K. **British Embassy** ✉ Lange Voorhout 10, The Hague ☎ 070/427–0427.
🏚 U.S. **U.S. Embassy** ✉ Lange Voorhout 102, The Hague ☎ 070/310–9209.

## EMERGENCIES
**Police, ambulance, and fire** (☎ 112 toll-free 24-hr switchboard for emergencies). The 24-hour help-line service **Afdeling Inlichtingen Apotheken** (☎ 020/694–8709) (*apotheken* means "pharmacy") can direct you to your nearest open pharmacy; there is a rotating schedule to cover evenings, nights, and weekends—details are also posted at your local *apotheken,* and in your area's regional newspaper. The **Centraal Doktorsdienst/Atacom** (Medical Center; ☎ 020/592–3434) offers a 24-hour English-speaking help line providing advice about medical symptoms. In the case

of minor accidents, phone **directory inquiries** (☎ 0900/8008) to get the number for the outpatients' department at your nearest *ziekenhuis* (hospital). **TBB** (☎ 020/570–9595 or 0900/821–2230) is a 24-hour dental service that refers callers to a dentist (or *tandarts*). Operators can also give details of pharmacies open outside normal hours.

For less-urgent police matters, call the **central number** (☎ 0900/8844), or call directory inquiries for your local station (⇨ Telephones, Directory & Operator Assistance). For car breakdowns and other car-related emergencies call the big automobile agency in Holland, the ANWB (⇨ Car Travel, Emergency Services).

Note that all numbers quoted above with the code 020 are for Amsterdam and surrounding area only, indicating that instead of a national central number for that service, help lines are centered on large towns, so also *see* Emergencies *in* the A to Z section in this guide's regional chapters.

## ETIQUETTE & BEHAVIOR
When visiting a Catholic or Protestant church service, you should not wear shorts. When visiting a mosque, women should wear long sleeves and pants or a knee-length skirt, and a scarf on their heads. If you are visiting a Dutch person's home, it is appropriate to bring a bouquet of flowers or a bottle of wine as a hostess gift. When greeting people, you should shake their hand and introduce yourself if you have not already done so. It is usual to greet family and close friends with a two-cheek or three-cheek kiss. Common phrases are: *goede dag* (good day), *graag* (please), and *dank U wel* (thank you).

## GAY & LESBIAN TRAVEL
Whether or not Amsterdam is the "Gay Capital of Europe," its reputation as being more tolerant of gays and lesbians than most other major world cities makes it a very popular mecca for gay and lesbian travelers. Legislation passed in April 2001 granted same-sex couples the right to marry when, previously, gay and lesbian couples could just register as partners. It's illegal for hotels to refuse accommodation

to gays and lesbians, and there are details available of those specifically gay-owned. The Gay & Lesbian Switchboard can provide information on hotels that are gay- and lesbian-friendly.

🔳 Local Contact Helpful gay and lesbian organizations include **COC National** ✉ Rozenstraat 8, Jordaan, Amsterdam ☎ 020/623-4596. COC's head office deals with all matters relating to gays and lesbians. The **local branch** ✉ Rozenstraat 14, Amsterdam ☎ 020/626-3087 is a busy meeting place, dealing with the social side, and has an info-coffee shop. Well-informed members of the **Gay & Lesbian Switchboard** ☎ 020/623-6565 dispense information and advice, and staff at **SAD Schorerstichting** ✉ PC Hooftstraat 5, 107117 BL Amsterdam ☎ 020/662-4206 provide STD tests as well as general information and HIV advice.

🔳 Gay- & Lesbian-Friendly Travel Agencies **Different Roads Travel** ✉ 1017 N. LaCienega Blvd., Suite 308, West Hollywood, CA 90069 ☎ 800/429-8747 or 310/289-6000 [Ext. 14 for both] 🖷 310/855-0323 ✑ lgernert@tzell.com. **Kennedy Travel** ✉ 130 W. 42nd St., Suite 401, New York, NY 10036 ☎ 800/237-7433 or 212/840-8659 🖷 212/730-2269 🌐 www.kennedytravel.com. **Now, Voyager** ✉ 4406 18th St., San Francisco, CA 94114 ☎ 800/255-6951 or 415/626-1169 🖷 415/626-8626 🌐 www.nowvoyager.com. **Skylink Travel and Tour/Flying Dutchmen Travel** ✉ 1455 N. Dutton Ave., Suite A, Santa Rosa, CA 95401 ☎ 800/225-5759 or 707/546-9888 🖷 707/636-0951; serving lesbian travelers.

## HEALTH

*Drogists* (pharmacists) sell toiletries and nonprescription drugs ( ⇨ *also* Emergencies). For prescription drugs go to an *apotheek* (pharmacy). While you are traveling in Holland, the Centers for Disease Control and Prevention (CDC) in Atlanta recommends that you observe health precautions similar to those that would apply while traveling in the United States.

🔳 Medical Care For inquiries about medical care, contact the national health service agency: **GGD Nederland** 🌐 www.gdd.nl.

### OVER-THE-COUNTER REMEDIES

You will find most standard over-the-counter medications, such as aspirin and acetaminophen, in the *drogisterij* (drugstore). You will have difficulty finding antihistamines and cold medications, like Sudafed, without a prescription.

## HOLIDAYS

*Nationale feestdagen* (national holidays) are New Year's Day (January 1); Good Friday; Easter Sunday and Monday; Koninginnedag (Queen's Day, April 30); Remembrance Day (May 4); Liberation Day (May 5); Ascension Day; Whitsunday (Pentecost) and Monday; and Christmas. During these holidays, banks and schools are closed, as are many shops, restaurants, and museums. Some businesses close for Remembrance Day, and on this day throughout Holland, there is a two-minute silent pause from 8 to 8:02 PM, and even traffic stops. Take note and please respect this custom.

## INSURANCE

The most useful travel-insurance plan is a comprehensive policy that includes coverage for trip cancellation and interruption, default, trip delay, and medical expenses (with a waiver for preexisting conditions).

Without insurance you'll lose all or most of your money if you cancel your trip, regardless of the reason. Default insurance covers you if your tour operator, airline, or cruise line goes out of business—the chances of which have been increasing. Trip-delay covers expenses that arise because of bad weather or mechanical delays. Study the fine print when comparing policies.

If you're traveling internationally, a key component of travel insurance is coverage for medical bills incurred if you get sick on the road. Such expenses aren't generally covered by Medicare or private policies. U.K. residents can buy a travel-insurance policy valid for most vacations taken during the year in which it's purchased (but check preexisting-condition coverage). British and Australian citizens need extra medical coverage when traveling overseas.

Always **buy travel policies directly from the insurance company**; if you buy them from a cruise line, airline, or tour operator that goes out of business you probably won't be covered for the agency or operator's default, a major risk. Before making any purchase, review your existing health and home-owner's policies to find what they cover away from home.

**⚏ Travel Insurers** In the United States: **Access America** ✉ 2805 N. Parham Rd., Richmond, VA 23294 ☏ 800/284-8300 🖷 800/346-9265 or 804/673-1469 ⊕ www.accessamerica.com. **Travel Guard International** ✉ 1145 Clark St., Stevens Point, WI 54481 ☏ 800/826-1300 or 715/345-1041 🖷 800/955-8785 or 715/345-1990 ⊕ www.travelguard.com. ⚏ In Australia: **Insurance Council of Australia** ✉ 56 Pitt St., Level 3, Sydney, NSW 2000 ☏ 02/9253-5100 🖷 02/9253-5111 ⊕ www.ica.com.au. In Canada: **RBC Insurance** ✉ 6880 Financial Dr., Mississauga, Ontario L5N 7Y5 ☏ 800/387-4357 or 905/816-2559 🖷 888/298-6458 ⊕ www.rbcinsurance.com. In New Zealand: **Insurance Council of New Zealand** ✉ 111-115 Customhouse Quay, Level 7, Box 474, Wellington ☏ 04/472-5230 🖷 04/473-3011 ⊕ www.icnz.org.nz. In the United Kingdom: **Association of British Insurers** ✉ 51 Gresham St., London EC2V 7HQ ☏ 020/7600-3333 🖷 020/7696-8999 ⊕ www.abi.org.uk.

## LANGUAGE

There are two official Dutch languages: Dutch, used across the country, and Fries (Frisian), used in the north. In Amsterdam, as in all the other major cities and towns, English is widely spoken. State schools teach English to pupils as young as eight, and with English TV, youngsters often have a smattering of authentic-sounding vocabulary before they even get into learning English at school. Not only is it the country's strong second language, but the general public is very happy to help English-speaking visitors, to the extent that even if you ask in Dutch, they answer cheerfully in English. Signs and notices often have duplicated information in English, if not more languages. Even in more remote villages you can usually find someone who speaks at least a little English.

## LODGING

Assume that hotels operate on the European Plan (EP, with no meals) unless we specify that they use either the Continental Plan (CP, with a Continental breakfast), Breakfast Plan (BP, with a full breakfast), or the Modified American Plan (MAP, with breakfast and dinner) or are all-inclusive (including all meals and most activities).

Accommodations in the incredibly popular Randstad region are at a premium, so **you should book well in advance.** The lodgings we review in this book are the cream of the crop in each price category. We always list the facilities that are available—but we don't specify whether they cost extra: when pricing accommodations, always ask what's included and what costs extra. Extra fees can be charged for everything from breakfast to use of parking facilities. For price categories, consult the price charts found under the Where to Eat and Where to Stay sections in Chapter 1 (Amsterdam) and under the About the Restaurants & Hotels sections in Chapters 2, 3, 4, 5, and 6.

Properties indicated by a ✕⌂ are lodging establishments whose restaurants warrant a special trip.

### APARTMENT & VILLA [OR HOUSE] RENTALS

If you want a home base that's roomy enough for a family and comes with cooking facilities, consider a furnished rental. These can save you money, especially if you're traveling with a group. Home-exchange directories sometimes list rentals as well as exchanges.

**City Mundo** has an excellent network, and whatever your requirements, this creative city specialist directory will try to hook you up to your ideal spot, whether that's in a windmill or a houseboat. The price drops the longer you stay, up to the maximum of 21 nights, with a minimum of 2 nights. Book online, at the group's Web site ( ⇨ Web Sites), where visuals and descriptions are constantly updated as new facilities come in.

It's also worth contacting **Holiday Link,** an agency that provides contacts and addresses for home-exchange holidays and house-sitting during holiday periods; bed-and-breakfasts; rentals of private houses in Holland; and budget accommodations. The company is part of **HomeLink International,** the worldwide vacation organization in more than 50 countries, so it knows what's what.

Get in touch with the VVV (tourist information offices) of the region you plan to travel to, as they all have extensive accommodations listings. They can book reservations for you, according to your specific accommodations requirements. Call the number below for the local office in the area you plan to visit.

🔳 International Agents **Hideaways International** ✉ 767 Islington St., Portsmouth, NH 03801 ☎ 800/843-4433 or 603/430-4433 🖷 603/430-4444 ⊕ www.hideaways.com, annual membership $185. **Villas International** ✉ 4340 Redwood Hwy., Suite D309, San Rafael, CA 94903 ☎ 800/221-2260 or 415/499-9490 🖷 415/499-9491 ⊕ www.villasintl. com.

🔳 Local Agents **Center Parcs** 🕮 Admiraliteitskade 40, 3063 ED Rotterdam ☎ 010/498-9898 or 0900/660-6600 [€0.20 per min] ⊕ www.centerparcs.nl. **City Mundo** ✉ Schinkelkade 47 II, 1075VK Amsterdam ☎ 020/676-5270 ⊕ www.citymundo.com. **Duinrell Holiday Cottages** ✉ Duinrell 1, 2242 JP Wassenaar ☎ 070/515-5258 🖷 070/515-5370 ⊕ www.duinrell.nl. **Holiday Link** 🕮 Postbus 70-155, 9704 AD Groningen ☎ 050/313-2424 ⊕ www.holidaylink.com. **Holland Tulip Parcs** ✉ Marijke Meustraat 112, 4818 LW Breda ☎ 076/520-0099 🖷 076/531-7920 ⊕ www.hollandtulipparcs.nl. **Landal Green Parks** 🕮 Box 910, 2270 AX Voorburg ☎ 070/300-3506 🖷 070/300-3515 ⊕ www.landalgreenparks.com. **VVV tourist offices** ☎ 0900/400-4040 [€0.55 per min]. **Zilverberk Parken** 🕮 Box 2067, 3800 CB Amersfoort ☎ 0900/8810 [€0.20 per min] or 033/465-6300 🖷 033/461-6003 ⊕ www.zilverberk.nl.

## BED & BREAKFASTS

You'll find a large choice of bed-and-breakfasts scattered throughout the country. Be sure to reserve in advance via Web or phone. Prices vary widely from €20 to €40 per person.

🔳 Reservation Services **Bed and Breakfast Directory** ✉ FreePost MID23985, Burton on Trent, DE13 7BR, England ⊕ www.bedandbreakfast-directory. co.uk. **Bed & Breakfast Holland** ☎ 020/615-7527 ⊕ www.bbholland.com. **Bed and Breakfast Service Nederland** ✉ Veilig Oord 60, 5531 XC Bladel ☎ 0497/330-300 🖷 0497/330-811 ⊕ www. bedandbreakfast.nl. **City Mundo** ✉ Schinkelkade 47 II, 1075 VK Amsterdam ☎ 020/676-5270 ⊕ www. citymundo.com. **Holiday Link** 🕮 Postbus 70-155, 9704 AD Groningen ☎ 050/313-2424 ⊕ www. holidaylink.com. **What's Wanted Group** ✉ Box 153, Hove, BN3 6UZ, England ⊕ www. allbedandbreakfast.com.

## CAMPING

Camping is a good way to find reasonably priced accommodations in an otherwise overcrowded resort, and camping gear can be rented at most resorts across Holland; contact your travel agent or the **ANWB** (Royal Dutch Touring Club) for details. Permits and memberships are not required for camping, but rates are cheaper if you book with one. Make sure you **stay only on authorized campsites**—if caught *vrij kamperen* (camping for free), or sleeping in your car, you face a €90 fine.

**You need your passport or alternative ID to register** on arrival at your campsite, unless you plan to stay on a Green campsite, for which you need ANWB's "Green" camping membership. Green sites are on farms where children can get involved feeding animals. Details on tented-only *natuurcampingen* (sites in protected environments) can also be obtained from the ANWB.

The ANWB publishes *Camping Gids Nederland* (Guide to Camping in Holland); although it is in Dutch, it lists the contact details of every site in Holland and has a lot of visuals. It's available from ANWB stores and larger bookshops across Holland for €9.95. Call the ANWB office for any questions about camping, to obtain "Green" campsite membership, or to find your nearest ANWB shop. When you dial, just hold the line for an information officer.

The local VVV (tourist information office) can also provide you with addresses of campsites around Holland. Call the VVV number below for sites in the area you plan to visit. Camp rates are seasonal, but for two people with a car and a tent expect to pay between €19 and €33, depending on where the campsite is and what facilities it offers.

🔳 Directory of Campgrounds **ANWB** (Royal Dutch Touring Club) ☎ 0800/0888 emergency number, 0800/0503 office number. **VVV Central Tourist Offices** ☎ 0900/400-4040 [€0.55 per min]. *See also* the A to Z section at the end of the appropriate regional chapter to find **VVVs** in the area you plan to visit.

## HOME EXCHANGES

**ⓘ Exchange Clubs HomeLink USA** ✉ 2937 N.W. 9th Terr., Wilton Manors, FL 33311 ☎ 800/638-3841 or 954/566-2687 📠 954/566-2783 ⊕ www. homelink.org; $75 yearly for a listing and online access; $45 additional to receive directories. **Intervac U.S.** ✉ 30 Corte San Fernando, Tiburon, CA 94920 ☎ 800/756-4663 📠 415/435-7440 ⊕ www. intervacus.com; $128 yearly for a listing, online access, and a catalog; $68 without catalog.

## HOSTELS

No matter what your age, you can **save on lodging costs by staying at hostels** (*jeugdherbergen*). In some 4,500 locations in more than 70 countries around the world, Hostelling International (HI), the umbrella group for a number of national youth-hostel associations, offers single-sex, dorm-style beds and, at many hostels, rooms for couples and family accommodations. Amsterdam is world famous for two beloved hostels: the Flying Pig Palace and the Stayokay Hostel in Vondelpark. Membership in any HI national hostel association, like the Dutch affiliation NJHC, or Nederlandse Jeugdherberg Centrale, is open to travelers of all ages and allows you to stay in HI-affiliated hostels at member rates; one-year membership is about $28 for adults (C$35 for a two-year minimum membership in Canada, £15 in the United Kingdom, A$52 in Australia, and NZ$40 in New Zealand); hostels run about $10–$25 (€11–€27.60) per night. Members have priority if the hostel is full; they're also eligible for discounts around the world, even on rail and bus travel in some countries. NJHC (Stayokay/ Nederlandse Jeudgherberg Centrale) has an excellent Web site with visuals and information about the many hostels on offer in Holland.

**ⓘ Organizations Hostelling International– Canada** ✉ 205 Catherine St., Suite 400, Ottawa, Ontario K2P 1C3 ☎ 800/663-5777 or 613/237-7884 📠 613/237-7868 ⊕ www.hihostels.ca. **Hostelling International–USA** ✉ 8401 Colesville Rd., Suite 600, Silver Spring, MD 20910 ☎ 301/495-1240 📠 301/495-6697 ⊕ www.hiusa.org. **NJHC** (Dutch Youth Hostel Association,) ⊠ Box 9191, 1006 AD Amsterdam ☎ 020/639-2929 📠 020/639-0199. **Stayokay (Nederlandse Jeugdherberg Centrale)** ☎ 010/264-6064 ⊕ www.stayokay.com. **YHA Australia** ✉ 422 Kent St., Sydney, NSW 2001 ☎ 02/9261-1111 📠 02/9261-1969 ⊕ www.yha.com.au. **YHA England and Wales** ✉ Trevelyan House, Dimple Rd., Matlock, Derbyshire DE4 3YH England ☎ 0870/870-8808, 0870/770-8868, 0162/959-2600 📠 0870/770-6127 ⊕ www.yha.org.uk. **YHA New Zealand** ✉ Moorhouse City, 166 Moorhouse Ave., Level 1, Box 436, Christchurch ☎ 0800/278-299 or 03/379-9970 📠 03/365-4476 ⊕ www.yha.org.nz.

## HOTELS

In line with the international system, Dutch hotels are awarded stars (one to five) by a governmental agency based on their facilities and services. Those with three or more stars feature en-suite bathrooms where a shower is standard, and a tub is a four-star standard. Rooms in lodgings listed in this guide have private bathrooms with showers unless otherwise indicated.

One Dutch peculiarity to watch out for is having twin beds pushed together instead of having one double. If you want a double bed (or *tweepersoonsbed*), you may have to pay more. Keep in mind that the star ratings are general indications and that a charming three-star might make for a better stay than a more expensive four-star. During low season, usually November to March (excluding Christmas and the New Year) when a hotel is not full, it is sometimes possible to **negotiate a discounted rate,** if one is not already offered. Prices in larger cities, particularly in the Randstad area, are significantly higher than those in outlying towns in rural areas, especially over the peak summer period. Room rates for deluxe and four-star rooms are on a par with those in other European cities, so in these categories, **ask for one of the better rooms,** since less-desirable rooms—and there occasionally are some—don't measure up to what you are paying for.

Most hotels quote room rates excluding breakfast. When you book a room, specifically **ask whether the rate includes breakfast.** You are under no obligation to take breakfast at your hotel, but most hotels expect you to do so. It is encouraging to note that many of the hotels we recommend offer a wide selection at their buffet breakfast instead of the simple, even skimpy Continental breakfasts.

Check out your hotel's location, and **ask your hotelier about availability of a room with a view,** if you're not worried about the extra expense: hotels in the historic center with a pretty canal view are highly sought after.

Always ask if there is an elevator (called a lift) or if guests need to climb any stairs. Even if you are fairly fit, you may find traditional Dutch staircases intimidating and difficult to negotiate. It's worth considering if you plan to stay in a listed monument. The alternative is to request a ground-floor room.

In older hotels, the quality of the rooms may vary; if you don't like the room you're given, request another. This applies to noise, too. Front rooms may be larger or have a view, but they may also have a lot of street noise—so if you're a light sleeper, **request a quiet room when making reservations.** Remember to **specify whether you care to have a bath or shower,** since many bathrooms do not have tubs. It is always a good idea to **have your reservation, dates, and rate confirmed by fax.** Note that many hotels in Holland do not have air-conditioning.

Aside from going directly to the hotels or booking a travel and hotel package with your travel agent, there are several ways of making reservations. The **Nederlands Reserverings Centrum** (the Dutch hoteliers' reservation service) handles bookings for the whole of Holland on its Web site for cancellations and reservations only; bookings are made online. The VVV (Netherlands Board of Tourism) offer the same services; branches of the VVV can be found in Schiphol Airport and Amsterdam Centraal Station, and regional VVV offices specialize in their own area. Contact the office based in the region you plan to travel to, or go to the area's VVV's Web site (listed under Visitor Information in the A to Z section found in the regional chapters of this book). Most agencies charge a booking fee, which starts at €9 per person.

A pleasant alternative to getting accommodations in a hotel is to stay at a bed-and-breakfast (B&B). The best way to track down B&B accommodations is through either creative city accommodations specialist City Mundo or Holiday Link, both of which deal with private accommodations and longer stays (⇨ Web Sites).

In summer, hotel rooms fill up quickly so book early. Spring and fall may also be fairly congested in the popular cities (Amsterdam, Maastricht, Utrecht).

🔢 **Local Contact City Mundo** ✉ Schinkelkade 47 II, 1075 VK Amsterdam ☎ 020/676-5270 ⊕ www. citymundo.com. **Holiday Link** 📠 Postbus 70-155, 9704 AD Groningen ☎ 050/313-2424 ⊕ www. holidaylink.com. **Nederlands Reserverings Centrum** (Dutch hoteliers' reservation service) ☎ 0299/ 689144 ⊕ www.hotelres.nl. **VVV Central Tourist Offices** ☎ 0900/400-4040 [€0.55 per min].

🔢 **Toll-Free Numbers Best Western** ☎ 800/528-1234 ⊕ www.bestwestern.com. **Choice** ☎ 800/424-6423 ⊕ www.choicehotels.com. **Hilton** ☎ 800/445-8667 ⊕ www.hilton.com. **Holiday Inn** ☎ 800/465-4329 ⊕ www.ichotelsgroup.com. **Inter-Continental** ☎ 800/327-0200 ⊕ www.ichotelsgroup.com. **Radisson** ☎ 800/333-3333 ⊕ www.radisson.com. **Sheraton** ☎ 800/325-3535 ⊕ www.starwood.com/ sheraton. **Westin Hotels & Resorts** ☎ 800/228-3000 ⊕ www.starwood.com/westin.

## MAIL & SHIPPING

For mail destined for outside the local area, use the *overige bestemmingen* slot in mailboxes. The national postal service's logo is PTT POST (white letters on a red oblong). The Dutch mail system can be slower than you'd expect, so allow about 10 days for mail to and from the United States and Canada and up to a week to and from the United Kingdom. For postal information within Holland call ☎ 0800/ 0417.

### POSTAL RATES

Airmail letters (lightweight stationery) to the United States and Canada cost €0.75 for the first 20 grams and €1.50 up to 50 grams. Always **stick the blue "priority" sticker on your envelope,** or write "priority" in big, clear letters to the side of the address. Postcards cost a universal €0.54, no matter where they are destined. Letters (for the first 20 grams) to the United Kingdom, as well as to any other EU country, cost €0.59. Letters sent within Holland cost €0.39 for the first 20 grams. You can buy *postzegels* (stamps) and postcards from tobacconists, the post office, the VVV, and souvenir shops.

## MEDIA

### IN ENGLISH

*Roundabout* is an English-language monthly magazine guide to what's going on culturally in Holland for visitors and residents, with the main emphasis on the Rotterdam area.

The *International Herald Tribune*, an English-language newspaper with general world news, is available daily in Holland from many newsagents, and the *Financieele Dagblaad* has a daily page devoted to English. Daily and weekly English-language newspapers, such as *Amsterdam Weekly* and *Amsterdam Times,* are available at bigger newsagents, but they are quite expensive, running at €5. Sunday papers have never taken off, but larger railway stations and Sunday-opening bookshops have international Sunday papers.

### BOOKS

For Holland's largest selection of books in English, head to **American Book Center** (⊠ Lange Poten 23 ☎ 070/364–2742), in The Hague; **Donner Bookstore** (⊠ Lijnbaan 150 ☎ 010/413–2070), in Rotterdam; or **Waterstone's Booksellers** (⊠ Kalverstraat 152, just off Spui ☎ 020/638–3821), in Amsterdam.

### MONEY MATTERS

The price tags in Holland' main cities are considered reasonable in comparison with those in neighboring countries. As you would expect, prices vary from region to region and are lower in the countryside than in the urban Randstad. Good value for money can still be had in many places, and as a tourist in this Anglophile country, you are a lot less likely to get ripped off in Holland than in countries where English is less-widely embraced.

Here are some sample prices: admission to the Rijksmuseum is €9; cheapest seats at the Stadsschouwburg theater run €12 for plays, €20 for opera; a movie ticket is €6.50–€9.50 (depending on time of show). Going to a Dutch nightclub might set you back €5–€20. A daily English-language newspaper is €5. An Amsterdam taxi ride (1⅓ km, or 1½ mi) costs about €4.55. An inexpensive hotel room for two, including breakfast, in Amsterdam, is about €65–€125; an inexpensive Amsterdam dinner is €20–€35 for two, and a half-liter carafe of house wine is €11. A simple sandwich item on the menu runs to about €2.50, a cup of coffee €2. A Coke is €1.40, and a half liter of beer is €2.95.

Prices throughout this guide are given for adults. Substantially reduced fees are almost always available for children, students, and senior citizens. For information on taxes, *see* Taxes.

### ATMS

The Dutch word for ATM is *Pinautomaat*; many locals call the machines simply "pin."

### CREDIT CARDS

Throughout this guide, the following abbreviations are used: **AE,** American Express; **DC,** Diners Club; **MC,** MasterCard; and **V,** Visa.

🔲 Reporting Lost Cards **American Express** ☎ 800/554-2639, 801/945-9450 [call collect], 020/504-8666 Global Assist in Holland. **Diners Club** ☎ 800/234-6377. **MasterCard** ☎ 0800/022-5821 in Holland. **Visa** ☎ 0800/022-3110 in Holland.

### CURRENCY

The single European Union (EU) currency, the euro, is now the official currency of the 11 countries participating in the European Monetary Union (with the notable exceptions of Great Britain, Denmark, Sweden, and Greece).At press time, 1 euro = 1.20 US$.

The euro system is classic; there are eight coins: 1 and 2 euros, plus 1, 2, 5, 10, 20, and 50 centimes, or cents, of the euro. All coins have one side that has the value of the euro on it and the other side with each country's own, unique national symbol. There are seven colorful notes: 5, 10, 20, 50, 100, 200, and 500 euros. Notes have the principal architectural styles from antiquity onward on one side and the map and the flag of Europe on the other and are the same for all countries.

## CURRENCY EXCHANGE

These days, the **easiest way to get euros is through ATMs.** An ATM is called a *Pinautomaat*; you can find them in airports, train stations, and throughout the city. ATM rates are excellent because they are based on wholesale rates offered only by major banks. It's a good idea, however, to bring some euros with you from home and always to have some cash and traveler's checks as backup. For the best deal when exchanging currencies not within the Monetary Union purview (the U.S. dollar, the yen, and the English pound are examples), compare rates at banks (which usually have the most favorable rates) and booths and look for exchange booths that clearly state "no commission." At exchange booths always confirm the rate with the teller before exchanging money. You won't do as well at exchange booths in airports or rail and bus stations, in hotels, in restaurants, or in stores. To avoid lines at airport exchange booths, **get some euros before you leave home.**

🖪 Exchange Services International Currency Express ✉ 427 N. Camden Dr., Suite F, Beverly Hills, CA 90210 ☎ 888/278-6628 orders 🖷 310/278-6410 ⊕ www.foreignmoney.com. Travel Ex Currency Services ☎ 800/287-7362 orders and retail locations ⊕ www.travelex.com.

GWK (*bureau de change*) ☎ 0900/0566 branches are located near railway stations throughout the country. There's an office at **Amsterdam Schiphol Airport** ☎ 020/653-5121.

## TRAVELER'S CHECKS

Do you need traveler's checks? It depends on where you're headed. If you're going to rural areas and villages, go with cash; traveler's checks are best used in cities and towns in the Randstad region and more popular destinations throughout the rest of the country. Lost or stolen checks can usually be replaced within 24 hours; to ensure a speedy refund, buy your own traveler's checks—don't let someone else pay for them, as irregularities like this can

cause delays. The person who bought the checks should make the call to request a refund.

## PACKING

When coming to Holland, be flexible: pack an umbrella (or two—the topography results in a blustery wind, which makes short work of a lightweight frame); bring a raincoat, with a thick liner in winter; and always have a sweater or jacket handy. For daytime wear and casual evenings, turtlenecks and thicker shirts under a sweater are ideal for winter. Unpredictable summer weather means that a long-sleeve cotton shirt and jacket could be perfect one day, whereas the next, a T-shirt or vest top is as much as you can wear, making it hard to pack lightly. Bring a little something for all eventualities and you shouldn't get stuck.

Men aren't required to wear ties or jackets anywhere, except in some smarter hotels and exclusive restaurants; jeans are very popular and worn to the office. Cobblestone streets make walking in high heels perilous—you don't want a wrenched ankle—and white sneakers are a dead giveaway that you are an American tourist; a better choice is a pair of dark-color, comfortable walking shoes.

In your carry-on luggage, pack an extra pair of eyeglasses or contact lenses and enough of any medication you take to last a few days longer than the entire trip. You may also ask your doctor to write a spare prescription using the drug's generic name, as brand names may vary from country to country. In luggage to be checked, **never pack prescription drugs, valuables, or undeveloped film.** And don't forget to carry with you the addresses of offices that handle refunds of lost traveler's checks. Check *Fodor's How to Pack* (available at online retailers and bookstores everywhere) for more tips.

To avoid customs and security delays, carry medications in their original packaging. Don't pack any sharp objects in your carry-on luggage, including knives of any size or material, scissors, nail clippers, and corkscrews, or anything else that might arouse suspicion.

To avoid having your checked luggage chosen for hand inspection, don't cram bags full. The U.S. Transportation Security Administration suggests packing shoes on top and placing personal items you don't want touched in clear plastic bags.

## CHECKING LUGGAGE

You're allowed to carry aboard one bag and one personal article, such as a purse or a laptop computer. Make sure what you carry on fits under your seat or in the overhead bin. Get to the gate early, so you can board as soon as possible, before the overhead bins fill up.

Baggage allowances vary by carrier, destination, and ticket class. On international flights, you're usually allowed to check two bags weighing up to 70 pounds (32 kilograms) each, although a few airlines allow checked bags of up to 88 pounds (40 kilograms) in first class. Some international carriers don't allow more than 66 pounds (30 kilograms) per bag in business class and 44 pounds (20 kilograms) in economy. In general, carry-on bags shouldn't exceed 40 pounds (18 kilograms). Most airlines won't accept bags that weigh more than 100 pounds (45 kilograms) on domestic or international flights. Expect to pay a fee for baggage that exceeds weight limits. Check baggage restrictions with your carrier before you pack.

Airline liability for baggage is limited to $2,500 per person on flights within the United States. On international flights it amounts to $9.07 per pound or $20 per kilogram for checked baggage (roughly $640 per 70-pound bag), with a maximum of $634.90 per piece, and $400 per passenger for unchecked baggage. You can buy additional coverage at check-in for about $10 per $1,000 of coverage, but it often excludes a rather extensive list of items, shown on your airline ticket.

Before departure, itemize your bags' contents and their worth, and label the bags with your name, address, and phone number. (If you use your home address, cover it so potential thieves can't see it readily.) Include a label inside each bag and **pack a copy of your itinerary.** At check-in, make sure each bag is correctly tagged with the destination airport's three-letter code. Because some checked bags will be opened for hand inspection, the U.S. Transportation Security Administration recommends that you leave luggage unlocked or use the plastic locks offered at check-in. TSA screeners place an inspection notice inside searched bags, which are resealed with a special lock.

If your bag has been searched and contents are missing or damaged, file a claim with the TSA Consumer Response Center as soon as possible. If your bags arrive damaged or fail to arrive at all, file a written report with the airline before leaving the airport.

**⨕ Complaints** U.S. Transportation Security Administration Contact Center ☎ 866/289-9673 ⊕ www.tsa.gov.

## PASSPORTS & VISAS

When traveling internationally, carry your passport even if you don't need one. Not only is it the best form of ID, but it's also being required more and more. As of December 31, 2005, for instance, Americans need a passport to reenter the country from Bermuda, the Caribbean, and Panama. Such requirements also affect reentry from Canada and Mexico by air and sea (as of December 31, 2006) and land (as of December 31, 2007). **Make two photocopies of the data page** (one for someone at home and another for you, carried separately from your passport). If you lose your passport, promptly call the nearest embassy or consulate and the local police.

U.S. passport applications for children under age 14 require consent from both parents or legal guardians; both parents must appear together to sign the application. If only one parent appears, he or she must submit a written statement from the other parent authorizing passport issuance for the child. A parent with sole authority must present evidence of it when applying; acceptable documentation includes the child's certified birth certificate listing only the applying parent, a court order specifically permitting this parent's travel with the child, or a death certificate for the nonapplying parent. Application forms and instructions are available on the Web site of the U.S. State Department's Bureau of Consular Affairs (⊕ travel.state.gov).

## ENTERING HOLLAND
All U.S., Canadian, and U.K. citizens, even infants, need only a valid passport to enter Holland for stays of up to 90 days.

## PASSPORT OFFICES
The best time to apply for a passport or to renew is in fall and winter. Before any trip, check your passport's expiration date, and, if necessary, renew it as soon as possible.

🔳 Australian Citizens **Passports Australia** Australian Department of Foreign Affairs and Trade ☎ 131-232 ⊕ www.passports.gov.au.

🔳 Canadian Citizens **Passport Office** ✉ To mail in applications: 70 Cremazie St., Gatineau, Québec ]8Y 3P2 ☎ 800/567-6868 or 819/994-3500 ⊕ www.ppt.gc.ca.

🔳 New Zealand Citizens **New Zealand Passports Office** ☎ 0800/22-5050 or 04/474-8100 ⊕ www.passports.govt.nz.

🔳 U.K. Citizens **U.K. Passport Service** ☎ 0870/521-0410 ⊕ www.passport.gov.uk.

🔳 U.S. Citizens **National Passport Information Center** ☎ 877/487-2778, 888/874-7793 TDD/TTY ⊕ travel.state.gov.

## SAFETY
Don't wear a money belt or a waist pack, both of which peg you as a tourist. Distribute your cash and any valuables (including your credit cards and passport) between a deep front pocket, an inside jacket or vest pocket, and a hidden money pouch. Do not reach for the money pouch once you're in public.

Most of the destinations in this guide are among the safest spots in Holland. Amsterdam is unlike any other modern metropolis: although it has had certain problems with crime, and with abuse of legalized prostitution and soft drugs, the serious crime rate is exceptionally low, so having your bike stolen is the worst thing most likely to happen to you. Still, in crowded intersections and dark alleys, it is always best to be streetwise and take double precautions for your safety; it may be best to keep your money in a money belt and not flaunt your expensive camera. As always, be wary of pickpockets in crowds and

while riding crowded city trams or trains and at ATMs. And use common sense when going out at night in large cities. Keep to well-lighted areas and take a taxi if you are going a long distance. It's a good idea to keep your valuables with you when you are out seeing the sights rather than leaving them in your hotel room.

## STUDENTS IN HOLLAND
Holland is a popular student destination, and in the university towns there are lots of facilities geared toward students' needs (housing, information, and so forth). Students with identification cards (such as an ISIC, or International Student Identity Card) are usually entitled to discounts in shops, clubs, museums, galleries, cinemas, and entertainment venues. The main division of the Universiteit van Amsterdam (UvA) can be found in historic buildings stretching from Spui to Kloveniersburgwal. The Vrije Universiteit (VU) is about half the size of UvA and is housed in one big building in the south of Amsterdam. The Rijksuniversiteit van Leiden is scattered across town, as is Rotterdam's Erasmus Universiteit. Delft's Technische Universiteit isn't a campus as such, but the majority of its buildings are in one area. Eindhoven also has a technical university, and Tilburg's university is well known for its economics department. In Enschede, the Universiteit Twente is named after the region; it is a technical university but also teaches social studies. Groningen has an enormous student population, as does Utrecht, whereas Maastricht's university is considerably smaller.

## LOCAL RESOURCES
The **Foreign Student Service** (FSS) promotes the well-being of foreign students, providing personal assistance and general information on studying in Holland. It also runs the International Student Insurance Service (ISIS) and organizes social activities. Accommodations agencies can help with finding a room, and for a small fee you can take part in accommodations agency lotteries (for multiple-night stays), usually held daily. Each university has a service and information center; UvA's center offers personal advice on studying and student life; contact individual universities

for information about their accommodations agencies and services, help lines, libraries, summer courses, student unions, and student welfare.

## STUDENT ACCOMMODATIONS

In addition to the YHA hostels, young visitors to Holland can stay at a youth hotel, or "sleep-in," which provides basic, inexpensive accommodations for young people. A list of these is available from the **NBT** (☎ 212/370–7360 in New York). In summer (and in some cases year-round), the **Vereniging voor Natuur en Milieu Educatie** (IVN; ✆ IVN, Postbus 20123, 1000 HC Amsterdam ☎ 020/622–8115 ⊕ www.ivn.nl) organizes work camps in scenic locations, popular among English-speaking visitors age 15–30. Another organization to consider for volunteer work in Holland is **Internationale Vrijwilligers Projecten** (✉ Willemstraat 7, 3511 RJ Utrecht ☎ 030/231–7721 ⊕ www.siw.nl/en).

## TRAVEL AGENCIES

To save money, **look into deals available through student-oriented travel agencies.** To qualify you'll need a bona fide student ID card. Members of international student groups are also eligible.

🔁 IDs & Services **British Council Education Centre** ✉ Weteringschans 85a, 1017 RZ Amsterdam ☎ 020/524–7676. **Erasmus Universiteit Rotterdam** ✉ Burgermeisteroudlaan 50 ☎ 010/408–1111. **Foreign Student Service** ✉ Oranje Nassaulaan 5, Amsterdam ☎ 020/671–5915. **Rijksuniversiteit Leiden** ✉ Rapenburg 70 ☎ 071/527–8011. **STA Travel** ✉ 10 Downing St., New York, NY 10014 ☎ 800/777–0112 24-hr service center, 212/627–3111 🖨 212/627–3387 ⊕ www.sta.com. **Technische Universiteit Delft** ✉ Julianalaan 134 ☎ 015/278–9111. **Travel Cuts** ✉ 187 College St., Toronto, Ontario M5T 1P7 Canada ☎ 800/592–2887 in U.S., 866/246–9762 or 416/979–2406 in Canada 🖨 416/979–8167 ⊕ www.travelcuts.com. **Universiteit van Amsterdam** ✉ Spui 21 ☎ 020/525–9111. **UvA Service and Information Center** ✉ Binnengasthuisstraat 9, Amsterdam ☎ 020/525–8080.

## TAXES

### HOTELS

The service charge and the 6% VAT (value-added tax) are included in the rate. Tourist tax is never included and is 5% extra.

### RESTAURANTS

In a restaurant you pay ⅂ . 6% VAT on food items, and .. all beverages, all of which are inc. the menu prices.

### VALUE-ADDED TAX

Referred to as the BTW in Holland, the Value-Added Tax (V.A.T.) runs 19% on clothes and luxury goods, 6% on basic goods. On most consumer goods, it is already included in the amount on the price tag, so you can't actually see what percentage you're paying.

To **get an V.A.T. refund,** you need to reside outside the European Union (EU) and you need to have spent €136 or more in the same shop on the same day (this is including tax). Provided that you personally carry the goods out of the country within 30 days, you may claim a refund at your point of departure from the EU. The simplest system is to **look for stores displaying Tax Free Shopping,** or Global Refund signs, like those at the Bijenkorf. Once you have made your purchases, go to their customer service department and **ask for a VAT or Tax Free form.** Normally you receive 15% back, but these refund service agents charge 5% commission. You then have these tax-refund forms stamped at customs at the airport where you finally depart from the European Union. It's also a good idea to carry your purchases in your hand luggage, in case customs wants to physically check what you've bought. Once stamped, the forms can be cashed at any bank in the airport, or you can opt to have the refund credited to your bank account.

🔁 V.A.T. Refunds **Global Refund Canada** ✆ Box 2020, Station Main Brampton, Ontario L6T 3S3 ☎ 800/993–4313 🖨 905/791–9078 ⊕ www.globalrefund.com.

## TELEPHONES

### AREA & COUNTRY CODES

The country code for Holland is 31. Here are area codes for major cities: Amsterdam, 020; Delft, 015; Eindhoven, 040; Groningen, 050; Leiden, 071; Maastricht, 043; Rotterdam, 010; Utrecht, 030. Essentially, the region around every town or city uses the same area code. To call Amster-

ou don't
en-digit
om else-
t the start of
he standard
other prefixes
numbers starting
numbers, but the
inic_     he prefix 0900 are
charged at    .tes (€0.35 a minute
or more), and 06 n.. .bers indicate mobile
(cell) phones.

When dialing a Dutch number from abroad, you drop the initial 0 from the local area code, so someone calling from New York, for example, to Amsterdam would dial 011 + 31 + 20 + the seven-digit phone number. From the United Kingdom, dial 00 + 31 + 20 + phone number. When you are dialing from Holland to someplace overseas, the country code is 00–1 for the United States and Canada, 00–61 for Australia, 00–64 for New Zealand, and 00–44 for the United Kingdom. All mobile and land-line phones in Holland are 10 digits long (some help lines and information centers, such as the rail inquiry line, have only 8 digits), with most area codes 3 digits and phone numbers 7 digits. Note that some smaller towns and villages have a 4-digit area code and a 6-digit local number.

## DIRECTORY & OPERATOR ASSISTANCE

To ask directory inquiries for a telephone number outside Holland, dial 0900/8418 (calls are charged at €1.15 an inquiry). For numbers within Holland, dial 0900/8008 (calls are charged at €1.15 an inquiry).

To reach an international operator, make a collect call, or dial toll free to a number outside Holland, dial 0800/0410; to speak to a local operator, or make a collect call within Holland, dial 0800/0101.

## LONG-DISTANCE SERVICES

AT&T, MCI, and Sprint access codes make calling long-distance relatively convenient, but you may find the local access number blocked in many hotel rooms. First ask the hotel operator to connect you. If the hotel operator balks, ask for an international operator, or dial the interna-

tional operator yourself. One way to improve your odds of getting connected to your long-distance carrier is to travel with more than one company's calling card (a hotel may block Sprint, for example, but not MCI). If all else fails, call from a pay phone. If you are traveling for a long period of time, consider renting a cell phone from a local company.

🖪 **Access Codes AT&T Direct** ☎ 0800/022-9111. **MCI WorldPhone** ☎ 0800/022-9122. **Sprint International Access** ☎ 0800/022-9119.

## PUBLIC PHONES & PHONE CARDS

To make a call, lift the receiver, wait until you hear a dial tone, a low-pitched constant hum, then insert a phone card, credit card, or the appropriate amount of coins. Dial the number, and as soon as your correspondent picks up the receiver, you are connected. To make an international call, dial 00 followed by the country code, then drop the first 0 of the area code ( ⇨ Area and Country codes, *above*).

Phone cards—*telefoon kaart* or *prepay kaart*—are used throughout Holland. Phone cards work only in booths affiliated with the card's company, so Telfort cards work only in blue Telfort booths, found on station platforms, and within towns; KPN cards can be used only in KPN booths, screened by green-edged glass. The cards can be purchased at the GWK—Holland Welcome Service, Wizzl Shops at train stations, at train ticket offices, phone stores, grocery stores, post offices, and major department stores.

Since the increase in cellular phones, the number of phone booths is decreasing. At every railway station there are pay phones, either in the ticket hall or on the platforms. There are clusters of pay phones around pedestrian squares, but the railway station phones are all Telfort and you can use only a Telfort card or coins, whereas the pay phones out on the street are KPN Telecom, where you need to use another card. Awkward, yes—and the reason is that the stations are the property of the NS (Nederlandse Spoorweg, or Dutch Train System), and so they have their own contract with Telfort, whereas public ground is owned by the government, which has a contract with former state firm KPN. The newest KPN phone booths also accept credit cards.

Telfort phone booths and public phones found in bars and cafés accept coins from €0.10 to €2.

Off-peak rates apply weekdays 8–8 and all weekend. Phone cards worth €5, €8, and €10 (approximately) can be bought from VVVs (branches of Holland Board of Tourism), post offices, train stations, newsagents, and tobacconists. Since hotels tend to overcharge for international calls, it is best to use a prepaid telephone card in a public phone.

## TIME

Holland is 1 hour ahead of Greenwich Mean Time (GMT). Daylight-saving time begins on the last Sunday in March, when clocks are set forward 1 hour; on the last Sunday in October, clocks are set back 1 hour. All clocks on Central European Time (CET) go forward and back on the same spring and autumn dates as GMT. Holland operate on a 24-hour clock, so AM hours are listed as in the United States and Britain but PM hours continue through the cycle (1 PM is 13:00, 2 PM is 14:00, etc.) When it's 3 PM in Amsterdam, it is 2 PM in London, 9 AM in New York City, and 6 AM in Los Angeles. A telephone call will get you the **speaking clock** (☎ 0900/8002) in Dutch.

## TIPPING

The following guidelines apply in Amsterdam, but the Dutch tip smaller amounts in smaller cities and towns. In restaurants a service charge of about 6% is included in menu prices. Tip 10% extra if you've really enjoyed the meal and gotten good service, and **leave the tip as change rather than putting it on your credit card.** If you're not satisfied, don't leave anything. Though a service charge is also included in hotel, taxi, bar, and café bills, the Dutch mostly round up the change to the nearest two euros for large bills and to the nearest euro for smaller ones. In taxis, round up the fare to 10% extra. Rest-room attendants expect only change, €0.25, and a cloakroom attendant in an average bar expects half a euro per coat (more in expensive hotels and restaurants).

## TOURS & PACKAGES

Because everything is prearranged on a prepackaged tour or independent vacation, you spend less time planning—and often get it all at a good price.

### BOOKING WITH AN AGENT

Travel agents are excellent resources. But it's a good idea to collect brochures from several agencies, as some agents' suggestions may be influenced by relationships with tour and package firms that reward them for volume sales. If you have a special interest, find an agent with expertise in that area. The American Society of Travel Agents (ASTA) has a database of specialists worldwide; you can log on to the group's Web site to find one near you.

Make sure your travel agent knows the accommodations and other services of the place being recommended. Ask about the hotel's location, room size, beds, and whether it has a pool, room service, or programs for children, if you care about these. Has your agent been there in person or sent others whom you can contact?

Do some homework on your own, too: local tourism boards can provide information about lesser-known and small-niche operators, some of which may sell only direct.

### BUYER BEWARE

Each year consumers are stranded or lose their money when tour operators—even large ones with excellent reputations—go out of business. So check out the operator. Ask several travel agents about its reputation, and try to **book with a company that has a consumer-protection program.** (Look for information in the company's brochure.) In the United States, members of the United States Tour Operators Association are required to set aside funds (up to $1 million) to help eligible customers cover payments and travel arrangements in the event that the company defaults. It's also a good idea to choose a company that participates in the American Society of Travel Agents' Tour Operator Program;

ASTA will act as mediator in any disputes between you and your tour operator.

Remember that the more your package or tour includes, the better you can predict the ultimate cost of your vacation. Make sure you know exactly what is covered, and beware of hidden costs. Are taxes, tips, and transfers included? Entertainment and excursions? These can add up.

🖪 Tour-Operator Recommendations **American Society of Travel Agents** (⇨ Travel Agencies). **CrossSphere–The Global Association for Packaged Travel** ✉ 546 E. Main St., Lexington, KY 40508 ☎ 800/682-8886 or 859/226-4444 🖷 859/ 226-4414 ⊕ www.CrossSphere.com. **United States Tour Operators Association** (USTOA) ✉ 275 Madison Ave., Suite 2014, New York, NY 10016 ☎ 212/ 599-6599 🖷 212/599-6744 ⊕ www.ustoa.com.

## TRAIN TRAVEL

Holland has a very compact network; the trains are among the most modern in Europe and are the quickest way to travel between city centers. Services are relatively frequent, with a minimum of two departures per hour for large cities for each routing. The carriages are modern and clean, and although many Dutch people complain about delays, the trains usually run exactly on time. Extra services are offered, such as the night train, which runs hourly all night, stopping at major cities and most staff speak English. Reserving a particular seat is not possible on Dutch trains, though. Stations in most towns are centrally located, usually within walking distance of major sights.

On the train you have the choice of *roken* (smoking) or *niet roken* (no-smoking), and first or second class, indicated with a large 1 or 2 painted on the outside of the train, for your reference as you get on, and at the end of each aisle. First-class travel costs about 50% more, which on local trains gives you a slightly larger seat in a compartment that is less likely to be full, but on long-distance trains you get wider seats, more legroom, and better ventilation and lighting. At peak travel times, first-class train travel is worth the difference.

The fastest trains on the Nederlandse Spoorwegen (or NS, Holland Railway) are the Thalys trains (www.thalys.com) operating on the main line from Amsterdam to The Hague and Rotterdam, through to Brussels and Paris, and the I.C.E. trains traveling from Amsterdam to Utrecht, Arnhem, and destinations across Germany. You pay a supplement for traveling on these trains, and reservations are made when you buy your ticket. There is little aisle and luggage space, though there is a space near the door where you can put large bags. To avoid having to squeeze though narrow aisles, **board only at your carriage** (look for the number on your ticket). Carriage numbers are displayed on their exterior. Next fastest are international trains, for which you do not have to pay a supplement. Intercity trains are novel in that they can come double-decker; they have a few more stops than the international trains and travel only within the country. *Sneltreins* (express trains) also have two decks but take in more stops, so they are a little slower. *Stoptreins* (local trains) are the slowest.

If you have a reduction pass (⇨ Cutting Costs, *below*), you are restricted from using it before 9 AM; further, because all trains serve commuters, you most likely won't get a seat if you travel during rush hour, which makes later travel doubly appealing.

To avoid long lines at station ticket windows when you're in a hurry, **buy tickets in advance.** With the exception of the Thalys and I.C.E. trains, all tickets can be purchased at the last minute—tickets for these trains can be bought up to one hour before departure and up to three months in advance (Thalys) or up to two months (I.C.E.).

Normal tickets are either *enkele reis* (one-way) or *retour* (round-trip). Round-trip tickets cost approximately 74% of two single tickets. They are valid only on the day you buy them, unless you ask specifically for a ticket with a different date, or not dated. If you buy a nondated ticket, **you must stamp the date on your ticket before you board the train** on your day of travel. Use one of the small yellow machines near the tracks. Just hold the ticket flat and slide it in the gap until you hear a short ring. Once stamped, your ticket is valid for the rest of the day. You can get on and off at will at stops in between your destinations until midnight.

Most main-line rail ticket windows are open Monday–Thursday 6 AM–11 PM, Friday 6 AM–11:45 PM, Saturday 7 AM–11:45 PM, and Sunday 7 AM–11 PM, and no credit cards, debit cards, or traveler's checks are valid for payment. If you don't have Dutch cash, the GWK money exchange has branches in or near most large stations.

If you forget to stamp your ticket in the machine, or you didn't make it in time to buy a ticket, you can seek out an inspector and pay the on-board fare, a stinging 70% more expensive than at the railway station counter. As in a tram or metro, you often travel in a train without anyone asking to check your ticket. Riders found without a valid ticket will be asked to buy a ticket at a higher rate.

Apart from using the ticket window in a station, you can **buy tickets at the yellow ticket machines** in the main hall of the railway station, or on the platforms. These machines accept cash and cards, if you have a four-digit PIN code. Each city is allocated a number (which is also the city's postal code), which you select from the list on the machine. For example, Amsterdam is 1000, Rotterdam is 3000, and Delft is 2600. Key this in, and then choose which of the following you want as flashing lights highlight each pair of options: first or second class; full fare or with a reduction; same-day travel or without a date stamp; and, finally, one-way or round-trip.

Note that in some Dutch cities (including Amsterdam, Rotterdam, The Hague, and Delft) there are two or more stations, although one is the principal station *Centraal*. **Be sure of the exact name of the station** from which your train will depart, and at which you wish to get out.

There is a refreshment service on faster trains, from intercities to the Thalys, with roller carts or a cafeteria or dining car. It is not advised to drink tap water on trains,

because the toilet facilities are cleaned only between journeys.

🚩 In Holland NS–Nederlandse Spoorwegen/Dutch Railways ☎ 0900/8008 ⊕ www.ns.nl.
🚩 From the U.K. British Rail ☎ 0845/748–4950.

## CUTTING COSTS

Train fares in Holland are lower than in most other European countries, but you can still **save money by looking into rail passes**—there are a host of special saver tickets that make train travel even cheaper. Be aware, however, that if you don't plan to cover many miles, then you may as well buy individual tickets; a *dagkaart* (unlimited travel pass for one day) costs €37.10 second class, €59.40 first class, but it is almost impossible to rack up enough miles to make it worthwhile.

Between July and the end of August, **check out the Zomertoer,** which allows second-class-only unlimited travel for 3 days within a 10-day period (€45 for one person and €59 for two people).

Once in Holland, **inquire about the Voordeel-urenkaart,** a reduction card available for all ages, which costs €49 and entitles the holder to a 40% discount on all first- and second-class tickets, when traveling after 9 AM. You need a residential address to apply for this card, as well as passport photos and ID. The card proper will take between four and six weeks to be processed and arrive on your doorstep, but you are issued a valid card for the interim time.

Holland is one of 17 countries in which you can **use a Eurailpass,** providing unlimited first-class travel in all 17 countries. If you plan to travel extensively, get a standard pass. Train travel is available for 15 days ($588), 21 days ($762), one month ($946), two months ($1,338), or three months ($1,654). Children aged 4–11 are charged half the adult fare, and children under 4 travel for free. You can also receive free or discounted travel on some ferry lines, and a Eurailpass Youth for second-class traveling at a lower fare is available to those under 26 ($414 for 15 days). If you plan to travel with one or more others, the Eurailpass Saver offers considerable discounts: 15 days is $498 per person.

**Use the Eurail Selectpass** if you can narrow down your travel: it offers unlimited first-class travel to three, four, or five countries, cutting the cost to you even further—Benelux (Belgium, Holland, and Luxembourg) counts as one. Fares are as follows: travel for 5 days ($438), 6 days ($476), 8 days ($552), 10 days ($624), or 15 days ($794) in a two-month period. There is a catch, though: the chosen countries must be connected by a direct rail or shipping line. As before, those under 26 can travel on a Eurail Selectpass Youth second class for less: $307 for five days. If two to five people travel on a Eurail Selectpass Saver together, the individual cost drops to $374 for five days.

**Order a free copy of the latest brochure, "Europe on Track,"** by calling **Eurail** (☎ 888/382–7245) in the United States to compare prices and options, or obtain all the information on their Web site. Whichever pass you choose, **remember to buy your Eurailpass or Eurail Selectpass before you leave** for Europe. You can buy the passes in Holland but at a *15% hike-up* compared with buying at home. You can get further information and order your tickets at the Rail Europe Web site.

Many travelers assume that the rail passes guarantee them seats on the trains they wish to ride, but **you need to book ahead,** even if you are using a rail pass. Seat reservations are required on most European high-speed trains and are a good idea on trains that may be crowded—particularly on popular summer routes.

**⑦ Information & Passes** All tickets for travel within Holland can be purchased at any Dutch rail station. International passes can be bought at the international window of larger stations. Eurailpasses and Eurail Selectpasses are available through **Eurail** ⊕ www.eurail.com and through the travel agencies of **Rail Europe** ⊠ 44 S. Broadway, No. 11, White Plains, NY 10601 ☎ 914/682–2999 ⊕ www. raileurope.com/us, and **CIT North America, Ltd.** ⊠ 15 W. 44th St., 10th fl., New York, NY 10036 ☎ 800/248–8687 ⊕ www.cit-rail.com.

## TRAIN TAXIS

When you buy your ticket from a station ticket office, you can buy a *trein-taxi* ticket from some stations for a standard €3.80 per person, per ride. It doesn't matter where you're going, so long as it's within the city limits. The fare is so cheap because it's shared—but with waiting time at a guaranteed maximum of 10 minutes after your call, you won't be hanging around long. Larger cities don't have trein-taxi service. Trein-taxis are ideal for getting to sights on the outskirts of smaller towns. **Ask at the ticket windows in smaller stations,** or ring the transport inquiry number ( ⇨ Train Information).

**⑦ Train Information** Holland-wide **Public Transport Information** ☎ 0900/9292 information officer including schedules and fares. For **lost and found** ☎ 030/235–3923 [hold the line for an operator] on train lines and in stations, ask for a form at the nearest station. **Nederlandse Spoorwegen** (Dutch Rail Customer Service) ☎ 0900/202–1163 [€0.10 per min].

## TRAVEL AGENCIES

A good travel agent puts your needs first. Look for an agency that has been in business at least five years, emphasizes customer service, and has someone on staff who specializes in your destination. In addition, **make sure the agency belongs to a professional trade organization.** The American Society of Travel Agents (ASTA) has more than 10,000 members in some 140 countries, enforces a strict code of ethics, and will step in to mediate agent-client disputes involving ASTA members. ASTA also maintains a directory of agents on its Web site; ASTA's TravelSense.org, a trip-planning and travel-advice site, can also help to locate a travel agent who caters to your needs. (If a travel agency is also acting as your tour operator, *see* Buyer Beware *in* Tours & Packages.)

**⑦ Local Agent Referrals American Society of Travel Agents (ASTA)** ⊠ 1101 King St., Suite 200, Alexandria, VA 22314 ☎ 703/739–2782 or 800/965–2782 24-hr hotline 📠 703/684–8319 ⊕ www. astanet.com and www.travelsense.org. **Association of British Travel Agents** ⊠ 68–71 Newman St., London W1T 3AH ☎ 020/7637–2444 📠 020/ 7637–0713 ⊕ www.abta.com. **Association of Canadian Travel Agencies** ⊠ 130 Albert St., Suite 1705, Ottawa, Ontario K1P 5G4 ☎ 613/237–3657 📠 613/ 237–7052 ⊕ www.acta.ca.**Australian Federation of Travel Agents** ⊠ 309 Pitt St., Level 3, Sydney, NSW

2000 ☎ 02/9264-3299 or 1300/363-416 🖷 02/9264-1085 ⊕ www.afta.com.au. **Travel Agents' Association of New Zealand** ✉ Tourism and Travel House, 79 Boulcott St., Level 5, Box 1888, Wellington 6001 ☎ 04/499-0104 🖷 04/499-0786 ⊕ www.taanz.org.nz.

🚩 **International Agents, Approved by Holland Board of Tourism American Express Travel** ✉ 200 Vesey St., Lobby Level, 3 World Financial Center, New York, NY 10285 ☎ 212/640-5130 🖷 212/640-9365. **Connoisseur Travel** ✉ 13315 W. Washington Blvd., Los Angeles, CA 90066 ☎ 310/306-6050 🖷 310/578-1860. **Priority Travel** ✉ 35 E. Wacker Dr., Chicago, IL 60601 ☎ 312/782-7340 🖷 312/558-9167. British agents: **Supranational Hotel Reservations** ☎ 0500/303030. Canadian agents: **Canada 3000 Tickets** ✉ TD Centre, 1201 Pender St. W, Vancouver, BC V6E 2V2 ☎ 604/609-3000. **Exclusive Tours (Merit Travel Group Inc.)** ✉ 145 King St. W, Toronto, Ontario M5H 1J8 🖷 416/368-8332.

## VISITOR INFORMATION

Learn more about foreign destinations by checking government-issued travel advisories and country information. For a broader picture, consider information from more than one country.

Each VVV (Netherlands Board of Tourism) within Holland has information principally on its own region; **contact the VVV of the area you plan to travel to,** and ask directly for information. Alternatively, **contact the Holland Board of Tourism** at home, or in Holland, for countrywide information. For specific VVV tourist offices for most cities and towns in Holland, consult Visitor Information in the A to Z section found in the regional chapters of this book.

🚩 **Holland Tourist Offices In Australia** ✆ Box 261, Bondi Junction 2022, NSW 1355 ☎ 029/387-6644 🖷 029/387-3962.

**In Canada** ✉ 25 Adelaide St. E, Suite 710, Toronto. Ontario M5C 1Y2 ☎ 416/363-1577 🖷 416/363-1470.

**In Holland** ☎ 070/370-5705 nationwide information. **VVV** ✉ Stationsplein 10, 1012 AB Amsterdam ☎ 0900/400-4040 regional specialists [€0.55 per min] ✉ Koningen Julianaplein 30, 2595 AA The Hague ☎ 0900/340-3505 regional specialists [€0.45 per min] ✉ Coolsingel 67, 3012 AC Rotterdam ☎ 0900/403-4065 regional specialists [€0.35 per min]. For regional tourist offices, *see* the A to Z sections at the end of each regional chapter in this book.

**In New Zealand** ✆ Box 3816, Auckland 1 ☎ 09/379-5399 🖷 09/379-5807.

**In the U.K.** ✆ Box 30783, London WC2B 6DH ☎ 0207/539-7950 🖷 0207/539-7953.

**In the U.S.** ✉ 355 Lexington Ave., 21st fl., New York, NY 10017 ☎ 212/557-3500 or 212/370-7360 🖷 212/370-9507 ⊕ www.goholland.com ✉ c/o Northwest Airlines, 11101 Aviation Blvd., Suite 200, Los Angeles, CA 90045 ☎ 310/348-9339 🖷 310/348-9344.

🚩 **Government Advisories Australian Department of Foreign Affairs and Trade** ☎ 300/139-281 travel advisories, 02/6261-1299 Consular Travel Advice ⊕ www.smartraveller.gov.au or www.dfat.gov.au. **Consular Affairs Bureau of Canada** ☎ 800/267-6788 or 613/944-6788 ⊕ www.voyage.gc.ca. **New Zealand Ministry of Foreign Affairs and Trade** ☎ 04/439-8000 ⊕ www.mft.govt.nz. **U.K. Foreign and Commonwealth Office** ✉ Travel Advice Unit, Consular Directorate, Old Admiralty Bldg., London SW1A 2PA ☎ 0870/606-0290 or 020/7008-1500 ⊕ www.fco.gov.uk/travel. **U.S. Department of State** ✉ Bureau of Consular Affairs, Overseas Citizens Services Office, 2201 C St. NW, Washington, DC 20520 ☎ 202/647-5225, 888/407-4747 or 317/472-2328 for interactive hotline ⊕ www.travel.state.gov.

## WEB SITES

Be sure to visit Fodors.com (⊕ www.fodors.com), a complete travel-planning site.

🚩 **Suggested Web Sites** The official site for Holland's Tourist Board is ⊕ www.holland.com. The official Amsterdam site is ⊕ www.amsterdam.nl. More information is found at ⊕ www.visitamsterdam.nl. A Holland-wide site is ⊕ www.visiteurope.com/holland. Other general sites are ⊕ www.visitholland.com and ⊕ www.amsterdamhotspots.nl. ⊕ www.channels.nl is a Web site that guides you through the city with the help of many colorful photographs. For more information on Holland, visit ⊕ www.goholland.com. Go on a virtual tour of Dutch museums at ⊕ www.tribute.nl/hollandmuseums.

Go to ⊕ www.citymundo.com to view City Mundo's creative city-specialist directory of accommodations. Make bookings online with Nederlands Reserverings Centrum (the Dutch hoteliers' reservation service) at ⊕ www.hotelres.nl. For budget accommodations, try ⊕ www.stayokay.com, which provides comprehensive information for Holland—just click on "English" to access all information. At ⊕ www.iyhf.org Hostelling International has a site for worldwide reservations. For information on car-breakdown rescue service, camping, biking, hiking, and water sports, go to ⊕ www.anwb.nl, the Royal Dutch Touring Club. Go to ⊕ www.raileurope.com for pan-Europe ticket sales, for U.S. residents, which also has links to sites for Australian, Canadian, New Zealand, and British residents; you'll find these at the top of the screen. At ⊕ www.weer.nl you can find out the weather forecasts for Holland (in Dutch but with figures and visuals so it's accessible). For a fun site where you can learn a bit of Dutch, go to ⊕ www.learndutch.org. The English-language Dutch magazine *Expats Magazine* has online articles about news and current cultural events at ⊕ www.expatsonline.nl. One of the most informative English-language Web sites about Holland is at ⊕ www.expatica.com. *Shark* is a free newspaper with alternative listings, and their site is at ⊕ www.underwateramsterdam.com.

# Amsterdam

## WORD OF MOUTH

"We LOVED, LOVED, LOVED Amsterdam! You always hear of the Red Light District and the coffee shops and the laissez-faire attitude, but you don't hear how open and friendly the people are, how lovely the canals and side streets, how wonderfully trendy the restaurants and cafés, how people are out strolling at all hours of the night and you feel safe everywhere.
"The standard reply we were given in Amsterdam, when we asked for anything, was always 'Of course!' How refreshing."

—MaureenB

Updated by
Steve Korver,
Nicole
Chabot, and
Kim Renfrew

**AMSTERDAM HAS AS MANY FACETS AS A 40-CARAT DIAMOND** polished by one of the city's gem cutters: the capital, and spiritual "downtown," of a nation ingrained with the principles of tolerance; a veritable Babylon of old-world charm; a font for home-grown geniuses such as Rembrandt and Van Gogh; a cornucopia bursting with parrot tulips and other greener—more potent—blooms; and a unified social zone that takes in cozy bars, archetypal "brown" cafés, and outdoor markets. While impressive gabled houses bear witness to the Golden Age of the 17th century, their upside-down images reflected in the waters of the city's canals symbolize and magnify the contradictions within the broader Dutch society. With a mere 730,000 friendly souls and with almost everything a scant 10-minute bike ride away, Amsterdam is actually like a village that happens to pack the cultural wallop of a megalopolis.

Today, Amsterdam bills itself as the business "Gateway to Europe." Hundreds of foreign companies have established headquarters here to take advantage of the city's central location in the European Union. The city is consequently hastening to upgrade its infrastructure and to create new cityscapes to lure photographers away from the diversions of the infamous Red Light District. For example, the Eastern Docklands—once a bastion for squatters attracted to its abandoned warehouses—has recently been transformed into a new hub of culture focused around the boardwalk, the re-invented Hotel Lloyd, and the acoustically perfect Muziekgebouw.

Still, it will take Amsterdam time to fully erase more than eight centuries of spicy, erratic history: Anabaptists running naked in the name of religious fervor in 1535; suicides after the 1730s crash of the tulip bulb market; riots galore, from the Eel Riot of the 1880s to the squatter riots a hundred years later; jazz trumpeter Chet Baker's swan dive from a hotel room window in 1988. Today, the city's love of debauchery is still on display during the festival of Queen's Day, when it transforms itself into a remarkably credible depiction of the Fall of Rome. And endless debates, about sin, students, gayness, sex and drugs, even, yes, about coffee shops.

# EXPLORING AMSTERDAM

By Steve
Korver

This chapter divides Amsterdam into seven fascinating explorations. Heading out from Amsterdam's Centraal Station, the main transport hub, you first discover the Nieuwe Zijde—the "New Side," comprising the western half of the Centrum (city center). You then head westward to the Grachtengordel West, or Western Canal Ring, and its fascinating and funky Jordaan neighborhood. This section deposits you at the next sector, which begins at the northwest end of Grachtengordel Oost, or the Eastern Canal Ring, famed for its 17th-century Golden Bend area. Continuing south, you head past Leidseplein square to Amsterdam's famous Museum District and, just beyond, De Pijp, the colorful district that sits shoulder to shoulder with Amsterdam Zuid, the poshest residential sector of Amsterdam (which has no historic sites). The chapter then heads back north to cover the eastern half of Amsterdam, beginning again at Centraal Station and taking in the historic Oude Zijde—the "Old Side," comprising the eastern half of the Centrum. You then move

Though it's much smaller than Paris or Rome, Amsterdam manages to pack as many pleasures and treasures within its borders as cities five times its size. But with so many attractions so closely packed together, it can be hard to decide what to see, and in what order. The itineraries below may give you some guidance as you explore Amsterdam—both the famous sights and those off the beaten path.

The city's "musts" include the **Het Koninklijk Paleis** (Royal Dam Palace); the **Schreierstoren** (Weeping Tower), from which Henry Hudson set sail in the *Half Moon* in 1609 to ultimately discover New York; **Museum het Rembrandthuis** (Rembrandt's House); the fascinating **Museum Amstelkring** (with its "attic" church); the **Begijnhof** (Beguine Court), the most peaceful courtyard in the city; the **Gouden Bocht** (Golden Bend), replete with stately burghers' mansions bearing stepped gables and Daniel Marot doorways; the **Anne Frankhuis** (Anne Frank House), that wrenching reminder of the horrors of war; and, of course, the incomparable **Rijksmuseum** (State Museum) and the world's largest collection of paintings by the legendary artist, the **Van Gogh Museum.** Diamonds galore fill the shops and factories of the historic **Joodse Buurt** (Jewish Quarter) east of the Zwanenburgwal.

**If you have 1 day** If you're prepared to be exhausted, it's possible to sample quite a few of Amsterdam's highlights in a single day. You should begin at the main rail terminus, Centraal Station, and head south along the (unfortunately quite tacky) Damrak street, turning right on Oudebrugsteeg for several blocks until you get to the Museum Amstelkring (at Oudezijds Voorburgwal 40), where you'll get a full blast of Golden Age splendor, thanks to spectacular period rooms and the famous "Our Dear Lord in the Attic" church. Afterward, backtrack to the Damrak, turn left, and continue south—noting the famous Beurs van Berlage stock exchange along the way—until you reach the seething hub of the Dam, the broadest square in the old section of town. Landmarked by the Nieuwe Kerk—site of all Dutch coronations—it is also home to the magical 17th-century Het Koninklijk Paleis, which fills the western side of the square. Its richly decorated marble interiors are open to the public when the queen isn't in residence. From the Dam, follow the busy pedestrian shopping street, Kalverstraat, south to the entrance to the Amsterdams Historisch Museum. Here you can get an enjoyable, easily digestible lesson on the city's past, including its freely accessible Schutters Gallery with its massive Golden Age group portraits.

Passing through the painting gallery of the Historisch Museum brings you to the entrance of the Begijnhof, a blissfully peaceful courtyard oasis. Behind the Begijnhof you come to an open square, the Spui, lined with popular sidewalk cafés, and to the Singel, the innermost of Amsterdam's concentric canals. Cut through the canals by way of the romantic Heisteeg alley and its continuation, the Wijde Heisteeg, turning left down the Herengracht to the corner of Leidsegracht. This part of the prestigious Gouden Bocht is the grandest stretch of canal in town.

Continue down the Herengracht to the Vijzelstraat and turn right to the next canal, the Keizersgracht. Cross the Keizersgracht and turn left to find the Museum van Loon, an atmospheric canal house, still occupied by the family that has owned it for centuries but open to the public. Turn back down Keizersgracht until you reach the very posh Nieuwe Spiegelstraat; take another right and walk toward Museumplein. Rising up in front of you is the redbrick, neo-Gothic splendor of the Rijksmuseum, housing the world's greatest collection of Dutch art, or, for now, at least its "Best of the Golden Age" selection (with its world-famed Rembrandts and Vermeers) found in the only wing not undergoing massive renovation in the coming years. When you leave the Rijksmuseum, head for Museumplein itself; to your right is Paulus Potterstraat (look for the diamond factory on the far corner), where you'll find the Van Gogh Museum, which contains a unique collection of the artist's work.

Continuing along Paulus Potterstraat, at the corner of Van Baerlestraat, you'll reach what used to be the Stedelijk Museum (the collection of modern art from Picasso to the present is now temporarily housed on the second and third floors of the former Post Group building, close to Centraal Station). Just around the corner of Van Baerlestraat, facing the back of the Rijksmuseum across Museumplein, is the magnificent 19th-century concert hall, the Concertgebouw. A short walk back up along Van Baerlestraat will bring you to the Vondelpark—acre after acre of parkland—where you can relax after your day of sightseeing.

If you have<br>**3 days** The most iconic sights in Amsterdam are the grand, crescent-shape waterways of the *Grachtengordel* (girdle or ring of canals), lined with splendid buildings and pretty, gabled houses. On your second day, take full advantage of these delights—wander off the main thoroughfares, saunter along the smaller canals that crisscross them, and sample the charms of such historic city neighborhoods as the Jordaan. Begin at busy Dam Square and circle around behind the royal palace to follow the tram tracks into the wide and busy Raadhuisstraat. Once you cross the Herengracht, turn right along the canal; at the bend in the first block you will see the Nederlands Theatermuseum, which occupies two gorgeous 17th-century houses. Return to the Raadhuisstraat and turn right, following it to the Westermarkt. Stop for a fish snack at the stall under the shadow of the tower of the Westerkerk, on the right, facing the next canal. This landmark is Rembrandt's burial place. Make a right past the church and follow the Prinsengracht canal to the Anne Frank House, where you can visit the attic hideaway in which Anne Frank wrote her diary.

The neighborhood to your left, across the canal, is the Jordaan, full of curious alleys and pretty canals, intriguing shops, and cafés that are perfect for dinner. At the intersection of the Prinsengracht and Brouwersgracht, turn and take a digestive stroll along the Brouwersgracht, one of the most picturesque canals in Amsterdam. Stop in at one of the Jordaan's charmingly grotty brown cafés for an after-dinner drink, then head back to your hotel via the romantically lighted canal rings.

On your third day, start by exploring "Rembrandt's neighborhood," Amsterdam's historic Jewish Quarter. Begin at its heart, Waterlooplein. Today the square is dominated by the imposing modern Muziektheater/Stadhuis (Music Theater/

Town Hall), which is surrounded by a large and lively flea market. East of Waterlooplein, on Jonas Daniël Meijerplein, is the Joods Historisch Museum, skillfully converted from a number of old synagogues. Just to the east of that, on the corner of Mr. Visserplein and Jonas Daniël Meijerplein is the stately Portugees Israelitische Synagoge. Its interior is simple but awe-inspiring because of its vast size and floods of natural light.

Venturing over to the sylvan Plantage neighborhood, you'll find that the varied flora cultivated in the greenhouses of the Hortus Botanicus is just across the canal. Then you might want to make a short diversion to the Verzetsmuseum, which explains the Dutch resistance to the occupying forces, passive and active, during the Second World War. But for something more lighthearted, especially if you have children in tow, proceed to the Artis Zoo (which was attractively laid out in parklike surroundings in the 19th century and has a well-stocked aquarium). Time permitting, take Tram 9 or 14 farther east along Plantage Middenlaan, to the Tropenmuseum, which has riveting displays on tropical cultures and a special children's section.

Alternatively, you can walk from the synagogue up Jodenbreestraat, where—in the second house from the corner by the Zwanenburgwal—you'll find the Museum het Rembrandthuis, the mansion where Rembrandt lived at the height of his prosperity, and which now houses a large collection of his etchings. Cross the bridge to St. Antoniesbreestraat and follow it to the Zuiderkerk, whose rather Asian-looking spire is the neighborhood's chief landmark. Take St. Antoniesbreestraat north to Nieuwmarkt. Take Koningsstraat to the Kromboomssloot and turn left, then right at Rechtboomssloot (both pretty, leafy canals), and follow it through this homey neighborhood, the oldest in Amsterdam, to Montelbaanstraat; turn left and cut through to the broad Oude Waal canal. Follow it right to the Montelbaanstoren, a tower that dates back to the 16th century and was often sketched by Rembrandt. Up Kalkmarkt from the tower is Prins Hendrikkade, which runs along the eastern docks.

Following Prins Hendrikkade east, you'll enter the modern world with a bang at the NEMO Science & Technology Center. A little farther on is the Nederlands Scheepvaartmuseum, where there is a fascinating replica of an old Dutch East India ship. Across the bridge on Hoogte Kadijk is the Museumwerf 't Kromhout, where wooden sailing boats are still restored and repaired. If, on the other hand, you go west along Prins Hendrikkade to Gelderskade, you can see the Schreierstoren, the tower where legend has it that women used to stand weeping and waiting for their men to return from sea. This is where Henry Hudson set sail for America in the 16th century—so it's a fitting farewell finale for your third day.

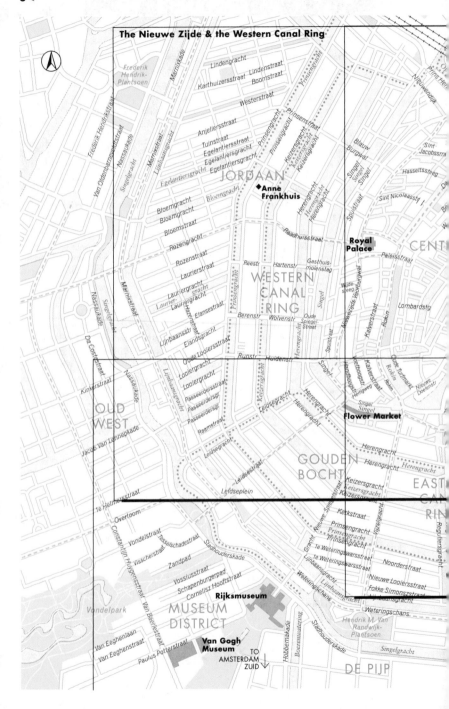

The Nieuwe Zijde & the Western Canal Ring

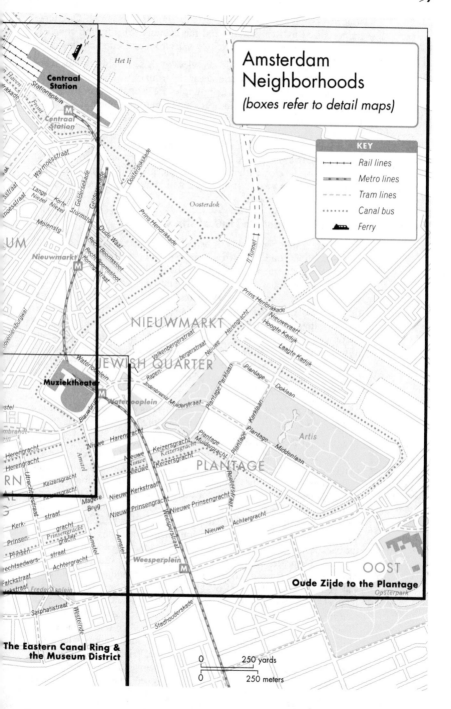

# Amsterdam Neighborhoods
*(boxes refer to detail maps)*

| KEY | |
| --- | --- |
| ┼┼┼┼ | Rail lines |
| ▬▬▬ | Metro lines |
| – – – | Tram lines |
| · · · · · | Canal bus |
| ⛴ | Ferry |

Centraal Station

Stationsplein

Het Ij

M Centraal Station

Oosterdoksdade

Oosterdok

Prins Hendrikkade

Warmoesstraat

Lange Niezel

Korte Niezel

Stormstd

Geldersekade

Molenstg

UM

Nieuwmarkt

M

Oude Waal

Rec Boomssloot

Recht Boomssloot

Kromm Straat

IJ Tunnel

Prins Hendrikkade

Nieuwevaart

Hoogte Kadijk

Herengracht

Laagte Kadijk

NIEUWMARKT

Valkenburgerstraat

bergerstraat

Nieuwe

JEWISH QUARTER

Rapen

Jodenbreestr Muiderstraat

Plantage-Parklaan

Plantage

Dokloan

Muziektheater

M

Waterlooplein

Plantage Kerklaan

Plantage

Artis

Plantage Middenlaan

stel

mbrandt

ein

Herengracht

Herengracht

Nieuwe Harengracht

Amstel

Nieuwe Keizersgracht

Nieuwe Keizersgracht

Keizersgracht

Plantage Muidergracht

PLANTAGE

Reelerstraat

RN

AL

Keizersgracht

Keizersgracht

Magere Brug

Nieuwe Kerkstraat

Nieuwe Prinsengracht

Nieuwe Prinsengracht

Weesperstraat

Nieuwe Achtergracht

Kerk-

Prinsen-

gracht

Prinsengracht

gracht

Prinsen- straat

rechtsedwars-

Achtergracht

Amstel

Weesperplein

M

OOST

Oosterpark

**Oude Zijde to the Plantage**

Falckstraat

straat Frederiksplein

Sarphatistraat

Westeinde

Stadhouderskade

**The Eastern Canal Ring & the Museum District**

0 — 250 yards

0 — 250 meters

south to cover two memorable neighborhoods, the Jewish Quarter—immortalized by Rembrandt—and the Plantage. Finally, you conclude with a tour of the sights of the city's waterfront and shipping district.

For a detailed and geographic overview of these neighborhoods, consult the "What's Where" section near the front of this book. And when it comes to street terms, a few helpful rules are in order. There are a number of address endings that indicate the form of thoroughfare: a *straat* is a street; a *laan* is a lane; a *gracht* or *sloot* is a canal, though some of these have been filled in to accommodate more road traffic; a *kade* is a canal-side quay; and a *dijk* is a dike, though in the urban environment this is not always obvious. House numbers are counted from nearest the center of the city, with the Dam as epicenter. Unfortunately, postal codes do not adhere to a system that will help you navigate from one neighborhood to another.

## The Nieuwe Zijde: The Western Half of the Centrum

A city with a split personality, Amsterdam is both a historic marvel and one of the most youthful metropolises in the world—and you'll see both sides in this first, introductory tour. In fact, a full blast of its two-faced persona will be yours simply by walking into Amsterdam's heart (if not soul): the Dam. For, as the very center of the *Centrum,* or center city, this gigantic square has hosted many singular sights, from the coronation of kings and queens, to stoned hippies camping out under the shadow of its surrealistically phallic National Monument. The Dam is just one showpiece of the western side of the historic center, known as the Nieuwe Zijde (New Side), a neighborhood just west of the Oude Zijde sector and taking up the area between Damrak (and its Rokin extension) and the Singel canal.

*Numbers in the text correspond to numbers in the margin and on the Nieuwe Zijde and the Western Canal Ring map.*

a good
walk

Beginning at **Centraal Station** ❶ ▶, wander straight up the once-watery Damrak while erasing with your mind's eye all the tourist tack and neon that disgrace the formerly epic buildings on the right. No such technique is required at the first prominent building on the left: the former stock exchange, **Beurs van Berlage** ❷, considered the most important piece of Dutch architecture from the 20th century. Once you have entered the **Dam** ❸, you will be quick to realize that this freshly scrubbed square—with its centerpiece, the National Monument (which has long attracted the backpacking community to sit beneath its granite shadow)—has been the city's center for centuries. On the right lies the square's most imposing building in both stature and history: the monumental **Het Koninklijk Paleis te Amsterdam** ❹ (Royal Palace), which is flanked to the right by the **Nieuwe Kerk** ❺—the certainly not new "New Church." Less ancient features of the square are the huge and bustling department store Bijenkorf (which appropriately means "beehive") and the famous diamond outlet Cassans. Ignore the middle-of-the-road walking-and-shopping streets that come out in front of the Royal Palace—the Kalverstraat to the left and its slightly more lowbrow Nieuwendijk to the right—to take the Mozes en Aäronstraat, which runs on the palace's right side.

The Neo-Gothic Magna Plaza—the former post office, which has been transformed into a specialty shopping plaza—will force you to take a left. Take the second right, Paleisstraat, but not before admiring the massive load that Atlas is carrying on the top of the Royal Palace's rear, and then perhaps glancing down Nieuwezijds Voorburgwal, once the country's Fleet Street but whose current bars and cafés form a magnet to the arty, hip drinking scene.

Then take the first left to walk down Spuistraat. If you see a huge building on the right with a huge punk-rocky mural on its facade, you are on the right track: this is the squat Vrankrijk, which has been the focal point of radical politics, music, and cheap beer for decades. Keep going until you get to Rosmarijnsteeg on the left. Proceeding down here and crossing Nieuwezijds Voorburgwal will drop you at the front door of the **Amsterdams Historisch Museum** ❻—certainly one of the city's best museums. If you choose to save it for later, take the alley, Sint Luciensteeg, to its left. Walking onward will connect you to the busiest shopping street of the Netherlands, the previously mentioned Kalverstraat (Calf Street), named after its former function as a cattle market. Turn right and walk a minute until you get to No. 92, where you can enter the Amsterdams Historisch Museum's courtyard café, the David & Goliath, with its central lime tree, planted for Queen Wilhelmina's coronation. In an adjacent passage across the courtyard is a grand enfilade of 17th-century civic guard portraits, on display here because some were too big to fit inside the museum.

Next, you'll enter Amsterdam's largest and most ancient *hofje* (almshouse): the tree-filled **Begijnhof** ❼. Although this painfully picturesque courtyard with its encircling houses and their pert little gardens is no longer home to nuns, its still entirely female residents do enjoy their quiet, and therefore the two entranceways regularly alternate their opening hours. (These are getting more and more irregular, since some residents are battling to close the doors completely—as of press time, the doors were open only between 8 and 11 AM daily.) If the entrance on the right along the Schutters Gallery's street extension, Gedempte Begijnensloot, is closed, head straight to the **Spui** ❽ square, following the wall on the right to get to the other arched entranceway. This route was once impossible when this street and square were moats protecting the honor of the Begijnhof's holy residents.

Once you are able to pull yourself away from this delightful part of Amsterdam, exit Spui to the southeast down Voetboogsteeg, whose entrance is immediately recognizable by the Arts and Crafts extravagances gracing the Art Nouveau Helios building (which won its architect, G. A. van Arkel, a bronze medal at the 1900 Paris World Fair) on the left and the more restrained grandeur of the University of Amsterdam's Maagdenhuis on the right (its name, Virgin House, refers to the orphans who lived here between 1629 and 1953).

Voetboogsteeg (Foot Restraint Alley) will connect you with Heiligeweg (Holy Road), the tiny remains of the Miracle of Amsterdam pilgrimage route that used to follow Leidsestraat and Overtoom out of the city and

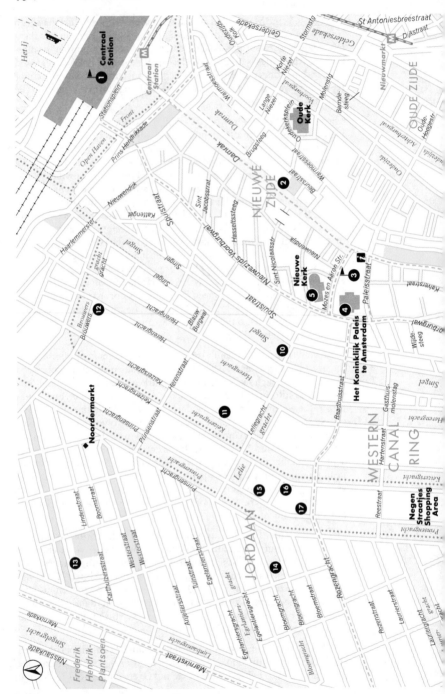

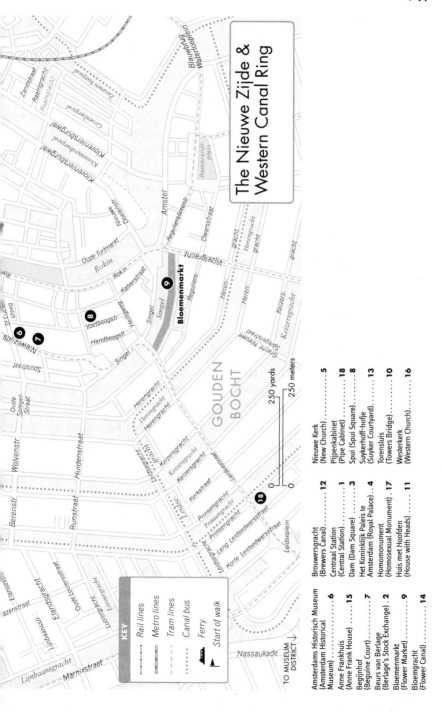

# The Nieuwe Zijde & Western Canal Ring

## KEY

| | |
|---|---|
| —— | Rail lines |
| ■■■■ | Metro lines |
| - - - | Tram lines |
| ••••• | Canal bus |
| ••••• | Ferry |
| ▲ | Start of walk |

250 yards

250 meters

GOUDEN BOCHT

Bloemenmarkt

TO MUSEUM DISTRICT ↓

Amsterdams Historisch Museum
(Amsterdam Historical
Museum) .......... **6**

Anne Frankhuis
(Anne Frank House) ..... **15**

Begijnhof
(Beguine Court) .......... **7**

Beurs van Berlage
(Berlage's Stock Exchange) . **2**

Bloemenmarkt
(Flower Market) .......... **9**

Bloemgracht
(Flower Canal) .......... **14**

Brouwersgracht
(Brewers Canal) .......... **12**

Centraal Station
(Central Station) .......... **1**

Dam (Dam Square) .......... **3**

Het Koninklijk Paleis te
Amsterdam (Royal Palace) .. **4**

Homomonument
(Homosexual Monument) . **17**

Huis met Hoofden
(House with Heads) ..... **11**

Nieuwe Kerk
(New Church) .......... **5**

Pipenkabinet
(Pipe Cabinet) .......... **18**

Spui (Spui Square) .......... **8**

Suykerhoff-hofje
(Suyker Courtyard) .......... **13**

Torensluis
(Towers Bridge) .......... **10**

Westerkerk
(Western Church) .......... **16**

into Europe. A rather nasty dominatrix type greets you over an arched entranceway whose inscription translates as "wild beasts must be tamed." And indeed, this once led into the Rasphuis (Shaving House) prison, which was quite the tourist attraction in its Golden Age heyday, when folks came to watch the prisoners shaving Brazilian hardwood for the use in paint. Nowadays, you might just want to pop through here to enjoy the view from the top of the Kalvertoren shopping complex.

Head south down Heiligeweg toward Koningsplein, an innocent-enough-looking square of sorts that has the sporadic habit of breaking out in riot: once in 1696 to protest the taxing of funerals and once in 1876 when the annual circus was canceled (Amsterdammers sure know how to fight for their rights). Turn left down the far side of the Singel to browse through the floating and fragrant **Bloemenmarkt** ⑨ flower market.

TIMING    Though you could potentially walk this route in a half hour, you should plan on spending at least three or four hours discovering all the sights. De Koninklijk Paleis (whose interior is closed for renovation until 2008) and the Nieuwe Kerk are known for their variable hours, so calling ahead might ease any potential heartbreak; Beurs van Berlage is closed on Monday. If you plan to do some shopping, keep in mind that shops are closed Monday mornings—although the whole of Kalverstraat has recently embraced, after much residual Calvinist procrastination, the concept of "Sunday shopping."

HOW TO GET    The Nieuwe Zijde is conveniently accessible by the city transportation
THERE    systems or by foot from Central Station where most tram and metro routes terminate. Trams 13, 14, and 17 go by Magna Plaza and then along Rozengracht through the Jordaan. Trams 1, 2, and 5 follow Nieuwezijds Voorburgwal and up Leidsestraat towards Vondelpark. Note that with all the current construction around Centraal Station and along the route of the projected new subway line being built that some routes may change. However, the maps posted at the stops are easy to decipher and will be updated with any changes.

## What to See

⑥ **Amsterdams Historisch Museum** (Amsterdam Historical Museum). Any city
FodorśChoice    that began in the 13th century as a sinking bog of a fishing village and
★    eventually became the 17th-century's most powerful trading city has a fascinating story to tell, and this museum does it superbly. It's housed in a rambling amalgamation of buildings, which was used as an orphanage in 1580 and then reopened as a museum in 1975. Although rich with art, models, and plain old treasures, the museum also employs a lot of state-of-the-art technologies: many will delight in the five different **speaking dollhouses** that tell of daily life through the centuries and a "white car" (a small car originally formulated to be a utopian form of urban transportation in the 1960s) in which you can cruise the city's streets. Budding musicians can even have a go on an old church carillon in one of the building's towers.

On the ground level are the old Boys' and Girls' Courtyards, separated by a loggia. In the boys' section, now the terrace of the **David & Goliath Café**, are rows of wooden lockers once used by the orphans for their meager possessions, now adorned with photos and artworks depicting Amsterdam's cultural life. Exiting the opposite end will lead you toward **Schutters Gallery**. This atrium—which used to be a narrow canal that separated the boy orphans from the girl orphans—is filled with huge, historic portraits of city militias (some of their red eyes make one suspect that marijuana has always been freely available in this city). Although Rembrandt painted more than a few portraits of the city Civic Guard members, pride of place here is given to works by Dirck Barendsz and Cornelis Anthonisz, notably the latter's *Meal of the 17 Guardsmen of Company H.* Elsewhere, be sure to take in the grand Regents' Chamber, adorned with a magnificent 1656 ceiling painting; the many relics and religious banners dealing with the "Miracle of Amsterdam" and the great religious fervor that rocked the 14th-century city; paintings of the great Golden Age, along with 17th-century city maps and dour Burgomeister portraits; and a stirring photographic panoply that captures the triumphs and tragedies of the modern-day metropolis. ✉ *Kalverstraat 92 and Nieuwezijds Voorburgwal 357, Nieuwe Zijde* ☎ *020/523–1822* ⊕ *www.ahm.nl* 🎫 *€6* ⊗ *Weekdays 10–5, weekends 11–5.*

❼ **Begijnhof** (Beguine Court). Here, serenity reigns just a block from the screeching of trams stopping next to the bustling **Spui** square. The richly scenic Begijnhof is the tree-filled courtyard of a residential hideaway, built in the 14th century for the Begijntes, a lay Catholic sisterhood. Created as conventlike living quarters for unmarried or widowed laywomen—of which there were many as a result of the Crusades' efficiency in killing off surplus men—this hof, or almshouse, required them to follow three simple rules: no hens, no dogs, no men. Rent was paid in the form of caring for the sick and educating the destitute. One resident, Cornelia Arens, so loved this spot that she asked to be buried in the gutter here in 1654—so out of respect, don't tap-dance on the slab of red granite on the walkway on the left side of De Engelse Kerk.

FodorśChoice
★

★ ❷ **Beurs van Berlage** (Berlage's Stock Exchange). Completed in 1903, the Stock Exchange is considered Amsterdam's first modern building. In 1874, when the Amsterdam Stock Exchange building on the Dam showed signs of collapse, the city authorities held a competition for the design of a new one. Fortunately, the architect initially chosen was caught copying the facade of a French town hall, so the commission was awarded to local boy H. P. Berlage. The building that Berlage came up with proved to be a template for its new century. Gone were all the ornamentations of the 19th-century "Neo" styles. The new Beurs, with its simple lines and the influence it had on the Amsterdam School architects who followed Berlage, earned him the reputation of being the "Father of Modern Dutch Architecture." In 2003, a freely accessible café was opened, complete with stunning mosaics in which to enjoy some scenic coffee slurping (Mon.–Sat. 10–6 PM). ✉ *Damrak 277, Nieuwe Zijde* ☎ *020/ 530–4141* ⊕ *www.beursvanberlage.nl* 🎫 *Varies based on exhibition* ⊗ *Varies based on exhibition.*

❾ **Bloemenmarkt** (Flower Market). Even if you don't want to stock up on bulbs, fresh cut flowers, or peyote home-grow kits here, you should drop by this tourist-friendly site because it's the last of the city's floating markets. In days gone by, merchants would sail up the Amstel loaded down with blooms from the great tulip fields to delight patroons and housewives. Today, the flower sellers stay put, but their wares are still offered on stalls-cum-boats. ⊠ *Singel (between Muntplein and Koningsplein), Nieuwe Zijde* ☉ *Mon.–Sat. 9:30–5.*

⌐ ★ ❶ **Centraal Station** (Central Station). The main hub of transportation in the Netherlands, this building was designed as a major architectural statement by P. J. H. Cuypers. Although sporting many Gothic motifs (including a unique wind vane disguised as a clock in its left tower), it is now considered a landmark of Dutch Neo-Renaissance style. (Cuypers also designed the city's other main gateway, the Rijksmuseum, which lies like a mirrored rival on the other side of town). The building of the station required the creation of three artificial islands and the ramming of 8,600 wooden piles to support it. Completed in 1885, it represented the psychological break with the city's seafaring past, as its erection slowly blocked the view to the IJ river. Other controversy arose from all its Gothic detailing, which was considered by uptight Protestants as a tad too Catholic—like Cuypers himself—and hence earned the building the nickname the "French Convent" (similarly, the Rijksmuseum became the "Bishop's Castle"). With more than 1,500 trains passing through daily, Centraal Station long ago learned to live with the guilt. And you should certainly not feel guilty about fighting your way through the street performers and backpackers who litter its doorways. ⊠ *Stationsplein, Nieuwe Zijde* ☎ *0900–9292 (public transport information).*

❸ **Dam** (Dam Square). Home to the Koninklijk Paleis and the Nieuwe Kerk, Amsterdam's official center of town is the Dam, which traces its roots to the 12th century, when wanderers from central Europe came floating in their canoes down the Amstel River and thought to stop to build a dam. A city began to evolve when a market was allowed in 1300, and soon this muddy mound became the focal point of the small settlement of Aemstelredamme and the location of the local weigh house. Folks came here to trade, talk, protest, and be executed. Ships once sailed right up to the weigh house, along the Damrak. But in the 19th century the Damrak was filled in to form the street leading to Centraal Station, and King Louis Napoléon had the weigh house demolished in 1808 because it spoiled the view from his bedroom window in the palace across the way. Regardless, the Dam, with its fresh and glistening white cobblestones, remains the city's true center.

The **National Monument,** a towering white obelisk in the center of the square, was erected in 1956 as memorial to the Dutch victims of World War II. A disconcerting modernist statement, it was designed with De Stijlian echoes by the architect J. J. P. Oud (who felt that De Stijl minimalism was in keeping with the monument's message). Every year on May 4, it's the national focal point for Remembrance Day, when the queen walks from the adjacent Koninklijk Paleis to the monument to lay flowers. The monument's urns imbedded in its rear contain earth from all the Dutch provinces and its former colonies (Indonesia, Suriname, and the Antilles). Oud designed the steps to be welcoming as seating; today, tourists still employ it as a favored rest spot from which to watch the world go by. ✉ *Follow Damrak south from Centraal Station; Raadhuisstraat leads from Dam to intersect main canals Nieuwe Zijde.*

❹ **Het Koninklijk Paleis te Amsterdam** (Royal Palace, Amsterdam). The Royal
**Fodor'sChoice** Palace is probably Amsterdam's greatest storyteller. But from the out-
★ side, it is somewhat hard to believe that this gray-stained building—with its aura of loneliness highlighted by the fact that it is one of the city's few freestanding buildings—was once called the "Eighth Wonder of the World" when it was built between 1648 and 1665 as the largest non-religious building on the planet, and that it is still used by the royal family for the highest of state occasions. From the inside, its magnificent interior inspires another brand of disbelief: this palace was actually built as a mere city hall—albeit one for a city drunk with cockiness for having created in a mere 100 years the richest and busiest harbor in the world.

The prosperous burghers of the 17th-century Golden Age, wanting something that could boast of their status to all visitors, hired the leading architectural ego of his day, Jacob van Campen. Van Campen's first problem was to create a surface on the blubbery former riverbed that was solid enough to build on. He used the standard local technique of driving wooden piles down to the solid subsurface—a method that inspired Erasmus to comment that Amsterdammers were the only people he knew who lived on treetops. What was less standard was the sheer total, 13,659—a number that is still pounded permanently into the minds of every Dutch schoolchild by the formula of adding 1 to the beginning and 9 to the end of the number of days of the year.

As the building rose, artists and sculptors with such immortal names as Ferdinand Bol, Govert Flinck (both students of Rembrandt, whose own sketches were rejected), and Jan Lievens were called in for the decorating. In the building's public entrance hall, known as the **Burgerzaal,** the world was placed quite literally at one's feet: two maps inlaid in the marble floor show Amsterdam as the center of the world, and the heavens painted above also present the city as the center of the universe.

The building has remained the Royal Palace ever since, and today plays host to Queen Beatrix (who required a few years to get over her fear of Amsterdam, after her 1966 wedding was disrupted by Provos throwing smoke bombs at her wedding carriage and her 1980 coronation was derailed by riots on the Dam). Unfortunately, like many things in town, the palace is closed for renovations until sometime in 2008. ✉ *Dam, Nieuwe Zijde* ☎ *020/620–4060* ⊕ *www.koninklijkhuis.nl* 🎫 *€4.50* ☾ *Oct.–Dec., Tues.–Thurs. and weekends 12:30–5; July–Sept., daily 11–5; occasionally closed for state events.*

★ ❺ **Nieuwe Kerk** (New Church). Begun in the 14th century, the Nieuwe Kerk is a soaring Late Gothic structure whose spire was never completed because the authorities—preoccupied with the building of Het Koninklijk Paleis, the city palace next door—ran out of money. Whereas the Oude Kerk had the blessing of the Bishop of Utrecht, the Nieuwe Kerk was supported by the local well-to-do merchant class, which resulted in an endless competition between the two parochial factions. At one point the Oude Kerk led the race with a whopping 38 pulpits against the Nieuwe

Kerk's 36, but first prize should go to Nieuwe Kerk for its still-existing pulpit sculpted by Albert Vinckenbrinck, which took him 19 years to complete. Other features include the unmarked grave of the poet Vondel, known as the "Dutch Shakespeare," and the extravagantly marked grave of Admiral Michiel de Ruyter, who daringly sailed his invading fleet up the river Medway in England in the 17th century, to become this country's ultimate naval hero. The Nieuwe Kerk has also been the National Church since 1815, when it began hosting the inauguration ceremony for monarchs. Since this does not occur that often, the church has broadened its appeal by serving as a venue for organ concerts and special—and invariably excellent—exhibitions, which attract a half-million visitors a year. These exhibitions have covered everything from Dutch photography to Moroccan treasures. ⊠ *Dam, Nieuwe Zijde* 🕾 *020/628–6909* ⊕ *www.nieuwekerk.nl* ⊠ *Admission varies according to exhibition* ☉ *During exhibitions Sun.–Wed., Fri., and Sat. 10–6, Thurs. 10–10. In between exhibitions hrs vary.*

**❽ Spui** (Spui Square). This beautiful and seemingly relaxed tree-lined square hides a lively and radical recent past. Journalists and bookworms have long favored its many cafés, and the Atheneum News Center (Nos. 14–16) and its adjoining bookstore are quite simply the city's best places to peruse an international array of literature, magazines, and newspapers. More cultural browsing can be enjoyed on the Spui's book market on Friday and its art market on Sunday.

> **need a break?** Several of the bar-cafés and eateries on Spui square are good places to take a break, including the ancient **Hoppe** (⊠ Spui 18–20, Nieuwe Zijde 🕾 020/420–4420), which has been serving drinks between woody walls and on sandy floors since 1670. If you just want to eat and run, try **Broodje van Kootje** (⊠ Spui 28, Nieuwe Zijde 🕾 020/623–7451) for a classic Amsterdam *broodje* (sandwich).

## City of 400 Bridges: The Western Canal Ring & the Jordaan

One of Amsterdam's greatest pleasures is also one of its simplest: strolling along the canals. The grand, crescent-shape waterways of the Grachtengordel (canal ring), which surround the old center, are made up of Prinsengracht, Keizersgracht, and Herengracht (Prince, Emperor, and Gentlemen canals), all of which are lined with grand gabled houses built for the movers and shakers of the 17th-century Golden Age. Commentators point to the fact that the Herengracht has always been the top address of the three as proof positive of the Netherlandish admiration for humility. Almost equally scenic are the intersecting canals and streets originally built to house and provide work space for artisans and workers, but which are now magnets to discerning shoppers, diners, and drinkers. The construction of the canal girdle that began at the dawn of the 17th century proceeded from west to east. This tour covers the first half-completed section between Brouwersgracht and Leidsegracht; some of its principal highlights are the Anne Frank House, the Westerkerk, and Noordermarkt, but you'll also get to see a panoply of canal-side mansions.

# MERCHANTS & MASTERPIECES: THE SPLENDOR OF THE BURGHER BAROQUE

**M**EN IN BLACK? *As much as Rembrandt's dour, frowning, and Calvinist portraits of town governors may be the image first conjured up by Holland's Golden Age, it should not be the last. A closer look at Dutch 17th-century painting shows that Holland was far from a country where people dressed only in black, wore wooden shoes, and interior decoration flowed in a minor key. Rather, befitting the boom economic years of the second half of the 17th century, Vermeer's sunlighted conversation pieces, Gabriel Metsu's music scenes, and Gerard Terborch's tea parties depict settings fitted out with all the fixings of true bourgeois splendor: alabaster columns, Delftware tiles, Turkish carpets, bouquets of Semper Augustus tulips (often as costly as jewels), farthingale chairs, tables inlaid with ivory, Venetian mirrors, ebony-framed paintings, and parrots from India. Strikingly, all this feather-bed luxury is still on view today in Amsterdam's historic mansions, such as the Museum Willet-Holthuysen, the Museum Amstelkring, the Bartolotti House, and other grachtenhuis (canal houses).*

This Baroque splendor was the result of Amsterdam's transformation into a consumer's paradise in the mid-17th century. Growing fat on the trade of cheese from Friesland, furs from Russia, cattle from Denmark, wine from France, spices from India, and the slave trade from the Java Seas, the rising Dutch burgerij, or burgher class, promptly developed a taste for frills and furbelows. Rose brick gave way to gleaming marble walls; the banketjestukken (breakfast pieces) paintings of the 1620s, often depicting a herring or two and a wineglass, were dropped in favor of the pronkstuk ("showpiece") still life—lobsters and venison set among tall goblets, bowls with strawberries, pewter ware, and silver jugs,

all brushed with the sensuality of innuendo.

Not surprisingly, the paintings merchants wanted to hang on their silver-leathered walls depicted the realities of daily life: milkmaids, drunkards, henpecked husbands, genteel music lessons, and elegant parties in tea salets (salons)—not muses and madonnas. All the while, preachers did their best to denounce Queen Money from their pulpits: the Dutch had to remember to be Deugdzaam (virtuous) and Deftzig (to act with propriety and reason). Even landscape paintings should be "cozy." In architecture, Mannerist taste for outlandish and overdone ornament—a holdover from the 16th-century Flemish Renaissance—was tempered by a new style of Italian Classicism, which toned down the clutter of design. Woe betide the burgomaster who did not practice moderation. Look at what happened to poor Rembrandt, who had married above his station, bought one of the grandest houses in the city, and decorated it to the nines, only to default on his mortgage and then liquidate his entire estate.

In the end, the "embarrassment of riches" gave Golden Age art its unique luster. Vermeer may essentially show us private individuals wrapped up in their own thoughts, but what enchants us is his wonderful depiction of an interior space, where his brush lovingly delineates everything from the textures of the deep pile of the Utrecht velvet cushion on a chair to the luxurious sheen of a woman's Lyons silk dress, from Delft tilewares to gleaming pewter chandeliers. The 17th-century Dutch may have come down with a case of advanced consumption—the mercantile, not physical, variety—but their art remains all the richer for it.

The area behind this stretch was set aside for houses for workers, many of whom were involved in this immense project, and for some of the city's smellier industries such as tanning and brewing. This area—bound by Brouwersgracht, Lijnbaansgracht, Looiersgracht, and Prinsengracht—was to evolve into the city's most singular neighborhood, the Jordaan (pronounced Yoarh-*dahn*). There are various theories on the origins of its name: as the other, more slummy side of the River Jordaan formed by Prinsengracht, or as a mutation of the French word *jardin* (garden), which can be regarded as either a literal reflection of its long-lost richness in gardens (still witnessed by its many streets and canals named after flowers and trees) or simply a sarcastic reference to its once oppressively nonfragrant reality.

Since the 1980s, the Jordaan has moved steadily upmarket, and now it is one of the trendiest parts of town. Its 1895 population of 80,000, which made it one of the densest in Europe, has declined to a mere 14,000. Today, you have a much better chance of hearing the spicy local dialect in Purmerend or Almere, where much of the original population has moved. But in many ways, the Jordaan will always remain the Jordaan, even though its narrow alleys and leafy canals are now a wanderer's paradise lined with quirky boutiques, excellent restaurants, and galleries—especially along the streets of Tweede Anjeliersdwarstraat, Tuinstraat, and Egelanteirsstraat.

*Numbers in the text correspond to numbers in the margin and on the Nieuwe Zijde & the Western Canal Ring map.*

**a good walk**

Exit the **Dam** ▶ ❹ on the tiny Eggertstraat—once called "Despair Alley," when it served as the church graveyard for suicides and the executed—on the right of **Nieuwe Kerk** and turn left onto Gravenstraat (Grave Street), which follows the church's rear walls. Cross the major artery Nieuwezijds Voorburgwal, minding that you do not get gravebound yourself by a cab or tram at this notoriously dangerous intersection. Enter the narrow Molensteeg and keep going straight to the bridge, **Torensluis** ❿, over the Singel, dotted with cafés to take advantage of the views up and down the canal.

Oude Leliestraat crosses the Herengracht and becomes the lovely Leliegracht, which has some excellent specialty bookstores. Be sure to stop and admire the unmissable building on the southwest corner of Keizersgracht (No. 174). This former insurance office—note the painting of the guardian angel near its top beneath its nonfunctional clock—was built by Gerrit van Arkel and is one of the city's few examples of *Nieuwkunst,* the Dutch version of Art Nouveau architecture. Formerly occupied by Greenpeace, who set sail to another location closer to the water, there are now plans afoot to transform this classic building into a classic hotel, so stay tuned. After studying this building, head north and take a right on Keizersgracht's odd-numbered side, where one can admire one of the finest Baroque examples of the Amsterdam renaissance, the **Huis met Hoofden** ⓫, or House with Heads, at No. 123. Continue north and at the end of the block, make a right on Herenstraat—a street lined with interesting shops—crossing Herengracht to head north on the east side of the canal. Continue straight to goggle at the gables of various canal-side houses before crossing the bridge over the lovely (and photogenic) **Brouwersgracht** ⑫. Continue along this canal westward for four blocks to then cross back at the bridge over Prinsengracht and proceed down its left bank. No. 7 was formerly the location of the clandestine Augustine chapel "De Posthoorn," which was attached by a secret corridor to the still existing café 't Papeneiland, which you can see across the canal on the corner with Brouwersgracht.

Cross over Prinsengracht, heading south to find **Noordermarkt.** Here, take the Noorderkerkstraat, which runs along the west side of the church to the once watery Lindengracht, host to a food and clothing market every Friday and Saturday. Hang a left and pause at the next intersection to imagine the bridge that once crossed here and hosted the once popular folk sport of eel pulling. This weekend pursuit involved hanging a slippery eel from a rope tied to the bridge and attempting to yank it off from a tippy boat below. One day in 1885, police tried to untie the rope, and the notorious Eel Riot ensued.

Continuing down Lindengracht a block or so will get you to the entrance to one of the city's most tranquil courtyards, the **Suykerhoff-hofje** ⑬ (at Nos. 149–163). Then turn left down 2e Lindendwarsstraat and you can have a straight "locals' walk"—with the street changing names at every block—all the way to Egelantiersgracht, about a six-block walk. About four blocks in this direction, keep your eyes peeled for the quirky building adornments provided by the Jordaan's artier residents and perhaps poke your head inside another courtyard, the Claes Claesz-hofje. Two blocks south is **Bloemgracht** ⑭, one of the stateliest of canals.

Take the shortest of jags to proceed left and find Prinsengracht, past No. 158, which was home to Kee Strikker, the woman who broke Vincent van Gogh's heart, while noting the crowds across the canal invariably lining up outside the **Anne Frankhuis** ⑮ (Anne Frank House). You may also notice that that side of the canal is about three feet higher than the side you are on in the Jordaan—only the richer Grachtengordel residents could afford the required sand. You certainly won't miss the church tower of Anne's neighbor, **Westerkerk** ⑯, behind which is the square of Westermarkt, the home to both the pink granite slabs that form the **Homomonument** ⑰ and onetime residence of 17th-century philosopher ("I think, therefore I am") René Descartes (No. 6).

After exploring this Jordaan-defining area—even though officially it is on the wrong side of Prinsengracht—cross Rozengracht and proceed down the right bank of Prinsengracht. Take note that the side streets you see across Prinsengracht are part of the **Nine Streets** specialty shopping and dining neighborhood. If you proceed right up Elandsgracht, you will first pass Johnny Jordaanplein with its bronze busts of Jordaan's revered singers Johnny Jordaan and Tante Leen and accordionist Johnny Meijer, who all gained a degree of immortality performing songs of lost love and beer in the local bars.

A still existing maze—but one that facilitates losing oneself in past ages of a kinder, gentler nature—is the rambling downscale antiques market, **Rommelmarkt** (daily 11–5), on Elandsgracht's southern parallel, Looiersgracht, at No. 38. From here, you can reconnect with Prinsengracht. Taking a right here brings you to the relatively banal entrance between Nos. 338 and 340 that once led to a Golden Age pleasure garden complete with mechanical figures of famous people (a Madame Tussaud's of sorts of its day) and a hedge labyrinth. However, pipe smokers or folks who just want a whiff of Amsterdam's long and obsessive relationship with tobacco will want to take this route farther up Prinsengracht to get to the **Pijpenkabinet** ⑯ (Pipe Cabinet).

If you'd rather not make this 10-block detour, just head straight over the bridge—which marks the Jordaan and your reentry into the generally more rarified air of the Grachtengordel—and turn left down Prinsengracht's eastern side and then right down Berenstraat into the very browsable heart of the **Nine Streets** specialty shopping area (perhaps checking out those artist-made books at Boekie Woekie at No. 16).

TIMING  It's difficult to say how long this walk will take, because it leads you through areas that invite wandering and the exploration of side streets. At a brisk and determined pace, you can manage the route in about two or three hours. Allow a minimum of an hour for the Anne Frank House, and try to get there early to beat the 10- to 20-minute lines that invariably form by midday.

The best time for canal walks is in late afternoon and early evening—or, if you're a reveler, early in the morning when the darkness gives the water a deep purple color before the dawn mist rolls in. If you're planning to go shopping in the Jordaan or the Nine Streets quarter, remember that shops in the Netherlands are closed Monday morning; however, that's the only time that the unmissable Noordermarkt flea market and the adjoining textile market along Westerstraat take place. With its many restaurants and cafés, the Jordaan is also a prime spot for evening frolicking.

HOW TO GET  The western edge of Amsterdam's "village," the Jordaan, is just a few
THERE  minutes stroll from the Dam square and Centraal Station. However, Trams 13, 14, and 17 follow Rozengracht and Trams 3 and 10 follow Marnixstraat to Haarlemmerplein.

## Sights to See

⑮  **Anne Frankhuis** (Anne Frank House). With her diary having sold more
Fodor'sChoice  than 30 million copies, Anne Frank is by far the most successful and fa-
★  mous author of the 20th century, testimony to the inspiring story of a girl who died at age 15 in a tragic denouement of the two-year saga now known to readers around the world. In the precious pages of *The Diary of Anne Frank* (published in 1947 as *The Annex* by her father after her death) the young Anne kept her sad record of two increasingly fraught years living in secret confinement from the Nazis. Along with the Van Daan family, the Frank family felt the noose tighten, so decided to move into a hidden warren of rooms at the back of this 1635-built canal house. Anne's diary has now been translated into more than 50 languages, making Anne the international celebrity she always dreamed of being. ✉ *Prinsengracht 263, Jordaan* ☎ *020/556-7100* ⊕ *www.annefrank. nl* 💶 *€7.50* ☽ *Sept.–Mar., daily 9–7; Apr.–Aug., daily 9–9.*

★ ⑭ **Bloemgracht** (Flower Canal). Lined with suave "burgher" houses of the 17th century, this canal was once so stately it was called the "Herengracht of the Jordaan" (Gentlemen's Canal of the Jordaan). In due course, it became a center for paint manufactories, which made sense, because Egelantiersgracht, an address favored by Golden Age artists, is just one canal to the north. Although modern intrusions have been made, Bloemgracht is still proudly presided over by "De Drie Hendricken," three houses set at Nos. 87 to 91. These 1642 mansions, built by Hendrick de Keyser (hence their nickname) and restored by the De Keyser Foundation, allure with their stepped gables, paned windows, and gable stones, carved with a farmer, a city settler, and a sailor. ⊠ *Between Lijnbaansgracht and Prinsengracht, Jordaan.*

⑫ **Brouwersgracht** (Brewers Canal). One of the most photographed spots
Fodor'sChoice  in town, this pretty, tree-lined canal at the northern border of the Jor-
★   daan district is bordered by residences and former warehouses of the brewers who traded here in the 17th century when Amsterdam was the "warehouse of the world." Without sacrificing the ancient vibe, most of the buildings have been converted into luxury apartments. Of particular note are the houses at Nos. 188 to 194. The canal is blessed with long views down the main canals and plenty of sunlight, perfect for photoops. The Brouwersgracht runs westward from the end of the Singel (a short walk along Prins Hendrikkade from Centraal Station) and forms a cap to the western end of the Grachtengordel. ⊠ *Jordaan.*

⑰ **Homomonument** (Homosexual Monument). This, the world's first memorial to persecuted gays and lesbians, was designed by Karin Daan, who employed three huge triangles of pinkish granite—representing past, present, and future—to form a larger triangle. On May 4 (Remembrance Day), there are services here commemorating the homosexual victims of World War II, when thousands were killed (the 50,000 sentenced were all forced to wear pink triangles stitched to their clothing). Flowers are laid daily for lost friends, especially on the descending triangle that forms a dock of sorts into Keizersgracht. Particularly large mountains of flowers form on December 1 (World AIDS Day). Signs will lead you to the "Pink Point of Presence," (☎ 020/428–1070 ⊕ www.pinpoint.org) one of the stalls along the east side of Westermarkt, which acts as an information point to visiting gays and lesbians. It is open daily noon–6 March through December; and Fri.–Sun. noon–6 PM January through February. ⊠ *Westermarkt, Jordaan.*

★ ⑪ **Huis met Hoofden** (House with Heads). The Greek deities of Apollo, Ceres, Mars, Minerva, Bacchus, and Diana welcome you—or rather, busts of them do—to this famous example of Dutch Neoclassic architecture, one of the grandest double houses of 17th-century Amsterdam. Delightfully graced with pilasters, pillars, and a step gable, the 1622 mansion is attributed to architect Pieter de Keyser, son of the more famed Hendrick. The heads adorn the entry facade and represent classical deities and are not, as a local tale has it, the concrete-coated skulls of six thieves decapitated by a vigilant but conflicted maid who ended up marrying the seventh. The house is now headquarters to the Monumentenzorg—custodian to many of the city's public monuments—and is not open to the public. ✉ *Keizersgracht 123, Western Canal Ring* ☎ *020/522–4888* ⊕ *www.bmz.amsterdam.nl.*

need a break? The city's most cherished slice of apple pie can be had at **Winkel** (✉ Noordermarkt 43, Jordaan ☎ 020/623–0223). For a funky setting and perhaps an inspired designer sandwich, head to **Finch** (✉ Noordermarkt 5, Jordaan ☎ 020/626–2461).

**⓲ Pijpenkabinet** (Pipe Cabinet). Considering Amsterdam's rich history of tobacco trading and its population's long tradition of rolling its own "shag," there should actually be a much larger museum dedicated to this subject. Perhaps this theoretical museum could relate such local facts as how urine-soaked tobacco was hailed as an able aphrodisiac in the 16th century, how "tobacco-smoke enema applicators" were used until the mid-19th-century in attempts to revive those found unconscious in the canals, and how Golden Age painters employed tobacco and its smoke as a metaphor for the fleeting nature of life. But as things stand, there is only this focused collection of more than 2,000 pipes, which aims to tell the tale of the Western European tradition of "sucking"—as the local parlance used to describe it. You might also want to check out the library or buy a pipe in the Smokiana shop. ✉ *Prinsengracht 488, Western Canal Ring* ☎ *020/421–1779* ⊕ *www.pijpenkabinet.nl* 🎫 €5 ☉ *Wed.–Sat. noon–6.*

**⓭ Suykerhoff-hofje.** For a moment of peace, enter this hof and take in its abundantly green courtyard, whose houses opened their doors in 1670 to Protestant "daughters and widows" (as long as they behaved and exhibited "a peace-loving humor") and provided each of them with free rent, twenty tons of turf, ten pounds of rice, a vat of butter, and some spending money each year. ✉ *Lindengracht 149–163, Western Canal Ring.*

**⓰ Torensluis** (Towers Bridge). Charming views down the Singel are yours from one of the café seats that line this broad bridge, originally built over a 17th-century sluice gate bookended with towers (hence the name), and still one of the widest in Amsterdam. If you do stop at one of the charming terraces here, let the knowledge of the bridge's ancient function as a lockup for drunks—dug deep in its foundations—keep you sufficiently sober. Note the bridge's statue of Multituli, the 19th-century writer who questioned Dutch colonial policies, before heading to the museum devoted to this author nearby at Korsjespoortsteeg 20. ✉ *Singel between Torensteeg and Oude Leliestraat, Western Canal Ring.*

★ **⓰ Westerkerk** (Western Church). Built between 1602 and 1631 by the ubiquitous Hendrick de Keyser and presumed the last resting place of Rembrandt, the Dutch Renaissance Westerkerk was the largest Protestant church in the world until Christopher Wren came along with his St. Paul's Cathedral in London. Its tower—endlessly mentioned in Jordaan songs—is topped by a gaudy copy of the crown of the Habsburg emperor Maximilian I (or, rather, to avoid a potential bar brawl, a later model of the crown used by Rudolph II). Maximilian gave Amsterdam the right to use his royal insignia in 1489 in gratitude for help from the city in his struggle for control of the Low Countries, and the crown's "XXX" marking was quickly exploited by the city's merchants as a visiting card of quality. More recently, Amsterdam's notoriety and the phallic nature of the quickly disappearing *Amsterdammertje* parking poles (which bear a XXX logo, a common civic insignia) has led many to speculate that the poles' markings suggest "Triple-X Rated." Now you know differently. . . . ⊠ *Prinsengracht 281 (corner of Westermarkt), Jordaan* ☎ *020/624–7766* ⊕ *www.westerkerk.nl* ☉ *Tower June–Sept., Tues., Wed., Fri., and Sat. 2–5; interior Apr.–Sept., weekdays 11–3; tower by appointment 020/689–2565* 💷 *€5.*

**need a break?** Along Westermarkt's southerly side is an excellent fish stall where you can sample raw herring or smoked eel (if you're so inclined). An equally traditionally Dutch way of keeping eating costs down is to pack one's belly with pancakes. The **Pancake Bakery** (⊠ Prinsengracht 191, Jordaan ☎ 020/625–1333) is one of the best places in Amsterdam to try them, with a menu that offers a near infinite range of topping possibilities—from the sweet to the fruity to the truly belly-gelling powers of cheese and bacon. If you're more thirsty than hungry, head to the brown café **Café Chris** (⊠ Bloemstraat 42, Jordaan ☎ 020/624–5942), up on the next corner, which has been pouring beverages since 1624. Its coziness is taken to absurd lengths in its tiny men's bathroom, whose cistern's position outside the door means that pranksters can easily shock you out of your reveries with a quick pull of the flusher. Be warned.

## Beyond the "Golden Bend": The Eastern Canal Ring & De Pijp

Amsterdam's 17th-century Golden Age left behind a tidemark of magnificent buildings lining its lovely canals. This is most striking along the famous Gouden Bocht (Golden Bend), where elaborate gables, richly decorated facades, finely detailed cornices, colored marbles, and heavy doors created an imposing architecture that suits the bank headquarters of today as well as it did the grandees of yore. This tour takes in such time-burnished marvels, but—to an even greater degree than with the tour of the Western Canal Ring and the Jordaan—this remains a city area of contrasts. Amsterdam's richest stretches of canals, the Eastern Canal Ring, which still glitters with the sumptuous pretensions of a Golden Age past, are a stark contrast to the more "street" (albeit quickly gentrifying) realities of the De Pijp district.

De Pijp ("The Pipe"), named for its narrow streets and towering gables, has been an "up-and-coming" neighborhood pretty much since it was built in the late 19th century to house working-class families. The cheap rent here now also attracts students, artists, and wacky radicals. This was once a place dense with brothels, where Eduard Jacobs sang his absurd but sharply polemical songs about pimps, prostitutes, and the disenfranchised (thereby laying the groundwork for the typically Dutch form of cabaret that is still popularly practiced by the likes of Freek de Jong and Hans Teeuwen). From his De Pijp grotto, the writer Bordewijk de-

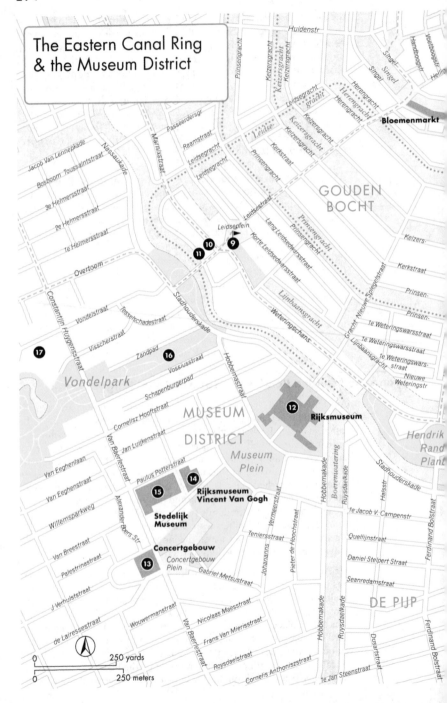

The Eastern Canal Ring
& the Museum District

KEY

- - - — *Metro lines*

- - - — *Tram lines*

...... — *Canal bus*

▶ — *Start of walk*

picted Amsterdam during World War I as a "ramshackle bordello, a wooden shoe made of rock"; Piet Mondriaan began formulating the revolutionary art of De Stijl in an attic studio on Ruysdaelkade (No. 75).

Later, waves of guest workers from Turkey and Morocco and immigrants from the former colonies of Suriname and Indonesia began arriving and were fundamental in revitalizing the area around Albert Cuyp Market—the largest outdoor market in the Netherlands—with shops, restaurants, and family values. By the 1980s, De Pijp was a true global village, with more than 126 nationalities. With a new underground Metro line destined—or doomed, depending on whom you talk to—to run through here by 2011, yet more upmarket investors are now appearing. But regardless, the Pijp remains a prime spot for cheap international eats and pub-crawling at local bars and cafés.

*Numbers in the text correspond to numbers in the margin and on the Eastern Canal Ring & the Museum District map.*

a good walk

The Muntplein, with the Dutch Renaissance **Munt Toren** ❶ ☞ (Mint Tower) as its focal point, is chaotic—but for a reason. From here you can enter the floating **Flower Market** to the south, witness the walking-and-shopping **Kalverstraat** to the west, or admire the facade to the north of Hotel de L'Europe (which Alfred Hitchcock used as a vertigo inducer in *Foreign Correspondent*).

By taking the road to the right of the tower, you can head to the **Torture Museum** (✉ Singel 449, Eastern Canal Ring ☎ 020/320–6642), with its iron maidens and other devices. It's open daily 10 AM–11 PM. If you'd rather stick temporarily with the chaos, however, you can follow the torturous crowds up Reguliersbreestraat's right side, past Easyeverything—a 24-hour cybercafé whose 650 monitors made it the world's largest for a short time in 2000—and the truly grand **Tuschinski Cinema** ❷, a theater that fuses art deco with a pure eclectic enthusiasm. For contrast, you might want to glance across the street from here to Nos. 31–33 and admire a classic piece of Functionalist-Constructivist architecture from 1934, which was originally a cinema; it has now been re-invented as the ultra-posh and trendy club-restaurant Cineac (☎ 020/530–6888 ⊕ www.cineac.nl). But before deciding that the Dutch have impeccable taste, wait until you witness the neon and touristic atrocities in **Rembrandtplein**, where things have changed a lot since it was the city's butter market. Something has gone terribly wrong here, the first clue of which may be the cheap iron (rather than bronze) statue of a cavalier Rembrandt in its center. But in the midst of the infinite middle-of-the-road cafés, clubs, and restaurants, there are some truly classy landmarks: **De Kroon** (No. 17), a shockingly spacious grand café complete with zoological specimens and a balcony, and **Schiller** (No. 26), with an amazing art deco interior that still evokes the bohemian types that used to hang out here.

After loading up on coffee at one of these establishments, exit the square through the enjoining smaller square Thorbeckeplein (you may first want to divert to the right up the very gay-friendly Reguliersdwarsstraat to pick out a restaurant or nightclub for later). The first canal you come to is Herengracht, and to the right lies the opulent Golden Bend, **Gouden**

**Bocht,** with some of the city's most impressive Golden Age residential monuments. On this corner you'll also notice the dark imposing Gebouw de Bazel. If you're more interested in looking at the life behind the facades, head left to **Willet-Holthuysen Museum** ❸. Then again, if there's a crack in the clouds, you may want to just hurry straight up Reguliersgracht to the intersection with Keizersgracht, where from the bridge an additional 15 bridges can be viewed.

From here hang a right to reach the majestically opulent interiors on display at **Museum van Loon** ❹. Almost directly across from here is the relatively new FOAM, or Photography Museum Amsterdam (✉ Keizersgracht 609, Canal Ring East ☎ 020/551–6500 ⊕ www.foam.nl ⊗ 10–5 Mon.–Wed., Sat., Sun., 10–9 Thurs.–Fri.), which has remarkably consistent Amstercentric exhibitions. Before backtracking east to Reguliersgracht to make the right that will get you to **Amstelveld** ❺, a tranquil square, perhaps first pause to observe the Amsterdam School bridge to the west crossing Vijzelstraat.

Sit awhile here at Amstelveld's famed café, now working under the new name of Janvier Proeflokaal (✉ Amstelveld 12 Canal Ring East ☎ 020/ 626–1199 ⊕ www.janvier.nu)—the adjacent blocks and Reguliersgracht combine to form one of the prettiest canal scenes in the city. As you approach Amstelveld square, you will see on its first corner a wooden church that includes the café Janvier Proeflokaal, with an exceedingly pleasant terrace, which looks across Prinsengracht to "De Duif" (No. 756); it arose in 1796 as one of the first openly Catholic churches after the Altercation in 1578. You may want to check whether its renovation is complete before taking Kerkstraat, running along Amstelveld's north side, to the east and crossing the excellently diverse shopping and eating strip of Utrechtsestraat. Continue until you reach the mighty river Amstel. Crossing it, the **Magere Brug** ❻, or Skinny Bridge, is the most photographed bridge in the city.

If you find yourself getting hungry and/or wanting to check out Amsterdam's most multicultural neighborhood, **De Pijp,** backtrack down Kerkstraat and turn left down Utrechtsestraat, follow its split to the right, cross the bridge, and take the second right to enter Europe's biggest and busiest day market, **Albert Cuypmarkt** ❼. Take the walking side street, 1e Sweelinckstraat, to the left toward the green peace of **Sarphatipark,** on whose opposite end you can connect with another charming walking and terrace street, 1e Van der Helststraat, which will bring you back down to the market. Heading straight will lead you through Gerard Douplein with its three funkily mosaic pillars, past Stichting Dodo (No. 21) on the right (where you can pause to invest in some laughably cheap secondhand Euro-bric-a-brac) before turning left on Daniel Stalpertstraat, which will get you to the Marie Heinekenplein. Turning right on Ferdinand Bol and right again on Stadshouderskade will take you to the front door of the **Heineken Brouwerij** ❽), a former brewery whose tour remains a must-do for some, a must-avoid for others. If you'd rather have a beer in a more relaxing atmosphere, there are lots of choices along the restful, tree-lined, and almost Parisian-flavor Frans Halstraat, which runs as Ferdinand Bolstraat's western parallel. *Proost!*

TIMING  If done briskly, this tour can be completed in an hour and half. Keep in mind, though, that Albert Cuypmarkt is a ghost town on Sunday, and the Museum van Loon does have particularly antisocial hours.

HOW TO GET
THERE  Trams 16, 24, and 25 follow Vijzelstraat through the canal ring and into the southern district of De Pijp. Tram 4 runs more to the east along Utrechtsestraat towards the RAI convention center.

## Sights to See

❼ **Albert Cuypmarkt** (Albert Cuyp Market). As the biggest and busiest street market in Europe, Albert Cuypmarkt—named after a Golden Age painter like the majority of the streets in De Pijp—welcomes 20,000 shoppers daily during the week and double that number on Saturday. Although you can come here for all your fresh food, textiles, and sundries, the atmosphere alone makes a visit worthwhile. With a decades-long waiting list for a permanent booth, things can get dramatic—if not occasionally violent—at 9 every morning on the corner of 1e Sweelinckstraat, where the lottery for that day's available temporary spaces take place. ⊠ *Albert Cuypmarkt between Ferdinand Bolstraat and Van Woustraat, De Pijp* ⊙ *Mon.–Sat. 9–5.*

❺ **Amstelveld.** One of the most tranquil corners in the Grachtengordel canal ring, Amstelveld square is landmarked by its **Amstelkerk,** a wooden church that arose in 1668 as one of the first openly Catholic churches after the Altercation in 1578. A Neo-Gothic face-lift was given to the interior in 1840, and the edifice was fitted out with community offices in the 1960s. Services are still held within its nave, however, where its liberal pastor is noted for pulling in the crowds. There's also an exceedingly pleasant terrace in the café Janvier Proeflokaal, which looks across Prinsengracht to "De Duif" (No. 756) and takes in many of the scenic pleasures—gabled houses, houseboats, canals. ⊠ *Bounded by Kerkstraat, Prinsengracht, Reguliersgracht, and Utrechtsestraat, Eastern Canal Ring.*

★ **Gouden Bocht** (Golden Bend). This stretch of the Herengracht—which indeed bends—between the Vijzelstraat and the Leidsegracht contains some of Amsterdam's most opulent Golden Age architecture. These buildings were the homes of the financial and political elite of the 17th and 18th centuries; in the late 19th century, most of them were converted into offices for banks and other financial institutions. Among the notable addresses on this stretch are "the most beautiful house in Amsterdam," No. 475 (a Louis XIV–style mansion designed by Hans Jacob Husly in 1703); 485 (Jean Coulon, 1739); 493 and 527, also in the Louis XVI style (1770); and 284 (Van Brienen House, 1728), another ornate Louis XVI facade. Interestingly, when initially laid out, the great canals, including Herengracht, had no trees, making the city look more than ever like a "Venice of the North." With time, elms were planted, in part to allow for their roots to stabilize the canal foundations. ⊠ *Bounded by Vijzelstraat and Leidsestraat, Eastern Canal Ring.*

❽ **Heineken Brouwerij** (Heineken Brewery). Founded by Gerard Heineken in 1864, the Heineken label quickly become one of Amsterdam's (and therefore the world's) most famous beers. As this factory couldn't keep

# THE CROWNING TOUCH: GABLES & GABLE STONES

**THE INFINITE ARRAY OF GABLES** of Amsterdam's houses, historic and modern, dominates the city's picture-postcard image and is a carefully preserved asset. The lack of firm land meant that Amsterdam houses were built on narrow, deep plots, and one of the few ways to make a property distinctive was at the top, with a decorative gable. The simplest and earliest form is the spout gable in the shape of an inverted funnel. When houses were still made of wood, this protective front could simply be nailed on. Another early form was the step gable, usually a continuation of the masonry of the facade, which rises to a pinnacle. This form was also used in Flemish architecture, as seen in the Belgian city of Bruges. The neck gable was the next development, a brick frontage in the form of a decorated oblong, hiding the angled roof behind. Bell gables are an elaboration of this, with more elaborate carved stone or decorative moldings. Another eye-catching element is the gable stone. These plaster or stone tablets placed above doors or built into walls were houses' identity tags before house numbers were introduced early in the 19th century. The gable stones are simple reliefs, sometimes brightly painted, which usually depicted the craft or profession of the inhabitants. For example, an apple merchant might have a depiction of Adam and Eve. To see a whole selection of rescued gable stones, pop into the Begijnhof courtyard or go to the St. Luciensteeg entranceway of the Amsterdam Historical Museum.

up with the enormous demand (today, most production rolls on in vast plants in The Hague and Den Bosch), it was transformed into a "Heineken Experience," an interactive center that offers tours of the more-than-century-old facilities. Everything from vast copper vats to beer-wagon dray horses is on view, and if you've ever wanted to know what it feels like to be a beer bottle, the virtual reality ride will clue you in. Others may enjoy the option to drink many beers in a very short time (note this tour is open only to visitors over the age of 18). ⊠ *Stadhouderskade 78, De Pijp* ☎ *020/523–9666* ⊕ *www.heinekenexperience.com* ⚑ *€10* ☉ *Tues.–Sun. 10–6.*

**⑥ Magere Brug** (Skinny Bridge). Of Amsterdam's 60-plus drawbridges, the Magere (which derives from "meager" in Dutch) is the most famous. It was purportedly built in 1672 by two sisters living on opposite sides of the Amstel, who wanted an efficient way of sharing that grandest of Dutch traditions: the *gezellig* (socially cozy) midmorning coffee break. Nowadays, it's spectacularly lit with electric lights at night, and often drawn up to let boats pass by. Many replacements to the original bridge have come and gone, and this, dating to 1969, is but the latest. ⊠ *Between Kerkstraat and Nieuwe Kerkstraat, Eastern Canal Ring.*

Fodor's Choice ★

**①** **Munt Toren** (Mint Tower). This tower received its name in 1672, when French troops occupied much of the surrounding Republic and Amsterdam was given the right to mint its own coins here for a brief two-year period. Although the spire was added by Hendrick de Keyser in 1620, the medieval tower and the adjoining guardhouse were part of a gate in the city's fortifying wall from 1490. The guardhouse, which now houses a Dutch porcelain shop, has a gable stone above its entrance, which portrays two men and a dog in a boat. This is a symbolic representation of the city, where warrior and merchant bonded together by loyalty—that would be the dog—are sailing toward the future. The tower's carillon of 38 bells was originally installed in 1666 by the famed Hemony Brothers. Although it is now automated to play every 15 minutes, a live recital often takes place on Friday between 3 and 4. ⊠ *Muntplein, Eastern Canal Ring.*

**②** **Tuschinski Cinema.** Although officially the architect of this "Prune Cake"— as it was described when it first opened in 1921—was H. L. De Jong, the financial and spiritual force was undoubtedly Abram Icek Tuschinski (1886–1942), a Polish Jew who after World War I decided to a build a theater that was "unique." And because interior designers Pieter de Besten, Jaap Gidding, and Chris Bartels came up with a dizzying and dense mixture of Baroque, Art Nouveau, Amsterdam School, Jugendstil, and Asian influences, it is safe to say that he achieved his goal. It began as a variety theater welcoming such stars as Marlene Dietrich, but it soon became a cinema, and to this day viewing a film from one of the extravagant private balconies remains an unforgettable experience—especially if you order champagne. Sobering note: Tuschinski died in Auschwitz. ⊠ *Reguliersbreestraat 26–28, Eastern Canal Ring* ☎ *0900–1458.*

**③** **Willet-Holthuysen Museum.** Few patrician houses are open to the public along the Herengracht, so make a beeline to this mansion to see Grachtengordel (Canal Ring) luxury at its best. In 1895, the widow Sandrina Louisa Willet-Holthuysen donated the house and contents—which included her husband's extensive art collection—to the city of Amsterdam. You can now wander through this 17th-century canal house, now under the management of Amsterdams Historisch Museum, and discover all its original 18th-century interiors, complete with that era's mod-cons from ballroom to *cabinet des merveilles* (rarities cabinet). You can air out the aura of Dutch luxury by lounging in the French-style garden in the back. ⊠ *Herengracht 605, Eastern Canal Ring* ☎ *020/523–1822* ⊕ *www.willetholthuysen.nl* ☒ *€4* ☉ *Weekdays 10–5, weekends 11–5.*

FodorśChoice
★

## Van Gogh & Company: From Leidseplein to the Museum District

With art, like all good things in life, moderation is the key . . . but you'll need to make an exception here. Amsterdam's acclaimed density of artistic masterpieces is concentrated around Museumplein, and the sheer quantity of quality here can be frankly overwhelming. This single square mile offers a remarkably complete lesson in the history of Western art: from the realistic but symbolically obtuse depictions offered by the masters of the Golden Age in the Rijksmuseum, to the artistic revolution of the end of the 19th century when artists—such as Van Gogh (and his colleagues on view in the Van Gogh Museum)—had to reinvent the relevance of painting in a photographic age, through to all the ensuing evolutions and revolutions of the 20th century documented in the Stedelijk Museum.

Unfortunately, this area is currently going through renovation chaos: the Rijksmuseum is only partially open until at least 2008, and the Stedelijk has found a wonderful new temporary home in a former post office near Central Station until at least the end of 2006. So, before you visit either place, be sure to call ahead.

This area of the "Old South," built as a very posh residential area for the rich at the end of the 19th century, harbors both vast expanses of green to neutralize the eyeballs and the city's best upmarket shopping opportunities to feed one's baser instincts; the former found in the city's beloved Vondelpark, the latter in the antique and couture shops along posh Nieuwe Spiegelstraat. And certainly this tour's starting point of the Leidseplein—just to the northwest of the Museum District proper—with its richness in performance and music venues, offers evening entertainment that may soothe any other senses that may feel neglected.

*Numbers in the text correspond to numbers in the margin and on the Eastern Canal Ring & the Museum District map.*

**a good walk**

We begin in **Leidseplein** ❾ ►, which might seem like a lowbrow start to a tour of some of world's greatest art treasures. But if you ignore the sports bars, the faux Irish pubs, and the side streets filled with tourist-preying eateries, you'll actually find yourself in the city's central zone for the performing arts—and this doesn't even include the street performers serenading the terraces. Theatergoers flock here for the offerings at the great **Stadsschouwburg** ❿ theater. Looming over the southwest corner of Leidseplein is the magical castle-like structure of the **American Hotel** ⓫.

Exit Leidseplein via its southeast extension, the Kleine Gartmanplantsoen, which features bronze lizards in the grass parkette on the left, and the political and cultural center–café, De Bali (No. 10) on the right, beside which are large Greek pillars whose mantle is emblazed with the Latin for "Wise men do not piss in the wind." This is the entrance to Max Euweplein, whose surrounding buildings used to be a prison complex that held Nazi resisters during the occupation (but are now dubiously modernized and house, among other ventures, a casino). But the square does have a huge chess set—in tribute to Max Euwe, who as a world champion became the nation's chess hero—and also provides a quick conduit to the gloriously green Vondelpark, this tour's end point.

But to stay on the culture trail continue down Weteringschans, past the Paradiso, until you see the *Night Watch*'s home, the **Rijksmuseum** ⓬, on the right. Here you may choose to go left down the antiques gallery–rich **Spiegelstraat,** or recall it for later as a handy passage back to the historic center of town. Otherwise, there might be a violinist or some Mongolian throat-singers on hand to accompany you as you take the acoustically rich arched passage under the museum to reach the freshly revamped **Museumplein** (Museum Square), whose new sense of space is quite at odds with the city's famed crampedness. Visible straight across the wading pool—which can miraculously turn to ice overnight in the heat of summer (thanks to some high-tech wizardry)—is the classical music mecca of the **Concertgebouw ⑬**, cherished by musicians the world over for its superlative acoustics. The round titanium-roofed building visible to its right is the new wing of the **Rijksmuseum Vincent Van Gogh (better known as the Van Gogh Museum) ⑭**, whose neighbor is the yet more modern **Stedelijk Museum ⑮**, usually home to the city's largest collection of contemporary art but currently planning to take its show on the road during renovations. From here you can go to the right down Van Baerlestraat to get to the city's green lungs of **Vondelpark ⑯**, perhaps pausing to window-shop along the cross street **PC Hooftstraat**, the nation's poshest high-end designer fashion strip. Film lovers will be sure to check out the park's **Nederlands Filmmuseum ⑰**, set in a lovely 19th-century pavilion.

TIMING  Merely walking this tour will take you less than an hour. However, truly absorbing all the art treasures along this route would require an additional two weeks. If you'd rather not bring a sleeping bag with you, then plan to spend a couple of hours in the Rijksmuseum and the Van Gogh Museum, and then take another hour to wander through the Stedelijk Museum. After seeing infinite representations of light fall, you can see the real thing in Vondelpark—where just before twilight when it's sunny, you can witness the unique quality of light that has played muse for the country's artists for centuries.

HOW TO GET THERE  From the central square of the Dam it takes about a quarter hour to hike the Leidsegracht or Leidsestraat to reach the southern sector of Amsterdam and the museum district. However, Nieuwe Spiegelstraat is a much more direct and relaxed route towards Museumplein. However, you can take Trams 1, 2, and 5 direct to Leidseplein or Trams 2 and 5 direct to Museumplein, although Trams 3, 12, 16, and 24 will deposit you at the Concertgebouw. The canals will also get you to the Rijksmuseum, courtesy of the Museumboot and its stop on the Singlegracht.

## Sights to See

**⑫ American Hotel.** The architecture of this landmark might drive a professional art historian a little batty. Designer Willem Kromhout grafted Neo-Gothic turrets, Jugenstil gables, art deco stained glass, and an Arts & Crafts clock tower onto a proto–Amsterdam School structure, and the result is somewhere between a Venetian palazzo (after all, it does overlook the Singelgracht and has its own boat landing) and a Dutch castle. No matter: this 1902 edifice is a charmer. Inside is the famed art deco–style Café Americain, where Mata Hari held her wedding reception. However, this café lost all its street credibility when it banned hippies in the '60s. ✉ *Leidsekade 97, Museum District* ☎ *020/556–3232* 🌐 *www.amsterdam-american.crowneplaza.com.*

★ **⑬ Concertgebouw** (Concert Building). The Netherlands' premier and globally acclaimed concert hall has been filled since 1892 with the music of the Royal Concertgebouw Orchestra and an endless stream of international artists. You'll recognize the building at once, if not by its nese classicist facade then by the golden lyre at its peak. Designed . Al van Gendt to be one of Amsterdam's most sumptuous examples of the Neo-Renaissance style, it continues to charm many of its 800,000 visitors per year. Indeed, this rates as the most visited concert hall in the world. There are two concert halls in the building, the Kleine (Small) and the Grote (Large), the latter being the most acoustically perfect on the planet, according to many pundits. The entrance is through the glass extension along the side. There are no tours of the building, so you'll need to buy a ticket to a concert to see beyond the broad lobby. Or, if you visit on a Wednesday before 12:30, from September to June, you can attend a free lunchtime concert. ⊠ *Concertgebouwplein 2–6, Museum District* ☎ *020/675–4411 24-hr concert schedule and hot line, 020/ 671–8345 box office* ⊕ *www.concertgebouw.nl.*

**need a break?**

For Concertgebouwgoers, a posh, popular, and freshly renovated pre- and post-concert dining location is **Bodega Keyzer** (⊠ Van Baerlestraat 96, Museum District ☎ 020/671–1441), whose French-inspired dishes, old-world interior, and uniformed waiters breathe with an appropriately rarified air.

**❾ Leidseplein** (Leidse Square). In medieval times, Leidseplein was the parking lot for horse-drawn carts since they were banned from the city center—an enlightened policy that today's city planners might learn from. Today, Leidseplein is where tourists come to park their behinds on the terraces and absorb the infinite crowds and street performers. Though it's difficult to imagine, this was long a top hangout for artists and intellectuals, and where Communists and Fascists came to clash between the wars. After World War II, bohemian frolicking took place in still somewhat evocative cafés like Reijnders (Leidseplein 6), the former resistance hangout Eijlders (Korte Leidsedwarsstraat 47), and the one within the impressively art deco American Hotel.

**need a break?**

Leidseplein and its surroundings are dense with café-break opportunities. The well-read and politically engaged crowd gathers around the café **De Balie** (⊠ Kleine Gartmanplantsoen 10, Museum District ☎ 020/553–5130). The theatrical crowd can be witnessed at **Café Cox** (⊠ Marnixstraat 429, Museum District ☎ 020/620–7222), part of the Stadsschouwburg building. The lounging American can find a familiar home at **Boom Chicago Lounge** (⊠ Leidseplein 12, Museum District ☎ 020/530–7300), which also provides a terrace option.

★ **⓱ Nederlands Filmmuseum.** One of the highlights of Vondelpark is the Netherlands Film Museum, which occupies an elegant 19th-century entertainment pavilion, first opened to the public in 1881 as a café. Here you'll find on display such historic treasures as Amsterdam's first movie theater, the **Cinema Parisien**, replete with its 1910 art deco interior, a film poster collection, and an adjacent public library (⊠ Vondelstraat 69–71 ☎ 020/589–1435 ☉ 1–5 Tues.–Fri.). The shows that play daily in its two cinemas draw on material from all over the world as well as from its substantial archives (which include such gems as hand-tinted silent movies). On Thursday in summer, there are free outdoor screenings beginning at dusk.

Even if you're not into film, check out the museum's very popular Café Vertigo, whose terrace tables offer grand views of Vondelpark. It's right near the Roemer Visscherstraat entrance. ⊠ *Vondelpark 3, Museum District* ☎ *020/589-1400* ⊕ *www.nfm.nl* ✉ *Free* ☽ *Mon.–Fri., 9 AM–10:30 PM, Sat.–Sun. hour before screenings.*

**⑫ Rijksmuseum** (State Museum). The Netherlands' greatest museum, the Rijksmuseum is home to Rembrandt's *Night Watch,* Vermeer's *The Kitchen Maid,* and a near infinite selection of world-famous masterpieces by the likes of Steen, Ruisdael, Brouwers, Hals, Hobbema, Cuyp, Van der Helst, and their Golden Age ilk. This national treasure, however, will be largely closed until summer 2008 for extensive renovation and rebuilding, following the plans of Seville's architect duo Antonio Cruz and Antonio Ortiz. Only the South Wing—which has now through corporate sponsorship been renamed the Philips Wing—will remain reliably open to house a "Best of" selection. However, with a new exhibition space in Schiphol Airport (Rijksmuseum Amsterdam Schiphol, Holland Boulevard between piers E and F, ☎ 020/653–5036, Mon.–Fri. 7 AM–8 PM, admission free), and promises of several "roaming" exhibits, visitors can still get an ample dose of Golden Age glory (as long as they call ahead or check the Web site).

The central figure of Rembrandt's *Night Watch* is Frans Banningh Cocq. His militia buddies who surround him each paid 100 guilders to be included—quite the sum in those days, so a few of them complained about being lost in all those shadows. It should also be noted that some of these shadows are formed by the daylight coming in through a small window. Daylight? Indeed, the *Night Watch* might be better described as the *Day Watch,* but it received its name when it was obscured with soot—imagine the restorers' surprise. ⊠ *Stadhouderskade 42; Entrance during renovations: Jan Luijkenstraat 1, Museum District* ☎ *020/674–7000* ⊕ *www.rijksmuseum.nl* ✉ *€9* ☽ *Daily 10–5.*

**need a break?** After walking through miles of art, there's nothing more invigorating than indulging in the fish-protein infusions on offer at the fish stall on the Rijksmuseum's front east side. **Altena** (⊠ Jan Luijkenstraat/ Stadhouderskade, Museum District) also has the bonus of a proprietor who will gladly talk you through the finer points of sliding a raw herring down your throat. On Museumplein, one can sit down on the patio of **Cobra Café** (⊠ Hobbemastraat 18, Museum District ☎ 020/470–0111) for a snack from the acclaimed menu, or choose a spot of your own after stocking up at the Albert Heijn supermarket under the grass slope across from the Concertgebouw.

**⑭ Rijksmuseum Vincent Van Gogh** (Vincent Van Gogh Museum). Opened in 1973, this remarkable light-infused building, based on a design by famed De Stijl architect Gerrit Rietveld, venerates the short, certainly not sweet, but highly productive career of everyone's favorite tortured 19th-century artist. First things first: Vincent was a Dutch boy, and therefore his name is not pronounced like the "Go" in Go-Go Lounge but rather like the "Go" uttered when one is choking on a whole raw herring.

Although some of the Van Gogh paintings that are scattered throughout the world's high-art temples are of dubious provenance, this collection's authenticity is indisputable: its roots trace directly back to brother Theo van Gogh, Vincent's artistic and financial supporter. The 200 paintings and 500 drawings on display here can be divided into his five basic periods, the first beginning in 1880 at age 27 after his failure in finding his voice as schoolmaster and lay preacher. These early depictions of Dutch country landscapes and peasants—particularly around the Borinage and Nuenen—were notable for their dark colors and a refusal to romanticize (a stand that perhaps also led in this period to his various failures in romance). The *Potato Eaters* is perhaps his most famous piece from this period. ⊠ *Paulus Potterstraat 7, Museum District* ☎ *020/570–5200* ⊕ *www.vangoghmuseum.nl* 🎫 *€10* ☼ *Sat.–Thurs. 10–6, Fri. 10–10.*

**❿ Stadsschouwburg** (Municipal Theater). Somehow managing to retain its central dominance on a square given over to neon and advertising, the Stadsschouwburg has been here since 1784. The Stadsschouwburg actually burned and had to be rebuilt several more times before receiving its current Neo-Renaissance facade and lushly Baroque horseshoe interior in 1890. The decades that followed saw the general state of the nation's theater scene descend into staidness until 1968 when, during a performance of the *Tempest,* the actors were showered with tomatoes. Part of a nationwide protest, the "tomato campaign" expressed the discontent with established theater's lack of social engagement. It resulted in more subsidies for newer theater groups—many of which now form the old guard who regularly play here.

Although the majority of the programming is in Dutch, it should be said that contemporary Dutch theater is marked by a strong visual—and often hilariously absurdist—sense. There's also a constant stream of visiting international theater and dance companies. ⊠ *Leidseplein 26, Museum District* ☎ *020/624–2311* ⊕ *www.stadsschouwburgamsterdam.nl.*

**★ ⓯ Stedelijk Museum** (Municipal Museum). Hot and happening modern art of this century and the last has one of the world's most respected homes here at the Stedelijk, which occupies a wedding-cake Neo-Renaissance structure first opened in 1895. It's a home that is undergoing renovation, however: beginning in 2006 and lasting at least until 2008, the museum will be undergoing massive refurbishment and addition of a new wing by globally acclaimed local architects Benthem/Crouwel, all of which undoubtedly will disrupt accessibility for several years to come. So it's best to call ahead or check the Web site to avoid disappointment (or to be directed to the many planned exhibitions in temporary spaces).

Until at least late 2006, the Stedelijk is in a marvelous temporary location near Central Station: Post CS (Oosterdokskade 5). It even overshadows its usual digs—in part thanks to the hip café-bar-restaurant **11**

(✉ 11th floor ☎ 020/625–5999 ⊕ www.ilove11.nl) that harbors breathtaking views of the city.

The Stedelijk began to cover its present course only after World War II. It now has a collection of paintings, sculpture, drawings, prints, photography, graphic design, applied arts, and new media that numbers 100,000 pieces. Although this stunning collection includes many works by such ancients of modernism as Chagall, Cézanne, Picasso, Monet, and Malevich, there is a definite emphasis on the post–World War II period: with such local CoBrA boys as Appel and Corneille; American Pop artists as Warhol, Johns, Oldenburg, and Liechtenstein; Abstract Expressionists as de Kooning and Pollock, and contemporary German Expressionists as Polke, Richter, and Baselitz. Still, many head here to find the homegrown masterworks of the De Stijl school, including the amazing *Red Blue Chair* Gerrit Rietveld designed in 1918, and the noted Mondriaan canvases on display, including his 1920 *Composition in Red, Black, Yellow, Blue, and Grey.* ✉ *Paulus Potterstraat 13, Museum District* ☎ *020/573–2911* ⊕ *www.stedelijk.nl* 🎫 €9 ⊙ *Daily 10–6.*

☼ 🅰 **Vondelpark.** On sunny days, Amsterdam's "Green Lung" is the most densely populated section of the city. From all walks of life, Vondelpark becomes *the* place where sun is worshiped, joints are smoked, beer is quaffed, picnics are eaten, bands are grooved to, dogs are walked, balls are kicked, lanes are biked and roller-skated on, and bongos are bonged. By evening, the park has invariably evolved into one large outdoor café. But the chaos is relatively tame and the appeal now much broader compared with that of the summer of 1973, when more than 100,000 camping youths called it home and airlines such as KLM saw bigger profits in advertising tickets to "Hippie Park" instead of its dull surroundings, "Amsterdam."

Such a future was certainly not envisioned in 1865 when Vondelpark was laid out as a 25-acre "walking and riding park" to be enjoyed by the residents of the affluent neighborhood that was arising around it. It soon expanded to cover some 120 acres. In the process, it was renamed after Joost van den Vondel, the "Dutch Shakespeare." Landscaped in the informal English style, the park is an irregular patchwork of copses, ponds, children's playgrounds, and fields linked by winding pathways. Between June and August, one of the park's focal points is the open-air theater where free concerts, plays, comedy, and children's programs are performed Wednesday–Saturday. Children, when they've grown bored with the many playing facilities, will invariably drag their parents to the llama field for some petting action or go in search of the 400 parrots (apparently the progeny of two escaped pets) that miraculously survive every winter. Plant-lovers can follow their noses to the formal and fragrant rose garden. ✉ *Stadhouderskade, Museum District.*

## The Oude Zijde: The Eastern Half of the Centrum

As the oldest part of Amsterdam, the Oude Zijde (Old Side) has been very old and very Dutch for a long time. It stands to reason, then, that you'll find, in this mirror quadrant to the Nieuwe Zijde, the entire galaxy of Amsterdam here—everything from the archaeological treasures of the Allard Pierson Museum to the famous "Our Lord in the Attic" chapel to, well, acres of bared female flesh. Yes, here within the shadow of the city's oldest church is the most famous Disneyland of Sex in the world: the Red Light District. Within it, most of the city's 13,000 professionals ply their trade and help generate an estimated half-a-billion sex-trade euros in revenue per year. Although a union, Rode Draad, has been representing sex-for-hire workers since 1984 and the tax man has long finagled a means to take his cut, it's only since 2000 that it has all become perfectly legal—including bordellos, clubs, and sex shops. And pragmatic it is indeed: you may be amazed to find that the area has been grouped according to "predilections" and thereby organized into sections (the turf around the area's ancient heart of the Oude Kerk, for instance, has been staked out by Africans). Although ultimately sleazy, especially in the Walletjes ("little walls")—also called De Wallen and defined by Oudezijds Voorburgwal and Oudezijds Achterburgwal north of Damstraat and their interconnecting streets—this area is also the oldest and once poshest part of town. Edit out the garish advertising and the breasts hypnotically sandwiched against the red-neon framed windows, and you have some very pretty buildings indeed. But have no fear: this area is also blessed with the city's Chinatown and large sections—as the vast majority of this tour will attest—of pure, unadulterated old worldness.

*Numbers in the text correspond to numbers in the margin and on the Oude Zijde, Plantage & Waterfront map.*

<table>
<tr><td>a good<br>walk</td></tr>
</table>

On exiting Centraal Station you'll see a Catholic church to the left, **Sint Nicolaaskerk** ☞, at which you may want to stop and check the times of its Gregorian chant vesper services in case you get the urge to purge your soul after this tour. In fact, for this tour you should try to take on the easygoing and forgiving nature of St. Nick, who, as the proto-Santa, was patron saint not only to children but also to thieves, prostitutes, and sailors—not to mention the city of Amsterdam. Sailors have long walked by this church on their way to the stress relief traditionally on offer on the **Zeedijk** ❶. (Perhaps that is why "doing the St. Nicolas" became standard local slang for engaging in the sex act.) Before turning left onto the Zeedijk, you may want to note that walking straight would connect you with the **Warmoesstraat** ❷ or that making a quick right would allow you to pay tribute to that melancholic sailor of jazz notes, crooning trumpet player Chet Baker, who made his final decrescendo from a window of the Prins Hendrick Hotel (Prins Hendrikade 53) in 1988. While walking up the infamous Zeedijk, dart up the side canal Oudezijds Kolk for a gander at the famous landmark **Schreierstoren** ❸, from where Henry Hudson began his journey that would lead him to New Amsterdam (the island otherwise known as Manhattan).

Zeedijk is capped by the **Nieuwmarkt** ❹ square, with the evocatively turreted De Waag as its medieval centerpiece. Although the religiously named streets to the right, Monnikenstraat and Bloedstraat (Monk and Blood streets), will ironically lead you to the carnal heart of the **Red Light District,** if you're more culturally inclined you should proceed to the op-

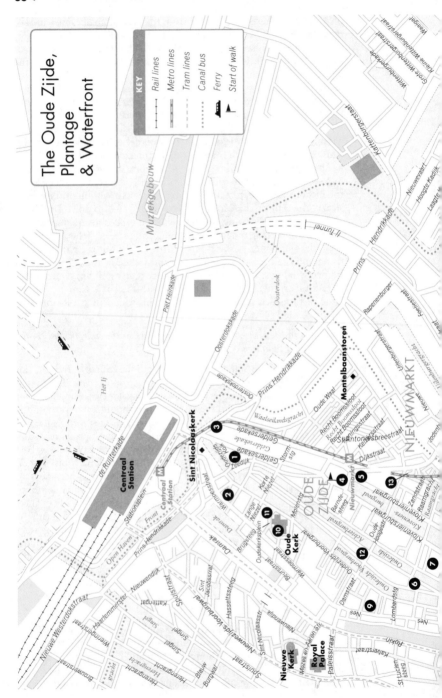

The Oude Zijde, Plantage & Waterfront

KEY

Rail lines
Metro lines
Tram lines
Canal bus
Ferry
Start of walk

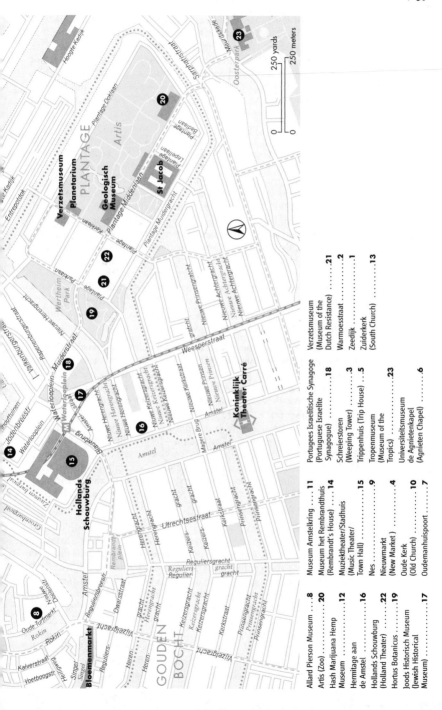

250 yards

250 meters

Allard Pierson Museum .....**8**
Artis (Zoo) .............**20**
Hash Marijuana Hemp
Museum ...............**12**
Hermitage aan
de Amstel .............**16**
Hollands Schouwburg
(Holland Theater) .......**22**
Hortus Botanicus .........**19**
Joods Historisch Museum
(Jewish Historical
Museum) ...............**17**

Museum Amstelkring ....**11**
Museum het Rembrandthuis
(Rembrandt's House) ....**14**
Muziektheater/Stadhuis
(Music Theater/
Town Hall) .............**15**
Nes .....................**9**
Nieuwmarkt
(New Market ) ...........**4**
Oude Kerk
(Old Church) ...........**10**
Oudemanhuispoort .......**7**

Portugees Israelitische Synagoge
(Portuguese Israelite
Synagogue) .............**18**
Schreierstoren
(Weeping Tower) .........**3**
Trippenhuis (Trip House) ...**5**
Tropenmuseum
(Museum of the
Tropics) ...............**23**
Universiteitsmuseum
de Agnietenkapel
(Agnieten Chapel) .......**6**

Verzetsmuseum
(Museum of the
Dutch Resistance) .......**21**
Warmoesstraat ...........**2**
Zeedijk ..................**1**
Zuiderkerk
(South Church) ..........**13**

posite side of the square and head straight up the left side of Kloveniersburgwal to the **Trippenhuis** ❺, the grand Trip House mansion. At the next intersection, on the southwest corner with Oude Hoogstraat, is the Oost Indische Huis, the former offices of the East India Trading Company, which once smelled of exotic spices but now, as part of the University of Amsterdam, exudes the fevered sweat of political science students. You might want to pop into its richly ornate courtyard, accessible via Oude Hoogstraat 24, where sailors once came to sign up for voyages. Continuing straight down Kloveniersburgwal's left bank, cross the first bridge to the right, perhaps pausing to browse through the many excellent English-language books on offer at the Book Exchange (Kloveniersburgwal 58), before proceeding straight down Rusland. For a sense of some traditional religion, make the first right down Oudezijds Achterburgwal to No. 185, the **Spinhuis**, once the location of the Convent of 11,000 Virgins. After circling this building via the small alleys that surround it, return to Rusland and cross the bridge on the right. Proceed straight down Sint Agnietenstraat, where you can make a right down Oudezijds Voorburgwal, following the curved Amsterdam School wall with its myth-drenched sculptures, past the entrance of Café Roux with its Karel Appel mural in its entranceway, and then right into the entrance of the courtyard belonging to the historically dense **Grand Hotel.** Under the name Prinsenhof, this acted as a City Hall between 1652 and 1655 and 1808 and 1988 and has welcomed such bold-face names as William of Orange and Michael Jackson.

Backtracking up Oudezijds Voorburgwal will lead you past the **Universiteitsmuseum de Agnietenkapel** ❻, or University Museum's Agnieten Chapel. A short jaunt to the left lets you cross another bridge; staying to the left, take the archway almost immediately on the right, which will lead you through sliding glass doors into the covered book market **Oudemanhuispoort** ❼, where trading has occurred since 1757. After browsing through this now more youth-oriented corridor—this is the heart of the University of Amsterdam—turn right down Kloveniersburgwal, where almost immediately you'll turn left over a drawbridge down Staalstraat. This is a relentlessly scenic specialty-shopping street and favored filming location, where you can stop to absorb the modern Dutch design delights in Droog & Co. at Staalstraat 7a/7b before heading to Waterlooplein flea market.

Continuing straight past the chic Grand Café Jaren on the left, take the right, before crossing the bridge over the canal, down Oude Turfmarkt past the archaeological **Allard Pierson Museum** ❽. Then take the first right down Langebrugsteeg, to the entrance on the left to the theatrical and the old Spinoza stomping ground of the **Nes** ❾, where on the corner you may want to pause to see what's on offer at the Appenzeller Gallery, a contemporary jewelry and design hot spot. Following the Nes will eventually connect you with the city's main square, the **Dam.** Here, cross the street and take the first alley, Pijlsteeg, to the right running alongside the nearest side of Hotel Krasnapolsky. Beyond the two sliding glass doors is the entrance to Wynand Fonkink Proeflokaal, an ancient "Tasting Local" and distillery (check out those oak caskets through the windows of No. 41) where one can indulge in a startling array of Dutch Courage in preparation for the full dose of Red Light awaiting you at the end of the alley along the Oudezijds Voorburgwal. Turning left down here will have you reaching the reassuringly religious **Oude Kerk ⑩** in no time, beyond which lies the **Museum Amstelkring ⑪** and its celebrated "Our Lord in the Attic" chapel—a must-see for art lovers.

If you want a more leisurely—but no less scholarly—cruise of humanity's darker sides, turn right, then immediately left down Oude Doelenstraat to reach Oudezijds Voorburgwal's parallel canal, Oudezijds Achterburgwal, on which you turn left. Sticking to the left bank of this canal will have you passing such unique institutions as the **Hash Marijuana Hemp Museum ⑫**; the infamous Casa Rosa nightclub at Nos. 106–8; and the **Erotic Museum.** If bicycle-powered dildos and other amazing arcana are not your thing, you may forgo the last institution—and the lore-rich erotic "theater," **Bananenbar,** across from it—and take the faithful escape route right before it to the left, Oude Kennissteeg.

TIMING    This tour will take two to three hours. If you want to enjoy the Red Light District's namesake lighting, mid- to late afternoon might be a good time to start. Such religious institutions as the Oude Kerk and Museum Amstelkring are closed for services on Sunday morning. The Allard Pierson Museum is closed Monday, and you should also note that the more "fringe" museums start and end their days somewhat later than most public museums.

HOW TO GET    You can easily walk to the Oude Zijde from Centraal Station or simply
THERE    hop on Tram 4, 9, 16, 24, or 25 to the Dam square, then stroll along Damstraat. Another way to access the neighborhood is Tram 9 or 14, or use the metro directly to Nieuwmarkt or Waterlooplein.

## Sights to See

**❽ Allard Pierson Museum.** Once the repository of the nation's gold supply, this former National Bank with its stern Neoclassical facade is now home to other treasures. Dynamite helped remove the safes and open up the space for the archaeological collection of the University of Amsterdam in 1934, and the museum traces the early development of Western civilization, from the Egyptians to the Romans, and of the Near Eastern cultures (Anatolia, Persia, Palestine) in a series of well-documented displays. The Egyptian section is particularly well done, with scale models of pyramids, some rather gruesome mummies that look as if they escaped from a B-movie studio lot, and computers that translate your name into hieroglyphics. ⊠ *Oude Turfmarkt 127, Oude Zijde* ☎ *020/525–2556* ⊕ *www.uba.uva.nl/apm* ⊠ *€5* ⊙ *Tues.–Fri. 10–5, weekends 1–5.*

**⑫ Hash Marijuana Hemp Museum.** One would think that more effort could have gone into the name of this institution—lateral thinking being one of the positive effects of its subject. But regardless, here's your chance to suck back the 8,000-year history of hemp use. The use of pot as medicine was first recorded in the Netherlands in 1554 as a cure for earaches. By this time, its less potent form, hemp, had long been used—as it would until the late 19th century—as the fiber source for rope, and hence was fundamental to the economics of this seafaring town. Besides elucidating certain points in history, a variety of displays educates about such things as smuggling and joint-rolling techniques. A cultivation zone offers handy hints for the green thumb in your family. And, predictably, there's an endless collection of bongs from around the world. ⊠ *Oudezijds Achterburgwal 148, Oude Zijde* ☎ *020/623–596* ⊕ *www. hashmuseum.com* ☜ *€6* ⊙ *Daily 11–10.*

**⑪ Museum Amstelkring** (Our Lord in the Attic Museum). With its elegant gray-and-white facade and spout gable, this appears to be just another canal house, and on the lower floors it is. The attic of this building, however, contains something unique: the only surviving *schuilkerken* (clandestine church) that dates from the Reformation in Amsterdam, when open worship by Catholics was outlawed. Since the Oude Kerk was then relieved of its original patron, St. Nicholas, when it was de-catholicized, this became the church dedicated to him until the Sint Nicolaaskerk was built. The chapel itself is a triumph of Dutch classicist taste, with magnificent marble columns, gilded capitals, a colored-marble altar, and the *Baptism of Christ* (1716) painting by Jacob de Wit presiding over all. Sunday services and weddings are still offered here. ⊠ *Oudezijds Voorburgwal 40, Oude Zijde* ☎ *020/624–6604* ⊕ *www.museumamstelkring. nl* ☜ *€7* ⊙ *Mon.–Sat. 10–5, Sun. 1–5.*

*Fodor's Choice* ★

**⑨ Nes.** Originating as a boggy walkway along the Amstel River when Amsterdam was an ever-sinking fishing village, the Nes is now a refreshingly quiet corridor filled with theaters. At the end of the 14th century, the Nes began evolving into a long strip of monasteries and convents before the Altercation of 1578 (or Protestant takeover) saw their eventual decline as Amsterdam became more concerned with commercial pursuits and as it marched toward its Golden Age. The Nes's spiritual life—which had largely made way for tobacco storage and processing—had a slight renaissance when the philosopher Spinoza (1623–77) moved here to escape the derision he was receiving from his own Jewish community for having fused Jewish mysticism with Descartian logic, concluding that body and soul were part of the same essence. Although the still-existing Frascati theater (Nos. 59–65) began life as a coffeehouse in the 18th century, it was not until the 1880s that the Nes began to bloom with cafés filled with dance, song, and operetta performances; stars often represented the less uptight segment of the Jewish community. Adjacent to the southern end of the Nes is **Gebed Zonder End,** the "Prayer Without End" alleyway, which got its name because it was said you could hear prayers from behind the walls of the convents which used to line this alley. ⊠ *Between Langebrugsteeg and Dam, Oude Zijde.*

**need a break?**

As to be expected from a theatrical neighborhood, the Nes offers some prime drinking holes, where you can also choose to have a leisurely meal. Fans of Belgian beer should certainly stop at the patio of **De Brakke Grond** (⊠ Nes 43, Oude Zijde ☎ 020/626–0044), part of the Flemish Cultural Center, to partake in one or two of the dozens of options. Coincidentally, on the "Prayer with End" alley, which runs parallel to Nes's south end, is **Captain Zeppos** (⊠ Gebed Zonder End 5, Oude Zijde ☎ 020/624–2057), which is named after a '60s Belgian TV star; this former cigar factory is soaked with jazzy old-world charm.

**❹** **Nieuwmarkt** (New Market). Home to the striking Waag gatehouse—where Rembrandt came to watch Professor Tulp in action before painting *The Anatomy Lesson*—and also to some of the most festive holiday celebrations in town, the Nieuwmarkt has been a marketplace since the 15th century. In those days, de Waag—or Sint Antoniespoort (St. Anthony's Port) as it was then known—formed a gateway in the city defenses. It was not until 17th-century expansion that the current form of Nieuwmarkt was established and farmers from the province of Noord-Holland began setting up stalls to make it a bustling daily market. The **Kruidenwinkel van Jacob Hooy & Co.** (✉ Kloveniersburgwal 12, Oude Zijde), Amsterdam's oldest medicinal herb and spice shop, and a small row of vegetable stalls are the only vague reminders of those times.

The **Waag** (Weigh House) in the center of the square was built in 1488, and functioned as a city gate, Sint Antoniespoort, until the early 17th century. During those centuries, the gate would be closed at exactly 9:30 PM to keep out not only the bandits but also the poor and the diseased who built shantytowns outside the wall. When the city expanded, it began a second life as a weighing house for incoming products—in particular such heavier goods as tobacco bales, ship artillery, and anchors—after a renovation added a tower and covered the inner courtyard. The top floor of the building came to accommodate the municipal militia and several guilds, including the masons who did the evocative decorations that grace each of the towers' entrances. One of its towers housed a teaching hospital for the academy of surgeons of the Surgeons' Guild. The Theatrum Anatomicum (Anatomy Theater), with its cupola tower covered in painted coats of arms (many of which disconcertingly reflect many of the doctors' original trade as barbers), was the first place in the Netherlands to host public dissections. For obvious reasons, these took place only in the winter. It was here that Rembrandt sketched Professor Tulp in preparation to paint his great *Anatomy Lesson*. Now the building is occupied by a café-restaurant with free Internet service and the **Society for Old and New Media** (⊕ www.waag.org). ✉ *Bounded by Kloveniersburgwal, Geldersekade, and Zeedijk, Oude Zijde.*

| need a break? | You may want to sniff out your own favorite among the many café-restaurants that line this square. Many will opt for the previously mentioned **In De Waag** (✉ Nieuwmarkt 4, Oude Zijde ☎ 020/422–7772), which highlights its epic medieval roots with candlelight. An arty and studenty option is **Lokaal 't Loosje** (✉ Nieuwmarkt 32–34, Oude Zijde ☎ 020/627–2635), which is graced with tile tableaus dating from 1912. |
|---|---|

**★ ❿** **Oude Kerk** (Old Church). The Oude Kerk is indeed Amsterdam's oldest church and has been surrounded by all the trappings of humanity's oldest trade (i.e., prostitution) for the vast majority of its history—a history that has seen it chaotically evolve from single-nave chapel to hall church to a cross basilica. It began as a wooden chapel in 1306 but was built for the ages between 1366 and 1566 (and fully restored between 1955 and 1979), when the whole neighborhood was rife with monasteries and convents. It is now a wholly unique exhibition space for modern-art exhibitions and the annual World Press Photo competition. Its carillon gets played every Saturday between 4 and 5. ⊠ *Oudekerksplein 23, Oude Zijde* ☎ *020/625–8284* ⊕ *www.oudekerk.nl* 🏷 *€4.50* ⊙ *Mon.–Sat. 11–5, Sun. 1–5.*

**❼ Oudemanhuispoort** (Old Man's House Alley). Landmarked by its famous chiseled pair of spectacles (set over the Oudezijds Achterburgwal pediment)—a sweet reference to old age—this was once a pensioners' house, an "Oudemannenhuis," first built in 1754. Today, bikes, not canes, are in evidence, as this former almshouse is now part of the University of Amsterdam. One charming relic from its founding days is the covered walkway, lined with tiny shops whose rents helped subsidize the 18th-century elderly. Adorned with red shutters, the stalls now house an array of antiquarian booksellers and lead on to Kloverniersburgwal, where a statue of Mother Amsterdam protecting two elders, sculpted by Anthonie Ziessenis in 1786, stands. ⊠ *Between Oudezijds Achterburgwal, and Klovniersburgwal, Oude Zijde.*

**★ ❸ Schreierstoren.** Famous as the point from which Henry Hudson set sail to America, this is Amsterdam's most distinctive fortress tower. Although today it's home to a rather frolicsome marine-theme jazz café, it began its life in 1486 as the end point of the city wall. The term *schreien* suggests the Dutch word for "wailing," and hence the folklore arose that this "Weeping Tower" was where women came to cry when their sailor husbands left for sea and to cry again when they did not return (perhaps followed by the short walk to the Red Light District to begin life as a merry widow?). But the word *schreier* actually comes from an Old Dutch word for a "sharp corner"—and, indeed, the building's rounded harbor face, which looks over the old **Oosterdok** (Eastern Dock), forms a sharp corner with its straight street face. A plaque on the building tells you that it was from this location that Henry Hudson set sail on behalf of the Dutch East India Company to find a shorter route to the East Indies. In his failure, he came across Canada's Hudson's Bay Company and later—continuing his bad-luck streak—New York harbor and the Hudson River. ⊠ *Prins Hendrikkade 94–95, Oude Zijde.*

**★ ❺ Trippenhuis** (Trip House). As family home to the two Trip brothers, who made their fortune in gun dealing during the 17th-century Golden Age, this noted house's buckshot-gray exterior and various armament motifs—including a mortar-shape chimney—are easily explained. But what's most distinctive about this building is that its Corinthian-columned facade actually hides two symmetrical buildings (note the wall that bisects the middle windows), one for each brother. It went on in the 18th century to house both the Rijksmuseum collection and the Royal Dutch Academy of Sciences before the latter became its sole resident. Be sure to look across the canal to No. 26, the door-wide white building topped with golden sphinxes and the date of 1696, which is known as both the "Little Trip House" and the "House of Mr. Trip's Coachman." The story goes that the smarty-pants coachman once remarked that he would be happy with a house as wide as the Trippenhuis door; not to be outsmarted, Mr. Trip went on to build just that with the left-over bricks. Or so the story goes; the Little Trip House is actually much bigger than it looks, and its completion date was long after either brother died. ✉ *Kloveniersburgwal 29, Oude Zijde.*

★ ❻ **Universiteitsmuseum de Agnietenkapel** (University Museum Agnieten Chapel). One of Amsterdam's few surviving medieval convents, this Gothic chapel was built in the 1470s. However, it has been emphasizing the secular since 1632, when it became part of the original University of Amsterdam, and thereby rates as the country's oldest lecture hall. Imagine bringing an apple to the likes of Vossius and Barlaeus, two greatly celebrated Renaissance scholars who both taught here. The grand interior solemnly sports stained-glass windows, an impressive Renaissance ceiling painting, and more than 40 paintings of humanists, including everyone's favorite, Erasmus. A renovation around 1919 saw the introduction of some elements of the Amsterdam School to its exterior. Sadly, the building is currently closed for more renovations, which should be completed in 2007. In the meantime, though, you can call and arrange a viewing of a temporary exhibition set up at Herengracht 182. ✉ *Oudezijds Voorburgwal 231, Oude Zijde* ☎ *020/525–3339* 💲 *Free* ⊙ *Mon.–Sat. 9–5.*

❷ **Warmoesstraat.** This densely touristy strip of hostels, bars, and coffee shops began life as one of the original dikes along the Amstel before evolving into the city's richest shopping street (a sharp contrast to its fallen sister, Zeedijk). It's here that the famous 17th-century poet Vondel once did business from his hosiery shop at No. 101, and where Mozart's dad tried to unload tickets for his son's concerts in the posh bars. It entered a decline in the 17th century when the proprietors forsook their above-store lodgings for the posher ones arising on the canal ring; sailors and their caterers started to fill in the gaps. In the 19th century, it evolved, along with its extension **Nes,** into the city's primary drinking and frolicking zone. Karl Marx was known to set himself up regularly in a hotel here not only to write in peace but to have the option to ask for a loan from his cousin-in-law, Gerard Philips, founder of that capitalist machine Philips.

Thanks to a recent revamp, Warmoesstraat is beginning to lose some of its Sodom and Gomorrah edge. Between the tourist traps, there are such hip hangouts as the Hotel Winston; restful oases serving stellar quiche such as De Bakkerswinkel (No. 69); and worthwhile specialty stores, such as Geels and Co. (No. 67), with its infinite selection of coffees and teas. There's even a squatted gallery, the beautifully spacious W139 (No. 139), dedicated to the very outer edges of conceptual art. ✉ *Between Dam and Nieuwe Brugsteeg, Oude Zijde.*

❶ **Zeedijk.** Few streets have had a longer or more torrid history; until recently known as the Black Hole of Amsterdam (because of its concentration of drug users), the Zeedijk is now on the up-and-up. As the original dam created to keep the sea at bay, Zeedijk has been around since Amsterdam began life as a fishing hamlet. The building of this dike in 1380 probably represented the first twitchings of democracy in these parts as individual fishing and farming folks were united to make battle against the sea. Less noble democratic forces saw it quickly specialize in the entertaining of sailors—a service it ended up providing for centuries. A more bohemian edge came into the mix in the last century when it provided a mecca for world-class jazz musicians who came to jam in its small clubs and cafés after their more official gigs in the Concertgebouw. One of the more popular was the still-existing Casablanca (No. 26), which regularly saw the likes of local heroes such as Kid Dynamite and Teddy Cotton and more international names such as Erroll Garner, Gerry Mulligan, and Count Basie. However, other, dingier dens began a lucrative sideline in heroin. By the 1970s, the area had become known throughout the country for its concentration of drug traffickers, where the only tourists were those attached to heavily guided "criminal safaris." But recently Zeedijk has gone through a radical gentrification. Although certainly not sterile of its past, it's now much easier to accept the stray, dubious-looking character as merely part of the street's scenery as opposed to its definition.

Café Maandje at No. 65 evokes the 1930s, when the first openly gay drinking and dancing dens in the city began popping up here. Its window maintains a shrine to its former proprietor and the spiritual forebear of lesbian biker babes everywhere: Bet van Beeren (1902–67). Although the café opens only on the rarest of occasions, a model of its interior can be viewed at the Amsterdams Historisch Museum. The rest of the street is a quirky mixture of middle-range Asian restaurants, brown cafés with carpeted tables, specialty shops and galleries, and the occasional Chinese medicinal shop. The Chinese community is in full visual effect at the end of the street, where recently the gloriously colorful pagoda-shape **Fo Kuang Shan Buddhist Temple** (No. 118) arose. ⊠ *Oude Zijde Kolk (near Centraal Station) to Nieuwmarkt, Oude Zijde.*

> **need a break?**
>
> Zeedijk offers five of the best quick snack/meal stops in town. The most revered is auspiciously placed across from the Buddhist Temple: **Nam Kee** (⊠ Zeedijk 111–113, Oude Zijde ☎ 020/624–3470) is a speedy and cheap Chinese spot whose steamed oysters are so sublime that they provided the title and muse for a local author's novel. **Snackbar Bird** (⊠ Zeedijk 72, Oude Zijde ☎ 020/420–6289) offers wok-fried-in-front-of-your-eyes dishes from Thailand; for a more lingering or less cramped meal, you might want to try its restaurant across the street. The ultimate Dutch snack, raw herring, can be enjoyed at the fresh-fish shop **Huijsmans Cock** (⊠ Zeedijk 129, Oude Zijde ☎ 020/624–2070), which also offers deliciously nutty whole wheat buns. A Zeedijk fave, **Cafe Latei** (⊠ Zeedijk 143, Oude Zijde ☎ 020/625–7485) combines a dense interior of quality kitsch (much of it for sale) with the serving of coffee and healthful snacks.

## East of the Amstel: From the Jewish Quarter to the Plantage

Although Amsterdam has been Calvinist, Protestant, and Catholic for varying chunks of its history, it has been continuously considered a secondary Jerusalem of sorts by migrating populations of Jews ever since the medieval era. In fact, the city came to be known as Mokum (the Hebrew word for "place"), as in *the* place for Jews. And when the Jewish population arrived, so did much of Amsterdam's color and glory. Just witness the legendary diamond trade and feast your eyes upon Rembrandt's *Jewish Bride* in the Rijksmuseum, just one of many canvases the artist painted when, searching for inspiration and Old Testament ambience, he deliberately set up a luxurious household near the heart of the Jewish Quarter.

Since the 15th century, the **Joodse Buurt** (Jewish Quarter) has traditionally been considered the district east of the Zwanenburgwal. The Quarter got its start thanks to the Inquisition, which was extremely efficient in motivating many Sephardic Jews to leave Spain in 1492. Over the next hundred years, their descendants slowly found their way to Amsterdam, where they could reestablish a semblance of their traditional lifestyle. The war with Spain inspired the 1597 Union of Utrecht, which, although formulated to protect Protestants from the religious oppression that came with Spanish invasions, essentially meant that all religions were tolerated. This provided a unique experience for the Jews, for here, unlike elsewhere in Europe, they were not forced to wear badges and live in ghettos. They were still, however, restricted—just like all the other non-Calvinists—from joining guilds and being registered as tradesmen. The only exceptions were in the up-and-coming trades where no guild Mafia had arisen, such as diamond cutting and polishing, sugar refining, silk weaving, and printing. These slim advantages also helped attract many Yiddish-speaking Ashkenazi Jews from Eastern Europe escaping pogroms. The 17th-century Golden Age and the rise of capitalism saw the weakening of the hardcore Calvinist grip on daily life, and only the Catholics remained barred from open worship. This accounts for the existence of 17th-century synagogues in the city and not of Catholic churches. Rembrandt came to the neighborhood at this time to take advantage of the proximity of all the "biblical faces" that he could employ in his religious paintings.

But it was only in 1796, inspired by the ideals of the French Revolution, that the guilds were finally banned and equal rights instilled. However, although there were always many rich Jewish merchants, poverty was still the essential lot of most Jews until the end of the 19th century, when the rise of the diamond industry meant the spreading of the community away from the old Jewish Quarter. By 1938, 10% of Amsterdam's population was Jewish, and they had imprinted their influence onto the city's culture as well as its slang (the Yiddish word *mazzel*, meaning "luck," remains a standard farewell here). What remains much more painfully ingrained in the city's psyche, however, is what happened during the Nazi occupation when the Jewish population was reduced to one-seventh of its size. There were many examples of bravery and the opening of homes to hide Jews, but there are many more—and less often told—stories of collaboration. Although the current Jewish population has risen to 20,000, they are now generally dispersed throughout the city, and it is really only the monuments that speak.

The devastation of the war, and the later demolition to make room for the Stadhuis/Muziektheater (City Hall/Music Theater) and the Metro, means the neighborhood is marked by a somewhat schizophrenic hodge-podge of the old and new. The adjacent, more residential neighborhood of **Plantage** to the east, which began as a sort of recreation park for the rich before houses for them arose in the 19th century, offers a more co-gent and restful atmosphere, with its wide boulevards.

*Numbers in the text correspond to numbers in the margin and on the Oude Zijde, Plantage & Waterfront map.*

**a good walk**

While trying to imagine the original 17th-century housing, walk east up Sint Antoniebreestraat from **Nieuwmarkt** ❹ ⏵, which was left as a ghost town for years after the occupation.

Across the street lies one of the neighborhood's few wholly successful infusions of modernity, the Theo Bosch–designed Pentagon Apartments, where to its right between Nos. 130 and 132 you can enter through a skull and crossbones–adorned gateway to the courtyard of the **Zuider-kerk** ⓭, the "Southern Church." Here, you can climb its 17th-century tower—certainly one of the most beautiful in all Holland—or see mod-els of Amsterdam's many future building projects. You can also linger on the bridge where Sint Antoniebreestraat turns into Jodenbreestraat; to the left, beside the disconcertingly crooked café, you can take in the view down Oudeschans toward the harbor. Turning around, you'll see across the street some stairs leading down to the **Waterlooplein** flea mar-ket. The first café-outfitted building on the left corner (Jodenbreestraat 2) is marked with the Hebrew date of 5649 (1889) and adorned with caryatids doing Atlas's dirty work. The house that previously stood here was rented to the art dealer Hendrick Uylenburg, with whose painting school a fresh-faced Rembrandt became aligned after he'd arrived from Leiden. Rembrandt ended up becoming much more aligned with Uylen-burg's niece Saskia; he married her and eventually bought the red-shut-tered house next door, today the famous **Museum het Rembrandthuis** ⓮.

Ignore the entrance to the Holland Experience—unless, of course, a cer-tain herb inspires you to take in a 3-D tour of Holland's stereotypes—to the left of Rembrandt's former digs and continue down Jodenbreestraat to take the first left after the Amsterdam Academy of Arts' Dance and Theater School. Along Nieuwe Uilenburgerstraat at No. 91, you can ad-mire the facade of a former synagogue that was built in 1766. A straight backtrack will get you to the flea market Waterlooplein. The white build-ing looming ahead is the multitask city hall–music theater, **Muziektheater/ Stadhuis** ⓯. After absorbing the surrounding chaos of carpets and stalls filled with vintage clothing and Euro-knickknacks, exit Waterlooplein via its northeast corner, where you can cross the street at the imposing church of **Mozes en Aäronkerk**. Head south and continue toward the upcoming bridge, **Blauwbrug**, to admire the view down the Amstel River. The "Blue Bridge," built in 1883, was named after its predecessor, a blue wooden bridge, so don't be distressed that it lacks its namesake color. Disconcerting is the fact that during Nazi occupation it was tangled in barbed wire to isolate the Jewish Quarter. If you want to visit **Hermitage aan de Amstel** ⓰ the outpost of that famed Russian museum, take a left before crossing Blauwbrug and proceed up to Nieuwe Herengracht.

Otherwise, turn back from the bridge and take the forking street to the right, Nieuwe Amstelstraat, a walking street where disused tram tracks mark the entrance to a complex of four synagogues that form the **Joods Historisch Museum** ⑰ (Jewish Historical Museum). From here cross the street at Mr. Visserplein—named after a Jewish resistance leader and now sporting a surreal children's playground called TunFun underneath it— toward the rows of tiny houses around the **Portugees Israelitische Synagoge** ⑱. To the right of the square, Jonas Daniel Meijerplein, is a statue of a husky dock worker, *De Dokwerker*. The statue commemorates the February Strike of February 25, 1941, when dock and transport workers protested the first *razzia* ("roundup") of Jews, with whom they felt united by common union and socialist ideals that had taken hold in the city in the previous decades. Taking Muiderstraat to the left of the synagogue complex, you'll soon see the glass structures of the **Hortus Botanicus** ⑲ botanical gardens. Hang left down Parklaan and right down the former diamond mecca of Henri Polaklaan. The street ends at the **Artis** ⑳ planetarium-zoo, and if you head left, you will come to the World War II resistance subterfuges (used to subvert the occupying Nazis) on display at the excellent **Verzetsmuseum** ㉑ (Resistance Museum).

Reversing down Plantage Kerklaan and then making a right after crossing Plantage Middenlaan will get you to the **Hollands Schouwburg** ㉒, a former theater that is now a memorial to the Jews collected there to await transportation to their fate in the concentration camps. Reversing to continue east down Plantage Middenlaan will get you to the Plantage Westermanplantsoen park on the right, where there's a war monument to the artists' resistance movement and superhero Gerrit van der Veen. Continuing on the same route, you'll eventually reach the imposing **Tropenmuseum** ㉓ (Tropics Museum) and the picnicking opportunities available in **Oosterpark**—perhaps after picking up supplies at the multicultural street market on Dapperstraat.

TIMING To see only the buildings along the main route, plan to spend an hour and a half. Detours to the Tropenmuseum will need an extra 20 minutes' traveling time. Museums along this route need at least a 30-minute visit, though Rembrandthuis, the Jewish Historical Museum, and the Tropenmuseum (whose children's section has very specific visiting times) deserve longer. Also note that the Waterloo flea market does not operate on Sunday.

HOW TO GET THERE Trams 9 and 14 will deposit you in the heart of the Plantage, near the Artis zoo and Hortus Botanicus. Metro stop Waterlooplein is also a stone's throw from here. Buses 22, 42, and 43 stop at the Scheepvaart Museum. Tram 6 runs from near Artis and loops around the city via Weteringschans before heading south after Leidseplein.

### Sights to See

⑳ **Artis** (Amsterdam Zoo). Short for Natura Artis Magistra ("Nature Is the Teacher of the Arts"), Artis was mainland Europe's first zoo and is the world's third oldest. Built in the mid-19th century, the 37-acre park is home to a natural-history museum, a zoo with an aviary, a planetarium, and an aquarium. The aquarium does this coastal country proud, with some 500 species on view in both freshwater and saltwater tanks; the highlight is a cross section of a canal complete with eels and sunken bicycles. As for the zoo proper, a few of its exhibits are cramped, but others are long on inspiration, including the toy ruin, where owls can peer out at you as if on sabbatical from a Hieronymus Bosch painting or, for that matter, a Harry Potter book. A recent expansion, including a new restaurant, has made the zoo bigger and better. In short: it's great for kids of all ages. A special Artis Express canal boat from the Centraal Station is a great alternative for getting here. ✉ *Plantage Kerklaan 40, Jewish Quarter and Plantage* ☏ *020/523–3400* ⊕ *www.artis. nl* 🎟 *€16* ⊙ *Zoo Oct.–May, daily 9–5; June–Sept., daily 9–6; planetarium times vary depending on program.*

**⑯ Hermitage aan de Amstel.** Although the full acre's worth of exhibition space will not to be completed until 2007, this outpost of the famed Russian art museum in St. Petersburg already has more than enough room for stunning exhibitions culled from perhaps the most famous art collection in the world. Some of the subjects they have already covered are: Venetian painters, Ancient Greek jewelry, and the treasures of Tsar Nicolas and his wife Alexandra. Be sure to go for a wander in the 17th century Amstelhof courtyard that surrounds this 19th century building. ✉ *Gebouw Neerlandia, Nieuwe Herengracht 14* ☏ *020/626–8168* ⊕ *www.hermitage.nl* 🎟 6 ⊙ *Daily 10–5.*

**㉒ Hollands Schouwburg** (Holland Theater). Between 1892 and 1941, this was *the* theater for Dutch theatrical performances, which came courtesy of such luminaries as writers Herman Heyermans and Esther de Boervan Rijk and such singer-entertainers as Louis Davids (the "Little Big Man"). In 1941, the Nazis shortly deemed it a Jewish-only theater before deciding in 1942 to use it as a central gathering point for the deportation of the city's Jews, first to the national gathering point of Westerbork and then to concentration camps in Germany. In the end, somewhere between 60,000 and 80,000 human souls passed through here for this purpose. In 1993, the Jewish Historical Museum renovated it to include a memorial room displaying the 6,700 family names of the 104,000 Dutch Jews deported and murdered and an upstairs exhibition room that tells the story of the occupation through documents, photographs, and videos. But it is the large and silent courtyard that is perhaps this monument's most effective remembrance. ✉ *Plantage Middenlaan 24, Jewish Quarter and Plantage* ☏ *020/626–9945* ⊕ *www. jhm.nl* 🎟 *Free* ⊙ *Daily 11–4.*

**★ ⑲ Hortus Botanicus.** This wonderful botanical garden was originally laid out as an herb garden for doctors and pharmacists in 1682 before it began collecting exotic plants from the East India Company's foreign fields of plunder. Today it's a labyrinth of ornamental gardens and greenhouses set to a variety of climates (desert, swamp, tropical, and subtropical) where a total of 8,000 species are represented—including one of the oldest potted plants in the world, a 300-year-old Cycas palm. Its café-terrace is one of the most peaceful in the city, and buying a coffee here is *alone* worth the price of admission. In fact, you can add some historical resonance to your sipping with the knowledge that Hortus harbors the descendants of the first coffee plants of Europe. A Dutch merchant stole one of the plants from Ethiopia, presented it to this Hortus in 1706, which in turn sent a clipping to a botanist in France, who finally saw to it that further clippings reached their destination of Brazil . . . where an industry was born. ✉ *Plantage Middenlaan 2a, Jewish Quarter and Plantage* ☎ *020/ 625–9021* ⊕ *www.hortus-botanicus.nl* 🎫 *€6* ☉ *Sept.–June, weekdays 9–5, weekends 10–5; July–Aug., weekdays 9–9, weekends 10–9.*

**⑰ Joods Historisch Museum** (Jewish Historical Museum). Four Ashkenazi synagogues (or *shuls*, as they are called in Yiddish) dating from the 17th and 18th centuries were skillfully combined with glass-and-steel constructions in 1987 into this impressive museum for documents, paintings, and objects related to the four-century history of the Jewish people in Amsterdam and the Netherlands. World War II plunder saw to it that the number of objects of a priceless and beautiful nature is limited, but the museum is still rich with a collection of unusual pieces ranging from the ceremonial to the domestic, from the antique to the modern. The museum also features a resource center and one of the city's few purely kosher cafés. Whether or not you tour the collections, check out the excellent tours of the Jewish Quarter conducted by this museum. Just outside the doors is the market at Waterlooplein, where the Jewish community once thrived, and which hosts the famous flea market, as lively as it was in the 17th century. The current Jewish community itself exists largely beneath the surface of Amsterdam, many of its constituents placing Dutch identity before Judaism. ✉ *Nieuwe Amstelstraat 1, Jewish Quarter and Plantage* ☎ *020/531–0310* ⊕ *www.jhm.nl* 🎫 *€6.50* ☉ *Daily 11–5.*

**need a break?** While in a refreshingly tourist-free zone, why not check out a friendly local brown café? **Eik & Linde** (✉ Plantage Middenlaan 22, Jewish Quarter and Plantage ☎ 020/622–5716) is one of the archetypal Amsterdam institutions famed for their brown walls, the result of decades of cigarette and pipe smoking by the patrons. This particular place is noted in recent Jewish history as the radio broadcast location where Ischa Meijer, interviewer extraordinaire, encouraged his Jewish guests to confront their own personal stories associated with the Holocaust.

**⑭ Museum het Rembrandthuis** (Rembrandt's House). One of Amsterdam's
**Fodor'sChoice** more remarkable relics, this house was bought by Rembrandt, flush with
★ success, for his family and is where he lived and worked between 1639 and 1658. Rembrandt chose this house on what was once the main street of the Jewish Quarter because he thought he could then experience daily and firsthand the faces he would use in his Old Testament religious paintings. Later Rembrandt lost the house to bankruptcy when he fell from popularity after the death of Saskia, his wife. When he showed a quick recovery—and an open taste for servant girls—after her death, his uncle-in-law, once his greatest champion, became his biggest detractor. Rembrandt's downfall was sealed: he came under attack by the Amsterdam burghers, who refused to accept his liaison with his amour, Hendrickje. ✉ *Jodenbreestraat 4–6, Jewish Quarter and Plantage* ☎ *020/520–0400* ⊕ *www.rembrandthuis.nl* 🎫 *€7.50* ☉ *Mon.–Sat. 10–5, Sun. 11–5.*

# TOURS AROUND AMSTERDAM

## Bicycle Tours

From April through October, guided 1½- to 3-hour bike trips through the central area of the city are available through **Yellow Bike** (✉ Nieuwezijds Kolk 29, Centrum ☎ 020/620–6940 ⊕ www. yellowbike.nl).

**Let's Go** (✉ VVV Netherlands Board of Tourism, Centraal Station, Centrum ⊕ www.letsgo-amsterdam.com) tours (contact the VVV for further details) takes you out of the city center by train before introducing you to the safer cycling of the surrounding countryside. Its tours include Edam and Volendam, Naarden and Muiden, and, in season, a Tulip Tour.

## Boat Tours

The quickest, easiest, and (frankly) most delightful way to get your bearings in Amsterdam is to take a canal-boat cruise. Trips last from 1 to 1½ hours and cover the harbor as well as the main canal district; there is a taped or live commentary available in four languages. Excursion boats leave from rondvaart (excursion piers) in various locations in the city every 15 minutes from March to October, and every 30 minutes in winter. Departures are frequent from Prins Hendrikkade near the Centraal Station, along the Damrak, and along the Rokin (near Muntplein), at Leidseplein, and Stadhouderskade (near the Rijksmuseum). For a tour lasting about an hour, the cost is around €8.50, but the student guides expect a small tip for their multilingual commentary. For a truly romantic view of Amsterdam, opt for one of the special dinner and candlelight cruises offered by some companies, notably Holland International. A candlelight dinner cruise costs upward of €25. Trips for all boat tours can also be booked through the tourist office.

The following companies operated canal cruises: **Amsterdam Canal Cruises** (✉ Nicolaas Witsenkade, opposite the Heineken Brewery, De Pijp ☎ 020/626–5636). **Holland International** (✉ Prins Hendrikkade, opposite Centraal Station, Centrum ☎ 020/622–7788). **Meyers Rondvaarten** (✉ Damrak 4, Dam ☎ 020/623–4208). **Rederij Lovers** (✉ Prins Hendrikkade 26 a, opposite Centraal Station, Centrum ☎ 020/530–1090). **Rederij P. Kooij** (✉ Rokin, near Spui, Centrum ☎ 020/623–3810). **Rederij Noord/Zuid** (✉ Stadhouderskade 25, opposite Parkhotel, Leidseplein ☎ 020/679–1370). **Rederij Plas** (✉ Damrak, quays 1–3, Dam ☎ 020/624–5406).

Several boat trips to museums are also available. **Canal bus** (✉ Nieuwe Weteringschans 24, Leidseplein ☎ 020/623–9886 ⊕ www.canal.nl), which makes six stops along two different routes between Centraal Station and the Rijksmuseum, costs €16, including tickets and/or reductions for museums. **Museumboot Rederij Lovers** (✉ Stationsplein 8, Centrum ☎ 020/530–1090) makes seven stops near 20 different museums. The cost is €14.25 for a day ticket that entitles you to a 50% discount on admission to the museums.

The Canal Bike Waterfiets is a peddle-powered boat that seats up to four for €28 per hour. You can tour the Grachtengordel ring of canals at your own pace. For one or two people, the hourly fee is €8 per person, and for three to four persons, it costs €7 per person, per hour. Rental hours are between 10 and 6:30 daily. There are five landing stages throughout the city, with two of the most popular ones located across from the Rijksmuseum and across from the Westerkerk.

## Bus Tours

Afternoon bus tours of the city operate daily. Itineraries vary, and prices range from €17 to €47. A 2½-hour city tour that includes a drive through the suburbs is offered by *Key Tours* (✉ Dam 19, Dam ☎ 020/623–5051). However, it must be said that this city of narrow alleys and canals is not best appreciated from the window of a coach. Also, a number of visitors feel unhappy that part of some tours involves a visit to a diamond factory, where they feel pressured into listening to a sales pitch. The same bus companies operate scenic trips to attractions outside the city.

## Walking Tours

The Amsterdam Tourist Board (VVV) maintains lists of personal guides and guided walking and cycling tours for groups in and around Amsterdam and can advise you on making arrangements. You can also contact **Guidor, Nederlandse Gidsen Organisatie** (Dutch Guides Organization, ✉ Hemsbrugstraat 11 ☎ 020/624–6072 or 020/627–0006 ⊕ www.guidor.nl). The costs are from €152 for a half day to €250 for a full day. The tourist office also sells brochures outlining easy-to-follow self-guided theme tours through the central part of the city. Among them are "A Journey of Discovery Through Maritime Amsterdam," "A Walk Through the Jordaan," "Jewish Amsterdam," and "Rembrandt and Amsterdam."

The following companies offer walking tours focusing on art and architecture: **Archivisie** (✉ Postbus 14603, 1001 LC ☎ 020/625–8908). **Artifex** (✉ Herengracht 342, 1016 CG, Grachtengordel ☎ 020/620–8112). **Arttra Cultureel Orgburo** (✉ Staalstraat 28, 1011 JM, De Wallen ☎ 020/625–9303 ⊕ www.arttra.com).

For walking tours of the Jewish Quarter, contact **Joods Historisch Museum** (✉ Jonas Daniel Meyerplein 2–4, Postbus 16737, 1001 RE, Plantage ☎ 020/626–9945 🖷 020/624–1721). **Yellow Bike** (✉ Nieuwezijds Kolk 29, Centrum ☎ 020/620–6940 ⊕ www.yellowbike.nl) organizes two-hour walking tours of the Jordaan and the Red Light District.

Probably the best deal in town is **Mee in Mokum** (✉ Hartenstraat 18, Jordaan ☎ 020/625–1390, call between 1 and 4), which offers walking tours led by retired longtime residents. For a mere €2.50, you are given an entertaining three-hour educational tour of the inner city or the Jordaan, focusing on architecture and surprising facts. These tours are also popular with Amsterdammers who wish to discover new things about their city. The admission fee entitles you to reduced fees to a choice of museums and a reduction in the price of a pancake at a nearby restaurant. Tours are held daily and start promptly at 11 AM. You must reserve at least a day in advance. Tours are limited to eight people; private arrangements can also be made for other times of the day.

need a
break?

Beware: the slant of **Café Sluyswacht** (⌧ Jodenbreestraat 1, Jewish
Quarter and Plantage ☎ 020/65–7611) can end up causing nausea
after one too many beers on its patio overlooking Oudeschans. For
more stable fare, just across the street from askew Café Sluyswacht
are the designer sandwiches at **Dantzig** (⌧ Zwanenburgwal 15,
Jewish Quarter and Plantage ☎ 020/620–9039), to be enjoyed either
on its patio looking over Waterlooplein or within its modern interior
of mosaics.

**⓯ Muziektheater/Stadhuis** (Music Theater/Town Hall). Universally known
as the Stopera—not just from the combining of "Stadhuis" (Town Hall)
and "Opera" but from the radical opposition expressed during its construction—this brick-and-marble complex when viewed from the south
resembles, as a local writer once described it, a "set of dentures." Another writer grumbled that its "two for one" nature was a tad too typical of the bargain-loving Dutch. Discontent with this modern complex
actually began before the first stone was in place, when locals protested
the razing of the 16th- and 17th-century houses in the old Jewish Quarter and around Nieuwmarkt to make way for it. Regardless, the 300
million-guilder building was completed, and today boasts an impressive
interior architecture complete with stunning acoustics. The Muziektheater
is now home base for the Nederlands Opera and the National Ballet and
the ballet orchestra. It is also a much-favored stage for other internationally renowned touring companies of both classical and avant-garde
tendencies. Tours of the backstage areas are run once a week (Saturday
at noon) or by prior arrangement. From September to May, the Boek-
manzaal is host to a free Tuesday lunch concert. ⌧ *Waterlooplein 22,
Jewish Quarter and Plantage* ☎ *020/625–5455* ⊕ *www.stopera.nl*
🎫 *Tours €4.50* ☉ *Mon.–Sat. 10–6; tours Sat. at noon or by arrangement; call 020/551–8103.*

**⓲ Portugees Israelitische Synagoge** (Portuguese Israelite Synagogue). With
Jerusalem's Temple of Solomon as inspiration, Elias Bouwman and
Danield Stalpaert designed this noted synagogue between 1671 and
1675. Its square brick building within a courtyard formed by brick houses
was commissioned by the Sephardic Jewish community that had emi-
grated via Portugal during the preceding two centuries. On its completion it was the largest synagogue in the world, and its spare, elegantly
proportioned wood interior has remained virtually unchanged through
the centuries. It is still magically illuminated by candles in two immense
candelabra during services. The surrounding buildings that form a
square around the synagogue house the world-famous Ets Haim ("Tree
of Life") library, one of the oldest in the world, and the winter synagogue for use on those draftier days. ⌧ *Mr. Visserplein 3, Jewish Quarter and Plantage* ☎ *020/624–5351, www.esnoga.com* 🎫 *€6.50*
☉ *Apr.–Oct., Sun.–Fri. 10–4; Nov.–Mar., Sun.–Thurs. 10–4, Fri. 10–3.*

**☾ ㉓ Tropenmuseum** (Museum of the Tropics). The country's largest anthropological museum, while honoring the Netherlands' link to Indonesia
and the West Indies, does a good job of covering many other non-Western cultures. Its skylighted and tiered interior, rich with wood, marble,
and gilt, harbors not only endless pieces of antiquity, art, and musical

instruments but also many displays and dioramas depicting everyday life. In the space of a couple of hours, you can wander through villages in Java, the Middle East, India, Africa, and Latin America (where you'll also find the city's smallest Internet café, El Cybernetico). There's also a great patio where you can enjoy food from the globe-embracing café.

In the children-friendly **Tropenmuseum Junior** (⊕ www. tropenmuseumjunior.nl), children can participate directly in the life of another culture through special programs involving art, dance, song, and sometimes even cooking. Adults may visit the children's section but only under the supervision of a child age 6–12. ⊠ *Linnaeusstraat 2, Plantage* ☎ *020/568–8215* ⊕ *www.tropenmuseum.nl* ☒ *€7.50, Tropenmuseum Junior €2 extra* ⊙ *Daily 10–5. Kindermuseum activities Wed. at 11, 1:30, and 3:15, weekends at 11:30, 1:30, and 3:15.*

**㉑ Verzetsmuseum** (Museum of the Dutch Resistance). The stirring and suspenseful story of the Dutch resistance to the occupying forces, passive and active, during World War II, is on display here. This museum, which began in another location, was originally set up by resistance members themselves—many of whom were Communist, the only political party at the time to make Nazi resistance part of its platform. Since taking up residence in the Plancius building (whose music-themed facade denotes its history between 1875 and the occupation as the home to Jewish choir and stage companies), the museum has moved toward embracing all the multimedia gizmos and broadening its vision to take on Dutch collaborators and the plain indifferent. But the highlights remain the original selection of the sneaky gadgets, ingenious hiding techniques, and the bicycle-powered printing presses that pumped out fake ID papers and such now-established publications as *De Parool* ("Password") and *Vrij Nederland* ("Free the Netherlands"), which began as illegal underground newsletters. ⊠ *Plantage Kerklaan 61, Jewish Quarter and Plantage* ☎ *020/620–2535* ⊕ *www.verzetsmuseum.org* ☒ *€5* ⊙ *Tues.–Fri. 10–5, Sat.–Mon. noon–5.*

**★ ⓭ Zuiderkerk** (South Church). Gorgeous enough to have inspired both Sir Christopher Wren and Monet, this famous church was built between 1603 and 1611 by Hendrick de Keyser, one of the most prolific architects of Holland's Golden Age. Legend has it this church hypnotized the great British architect Wren, who went on to build London's St. Paul's Cathedral (which spitefully superseded Keyser's own Westerkerk as the world's largest Protestant church); centuries later, Monet committed the Zuiderkerk to canvas. It was one of the earliest churches built in Amsterdam in the Renaissance style and was the first in the city to be built for the Dutch Reformed Church. ⊠ *Zuiderkerkhof, Jewish Quarter and Plantage* ☎ *No phone* ⊕ *www.zuiderkerk.amsterdam.nl* ☒ *Free* ⊙ *Church Mon. 11–4; Tues., Wed., and Fri. 9–4; Thurs. 9–8.*

# WHERE TO EAT

By Steve Korver

Until a decade or two ago, it seemed that eating in Amsterdam was tinged more with the flavor of Calvinism than with any culinary influence. Luckily today, the Dutch embrace cuisine from all corners of the globe. International urban eating trends, although perhaps arriving more slowly in Amsterdam than other places, now make it highly probable that you'll encounter, on a walk through the city, sushi shacks, soup shops, noodle joints, and organic bakeries selling hearty Mediterranean breads. Many of the city's former industrial- and harbor-related buildings are being transformed into distinctive or trendy dining establishments.

If you're the type who likes to make your own discoveries, here are a few tips to keep in mind. In general, except as a lark, avoid the tourist traps around Leidseplein, Rembrandtplein, the Damrak, and the Red Light District. Cheap global eats are concentrated in the De Pijp district. A broad selection of middle-range eateries can be found around Nieuwmarkt, the Jordaan, and Utrechtsestraat. To find posher purveyors for a true blowout, head to Reguliersdwarsstraat or the Nine Streets (the interconnecting streets of the canal girdle between Raadhuisstraat and Leidsestraat) areas.

Note: For a rundown of the best of Amsterdam's famous atmosphere-soaked "brown cafés"—where there is traditionally more imbibing than dining—see Chapter 4, Nightlife & the Arts.

| WHAT IT COSTS In euros | | | | |
| --- | --- | --- | --- | --- |
| | **$$$$** | **$$$** | **$$** | **$** | **¢** |
| AT DINNER | over €30 | €22–€30 | €15–€22 | €10–€15 | under €10 |

Prices are per person for a main course and include part of the 15% service charge.

## Nieuwe Zijde & Spui

The historical center's "new side" has the history but none of the neon of the "old side." It's the intellectual heart of Amsterdam and ground central for roaming hipsters, who often load up at a restaurant around Spui square before washing it down with some nightlife in an ancient bar or the latest lounge.

### Dutch

**$$$–$$$$** ✕ **D' Vijff Vlieghen.** The "Five Flies" is a rambling dining institution that FodorśChoice takes up five adjoining Golden Age houses. Yet the densely evocative ★ Golden Age vibe—complete with bona fide Rembrandt etchings, wooden *jenever* (Dutch gin) barrels, crystal and armor collections, and an endless array of old-school bric-a-brac—came into being only in 1939. You'll find business folk clinching deals in private nooks here, but also busloads of tourists who have dibs on complete sections: book accordingly. The overpriced menu of new Dutch cuisine emphasizes local, fresh, and often organic ingredients in everything from wild boar to purely vegetarian dishes; try the fillet of lamb rolled in herbs and enveloped in phylllo pastry, or the crispy fried bass with young leeks. Lack of choice is not an issue here: the menus, the wine list, and the flavored jenever are—like the decor—all of epic proportions. ⊠ *Spuistraat 294–302, Nieuwe Zijde and Spui* ☎ *020/530–4060* 🏛 *Jacket and tie* ▤ *AE, DC, MC, V* ⊘ *No lunch.*

★ **$$–$$$$**   ✕ **De Poort.** Recently restored in the Old Dutch style (complete with polished woods and ceiling paintings), De Poort—part of the Die Poert van Cleve hotel complex—is, in fact, officially Old Dutch. Its roots as a steak brasserie stretch back to 1870, when it awed the city as the first place with electric light. By the time you read this, De Poort will have served well over 6 million of its acclaimed juicy slabs, served with a choice of accompaniments. The menu is supplemented with other options such as smoked salmon, a traditional pea soup thick enough to eat with a fork, and a variety of seafood dishes. ✉ *Nieuwezijds Voorburgwal 176–180, Nieuwe Zijde and Spui* ☎ *020/622–6429* ▤ *AE, DC, MC, V.*

**$$$**   ✕ **De Roode Leeuwe.** Evoking a sense of timeless classicism along a strip that is decidedly middle-of-the-road, De Roode Leeuw is a brasserie with the city's oldest heated terrace and an impressive champagne list. You'll find poshed-up native fare served up here with even posher silverware, be it eel (caught fresh from the nearby IJsselmeer before being stewed) in a creamy herb sauce, or Zeeland mussels steamed and served with French fries and salad. Besides attracting passing tourists, the restaurant has also built up a sizable local following ever since it received the coveted "Neerlands Dis" (Netherlands' Dish) award. ✉ *Damrak 93, Nieuwe Zijde and Spui* ☎ *020/555–0666* ⚱ *Reservations essential* ▤ *AE, DC, MC, V.*

¢   ✕ **Keuken van 1870.** This former soup kitchen, where sharing tables is still the norm, offers the best and most economic foray into the world of traditional Dutch cooking. The kitchen serves such warming singularities as *hutspot* (a hotchpotch of potatoes, carrots, and onions), its more free-ranging variant stamppot (a stew made with potatoes, greens, and chunks of cured sausage), *erwtensoep* (a sausage-fortified, extremely thick pea soup), and, naturally, a full range of meat, fish, vegetable, and potato plates. After a spell of bad luck—namely bankruptcy—the restaurant has reopened under a new owner with a scrubbed new interior and the promise that they will continue to serve a daily three-course meal for a measly €7.50. Bless 'em. ✉ *Spuistraat 4, Nieuwe Zijde and Spui* ☎ *020/620–4018* ▤ *no credit cards* ⊙ *No lunch. Closed Sun.*

## French

**$$$**   ✕ **De Silveren Spiegel.** Despite appearances, this precariously crooked building near the solid Round Lutheran Church is here to stay. Designed by the ubiquitous Hendrik de Keyser, it has managed to remain standing since 1614, so it should last through your dinner of contemporary Dutch cuisine. In fact, take time to enjoy their use of famous local ingredients, such as succulent lamb from the North Sea island of Texel and honey from Amsterdam's own Vondel Park. There are also expertly prepared fish plates, such as roasted fillet of red snapper with pickled cherry tomatoes and a puree of white bean and fennel. The full five-course menu will set you back €55. Lunch is available by reservation only (phone a day ahead ✉ *Kattengat 4–6, Nieuwe Zijde and Spui* ☎ *020/624–6589* ⚱ *Reservations essential* ▤ *AE, MC, V* ⊙ *Closed Sun.*

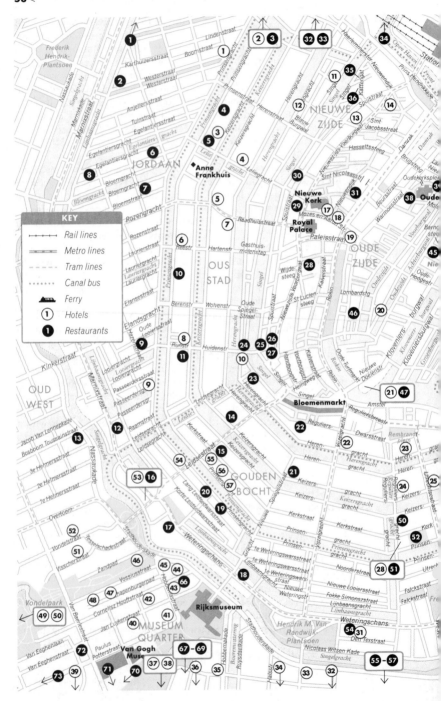

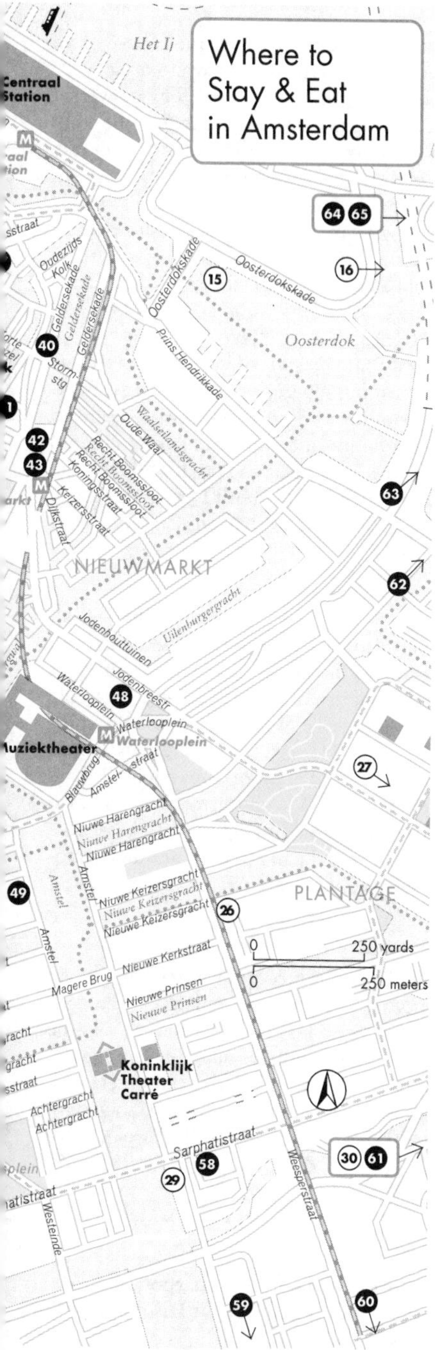

Where to Stay & Eat in Amsterdam
Het Ij
Centraal Station
Oosterdokskade
Oosterdok
Prins Hendrikkade
Oudezijds Kolk
Geldersekade
Storm stg
Waalseilandsgracht
Oude Waal
Recht Boomssloot
Koningsstraat
Keizersstraat
Dijkstraat
NIEUWMARKT
Uilenburgergracht
Jodenhouttuinen
Jodenbreestr
Waterlooplein
Muziektheater
Blauwbrug
Amstelstraat
Nieuwe Herengracht
Nieuwe Keizersgracht
Amstel
PLANTAGE
Nieuwe Kerkstraat
Magere Brug
Nieuwe Prinsen
0 250 yards
0 250 meters
Koninklijk Theater Carré
Achtergracht
Sarphatistraat
Weesperstraat
Westeinde

**Restaurants**

Amsterdam 32
An 54
Bakkerswinkel 38
Bagels and Beans 72
Balti House 55
Balraj 33
Bazar 56
Bird 41
Blauw aan de Wal 45
Blue Pepper 13
Bojo 20
Bond 70
Brasserie van Baerle 71
Breitner 49
Café Americain 16
Café Bern 43
Café de Reiger 6
Café Luxembourg 27
Christophe 5
Cinema Paradiso 2
De Belhamel 3
De Koe 12
De Kas 60
De Oceaan 64
De Poort 29
De Roode Leeuw 31
De Silveren Spiegel 35
De Vliegende Schotel 8
D'Vijff Vlieghen 25
Eat Mode 40
Excelsior 47
Goodies 24
Green Planet 30
Griekse Taverna 67
Groene Lantaarn 7
Harkema 46
In de Waag 42
Janvier 52
Kam Yin 37
Kantjil en de Tijger 26
Keuken van 1870 36
Kilimanjaro 62
La Vallade 59
Le Garage 68
Levant 18
Los Pilones 15
Lust 11
Mamouche 57
Moeders Pot 1
Odessa 65
Pancake Bakery 4
Pianeta Terra 23
Plancius 63
Pulpo 73
Pygma-Lion 21
Rose's Cantina 22
Sa Seada 61
Sama Sebo 66
Segugio 53
Sluizer 51
Song Kwae 44
Soup en Zo 48
Supperclub 28
Tapasbar a la Plancha 9
Tempo Doeloe 50
Tibet 39
Vakzuid 69
Van de Kaart 19
VandeMarkt 58
Van Puffelen 10
Wagamama 17
Walem 14
Wilhelmina-Dok 34

**Hotels**

Aalders 40
Albus Grand 22
Ambassade 10
Amstel Botel 15
Amsterdam-American 53
Amsterdam Wiechmann 9
Apollo First 39
Arena 30
Armada 25
Asterisk 31
Avenue 13
Bilderberg Jan Luyken 42
College Hotel 35
Dam Square 17
Di-Ann 7
Dikker and Thijs Fenice 54
Dylan Amsterdam 8
Fantasia 26
Fita 43
Flying Pig Palace Hostel 14, 48
Grand Amsterdam Sofitel Demeure 20
Gresham Memphis 37
Hans Brinker 57
Hegra 2
Het Canal House 3
Hotel Amsterdam De Roode Leeuw 18
Hotel de L'Europe 21
InterContinental Amstel Amsterdam 29
Keizersgracht 1
Le Meridien Apollo 34
Lloyd Hotel 16
Marcel's Creative Exchange 55
Museum Square 38
Museumzicht 41
Nadia 5
NH Grand Hotel Krasnapolsky 19
NH Schiller 23
Okura Amsterdam 32
Park 45
Piet Hein 47
Prinsen 52
Prinsengracht 28
Pulitzer 6
Quentin England 51
Rembrandt 27
Renaissance Amsterdam 12
Sander 50
Seven Bridges 24
Seven One Seven 56
Singel 11
Smit 44
Stadhouder 33
Stayokay Amsterdam Vondelpark 46
't Hotel 4
Toro 49
Washington 36

### Eclectic

**$$$$** ✕ **Supperclub.** The concept is simple but artful. Over the course of an
**Fodor'sChoice** evening, diners casually lounge on white mattresses in a white space while
★ receiving endless courses of food (and drink . . . ) marked by irreverent
flavor combinations. DJs, VJs, and live performances enhance the club-
like, relentlessly hip vibe. Once purely an underground endeavor, the
Supperclub is set to go global with branches already in Rome and San
Francisco. They've even taken their concept to Amsterdam's waterways with their own cruise ship (www.supperclubcruise.nl). Supperclub's
popularity suggests that one should really go only in large groups;
otherwise you may run the risk of being overwhelmed by one of the same.
⊠ *Jonge Roelensteeg 21, Nieuwe Zijde and Spui* ☎ *020/344–6400*
⚐ *Reservations essential* ⊟ *AE, DC, MC, V* ⊗ *No lunch.*

★ **¢–$** ✕ **Café Luxembourg.** One of the city's top grand cafés, Luxembourg has
a stately interior and a view of a bustling square, both of which are maximized for people watching. Famous for its brunch, its classic café menu
includes a terrific goat cheese salad, dim sum, and excellent Holtkamp
*krokets* (croquettes, these with a shrimp or meat and potato filling). The
"reading table" is democratically packed with both Dutch and international newspapers and mags. ⊠ *Spuistraat 24, Nieuwe Zijde and Spui*
☎ *020/620–6264* ⊟ *AE, DC, MC, V.*

### Indonesian

★ **$$–$$$** ✕ **Kantjil en de Tijger.** The interior of this large and spacious Indonesian
restaurant is a serene take on Jugendstil (a sort of Austrian art nouveau).
Although you can order à la carte, the menu is based on three different
*rijsttafel* (rice tables), with an abundance of meat, fish, and vegetable
dishes varying in flavor from coconut-milk sweet to distressingly spicy
(tip: the sweet and light local *witbier* beer is an excellent antidote). Groups
often come here to line their bellies before a night of drinking in the bars
around the nearby Spui and Nieuwezijds Voorburgwal. You can also
opt to hit the counter at the adjacent Kantjil To Go (Nieuwezijds Voorburgwal 352, open noon–9 PM daily) for cheap boxes of noodley good-
ness. ⊠ *Spuistraat 291/293, Nieuwe Zijde and Spui* ☎ *020/620–0994*
⊟ *AE, DC, MC, V* ⊗ *No lunch.*

### Vegetarian

**¢–$** ✕ **Green Planet.** You know this is a serious mecca for vegetarians when
90% of the kitchen's ingredients are organic, the resident cat is a dedicated veg (in both diet and manner), and it's the only restaurant in the
country that employs biodegradable packaging for takeout. The equally
noble menu covers everything from wraps to stir-fries but enters true
profundity when it comes to the lasagna and the carrot-orange soup with
fresh thyme. Followers of the Atkins diet should avoid this place like
the plague. ⊠ *Spuistraat 122, Nieuwe Zijde and Spui* ☎ *020/625–
8280* ⊟ *No credit cards* ⊗ *Closed Mon.*

## Oude Zijde

The city's "old side" of its historical center, although harboring the decidedly nonedible neon grotesqueries of the Red Light District, is also

host to many bargain Asian restaurants and the fine delicacies of some of Amsterdam's most esteemed eateries.

## Chinese

¢–$ ╳ **Kam Yin.** Representative of the many Suriname snack bars found throughout the city, Kam Yin offers this South American country's unique fusion of Caribbean, Chinese, and Indonesian cuisines that arose from its history as a Dutch colony. Perhaps the most popular meal is the *roti*, a flat-bread pancake, which comes with lightly curried potatoes and vegetable or meat additions. If you come for lunch, try a *broodje pom*, a bun sandwich filled with a remarkably addictive mélange of chicken and cassava root (mmmmm, root vegetable). Basic, clean, convivial, and noisy, Kam Yin shows extra sensitivity with its speedy service, long hours (daily noon–midnight), and a doggy-bag option. ⊠ *Warmoesstraat 6–8, Oude Zijde* ☎ *020/625–3115* ▤ *No credit cards.*

¢–$ ╳ **Tibet Restaurant.** Come here for budget prices or late-night hours (daily 1:30 PM–1:30 AM), but don't expect the Dalai Lama to drop by. Although you can get some authentic dishes here, like *momo* dumplings and various pork offerings that come either in spicy "folk-style" chunks or milder "family-style" shreds, the majority of the menu is ironically dedicated to standard Chinese Szechuan fare. ⊠ *Lange Niezel 24, Oude Zijde* ☎ *020/624–1137* ▤ *MC, V.*

## Contemporary

$$–$$$ ╳ **Blauw aan de Wal.** In the heart of the Red Light District is a small alley that leads to this charming oasis, complete with the innocent chirping of birds. "Blue on the Quay" is set in a courtyard that once belonged to the Bethanienklooster monastery; it now offers a restful ambience with multiple dining areas (one is no-smoking), each with a unique and serene view. Original wood floors and exposed-brick walls hint at the building's 1625 origins, but the extensive and inspired wine list, and the open kitchen employing fresh local ingredients in its Mediterranean-influenced cuisine, both have a contemporary chic. After starting with a frothy pea soup with chanterelle mushrooms and pancetta, you may want to indulge in a melt-in-the-mouth, herb-crusted lamb fillet. ⊠ *Oude Zijde Achterburgwal 99, Oude Zijde* ☎ *020/330–2257* ▤ *AE, MC, V* ◷ *Closed Sun. No lunch.*

## Dutch

$ ╳ **Café Bern.** This dark and woody café, as evocative as a Jan Steen 17th-century interior, has been serving the same cheese fondue for decades, and for good reason: it's just about perfect, especially if you enhance digestion—and the frolic factor—with plenty of orders from the fully stocked bar. Just start shredding the accompanying French stick and start dunking those bread bits into that wonderfully gooey mess. Like the Dutch, you, too, may be inspired to establish cheese fondue as your own celebratory meal of choice. ⊠ *Nieuwmarkt 9, Oude Zijde* ☎ *020/622–0034* ♨ *Reservations essential* ▤ *No credit cards* ◷ *No lunch.*

Fodor'sChoice ★

¢ ╳ **Bakkerswinkel.** This genteel yet unpretentious bakery/tearoom evokes an English country kitchen, one that lovingly prepares and serves breakfasts, high tea, hearty-breaded sandwiches, soups, and divine (almost

Fodor'sChoice ★

manly) slabs of quiche. The closely clustered wooden tables don't make for much privacy, but this place is a true oasis if you want to indulge in a healthful breakfast or lunch. It opens at 8 AM daily, and there's a second location, complete with garden patio, in the Museum District. ⊠ *Warmoestraat 69, Oude Zijde* ☎ *020/489–8000* ▭ *No credit cards* ☽ *No dinner. Closed Mon.* ⊠ *Roelef Hartstraat 68* ☎ *020/662–3594* ▭ *No credit cards* ☽ *No dinner. Closed Mon.*

### French

★ **$$$$** ✕ **Excelsior.** When only the poshest and most classically elegant will do, take your primped-up selves here. The tinkling of a grand piano, solicitous waiters, knowledgeable sommeliers, towering dessert trolleys, and preparation carts all waltz together here in a setting of towering palms, tall candelabras, shimmering chandeliers, and stunning views over the Amstel River. The menu here is traditional French, but the inspired chef, Jean-Jacques Menanteau, also knows some twists, such as a sublime lobster bisque and a grilled turbot with shrimp and Parmesan risotto. If you're feeling adventurous, opt for his fixed-price 5-course *menu excelsior,* for €80 (+€42.50 wine arrangement) which features not only seasonal specialties (think truffles) but occasionally also the acclaimed dishes he creates from such unprepossessing meats as liver and kidney. There are also four more fixed-priced menus to choose from. ⊠ *Hotel de l'Europe, Nieuwe Doelenstraat 2–8, Oude Zijde* ☎ *020/531–1705* ⋔ *Jacket and tie* ▭ *AE, DC, MC, V* ☽ *No lunch Sat. and Sun.*

**$–$$** ✕ **Harkema.** This new brasserie along the city's premier theater strip has infused a former tobacco factory with light, colour and general design savvy. Their kitchen, which is open between 11 AM and midnight daily, pumps out reasonably priced lunches and French classics, and a wall of wine is on hand to appeal to all tastes. ⊠ *Nes 67, Oude Zijde* ☎ *020/428–2222* ▭ *MC, V.*

**$$** ✕ **In de Waag.** The lofty, beamed interior of the historic Waag (weigh house) has been converted into a grand café and restaurant. Although the reading table houses computer terminals with free Internet access, a strict dinner lighting policy of "candles only"—from a huge wooden candelabra, no less—helps maintain the building's medieval majesty. The menu is heartily Burgundian with such entrées as baked fillet of salmon with braised endives and Noilly Prat sauce or tournedos of entrecôte with roasted beets. The long wooden tables make this an ideal location for larger groups, and if you happen to belong to a party of eight, you should definitely book the spookily evocative tower room. Daytime hunger pangs are also catered to from 10 AM, when you can enjoy a sandwich, a salad, or a snack on the spacious terrace. ⊠ *Nieuwmarkt 4, Oude Zijde* ☎ *020/422–7772* ▭ *AE, DC, MC, V.*

### Pan-Asian

¢ ✕ **Eat Mode.** One can easily imagine this sleek steel- and Formica-rich snack bar, dedicated to the more popular dishes of Asia, set on a Tokyo subway platform. So it just adds to the charm that it is, in fact, on Amsterdam's oldest street. Order some cheap but tasty yakitori, sushi, noodles, or whatever is on the specials menu that day, and then wait for your number to be called out. ⊠ *Zeedijk 105-7, Oude Zijde* ☎ *020/330–0806* ▭ *No credit cards.*

### Thai

**$-$$  ✕ Bird.** After many years of success operating the chaotic and tiny Thai snack bar across the street, Bird's proprietors opened this expansive 100-seat restaurant. Now they have the extra kitchen space to flash-fry their options from an expanded menu, and enough room to place the chunky teak furnishings they had imported from Thailand. The best tables—where you can enjoy coconut-chicken soup with lemongrass followed by fruity curry with mixed seafood—are at the rear overlooking the canal. ⊠ *Zeedijk 72–74, Oude Zijde* ☎ *020/620–1442* ▤ *AE, DC, MC, V.*

**¢-$  ✕ Song Kwae.** Perhaps influenced by their Chinese competitors, this buzzing joint offers speedy service and high-quality food for a budget price. Alongside the traditional red and green Thai curries and the stir-fry options, there are specialties such as green papaya salad with crab and *potek*, a searingly spicy mix of meats and fish. In the summer, the seating spills over onto the street with its views of Nieuwmarkt. They have also just opened a nearby sister restaurant Song Kwae Sukiyaki that specializes in the always socially convivial fondue. ⊠ *Kloveniersburgwal 14, Oude Zijde* ☎ *020/624–2568* ▤ *AE, DC, MC, V* ⊠ *Binnenbantammerstraat 11 Oude Zijde* ☎ *020/422–2444* ▤ *AE, DC, MC, V.*

### Vegetarian

**¢  ✕ Soup en Zo.** Only in the last few years, perhaps because *Seinfeld* is still catching up here, has the concept of speedy soup purveyors hit Amsterdam. "Soup etc." leads the pack by being particularly speedy (at least between 10 and 7:30 daily), as well as health conscious. Four soups are available daily, served with chunky slices of whole-grain breads, and the menu also offers salads and exotic fruit juices imported from Brazil as frozen fruit pulp. Once you're fortified, you can rush back to searching for bargains at the Waterlooplein flea market or window shopping for arts and antiques around its second, Museum District location. ⊠ *Jodenbreestraat 94a, Oude Zijde* ☎ *020/422–2243* ▤ *No credit cards* ⊠ *Nieuwe Spiegelstraat 54, Museum District* ☎ *020/330–7781* ▤ *No credit cards.*

## Western Canal Ring

The intrinsically posh sector of the Grachtengordel ring and its intersecting streets is a foodie paradise. Meals here come equipped with the potential for an after-dinner romantic walk to aid the digestion.

### Contemporary

**¢  ✕ Lust.** Before you get the wrong idea: "lust" is a much softer word in Dutch and suggests a calmer desire best translated as "appetite." And if you've worked up a lunchy one while wandering the Nine Streets specialty shopping area, this is a truly satiating place for healthful club sandwiches, bagels (try one with the sublime tuna spread), fruit shakes, stir-fries, pastas, and salads. There's a limited dinner menu, too, with entrées costing about €15. Be sure to visit to the wacky washroom before you leave. ⊠ *Runstraat 13, Western Canal Ring* ☎ *020/626–5791* ▤ *No credit cards* ⊙ *No dinner.*

### Continental

**$$** ✕ **De Belhamel.** Set on the edge of the Jordaan, this restaurant is blessed with art nouveau detailing and wallpaper that is so darkly evocative of fin-de-siècle living it may inspire a thirst for absinthe and Symbolist poetry. But the views of the Herengracht canal and the attentive and friendly service help create a more purely romantic setting in which to settle down and enjoy the French-inspired menu. In the winter, hearty game dishes (such as venison with a red-wine and shallot sauce) are featured; in summer, lighter fare is offered, and the seating spills out into the street. ⊠ *Brouwersgracht 60, Western Canal Ring* ☎ *020/622–1095* ▤ *AE, MC, V* ☉ *No lunch.*

**$$** ✕ **Van Puffelen.** The woody and ancient Van Puffelen, on a particularly mellow stretch of canal, offers both a startling array of herbed and spiced jenevers in its role as a *proeverij* ("tasting house") and, in addition, a huge restaurant section in which to settle the belly. The menu is of the modern café variety, but it's the weekly changing specials (a 3-course dinner costs €19.50, and is served Sun.–Wed.) that draws so many regulars. Red meat tends to be done rare here. If the main dining room gets too boistero, you can always escape to the more secluded and intimate mezzanine or, in the summer, the terrace. Reservations are essential for the restaurant (also essential is a visit to the "liquor vat" washrooms). ⊠ *Prinsengracht 375–377, Western Canal Ring* ☎ *020/624–6270* ▤ *AE, DC, MC, V* ☉ *No lunch Mon.–Wed.*

### Dutch

**¢–$** ✕ **Pancake Bakery.** It's hard to go wrong when going out for Dutch pancakes in Amsterdam. But the quaint Pancake Bakery rises above the pack of similar eateries with its medieval vibe, canal-side patio, and a mammoth menu with over 70 choices of sweet and savory toppings. There are also omelettes, and a convincing take on the folk dish of *erwtensoep* (a superthick, smoked sausage-imbued pea soup). ⊠ *Prinsengracht 191, Western Canal Ring* ☎ *020/625–1333* ▤ *AE, MC, V.*

### French

**$$$$** ✕ **Christophe.** When Algerian-born Frenchman Jean-Christophe Royer opened his canal-side *eettempel* (eating temple) in the 1980s, it was almost immediately lauded for both its William Katz–designed interior, which evokes this artist's acclaimed ballet scenery, and Royer's own culinary vision, which embellishes French haute cuisine with Arabic and African influences. In short: Christophe's cooking awards are well deserved. The ever-changing menu—always loaded with vegetarian options—may include entrées such as roasted lobster with soft garlic and small "la ratte" potatoes, or sweetbreads of veal with rosemary, asparagus and compote of preserved lemon. ⊠ *Leliegracht 46, Western Canal Ring* ☎ *020/625–0807* ⌕ *Reservations essential* 🏛 *Jacket required* ▤ *AE, DC, MC, V* ☉ *Closed Sun. and Mon., 1st wk in Jan., and 2 wks in July and Aug. No lunch.*

### Italian

**$$** ✕ **Pianeta Terra.** Marble-clad, intimate, and softly lit, this restaurant has a menu that embraces the whole Mediterranean region (and that pays respect to vegetarians and organic farmers). The daily set menus are a sure bet, and may include carpaccio of swordfish with Pecorino cheese, octopus and mussels prepared in a traditionally Moroccan *tagine* (clay pot), or a dish employing pasta, which, like the bread, is made on the premises from only organic ingredients. ⊠ *Beulingstraat 7, Western Canal Ring* ☎ *020/626–1912* ⌂ *Reservations essential* ▤ *AE, DC, MC, V* ☯ *No lunch.*

★ **$–$$** ✕ **Goodies.** Free of all pretension, this spaghetteria is merely out to serve fresh homemade pastas, healthful salads, and tasty meat and fish dishes of the highest quality for the friendliest of prices. You will, however, be packed like a sardine at the wooden tables and benches (moved onto the street during warm weather). By day, Goodies switches modes and becomes a popular café serving filling sandwiches on wedges of hearty bread, plus salads and deliciously thick fruit shakes. Reservations are essential for dinner. ⊠ *Huidenstraat 9, Western Canal Ring* ☎ *020/625–6122* ▤ *AE, MC, V.*

## Leidseplein: Center Canal Ring

Leidse "square" is the heart of Amsterdam's nightlife. Although the connecting streets are packed with middle-of-the-road restaurants, there are a number of culinary treasures to be found in and around the central canal belt.

### Contemporary

**$–$$** ✕ **Walem.** As if ripped from the pages of *Wallpaper* magazine, this sleekly hip and trendy all-day grand café serves elegant breakfast and brunch options—as well as plenty of both cappuccino and champagne. Dinnertime is fusion time, as the chefs create salads of marinated duck and chicken, crispy greens, and buckwheat noodles; or slather a roast duck with bilberry sauce and serve it with a hotchpotch of arugula. In the summer, you can relax in the formal garden or on the canal-side terrace, and late at night, guest DJs spin hip lounge tunes for an appreciative crowd. ⊠ *Keizersgracht 449, Leidseplein* ☎ *020/625–3544* ▤ *AE, MC, V.*

**¢–$** ✕ **De Koe.** Downstairs at "The Cow," the cooks crowded into the tiny kitchen manage to pump out wonderfully prepared dishes. Despite the restaurant's name, the ever-changing menu tends to favor less beef and more fish and ostrich (including dishes made with truffle sauce). The crowd here is largely local, casual and friendly short: you won't see any yuppies here. Upstairs from the café is an equally earthy and popular bar. ⊠ *Marnixstraat 381, Leidseplein* ☎ *020/625–4482* ▤ *AE, DC, MC, V* ☯ *No lunch.*

### Continental

**$$–$$$** ✕ **Café Americain.** Though thousands of buildings in Amsterdam are designated historic monuments, few like the Americain have their *interiors* landmarked as well. And for good reason: it's an art deco display of arched ceilings, stained glass, leaded-glass lamps, wall paintings, and a huge antique reading table (Mata Hari had her wedding reception here). Though the food is less notable than the décor (the menu offers everything from light snacks to full dinners), the coffee and cakes are always excellent. ⊠ *American Hotel, Leidsekade 97, Leidseplein* ☎ *020/624–5322* ⌂ *Reservations not accepted* ▤ *AE, DC, MC, V.*

## Indonesian

**$$–$$$**   ✕ **Blue Pepper.** One of the more widely acclaimed of recent newcomers
**Fodor'sChoice**   in town, this blue-toned Indo features the inspired cooking of chef
★   Sonja Pereira, whose previous restaurant won her a Michelin star. Blue
Pepper will undoubtedly follow suit; here, you can order just about anything and rest assured that it will be excellent. If you're lucky, the ever-
changing menu might include Kambing kecap where pan-fried tender
pieces of lamb are cooked with lime leaves, lemon grass, garlic, soy sauce
and chilli peppers. Unlike many other Indonesian restaurants, you won't
have a thousand different dishes piled on your plate here—just a few
obsessively prepared ones. There are full prix-fixe dinners (€40–55) and
a savvy selection of wines. Be warned: the price of a main course is de-
ceiving here since you'll always be inspired to spend more than you
planned. ⊠ *Nassaukade 366, Leidseplein* ☎ *020/489–7039* 🚗 *AE,
DC, MC, V* ☉ *No lunch.*

**¢–$**   ✕ **Bojo.** There are plenty of mediocre late-night eateries around the Lei-
dseplein, but the bambooed Bojo—stands out for its huge portions of
enjoyable food. You'll find everything here, from *saté* (skewered and bar-
becued meats) to vegetarian *gado-gado* (where raw vegetables are
drowned in a spicy peanut sauce) to the monumental rice table where
dozens of different small side dishes are served. It's open until 2 AM during the week and 4 AM on the weekend. ⊠ *Lange Leidsedwarsstraat 51,
Leidseplein* ☎ *020/622–7434* 🚗 *AE, DC, MC* ☉ *No lunch weekdays.*

## Japanese

**¢–$**   ✕ **Wagamama.** Though it may sound like an Italian restaurant run by
a large-bottomed matriarch, this is actually a slick, minimalist London-
based chain re-creating the centuries-old traditions of Japanese ramen
shops. It's fresh, fast, and fairly cheap; just fill out a menu and hand it
to one of the waitstaff. Moments later, a hearty bowl of noodles and
broth supplemented with your choice of meats, fish, and vegetables will
arrive. Further empowerment comes in the form of fruit and/or vegetable
shakes. There's a newly opened second location by the World Trade Center (Zuidplein 12, Amsterdam South, 020/620–3032). ⊠ *Max Euweplein 10, Leidseplein* ☎ *020/528–7778* 🚗 *AE, MC, V.*

## Mediterranean

**$$$**   ✕ **Van de Kaart.** This sub-canal-level newcomer with its peaceful dining
room offers a savvy and stylish balancing of Mediterranean tastes. Though
the menu is in continual flux, it may include shrimp sausages, octopus
with a salad of couscous, basil, and black olives, or a galantine of organic
chicken with shitake mushrooms. You can also opt for one of three sur-
prise menus with matching wines (€37.50 for three courses, €44.50 for
four courses, and €52.50 for five courses). Wine arrangements cost €5.50
per glass. ⊠ *Prinsengracht 512sous, Leidseplein* ☎ *020/625–9232* 🚗 *AE,
DC, MC, V* ☉ *No lunch Sat—Tues. Closed Sun.*

## Mexican

**¢–$**   ✕ **Los Pilones.** Given how far Amsterdam is from Mexico, it may take
a little courage for you to try this eatery's cactus salad (even though the
main ingredient is happily de-spiked), or the popular Day of the Dead

dish, enchiladas with mole (pronounced moh-*lay*, and featuring a spicy chocolate-chile sauce rather than blind rodents). But even if these aren't the most authentic Mexican dishes you'll ever eat, the charming young staff and casual environment here are winners. Even better, the selection of tequilas is deliciously ample, and the margaritas have all the requisite bite and zest. ✉ *Kerkstraat 63, Leidseplein* ☎ *020/320–4651* 🖃 *AE, DC, MC, V* ⊘ *No lunch. Closed Mon.*

### Turkish

**$$** ✕ **Levant.** Welcome to Istanbul Junior, where in a simple and modern setting, you can indulge in grilled meats and meze—and the appropriate firewaters to wash them down with—while your children are invariably entertained by the extraordinarily warm staff. This hidden treasure comes with an even more hidden treasure of a canal-side terrace (from which, on your way out, you can pay your respects to the bustling kitchen staff). Reservations are especially recommended. ✉ *Weteringschans 93, Leidseplein* ☎ *020/662–5184* 🖃 *MC, V* ⊘ *Closed Sun. No lunch.*

## Eastern Canal Ring, Rembrandtplein & De Pijp

The eastern sector of the Grachtengordel canal ring and the nightclub-rich Rembrandtplein come equipped with some of the city's poshest restaurants. But for a less rarified air, head to the excellent and economic ethnic eateries that dot the more casual De Pijp neighborhood.

### African

**$–$$$** ✕ **Pygma-Lion.** The rather expensive dinner menu here reflects the exotic side of South African cuisine, by offering such exotic meats as crocodile, zebra (served as a minced sausage), and antelope along with a vast array of vegetarian options. The minimalist interior is actually quite small so expect your conversations to be overheard by your proximate dining neighbours. ✉ *Nieuwe Spiegelstraat 5a, Eastern Canal Ring* ☎ *020/420–7022* 🖃 *AE, MC, V* ⊘ *Closed Mon.*

### Continental

**$$** ✕ **Janvier.** Located in a wooden church that once served as a stable for Napoléon's horses, Janvier has a patio overlooking a scenic square that's a perfect place to linger over wine (there are 15 varieties offered by the glass). The lunch menu includes salads, soups and sandwiches, while dinner brings choices like saltimbocca, chicken cordon bleu and various fondues. ✉ *Amstelveld 12, Eastern Canal Ring* ☎ *020/626–1199* 🖃 *AE, DC, MC, V.*

**$–$$** ✕ **Sluizer.** Sluizer is actually a twin restaurant with a bistrolike atmosphere that once upon a time served meat on one side and fish on the other. Now it's all united, and both areas remain simply decorated and unpretentious. Sluizer is known for simple, good food prepared without an excess of either fanfare or creativity. Because the prices are right and the service swift, it is crowded every night with a predominantly business and pre-theater crowd. ✉ *Utrechtsestraat 43–45, Eastern Canal Ring* ☎ *020/622–6376 (meat), 020/626–3557 (fish)* 🖃 *AE, DC, MC, V* ⊘ *No lunch weekends.*

## French

★ $$$-$$$$ ✕**Breitner.** Whether for romance or the pure enjoyment of fine contemporary dining, Breitner gets high marks. With a formal interior of rich red carpeting and muted pastel colors, and a view across the Amstel River that takes in both the Muziektheater-Stadhuis (Music Theater–City Hall complex) and the grand Carre Theater, this spot serves French-inspired dishes, many of which pack a flavorful punch. The seasonal menu may include such starters as baked quail with goose liver and bacon, and entrées such as skate with Indonesian-style vegetables or smoked rib of beef with a sauce of whole-grain mustard and marinated vegetables. Foie gras, fabulous desserts, and an innovative wine list allow you to step into the realm of pure decadence. As to be expected, the service is flawless and the patrons do their part to reflect Breitner's high standards by dressing smartly. ⊠ *Amstel 212, Eastern Canal Ring* ☎ *020/627–7879* ⚏ *Reservations essential* ▭ *AE, DC, MC, V* ☉ *Closed Sun. No lunch.*

## Indian

$-$$ ✕**Balti House.** If you find yourself craving curry, the dishes at this excellent purveyor of Indian cuisine have an actual subtle variance in flavors as opposed to unsubtle variance in tongue-blistering potential. Some of their more addictive choices are any one of their soups or tandooris, the butter chicken, the garlic *nan* bread and the homemade *kulfi* ice cream. The patio's a lovely place to sit when the sun is out, ⊠ *Albert Cuypstraat 41, De Pijp* ☎ *020/470–8917* ▭ *AE, MC, V* ☉ *No lunch.*

## Indonesian

$$-$$$$ ✕**Tempo Doeloe.** For decades, this has been a safe and elegant—albeit somewhat cramped—place to indulge in that spicy smorgasbord of the gods, the Indonesian rice table. Stay alert when the waitstaff point out the hotness of the dishes; otherwise you might wind up having to down several of gallons of antidotal *witbier* (a sweet local wheat beer). Tempo's more informal neighbor, **Tujuh Maret** (Utrechtsestraat 73, 020/427–9865), offers a cheaper but no less tantalizing alternative (with takeout as an option). ⊠ *Utrechtsestraat 75, Eastern Canal Ring* ☎ *020/625–6718* ⚏ *Reservations essential* ▭ *AE, DC, MC, V* ☉ *No lunch.*

## Italian

$$-$$$ ✕**Segugio.** Two local and long-respected Italian chefs came together a few years ago to open this temple to the taste buds—and they brought some of their ancient family recipes with them. The Venetian-style stucco walls give the dining room a rustic and genuine feel. In the summer you can have aperitifs on the patio, and in the winter you can request a table by the open fire. Foodies can try the chefs' five-course menu for €52.50. But making a choice from the main menu—perhaps sublime risotto of the day, or a roasted rabbit hopped up with capers and olives—is usually fail-safe, too. ⊠ *Utrechtsestraat 96, Eastern Canal Ring* ☎ *020/330–1503* ▭ *AE, MC, V.*

## Japanese

$-$$ ✕**An.** This long-popular Japanese eatery once only offered only takeout; now, with a new space for tables and a liquor license, you can linger over an evening meal along with some excellent plum wine (*umeshuu*). Although the menu focuses on sushi, An also offers fantastic baked tofu (*atsuage*) and some super-delicious *gyoza* dumplings. You may still choose to forgo dining in the oddly Mediterranean–style dining room and takeout on a nearby bench on the Amstel or within the green expanses of Saraphatipark. ⊠ *Weteringschans 76, Eastern Canal Ring* ☎ *020/624–4672* ⊟ *No credit cards* ☉ *Closed Sun. and Mon.; no lunch.*

### Middle Eastern

$  ✕ **Bazar.** A golden-angel capped church provides the singular setting for this relatively new and Arabic kitsch-addled restaurant. Cheap and flavorful North African cooking covering the range from falafel to mixed grilled meats is served up here in an atmosphere of convivial chaos. Since it's located alongside the country's largest outdoor market, Bazar is also the perfect place to break for coffee in between rounds of market wandering. ⊠ *Albert Cuypstraat 182 De Pijp* ☎ *020/675–0544* ⊟ *AmEx, DC, MC, V.*

### Moroccan

$$  ✕ **Mamouche.** All signs of this location's past as a Hell's Angels bar have been erased; it's now a North African teahouse that takes almost Parisian delight in detail. Romantic and posh, this spot has been a hit with locals ever since it opened in 2002, offering dishes such as couscous with saffron-baked pumpkin. Chocoholics will say a heartfelt amen when rounding off their meal with the Ahram, a dark, mysterious pyramid embellished with a nut caramel sauce. ⊠ *Quelijnstraat 104, De Pijp* ☎ *020/673–6361* ⊟ *AE, DC, MC, V* ☉ *Closed Mon. No lunch.*

### Tex-Mex

$$  ✕ **Rose's Cantina.** Rose's does what it can to fill the Tex-Mex void in the Amsterdam dining market serving up heaping portions of mediocre food alongside daredevil margaritas. If you've got sensitive ears, consider bringing earplugs with you; the noise levels careen up the decibel scale. In summer you can sit in the gardens facing the backs of the stately mansions on the Herengracht. ⊠ *Reguliersdwarsstraat 38, Rembrandtplein* ☎ *020/625–9797* ⊟ *AE, DC, MC, V* ☉ *No lunch.*

## Jordaan

The Jordaan is Amsterdam's most colorful and authentic neighborhood, so it is no surprise that it has some of the most colorful and authentic—whether Italian or Indian—restaurants. Afterward, you can order your digestive at a friendly local bar.

### Dutch

$$–$$$  ✕ **Groene Lantaarn.** Traditionally Swiss, cheese fondue has long been the party dish of choice for the Dutch, and this place offers a beautiful Old World setting to enjoy this or another of many cheese delights. The menu documents fondue's evolution and infinite global variants, offering such options as the communal deep-frying of meats and the shared steaming of dim sum. Of fundamental importance: the bar is fully stocked with a variety of grease-cutting choices. ⊠ *Bloemgracht 47, Jordaan* ☎ *020/*

620–2088 ⚐ *Reservations essential* ▭ *AE, MC, V* ⊘ *Closed Mon.–Wed. No lunch.*

¢ ✕ **Moeders Pot.** "Mother's Pot" does not refer to a beer-swilling matriarch (nor to your mother's lesbian lover as the local parlance would interpret it) but rather to those local old-school home-cooking recipes that deem that each meat, potato, and vegetable should rightly have the life completely fried out of it. But don't be frightened: rarely will you find such mass amounts of staple foods costing less or an interior more charmingly kitsch-ified. And since one man does all the work here, please be sensitive to the fact that he might have to rush off to flip a steak in mid-order. If you want your local cuisine served up quickly and Cultural, head here. ⊠ *Vinkenstraat 119, Jordaan* ☎ *020/623–7643* ▭ *No credit cards* ⊘ *No lunch. Closed Sun.*

## Continental

★ **$–$$** ✕ **Amsterdam.** Getting here requires going west of the Jordaan, and beyond the Westergasfabriek cultural complex. Like that neighbor (which began its days as a gas factory), this spot is an industrial monument—for a century, this plant pumped water from coastal dunes. Now, under a sky-high ceiling, one can dine on honestly rendered French and Dutch dishes—from ribeye béarnaise and steak tartare to wonderful fish dishes like grilled tuna with ratatouille—in a bustling atmosphere favored by families and larger groups. If it's too noisy for you, seek refuge on the peaceful terrace. ⊠ *Watertorenplein 6, Jordaan* ☎ *020/682–2666* ▭ *AE, DC, MC, V.*

★ **$$** ✕ **Café de Reiger.** This excellent neighborhood brown café ("brown" because of its ancient woody, nicotine-stained nature) has a long history—reflected in its tile tableaux and century-old fittings—of being packed with boisterous drinkers and diners. The Dutch fare is of the bold meat-potato-vegetable variety, always wonderfully prepared and sometimes even with an occasional adventurous diversion, such as the sea bass tastily swimming in a sauce of fennel and spinach. At lunchtime there is a menu of sandwiches and warm snacks. ⊠ *Nieuwe Leliestraat 34, Jordaan* ☎ *020/624–7426* ⚐ *Reservations essential* ▭ *AE, MC, V.*

## Indian

**$** ✕ **Balraj.** For a quarter of a century, Balraj has been a favorite of curry connoisseurs. The ambience is unremarkable—though the restaurant is clean and the plastic flowers are always impeccably fresh. The friendly fellows who serve delicious snacks, soups, and meals from their homeland, however, are a pleasure to interact with. You'll break out in the happiest of sweats when indulging in the chicken Madras, which you can wash down with sweet cardamom tea. ⊠ *Haarlemmerdijk 28, Jordaan* ☎ *020/625–1428* ▭ *No credit cards* ⊘ *No lunch.*

## Italian

**$$** ✕ **Cinema Paradiso.** This former art-house cinema has been reinvented as a designer eatery serving excellent starters—both their *bresaola* (an antipasto of air-dried salted beef that has been aged for two months, sliced thin, and then moistened with olive oil and lemon) and *gambas* (prawns) are pure manna. But for the Full Montini, you can also choose from a wide array of simple pastas and pizzas. The restaurant doesn't take reservations, but you can linger at the pleasant bar while you wait (sometimes for quite a stretch) for a table. ⊠ *Westerstraat 186, Jordaan* ☎ *020/623–7344* ▤ *AE, MC, V* ⊘ *Closed Mon. No lunch.*

### Spanish

**$**   ✕**Tapasbar a La Plancha.** With its perfect quiche-like egg-and-potato tortilla and garlicky gamba prawns, Plancha has some of the best tapas in town. Once you communicate with the super-friendly staff (preferably in Spanish) you'll quickly realize that it's also one of the most authentically Latin places in town. This place is very popular with neighborhood locals and so tiny that the bull's head over the bar barely fits, but you can snag a spot by booking ahead or dropping by during a quieter time during their long hours (till 1 AM on weekdays and 3 AM on weekends). ⊠ *1e Looiersdwarsstraat 15, at Looiersgracht, Jordaan* ☎ *020/ 420–3633* ▤ *MC, V* ⊘ *Closed Mon.*

### Vegetarian

**¢–$**   ✕**De Vliegende Schotel.** The Flying Saucer has been providing tasty and inexpensive vegetarian fare for a couple of decades now. With buffet-style ordering and an innately left-wing squatter's aesthetic, this is alternative Amsterdam at its best, one that you will grow to appreciate all the more if you wash your dinner down with some organic beer or wine. If the dining room's full or your need for spelt hits you around lunchtime, the more kitschy but no less vegan-friendly De Bolhoed (Prinsengracht 60, 020/626–1803), complete with patio, is but a short stroll away. ⊠ *Nieuwe Leliestraat 162, Jordaan* ☎ *020/625–2041* ▤ *AE, MC, V* ⊘ *No lunch.*

## Museum District & South Amsterdam

Monuments to culture, acres of lush greenery, and residences for the rich combine to make this area rich with high-end culinary favorites.

### Contemporary

**$$$–$$$$**   ✕**Le Garage.** This former garage is now a brasserie of red-plush seating and kaleidoscopically mirrored walls—handy for local glitterati who like to see and be seen. This is the home of the celebrity "Crazy Chef" Joop Braakhekke, whose busy schedule of TV appearances necessitates his leaving his kitchen in other—very capable—hands. The food is invariably excellent and uses French haute cuisine as the basis on which to embrace the world. Particularly sublime is the Flemish *hennepotje,* a starter pâté of chicken, snails, and rabbit, and the Moroccan *pastilla d'anguille,* which seals a mélange of duck liver and eel in a thin pastry dough. Although champagnes, fine wines, and caviar accent the essential poshness of it all, the daily set lunch menu is quite reasonably priced. They now also have a sister establishment, En Pluche (471–4695) next door serving "global street foods" and fancy cocktails. ⊠ *Ruysdaelstraat 54, Museum District and South Amsterdam* ☎ *020/679–7176* ⌲ *Reservations essential* 🏛 *Jacket and tie* ▤ *AE, DC, MC, V* ⊘ *No lunch weekends.*

**$$–$$$**   ✕**Brasserie van Baerle.** If it's Sunday and you want to brunch on the holiest of trinities—blini, caviar, and champagne—look no further than this brasserie. The elegant modern decor and the professional yet personal service attracts a business crowd at lunch, as well as late-night diners still on an aesthetic roll after attending an event at the nearby Concert Building. The imaginative chef knows how to put on an inspired show with a fusion menu that includes both light and spicy Asian salads and heavier fare such as veal tartlet with sweetbreads, tongue, and winter truffles. There's outdoor dining when the weather cooperates. ⊠ *Van Baerlestraat 158, Museum District and South Amsterdam* ☎ *020/ 679–1532* ▤ *AE, DC, MC, V* ✆ *Closed Sat.*

### Eclectic

**$$–$$$** ✕ **Vakzuid.** This sprawling bar-café-lounge-restaurant is in Section South of the still-new-looking 1928 Olympic Stadium, an architectural monument designed by one of the founders of De Stijl, Jan Wils. Vakzuid fits right in with its contemporary take on the functionally modern. There's a huge, sunny patio (accessible by water taxi) with plush comfortable seating and umbrellas; a solo-friendly bar specializing in coffee and designer sandwiches by day and cocktails and sushi by night; a comfortable lounge area with a view over the track field; and a raised restaurant section with an open kitchen serving a fusion of Mediterranean and Asian cooking. Thursday through Saturday evenings sees this spot transform into something resembling a nightclub, complete with noise, smoke, bouncers, and DJs. Reservations are essential for the restaurant ⊠ *Olympisch Stadion 35, Museum District and South Amsterdam* ☎ *020/570– 8400* ▤ *AE, DC, MC, V.*

**¢** ✕ **Bagels and Beans.** This low-key, bustling hot spot is just what the good Jewish doctor ordered: a wealth of fresh-made bagel choices, along with fresh juices and piping-hot coffee. There are two other locations (at Ferdinand Bolstraat 70 in the Pijp, and Keizersgracht 504 near Leidseplein), but the Museum District location wins out with its remarkably pleasant and peaceful back patio. ⊠ *Van Baerlestraat 40, Museum District and South Amsterdam* ☎ *020/675–7050* ▤ *AE, DC, MC, V* ✆ *No dinner.*

### Greek

**$** ✕ **Griekse Taverna.** You won't find souvlaki or gyros here; nor will you find the activity of plate throwing as a *digestif* (as you will as the neighboring I Kriti [Balthasar Floriszstraat 3, 020/664–1445 ]). But this woody and comfortable taverna does win points for its late hours (it's open until midnight) and its excellent, affordable, and fresh herbed starters (€4.80/plate), which are brought to your table en masse for you to choose from. Since these easily make a full meal, you won't have to worry about choosing one of their grilled main dishes until your inevitable next visit. ⊠ *Hobbemakade 64/65, Museum District/De Pijp* ☎ *020/ 671–7923* ▤ *No credit cards.*

### Indonesian

**$$** ✕ **Sama Sebo.** This small, busy, and relaxed neighborhood restaurant acts as a good, albeit not too adventurous, Intro to Indo course. Near Museumplein, for the last 30 years Sama Sebo has been dishing out *rijsttafel*, a feast with myriad exotically spiced small dishes, in an atmosphere characteristically enhanced by rush mats and shadow puppets.

There are also simpler dishes such as *bami goreng* (spicy fried noodles with vegetables and meat options) and *nasi goreng* (same, but with the noodles replaced by rice). At the bar, you can wait for your table while having a beer and getting to know the regulars. ⊠ *P. C. Hooftstraat 27, Museum District and South Amsterdam* ☎ *020/662–8146* ☰ *AE, DC, MC, V* ⊙ *Closed Sun.*

### Mediterranean

**$$** ✕ **Bond.** Bond. Jan Bond. With its golden ceiling above and lush lamps, sofas, and sounds below, Bond is equally as double-oh-so-'70s as it is comfortably experimental. Ditto for the dinner menu, which darts from braised rabbit to steak grilled with heirloom mushrooms to fish roasted with corn, wild parsnips, and oranges. Being close to the similarly gilded Concert Building, Bond can also be a great location for, say, a post-Rossini martini. Lunchtime sees things a tad more restrained, with choices running more along the lines of club sandwiches and decidedly non-McDonalds-like caesar salads. ⊠ *Valeriusstraat 128b, Museum District and South Amsterdam* ☎ *020/676–4647* ☰ *No credit cards.*

**$$** ✕ **Pulpo.** This trendy hot spot suggests a simple Italian trattoria at first glance—until, that is, you notice the '70s shag carpeting covering the walls. The surprises continue, thanks to Pulpo's remarkable friendliness and great price/quality ratio. So, settle back, groove to jazzy tunes, and splash some Mediterranean sunshine down with a glass of fine Italian wine. The main courses are simple but always top-notch—few can resist the signature marinated squid with *rucola* (arugula) and lime, or the ever-popular candied duck. And if you arrive before 6:45 PM, a three-course, preconcert menu will set you back only €26 ⊠ *Willemsparkweg 87, Museum District and South Amsterdam* ☎ *020/676–0700* ☰ *AE, DC, MC, V* ⊙ *Closed Mon. No lunch Sun.*

## East of Amstel

Head away from the historical center, east of the Amstel River, and toward the tranquil neighborhood known as the Plantage for a truly leisurely meal.

### Eclectic

★ **$$** ✕ **Plancius.** With its arty but calming leather-walled interior, Plancius offers a refreshing sense of space after the chaos of the Artis zoo or the cramped exhibits at the Resistance Museum. After breakfast and lunch service, things get kicked up a notch in the evenings, when a fashionable and convivial crowd comes to hobnob. The superb menu is adventurous, mixing and matching everything from Italian *panzarotti* (a folded-over pizza of sorts) to Indian dal-lentil soup to fish steaks with teriyaki and tahini sauce. Everything is made from scratch, right down to the tapenade. ⊠ *Plantage Kerklaan 61a, East of Amstel* ☎ *020/ 330–9469* ☰ *AE, MC, V.*

### French

★ **$$$–$$$$** ✕ **De Kas.** This 1926-built municipal "greenhouse" (not to be confused with a coffee shop of the same name) must be the ultimate workplace for chefs: they can begin the day picking the best and freshest of homegrown produce before building an inspired French-based menu around them. For diners it's equally sumptuous, especially since the setting harbors two such very un-Dutch commodities as maximum light and a giddy sense of vertical space thanks to the glass roof. The frequently changing menu always consists of a selection of small starters, followed by a main course and a dessert; you can also opt for the whole hog on the chef's table, which will set you back €125, including wine. Reservations are essential since this place was quick to chart high in the culinary orbit when it opened in 2002. And don't miss out on their house cocktail: campagne with lemon basil. i ⊠ *Kamerlingh Onnelaan 3, East of Amstel* ☏ *020/462-4562* ▭ *AE, DC, MC, V* ⊘ *Closed Sun. No lunch Sat.*

**$$$** ✕ **La Vallade.** A candlelit, cozy atmosphere and revered French country cooking inspire many to take Tram 9 to this outlying restaurant on the Ringdijk, the city's perimeter dike. Every night a new four-course menu is posted, for just €30, the only constant being a diverse cheese board. A lovely terrace in the summer slightly increases the chances of being able to book a table. ⊠ *Ringdijk 23, East of Amstel* ☏ *020/665-2025* ▭ *No credit cards* ⊘ *No lunch.*

### Italian

**$$–$$$** ✕ **Sa Seada.** Named after a Sardinian dish, this slightly out-of-the-way newcomer near Ooster Park has some of the best pizza and calzones in town (including one particularly *delizioso* number with ricotta cheese) and also sports a great patio if the indoor coziness gets a little cramped. It's just a shame that European Union regulations no longer allow the importing of the famed Sardinian worm cheese. It's not only a crime against cheese plates everywhere but also prevents this place from being the ultimate in authenticity. But here we can blame the EU, and not this wonderful little treasure. ⊠ *1e Oosterparkstraat 3–5, East of Amstel* ☏ *020/663-3276* ▭ *AE* ⊘ *Closed Tues. No lunch.*

### Mediterranean

**★ $$** ✕ **VandeMarkt.** "From the Market" truly defines the food here: each course of the day's three- (€36) or four- (€43) course feast is made from the freshest ingredients found at the market that morning. As such, the menu might include anything from a lobster bisque with prawn wontons to wild duck with sage sauce. (Often, dishes exhibit pan-Mediterranean and Moroccan influences, with sauces infused by nuts and chickpeas.) The setting is sleek and up-to-the-minute trendy, with simple pine floors and tables contrasting with brightly colored walls. ⊠ *Schollenbrugstraat 8–9, East of Amstel* ☏ *020/468-6958* ⌂ *Reservations essential* ▭ *AE, DC, MC, V* ⊘ *Closed Sun. No lunch.*

## Station & Docklands

Amsterdam's historical harbor is getting the finishing touches on what is hoped to be an image-polishing boardwalk that will perhaps evolve into the city's premier entertainment zone. And naturally, many industrial buildings have been transformed into dining hot spots. And at least until 2007, you can snack, drink or dine atop Post CS, the temporary home for the Stedelijk Museum of Modern Art, at café-bar-restaurant-club 11 (Oosterdokskade 3–5, 020/625-5999, www.ilove11.nl).

## African

**$–$$** ✕ **Kilimanjaro.** This relaxed and friendly pan-African place serves dishes from all over the continent—including one that may well inspire the outburst from the hammier among us: "this is darn crocodilicious!"—but focuses in on the often vegetarian *enjera* pancake-based meals of Ethiopia (which you famously eat with your hands). Have a seat on the summer patio, order either a *mongooza* beer (served in a calabash) or a fruity cocktail (species: exotic), and then later round off your meal with a freshly hand-ground Ethiopian coffee served with popcorn before taking a digestive stroll around the harbor. ✉ *Rapenburgerplein 6, Station and Docklands* ☎ *020/622–3485* ▭ *AE, DC, MC, V* ✆ *Closed Mon. No lunch.*

## Contemporary

**$$–$$$** ✕ **Odessa.** This floating restaurant—it's actually an expat Ukrainian trawler—attracts hipsters and boaties alike. Although you'll pay a pretty price for its international fusion meals, you can get a three-course dinner for €27.50, as well as water views of some acclaimed local architecture. In the summer, the deck is open to diner, s and on sporadic Sundays there are all-you-can-eat barbecues. Dancing begins after dark. ✉ *Veemkade 259, Station and Docklands* ☎ *020/419–3011* ▭ *AE, DC, MC, V* ✆ *No lunch.*

**$$** ✕ **De Oceaan.** "The Ocean" is suitably located on the city's Borneo island with an outlook over old ships. No matter that those plucky Dutch long ago transformed this bay of seawater into a freshwater lake; saltwater fish still make up the bulk of the ever-changing menu, which hops erratically across the globe for inspiration. You may choose to aid digestion by taking a walk along the very odd Schipstimmermanstraat (filled with wacky modern residential architecture), as this restaurant is in the heart of a modern architecture mecca. It also offers a less-fishy-oriented breakfast. ✉ *RJH Fortuynplein 29, Borneo Island, Station and Docklands* ☎ *020/419–0020* ▭ *MC, V* ✆ *No lunch on weekdays.*

## Continental

**★ $–$$** ✕ **Wilhelmina-Dok.** Getting to this former haven dock involves seafaring—you take a fun ferry ride along the Noordzeekanaal (North Sea Canal) departing from a dock directly behind Centraal Station. Set on two levels, this cube-form, large-windowed restaurant looks across the IJ river to Amsterdam's redeveloped docklands—a view totally unblocked when sitting at the picnic tables put out in the summer. And the changing daily menu fits the setting: rich in fish (from soup offerings to grilled choices) yet still kid-friendly enough to serve spaghetti with safely blunt-nosed scissors. A heavily laden dessert trolley offers to energize you for the voyage back to town. The establishment also serves sandwiches and soups during the day, and sometimes organizes music and film nights in the summer. Note that there is ferry service every 10 minutes to IJplein in Amsterdam-Noord from Steiger 8 (Pier 8). Turn right off the ferry, follow the banks of the canal, and you will find the restaurant in five minutes. You can also take the restaurant's own boat from Steiger 9 (Pier 9), but you'll have to call in advance. ✉ *Noordwal 1, Amsterdam-Noord, Station and Docklands* ☎ *020/632–3701* ▭ *AE, MC, V* ✆ *Closed Jan.*

# WHERE TO STAY

Updated by
Nicole Chabot

If you consider your hotel an integral part of your travel experience—not simply somewhere to spend the night—then staying in one of Amsterdam's registered historic monuments-turned-guesthouses is a true thrill. These lovely gabled buildings, which often overlook canals and have carefully tended gardens, allow you to intimately experience this city's rich sense of history—from the inside.

Of course, not everyone likes the idea of beaming themselves back to the 17th century over morning coffee, so it's good that Amsterdam is equally famous for its sleekly modern, ultra-designed hotels catering to savvy business types.

The city's larger hotels, including the expensive international chains, are clustered around Centraal Station, at Dam Square, and near Leidseplein. If you'd rather wake to birdsong and enjoy breakfast in the garden, there are many refined hotels to choose from around the leafy, quiet streets in South Amsterdam and its Museum District. There are also several charming, small, family-run hotels next to the Vondelpark, which are relatively inexpensive despite their prime location. Hotels in the Jordaan area—a maze of small streets, narrow canals, and hidden *hofjes* (almshouses/courtyards)—tend to have small, cozy rooms and extremely friendly staff.

We always list the facilities that are available—but we don't specify whether they cost extra. For instance, although Amsterdam is a biker/pedestrian's paradise, it is a driver's nightmare, and few hotels have parking lots (those that do charge accordingly). In fact, cars are perhaps best abandoned in one of the city's multistory lots for the duration of your stay. Many hotels operate on the European Plan (with no meals) and some on the Continental Plan (with a Continental breakfast). Breakfast (*ontbijt*) can vary from packaged juice, coffee, rolls, and butter to a generous buffet.

| WHAT IT COSTS In euros | | | | |
|---|---|---|---|---|
| **$$$$** | **$$$** | **$$** | **$** | **¢** |
| HOTELS   over €230 | €165–€230 | €120–€165 | €75–€120 | under €75 |

Prices are for two people in a standard double room in high season, including the 6% VAT.

## The Canal Rings

Most Grachtengordel (canal ring) lodgings come with all the Golden Age trimmings. As for neighborhoods, these canal-side hotels are listed as either in the Western Canal Ring, which is northwest of the Golden Bend area, or the Eastern Canal Ring, which is southeast of the Golden Bend area.

**$$$$** ✕🍴📺 **Dylan Amsterdam.** Known for her chic London proper⌐ **Fodor'sChoice** Hempel opened this Amsterdam outpost as the city's fir ★ hotel. It's located at (and incorporates a stone-arch entra⌐ the site of the historic Municipal Theater, which was destroyed by a fire in the 17th century. Today, the elegant rooms here are decorated with lacquered trunks, mahogany screens, modernist hardwood tables, and luxurious upholstery. One suite commands a view of the canal; many other rooms overlook a serene central courtyard. All have super-modern bathrooms. The hotel's restaurant now offers an acclaimed Asian-Western menu (try the lobster Fabergé with creamy lemongrass sauce) in a vogueish setting that functioned as a bakery between 1787 and 1811. ⊠ *Keizersgracht 384, 1016 GB, Western Canal Ring* ☎ *020/530–2010* 🖷 *020/530–2030* ⊕ *www.dylanamsterdam.com* ➷ *22 rooms, 19 suites* ⟁ *Restaurant, café, dining room, room service, IDD phones, fans, in-room data ports, in-room fax, in-room safes, minibars, cable TV with movies, WiFi, in-room VCRs, massage, boating, bicycles, bar, lounge, babysitting, dry cleaning, laundry service, concierge, Internet, business services, meeting rooms, some pets allowed, no-smoking rooms; no a/c in some rooms* ▭ *AE, DC, MC, V.*

★ **$$$–$$$$** 📺 **Pulitzer.** A clutch of 17th- and 18th-century houses—25 in all—were combined to create this rambling hotel sprinkled with landscaped garden courtyards which featured in the blockbuster movie *Ocean's Twelve*. It faces the Prinsengracht and the Keizersgracht canals and is just a short walk from both the Dam Square and the Jordaan. The place retains a historic ambience: most guest rooms—which are surprisingly spacious compared with its labyrinth of narrow halls and steep stairs—have beam ceilings and antique stylings. An appropriately historical sound track is provided every half hour when the nearby Westerkerk chimes the time. Modern touches include heated bathroom floors and wireless Internet in some rooms. ⊠ *Prinsengracht 315–331, 1016 GZ, Western Canal Ring* ☎ *020/523–5235* 🖷 *020/627–6753* ⊕ *www.luxurycollection. nl* ➷ *230 rooms, 3 suites* ⟁ *Restaurant, café, coffee shop, room service, IDD phones, in-room data ports, some in-room safes, some in-room kitchenettes, minibars, cable TV, some WiFi, gym, massage, boating, bicycles, bar, lobby lounge, piano bar, babysitting, dry cleaning, laundry service, concierge, Internet, business services, convention center, meeting rooms, car rental, travel services, some pets allowed, no-smoking floors* ▭ *AE, DC, MC, V.*

★ **$$$$** 📺 **Seven One Seven.** Designer and former proprietor Kees van der Valk (who has now retired to warmer climes) was a fashion designer who savvily applied his discerning eye to the décor of this hotel. Men's suiting fabrics have been used to upholster the overstuffed armchairs and sofas, and guest rooms—each of which is named for a different composer, artist, or writer—are filled with classical antiquities, framed art, flowers, and candles. Breakfast can be served in the suites or downstairs in the Stravinsky Room, where coffee, tea, cakes, wine, and beer are available for the asking throughout the day and evening. There's also a plush library and a pretty back patio. ⊠ *Prinsengracht 717, 1017 JW, Western Canal Ring* ☎ *020/427–0717* 🖷 *020/423–0717* ⊕ *www.717hotel.nl* ➷ *8 suites* ⟁ *Dining room, IDD phones, fans, in-*

room data ports, in-room safes, minibars, cable TV, WiFi, lounge, dry cleaning, laundry facilities, laundry service, concierge, Internet, business services, meeting room, some pets allowed (fee) ⊟ AE, DC, MC, V ⏐O⏐ CP.

**$$$**
**Fodor'sChoice**
★

🏨 **Ambassade.** Ten 17th- and 18th-century houses have been folded into this hotel on the Herengracht near the Spui square, whose Friday book market might explain the Ambassade's popularity with book-world people: Doris Lessing, John Le Carré, Umberto Eco, and Salman Rushdie are regulars, and novelist Howard Norman set part of his book *The Museum Guard* here. Two lounges—one of which functions as breakfast room—and the library are elegantly decorated with Oriental rugs, chandeliers, clocks, paintings, and antiques. The canal-side rooms are spacious, with large floor-to-ceiling windows and solid, functional furniture. The rooms at the rear are quieter but smaller and darker; attic rooms have beamed ceilings. Service is attentive and friendly, and if by the smallest of chances you do end up getting out of sorts, you can always seek refuge in the flotation tanks. ✉ *Herengracht 341, 1016 AZ, Western Canal Ring* ☏ *020/555–0222* 🖷 *020/555–0277* ⊕ *www.ambassade-hotel. nl* ⇌ *51 rooms, 8 suites, 1 apartment* ⚬ *Room service, IDD phones, fans, in-room data ports, in-room safes, cable TV, floating and massage, bicycles, lobby lounge, lounge, babysitting, dry cleaning, laundry service, concierge, Internet, business services, meeting rooms, car rental, travel services, parking fee; no a/c* ⊟ *AE, DC, MC, V.*

**$$–$$$$**
**Fodor'sChoice**
★

🏨 **Het Canal House.** A lot of love has gone into the refurbishment of this 1640 canal-house hotel. It's a beautiful old home with high plaster ceilings, antique furniture, old paintings, and a backyard garden bursting with plants and flowers. Every room is unique in size and décor, but you can probably count on a grandmotherly quilt on the bed—and there isn't a television set in sight (although, oddly for this sort of setup, there is an elevator). The elegant chandeliered breakfast room with burled-wood grand piano overlooks the garden, and there is a small bar in the front parlor. Wandering the halls is a treat. ✉ *Keizersgracht 148, 1015 CX, Western Canal Ring* ☏ *020/622–5182* 🖷 *020/624–1317* ⊕ *www. canalhouse.nl* ⇌ *26 rooms* ⚬ *Dining room, IDD phones, fans, some cable TVs, bar, laundry service, Internet, business services, some pets allowed, no-smoking rooms; no a/c* ⊟ *AE, DC, MC, V* ⏐O⏐ *CP.*

**$$**

🏨 **'t Hotel.** Guests return year after year to this romantic canal-side hotel in the Jordaan. It occupies an 18th-century house and is a registered monument (which means no elevator). Rooms here are larger than those in similar historic lodgings; those in the rear are especially quiet. Room number eight on the top floor has a garden view. Antiques and hats are for sale in a small shop within the hotel. ✉ *Leliegracht 18, 1015 DE, Western Canal Ring* ☏ *020/422–2741* 🖷 *020/626–7873* ⊕ *www.thotel. nl* ⇌ *8 rooms* ⚬ *Dining room, IDD phones, fans, in-room data ports, in-room safes, refrigerators, cable TV, WiFi, dry cleaning on request, laundry service on request, Internet, business services, no-smoking rooms; no a/c* ⊟ *AE, MC, V* ⏐O⏐ *CP.*

★ **$$–$$$**

🏨 **Prinsengracht Hotel.** With vast town-house windows overlooking the houseboat-graced Prinsengracht Canal, these three 18th-century canal houses are a popular choice. When the weather is fine, it's delightful to breakfast in the hotel's garden, which also has its own small guesthouse, a simple affair that sleeps up to four. Front rooms have a view of the Prinsengracht; back rooms overlook the garden. A short walk takes you to the Rembrandtplein, the Flower Market, and the shopping area by the Kalverstraat. ✉ *Prinsengracht 1015, 1017 KN, Western Canal Ring* ☎ *020/623–7779* 🖷 *020/623–8926* ⊕ *www.prinsengrachthotel.nl* ⊷ *34 rooms* ⟂ *Dining room, room service, IDD phones, fans, in-room safes, cable TV, WiFi, lobby lounge, dry cleaning, laundry service, Internet, business services, no-smoking floor; no a/c* ⊟ *AE, DC, MC, V.*

**¢–$$** 🖽 **Armada.** A superb canal-side location at the corner of the Utrechtsestraat—where there's excellent shopping and dining—is the main draw here. The rooms are simple, and some have shared bathrooms. The breakfast room has an aquarium, and—in 17th-century style—small Oriental carpets covering the tables. ✉ *Keizersgracht 713, 1017 DX, Eastern Canal Ring* ☎ *020/623–2980* 🖷 *020/623–5829* ⊷ *26 rooms, 8 with shared bath* ⟂ *Dining room, cable TV, lobby lounge, no-smoking rooms* ⊟ *AE, DC, MC, V* ⦿ *CP.*

**$** 🖽 **Keizersgracht.** Appealing to youthful and budget-minded travelers, this hotel sits along its namesake canal, and is a five-minute walk from Centraal Station. The lodgings here are Spartan, but the staff is friendly and helpful, there's an elevator, and all rooms have private bathrooms. There's a downstairs bar where you can socialize, watch TV, and play pool, pinball, or video games. Light meals and snacks can be ordered throughout the day. ✉ *Keizersgracht 15–17, 1015 CC, Western Canal Ring* ☎ *020/625–1364* 🖷 *020/620–7347* ⊷ *26 rooms* ⟂ *Dining room, Internet, no-smoking rooms, bar; no a/c, no room phones, no room TVs* ⊟ *AE, DC, MC, V.*

**¢–$** 🖽 **Hegra.** In a 17th-century building on the Herengracht canal, this hotel embodies what the Dutch call *klein maar fijn* (small but good). Rooms are unpretentious but comfortable, and the ones in front have a canal view. Some have shared baths. The absence of amenities is offset by the cordiality of the family that runs the property, the great location (with a proximity to the Anne Frank House, shopping streets and the major art museums), and the relatively gentle price tag. ✉ *Herengracht 269, 1016 BJ, Western Canal Ring* ☎ *020/623–7877* 🖷 *020/623–8159* ⊷ *11 rooms, 2 with shared bath* ⟂ *No a/c, no room phones, no room TVs* ⊟ *AE, DC, MC, V* ⦿ *CP.*

## De Pijp & Amsterdam South

Both budget and posh, the homey and the businesslike, accommodations come together in the more quiet residential neighborhoods of De Pijp and the high-toned Oud Zuid (Old South). They are set a mere 15-minute canal ride away from Centraal Station, but far enough removed from center-city crowds.

**$$$$** ✕🖽 **Le Méridien Apollo.** Amsterdam is often called the "Venice of the North" and situated, as it is, at the confluence of five canals, the Apollo nearly lives up to this title itself. A modernist palace framed by lovely trees, it's in the swank and suave Apollolaan district, known for its elegant shops and within easy distance of the RAI congress center and the Museum Quarter. Guest rooms are luxurious and Le Méridien modern, a bit generic with lots of polished wood, bright textiles, and light accent pieces. Downstairs, the tangerine and terra-cotta–hued La Sirene offers a French-Mediterranean menu crafted by the famous Parisian chef Michel Rostang. Few can resist feasting on fish on the restaurant's beautiful canal-side terraces (higher-priced rooms also offer great views of the canals). As *un touche finale*, the hotel even has its own private marina. ⊠ *Apollolaan 2, 1077 BA, Amsterdam South* ☎ *020/673–5922* 🖶 *020/570–5744* ⊕ *www.apollo.lemeridien.com* 🛏 *219 rooms, 18 suites* 🍴 *Restaurant, room service, IDD phones, in-room data ports, in-room safes, minibars, cable TV with movies, gym, dock, boating, bicycles, bar, lounge, shop, babysitting, laundry service, concierge, Internet, business services, convention center, meeting rooms, car rental, travel services, parking (fee), no-smoking floors* ▭ *AE, DC, MC, V.*

★ **$$$$** ✕🏨 **Okura Amsterdam.** This hotel is a prominent landmark in the capital, not least because it sports the largest barometer in the Netherlands; every day after the sun goes down, the building forecasts the next day's weather by changing color. Inside, there's a cavernous, dramatic lobby with inch-thick carpeting, and two marvelous, Michelin-starred restaurants to choose from: Yamazato (serving Japanese food that's touted as the best in the city), and the classic French Le Ciel Bleu. One interesting extra that's sure to help you get back on your feet if you've arrived after a long flight is the hotel's jet-lag program, which uses light therapy to help you adjust to your new surroundings. There is WiFi throughout the property. ⊠ *Ferdinand Bolstraat 333, 1072 LH, De Pijp* ☎ *020/678–7111* 🖶 *020/671–2344* ⊕ *www.okura.nl* 🛏 *301 rooms, 34 suites* 🍴 *4 restaurants, room service, IDD phones, in-room data ports, in-room safes, some kitchenettes, minibars, some microwaves, some refrigerators, cable TV with movies, indoor pool, gym, hair salon, hot tub, massage, sauna, dock, boating, bicycles, mountain bikes, 2 bars, lounge, shops, babysitting, some laundry facilities, laundry service, concierge, Internet, business services, convention center, meeting rooms, car rental, travel services, parking (fee), no-smoking floors* ▭ *AE, DC, MC, V.*

**$$–$$$** 🏨 **Apollo First.** The big neon sign here seems more suitable for a cinema, but once inside this family-run hotel you'll find yourself surrounded by quiet elegance. Black walls, gold trim, overstuffed chairs, and glittering chandeliers and sconces make the lobby a modern jewel box. Upstairs, you'll want to opt for a room at the back: quieter, these chambers allow you to fully savor the tranquility of the hotel's sylvan garden terrace. A few steps out the door the chic shops of the Apollolaan start; you're also within walking distance of Museum Square. Pets are allowed as long as you ask the hotel in advance. ⊠ *Apollolaan 123, 1077 AP, Amsterdam South* ☎ *020/577–3800* 🖶 *020/675–0348* ⊕ *www.apollofirst.nl* 🛏 *40 rooms, 3 suites* 🍴 *Café, dining room, room service, IDD phones, fans, in-room data ports, in-room safes, some in-room kitchenettes, cable TV, WiFi, boating, bar, lobby lounge, piano, shop, dry cleaning, laundry service, concierge, Internet, business services, meeting room, car rental, travel services, no-smoking rooms; no a/c* ▭ *AE, DC, MC, V.*

**¢–$** 🏨 **Stadhouder.** The Canalboat service stops right in front of this simple, well-kept hotel, in a century-old canal house just a few minutes' walk from the Museum District. Though facilities are limited, there is an elevator, unusual for hotels in this price category—and necessary, given the steep and narrow *trappenhuis* (walk-up) stairway. The lovely mother–daughter team that owns the hotel (Lydia and Danielle De Graaf) have, with their friendly dog, created a cozy atmosphere; the delightful breakfast room is filled with blue-and-white Delft-style pottery and red flowers. There is an additional 5% charge if you pay with a credit card. ☒ *Stadhouderskade 76, 1072 AE, De Pijp* ☎ *020/671–8428* 🖷 *020/664–7410* 📠 *21 rooms, 10 with shared bath.* 🛆 *Dining room, some in-room fans, cable TV; no a/c, no room phones* 🖃 *AE, DC, MC, V* ¶○¶ *CP.*

## The Eastern Docklands

★ **$–$$$$** 🖻 **Lloyd Hotel.** From the outside, the art deco–style Lloyd Hotel looks slightly severe, but its appearance fits with its history. Built in 1921 as a hotel for eastern European immigrants, it became a prison, then a detention center, before finally emerging as a living/working space for artists. In November 2004, it reopened as one of the city's most cutting-edge hotels. The vast café-cum-lobby is effortlessly stylish, with colossal white walls and plenty of natural light streaming in through windows; and its 120 rooms are quirkily and almost all uniquely designed; with unusual furniture that has been featured in many architectural and fashion magazine spreads. One of the funkiest lodging choices is the "rough music room," with its log cabin-style plank walls, its bed big enough for eight, and its screaming lime-green, plastic-clad bathroom. Most rooms have extra large tables, grand pianos, and kitchens. The hotel includes a cultural embassy, which, according to hotel literature, "offers a total service package, giving personal advice, obtaining tickets for theatrical performances, or arranging an informal encounter with a kindred spirit." Clearly, the Lloyd is unconventional. ☒ *Oostelijke Handelskade 34, 1019 BN, Eastern Harbour Area* ☎ *020/561–3636* 🖷 *020/561–3600* ⊕ *www.lloydhotel.com* 📠 *110 rooms, 16 with shared bath* 🛆 *Restaurant, café, room service, in-room data ports, some in-room kitchens, cable TV with movies, bar, lounge, some pianos, shop, dry cleaning, laundry service, concierge, Internet, meeting rooms, parking (fee), no-smoking rooms; no a/c.*

## Jordaan

While wandering this most singular of neighborhoods, you may decide it's your favorite in the city—so why not stay in it? The bells from the Westertoren take you back in time; sleepy little canals and narrow cobblestone streets with lopsided 17th-century houses give the area a special charm. On the surface, the neighborhood still looks very much as it did when Anne Frank lived here, although behind the weather-worn exteriors it now sports numerous fascinating boutiques and antique shops.

★ **$$** 🖻 **Amsterdam Wiechmann.** A favorite with rock musicians—of both the punk (Sex Pistols) and country (Emmy Lou Harris) persuasions—the Wiechmann's main claim to fame is announced by a gold record displayed in the lobby, the pride and joy of the owner, John Boddy. There are delightful personal touches, like a teapot collection and framed

Delft blue tiles, throughout the lobby and adjoining breakfast room, and fresh flowers are everywhere. The maze of hallways through the hotel's three buildings lead to guest rooms of wildly varying sizes; these are plainly decorated but enlivened by quilted bedspreads and floral drapes. Some have bedside tables covered by rugs (an old Dutch tradition). It's worth the extra money to get a room with views over the canal. Although the hotel's facilities could use some upgrading, it does have wireless Internet access and a sense of charm that's hard to beat. ⊠ *Prinsengracht 328–332, 1016 HX, Jordaan* ☎ *020/626-3321* 🖷 *020/626-8962* ⊕ *www.hotelwiechmann.nl* 🛏 *37 rooms, 1 suite* ⚙ *Dining room, IDD phones, fans, in-room data ports, in-room safes, cable TV, WiFi, bar, lounge, concierge, Internet, business services; no a/c* ⊟ *MC, V* ⦿| *CP.*

¢–$$    🏨 **Di-Ann.** Just a few minutes' walk from the Westertoren, Anne Frankhuis, and the Royal Palace, this friendly hotel occupies a gorgeously historic building, replete with gable roofs, Romanesque balconies, and half-moon windows. Perched above a ground floor filled with shops, overlooking the regal Herengracht, and several blocks from the hectic Dam square, the Di-Ann is right in the middle of all the action (perhaps too so: delicate sleepers should opt for a room in the rear). When you enter, you need to climb a traditional narrow, steep staircase, so if you have any mobility problems, this isn't the hotel for you. Some of the attractively modern guest rooms have balconies, and those in the rear overlook a garden. Other rooms have views of the Westertoren, Royal Palace, or the canal. The breakfast room allures with crown moldings, chandelier, and flowered wallpapers. ⊠ *Raadhuisstraat 27, 1016 DC Jordaan* ☎ *020/623-1137* 🖷 *020/624-3598* ⊕ *www.diann.nl* 🛏 *33 rooms* ⚙ *Dining room, IDD phones, some in-room fans, in-room data ports, in-room safes, cable TV, WiFi; no a/c* ⊟ *AE, DC, MC, V* ⦿| *CP.*

★ ¢–$$    🏨 **Nadia.** The exterior of this 19th-century building is an architectural extravaganza, complete with kiosk corner turret, Art Nouveau–y portals, and redbrick trim. Inside, rooms are white, modern, and casual, and some have adorable views overlooking the canals (sleepers bothered by noise should opt for rooms in the rear). The breakfast room is idyllic, bathed in a rosy orange glow, and topped by a chandelier, with leafy views out the windows. The friendly staff will encourage you to help yourself to a welcome drink when you arrive. Like the Di-Ann, this enjoys a great location for seeing the sights. ⊠ *Raadhuisstraat 51, 1016 DD Jordaan* ☎ *020/620-1550* 🖷 *020/428-1507* ⊕ *www.nadia.nl* 🛏 *52 rooms* ⚙ *Dining room, room service, IDD phones, fans, refrigerators, cable TV, babysitting, concierge, Internet, no-smoking rooms; no a/c* ⊟ *AE, MC, V* ⦿| *CP.*

## Leidseplein

It can be noisy in the city's busiest square, but then again sometimes it pays to be centrally located.

★ $$–$$$$    🏨 **Amsterdam-American.** Housed in one of the city's most fancifully designed buildings—one that is said to form the missing link between Art Nouveau and the Amsterdam School—the American (the name everyone knows it by) is a beloved Amsterdam landmark. Directly on Leid-

seplein, this 1902 castle-like structure is an agglomeration of Neo
Gothic turrets, Jugenstil gables, art deco stained glass, and an Arts &
Crafts clock tower. Gloriously overlooking the Singelgracht canal (one
reason why the hotel has its own boat landing), this place is near everything—nightlife, dining, sightseeing, and shopping. Guest rooms are sizable, bright, and furnished in a modern art deco style, and you have a
choice between canal and bustling-square views—the latter option having the bonus of small balconies. Newlyweds might want to indulge in
the Mata Hari Honeymoon Suite, named after the spy fatale who celebrated her own wedding here. ⊠ *Leidsekade 97, 1017 PN, Leidseplein*
☎ *020/556–3000* 🖷 *020/556–3001* ⊕ *www.amsterdamamerican.com*
🛏 *174 rooms, 16 suites* ♿ *Restaurant, IDD phones, in-room data*
*ports, in-room safes, minibars, cable TV with movies, gym, sauna, bar,*
*dry cleaning, laundry service, concierge, Internet, business services,*
*meeting rooms, no-smoking floors* ▭ *AE, DC, MC, V.*

★ **$$$$** 🏨 **Park.** At first glance, the Park looks like everyone's dream of a grand
Netherlandish hotel: it's topped by a picturesque pepper-pot tower, and
its 18th-century building set with regal windows is mirrored charmingly
in the Singel river. But though this stately Amsterdam fixture has one
foot in history, the other is firmly entrenched in today, thanks to its mod-
ern-luxe décor and amenities (many rooms have air-conditioning and
minibars, and there are meeting rooms and Internet access for business
travelers). The neon lights of Leidseplein's shops, casino, and clubs are
around the corner, and the sylvan glades of Amsterdam's gorgeous Vondelpark are just across the road, beckoning you to take an early morning jog. The major art museums are also within walking distance.
⊠ *Stadhouderskade 25, 1071 ZD Leidseplein* ☎ *020/671–1222* 🖷 *020/*
*664–9455* ⊕ *www.park.lemeridien.com* 🛏 *187 rooms, 6 suites* ♿ *Restau-*
*rant, room service, some in-room safes, some in-room minibars, cable*
*TV, hair salon, bar, lounge, shops, laundry service, concierge, Internet,*
*business services, meeting rooms, parking (fee), no-smoking rooms; no*
*a/c in some rooms* ▭ *AE, DC, MC, V.*

**$$–$$$$** 🏨 **Dikker and Thijs Fenice.** "Lavish," "classical," and "cozy" are some
**Fodor'sChoice** of the adjectives typically used to describe this hotel, which has a regal
★ address on the Prinsengracht canal. The hotel, first opened as a shop in
1895, has been renowned for fine dining since its founder, A. W. Dikker,
entered into a partnership in 1915 with H. Thijs, who had apprenticed
with the famous French chef Escoffier. The busy location—happily, all
the majestic sash windows are double-glazed—is convenient to the
major shopping areas and one block from the Leidseplein, nightlife
center of the city. The art deco–style rooms are fully modernized, although
they retain a regal ambiance with dark-wood furniture, scarlet uphol-
stery, and gilt-edged mirrors. Room 408 has a wonderful beamed ceil-
ing. Of the upper-price hotels, this is one of the few that includes
breakfast in the basic room rate. ⊠ *Prinsengracht 444, 1017 KE, Lei-*
*dseplein* ☎ *020/620–1212* 🖷 *020/625–8986* ⊕ *www.dtfh.nl* 🛏 *42*
*rooms* ♿ *Restaurant, room service, in-room data ports, minibars, cable*
*TV with movies, WiFi, bicycles, bar, babysitting, dry cleaning, laundry*
*service, concierge, Internet, business services, some pets allowed, no-smok-*
*ing rooms; no a/c in some rooms* ▭ *AE, DC, MC, V* 🍽 *CP.*

$ ▥ **Marcel's Creative Exchange Bed & Breakfast.** How would you like to stay in a renovated 17th-century home decorated with fine antiques and original works of art, located in the heart of the city and all for a sweetly gentle price? The owner is fascinating, with mucho worldwide artistic connections and will share his information about the city and the art scene like a personal mentor. Yes, this is all possible, but the catch is that you have to be interesting enough to pass muster—exclamation point—with the host. Internationally renowned artist/designer Marcel van Woerkom has been renting rooms in his house since 1970 and has since hosted royalty, travelers, and artists from a variety of disciplines. All guests surely drool over the moderne interiors with their furniture from Charles and Ray Eames, Alvar Alto, Philippe Starck, and Marcel Breuer. Because of the location on the Leidsestraat next to De Uitkijk, Amsterdam's oldest existing art cinema (Marcel is one of the owners), you're right in the thick of things and can watch the city from a balcony. ⊠ *87 Leidsestraat, 1017 NX, Leidseplein* ☎ *020/622–9834* ⚐ *020/772–7446* ⊕ *www.marcelamsterdam.com* ⏎ *3 rooms; 1 suite, 2 with shared bath* ⚒ *IDD phones, some in-room fans, some in-room refrigerators, cable TV, concierge, Internet, business services, meeting room, no-smoking rooms; no a/c* ▭ *V.*

¢ ▥ **Hans Brinker.** Housed in a brick building that was a monastery about half a century ago, this hostel has rooms that are no-frills but sparkling clean, with white walls and blue floors. The dorms have bunk beds, the private rooms have bathroom facilities. As basic as it all is, it's never boring. You can boogie in the disco, drink at the bar, enjoy incredibly cheap meals (guests only) in the restaurant and surf the Net on one of the hostel's three computers. From five to six, you'll find your fellow backpackers guzzling beer in the bar during Happy Hour. And it's all "happening" at Leidseplein, just around the corner. What more could you want? Whole smoking floors are available. ⊠ *Kerkstraat 136, 1017 GR, Leidseplein* ☎ *020/622–0687* ⚐ *020/638–2060* ⊕ *www. hans-brinkerhotel.com* ⏎ *120 rooms, all with shared bath, 500 beds* ⚒ *Restaurant, bar, nightclub, no-smoking rooms; no a/c, no room phones, no room TVs* ▭ *MC, V* ¶◎¶ *CP.*

## Museum District & Vondelpark

If you've come to Amsterdam for its reputation as the city of the arts, then you simply must book a room in this quarter. All the city's top museums are here, the priciest shopping neighborhood is just around the corner, and the lovely green Vondelpark is just to the west. Little wonder that this entire area has been colonized by fine hotels.

★ $$$$ ▥ **Gresham Memphis.** Classically proportioned, mansard-roofed, and ivy-covered—what more do you want from an Amsterdam hotel facade? This elegant, exceptionally spacious hotel was once the private residence of Freddy Heineken, of brewery fame. Formerly decorated in a classical style, the entire hotel was renovated in 2003 to give it a fresh, modern, and airy look, so if you want Vermeer-style interiors, this isn't the place for you. But the new design is energizing, not to say empowering (lots of businesspeople stay here): the breakfast room is bright and welcoming, the bar-lounge is sleek contempo, the guest rooms modern and tranquil. As formal but not as expensive as the deluxe hotels, and embraced by a serene residential neighborhood, the Memphis is near the Concertgebouw. Extra beds are available, and children under 12 are welcome at no additional charge. The large bar has comfortable armchairs and tables and serves light meals. ⊠ *De Lairessestraat 87, 1071 NX, Museum District* ☎ *020/673-3141* 🖷 *020/673-7312* ⊕ *www. memphishotel.nl* ⇨ *65 rooms, 9 suites* ♻ *Café, dining room, room service, IDD phones, fans, in-room data ports, some in-room safes, minibars, refrigerators, cable TV with movies, WiFi, exercise equipment, bar, lobby lounge, dry cleaning, laundry service, concierge, Internet, business services, meeting room, no-smoking floors* ▭ *AE, DC, MC, V.*

★ **$$$–$$$$** ✕▦ **The College Hotel.** This brand-new hotel—which nevertheless occupies an 1895 school building—was opened in May 2005. It's owned by an educational institute, the ROC of Amsterdam, and operated as a training ground for students of the hotel management program (which accounts for the fresh-faced staff). The building has wide, grand corridors and stairwells, and the rooms have high ceilings, carpets you can sink into, and gleaming bathrooms. The in-house restaurant is one of only a few that serve New Dutch cuisine; you can try warm smoked eel here, with radish, apple syrup, and grated lemon. ⊠ *Roelof Hartstraat 1, 1071 VEMuseum District* ☎ *020/571–1511* 🖷 *020/571–1512* ⊕ *www. thecollegehotel.com* ⇨ *38 rooms, 2 suites* ♻ *Restaurant, room service, IDD phones, in-room data ports, in-room safes, minibars, cable TV with movies, some in-room VCRs, WiFi, massage, boating, bicycles, mountain bikes, bar, lounge, shop, babysitting, dry cleaning, laundry service, concierge, Internet, business services, meeting rooms, car rental, travel services, parking (fee), no-smoking floor* ▭ *AE, MC, V.*

**$–$$$** ▦ **Museum Square.** Small and refined, with a cherry brick and white facade, this hotel is within walking distance of the Concertgebouw and the major art museums, as well as a large selection of good restaurants and trendy brasseries. The Vondelpark is very nearby, but you can enjoy your own little piece of private heaven in the hotel's tranquil Japanese garden. Rooms are light, airy, and attractively furnished. ⊠ *De Lairessestraat 7, 1071 NR Museum District* ☎ *020/671–9596* 🖷 *020/671–1756* ⊕ *www.amsterdamcityhotels.nl* ⇨ *34 rooms* ♻ *Dining room, IDD phones, fans, in-room safes, minibars, cable TV with movies, WiFi, bar, babysitting, dry cleaning, laundry service, Internet, no-smoking floors; no a/c in some rooms* ▭ *AE, DC, MC, V* †◯▮ *CP.*

**$$–$$$** ▦ **Toro.** In a prim and proper 19th-century-style villa on the southern border of the Vondelpark, this hotel offers a relaxing atmosphere. The views of the park and a small lake, and an interior tastefully dotted with antiques, oil paintings, and chandeliers provide a special homelike environment that is rare in Amsterdam. Rooms are bright and spacious, and some have balconies. Set near the area of the park far from the museum quarter and its shops, slightly outside the city center in a chic residential area, the hotel is, nevertheless, convenient to tram lines and lends itself to a lovely stroll through the park from the heart of Amsterdam. ⊠ *Koningslaan 64, 1075 AG, Vondelpark* ☎ *020/673-7223* 🖷 *020/ 675-0031* ⊕ *www.hoteltoro.nl* ⇨ *22 rooms* ♻ *Dining room, room ser-*

*vice, IDD phones, in-room data ports, in-room safes, minibars, cable TV, some in-room VCRs, bicycles, bar, lounge, babysitting, dry cleaning, laundry facilities, concierge, Internet, business services, some pets allowed (fee), no-smoking rooms* ▭ *AE, DC, MC, V.*

★ **$$$–$$$$** 🏨 **Bilderberg Jan Luyken.** This small, formal, and stylish town house hotel offers a peaceful sanctuary, complete with serene garden and restrained art nouveau stylings. Located in a trio of quaint 19th-century five-story town houses, its exterior is fitted out with wrought-iron balconies, cute gables, and the usual ugly roof extension. The interior décor is largely *Wallpaper*-modern—tripod lamps, "paper" steel ashtrays, Knoll-ish chairs. Guest rooms can be on the snug side, and service and housekeeping leave a bit to be desired, according to some readers. The hotel is just one block away from the Museumplein and fashionable shopping streets; perhaps this explains its popularity with musicians in town who play the nearby Concertgebouw. There's a lovely little "relaxation" room with a tanning lounge, Turkish bath, and hot tub, and the hotel's trendy bar, Wines and Bites, serves high-quality wine along with snacks and lunches. ✉ *Jan Luykenstraat 58, 1071 CS, Museum District* ☎ *020/573–0730* 🖷 *020/676–3841* ⊕ *www. janluyken.nl* ⤴ *62 rooms* ⟁ *Dining room, room service, IDD phones, in-room data ports, in-room safes, minibars, cable TV, some in-room VCRs, WiFi, massage, spa, steam room, boating, bicycles, mountain bikes, wine bar, babysitting, dry cleaning, laundry service, concierge, business services, car rental, travel services, no-smoking floors* ▭ *AE, DC, MC, V.*

★ **$$–$$$** 🏨 **Prinsen.** P. H. H. Cuijpers, the architect of the Rijksmuseum and Centraal Station, also created the adorable building occupied by this hotel. A chalet roof, dormers, bay window, jigsaw trim, neoclassical columns, and sculpted reliefs of cats (one showing a kitty chasing mice) all decorate the exterior, which was built around 1870. The storybook feeling, however, ends as soon as you step in the door: the interiors have all been gutted and renovated. Many of the bedrooms are still cheery and gracious, though, and on the ground floor, there's a bright yellow breakfast room overlooking a lovely garden. On a quiet street next to the Vondelpark, the hotel makes all its guests very welcome and is particularly gay-friendly. ✉ *Vondelstraat 36–38, 1054 GE, Vondelpark* ☎ *020/616–2323* 🖷 *020/616–6112* ⊕ *www.prinsenhotel.nl* ⤴ *45 rooms, 1 suite* ⟁ *Dining room, IDD phones, in-room safes, cable TV, bar, laundry service; no a/c* ▭ *AE, DC, MC, V* ⦿ *CP.*

★ **$$** 🏨 **Smit.** Despite its location, at the foot of the exclusive P. C. Hooftstraat and south entrance to the Rijksmuseum, this hotel is anything but pretentious. It's a lively and friendly place and a good choice for those who want to enjoy the Leidseplein nightlife. The neighboring restaurant is open for lunch and snacks but closes at 6 PM. The rooms are very plain and the recently remodeled bathrooms are relatively spacious. Some of the rooms facing the tram lines are less quiet. ✉ *P. C. Hooftstraat 24, 1071 BX, Museum District* ☎ *020/671–4785* 🖷 *020/662–9161* ⊕ *www. hotelsmit.com* ⤴ *63 rooms* ⟁ *Café, dining room, IDD phones, in-room data ports, in-room safes, cable TV, some pets allowed, no-smoking floors; no a/c* ▭ *AE, DC, MC, V* ⦿ *CP.*

**$–$$** 🏨 **Aalders.** Occupying a cozy, charming town house, this busy little hotel has reasonably sized rooms with large windows on a quiet street. All rooms have shower or bath; double rooms have twin beds. Breakfast is served in a large and beautiful second-floor room. ⊠ *Jan Luykenstraat 13–15, 1071 CJ, Museum District* ☎ *020/662–0116* 🖷 *020/673–4698* ⊕ *www.hotelaalders.nl* ➟ *28 rooms* ᗡ *Café, dining room, IDD phones, fans, cable TV, WiFi, bar, laundry service, Internet, travel services, no-smoking floors; no a/c* ⊟ *AE, DC, MC, V* ☼ *Closed Dec. 11–27* ⊙| *CP.*

**$$$** 🗖 **Fita.** The couple who run this property, Hans and Loes de Rapper, place an emphasis on the spic-and-span. Therefore, this peaceful hotel, which is in a gracious, turn-of-the-20th-century, five-story townhouse, is not only dustless but is off-limits to smokers. In the morning, you can enjoy fresh-baked bread and homemade jam, along with freshly squeezed orange juice, at the buffet breakfast. Another plus: you won't be charged for telephone calls within Europe and to the United States. The Rijksmuseum, Van Gogh Museum, Stedelijk Museum, and Concertge-bouw are literally around the corner. ⊠ *Jan Luykenstraat 37, 1071 CL, Museum District* ☎ *020/679–0976* 🖷 *020/664–3969* ⊕ *www.hotelfita. com* ➟ *16 rooms* ᗡ *Dining room, IDD phones, fans, cable TV, WiFi, babysitting, dry cleaning, laundry service, Internet, car rental, some pets allowed, no-smoking rooms; no a/c* ⊟ *AE, DC, MC, V* ☼ *Closed Dec. 15–Jan. 15* ⊙| *CP.*

★ **$$** 🗖 **Piet Hein.** Salons don't come any sleeker than the ones inside this or-nate brick Vondelpark mansion, with their cube-shaped chairs, gleam-ing Swedish woods, sisal-like carpeting, white-on-white hues, and bright bursts of navy blue, perhaps in homage to Piet Hein, the legendary 17th-century Dutch privateer and vice admiral. Other maritime touches in-clude paintings of sailing ships, navy blue carpets with patterns of seaman's knots, and cozy rooms that make you feel like you're in a ship's cabin. Some bedrooms here are so sprightly done up you will feel ten years younger. Real color lies outside the windows, as front rooms have fine views of the park (always in demand—even booking far in advance doesn't guarantee you one of these rooms). Those in the back look over a garden. The P. C. Hooftstraat, the Concertgebouw, and the city's major art museums are nearby. ⊠ *Vossiusstraat 52, 1071 AK Museum District* ☎ *020/662–7205* 🖷 *020/662–1526* ⊕ *www.hotelpiethein.nl* ➟ *60 rooms* ᗡ *Dining room, room service, IDD phones, in-room safes, cable TV, bar, lobby lounge, babysitting, dry cleaning, laundry ser-vice, Internet, business services, car rental, travel services, no-smoking rooms; no a/c in some rooms* ⊟ *AE, DC, MC, V* ⊙| *CP.*

**$–$$** 🗖 **Washington.** Just a stone's throw from the Museumplein, this hotel
**Fodor'sChoice** often attracts international musicians in town to perform at the nearby
★ Concertgebouw—except perhaps those who play the cello (there's a steep staircase here, hard to navigate with bulky baggage). The owner Mr. Boelhouwer is helpful and will lend from his collection of guidebooks. The breakfast room and lounge are filled with antiques and marvelous brass chandeliers, and the hotel is meticulously polished and sparkling clean. The rooms are simply and charmingly decorated in white and pas-tel shades. Large windows let in a flood of light. There are also five com-fortable and cozy apartments with their own kitchens; some also have living rooms, bathtubs, and and pianos. ⊠ *Frans van Mierisstraat 10, 1071 RS, Museum District* ☎ *020/679–7453* 🖷 *020/673–4435* ⊕ *www.*

*hotelwashington.nl* ⟿ *17 rooms, 4 with shared bath, 5 apartments* ♨ *Dining room, room service, IDD phones, cable TV, WiFi, beer garden, lobby lounge, lounge, some pianos, some laundry facilities, laundry service, Internet, business services; no a/c* ▭ *AE, DC, MC, V* ❢◯❢ *CP.*

**¢–$**    ▦ **Museumzicht.** The name "Museum View" is accurate: this hotel is directly across the street from the Rijksmuseum. The owner formerly had an antiques shop, so the house is filled with wonderful objects such as art deco wardrobes, tables and chairs, '50s lamps, and Lloyd Loom chairs. The breakfast room–lounge has a Murano glass chandelier and art deco pottery on the chimney walls. Elsewhere hang 19th and 20th century landscpaes and portraits. The rooms are simple but delightful, with pastel-striped wallpaper and little etchings. The hotel is on the top floors of the building, and guests must climb a narrow and steep stairway with their luggage to the reception desk and to the rooms—the owners highly recommend traveling light. ✉ *Jan Luykenstraat 22, 1071 CN, Museum District* ☎ *020/671–2954* 🖷 *020/671–3597* ⟿ *14 rooms, 3 with shower* ♨ *Dining room, fans, babysitting; no a/c, no room TVs* ▭ *MC, V* ❢◯❢ *CP.*

**$**    ▦ **Quentin England.** The intimate Quentin England is one of a series of adjoining buildings dating from 1884, each of which is built in an architectural style of the country whose name it bears. A connoisseur's delight—adorned with a Tudor gable and five-step gable—the Quentin occupies the England and Netherlands buildings. Rooms are simple and vary greatly in size but are cozy and clean. The tiny breakfast room is particularly enchanting, with flower boxes on the windowsills, dark-wood tables, and fin-de-siècle decorations. Behind the reception desk is a small bar and espresso machine (perhaps on loan from the neighboring Italian building?). The hotel offers tremendous character and attention in place of space and facilities. There is an additional 5% fee for using a credit card. ✉ *Roemer Visscherstraat 30, 1054 EZ, Vondelpark* ☎ *020/616–6032* 🖷 *020/685–3148* ⊕ *www.quentinhotels.com* ⟿ *40 rooms, 3 with shared bath* ♨ *Café, dining room, IDD phones, cable TV, some pets allowed; no a/c* ▭ *MC, V.*

**$$**    ▦ **Sander.** Inexpensive, and perfectly situated for museum-going, the Hotel Sander offers rooms best described as traditionally Dutch: comfortable and simple. Seating areas in window bays give some rooms additional charm. The bar and breakfast room open out onto a garden. The hotel is also particularly gay-friendly. ✉ *Jacob Obrechtstraat 69, 1071 KJ, Museum District* ☎ *020/662–7574* 🖷 *020/679–6067* ⊕ *www.hotel-sander.nl* ⟿ *20 rooms* ♨ *Dining room, snack bar, IDD phones, some in-room fans, in-room safes, cable TV, bar, lobby lounge, laundry service, Internet, business services; no a/c* ▭ *AE, MC, V* ❢◯❢ *CP.*

**★ ¢**    ▦ **Flying Pig Palace Hostel.** For those backpackers who like to chill out and save a load of money, the Pig Palaces—there is one in the city center and another in the posher neighborhood of Vondelpark—are the favored choice of "piggies" everywhere. The admittance policy is strict: if you're not a backpacker aged 16 to 35, you'll have to look elsewhere. Not only breakfast and sheets are included in the price, but also free Internet and e-mail service and the use of in-line skates (so lace up and explore the park, or join the once-weekly night skate throughout the city). There's a bar claiming to serve the cheapest beer in town, and you can cook with other guests in the kitchen. If you're traveling with an amour or don't mind sharing with a friend, the best deal is to book a queen-size bunk bed in one of the dorms. The downtown hostel is slightly more expensive, but it hosts a disco twice a week and rents in-line skating equipment. It has no private baths, however. ☒ *Vossiusstraat 46, 1071 AJ, Vondelpark* ☎ *020/400–4187* 🖷 *020/421–0802* ⊕ *www. flyingpig.nl* ⮰ *4 rooms, 20 dormitories* ⚘ *Dining room, some room TVs, bar, lounge, no-smoking floors; no a/c, no room phones, no kids under 16* ▭ *AE, MC, V* ⵀ *CP* ☒ *Flying Pig Downtown: Nieuwendijk 100, 1012 MR, Nieuwe Zijde* ☎ *020/420–6822* 🖷 *020/421–0802* ⮰ *4 rooms, 20 dormitories* ⚘ *Bar; no a/c, no room phone, no room TVs* ⚘ *Reservations not accepted* ▭ *AE, MC, V* ⵀ *CP.*

★ ¢–$  🏨 **Stayokay Amsterdam-Vondelpark.** Word of mouth has made this hostel so popular that over 75,000 backpackers stay here every year. Hidden on a small side path within the Vondelpark, the location is almost like being in a secret forest, despite being only minutes away from the hustle and bustle of the city. Put your bike in the hostel's covered shed, breakfast on the terrace and ogle the parrots in the trees, then do a few rounds of the park (a great place to connect with new people). Accommodations range from rooms that sleep two to dormitories for twenty, and sheets are included in the price. In the spacious lounge, you can use the Internet, watch TV, play pool, or get acquainted with backpackers from around the world. Some rooms are available for those with disabilities. There are no private baths, but there's wireless Internet access throughout the property, and the hostel can arrange Euroline tickets. This is probably the cleanest hostel anywhere—your mom would definitely approve. ☒ *Zandpad 5, 1054 GA, Vondelpark* ☎ *020/589–8996* 🖷 *020/589–8955* ⊕ *www.stayokay.com* ⮰ *100 rooms, 536 beds* ⚘ *Restaurant, WiFi, laundry facilities, boating, bicycles, bar, laundry facilities, Internet, travel services, no-smoking floors; no a/c, no room phones, no room TVs* ▭ *AE, MC, V* ⵀ *CP.*

## Nieuwe Zijde

If you want to stay in the heart of Amsterdam, the "New Side" is ground zero. Crowds centered around the Dam square mean you'll have plenty of company.

$$$$  🏨 **NH Grand Hotel Krasnapolsky.** Until the Hilton came along, this hotel was Holland's biggest. As you'll see when you take a table in the Kras's soaringly beautiful Wintertuin (Winter Garden), Amsterdam's loveliest place for luncheon, it was also one of the best. Sitting in this masterpiece of 19th-century allure, replete with potted palms, greenhouse roof, Victorian chandeliers, and buffet tables stocked with cakes and roses, will make you feel like a countess or duke. Sadly, the rest of this 1866 landmark isn't as impressive. Unfortunately, a mishmash of revamping over the years was done with a progressively penurious attitude toward living space. Last renovated in 2003, the guest rooms—now numbering more than 468—vary greatly in size and tend toward disappointingly serviceable functionality. There are some memorable dining spots here, however; you can linger over a *jenever* gin cocktail at

the Proeflokaal Wynand Fockink (Tasting House Wynand Fockink), dine in France or feast on Japanese delights at the Edo teppanyaki restaurant. ✉ *Dam 9, 101 JS, Nieuwe Zijde* ☎ *020/554–9111* 🖷 *020/622–8607* ⊕ *www.nh-hotels.com* ⏎ *426 rooms, 7 suites, 35 apartments* ♿ *3 restaurants, room service, IDD phones, some in-room fans, in-room data ports, some in-room faxes, in-room safes, some in-room hot tubs, some in-room kitchenettes, minibars, some in-room microwaves, some in-room refrigerators, cable TV with movies, some in-room VCRs, exercise equipment, hair salon, spa, boating, bicycles, mountain bikes, bar, lounge, shops, babysitting, dry cleaning, some laundry facilities, laundry service, concierge, Internet, business services, convention center, meeting rooms, car rental, travel services, parking (fee), no-smoking floors; no a/c in some rooms* ▤ *AE, DC, MC, V.*

**$$$$** ✕🏨 **Hotel Amsterdam–De Roode Leeuw.** On the corner of Dam Square and across from the city's leading department store, De Bijenkorf is a cut above many others on the Damrak. The guest rooms on the elegant 18th-century facade have soundproof windows to buffer the outside world, and rooms at the back or on the "executive floor" are also safe bets. Rooms that accommodate three people and extra beds are available, and the hotel's restaurant, De Roode Leeuw, has built up a sizable following thanks to its heated terrace, Dutch haute cuisine, and encyclopedic champagne list. The restaurant is the recipient of the coveted *Neerlands Dis* (Netherlands' Dish) award, and serves up a succulent roast Gelderland chicken in tarragon sauce, as well as an array of stampots made with smoked sausage, beef steak, and bacon. ✉ *Damrak 93–94, 1012 LP, Nieuwe Zijde* ☎ *020/555–0666* 🖷 *020/620–4716* ⊕ *www. hotelamsterdam.nl* ⏎ *79 rooms* ♿ *Restaurant, café, IDD phones, in-room data ports, in-room safes, minibars, cable TV, shop, babysitting, dry cleaning, laundry service, concierge, Internet, business services, 2 meeting rooms, car rental, no-smoking floor* ▤ *AE, DC, MC, V.*

★ **$$$** 🏨 **Dam Square.** Just around the corner from the Royal Palace, this hotel is a surprisingly quiet oasis, due to its location on a narrow, pedestrians-only street. The Amsterdam School–style building is adorned with storybook-ornate brick and stone trim and a gabled roof; inside, rooms are modern and comfortable with terra-cotta and dark green furnishings. The building once housed a liquor distillery, and you can still enjoy a visit to the tasting house next door. A nice plus here is the hotel's level of service—at times, the staff coddles you. It's no surprise that visitors return again and again. ✉ *Gravenstraat 12–16, 1012 NM, Nieuwe Zijde* ☎ *020/623–3716* 🖷 *020/638–1156* ⊕ *www.tulipinndamsquare. com* ⏎ *38 rooms, 1 suites* ♿ *Dining room, IDD phones, in-room data ports, room TVs with movies, lounge, laundry facilities, laundry service, Internet, no-smoking rooms, bar* ▤ *AE, DC, MC, V* ⦿ *CP.*

**$$** 🏨 **Avenue.** Occupying several historic buildings—one a listed monument that used to be a warehouse for the United East India Company—this hotel recently underwent renovation. Its rooms, though small, are comfortable, and are furnished in a bright, cheerful contemporary style. Double window glazing and extra-thick ensure that you won't be disturbed by street noise or rambunctious neighbors. The large and varied breakfast buffet gets consistent raves. ✉ *Nieuwezijds Voorburgwal 33, 1012*

RD, Nieuwe Zijde ☎ 020/530–9530 🖷 020/530–9599 ⊕ wℳ hotel.nl ⥲ 80 rooms ㋡ IDD phones, some in-room fans, so kitchenettes, 1 room with refrigerator, cable TV with movies, conciℯℊℴ⸴ no a/c, no room phones ▤ AE, DC, MC, V ⑂⍥⑂ CP.

**$$–$$$**    🏨 **Singel.** The three renovated 17th-century canal houses that comprise this property are charmingly lopsided and quirky-looking, with cheerful, striped window canopies. The historic exterior belies the modern furnishings and comforts you'll discover within, however, which include an elevator, And express ironing and shoeshine service. If you want a view of the Singel canal, book a front or side room. From the hotel, it's just a short stroll to the Kalvertoren and Magna Plaza shopping malls, as well as the Dam Square. ⊠ Singel 13–17, 1012 VC, Nieuwe Zijde ☎ 020/626–3108 🖷 020/620–3777 ⊕ www.singelhotel.nl ⥲ 32 rooms ㋡ Dining room, room service, IDD phones, no a/c, fans, in-room safes, cable TV, bar, lounge, babysitting, laundry service, no-smoking floors; no a/c ▤ AE, DC, MC, V ⑂⍥⑂ CP.

**¢–$**    🏨 **Asterisk.** A touch of the 19th century still hovers about this very friendly hotel. Some guest rooms feature decorative ceiling moldings and chandeliers. Major art museums, the Leidseplein, the Flower Market, and the Rembrandtsplein are all within walking distance of the hotel, which is on a quiet street. For children, cots and high chairs are available if you request them in advance. The main building has an elevator. Breakfast is included in the price only if you pay cash in advance. ⊠ Den Texstraat 16, 1017 ZA, Nieuwe Zijde ☎ 020/626–2396 🖷 020/638–2790 ⊕ www.asteriskhotel.nl ⥲ 40 rooms; 7 with shared bath ㋡ Dining room, IDD phones, in-room safes, cable TV, lobby lounge, Internet, business services; no a/c ▤ MC, V.

## Oude Zijde

The adjacent Red Light District may cast a less-than-rosy glow, but the Old Side, for the most part, remains one of the city's most historic neighborhoods.

**$$$$**    ✕🏨 **Grand Amsterdam Sofitel Demeure.** For captivating elegance, nothing
**Fodor'sChoice**    tops the facade of the Grand, with its Neoclassical courtyard, white sash
★    windows, carved marble pediments, and roof abristle with chimneys and gilded weather vanes. If it seems lifted from a Rembrandt painting, that's because this hotel's celebrated city-center site has a long and varied history: it was built in the 14th century as a convent, then went on to house the offices of the Amsterdam Admiralty. After being rezoned by Napoléon, it became Amsterdam's city hall from 1808 to 1988, and then finally reopened in 1992 as one of the city's most deluxe hotels, where guests like Mick Jagger and President Jacques Chirac of France have made their home-away-from-home. The guest rooms here feature traditional-luxe furniture, fine fabrics, and quiet hues, plus every manner of business mod con. The Café Roux, an oak-and-black-trim art deco -ish brasserie, sports a Karel Appel mural and some of the most stylish French dishes in town. The Admiralty, a more casual nook that opens out onto a glorious garden, is a great place to enjoy afternoon tea. ⊠ Oudezijds Voorburgwal 197, 1012 EX, Oude Zijde ☎ 020/555–3111 🖷 020/555–3222 ⊕ www.

*TheGrand.nl* 129 rooms, 37 suites, 16 apartments Restaurant, room service, IDD phones, some in-room fans, in-room data ports, in-room safes, some in-room kitchenettes, minibars, some in-room microwaves, some in-room refrigerators, cable TV with movies, some in-room VCRs, indoor pool, massage, sauna, steam room, bicycles, mountain bikes, lobby lounge, babysitting, dry cleaning, laundry service, concierge, Internet, business services, meeting rooms, car rental, travel services, parking (fee), no-smoking floors AE, DC, MC, V.

★ **$$$$** **Hotel de l'Europe.** Owned by Freddy Heineken's daughter, Charlene de Carvalho, this quiet, gracious, and plush hotel has a history extending back to 1638 (although its delightful, storybook facade dates only to the 19th century). Overlooking the Amstel River, the Muntplein, and the Flower Market, it may be familiar to those who remember the setting of Hitchcock's *Foreign Correspondent*. The chandeliered lobby leads off to the lounge, aglow with gold-trimmed ceiling coves and blackamoor lamps—the perfect setting for high tea (served in full glory here). Guest rooms are furnished with reserved, classical elegance: the city-side rooms are full of warm, rich colors; riverside rooms are in brilliant whites and have French windows. All have Victorian-style draperies as canopies over the beds. The restaurant's fine French food is ooh-la-la. ⊠ *Nieuwe Doelenstraat 2–8, 1012 CP, Oude Zijde* ☎ *020/531–1777* 🖷 *020/531–1778* ⊕ *www.leurope.nl* 77 rooms, 23 suites 2 restaurants, room service, IDD phones, in-room data ports, in-room safes, some in-room hot tubs, some in-room kitchenettes, minibars, some in-room refrigerators, cable TV with movies, WiFi, indoor pool, gym, massage, sauna, hot tub, bicycles, bar, lobby lounge, lounge, library, babysitting, dry cleaning, laundry service, concierge, Internet, business services, convention center, meeting rooms, some pets allowed, no-smoking floors AE, DC, MC, V.

**$$$–$$$$** **Renaissance Amsterdam.** It's not every day that a 17th-century church is part of a hotel, but an underground passage connects the Renaissance with the domed Koepelkerk, an erstwhile Lutheran church that now serves as this hotel's conference center. Smack dab in the middle of the Centrum (city center), between Dam Square and Centraal Station, this ultramodern hotel's top floors provide panoramic views of the city. Another high point is the hotel's highly popular fitness center, Splash, where you can have a complete workout or relax with a massage, steam bath, whirlpool, or sauna. The soaring lobby is basically modern, trimmed out with wood and equipped with wireless Internet access. ⊠ *Kattengat 1, 1012 SZ, Oude Zijde* ☎ *020/621–2223* 🖷 *020/627–5245* ⊕ *www.renaissancehotels.com* 375 rooms, 6 suites, 24 apartments Restaurant, café, dining room, room service, IDD phones, some in-room fans, in-room data ports, some in-room kitchenettes, minibars, some in-room microwaves, some in-room refrigerators, cable TV with movies and video games, some WiFi, gym, health club, sauna, dock, bar, lobby lounge, lounge, babysitting, dry cleaning, laundry service, concierge, Internet, business services, convention center, meeting rooms, parking (fee), some pets allowed, no-smoking floors AE, DC, MC, V.

**$** **Amstel Botel.** This floating hotel, moored near Centraal Station, is an appropriate lodging in watery Amsterdam. However, it is more *Love*

*Ferry* than *Love Boat*. The clean and modern rooms are cabinlike, but the portholes have been replaced by windows that provide fine views of the city across the water. If you want a room with a view, try to avoid rooms on the land side of the vessel, which look out on a building site. ⊠ *Oosterdokskade 2–4, 1011 AE, Oude Zijde* ☎ *020/626–4247* 🖷 *020/639–1952* ⊕ *www.amstelbotel.nl* 🛏 *175 rooms* ♿ *Dining room, IDD phones, in-room safes, cable TV with movies, billiards, bar, Internet, no-smoking rooms; no a/c* ☐ *AE, DC, MC, V.*

## The Plantage

The small tranquil neighborhood known as the Plantage is a great choice if you want a more relaxed stay. The Hortus Botanicus, Artis Zoo, and the Tropenmuseum dominate this *Oost* (East) Amsterdam area. The Tropenmuseum backs on to the Oosterpark neighborhood, which is bordered by the Linneausstraat, Populierenweg, Amstel River, and Mauritskade. It's a mainly residential area with the exception of the busy Wibautstraat.

**$$$$**
**FodorsChoice**
★

✕🖾 **InterContinental Amstel Amsterdam.** Elegant enough to please a queen, extroverted enough to welcome Madonna, the Rolling Stones, and Michael Jackson, this grand dowager has wowed all onlookers since it opened its doors in 1867. With its palatial five stories, sash windows, and historic roof dormers, this lily was gilded in 1992 with a renovation by Pierre Yves Rochon of Paris. You'll feel like a visiting dignitary when entering the magnificent lobby, with its grand double staircase that demands you glide, not walk, down it. The guest rooms are the most spacious in the city (though they shrink considerably on the top floor), and the décor features Oriental rugs, brocade upholstery, Delft lamps, and a color palette of warm tones inspired by Makkum pottery. Fresh tulips are placed in all of the rooms, and the bathrooms spoil guests with showerheads the size of dinner plates. The generous staff-to-guest ratio, the top-notch food—in particular, at the award-winning La Rive restaurant—the riverside terrace, the Amstel Lounge (perfect for drinks), and the endless stream of extra "little touches" (such as yacht service), will make for a truly baronial experience. ⊠ *Professor Tulpplein 1, 1018 GX, Plantage* ☎ *020/622–6060* 🖷 *020/622–5808* ⊕ *www. intercontinental.com* 🛏 *55 rooms, 24 suites* ♿ *2 restaurants, room service, IDD phones, in-room data ports, some in-room faxes, in-room safes, some in-room kitchenettes, minibars, some in-room microwaves, some in-room refrigerators, cable TV with movies and video games, in-room VCRs, indoor pool, exercise equipment, gym, health club, hair salon, hot tub, massage, sauna, steam room, Turkish bath, bicycles, bar, lobby lounge, lounge, shop, babysitting, dry cleaning, laundry service, concierge, Internet, business services, convention center, meeting rooms, parking (fee), no-smoking floor* ☐ *AE, DC, MC, V.*

★ **$$–$$$$**
🖾 **Arena.** This grand complex in a former 19th-century Roman Catholic orphanage consists of the hotel, a café-restaurant, a patio, a back garden, and a dance club (complete with frescoed walls that reflect its former function as a clandestine church). For those who like spare minimal style the hotel is strikingly austere—as if it were torn from the pages of *Wallpaper* magazine. The lobby is minimalist black with an impressive

cast-iron staircase leading to the rooms. The hotel used the hottest young Dutch architects and designers to supervise the recent renovation, which has helped erase the shadow of its past as a youth hostel. Rooms—some of which are split-level to form a lounge area—are furnished with modernist furniture by Gispen, Eames, and Martin Visser. There is wireless Internet access in the café. ⊠ *'s-Gravesandestraat 51, 1092 AA, Plantage* ☎ *020/850–2410* 🖷 *020/850–2405* ⊕ *www.hotelarena.nl* 📞 *121 rooms, 6 suites* ♻ *Restaurant, café, room TVs with movies, some WiFi, bar, lounge, dance club, nightclub, laundry facilities, concierge, Internet, business services, meeting rooms, parking (fee), no-smoking rooms; no a/c* ⊟ *DC, MC, V* ⊙ *CP.*

$  ▥ **Fantasia.** Peace and quiet await you at this small, friendly family hotel, occupying a circa 1733 canal house not far from the Plantage. Ornamental cows are found everywhere in the hotel (there's a history of farming in the owner's family). There's a room to suit everyone, from a small attic room (complete with bath) to a family room that sleeps four; there's also a pleasant hotel garden where you can relax and pet the resident dog. ⊠ *Nieuwe Keizersgracht 16, 1018 DR, Plantage* ☎ *020/623–8259* 🖷 *020/622–3913* ⊕ *www.fantasia-hotel.com* 📞 *19 rooms, 2 with shared bath* ♻ *Dining room, IDD phones, some in-room fans, beer garden, concierge, Internet, business services, meeting rooms, no-smoking rooms; no a/c, no room phones, no room TVs* ⊟ *AE, MC, V* ⊙ *CP.*

★ $  ▥ **Rembrandt.** Because it is close to the University of Amsterdam, the Artis zoo, Hortus Botanicus, and Tropenmuseum, the Hotel Rembrandt is often populated with academics and museum people—which explains the library of 1,800 books that you can browse. The rarified air is particularly thick in the remarkable breakfast room: the 18th-century paintings and exquisitely painted woodwork on the ceiling, and the wood paneling and beams carved in and dated 1558, were transported to their current location in the 19th century. Most of the rooms at the back of the hotel facing the garden are quiet, though there's now double glazing at the front of the property. Duplex Room 21, in the front, can accommodate a family of six, and six rooms can house three or four. All are immaculately clean. ⊠ *Plantage Middenlaan 17, 1018 DA, Plantage* ☎ *020/627–2714* 🖷 *020/638–0293* ⊕ *www.hotelrembrandt.nl* 📞 *16 rooms, 1 suite* ♻ *Dining room, IDD phones, in-room data ports, Cable TV with movies, lobby lounge, library, babysitting, concierge, Internet, business services, meeting rooms; no a/c* ⊟ *AE, MC, V* ⊙ *CP.*

## Rembrandtplein

Rembrandtplein may be a glaring tribute to neon and nightclubs, but its location is close to everything.

$$–$$$  ▥ **Albus Grand.** The Albus Grand's exterior has been graciously designed to conjure up the look of yesteryear. Inside, seven floors offer rooms of a comfortable size. Even the street-side rooms, which overlook the Munt tower and Flower Market, are remarkably quiet because of their double-paned windows. The hotel lobby and guest rooms are tastefully decorated with wicker chairs and contemporary paintings from the owners' collection. The buffet in the light and cheerful breakfast room

serves Dutch specialties as well as more run-of-the-~
straat 49, 1017 HE, Rembrandtplein ☎ 020/530–620(
⊕ www.albusgrandhotel.com ⌁ 74 rooms ⚿ Restau~
IDD phones, some in-room fans, some in-room data
with movies, lobby lounge, babysitting, laundry servic~
ness services, no-smoking floors; no a/c ⊟ AE, DC, M~

**$$$** ✕ 🖃 **NH Schiller.** Frits Schiller built this hotel in 1912 in t~ ~rt nouveau variant known as Jugendstil. He may have been an artist of modest ability, but a huge number of his paintings, whose colors inspired the inventive decor of the modernized rooms, are proudly displayed throughout the hotel. His friends, bohemian painters and sculptors, came to the Schiller Café, which became a famous meeting place and is still an informal and popular bar with Amsterdammers. From the lobby lounge you can check your e-mail to the hum of the espresso machine from the Brasserie Schiller. A winter film series is held on Sunday afternoons in the restaurant, with cocktails and dinner included. Rooms are conveniently stocked with coffeemakers, trouser presses, and hair dryers; six have two double beds and are big enough for families. ⊠ Rembrandtplein 26–36, 1017 CV, Rembrandtplein ☎ 020/554–0700 🖷 020/626–6831 ⊕ www.nh-hotels.com ⌁ 91 rooms, 1 suite ⚿ Restaurant, café, dining room, room service, IDD phones, some in-room fans, in-room data ports, in-room safes, some in-room minibars, cable TV with movies, WiFi, some in-room VCRs, bar, lobby lounge, babysitting, dry cleaning, laundry service, concierge, Internet, meeting rooms, no-smoking floors; no a/c ⊟ AE, DC, MC, V.

**$–$$$** 🖃 **Seven Bridges.** One of the famous canal sights in Amsterdam is the
**Fodor's**Choice lineup of seven consecutive bridges that can be seen gracing Reguliers-
★ gracht. This atmosphere-y little retreat, which looks over these bridges, also takes its name from them. Occupying an 18th-century house in the heart of "Golden Bend" country (yet just a few blocks from Rembrandtplein), this hotel offers uniquely stylish guest rooms, all meticulously decorated with dark woods, Oriental rugs, handcrafted and inlaid bed frames, and art deco tables. The proud owner scouts the antiques stores and auction houses for furnishings, and all have thorough documentation. The top-floor, beam-ceilinged rooms are the smallest and are priced accordingly; the first-floor room No. 5 is practically palatial, with its own private terrace. Although there's no common area or salon, you can have breakfast delivered to your room. Nail down your reservation well in advance. ⊠ Reguliersgracht 31, 1017 LK, Rembrandtplein ☎ 020/623–1329 🖷 020/624–7652 ⊕ www.sevenbridgeshotel.nl ⌁ 8 rooms ⚿ IDD phones, some in-room fans, cable TV, WiFi, Internet, no-smoking rooms; no a/c ⊟ AE, MC, V ⧀ CP.

# NIGHTLIFE & THE ARTS

By Steve
Korver

**NIGHTLIFE AND THE ARTS HAVE ALWAYS WALKED HAND IN HAND** in Amsterdam. If you want proof, just have a look at the Golden Age paintings by Jan Steen and his colleagues that grace the walls of the Rijksmuseum, many of which depict feisty bar scenes. Locals have apparently always known that there's nothing like a beer after a long day of more noble and artistic pursuits.

Fasten your seat belts: Amsterdam's nightlife can have you careening between smoky coffee shops, chic wine bars, mellow jazz joints, laid-back lounges, and clubs either intimate or raucous. The bona fide local flavor can perhaps best be tasted in one of the city's ubiquitous brown café-bars—called "brown" because of their woody walls and nicotine-stained ceilings. Here, both young and old, the mohawked and the merely balding, come to relax, rave, and revel in every variety of coffee and alcohol.

The nightlife scene is centered on two of Amsterdam's main squares. Leidseplein, rich with cafés and discos that attract younger visitors to the city, also has the city's two major live venues, Melkweg and, around the corner, Paradiso. The Melkweg even got a new neighbor in 2005: Sugar Factory is developing its own specialized brand of nightlife where art, dance, theater, and good ol' fashioned DJ-driven clubbing all come together in the same night. The area around Rembrandtplein, whose cafés cater to a more local crowd, has the trendier nightspots and many of Amsterdam's gay venues (the latter being particularly concentrated along Reguliersdwarsstraat). Warmoesstraat and other streets in the Red Light District provide the spicy setting for leather-oriented gay bars and the more throbbing rock clubs. The lounge phenomenon, although a bit late in arriving, is now in full bloom, offering a kinder, gentler club vibe.

## Bars

Although brown cafés are probably the most authentically "local" places to stop in for a coffee or something stronger, there are also plenty of other watering holes in Amsterdam that embrace a more international vibe. In these places, the old-style woody décor has been replaced with sleek minimalist furniture, and music from all over the world can be heard on the stereo, or being spun by DJs.

The youthful, late-houred, and grottolike **Absinthe** (⊠ Nieuwezijds Voorburgwal 171, Nieuwe Zijde and Spui ☎ 020/–623–4413, www. absinthe.nl) offers the option of true hallucinations if you happen to overindulge in their liquid namesake, rumored to be the trigger for Van Gogh's act of self-mutilation. And no worries: this is a legal recipe. The trendy, sleekly minimal, and cheekily no-signed **Bar With No Name** (⊠ Wolvenstraat 23, Grachtengordel West ☎ 020/320–0843) ironically attracts a lot of commercial arts and advertising types. It also happens to be open all day for great breakfasts, lunches, and dinners. The theatrical crowd can be witnessed eating, drinking, and being generally merry at **Café Cox** (⊠ Marnixstraat 429, Museum District ☎ 020/523–7851), part of the Stadsschouwburg building.

As to be expected from a theatrical neighborhood, the Nes offers some prime drinking holes. Fans of Belgian beer should certainly stop at the patio or the clean interior of **De Brakke Grond** (⊠ Nes 43, Oude Zijde ☎ 020/626–0044), part of the Flemish Cultural Center, to partake in one or two of the dozens of options. **De Buurvrouw** (⊠ St. Pieterspoortsteeg 29, Oude Zijde ☎ 020/625–9654) is a small sawdust- and kitsch-strewn haven where students and alternative types don't mind yelling over the latest in loud guitars and funky beats. The always welcoming and cozy **De Still** (⊠ Spuistraat 326, Nieuwe Zijde and Spui ☎ 020/427–6809) is for the whiskey obsessive with ambitions to try as many as possible of the 600 varieties on offer here.

## Brown Cafés

Coffee and conversation are the two main ingredients of *gezelligheid* (a socially cozy time) for an Amsterdammer, and upon occasion a beer or two (with perhaps a *jenever* [Dutch gin] added to the mix) as the evening wears on. The best place for these pleasures is a traditional brown café, or *bruine kroeg*. Wood paneling, wooden floors, comfortably worn furniture, and walls and ceilings stained with eons' worth of tobacco smoke give the cafés their name—though today a little artfully stippled paint achieves the same effect. The Jordaan district is a particularly happy hunting ground for this phenomenon.

Intensely evocative if out of the way, **Bierbrouwerij 't IJ** (⊠ Funenkade 7, East of Amstel ☎ 020/622–8325) is a microbrewery perched under a windmill and is open Wednesday–Sunday 3–8. **Café Chris** (⊠ Bloemstraat 42, Jordaan ☎ 020/624–5942) has been pouring beverages since 1624 when it was used as the local bar for the builders of the Western Church. Its coziness is enhanced by having the smallest washrooms in town. Beware: the slant of **Café Sluyswacht** (⊠ Jodenbreestraat 1, Jewish Quarter and Plantage ☎ 020/625–7611) can end up causing nausea after one too many beers on its patio overlooking Oudeschans. Once the tasting house of an old family distillery, **De Admiraal** (⊠ Herengracht 319, Grachtengordel East ☎ 020/625–4334) still serves potent liqueurs—many with obscene names. **De Doktertje** (⊠ Rozenboomsteeg 4, Nieuwe Zijde and Spui ☎ 020/626–4427), or "the Doctor," has been prescribing beers and liquors for what ails you for centuries from the tiniest brown bar in the country. A true classic.

Decidedly ancient and brown, **De Engelse Reet** (⊠ Begijnensteeg 4, Nieuwe Zijde and Spui ☎ 020/623–1777) is like stepping back into some lost age when beer was the safest alternative to drinking water. Like many cafés in the Jordaan, **De Prins** (⊠ Prinsengracht 124, Jordaan ☎ 020/624–9382) is blessed with a canal-side patio. **De Reiger** (⊠ Nieuwe Leliestraat 34, Jordaan ☎ 020/624–7426) has a distinctive Jugendstil bar and serves highly touted food. If you want to hear the locals sing folk music on Sunday afternoon, stop by **De Twee Zwaantjes** (⊠ Prinsengracht 114, Jordaan ☎ 020/625–2729). A busy, jolly brown café, **In de Wildeman** (⊠ Kolksteeg 3, Nieuwe Zijde and Spui ☎ 020/638–2348) attracts a wide range of types and ages.

**Fodor'sChoice**
★

Set with Golden Age chandeliers, leaded-glass windows, and the patina of centuries, the gloriously charming **'t Smalle** (⊠ Egelantiersgracht 12, Jordaan ☎ 020/623–9617) is one of Amsterdam's most delightful spots. The after-work crowd always jams the waterside terrace here, but opt instead for the historic interior, once home to one of the city's first jenever distilleries. It is not surprising to learn that a literal copy of this place was created for Nagasaki's Holland Village in Japan. One of Amsterdam's most famous *proeflokaal* ("tasting houses"), **Wynand Fockink**

★

(✉ Pijlsteeg 31, Oude Zijde ☎ 020/639–2695) offers top tasting options for Dutch jenever between 3 and 9 PM daily in a more cramped yet equally evocative locale.

## Cabarets
**Boom Chicago** (✉ Leidseplein 12, Leidseplein ☎ 020/423–0101 ⊕ www.boomchicago.nl), at the Leidseplein Theater, belongs to a bunch of zany ex-pat Americans who opened their own restaurant-theater to present improvised comedy inspired by life in both Amsterdam and the world. Dinner and seating begin at 7, with show time at 8:15. On weekends there are also late shows. **Kleine Komedie** (✉ Amstel 56–58, East of Amstel ☎ 020/624–0534) has for many years been the most vibrant venue for cabaret and comedy (mainly in Dutch).

## Casino
The **Holland Casino Amsterdam** (✉ Max Euweplein 62, Leidseplein ☎ 020/521–1111) is part of the Lido complex near Leidseplein. One of the largest casinos in Europe (it's more than 90,000 square feet), it offers everything from your choice of French or American roulette to computerized bingo, as well as the obligatory slot machines to eat up your supply of loose euros. On your way out of town via Schiphol airport, Holland Casino has lounges tucked away in many of the wings of the airport leading to your gate.

## Cocktail Bars & Grand Cafés
Exceedingly popular, the riverside **Café de Jaren** (✉ Nieuwe Doelenstraat 20, Oude Zijde ☎ 020/625–5771) is a large, airy multilevel bar/café/restaurant with a lovely terrace overlooking the Amstel. Part of the Nederlands Filmmuseum, **Café Vertigo** (✉ Vondelpark 3, Museum District ☎ 020/612–3021) has a stunningly scenic terrace for watching the chaos that is Vondelpark.

**De Kroon** (✉ Rembrandtplein 17, Rembrandtplein ☎ 020/625–2011) is a grand café with intimate seating arrangements and a U-shaped bar surrounding old-style wooden museum cases filled with zoological specimens. The bar attracts a fashionable yuppie clientele in the evenings. **Luxembourg** (✉ Spui 22–24, Nieuwe Zijde and Spui ☎ 020/620–6264) has an art deco–style interior and a glassed-in terrace for people-watching on Spui square. One of Rembrandtplein's few redeeming features, **Schiller** (✉ Rembrandtplein 26, Rembrandtplein ☎ 020/624–9846), part of the hotel of the same name, has a faded glory and a real sense of history thanks to a wooden fin-de-siècle interior that other grand cafés would sell their souls for. This remains a favorite with the media crowd.

## Coffee Shops
Generally, the "coffee shops" where marijuana and hashish are smoked tend to be dim, grotty, and noxious places—but there are a few cleaner and more sophisticated establishments. If you're going to partake, be sure to use caution; the available product is of very high quality, if you're not used to it you may overreact, chemically speaking.

Hidden in a small alley, **Abraxas** (✉ Jonge Roelensteeg 12–14, Nieuwe Zijde and Spui ☎ 020/625–5763) supplements its smokeables with a menu of ganja cakes and shakes in an atmosphere that suggests a hip and multilevel home of a family of hobbits. **Barney's** (⊠ Haarlemmerstraat 102, Jordaan ☎ 020/625–9761) brings together two stand-alone concepts: a wide variety of smokeables and all-day breakfasts of the world. Artful mosaics provide background at the **Greenhouse** (⊠ Oudezijds Voorburgwal 191, Oude Zijde ☎ 020/627–1739), renowned for the "quality" of both its weeds and its seeds. Other locations: Waterlooplein 345 (No phone). **Kadinsky** (⊠ Rosmarijnsteeg 9, Nieuwe Zijde ☎ 020/624–7023) offers mellow jazz and scrumptious chocolate-chip cookies. The clientele at the **Other Side** (⊠ Reguliersdwarsstraat 6, Rembrandtplein ☎ 020/421–1014) is primarily gay.

## Dance & Rock Clubs

Since the heady '50s, Amsterdam has been the place where perhaps 90% of the world's musicians dream of playing some day. And happily for them, the city's venues are geared towards making such dreams come true (so much so that the town locals are often relegated to playing clubs on the national circuit). In particular, two legendary locations—the Melkweg and the Paradiso—have savvily kept their fingers on the pulse of every major musical trend since the late '60s. After the hippies, punk rock took over.

**Arena** (⊠ 's-Gravensandestraat 51, East of Amstel ☎ 020/850–2420 ⊕ www.hotelarena.nl), part of the Arena hotel complex, is popular for its hip roster of DJs and club nights, which take place in a reinvented, formerly clandestine church. The relatively new **Bitterzoet** (⊠ Spuistraat 2 ☎ 020/521–3001 ⊕ www.bitterzoet.com) has a packed program of DJs, bands, and even theater. Think "casual," "urban," and "jazzy."

**Jimmy Woo's** (⊠ Korte Leidsedwarsstraat 18, Leidseplein ☎ 020/626–3150 ⊕ www.jimmywoo.nl) is probably the hottest club in town for the rich, famous and wannabes thanks to its funky urban grooves and stellar sound system. **Korsakoff** (⊠ Lijnbaansgrach 161, Jordaan ☎ 020/625–7854 ⊕ www.korsakoff.nl) is a dark but friendly magnet for the pierced and tattooed among us who like their music industrially rough and ready.

★ The legendary **Melkweg** (⊠ Lijnbaansgracht 234, Leidseplein ☎ 020/531–8181 ⊕ www.melkweg.nl) has a broad programming policy that takes in everything from punk to house to world music. This Milky Way, named after the building's previous function as a milk factory, began as a hippie squat in the '60s before evolving with the times to provide a venue for the major trends that followed. Today it's a slickly operated multimedia center equipped with two concert halls, a theater, cinema, gallery, and café-restaurant. On any day of the week you may walk into an evening of rock, reggae, drum'n'bass, hip-hop, soul, hardcore, or any other imaginable genre.

★ The country's most famous concert venue, and former church, **Paradiso** (⊠ Weteringschans 6–8, Leidseplein ☎ 020/626–4521 ⊕ www.paradiso.nl), known as the "pop temple" for its vaulted ceilings and stained glass, began its days as a hippie squat allowed by the local government who hoped it might help empty the Vondelpark (then serving as a crash pad for a generation). To this day, the Paradiso remains an epic venue for both music's legends and up-and-comers, regardless of their genre. Most concerts are followed by a club night to the early hours that showcases the latest dance sounds.

If a small-scale club is what you're after, **Winston** (⊠ Warmoesstraat 129, Oude Zijde ☎ 020/623–1380 ⊕ www.winston.nl) is ambitious when it comes to programming—from spoken word to punk to DJs to the easiest of easy tunes. A favorite with tourists, **The Last Waterhole** (⊠ Korte Leidsedwarsstraat 49, Museum District ☎ 020/620–8904 ⊕ www. lastwaterhole.nl) usually features a blues and rock cover band of dubious distinction—but it remains a fun place to trade tales of the road.

Potential pleasure-palace extraordinaire, the **Westergasfabriek** (⊠ Haarlemmerweg 8-10, Amsterdam West ☎ 020/586–0710 ⊕ www. westergasfabriek.nl) is an arts and cultural center. Covering the historic 19th-century Western Gas Factory grounds, its site consists of 13 monumental buildings of various sizes and shapes, which play host to film and theater companies, fashion shows, corporate functions, movie shoots, art shows, operas, techno parties, and assorted festivals, plus bars, nightclubs, and restaurants. Visitors interested in all matters of culture should certainly check out how things are shaping up there.

## Gay & Lesbian Bars

Tankards and brass pots hanging from the ceiling in the woody **Amstel Taveerne** (⊠ Amstel 54, Rembrandtplein ☎ 020/623–4254) reflect the friendly crowd of Amsterdammers around the bar whose members burst into song whenever the sound system plays an old favorite. **April** (⊠ Reguliersdwarsstraat 37, Rembrandtplein ☎ 020/625–9572 ⊕ www.april-exit.com), which gets going only after 11, has a lounge in the front and a fabulous rotating bar in the back, which management opens when the place becomes particularly crowded on the weekends. April's late-night multilevel bar and disco. For a heavy cruise scene, the men-only and leather-rich **Cockring** (⊠ Warmoesstraat 96, Oude Zijde ☎ 020/623–9604 ⊕ www. clubcockring.com) does business well into the morning hours.

Amsterdam has few places where lesbians can meet and party. Women should check at the bars, the women/lesbian bookstore Xantippe Unlimited (Prinsengracht 290, Grachtengordel West, 020/623–5854), or the COC (Rozenstraat 8, Jordaan, 020/623–4596, www.coc.nl), a national organization that deals with all matters gay and lesbian, for women's parties and events. Amsterdam's best lesbian bar, **Saarein II** (⊠ Elandsstraat 119, Jordaan ☎ 020/623–4901), has a cozy brown-café atmosphere in the Jordaan and a relatively new "mixed" policy. Hence the "II." The lesbian perennial **Vive-la-Vie** (⊠ Amstelstraat 7, Rembrandtplein ☎ 020/624–0114 ⊕ www.vivelavie.nl) has a lively bar scene and is both men- and straight-friendly.

## Jazz Clubs

Amsterdam has provided a happy home-away-from-home for jazz musicians since the early '50s, when such legends as Chet Baker and Gerry Mulligan would wind down after their official show at the Concertgebouw by jamming at one or another of the many bohemian bars around the Zeedijk. For the last quarter century, the world-statured but intimate Bimhuis has taken over duties as the city's major jazz venue with an excellent programming policy that welcomes both the legendary jazz performer and the latest avant-garde up-and-comer.

In the smoky, jam-packed atmosphere of **Alto** (⊠ Korte Leidsedwarsstraat 115, Leidseplein ☎ 020/626–3249 ⊕ www.jazz-cafe-alto.nl), you can hear the top picks of local bands. **Bamboo Bar** (⊠ Lange Leidsedwarsstraat 64, Leidseplein ☎ 020/624–3993) has a long bar and cool Latin sounds. At **Bimhuis** (⊠ Piet Heinkade 3, Waterfront ☎ 020/623–1361 ⊕ www.bimhuis.nl), the best-known jazz place in town left its classic digs in 2005 in favor of the brand spanking new—and utterly wonderful—Muziekgebouw in the eastern docklands. Everyone, from old legend to the latest avant-gardist agrees: it's close to perfect.

Fodor'sChoice
★

Fans of more traditional jazz should check out the legendary **Cotton Club** (⊠ Nieuwmarkt 5, Oude Zijde ☎ 020/626–6192), named after its original owner, the Surinamer trumpet player Teddy Cotton. While the music is not usually live, its gregarious crowd is certainly lively.

### Lounges

Since it opened, **Bep** (⊠ Nieuwezijds Voorburgwal 260, Nieuwe Zijde and Spui ☎ 020/626–5649) has attracted a smart artist crowd for mellow afternoons and lively evenings. A group of artists runs **The Getaway** (⊠ Nieuwezijds Voorburgwal 250, Nieuwe Zijde and Spui ☎ 020/627–1427); it was one of the first lounges to become popular, and often spotlights funky DJs. **Lime** (⊠ Zeedijk 104, Oude Zijde ☎ 020/639–3020) is a slick and minimal lounge with a nicely unpretentious atmosphere. **Lux** (⊠ Marnixstraat 397, Nieuwe Zijde and Spui ☎ 020/422–1412) has a fantastic 1960s décor and an attractive young crowd.

Fodor'sChoice
★

## The Arts

*What's On in Amsterdam* is a comprehensive, albeit a tad dull, English-language publication distributed by the tourist office that lists art and performing-arts events around the city. You'd also do well to browse through the many fliers, pamphlets, booklets, and magazines—including the Dutch-language but still somewhat decipherable and certainly complete *Uitkrant*. Spring 2004 saw the debut of an English-language cultural listings and reviews weekly called—appropriately enough—*Amsterdam Weekly* that has already established itself an invaluable resource for visitors and natives alike. All of these are available at the **AUB Ticketshop** (⊠ Leidseplein, at Marnixstraat, Leidseplein ☎ 0900/0191 9–6 daily ⊕ www.aub.nl), open Monday–Saturday 10–7:30, Sunday noon–7:30. Tickets can also be purchased in person at the tourist information offices through the **VVV Ticketmaster** (⊠ Stationsplein 10, Centraal Station), open daily 10–5, or at theater box offices. Reserve tickets to performances at the major theaters before your arrival through the AUB Web site or by calling +31 (0)20/621–1288 from abroad.

### Music

There are two auditoriums, large and small, under one roof at the Netherlands' premier concert hall, the **Concertgebouw** (⊠ Concertgebouwplein 2–6, Museum District ☎ 020/671–8345 ⊕ www.

Fodor'sChoice
★

concertgebouw.nl). With its Viennese Classicist facade surmounted by a golden lyre, this hall draws 800,000 visitors to 650 concerts per year, many of whom flock here to enjoy Bach and Beethoven performed under nearly perfect acoustic conditions. In the larger of the two theaters, the **Grote Zaal,** Amsterdam's critically acclaimed **Koninklijk Concertgebouworkest** (Royal Concert Orchestra), whose recordings are in the collections of most self-respecting lovers of classical music, is often joined by international soloists. Visiting maestros also push the prices up but the range remains wide: expect to pay anything between €5 and €100. But throughout July and August, tickets for the Robeco Summer Concerts, which involve high-profile artists and orchestras, are an excellent bargain. The smaller hall, the **Kleine Zaal,** is a venue for chamber music and up-and-coming musicians and is the usual setting for the free lunchtime concerts on Wednesdays at 12:30. The architectural landmark and progenitor of the Amsterdam School, the **Beurs van Berlage** (✉ Damrak 213, Oude Zijde ☎ 020/521–7575 ⊕ www.beursvanberlage. nl) also has two concert halls—including the definitely unique glass-box "diamond-in-space" Amvest Zaal—with the Netherlands Philharmonic and the Netherlands Chamber Orchestra as the in-house talent. The brand new and already essential **Muziekgebouw** (✉ Piet Heinkade 1, Waterfront ☎ 020/788–2010 ⊕ www.muziekgebouw.nl) also plays home to legendary jazz club Bimhuis (*see* above) and a café with excellent views over the harbor in this up-and-coming neighborhood.

Skaters, joggers, cyclists, and sun worshippers gather in Vondelpark each summer to enjoy the great outdoors. However, between late May and September, they're joined by culture vultures, who head to the **Vondelpark Openluchttheater** (✉ Vondelpark, Museum District ☎ 020/673–1499 ⊕ www.openluchttheater.nl) for its program of music, theater, and children's events (theatrical events have, in fact, been held in the park since 1865). During the festival, Wednesdays offer a lunchtime concert and a midafternoon children's show; Thursday nights find a concert on the bandstand; there's a theater show every Friday night; various events (including another theater show) take place on Saturday; and theater events and pop concerts are held on Sunday afternoons.

### Opera & Ballet

★ The grand and elegant **Muziektheater** (✉ Amstel 3/Waterlooplein 22, Oude Zijde ☎ 020/625–5455 ⊕ www.muziektheater.nl) seats 1,600 people and hosts international opera, ballet, and orchestra performances throughout the year. It's also home to **De Nederlandse Opera** (Netherlands National Opera), **Het Nationale Ballet** (Netherlands National Ballet), and the newly established Holland Symphonia, all of whose repertoires embrace both the classical and the 20th century. Muziektheater's huge and flexible stage acts as a magnet to directors with a penchant for grand-scale décors, such as Robert Wilson, Willy Decker, and Peter Sellars. The red-and-gold plushness of **Stadsschouwburg** (✉ Leidseplein 26, Leidseplein ☎ 020/624–2311 ⊕ www.ssba.nl), home to the underrated **Nationale Reisopera** (National Travelling Opera), regularly hosts visiting companies.

## Dance

The grand and spacious **Muziektheater** (⊠ Waterlooplein 22/Amstel 3, Oude Zijde ☎ 020/625–5455 ⊕ www.muziektheater.nl) is not only home to the **De Nederlandse Opera** (Netherlands National Opera) and **Het Nationale Ballet** (Netherlands National Ballet), but also often hosts the **Nederlands Dans Theater** (National Dance Theater) which has evolved into one of the most celebrated of modern dance companies in the world under choreographers Jiri Kylian and Hans van Manen.

## Theater

The red-velvet **Stadsschouwburg** (⊠ Leidseplein 26, Leidseplein ☎ 020/624–2311) focuses primarily on Dutch theater but has occasional English and multicultural performances where understanding the language becomes less of an issue. For lavish, large-scale productions, the place to go is **Koninklijk Theater Carre** (⊠ Amstel 115–125, East of Amstel ☎ 0900/252–5255), originally built in the 19th century as permanent home to a circus.

Alternative "forms" of theater are *very* Amsterdam. The nightclub and "night theater" **Sugar Factory** (⊠ Lijnbaansgracht 238, Leidseplein ☎ 020/626–5006 ⊕ www.sugarfactory.nl) opened its doors in 2005 with the agenda to infuse late-night nightlife with theater, dance, art and poetry—often all on the same night. The former industrial shipyards **NDSM** (⊠ TT Neveritaweg 15, Amsterdam-North/Waterfront ☎ 020/330–5480 ⊕ www.ndsm.nl) have been reinvented as a "breeding ground for the arts" where regular theater performances and festivals can be found. And with a new ferry departing from behind Central Station, getting there has never been easier. Similarly, the former gas-factory complex **Westergasfabriek** (⊠ Haarlemmerweg 8-10, Amsterdam West ☎ 020/586–0710 ⊕ www.westergasfabriek.nl) (*see* Dance and Rock Clubs) will undoubtedly continue employing its singular performance spaces for a variety of shows and festivals that often embrace the more visual, and more avant-garde, of the entertainment spectrum.

# SHOPPING

Updated by
Nicole Chabot

**AS OLD AS AMSTERDAM IS,** some things never seem to change. The bustle and noise of crowds of shoppers in the area surrounding Dam Square is reminiscent of the cattle drives that only a few centuries ago thundered to market through the Kalverstraat (Calf's Street), now one of the major shopping streets. The city's mercantile roots go as far back as Rembrandt's day, when the maritime Dutch West India and East India companies were busy colonizing a trading empire so far-flung the sun never set on it entirely. The resulting plunder—spices from Java, porcelains from China, furs from Russia, rugs from Turkey—produced the first wave of shop-'til-you-drop Amsterdammers.

BARGAINS TO
BLOW-OUTS

Shopping hours in the Netherlands are regulated by law, with one night a week reserved for late shopping. In Amsterdam, department stores and many other shops are closed Monday mornings, and stay open Thursday evenings, which are famously known as *koopavonden* ("buying evenings"). Increasingly, following an easing of legislation governing shopping hours, you'll find main branches of major stores in the center of the city open on Sunday afternoon, but note that most stores are shuttered on Sunday. Purchases of €136 or more qualify for a tax refund; refer to our section on the V.A.T. (Value-Added Tax).

## Shopping Districts & Streets

If you are literally out to shop 'til you drop, Amsterdam will oblige. A "grand tour" route for all the main shopping areas threads itself through the city, running from Dam Square all the way down to De Pijp. But unless you've got bionic feet, it's better to break the following pilgrimage—running from north to south, with several detours east and west—into several sections. If not, you're bound to your hotel room weary and wiped out (although you may also be three pounds lighter).

The heart of the city center, or Centrum, **Dam Square** is home to two of Amsterdam's main department stores, the C & A and De Bijenkorf. Beyond the west side of the square sits one of Amsterdam's shopping spectaculars, the **Magna Plaza** (⊠ Nieuwezijds Voorburgwal 182, Nieuwe Zijde ⊕ www.magnaplaza.nl). Built inside the city's 19th-century post office—designed by Cornelis Hendrik Peters in "post-office Gothic" (sort of like London's House of Parliament)—this gigantic structure looks like a fairy-tale frontispiece.

FodorśChoice
★
If department stores aren't your speed, head west from the Dam to the heart of the Grachtengordel canal section and explore the **Negen Straatjes** ("The Nine Streets"), nine charming, tiny streets that radiate from behind the Royal Palace. Here, in a sector bordered by Raadhuisstraat and Leidsestraat, specialty and fashion shops are delightfully one-of-a-kind. Heading even farther to the west you enter the chic and funky sector of the **Jordaan,** where generation after generation of experimental designers have set up shop to show their imaginative creations.

Returning to the Centrum, two popular streets offer something for nearly all tastes and wallets. Stretching to the north from Dam Square and toward Centraal Station is **Nieuwendijk,** a busy pedestrian mall loved by bargain hunters. To the south of the Dam runs **Kalverstraat,** the city's main pedestrians-only shopping street, where much of Amsterdam does its day-to-day shopping. Running south to the Muntplein, this street is somewhat down-market but, remember, street-cred is important in this city. Here, too, you'll find the imposing **Kalvertoren shopping mall** (⊠ Kalverstraat, near Munt, Nieuwe Zijde), which is a covered shopping mall with a rooftop restaurant with magnificent views of the city. Running parallel to Kalverstraat is the **Rokin,** a main tram route lined with shops offering high-priced trendy fashion, jewelry, accessories, antiques, and even an old master painting or two. Near the bottom of Kalverstraat's big "C," **Leidsestraat** cuts south to the elegant Museum Quarter.

For possible antiques of the 22nd century, continue east of the Spiegelkwartier several blocks to find **Utrechtsestraat,** which offers a variety of opportunities for the up-to-date home shopper, with stores specializing in kitchen, interior, and design objects. Now head south across the Singel canal to the Museum Quarter, where, a few blocks east of the Rijksmuseum, you'll find the city's posh and prestigious **P. C. Hooftstraat,** generally known as the P. C. Home to chic designer boutiques, this is where diplomats and politicians buy their glad rags. Several blocks to the east, just beyond the Concertgebouw is **Van Baerlestraat,** lined with bookstores specializing in art, music, and language and clothing shops that are smart—but not quite smart enough to have made it to the adjoining P. C. Hooftstraat.

Remember, if you want to add the very latest stores to the lists below, check out the suggestions in the Holland's high-style monthly glossies, such as *Dutch, Residence, Elegance, Avenue, BLVD,* and the Dutch-language *Elle.*

## Markets

Whether hunting for treasures or trash (a busted Louis XVI ear trumpet was reportedly once spotted), you could get lucky at one of Amsterdam's flea markets. Even if you're not looking for anything in particular, you can unearth terrific finds, often at rock-bottom prices. Few markets compare with Amsterdam's **Waterlooplein** flea market, which surrounds the perimeter of the Stopera (Muziektheater/Town Hall complex) building. It's a descendant of the haphazard pushcart trade that gave this part of the city its distinct and lively character in the early part of the century. The flea market is open Monday–Saturday 9:30–5. The **Bloemenmarkt,** (along the Singel canal, between Koningsplein and Muntplein) is another of Amsterdam's must-see markets, where flowers and plants are sold from permanently moored barges. The market is open Monday–Sunday 8:30–6.

On Saturday 9–4, the **Noordermarkt** (which winds around Noorderkerk and along Lindengracht) hosts a fabric market; on Monday mornings, a flea market evocative of the old world takes over. **Nieuwmarkt** (at northern end of Kloverniersburgwal) hosts an organic farmers' market, with specialist stalls selling essential oils and other New Age fare alongside the oats, legumes, and vegetables. **Sunday art markets** are held in good weather from April to October in the Rembrandtplein area on Thorbeckeplein (10:30–6), and from April–November at in the Dam area at Spui square (10–6), which also hosts a *boeken market* on Friday (10–6) that's a used and antiquarian book–browsing paradise.

## Specialty Stores

### Antiques & Golden Age Art

A William and Mary–era harpsichord? One of the printed maps that figured prominently in Vermeer's *Lutenist?* An 18th-century bed-curtain tie-up? Or a pewter nautilus cup redolent of a Golden Age still-life? All these and more may be available in Amsterdam's famous array of antiques stores, the **Spiegelkwartier,** or Spiegel Quarter, centered around Nieuwe Spiegelstraat and its continuation, Spiegelgracht. But this section—with shops on both sides of the street and canal for five blocks, from the Golden Bend of the Herengracht nearly to the Rijksmuseum—often requires a House of Orange budget. For more gently priced antiques and curios, you might rather opt to tiptoe past the 18th-century tulipwood armoires and explore the **Jordaan,** an increasingly popular area for adventurous collectors. In stark contrast to the elegant stores in the Spiegel Quarter with their beautiful displays, the tiny, unprepossessing shops dotted along the Elandsgracht and connecting streets, such as the 1e Looiersdwarststraat, offer equally wonderful treasures, but you need to hunt for them. Those who take the time to carefully examine the backroom shelves, nooks, and crannies of a small shop may be rewarded with a big find.

## Art: Modern to Contemporary

Many of the galleries that deal in modern and contemporary art are centered on the **Keizersgracht** and **Spiegelkwartier,** and others are found around the Western Canal Ring and De Jordaan. Artists have traditionally gravitated to low-rent areas. The **De Baarsjes** neighborhood in the western part of the city is increasingly attracting small galleries that showcase exciting works of art. With a shabbiness reminiscent of the early days of New York's Soho, it's worth a detour for adventurous art-lovers. *Day by Day in Amsterdam,* published by the tourist office, is a reasonable source of information on current exhibitions; another is the Dutch-language publication *Alert,* which has the most comprehensive listings available. Opening times at galleries vary greatly. Many are closed between exhibitions, so it's a good idea to check out the magazine listings or call first for information.

## Books

True to its name, the **American Book Center** (⊠ Kalverstraat 185, Nieuwe Zijde ☎ 020/625–5537) is strongly oriented toward American tastes and expectations. As reputedly the largest English-language book emporium on the Continent, the selection is vast, but the prices are usually higher

★ than you'd pay on the other side of the ocean. **Antiquariaat Kok** (⊠ Oude Hoogstraat 14–18, Oude Zijde ☎ 020/623–1191) is an antiquarian heaven, with oodles of treasures on Amsterdam history. Another floor in the store holds one of Amsterdam's largest selections of second-hand books (the best titles are always out of print, right?). **Athenaeum Nieuwscentrum** (⊠ Spui 14–16, Nieuwe Zijde ☎ 624–2972) has the city's best selection of international magazines and newspapers; its sister bookstore next door offers the latest and greatest in international literature.

**Oudemanhuis Book Market** (⊠ Oudemanhuispoort, Oude Zijde) is a tiny, venerable covered book market in the heart of the University of Amsterdam that's been selling used and antiquarian books, prints, and sheet music for more than a century. **Scheltema** (⊠ Koningsplein 20, Eastern Canal Ring ☎ 020/523–1411) has six floors of books on every imaginable subject with plenty of room for marked-down remainders. It's one of Amsterdam's busiest and best-stocked international bookstores. There's a small café on the first floor. **Waterstone's** (⊠ Kalverstraat 152, Nieuwe Zijde ☎ 020/638–3821) has four floors of English-language books, from children's stories to computer manuals. There's a huge selection of U.K. magazines. For information on the Spui's Friday book market, *see* Markets.

## Ceramics & Crystal

You'll find a unique, comprehensive selection of glassware at **Breekbaar** (⊠ Weteringschans 209, Spiegelkwartier ☎ 020/626–1260). For superb porcelain, glass, and tiles from before 1800, visit **Frides Lamëris** (⊠ Nieuwe Spiegelstraat 55, Spiegelkwartier ☎ 020/626–4066). **De Glaswerkplaats** (⊠ Berenstraat 41, Western Canal Ring ☎ 020/420–2120) is a studio located in the Negen Straatjes area where you can order custom-made designs in fused glass, or stained glass.

## Children

★ You may be hypnotized by the magenta-dyed mustache that the eponymous shop owner sports at **Couzijn Simon** (⊠ Prinsengracht 578, Eastern Canal Ring ☎ 020/624–7691), but it's his toy treasures that will make your child as pop-eyed as some of the vintage dolls here. The shop is crammed with wonders: an 18th-century rocking horse as finely carved as an 18th-century sculpture; a four-foot-long wooden ice skate (a former store sign); a one-inch doll with tiny hinged limbs; vintage trains and collector teddy bears; and porcelain dolls dressed for a costume ball. Some of the toys here even date back to the mid-18th century, which was when this shop first opened as a pharmacy. In the back is a small garden and a cottage, now the atelier of Dutch painter Anton Hoeboeur, whose works are for sale. The delightful **De Beestenwinkel** (⊠ Staalstraat 11, Oude Zijde ☎ 020/623–1805) has nothing but animal toys in every price range. Specializing in mobiles from around the world, **Gone with the Wind** (⊠ Vijzelstraat 22, Nieuwe Zijde ☎ 020/423–0230) also sells unusual handcrafted wooden flowers and toys and spring-operated jumping toys.

## Diamonds & Jewelry

Diamonds are hardly ever a bargain. But compared to other cities, and thanks to Amsterdam's centuries-old ties to South Africa, they almost fall into that category here. The city's famous factories even allow one-stop shopping. The **Amsterdam Diamond Center** (⊠ Rokin 1–5, Nieuwe Zijde ☎ 020/624–5787) houses several diamond sellers. Set near the Rijksmuseum, **Coster Diamonds** (⊠ Paulus Potterstraat 2–8, Museum District ☎ 020/676–2222 ⊕ www.costerdiamonds.com) not only sells jewelry and loose diamonds but gives free demonstrations of diamond cutting so you can learn all about the "four Cs"—carat, color, clarity, and cut. You can see a replica of the most famous diamond cut in the factory—the Koh-I-Noor, one of the prize gems of the British crown jewels. After your tour, enjoy the petit café here. One of the international leaders in contemporary jewelry design is **Hans Appenzeller** (⊠ Grimburgwal 1, Nieuwe Zijde ☎ 020/626–8218). In the Negen Straatjes shopping area, **BLGK** (⊠ Hartenstraat 28, Western Canal Ring ☎ 020/624–8154) specializes in Byzantine-inspired silver and gold jewelry. **Bonebakker** (⊠ Rokin 88/90, Nieuwe Zijde ☎ 020/623–2294) is one of the city's oldest and finest jewelers and carries an exceptionally wide range of fine watches and silverware. They've been in business since 1792, and Adrian Bonebakker, the founder, was commissioned by King Willem II to design and make the royal crown for the House of Orange.

Fodor'sChoice ★

## Food & Beverages

CHEESE  **De Kaaskamer** stinks. Of cheese. Which just goes to show what a terrific selection it has. In addition to the usual Dutch suspects—Edam, Gouda, Old Amsterdam, and smoked cheeses, this family business also sells choices from France, Greece, Italy, and Switzerland. There's also a great assortment of accompanying cold cuts, olives, and freshly made sauces. (⊠ Runstraat 7, Western Canal Ring ☎ 020/623–3483)

CHOCOLATE  Chocoholics, take note. **Arti Choc** (⊠ Koninginneweg 141, Amsterdam Zuid ☎ 020/470–9805) not only sells handmade bonbons, but will also custom design just about anything you can imagine made from chocolate. **Australian Homemade Amsterdam** (⊠ Singel 437, Nieuwe Zijde ☎ 020/428–7533) uses natural ingredients to make chocolate and ice
★ cream. Amsterdam's best handmade chocolates come from **Puccini Bomboni** (⊠ Singel 184, Nieuwe Zijde ☎ 020/427–8341 ⊠ Staalstraat 17, Eastern Canal Ring ☎ 020/626–5474), where exotic combinations of chocolate and herbs (such as thyme and pepper) and spices are a specialty. The variety isn't enormous, but there are enough knockouts, including chocolates filled with calvados, Cointreau, rhubarb, and tamarind.

## Gifts & Souvenirs

The interior of **Baobab 1** (⊠ Elandsgracht 128, Jordaan ☎ 020/626–8398) is like something out of Ali Baba's cave of treasures or 1001 Nights. You'll find a rich trove of jewelry, statuary, and all kinds of objects from such locales as India and the Middle East.

You can't visit Holland and not buy a pair of *klompen*, can you? Lo-
Fodor'sChoice  cated in a former metro station, **De Klompenboer** (⊠ Sint Anthonies-
★ breestraat 51A, Nieuwmarkt ☎ 020/623–0632) sells toys upstairs and klompen downstairs. They have wooden shoes in the classic bright yellow/orange color, but also in red, blue, and natural wood in sizes to fit feet from two-year-olds to adults.

## Housewares

**Bebob Design Interior** (⊠ Prinsengracht 764, Eastern Canal Ring ☎ 020/624–5763) supplies collectors and galleries with hard-to-find historic designs of chairs, sofas, tables, office chairs, and lighting fixtures from top lines. **Capsicum** (⊠ Oude Hoogstraat 1, Oude Zijde ☎ 020/623–1016) makes fabricholics drool with its gorgeous weaves, prints, and colors; this is not your run-of-the-mill fabric store.

**Droog Design** (⊠ Staalstraat 7A & B, Nieuwmarkt ☎ 020/626–9809) is rapidly gaining an international reputation for its ground-breaking industrial and interior designs. Droog started out as a Dutch design collective, but now cutting-edge designers from all over the globe participate in their exhibitions. Their designers are among the most influential in contemporary design. The entire harbor district was given a shot in
★ the arm with the five-story showcase for home design, **Post Amsterdam** (⊠ Oosterdoksekade 5, Eastern Harbour Area, Eastern Docklands ☎ 020/421–1033). Don't be surprised to find the editors of top home design magazines browsing here for inspiration; this place is a show-

case for the hottest new trends. You can see the newest international collections, fresh from the big trade expositions—and afterward, enjoy a meal at the nearby restaurant/bar/club 11.

## Music

**Fodor'sChoice** Near the Concertgebouw, **Broekmans & Van Poppel** (⌧ Van Baerlestraat
★ 92–94, Museum District ☎ 020/675–1653) specializes in recordings, sheet music, and accessories for classical and antiquarian music. There's an antiques-store atmosphere at **Datzzit Verzamel—Muziek en Filmwinkel** (⌧ Prinsengracht 306, Eastern Canal Ring ☎ 020/622–1195). The merchandise includes music on 78s, vinyl, and CD, as well as film memorabilia.

**Concerto** (⌧ Utrechtsestraat 54–60, Eastern Canal Ring ☎ 020/626–6577) is filled with new and used records and CDs covering all imaginable genres. If you're looking for a particular recording, this should be your first stop.

## Shoes

★ Located in the Negen Straatjes area, **Antonia Shoes** (⌧ Gasthuismolen-steeg 18–20, Western Canal Ring ☎ 020/320–9433) offers two stores of hip footwear from top European designers for men and women. Extreme, classic, high heels, flat shoes—if it's available in footwear, they carry it, with handbags to match. There are styles for men, too. **Antonia Shoes** (⌧ Gasthuismolensteeg 16, Western Canal Ring ☎ 020/627–2433) sells bedroom slippers and Wellington boots. **Bally Shoes** (⌧ Leidsestraat 8–10, Eastern Canal Ring ☎ 020/622–2888) is a byword for good taste (and high prices) in women's shoes. **Jan Jansen** (⌧ Rokin 42, Nieuwe Zijde ☎ 020/625–1350) has the crème de la crème of shoes, with gorgeous color combinations and stunning designs. Famed Jansen is an artist/craftsman who designs and makes his special shoes in very small series, but he also has a manufactured line, Jan Jansen Sense, that is carried in shops worldwide. He's won numerous design awards and his shoes are in many museum collections.

# SIDE TRIPS: FOLKLORIC HOLLAND

Updated by
Kim Renfrew

If you want your postcards to come to life, head to the famous "folkloric" towns of Zuiderzee, Volendam, and Marken, where boys can still be seen wearing Hans Brinker costumes and sleepy little fishing ports are lost in time. This region is found in the province of Noord-Holland (whose southernmost sector includes Amsterdam). This particular region around the Zaan River and the IJsselmeer "sea" is called Zaanstreek and Waterland (despite there being water everywhere in the Netherlands). Naturally, it's a great area for watery pursuits like fishing, swimming, and sailing. A fun (even convenient) way to travel hereabouts is by water (*see* Guided Tours *in* Side Trips A to Z), making stops along the way.

*Numbers in the margin correspond to points of interest on the Side Trips from Amsterdam map.*

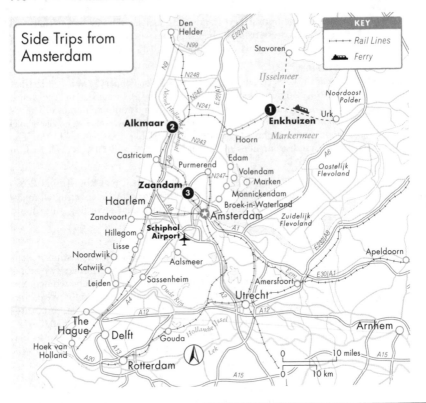

## Enkhuizen

**❶** *20 km (13 mi) northeast of Hoorn, 60 km (37 mi) northeast of Amsterdam. Take Routes N506 or N302.*

Near the former harbor town of Enkhuizen, about 19 km (12 mi) east of Hoorn, is perhaps the most famous of the "costume villages," the
★ ☺ **Zuiderzeemuseum.** It is one of the Netherlands' most complete outdoor museums, with streets, neighborhoods, and harbors created with historic buildings. There are 130 houses, shops, and workshops where the old crafts are still practiced. To reach the museum you have to take a boat from the main entrance, a romantic way to take a step back in time. Assorted historical treasures here include a 19th-century apothecary, cottages moved from the isle of Urk and the village of Zoutkamp, sail-making and herring shops, picturesque lime kilns from Noord-Holland, and a children's island that takes kids back to life in the former fishing village of Marken during the 1930s. The indoor Marine Hall museum, built in 1625 and once the property of the Dutch East India Company, houses permanent exhibitions depicting the rich history of the Zuiderzee (now the IJsselmeer). ✉ *Wierdijk 12–22, Enkhuizen* ☎ *0228/351–111* 💰 *€10; indoor museum only, €5.50* ☾ *Indoor museum Tues.–Sun. 10–5; outdoor museum Apr.–Oct., Tues.–Sun. 10–5, July–Oct, daily 10–6.*

# Alkmaar

**2** *45 km (13 mi) southwest of Enkhuizen, 40 km (25 mi) northwest of*
**Fodor's**Choice  *Amsterdam. Take Routes N302–A7/E22–N243–N242.*
★

As one of the "cheese towns," Alkmaar is most noted for its traditional cheese market—but it also has several hundred historical monuments, many windmills, and beautiful medieval courtyards—a concentration of all things Holland. The city has been on the map for more than 750 years, and is littered with monuments: the St. Lawrence Church—with its great centuries-old organ and tomb of Count Floris V; the Town Hall, a beautiful Gothic building from 1520; the Remonstraat Church; and the House of the Cannonball (bearing a vestige of Spanish invaders).

But the glory of Alkmaar is the **Waaggebouw,** or Weigh House, a 15th-century chapel with a tower added in 1597. As you stand below its ornate step gables, your eye is drawn upward by a labyrinth of receding planes that culminate in the weather vane. If the hour is about to strike, take a break to enjoy the chimes and watch the moving figures of mounted knights and trumpeters (the noon hour gets the biggest show). Then climb the tower for a view of the town: canals cross this way and that, and the former ramparts are outlined by gardens often ablaze with flowers. In the distance, windmills turn in the face of a breeze perfumed with the faint scent of the sea.

If you visit during a Friday morning, you're in for a real spectacle. The cheeses arrive at the market by barge, and are unloaded in a juggling act worthy of circus performers; the balls are pitched from the barge to barrows that look like stretchers. At this point pairs of colorfully attired men from the Porters' Guild (in existence for 400 years) carry the cheeses away, no mean feat, as the average weight is about 350 pounds per barrow. A "father" directs the activities of the 28 porters, who are divided into four groups, or *veems,* dressed alike in white shirts and trousers but distinguished by blue, red, green, or yellow straw hats. The actual selling of the cheeses takes place in a ring and is consummated by a handclasp that is as binding as a signed contract. The cheese market takes place from the first week in April to the first week in September on Friday mornings from 10 to 12:30. After the sale—the auction is done through traditional hand-clapping signals—the official weighing of the cheese is done at the Weigh House. All in all, it may be easier to buy your cheese at a supermarket, but it's lovely to get a glimpse of such old-world pageantry.

The local VVV (Tourist Information Office) organizes a walking tour of noteworthy sites. The 1½-hour tour costs €3.50. It starts at 12:30, except in September, when it starts at 11. Tickets can be purchased at the Alkmaar VVV office. If planning to explore on your own, pick up a map from the VVV.

The **Stedelijk Museum Alkmaar** focuses on the history of the region from Alkmaar's "Golden Age"—the 16th and 17th centuries—to the present day. There's an intriguing display of city life shown in detailed miniature dioramas. Paintings depict the Spanish siege of the city, portraits capture noblemen and militia leaders, and other historic artifacts make this a good starting point before exploring Alkmaar itself. ⊠ *Canadaplein 1* ☎ *072/511–0737* ⊕ *www.stedelijkmuseumalkmaar.nl* ⊠ *€3.40* ☉ *Tues.–Fri. 10–5, Sat. and Sun. 1–5.*

While attending the cheese market, you'll see the cheese being weighed at the Waaggebouw, which is also where you'll find **Dutch Cheese Museum.** Cheese has been produced in Noord-Holland for nearly 2,500 years, and here you can learn about past and present-day cheese making (farm versus factory). Twenty-four 16th-century panels depict women's regional costumes from all over Noord-Holland, and there are also some full-size replica outfits on display. ⊠ *Waagplein 2* ☎ *072/ 511–4284* ⊕ *www.kaasmuseum.nl* ⊠ *€2.50* ☉ *Apr.–end of Oct., Mon.–Thurs., Sat. 10–4, Fri. 9–4.*

## Zaandam

❸ *31 km (19 mi) southeast of Alkmaar, 16 km (10 mi) northwest of Amsterdam. Take Route N203 via Zaanse Schans (Zaandijk).*

Fodor'sChoice ★

During the 17th century Holland was renowned as the leading shipbuilding nation of the world, with Zaandam as its center. One of the many people who came here to learn the craft of shipbuilding was Peter the Great of Russia (whose statue now adorns the Damplein, the town marketplace). Today, modern shipyards stud the area—once immortalized in several canvases by Claude Monet—but set within the Zaanstreek region is a jewel: the **Zaanse Schans,** a living open-air museum. Here, time appears to have stood still, and you can easily immerse yourself in the 17th and 18th century. The village, built along the Zaan River, is filled with a great many working windmills and original Zaanse-style green wooden houses. Many have been restored as private homes, but a whole cluster are open to the public, and traditional crafts and businesses are still kept alive. You can see warehouses from the Dutch East India Trading Company and visit the workshop of a clog maker, the shops of a traditional cheese maker, a bakery museum, and the working windmills themselves. Each of these "mini museums" has its own low admission price. The Zaanse Schans presents a terrific skyline when viewed from the water, so avail yourself of the local VVV (Tourist Information Office) canal cruises. A mile or so north of Zaandam you come to Koog aan de Zaan, notable chiefly for the old (1751) **Het Pink windmill,** now a museum devoted to the history and construction of mills. ⊠ *Kraaienest, Zaandam* ☎ *075/616–8218* ⊕ *www.zaanseschans.nl* ⊠ *Free* ☉ *Daily 8–4.*

## Side Trips Essentials

### ARRIVING & DEPARTING
**By Car:** To reach Alkmaar from Amsterdam, take the A8 and A9 north. To get to Enkhuizen and its famous Zuiderzeemuseum, follow the A7 via Purmerend and Hoorn, then take the N302 in the direction of Enkhuizen. ANWB signs direct you to the museum.

**By Train:** Local trains operate every 15 minutes direct from Amsterdam to Alkmaar and Leiden, every half hour to Hoorn and Enkhuizen.

Call for **national train information** (☎ 0900/9292).

# AMSTERDAM ESSENTIALS

## Transportation to Amsterdam

### BY AIR

Located 17 km (11 mi) southeast of Amsterdam, **Luchthaven Schiphol** (pronounced "Shh-kip-hole") is the main passenger airport for Holland. With the annual number of passengers using Schiphol approaching 40 million, it is ranked among the world's top five best-connected airports. A hotel, a service to aid passengers with disabilities, parking lots, and a main office of the Netherlands tourist board (in Schiphol Plaza and known as "HTi"—Holland Tourist Information) can prove most useful. The comprehensive Schiphol telephone service, charged at €0.10 per minute, provides information about flight arrivals and departures as well as all transport and parking facilities.

🛈 Amsterdam Luchthaven (Airport) Schiphol ✉ 17 km (11 mi) southwest of Amsterdam ☎ 0900/0141 ⊕ www.schiphol.nl.

AIRPORT TRANSFER  The Schiphol Rail Link operates between the airport and the city 24 hours a day, with service to Centraal Station—Amsterdam's central railway station—or to stations in the south of the city. From 6:30 AM to 12:30 AM, a train departs from or arrives at Schiphol every 15 minutes; other hours, there is one train every hour. The trip takes about 15 minutes and costs €3.10. Trains leave from the platforms of Schiphol Station, found beneath Schiphol Plaza. They head into the city using one of three routes. The most popular is the NS Schiphollijn, which runs to Centraal Station (with two stops in west Amsterdam). Another route heads to the Amsterdam Zuid/WTC (South/World Trade Center) station in south Amsterdam, and another line heads to the RAI section, near the big convention center. From these south Amsterdam stations, Tram 5 goes to Leidseplein and the Museum Quarter; from RAI, Tram 4 goes to Rembrandtplein. Keep in mind that Schiphol Station is one of Holland's busiest—make sure you catch the shuttle to Amsterdam and not a train heading to The Hague! As always, when arriving at Amsterdam's Centraal Station, keep an eye out for any stray pickpockets. Other than taxis, you may wish to hop aboard a tram or bus to get to your hotel, so go to one of the **Gemeentevervoerbedrijf (GVB) Amsterdam Municipal Transport** booths found in front of the Centraal Station. Here you can find directions, fare information, and schedules.

Finally, there is a taxi stand directly in front of the arrival hall at Amsterdam Schiphol Airport. A service charge is included, but small additional tips are not unwelcome. New laws determine that taxi fares are now fixed from Schiphol to Amsterdam; depending on the neighborhood, a trip will cost between €25 and €30. When you're returning home, a ride to Schiphol from Amsterdam center city area, the Centrum, will cost €22. A new service that might be convenient for budget travelers who count every euro is the Schiphol Travel Taxi. The taxi needs to be booked at least 48 hours in advance and rides are shared, so the trip will take a bit longer as the taxi stops to pick up passengers.

**▲ Taxis & Shuttles** **KLM Shuttle** ☎ 020/653-4975. **Schiphol Rail Link** ☎ 0900/9292. **Schiphol Travel Taxi** ☎ 020/0900-8876.

## BY CAR

A network of well-maintained superhighways and other roads covers the Netherlands, making car travel convenient. Major European highways leading into Amsterdam from the borders are E19 from western Belgium; E25 from eastern Belgium; and E22, E30, and E35 from Germany. Follow the signs for *Centrum* to reach the center of the city. At rush hour, traffic is dense but not so dense as to become stationary.

The major car rental firms have convenient booths at Schiphol Airport, but the airport charges rental companies a fee that is passed on to customers, so you'll get a better deal at downtown locations.

Rates vary from company to company; daily rates start at approximately $50 for a one-day rental, $140 for a three-day rental, and $300 for a week's rental. This does not include collision insurance or airport fee. Tax is included and weekly rates often include unlimited mileage. As standard, cars in Europe are stick shift. An automatic transmission will cost a little extra.

**▲ Major Agencies** **Alamo** ☎ 800/462-5266, 0208/750-2800 in U.K. ⊕ www.alamo. com. **Avis** ☎ 800/230-4898, 800/272-5871 in Canada, 02/9353-9000 in Australia, 0800/655-111 in New Zealand, 0870/606-0100 in U.K. ⊕ www.avis.com. **Budget** ☎ 0144/ 227-6266 in the U.K. **Dollar** ☎ 800/800-3665, 800/800-6000 in U.K., 649/255-0620 in New Zealand ⊕ www.dollar.com. **Hertz** ☎ 800/654-3001, 800/263-0600 in Canada, 0870/844-8844 in U.K., 03/9698-2555 in Australia, 0800/654-321 in New Zealand ⊕ www.hertz.com. **National Car Rental** ☎ 800/227-7368, 020/8745-2800 in U.K. ⊕ www.nationalcar.com.

**▲ Local Agencies** **Avis** ✉ Nassaukade 380, Oud Zuid ☎ 020/683-6061. **Budget** ✉ Overtoom 121, Vondelpark ☎ 020/604-1349 ⊕ www.budget.com. **Hertz** ✉ Overtoom 333, Vondelpark ☎ 020/612-2441.

## BY TRAIN

The city has several substations, although one is the principal station, and is called the Centraal. **Be sure of the exact name of the station** from which your train will depart, and at which you wish to get out. Described in more detail below, train stations in Amsterdam (all preceded by the name Amsterdam) are Centraal, Sloterdijk, Muiderpoort, Amstel, Lelylaan, Zuid WTC (World Trade Center), Rai, Bijlmer, and Duivendrecht. There are about nine train stations in the center city, but only a few are of interest to visitors. All trains for national or international destinations depart from Centraal Station. Business travelers go to Station Rai for the RAI congress center and Station Zuid WTC (World Trade Center). There is a refreshment service on intercity trains, with roller carts or a cafeteria or dining car.

**▲ In the Netherlands** **NS-Nederlandse Spoorwegen/Dutch Railways** ☎ 0900/202-1163, 0900/202-1163, calls cost 10¢ per minute ⊕ www.ns.nl.

## Transportation Around Amsterdam

Everyone's dream of touring Amsterdam is to take a scenic hop on the Canal Bus, or go the two-wheel route with a bike, or just hoof it, as an eager army of bipeds does every year. Indeed, Amsterdam is relatively small as metropolises go and you can virtually connect all the main sites in a five-hour stroll. Happily, however, Amsterdam also has a full-scale bus and tram system—the GVB (city transport company)—that can whisk you from sector to sector, and attraction to attraction, throughout the city. Buses and trams run frequently; schedules and routes are posted at stops. In addition, somewhat surprisingly for this water-bound and centuries-old city, Amsterdam also has a subway, referred to as the metro, with lines running southeast and southwest. Once you understand the fanlike pattern of Amsterdam's geography, you will have an easier time getting around; most trams and buses begin and end their journeys at Centraal Station, sightseeing and shopping are focused at Dam Square and Museumplein, and the arts and nightlife are centered in the areas of Leidseplein, Rembrandtplein, and Waterlooplein. There are usually maps of Amsterdam's full transport network in individual shelters, and diagrams of routes are found on board.

The transit map published by GVB (Gemeentelijk Vervoer Bedrijf/City transport company) is very useful. It's available at the GVB ticket office across from the central railway station or at the VVV tourist information offices next door. It is also reprinted as the center spread in *Day by Day in Amsterdam*, the monthly guide to activities and shopping published by the tourist office. The map shows the locations of all major museums, monuments, theaters, and markets, and it tells you which trams to take to reach them. The GVB also has a very **useful site with transportation information** in English with route maps ⊕ www.gvb.nl. In addition, they publish folders in just about every language (including Japanese, Chinese, and Arabic) that explains everything about using public transport.

DE OPSTAPPER  A great new public transport option is the *Opstapper,* a transit van that traverses the elegant Prinsengracht—heart of the historic canal sector—between Centraal Station and the Music Theater. For a one-zone stamp on your strippenkaart, you can get on or off anywhere along the Prinsengracht. You can hail it on the street, or get on at its starting point in front of Centraal Station. There are no fixed stops. It passes within walking distance of the Anne Frank House, the Leidseplein, and maybe even your hotel. The buses run every ten minutes from 7:30 AM to 6:30 PM. There are eight seats and room for an additional eight standing passengers.

METRO  Amsterdam has a full-fledged subway system, called the metro, but travelers will usually find trams and buses more convenient for getting around, as most metro stops are geared for city residents traveling to the outer suburbs. However, the Amsterdam metro can get you from point A to point C in a quantum leap—for instance, from Centraal Station (at the northern harbor edge of the city) to Amstel Station (a train station at the southeastern area of the city, with connections to many buses and trams)—much faster than a tram, which makes many stops along the way. A strippenkaart is used the same way as for other public transport.

The same ticket can be used in buses, trams, and metros throughout Holland. *Enkele Reis* (single-ride tickets) are valid for one hour only and can be purchased from tram and bus drivers for €1.60. However, it is far more practical to buy a *strippenkaart* (strip ticket) that includes 2 to 45 "strips," or ticket units. The best buy for most visitors is the 15-strip ticket for €6.50. A 45-strip ticket costs €19.20. Although newer trams have ticket control booths, by tradition, Dutch trams and buses work on the honor system: upon boarding, punch your ticket at one of the machines in the rear or center section of the tram or bus. The city is divided into zones, which are indicated on the transit map, and it is important to punch the correct number of zones on your ticket (one for the basic tariff and one for each zone traveled).

The All Amsterdam Transport Pass costs €22 and entitles you to a day of unlimited travel on tram, bus, metro, and Canal Bus plus coupons worth about €133 for major attractions, snacks, etc. This pass can be purchased at the GVB ticket office in front of Centraal Station and at the main Canal Bus office at Prins Hendrikkade. The recently introduced electronic Amsterdam Culture Pass provides free and discount admissions to many of the city's top museums, plus a free canal round-trip, free use of public transport, and a 25% discount on various attractions and restaurants; savings can amount to more than €100. A one-day pass costs €33, two-days costs €43, and three-day costs €53. The pass comes with a booklet in Dutch, English, French, and German. It can be purchased at branches of the VVV (Netherlands Board of Tourism), the GVB (City Transport Company), both at Centraal Station, and through some hotels and museums.

🚩 **GVB** ✉ Prins Hendrikkade 108–114, Centrum ☎ 0900/9292 ⊕ www.gvb.nl.

## BY BIKE

To rent a bicycle, you'll pay from €8.50 per day, plus a deposit of about €50 per bike, and need a passport or other identification. The more days you rent, the cheaper the price, and rates by the week are even more competitive. Bikes can be rented at outlets near railway stations or by contacting rental centers. MacBike—the most popular rental firm in town—has various rental points around the city center; Bike City is near the Anne Frank House; Damstraat Rent-a-Bike is near the Dam Square.

Never leave your bike unlocked: there is a rapid turnover of stolen bikes no matter what quality or condition. Use a "D" lock, which can't be cut with the average thieves' tools, and lock your bike's frame to something that can't be shifted, such as a railing. Never buy a bicycle from someone on the street; it has probably just been stolen.

## BY TAXI

Vacant taxis on the move through the streets are often on call to their dispatcher. Occasionally, if you get lucky, they'll stop for you if you hail them but the regular practice is to wait by a taxi stand or phone them. Taxi stands are at the major squares and in front of the large hotels.

You can also call Taxicentrale, the main dispatching office. Fares are €2.90, plus €1.80 per kilometer (half mile). A 5-km (3-mi) ride will cost about €12. A new initiative in the city is the *Wieler Taxi* (bike taxi), which resembles a larger version of a child's pedal-car and isn't very practical in the rain.

A water taxi provides a novel, if pricey, means of getting about. Water taxis can be hailed anytime you see one cruising the canals of the city, or called by telephone. The boats are miniature versions of the large sightseeing canal boats, and each carries up to eight passengers. The cost is €75 for a half hour, including pick-up charge, with a charge of €60 each half-hour period thereafter. The rate is per ride, regardless of the number of passengers.

�· Taxi Companies **Taxicentrale** ☎ 020/677-7777. **Wielertaxi** ☎ 020/672-1149. **Water Taxi** ☎ 020/535-6363 ⊕ www.water-taxi.nl.

## Contacts & Resources

### EMERGENCIES

**Police, ambulance, and fire** (☎ 112 toll-free 24-hour switchboard for emergencies). The 24-hour help-line service **Afdeling Inlichtingen Apotheken** (☎ 020/694-8709) (*apotheken* means "pharmacy") can direct you to your nearest open pharmacy; there is a rotating schedule to cover evenings, nights, and weekends—details are also posted at your local *apotheken,* and in the city newspapers. The **Centraal Doktorsdienst/Atacom** (Medical Center; ☎ 020/592-3434) offers a 24-hour English-speaking help line providing advice about medical symptoms. In the case of minor accidents, phone **directory inquiries** (☎ 0900/8008) to get the number for the outpatients' department at your nearest *ziekenhuis* (hospital). **TBB** (☎ 020/570-9595 or 0900/821-2230) is a 24-hour dental service that refers callers to a dentist (or *tandarts*). Operators can also give details of pharmacies open outside normal hours. For less urgent police matters, call the **central number** (☎ 0900/8844). The city's **police headquarters** is at the crossing Marnixstraat/Elandsgracht and can be reached with Tram line 3, 7, 12, or 17.

### VISITOR INFORMATION

The VVV (Netherlands Board of Tourism) has several offices around Amsterdam. The office in Centraal Station is open daily 8–8; the one on Stationsplein, opposite Centraal Station, is open daily 9–5; on Leidseplein, daily 9–5; and at Schiphol Airport, daily 7–10.

�· Amsterdam Tourist Information **VVV–Netherlands Board of Tourism** ⊕ www. holland.com/amsterdam ⊠ Spoor 2/Platform 2, Centraal Station, Centrum ⊠ Stationsplein 10, Central Station ⊠ Leidseplein 1, corner Leidsestraat, Leidseplein ⊠ Schiphol Airport, Badhoevedorp ☎ 0900/400-4040 €0.55 per minute weekdays 9-5. Outside office hours, this line has an extensive voice-response program.

# Metropolitan Holland: Rotterdam & the Randstad

**2**

By Charlotte A. R. Vaudrey
Revised by Tim Skelton

**IN AND AROUND THE PROVINCE OF ZUID-HOLLAND** (South Holland), like filings around the end of a magnet, six major urban centers cluster in a horseshoe arc to the west and south of Amsterdam: Haarlem, Leiden, Delft, Gouda, Utrecht, and Rotterdam. Each of these centers has continued to develop, prosper, and grow independently from the capital—so extravagantly that the borders of each community nearly verge on the next. In fact, the whole of South Holland is now dubbed the Randstad ("Border City") because locals consider it one mammoth megalopolis—a movement begun three decades ago, when Leiden began to stretch a hand south to The Hague, and Delft found itself beginning to be compressed between The Hague and Rotterdam. More than 25% of Holland's 15 million residents now live in and around the 10 small- to large-size cities that are within 80 km (50 mi) of the capital. Randstad also means "Edge City," another term the Dutch use to describe the circle formed by the cities of Amsterdam, The Hague, Rotterdam, and Utrecht, since the cities lie on the same geologic ridge at the northwestern edge of the country. Whatever the terminology, this entire region is considered "The West."

Rotterdam is the industrial center of Holland and the world's largest port. The city's quaint statue of Erasmus was long ago overshadowed by some of the most forward-looking architecture to dazzle any European city. When Rotterdam's city center and harbor were completely destroyed in World War II, the authorities decided to start afresh rather than try to reconstruct its former maze of canals. The imposing, futuristic skyline along the banks of the Maas River has been developing since then. Today, say architectural pundits, we have seen the future, and it is Manhattan-on-the-Maas (as locals call it), thanks in large part to the efforts of major figures such as Rem Koolhaas, Eric van Egeraat, and UN Studio.

Elsewhere in the region, you can pursue the ghost of Frans Hals through the Golden Age streets of Haarlem; discover the great university and the church of America's Pilgrim Fathers based at Leiden; feast on Gouda in Gouda; explore the time-stained town center of Utrecht; and wander through the ancient cobbled streets of Delft, which once colored the world with its unique blue. Many other colors are on view in Holland's fabled tulip fields. Every spring, green thumbers everywhere make a pilgrimage to Lisse to view them at the noted tulip gardens known as the Keukenhof, and drive the Bollenstreek Route, which takes them through miles of countryside glowing with gorgeous hues and blooms. Though you would miss much of interest if you left Holland after visiting no more than this corner of the country, there is no other region that so well merits your time. Indeed, although it remains an area small enough to drive through in a day, it is also interesting enough to take weeks to explore.

## Exploring Rotterdam & the Randstad

The ring that encircles the Randstad incorporates most towns and sights and conveniently makes a circular drive or train trip ideal, avoiding the need for any doubling back. Rotterdam, as the crux in the cultural axis, lies farthest from Amsterdam, 73 km (45 mi) south of the capital, with slightly more to see on the eastern side of the area between the two cities.

## About the Restaurants & Hotels

Although this area of Holland is home to some of the country's most worldly restaurants, keep in mind that bars and Holland's famous *bruine kroeg* (brown cafés)—so called because of their time- and smoke-stained interiors—also offer house specials whose prices are usually cheap enough to keep students and young people coming in (look in particular for the *kleine kaart*, or lighter meal menu, usually offered in the bar area). Perennially popular dishes such as satay and pepper steak never come off the menu. Some bars with restaurants attached have theme nights, so in summer you can expect Javanese nights, with drummers, when the menu takes on Asian flavors.

Hotels in the Randstad region range from extensive elegant canal houses, to smaller hotels that create the feeling of living in a comfortable, private residence, to cross-country chains with anonymous decor. Happily, most large towns have one, or even several, deluxe hotels that exceed all expectations. Accommodation in Rotterdam—a big convention city—is at a premium, so book well in advance. Get in touch with the VVV (tourist offices) of the region you plan to travel to, as they have extensive accommodation listings. They can book reservations for you, according to your specific requirements. Assume all rooms have air-conditioning, TV, telephones, and private bath, unless otherwise noted. Assume hotels operate on the EP meal plan (with no meals) unless stated otherwise.

| WHAT IT COSTS In euros | | | | | |
|---|---|---|---|---|---|
| | **$$$$** | **$$$** | **$$** | **$** | **¢** |
| RESTAURANTS | over €30 | €22–€30 | €15–€22 | €10–€15 | under €10 |
| HOTELS | over €230 | €165–€230 | €120–€165 | €75–€120 | under €75 |

Restaurant prices are per person for a main course only, excluding tax (6% for food and 19% for alcoholic beverages) and service; note that if a restaurant offers only prix-fixe meals, it has been given the price category that reflects the full prix-fixe price. Hotel prices are for a standard double room in high season, including the 6% VAT.

## Timing

This part of Holland is at its best in late spring or early autumn. High summer means too many visitors, and touring in winter often puts you at the mercy of the weather (but even in summer, pack your umbrella). For flora lovers, mid- to late April is ideal for a trip around Haarlem and Leiden, as the fields are bright with spring bulbs. Many restaurants are closed Sunday (also Monday); museums tend to close Monday.

If you're into the arts, you might prefer to schedule your trip to catch one of the area's two world-renowned festivals: the International Film Festival Rotterdam, where 300 noncommercial films are screened in late January and early February, and the Festival Oude Muziek (Festival of Early Music), where 150 concerts are held in venues across Utrecht in late August.

**2**

There is no need to rent a car to journey through this region, as every location is accessible by public transport. Indeed, for many of the towns covered in this chapter, traffic and parking just make car rental a headache. Kinderdijk, Muiden, and Brielle do not have convenient train stations, but all three are on bus routes, bringing them easily within reach of the independent, carless traveler.

*Numbers in the text correspond to numbers in the margin and on the Metropolitan Holland, Haarlem, Leiden, Utrecht, and Exploring Rotterdam maps.*

**If you have**
**3 days**

Get an early start from Amsterdam and head west to nearby **Haarlem** ①–⑨ ▶, a Golden Age town made famous by art. Here, lying in the shadow of a nest of lovely medieval buildings in the heart of this 900-year-old city, you'll find the Frans Hals Museum, housing many of the roistering and unforgettable portraits of this 17th-century painter. Explore the famous Church of Sint Bavo—adorably framed by a flower market—the history-rich main square, the tapestried Town Hall, and the Renaissance-era Hallen exhibition halls, and end with the great old-master drawings on view at the Teylers Museum. After lunch, set off for ☒ **Leiden** ⑫–㉔, birthplace of Rembrandt and home base for the Pilgrim Fathers; as home to Holland's greatest university, the city is packed with cosmopolitan hotels, restaurants, and shops, offering a fine place to break your stay. Follow in Rembrandt's footsteps (about all you can do, since nearly all traces of him and his family have vanished hereabouts) and explore the quaint streets. If it's springtime, take the N208 out of town and through the bulb fields to **Lisse** ⑪, heart of Tulip Country and home to the famed Keukenhof Gardens. On your second morning journey south and take your car or tram (20 minutes) to nearby ☒ **Delft** ㉕–㊳, one of the most beautifully preserved historic towns in the country and the place that gave us Delftware and that mysterious master painter Vermeer. Happily, many streets and canals in the Centrum, the historic center, have a once-upon-a-time feel, and you may be tempted to set up your own easel in a minute. There are some patrician mansion-museums to explore here, and you can visit the city's renowned porcelain factory. On your third morning head 23 km (14 mi) southeast to **Rotterdam** ㊵–㊽. Start by going out to Delfshaven, then take a breathless trip around the Dubbelde Palmboom museum as you briskly take in the harbor. On your way back across town walk along the old harbor at Veerhaven, before crossing the Erasmus Bridge to the Kop van Zuid. A great museum is the famous Museum Boijmans van Beuningen, home to some legendary old-master paintings, including Pieter Bruegel the Elder's *Tower of Babel*. Take in Wilhelminaplein and the shops before jumping into a water taxi and crossing the river, this time across to the Oude Haven, where you should have time to see the Kijk-Kubus cube houses by Blaak railway station; then hop a train back to Amsterdam.

**If you have**
**6 days**

Extend the three-day itinerary above by starting with an overnight stay in ☒ **Rotterdam** ㊵–㊽ ▶, which will allow you to luxuriate in extra time. You could head to Het Park, an ideal antidote to the city's bustle, and, for a fantastic view, go up the Euromast, or go to the Architecture Institute to learn more about the Kop van Zuid and Blaak districts. In historic Delfshaven, go to the Pilgrim Fathers' Church, or explore the Oude Haven. Other museums in the city include specialty collections such as the city's historical museum, split between exhibitions in Het Schielandshuis and De Dubbelde Palmboom. In the Entrepot district you could pick up some shopping in the interior design district, along the marina. Climb on board a warship at the Maritiem Museum. See photography and art collections at the Witte de With Center for Contemporary Art. As you wander up Westersingel, take in the Sculpture Terrace and the biggest skate park in the city. If you want a mini-escape from urban bustle, visit the enormous Kinderdijk windmills, an easy day trip from Rotterdam that you can even visit by boat.

On the way back north, stop off in ⊞ **Gouda** 68, famed not only for its cheeses but also for its medieval City Hall and the magnificent stained glass in the Sint Janskerk. Opt to take the train or the A12 to ⊞ **Utrecht** 69 – 77, where you can climb the Gothic Domtoren, the highest church tower in the Netherlands, for a panoramic view of the countryside. Back on ground level, you can visit a delightful museum of music boxes, player pianos, and barrel organs, or learn about the history of train travel in the Spoorwegmuseum (Railway Museum). Explore the possibility of an afternoon trip to the **Kasteel de Haar** 78, Holland's most spectacular castle extravaganza. Return to Amsterdam either by car or—via Utrecht's railway hub—by train.

# HAARLEM TO DELFT

A route south of Amsterdam, running near the coast, takes you through the heart of metropolitan Holland, starting with Haarlem and ending at Rotterdam. Here, great city centers still bear witness to the Golden Age of the 17th century: Haarlem, with the glories of Sint Bavo's and the celebrated portrait skills of local Frans Hals; Leiden, where a child was baptized and left town two decades later to find fame and riches as Rembrandt van Rijn; and Delft, whose frozen-in-amber scene seems not so distantly removed from that painted in Vermeer's legendary *View of Delft*. Once past the bright lights of these town centers, you'll find the land stretches flat as far as the eye can see, though the coast west of Haarlem and Leiden undulates with long expanses of dunes, many of which are nature reserves. In spring, the farmland between these two towns is legendarily bright with tulips and other blooms. Venture down some unmarked roads and you can still find a storybook Holland of green meadows, hayracks, brimming canals, and—dare we say—a rosy-cheeked child or two.

## Haarlem

*20 km (12 mi) west of Amsterdam, 41 km (26 mi) north of The Hague.*

It is just a short hop from the ocean of annual color that is Holland's Bulb Route to this haven of perennial color. Haarlem's historic center is beautiful, dotted with charming *hofjes* (historic almshouse courtyards), and has a lively population—often the overspill of students who can't find lodgings in Amsterdam or Leiden. The city is also home to fine museums stuffed with art by masters of the Haarlem School, such as the renowned Teylers Museum, and the town center is adorned with the imposing Grote Kerk, often painted by the masters of the Golden Age. Lying between Amsterdam and the coastal resort of Zandvoort, Haarlem is close to the dunes and the sea and attracts hordes of beach-going Amsterdammers and Germans every summer. No matter that all traces of Haarlem's origins as a 10th-century settlement on a choppy inland sea disappeared with the draining of the Haarlemmermeer in the mid-19th century: the town itself hasn't lost its appeal.

If you arrive by train (just a 15-minute trip from the capital), take a look around before you leave the railway station—a fabulous art nouveau building dating from 1908. Head down Jansweg (to the left of the station as you exit) for several blocks, over the Nieuwe Gracht canal and into the city center, where, farther along on Jansstraat, you hit Haarlem's pulsing heart, the famous **Grote Markt.** Around this great market square the whole of Dutch architecture can be traced in a chain of majestic buildings ranging from the 14th to the 19th century. With a smile and a little bravado, you can enter most of them for a quick look. But all eyes are first drawn to the imposing mass of Sint Bavo's.

**❷** The Late Gothic Sint Bavo's church, more commonly called the **Grote Kerk,** or Great Church, dominates the square and was built in the 14th century, but severe fire damage in 1370 led to a further 150 years of rebuilding and expansion. St. Bavo was the patron saint of the community. This is the burial place of Frans Hals—a lamp marks his tombstone behind the brass choir screen. Here, too, is buried Laurens Coster, who in 1423 invented printing—sorry, Gutenberg—seemingly because the love-struck Coster was inspired when carved-bark letters fell into the sand below a tree he was etching with a valentine (a statue of Coster adorns the square outside). The imposing wooden vault shelters a whimsical historic sight. In the north transept, the Dog Whippers' chapel pays tribute to men who ejected snarling dogs from the sacred premises; note the carved capital on the left-hand arch that depicts a man whipping a dog. The church is the home of the Müller organ, on which both Handel and Mozart played (Mozart at age 10). Installed in 1738, and for centuries considered the finest in the world, this gilded and gleaming instrument has been meticulously maintained and restored through the years to protect the sound planned by its creator, the master organ builder Christian Müller. Between May and October the official town organists of Haarlem perform free concerts every Tuesday at 8:15 PM, and also occasionally on Thursday at 3 PM. You may be lucky enough to hear orchestras rehearsing for concerts as you tiptoe through. One thing is clear: there are few places where a Bach prelude or fugue sounds as magisterial. ⊠ *Grote Markt* ☎ *023/533–2040* ✉ *€2* ⊘ *Mon.–Sat. 10–4.*

**need a break?**

The spacious **Grand Café Brinkmann** (⊠ Brinkmannpassage 41 ☎ 023/532–3111), adorned with cherubic ceiling paintings, offers baguettes, pancakes, and other light snacks. Windows edged with art deco stained glass overlook the Grote Markt and Sint Bavo's church across the square.

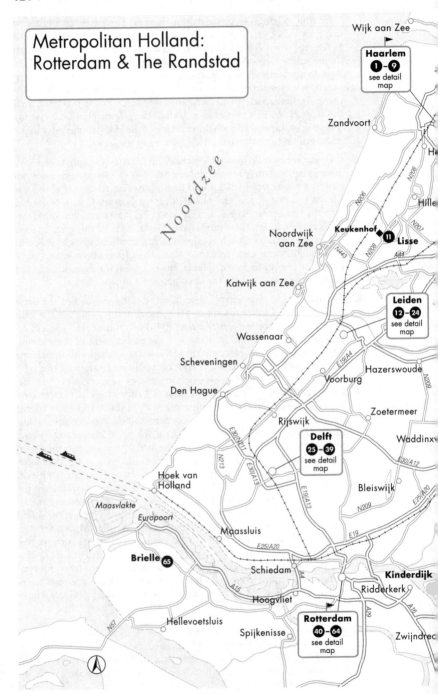

Metropolitan Holland:
Rotterdam & The Randstad

Wik aan Zee

**Haarlem**
**1**-**9**
see detail
map

Zandvoort

*Noordzee*

N206

Hille

N207

Noordwijk
aan Zee

**Keukenhof**♦ **11**
**Lisse**

N208

A44

Katwijk aan Zee

N443

**Leiden**
**12**-**24**
see detail
map

Wassenaar

Hazerswoude

Scheveningen

E19/A4

N209

Voorburg

Den Hague

Zoetermeer

Rijswijk

Waddinx

**Delft**
**25**-**39**
see detail
map

E30/N211

N213

E30/A13

E30/A12

Bleiswijk

Hoek van
Holland

E19/A13

N209

E25/A20

*Maasvlakte*

*Europoort*

Maassluis

E19

E25/A20

**Brielle 65**

Schiedam

**Kinderdijk**

A4

Ridderkerk

Hoogvliet

A29

A15

A16

Hellevoetsluis

**Rotterdam**
**40**-**64**
see detail
map

Zwijndrec

N57

Spijkenisse

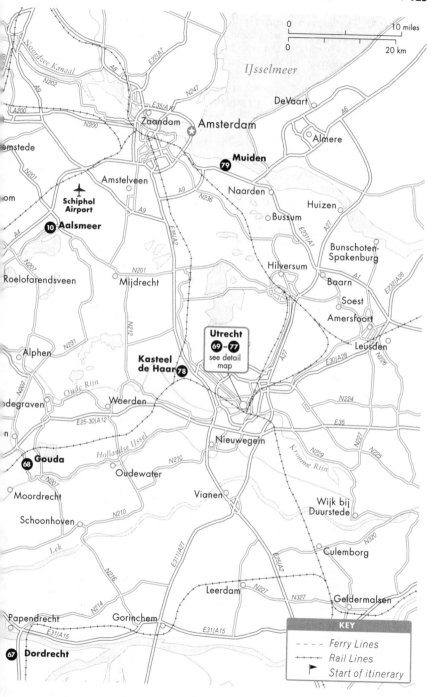

**KEY**

--- Ferry Lines

+++ Rail Lines

▶ Start of itinerary

❸ On the market square is the 14th-century **Stadhuis,** or Town Hall, originally a hunting lodge belonging to the Count of Holland, who permitted it to be transformed into Haarlem's Town Hall in the 14th century. The large main **Gravenzaal** (Count's Hall) is worth a visit—if you can sneak in between bouts of confetti throwing, as this has a goodly number of bridal parties ascending its steps on a regular basis—to study its collection of 16th-century paintings amassed by the Count of Holland. If you wish to tour the premises, call in advance to get permission, as rooms may be closed for civic functions. ⊠ *Grote Markt 2* ☏ *023/511–3000* 🖃 *Free* ⊙ *Weekdays 10–4 (when not closed for civic functions).*

Just off the Grote Markt, tucked into a small gabled town building above a shop, is the **Corrie ten Boomhuis** (Corrie ten Boom House) which honors a family of World War II resistance fighters who successfully hid a number of Jewish families before being captured themselves by the Germans in 1944. Most of the Ten Boom family died in the concentration camps, but Corrie survived and returned to Haarlem to tell the story in her book *The Hiding Place.* The family clock shop is preserved on the street floor, and their living quarters now contain displays, documents, photographs, and memorabilia. Visitors can also see the hiding closet, which the Gestapo never found, although they lived six days in the house hoping to starve out anyone who might be concealed here. The upstairs living quarters are not accessible through the shop, but via the side door of No. 19, down a narrow alley beside the shop. Meeting instructions giving the time of the next guided tour are posted on the door. ⊠ *Barteljorisstraat 19* ☏ *023/531–0823* ⊕ *www.corrietenboom.com* 🖃 *Donations accepted* ⊙ *Apr.–Oct., Tues.–Sat. 10–4; Nov.–Mar., Tues.–Sat. 11–3.*

❺ Overlooking the Grote Markt is the **De Hallen,** or The Halls museum complex, whose two buildings—the Vleeshal and the Verweyhal House—contain a variety of artworks, ranging from temporary special exhibitions to a permanent collection of modern art by artists from Haarlem and surrounding areas. A branch of the town's Frans Hals Museum, De Hallen has an extensive collection, with the works of Dutch impressionists and expressionists, including sculpture, textiles, and ceramics, as well as paintings and graphics. The **Vleeshal** (Meat Market) building is one of the most interesting cultural legacies of the Dutch Renaissance. Externally it is unique, for nowhere in the country is there such a fine sweep of stepped gables that invite you, had you a giant's stride, to clamber up to the pinnacle that seems to pierce the scudding clouds. It was built in 1602–03 by Lieven de Key, Haarlem's master builder. The ox heads that look down from the facade are reminders of the building's original function: it was the only place in Haarlem where meat could be sold, and the building was used for that sole purpose until 1840. Today it is used for exhibitions—generally works of modern and contemporary painting, glass, furniture, clocks, and sculpture. Just hope that your visit doesn't coincide with the weather illustrated by Karel Appel in *People in a Storm.* Note the early landscape work by Piet Mondriaan, *Farms in Duivendrecht,* so different from his later De Stijl shapes.

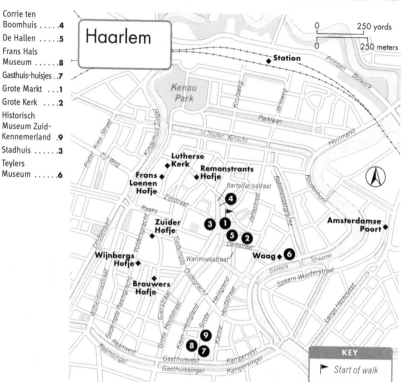

Haarlem

0       250 yards

0       250 meters

KEY

► *Start of walk*

The **Verweyhal Gallery of Modern Art** was built in 1879 as a gentle-men's club, originally named *Trou moet Blijcken* ("Loyalty Must Be Proven"). The building now bears the name of native Haarlem artist Kees Verwey, who died in 1995. The Verweyhal is used as an exhibi-tion space for selections from the Frans Hals Museum's enormous col-lection of modern and contemporary art. In addition to the works of Kees Verwey, the exhibition covers such artists as Jacobus van Looy, Jan Sluijters, Leo Gestel, Herman Kruyder, and Karel Appel. Note, too, a fine collection of contemporary ceramics. ⊠ *Grote Markt 16* ☎ *023/ 511-5775* ⊕ *www.dehallen.com* 🖃 *€4* ⊙ *Tues.–Sat. 11–5, Sun. noon–5.*

Leaving the Grote Markt by the eastern side, take Damstraat over to the river and the **Waag** (Weigh House). Built entirely of stone, and dat-ing to 1598, it was designed by Lieven de Key to weigh goods brought into the city via the Spaarne canal. Head north up the Spaarne em-

★ ❻ bankment to reach the **Teylers Museum,** the best sort of small museum, based on the wonderfully eclectic whims of an eccentric private collec-tor, in this case the 18th-century merchant Pieter Teyler van der Hulst. Founded in 1784, it's the country's oldest museum and has a mixture of exhibits, with fossils and minerals sitting alongside antique scientific instruments, such as a battery of 25 Leiden jars, dating from 1789 and used to store an electric charge. The museum itself is a grand old building with mosaic floors; its major artistic attraction is the legendary collection of drawings and prints by old masters, such as Michelangelo, Rembrandt, and Raphael, based on a collection that once belonged to Queen Christina of Sweden.

Unfortunately, only a few drawings are on display at any one time because of their fragility. There is also a collection of coins and medals and even a rare 31-tone Fokker organ. In the beautiful oval library, brass parabolic mirrors (dating from 1800) send the soft ticking of a watch right across the room; the Luminescence Cabinet is stocked with fluorescent and phosphorescent rocks and minerals that glow with extraordinary colors in the dark. Much of the collection is housed in beautiful wooden display cases in the original 18th-century museum building, while the drawing collection is in a discreetly extended modern wing. ✉ *Spaarne 16* ☎ *023/531–9010* ⊕ *www.teylersmuseum.nl* 💰 *€5.50* ☙ *Tues.–Sat. 10–5, Sun. noon–5.*

Not far from the Teylers Museum is the **Gravenstenenbrug**, a picturesque drawbridge across the Spaarne. Once you're on the far side of the canal, a short detour north along Spaarnwouderstraat takes you to the **Amsterdamse Poort** (Amsterdam Gate), the only remaining city gate, dating from around 1400; remains of the city wall can be seen at its base.

Walking between the Vleeshal and Sint Bavo Kerk, away from the Grote Markt, you come to Warmoesstraat—a very different thoroughfare from the street of the same name in Amsterdam. Here in Haarlem it is a quaint cobbled street, not a throbbing neon-lighted avenue. There are shops here, but they cater to the upper end of the market, with designer-wear stores, bespoke jewelers, little specialty shops (note the bead-and-button boutique), and bistros. As you walk down Warmoesstraat and its continuations to the Frans Hals Museum, don't miss the **Gasthuis-huisjes** on your left-hand side, nearly opposite the museum. This series of houses with identical step gables originally formed part of the St. Elizabeth hospital and was built in 1610. As you walk up Warmoesstraat, look at the short posts to restrict cars from parking: the usually rounded tops have been capped with flowerpots filled with geraniums and other brightly colored flowers—another indication of how locals prize flowers.

**❽** The **Frans Hals Museum**, set near the River Spaarne (from the Grote Markt, follow Warmoesstraat and its continuations, Schagchelstraat and Groot Heiligland), is named after the celebrated man himself and holds a collection of amazingly virile and lively group portraits by the Golden Age painter; these portraits depict the merrymaking civic guards and congregating regents for which Hals became world famous. The museum is in one of the town's smarter hofjes, in an entire block of almshouses grouped around an attractive garden courtyard, a setting that in itself is a gem of artistry. In the 17th century this was an old men's home, an *Oudemannenhuis*. The cottages now form a sequence of galleries for paintings, period furniture, antique silver, and ceramics. The focal point of the museum is a collection of 17th-century paintings that includes the works of Frans Hals and other masters of the Haarlem School.

You might find yourself overwhelmed by the visual banquet of Hals paintings, but take time to look in all the rooms branching off the main route, festooned with works by other masters. In the first room, you are greeted by a huge triptych commissioned for the visiting Prince of Orange's lodgings in the Prinsenhof. Note, too, the work of Dirck Hals, whose depictions of parties and revelry at musical get-togethers comes as a complete contrast to the more serious portraiture of his famous elder brother. Perplexing questions hang over some works, such as the painting where X-rays picked out a second face in the background (experts are not sure whether Hals painted either). But many of the works on display represent Frans Hals at his jovial best—for instance, the *Banquet of the Officers of the Civic Guard of St. Adrian* (1624–27) or the *Banquet of the Officers of the St. George Militia* (1616), where the artist cunningly allows for the niceties of rank (captains are more prominent than sergeants, who are more central than ensigns, and so on down the line) as well as emotional interaction, for Hals was the first painter to have people gaze and laugh at each other in these grand *schutter* (marksmen) portraits. In many instances, Hals leaves "class portrait" decorum well behind: in a group scene of the *Regentesses of the Old Men's Home* (1664) he appears to have taken revenge on their strict governance, immortalizing the women as a dour and frightening group. Nineteenth-century academicians later criticized Hals for his imprecise handling of details, but Hals was 80 when completing this portrait, and it was his *mouvementé*, nearly proto–Jackson Pollock, way with the brush that has made him the darling of 20th-century artists and art historians.

There is a wide array of works by Haarlem School masters on view, including Jan de Bray, Frans Jansz Post, Judith Leyster, Johannes Verspronck, Isaack van Ostade, Adriaen van Ostade, and Jacob van Ruysdael. But all the works are worthy of this museum, and details are eye-opening: Philips Wouwerman's gorgeous *Landscape with a Horseman* punctuates its dreamy setting with Dutch realism: a dog squatting grossly. As respite from nearly 250 canvases, step into the museum's courtyard—lovely, and planted with formal-garden baby hedges, of which you get only fleeting glimpses as you work your way through the galleries (most of the blinds are shut against the sunlight to protect the paintings). In one room, with curtains drawn for extra protection, is **Sara Rothè's Dolls' House**; nearby is an exquisitely crafted miniature version of a merchant's canal house. On leaving, *View of Haarlem* (1655) by Nicolaes Hals, Frans's son, bids you good-bye. Ask whether you can visit the restoration workshop (variable hours), where you can stand behind a glass wall and watch painters work painstakingly on a tiny patch of an old master that will occupy them for months. ⊠ *Groot Heiligland 62* ☎ *023/511–5775* ⊕ *www.franshalsmuseum.com* ⊠ €7 ☉ *Tues.–Sat. 11–5, Sun. noon–5.*

**❾** Located near the Frans Hals Museum, with two or three small temporary exhibitions a year, the town's history museum, the **Historisch Museum Zuid-Kennemerland** makes the most of its limited resources, offering a decent insight into the history of the city and the surrounding area. Video screenings (in English), models of the city, and touch-screen computers relate stories that take you back in history. There are fascinating old prints and maps, and some apparently random exhibits, including one of the earliest printing presses, dating from the 17th century. Also on view here is an incisive exhibition on modern Dutch architecture, **ABC Architectuur Centrum Haarlem,** with plans and photographs from city projects already finished and still in the planning stages (De Bruijn's Woonhuis is particularly ingenious). ⊠ *Groot Heiligland 47* ☎ *023/542–2427 Historisch Museum* ⊕ *www.hmzk.nl* ▧ *€1* ☉ *Tues.–Sat. noon–5, Sun. 1–5.*

In the lower, southwestern sector of the city, you'll find many of the historic hofjes (almshouse courtyards) that make Haarlem such a pleasant place. In and around Voldersgracht, Gasthuisstraat, Zuiderstraat, and Lange Annastraat, look for the Zuider Hofje, the Hofje van Loo, the Wijnbergs Hofje, and the Brouwershofje. Closer to the Grote Markt are the Remonstrants Hofje, the Luthershofje, and the Frans Loenen Hofje.

## Where to Stay & Eat

**$$–$$$** ✕ **Peter Cuyper.** In a 17th-century mansion that was once a bank, this small, gracious restaurant has a traditional beamed dining room that is brightened with flowers, crisp linens, and light filtering through the mullioned windows. Ask for a table with a view of the enclosed garden (open in summer) if you've missed out on a table outside. Try the turbot with wild morel mushroom gravy, or one of the delicious soups. The restaurant is convenient to both the Frans Hals and the Teylers museums. ⊠ *Kleine Houtstraat 70* ☎ *023/532–0885* ⌖ *Reservations essential* ▤ *AE, DC, MC, V* ☉ *Closed Sun. and Mon. No lunch Sat.*

**$–$$** ✕ **De Lachende Javaan.** Stepping into "The Laughing Javanese" off an old Haarlem street that hasn't changed in centuries, you are hit with a flash of color and pungent smells. You can sit upstairs at one of the window tables and look out over the sober gabled houses while eating *kambing saté* (skewers of lamb in soy sauce) and *kipkarbonaade met sambal djeroek* (grilled chicken with a fiery Indonesian sauce), but the menu options are enormous, so you can mix and match, choosing a meal of 12 small dishes if you want. ⊠ *Frankestraat 27* ☎ *023/532–8792* ▤ *AE, DC, MC, V* ☉ *Closed Mon. No lunch.*

★ **$–$$** ✕ **XO.** A very funky restaurant-bar, XO has chunky silver graphics, purple-and-gray walls, and oversize but softly lighted lamps. Throw in some fun touches—"king" chairs, complete with claw feet and red cushions; nifty recesses at the bar for extra intimacy; big stone candlesticks—and you've got an alluring setting for lunch and evening edibles. The dinner menu changes regularly but always contains mouthwatering and exquisitely presented dishes, such as cod filet baked in a sun-dried tomato-and-truffle crust, with black pasta, spinach, and a white-wine cream sauce. For a lunchtime snack try the imaginative bread rolls stuffed with marinated salmon, horseradish cream, or cucumber salad; or Greek bread with feta, grilled chicken, olives, tomatoes, and tzatziki. ⊠ *Grote Markt 8* ☎ *023/551–1350* ▤ *AE, MC, V.*

**¢–$$** ✕ **Jacobus Pieck.** One of Haarlem's best *eetlokaals* (dining spots), this attracts locals with its long bar, cozy tables, and lovely sun trap of a garden. The menu offers standards but with a twist: try the Popeye Blues

Salad—a wild spinach, blue cheese, and bacon number, with creamy mustard dressing for a lighter option—or, for dinner, a butterfish fillet with okra and sugar snaps in a Tuscan dressing. As you'll see, the food makes this restaurant-café very popular, so get here early or book ahead to snag a table. ⊠ *Warmoestraat 18* ☎ *023/532–6144* ⊟ *No credit cards* ☉ *Closed Sun. No dinner Mon.*

**$$–$$$** ▦ **Golden Tulip Lion d'Or.** This modern hotel is in a pretty 18th-century building just 50 yards from the railway station and within walking distance of major downtown sights. Rooms are spacious with good lighting and upscale chain-hotel-style furnishings. The bathrooms all have tubs as well as showers. Downstairs are meeting rooms, and a reasonably priced restaurant and bar. A jogging path runs behind the hotel. ⊠ *Kruisweg 34–36, 2011 LC* ☎ *023/532–1750* ⊟ *023/532–9543* ⊕ *www.goldentulip.com* ⋈ *32 rooms, 2 suites* ⚬ *Restaurant, cable TV, in-room data ports, bar, parking (fee), some pets allowed* ⊟ *AE, DC, MC, V* ⊙⧵ *BP.*

**¢–$** ▦ **Carillon.** This is an old-fashioned hotel with a friendly staff, set in the shadow of Sint Bavo's across the Grote Markt. Small rooms are spartan but fresh and comfortable, with impeccable bathrooms that include showers but not tubs. The central location and reasonable rates make it a top spot to accommodate a day of exploring and then a night out. The café-bar has a nice terrace on the square. ⊠ *Grote Markt 27, 2011 RC* ☎ *023/531–0591* ⊟ *023/531–4909* ⊕ *www.hotelcarillon.com* ⋈ *21 rooms, 15 with bath* ⚬ *Restaurant, cable TV, in-room data ports, bar; no a/c* ⊟ *AE, DC, MC, V* ⊙⧵ *CP.*

**¢** ▦ **Faber.** Within walking distance of the beaches of Zandvoort, this is a small family-style hotel with bright, tidy rooms and a summer terrace. It's run by two brothers, Hans and Martin, who make a point of making sure your stay is comfortable. Rooms book up very quickly in summer, so make reservations early. ⊠ *Kostverlorenstraat 15, 2042 PA Zandvoort* ☎ *023/571–2825* ⊟ *023/571–6886* ⊕ *www.hotel-faber.nl* ⋈ *32 rooms* ⚬ *Restaurant, cable TV, bar; no a/c* ⊟ *AE, MC, V* ⊙⧵ *CP.*

## Nightlife & the Arts

Haarlem hosts the **International Organ Competition** in even-numbered years for a week in July, giving people ample opportunity to hear the renowned Müller organ at full throttle.

Haarlem is more than a city of nostalgia, with the **Patronaat** (⊠ Zijlsingel 2 ☎ 023/532–6010) an excellent rock music venue: it's Haarlem's answer to the Melkweg in Amsterdam, though without the really big bands. For a mellower vibe, the **Grand Cafe Triple** (⊠ Botermarkt 21 ☎ 023/531–9688) is a jazz and blues bar that hosts free live events, such as jam sessions, most nights starting at 9 PM.

Bars often metamorphose into busy nightspots, such as **Mickie's** (⊠ Kruisstraat 22 ☎ 023/551–8661), which by day is a mellow café but at night is a rowdy nightclub with a DJ, serious lighting rigged up overhead, and enormous speakers to ensure the sound is loud.

For lots more bars and cafés head to Lange Veerstraat or the Botermarkt square.

**Theo Swagemakers** (⌂ Stoofsteeg 6 ☎ 023/532–7761 ⌨ €3.50) is a gallery that sells artwork by Swagemakers (1898–1994) himself, as well as other artists' work. It's open Thursday–Sunday 1–5. Other more commercial art galleries can be found along Koningstraat. On Frankestraat, look for art nouveau and art deco dealer **Kunsthandel Hermine Guldemond** (⌂ Frankestraat 39 ☎ 023/532–6603).

### The Outdoors

BEACHES **Zandvoort** is only 9 km (5½ mi) from Haarlem and has the area's biggest and best beach, always a favorite for sun-starved Amsterdammers. It can get crowded but is very expansive—if you wander south for 10 minutes or so, you can find isolated spots among the dunes; after about 20 minutes, you come to the nude, in places gay, sunbathing beach.

BICYCLING **De Volkenfietser** (⌂ Koningstraat 36 ☎ 023/532–5577) has bicycles for rent. You can also rent bicycles from **Peters** (⌂ Stationsplein 7 ☎ 023/531–7066).

### Shopping

The pedestrianized Barteljorisstraat has lots of chic chains, such as Vanilia, Esprit, and MEXX, as well as a number of street-wear shops for men, such as Man 2 Be. The top end of Kruisstraat has furniture shops, from antiques to designer, and a lot in between. Flowers can be found on Krocht, on the corner junction of Kruisstraat and Barteljorisstraat; the sumptuous displays echo the nearby tulip fields between Haarlem and the Keukenhof.

## Aalsmeer

**⑩** *14 km (9 mi) southeast of Haarlem, 14 km (9 mi) south of Amsterdam, 38 km (24 mi) northeast of The Hague.*

At Aalsmeer, about 19 km (12 mi) southwest of Amsterdam near Schiphol Airport, the **Bloemenveiling Aalsmeer** (Aalsmeer Flower Auction) is held five days a week from early to mid-morning. The largest flower auction in the world, it has three auction halls operating continuously in a building the size of several football fields. You walk on a catwalk above the rolling four-tier carts that wait to move on tracks past the auctioneers. The buying system is what is called a Dutch auction—the price goes down, not up, on a large "clock" on the wall. The buyers sit lecture-style with buzzers on their desks; the first to register a bid gets the bunch. Note that you can reach the auction hall by taking Bus No. 172 from the stop opposite the American Hotel, near Amsterdam's Leidseplein. ⌂ *Legmeerdijk 313* ☎ *0297/392185* ⊕ *www.vba.com* ⌨ *€4.50* ⊙ *Weekdays 7:30–11 AM.*

## Lisse & the Bulb Fields

**⑪** *15 km (9 mi) southeast of Haarlem, 30 km (19 mi) south of Amsterdam, 24 km (15 mi) northeast of The Hague.*

Fodor's Choice
★

How could you visit Holland and not tiptoe through the tulips? If you are in Amsterdam at the right time of year, it is easy to sample one of the best-known aspects of quintessential Holland—the bulb fields, in

# TULIPMANIA

**YOU MUST PREPARE YOURSELF FOR A SURPRISE**—*for a short period in spring, the landscape of Holland's fabled Tulip Country looks exactly like the color postcards you've seen. In a region set about 36 km (22 mi) south of Amsterdam, in the farmlands around the hub of Lisse, the fields stretch out as far as the eye can see on either side of the roads in a neat checkerboard pattern of brilliant color. The bluest of skies combine with the brilliantly colored living flower quilt to create a dazzling Technicolor world; colors appear clearer and brighter than you've ever experienced them. Little wonder that every April, buses, bikes, and tours packed with Hollanders and tourists drive down the Bloemen Route, attend the Bulb District Annual Parade (usually the last Saturday in April), visit the noted Keukenhof Gardens, and generally feast their eyes on the countryside, which looks like a 3-D Van Gogh painting—an unmissable trip for many travelers to Holland.*

an area around the town of Lisse, address to the famous Keukenhof Gardens. This flower-growing area to the southwest of Amsterdam is a modern-day powerhouse of Dutch production techniques, resulting in a blizzard of Dutch flowers falling on every corner of Earth in spring. For much of April, the bulb fields blaze with color: great squares and oblongs of red, yellow, and white look like giant Mondriaan paintings laid out on the ground (you're intrigued from the moment you see them from your airplane window). It is a spectacular sight, whether you travel through the fields by bike or bus, or pass by in the train on your way to Leiden.

Optimum viewing time used to depend on the weather during the final critical 10 days after the buds were fully formed. Now that much hardier strains are grown, your timing doesn't have to be perfect, but in general early to mid-March is still the best time to see crocuses, mid-March to early April is ideal for viewing daffodils and narcissi, and mid-April to early May is best for seeing the tulips and hyacinths (although the hyacinths tend not to last into May). By the middle of May the party is over, and most of the fields become no more than a sea of forlorn decapitated stems. Note that an early or late spring can move these approximate dates forward or backward by as much as two weeks, but for the most part you can bet that mid- to late April is the ideal time to be here. If the blooms don't cooperate, you can check out some of the great 17th-century Dutch floral still-life paintings in Amsterdam's Rijksmuseum.

Those paintings, in fact, should be discovered in any event, since they are telling evidence of "tulipmania," the astounding frenzy that broke out in 1630s Holland for the buying and cultivating of the tulip, recently imported from Turkey, which became a sort of 17th-century futures market. The rarest bulbs became more expensive than houses, only to have the whole market crash in due course, taking many fortunes with it. The first tulip bulbs were brought to Holland from Turkey in 1559. The name "tulip" was taken from *tulband*, the Dutch word for "turban," because of the blossom's appearance. In 1625 an offer of Fl 3,000 for two bulbs was turned down, but the speculation in bulbs became a mania during the years 1634–37, as irrational and popular as stock market speculation in the late 1920s, when fortunes were made—and lost—in a single day. One Semper Augustus bloom clocked in at today's equivalent of €4,000—little wonder the great artist of the time, Sir Peter Paul Rubens, was heard to lament that he could afford to buy only one tulip for his wife's birthday. Today, scientists diagnose the condition suffered by the rarest tulips illustrated in that era's books as viruses that caused abnormal (and beautiful) coloring or shape. The most famous aberration is the "black" tulip, which is really a very dark purple. This flower was immortalized in Alexandre Dumas's novel *The Black Tulip,* which deals with the saga to develop this strain in the 17th century.

The bulb fields extend from just north of Leiden to the southern limits of Haarlem, but the greatest concentration is limited to the district that begins at Sassenheim and ends between Hillegom and Bennebroek. The apparent artificiality of the sharply defined rectangular fields is not a concession to taste. It is part of the businesslike efficiency of an industry that has made tulip bulbs one of Holland's leading export commodities. Here it is the bulb, not the flower, that is the most important part of the plant. When the flowers are ripe, so to speak, they are cut off to divert the plants' energy back into the bulbs, leaving only the green stalks. The children play with the discarded blooms, threading them into garlands that they sell to passing motorists or making floral mosaics. If you're really serious about your tulips, be sure to visit the Hortus Botanicus in Leiden—it was here that Carolus Clusius, a leading botanist of the 17th century, promulgated the glamour and glory of this flower, and this garden remains a leading shrine for tulip-philes the world over. Another top destination is the annual **Bloemen Corso** (Bulb District Flower Parade), held on the last Saturday in April (except when Queen's Day—April 30—falls on a weekend, in which case it takes place the weekend before), a colorful procession filled with floats and marching bands along a 40-km (25-mi) route that extends from Noordwijk to Haarlem.

For a breathtaking bird's-eye view of Bloemen Corso, take to the skies and gaze down on the multihue pageant from above. Operating out of Rotterdam Airport, **Kroonduif Air** (☎ 010/415–7855 ⊕ www.kroonduif-air.nl) offers 60-minute scenic flights over the Bulb Fields in spring for €82 per person, based on a full plane load of three passengers.

Lisse is one of the hubs for the famed Bollenstreek Route (Bulb District Route), more popularly known as the **Bloemen Route.** Day-trippers from Amsterdam head here by taking the A4 southbound toward Leiden, then the N207 turn for Lisse, if venturing here by car. A quick route by public transport is to take the train from Amsterdam's Centraal Station to Leiden's Centraal Station and from there take Bus No. 54, aka the Keukenhof Express, which travels through Lisse when the gardens are open. Other modes of transport are to rent bikes from Haarlem or Leiden, or, more comfortably, take Bus No. 50 or 51 at the rail stations in either Haarlem or Leiden to disembark near a Van Gogh field you want to explore—Hillegom is a top village stop hereabouts. When the bulbs

are at their best, they are often "beheaded" (to ensure future gr
by armies of wood-shoed gardeners, who remind us that these bulb fie
are private property (so be circumspect about heading down any fiel
lanes). Tour companies and the local VVVs (tourist information offices)
also organize walking and bicycle tours, often including a visit to
Keukenhof. When you take a walking or bicycle tour, or independently
travel one of these ways following a map route, you get to experience
the subtle scents in the fields. You'll find roadside flower stalls selling
flowers, bulbs, and garlands.

The Bollenstreek was designed as a special itinerary through the heart
of the flower-growing region and laid out by the Dutch auto club,
ANWB. The circular route is marked with easy-to-follow, hexagonal,
dark-green (almost black)–on–white signs that read BOLLENSTREEK ROUTE.
It has no beginning or end, so you can start from anywhere. Starting
from **Leiden**, it circles north through **Rijnsburg** (site of one of Holland's
three major flower auction houses), where there is a colorful Flower Parade in August. The route takes you past the beach community of
**Katwijk**, and continues north through to the dunes beyond **Noordwijk**,
a vast, sandy nature reserve almost as big as the bulb district itself. Small
canals and pools of water are dotted about in between the dunes, providing a haven for birdlife. This is also a popular seaside resort, drawing Dutch, English, and German vacationers who rent rooms from
locals. You might want to make a brief stop along the way to see the
historic white church in **Noordwijkerhout**; although much of the church
has been restored, part of it was a ship that dates from the year 1000.
In the southern suburbs of **Haarlem**, the Bulb Route turns south once
more and passes through **Hillegom** and **Lisse**, the middlemost of the main
bulb towns, noted for its Keukenhof Gardens.

Continue south to **Sassenheim**, where there is an imposing 13th-century
ruined castle. From here, the loop is completed by heading to **Oestgeest**
and back to Leiden, but drivers should instead head west from Sassenheim on Carolus Clusiuslaan (at the northern edge of town) into the bulb
fields. After about a mile, head north again on Loosterweg, following
the zigs and zags of this country lane as it passes through the very heart
of fields overburdened with color. Presently you are back at Lisse again,
and can follow the signs for Keukenhof.

For six weeks from the end of March to the middle of May the 17-acre
**Keukenhof** (Kitchen Courtyard) park and greenhouse complex, founded
in 1950 by Tom van Waveren and other leading bulb growers, is one of
the largest living open-air flower exhibitions in the world. As many as
7 million tulip bulbs bloom every spring, either in hothouses (where they
may reach a height of nearly 3 feet) or in flower beds along the sides of
a charming lake. In the last weeks of April you can catch tulips, daffodils, hyacinths, and narcissi all flowering simultaneously. In addition
there are 50,000 square feet of more exotic blooms under glass. Unfortunately, Keukenhof is the creation of the leading Dutch bulb-grow-
ing exporters, who use it as a showcase for their latest hybrids. There
are many open gardens adorned with colorful flowers (even black tulips)
and gaudy frilled varieties. There is also a depressing lack of style—gar-

en after garden has bright floral mosaics, meandering streams, placid ools, too many paved paths, and hordes of people (more than 700,000 in average season). Any sense of history—Keukenhof's roots extend ....k to the 15th century when it was the herbal farm of one of Holland's richest ladies, the Countess Jacoba van Beieren—has been obliterated. Tulip time is famous here, but the grounds are occasionally opened for special shows at other times of the year. In the center of Lisse is a small museum devoted to the history of tulip growing, the **Museum voor de Bloembollenstreek.** For information about access to Lisse, by public transport, log on to www.9292ov.nl or call the main **info number** (☎ 0900/9292). ⊠ *Stationsweg 166a, Lisse* ☎ *0252/465–555* ⊕ *www.keukenhof.nl* 🎫 *€12.50* ☉ *Late Mar.–mid-May, daily 8–7:30.*

## Leiden

*35 km (22 mi) south of Haarlem, 45 km (28 mi) south of Amsterdam, 16 km (10 mi) northeast of The Hague.*

The town of Leiden owes its first importance to its watery geography—it stands at the junction of two branches of the Rhine—the "Old" and the "New." But as birthplace of Rembrandt and site of the nation's oldest and most prestigious university, Leiden has long continued to play an important part in Dutch history. A place where windmills still rise over the cityscape, Leiden offers the charm of Amsterdam with little of the sleaze. Despite its wealth and historical air, Leiden, it is often said, could not be pompous if it tried.

Cobbled streets, gabled houses, narrow canals overhung with lime trees, and antiques shops give the historic center a tangible feeling of history, and Leiden's university's academic buildings, the historic Waag (Weigh House) and the Burcht fortress, the stately mansions lining the Rapenburg—the most elegant canal in the town—and no fewer than 35 hofjes make it a rewarding place for a stroll. As you walk about, keep a watch for verses painted on lofty gables, a project started some 10 years ago. The proverbs, sayings, and poems now number more than 70, and are in a multitude of languages. Don't keep an eye out for any Rembrandt sightings: although he lived here for 20 years, Rembrandt left almost no trace of his life here—his birthplace was knocked down years ago (marked only by a plaque on a very modern wall). Even his actual birth date (1606 or 1607) is disputed. A Rembrandt "walk" is marked by the absence of any real site, although you can see where his sister Trintje lived and where his brother Adriaen worked as a cobbler.

With a university founded in 1575 (and a list of old boys including Descartes, U.S. president John Quincy Adams, and many a Dutch royal), Leiden's appeal is found in the mixture of musty-looking buildings, bicycles, brown cafés, and fresh-faced students, which gives the town zest and energy.

The historic center is marked by the Burcht, an 11th-century mound of earth with a fortification on top to control the confluence of the Old and New Rhine ("De Rijn," whence Rembrandt took his last name), which almost encircle it. Here there may have been a Roman colony, Lugdunum Batavorum, though no one knows for sure. The history of the town has been full enough without insisting on classical origins. The town's finest hour was in the 16th century, when the Spanish laid siege after the mayor, in a fashion typical of the age, rejected the surrender terms with a verse from the ancient Roman poet Cato. The siege went on and on, but relief came, incredibly, from the sea. The Dutch fleet sailed overland from lake to lake, breaking another dike every night so its advance could continue in the morning. On October 3, 1574, the ordeal was over, and the day has been marked by the distribution of loaves of bread and herring, as well as *hutspot* (stew) on that anniversary ever since. As a reward for its courage and steadfastness, William the Silent offered Leiden the choice between relief from taxes and the establishment of a university. With a sense of realism that has perhaps been overidealized, the rejoicing citizens concluded that tax relief would be only temporary at best, whereas a university would always be an asset. Leiden's professors were soon renowned all over Europe for their learning, their integrity, and their independence.

**a good walk**

Just a short stroll from the Stationsplein and the train station are the first of Leiden's many museums. Heading down Stationsweg, turn right just after crossing a small canal, to find the **Rijksmuseum voor Volkenkunde** ⑫ ▶, a museum with myriad marvels of African, Oceanic, Asian, American, and Arctic cultures, including a collection of Japanese artifacts so extensive that people make pilgrimages from Japan to view it. Head northwest from here and you'll hit the natural history exhibition, **Naturalis** ⑬, but if you're not a science buff, just head back directly over Stationsweg and continue on to Binnevestgracht to find the **Molenmuseum de Valk** ⑭, which allows you to study the innards of an 18th-century windmill. From here it is just a few blocks south to **Stedelijk Museum de Lakenhal** ⑮, a magisterial guildhall of the 17th century, replete with historic halls and a collection of fine old masters by Jan van Goyen, Lucas van Leiden, and others. Go west to Turfmarkt and head south over the Bostel bridge and left into Caeciliastraat. Bear slightly right at a small square, and you reach Leiden's famous collection of medical curios, the **Museum Boerhaave** ⑯. Retrace your steps to Turfmarkt, then continue south over the Rhine and left into Boommarkt, following the canal past the historic Waag (Weigh House), which occasionally hosts free art exhibitions. Beyond Stadhuisplein you reach the Korenbeurs Brug, or Cornmarket Bridge, an unusual covered affair from which there are magnificent views. North of the bridge are the **De Burcht** ⑰ fortification, the 14th-century Hooglandse or St. Pancas church, the small **Het Pilgrim Museum** ⑱, and the delightful St. Anna Almshouse, the oldest and one of the most beautiful in town. Head south to Breestraat, the narrow bustling street that forms the backbone of the old city. Around the front of the looming **Stadhuis** ⑲ (Town Hall), note the glorious 17th-century facade, all that remains of the original building, destroyed by fire in 1929.

Across from the Stadhuis, walk down narrow Pieterskerk Choorsteeg to the imposing mass of the **Pieterskerk** ⑳, the oldest house of worship in the city, where Thanksgiving Day services are offered every year by

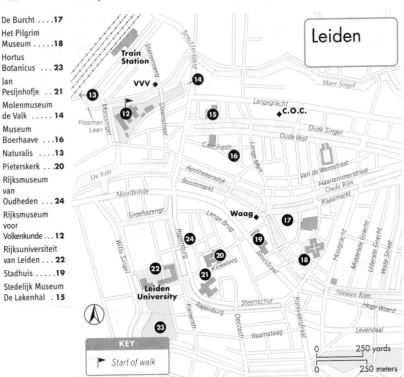

Americans to honor the Pilgrim Fathers who worshipped here. Opposite the church is the **Jan Pesijnhofje** ㉑, an almshouse founded in 1683 by a Delano ancestor of President Franklin Roosevelt. You are already in the student quarter, and the narrow street that continues southwest from the entrance of the almshouse leads across the charming Rapenburg Canal to the famous **Rijksuniversiteit van Leiden** ㉒ (Leiden University) area. Turn right here to reach the celebrated **Hortus Botanicus** ㉓ (Botanical Garden), which once showcased the greatest display of tulips in the tulip-mad 17th century. After viewing the gardens, continue north along the Rapenburg embankment and cross over at the next bridge to find the **Rijksmuseum van Oudheden** ㉔, which houses the largest archaeological collection in the land; then return several blocks eastward to Breestraat for your well-deserved time-out.

TIMING   It will take you 1½ to 2 hours to complete this walk, not including time spent in the museums.

## What to See

⓱ **De Burcht.** This medieval fortress, built around AD 1000, is perched high above the town on an ancient artificial mound, providing the best overviews of the city to be had. There is a defiant-looking carved lion at the entrance, with the words "Pugno Pro Patria" ("I fight for the Fatherland") underneath. It isn't a big lion, and it certainly isn't a big fortress, but it was here in 1574 that the town witnessed its finest hour: after a yearlong siege the population had been very close to being starved into submission when William broke down nearby dikes, flooding the ground around Leiden; whether the Spanish were more surprised than scared is not recorded, but it had the desired effect, because they fled as the water approached. William's timely arrival is remembered in the festival-like **Het Onzet van Leiden** (Relief of Leiden), an event celebrated every October 3, with much eating of hutspot, said to be what the starving townspeople fell on when they approached the then-deserted Spanish garrison. ⊠ *Nieuwe Rijn* 🎫 *Free.*

⓲ **Het Pilgrim Museum** (Leiden American Pilgrim Museum). This documentation center occupies a small 14th-century house furnished to illustrate what the Pilgrims' daily life was like before they left for the New World. Brief texts and 17th-century engravings tell the story of their extraordinary odyssey. You can get complete information here about the Pilgrim sites throughout the city, notably those at the Pieterskerk. ⊠ *Beschuitsteeg 9* 📞 *071/512–2413* ⊕ *www.pilgrimhall.org/ leidenmuseum.htm* 🎫 *€2* 🕑 *Wed.–Sat. 1–5.*

★ ㉓ **Hortus Botanicus** (Botanical Garden). Leiden University's renowned botanical garden is a leading shrine for tulip lovers the world over. Planted in 1594, the garden was meant to be a *hortus academicus* and was originally laid out by the greatest botanist of the age, Carolus Clusius, who had bounced around Europe surveying flowers and writing important studies for various societies and princely patrons, until an offer from the fledgling University of Leiden brought him to Holland. It is commonly reported that this garden was the first place tulip bulbs were planted in Holland, but this is far from the case. Dutch merchants with connections to Istanbul had decades before received bulbs as gifts, and before long they, and scholars like Clusius, were busy dispatching seeds to all corners of the land.

But it was here in Leiden that Clusius put the cap on a study of tulips, divining their schools and species, making distinctions between free-growing ones and hybrid cultivars, and bedding out his garden with wonderful displays of Couleren (single-color) and Marquetrian (multicolor) tulips, starting the enormous vogue for Rosen, Violetten, Bizarden, and numerous other species of tulip that came to rage in Holland in the following decades, leading to the Great Tulip Mania of the 1630s. Today, in addition to seeing the tulip beds of the original design, you can also find Clusius's garden laid out with extensive rose gardens, shrubs, and towering trees, as well as an orangery, a Japanese garden, and several hothouses full of orchids, giant water lily pads, and other rarities. ⊠ *Rapenburg 73* 📞 *071/527–7249* ⊕ *www.leidenuniv.nl/hortus* 🎫 *€4* 🕑 *Apr.–Oct., Mon.–Sun. 10–6; Nov.–Mar., Sun.–Fri. 10–4.*

㉑ **Jan Pesijnhofje.** This is just one of a number of Leiden's pretty hofjes. Centered on a tranquil garden and founded in the 17th century by a distant ancestor of President Franklin Delano Roosevelt, it marks the site where the Reverend John Robinson, spiritual head of the Pilgrims, lived and died (1625). Robinson had settled in Leiden a decade before his flock arrived on their *Mayflower,* but unfortunately fell ill before they departed for the wilder shores of America. Other Pilgrim sites nearby are the Pieterskerk and a plaque marking the Pilgrim Press on William Brewster Alley. Many of the city's hofjes are still used as residential accommodations for the elderly, so if you see a sign that says VERBODEN TOEGANG ("no entry"), respect their privacy. Other almshouses can be found at **Coninckshofje** (⊠ Oude Vest 15), **St. Stevenshof** (⊠ Haarlemmerstraat 48–50), and the **Groeneveldstichting** (⊠ Oude Vest 41). ⊠ *Pieterskerkhof 21.*

★ ⑭ **Molenmuseum de Valk** (De Valk Windmill Museum). Near the main train station, this enchanting windmill-turned-museum is the only survivor of 19 windmills that once lined the city walls. It began grinding grain in 1743 and is occasionally pressed back into service to produce wholewheat flour (which you can purchase at the mill shop). Perfectly preserved living quarters on the ground floor greet you as you clamber past massive millstones and head up seven stories to the top of the mill—stop on the way up to step out onto the "reefing stage," the platform than runs around the outside for a view of the city, where the gleaming canals remind us that they were once "paved with gold" (as thoroughfares used to ship the grain made at this windmill, and many others, to surrounding towns). Most afternoons from April to the end of September the sails of the windmill are put into operation—get your camcorders ready. ⊠ *2e Binnenvestgracht 1* ☎ *071/516–5353* ⊕ *http://home. wanadoo.nl/molenmuseum* 🖾 *€2.50* ⊗ *Tues.–Sat. 10–5, Sun. 1–5.*

⑯ **Museum Boerhaave.** Housed in the former Caecilia Hospital, this famed collection allows visitors to study five centuries of scientific and medical research. Highlights include Leeuwenhoek's original microscopes, early pendulum clocks crafted by Christiaan Huygens, and a reconstruction of a 17th-century "anatomy theater." ⊠ *Lange St. Agnietenstraat 10* ☎ *071/521–4224* ⊕ *www.museumboerhaave.nl* 🖾 *€6* ⊗ *Tues.–Sat. 10–5, Sun. noon–5.*

🐾 ⑬ **Naturalis.** The latest addition to Leiden's many science-oriented sights is this National Museum of Natural History. Displays include full-scale dinosaurs, minerals, and stuffed animals. Look out for a giant 2-foot crab. As a museum that especially appeals to children, there is a dedicated activity center for learning while playing. From the Volkenkunde museum, head northwest on the Plesmanlaan avenue and go under the railway tracks toward the A44; the first road on the right is Darwinweg, and Naturalis is on the Plesmanlaan avenue. ⊠ *Darwinweg 2* ☎ *071/568–7600* ⊕ *www.naturalis.nl* 🖾 *€9* ⊗ *Tues.–Sun. 10–6.*

⑳ **Pieterskerk** (St. Peter's Church). A stone's throw of the University of Leiden, the oldest church in the city is often surrounded by students sunning themselves in the church square. Dating from 1428, it is rarely used as a place of worship because its upkeep became overwhelming in the 1970s. Happily though, it hasn't been abandoned, but has diversified into hosting an extraordinary range of events, from fashion shows (with a catwalk stretching the magnificent length of the nave) to student examinations and graduation balls—it can even be rented for receptions for a bargain price. But history can still be found here. The grave of painter Jan Steen lies on one wall, and somewhere in an unmarked burial chamber Rembrandt's parents sleep on. More important to Americans (who gather here every Thanksgiving Day for a special service), one corner is devoted to the Pilgrim Fathers—Puritan refugees from English religious persecution—who often worshipped here. They had petitioned the city fathers in 1609 to relocate here from Amsterdam, which they found "torn by the spirit of controversy." Plaques inside and out pay tribute to the Reverend John Robinson, who was spiritual leader to this community of Puritans; his grave is here, because he grew ill before the Pilgrims set out on their momentous journey to the New World. A stroll from the church down Herensteeg brings you to a house (marked by a plaque) where William Brewster and his Pilgrim Press published the theological writings that clashed so strongly with the dogmas of the Church of England. ⊠ *Pieterskerkhof* ☎ *071/512–4319* ◫ *Free* ⊙ *Daily 1:30–4.*

★ ㉔ **Rijksmuseum van Oudheden** (National Museum of Antiquities). Leiden's most notable museum houses the largest archaeological collection in Holland. At vast expense, the layout and thematic grouping of antiquities have been overhauled, making the museum more aesthetically appealing and a delightful place to wander. Collections include pieces from ancient Egypt, the classical world, the Near East, and the Netherlands, from prehistory to the Middle Ages. Among the 6,000 objects on display, exhibits to look out for include the chillingly ghoulish collection of 13 ancient Egyptian human mummies, monumental Roman portraits, a complete set of Greek bronze armor from the 4th century BC, and the 3,500-year-old bronze "Sword of Jutphaas," discovered during dredging work in Nieuwegein, near Utrecht, and donated to the museum in 2005. In the entrance hall is the complete 1st century AD Nubian Temple of Taffeh, rescued from Egypt during the 1960s, when the Aswan Dam project drowned its original home. As you tour the galleries, you may encounter a "guide from antiquity" who will charmingly provide a "personal" perspective on the objects, which are further placed in context through elaborate scenery, scale models, film footage, and 3-D reconstructions. Temporary exhibitions are always exceptional here and meet the highest scholarly standards. ⊠ *Rapenburg 28* ☎ *071/516–3163* ⊕ *www.rmo.nl* ◫ *€7.50* ⊙ *Tues.–Fri. 10–5, weekends noon–5.*

> **need a break?**

**De Waterlijn** (⊠ Prinssekade 5 ☎ 071/512–1279) occupies one of the most attractive spots in town. Just past the end of the Rapenburg canal (which is itself lined with gracious buildings), this strikingly modern, glass-walled café on a moored boat offers views of old boats, gabled houses, and a windmill. The Dutch apple tart will please most.

▸ ⑫ **Rijksmuseum voor Volkenkunde** (National Museum of Ethnology). A leading showcase for the cultures of Africa, Oceania, Asia, the Americas, and the Arctic, this museum contains a fascinating collection of anthropological treasures. In particular, the Siebold Collection of Japanese art and artifacts is world famous; and the exhibits of Indonesia and Surinam artifacts—no doubt plundered during the Netherlands' colonization of these lands—are also most impressive. The building is large and you could happily get lost here without a floor plan. ☒ *Steenstraat 1* ☏ *071/516–8800* ⊕ *www.rmv.nl* 🎟 *€6.50* ☉ *Tues.–Sun. 10–5.*

**㉒ Rijksuniversiteit van Leiden** (Leiden University). Founded in 1575 in gratitude by William the Silent for Leiden's leading role in the Dutch Revolt against the Spanish, this university became one of the leading meccas of scholastic thought, drawing great thinkers and scientists of the 16th and 17th centuries, including the philosopher René Descartes. Today it is still one of the most respected academic establishments in the country, and the students preserve many time-honored traditions. The old university buildings are not open to the public—except for the celebrated Hortus Botanicus garden—but in the Academic Quarter, between the Rapenburg and Singel canals, students give Leiden a lively atmosphere.

**⑲ Stadhuis** (Town Hall). This was originally built in 1597, but the unattractive brick building you see today dates back to the 1930s, as the first structure was consumed by fire. All that was left was the beautiful front facade, which fortunately you can still see on Breestraat. Behind the Town Hall stands the sturdy 17th-century **Waag** (Weigh House), once the focus of the market square. Streets around here abound in names that end in "markt": Vismarkt (fish) to Botermarkt (butter) to Beestenmarkt (livestock).

**★ ⑮ Stedelijk Museum de Lakenhal** (Lakenhal Museum). Built in 1639 for the city's cloth merchants, this grand structure is adorned with decorations alluding to the manufacture of textiles. Leiden enjoyed a Golden Age of the late 16th and 17th centuries in both textiles and art. It was during this period that the city's artist community was most prolific, spawning three great painters of the time: Rembrandt, Jan van Goyen, and Jan Steen. Although few works by these artists remain in the city, this collection does have two early Rembrandts, though their rawness may come as a surprise to loyal followers. The museum has an impressive collection of paintings, furniture, and silver and pewter pieces, set in the sumptuous surrounds of a 17th-century Cloth Hall, a witness to Leiden's great importance in the wool trade. This is the building where the cloth was inspected and traded, and reconstructed guild rooms, replete with authentic antiques, show where the Guild Governors met. Galleries are hung with paintings by Gerrit Dou, Jan Steen, and Salomon van Ruysdael, as well as a grand collection of the works of Lucas van Leyden (another local boy made good), including his triptych, the *Last Judgment.* ☒ *Oude Singel 32* ☏ *071/516–5360* ⊕ *www.lakenhal.nl* 🎟 *€4* ☉ *Tues.–Fri. 10–5, weekends noon–5.*

## Where to Stay & Eat

**★ $$ ✕ Bistro La Cloche.** This chic, attractive French-Dutch restaurant, just off the Rapenburg canal on the small street leading to St. Peter's Church, is done up in soft pastels, with flowers everywhere. It has a pleasant though small street-side café, and quieter dining upstairs. Try their lovely crown of Dutch lamb with an herb crust and balsamic sauce, but leave room for one of their extraordinary desserts, such as the marzipan triangle stuffed with chocolate parfait and topped with Moreno cherry sauce. ⊠ *Kloksteeg 3* ☎ *071/512–3053* ⌦ *Reservations essential* ▤ *AE, DC, MC, V* ⊗ *Closed Sun.*

¢–$$ ✕ **Annie's Verjaardag.** A low-ceilinged, arched cellar, often full of chatty students, and a water-level canal-side terrace with great views, guarantee a special atmosphere no matter where you sit in this popular eatery. During the day, there is a modest selection of salads and sandwiches on baguettes, and at least one offering that is more substantial. After 6 you can choose from a fuller menu that includes cheese fondue, grilled trout, and spareribs. ⊠ *Hoogstraat 1a* ☎ *071/512–5737* ⌦ *Reservations not accepted* ▤ *MC, V.*

¢–$$ ✕ **M'n Broer.** Run by a pair of twins, "My Brother" is a cozy brasserie with a brown-café atmosphere. The kitchen serves up such hearty meals as seafood pie and roast duck with port sauce; the portions are generous, and the food is excellent. ⊠ *Kloksteeg 7* ☎ *071/512–5024* ⌦ *Reservations not accepted* ▤ *MC, V.*

$ ✕ **Entrekoos.** This restaurant shares a kitchen with its neighbor, 't Pannekoekenhuysje Oudt Leyden, but it has a totally different menu and a relaxed mood. The name is a phonetic Dutch pronunciation of *entrecôtes* (steaks), and a steak dinner, complete with vegetables, costs a mere €10. Despite the name, vegetarians are not neglected. ⊠ *Steenstraat 51* ☎ *071/513–5809* ▤ *AE, MC, V.*

¢–$ ✕ **'t Pannekoekenhuysje Oudt Leyden.** Besides pancakes, this Dutch-style restaurant has a small traditional menu with simple grilled and sautéed meats and fish. It shares a kitchen with its neighbor, Entrekoos. ⊠ *Steenstraat 49* ☎ *071/513–3144* ▤ *AE, MC, V.*

$$$ ▥ **Holiday Inn Leiden.** Just off the secondary highway between Leiden and The Hague and not far from the beaches at Katwijk, this is more a resort than a hotel. There is a vast interior garden lobby, and the decor of the guest rooms carries out the garden theme with bold colors and floral curtains. ⊠ *Haagse Schouwweg 10, 2332 KG* ☎ *071/535–5555* ⎁ *071/535–5553* ⊕ *www.holiday-inn-leiden.com* ⤳ *200 rooms* ⌂ *Restaurant, minibars, cable TV, in-room data ports, 5 tennis courts, pool, health club, sauna, bar, some pets allowed* ▤ *AE, DC, MC, V.*

★ $–$$ ▥ **De Doelen.** Placed right on the Rapenburg, the most elegant of Leiden's canals, this family-run hotel is in an old patrician mansion, dating from 1638. The communal rooms are gorgeous, wooden-beamed, and robustly decorated—traveling trunks, antique mirrors, and an enormous floral painting atop an ornate mantelpiece are some fetching accents. Guest rooms are comfortable, but it is worth paying more to get one of the deluxe species, on the first floor, which are more spacious, and have prettier, brighter furnishings. ⊠ *Rapenburg 2, 2311 EV* ☎ *071/512–0527* ⎁ *071/512–8453* ⊕ *www.dedoelen.com* ⤳ *16 rooms* ⌂ *Cable TV, in-room data ports, some pets allowed; no a/c* ▤ *AE, DC, MC, V.*

★ $–$$ ▥ **Nieuw Minerva.** Each one of the rooms in this glossy hotel, set in six 16th-century canal houses along De Rijn canal in the historical center of town, is individually decorated with great flair: the Red and White room is done in a country-gingham check, the Bridal Suite shines with an opulent four-poster in deepest red, and the Delft Blue room is decorated with traditional Delftware pottery. The Keukenhof room has old botanists' prints hanging above the bed, and bright flowery curtains and bedding. All of this means this place gives you a lot more than the average two-star. ⊠ *Boommarkt 23, 2311 EA* ☎ *071/512–6358* 📠 *071/514–2674* ⊕ *www.nieuwminerva.nl* ⟿ *36 rooms, 3 suites* ⚌ *Restaurant, cable TV, in-room data ports, 2 bars, some pets allowed; no a/c* ▭ *AE, DC, MC, V* ⦿ *CP.*

$ 🏨 **Mayflower.** This hotel, named, of course, after the Pilgrim Fathers' ship, is conveniently located on the Beestenmarkt, one of the main squares in Leiden. The rooms are light and pleasant, but the furnishings are somewhat outdated, with brown tiles in some bathrooms. It is, however, scrupulously clean, and boasts friendly service (rarer than you might expect). ⊠ *Beestenmarkt 2, 2312 CC* ☎ *071/514–2641* 📠 *071/512–8516* ⊕ *www.hotelmayflower.nl* ⟿ *25 rooms* ⚌ *Cable TV; no a/c* ▭ *AE, MC, V* ⦿ *CP.*

## Festivals

Many events and festivals take place in Leiden every year. The highlights include Leiden Jazz Week in January; the 10-day summer festival, the Leiden Lakenfeesten in July, which features music, street theater, and markets across town; and the celebration of the Relief of Leiden October 2–4.

## Nightlife & the Arts

The **Stadsgehoorzaal** (⊠ Breestraat 60 ☎ 071/513–1704 ⊕ www.stadsgehoorzaalleiden.nl) hosts musicians from all backgrounds, ranging from soloists supported by classical orchestras, to cabaret and jazz; this is one of the main venues for the Jazz Week festival. Every Thursday and Sunday jazz musicians from across Holland and beyond gather in a busy bar near De Burcht for aptly named sessions of "Jazz in De Burcht"—for information, contact **Societeit de Burcht** (⊠ Burgsteeg 14 ☎ 071/514–2389). Admission is free, but you're advised to hit the bar before the 10 PM kickoff, to be sure of a space to sit or lean.

If you feel like clubbing, head to **In Casa** (⊠ Lammermarkt 100 ☎ 071/512–4938), the biggest club in Leiden, with a capacity of 1,000. Cover charges start at €34. Call in advance to get information about which DJs are playing. Thursday focuses on 1970s and '80s beats, and Saturday is for '90s nights. Oddly enough, the club is closed most Fridays. The bar drawing the most hip twentysomethings is **Annie's Verjaardag** (⊠ Hoogstraat 1a ☎ 071/512–5737), which is one of Leiden's liveliest central spots.

## The Outdoors

BEACHES  Leiden's coastal resorts are at **Katwijk** and **Noordwijk**, in the dunes beside the North Sea.

BICYCLING  The place to rent a bicycle in Leiden is the **Fietspoint Oldenburger** (⊠ Stationsplein 3 ☎ 071/512–0068), next to the railroad station. They require a security deposit of €50 and legitimate ID.

CANOEING  A canoe may be the very best way to get a close view of the bulb fields that fill the countryside between Haarlem and Leiden. The **VVV Leiden tourist office** (⊠ Stationsweg 2d ☎ 0900/222-2333 ⊕ www.

leidenpromotie.nl) can provide help with boat rental, and h₍
out four different routes of varying lengths through the dune
regions. Ask, too, about the Singel sightseeing route through
canals and moats.

## Shopping

The old city center of Leiden proffers a wide variety of shops, with Haarlemmerstraat the street to head for if shopping is high on your agenda. Breestraat, which runs parallel to the Nieuwe Rijn canal, comes in a close second for choice, and the district between Pieterskerk and De Burcht holds the best antiques shops and boutiques. Shops stay open until 9 on Thursday *koopavond* (shopping night), and every last Sunday of the month is designated a special shopping day, with the majority of shops open. Leiden's bigger street markets are held in the city center on the Nieuwe Rijn on Wednesday and Saturday 9–6, and at Vijf Meiplein on Tuesday 9–2.

**'t Spieghel** (✉ Langebrug 91  ☎ 071/512–4958) has a gorgeous collection of antique French mirrors, most of which date from the period between 1850 and 1900. Many have gold-leaf or gilded frames. The shop is on the Langebrug (Long Bridge), which used to be a canal in the 17th century. So many bridges crossed the canal that from a distance it looked like one long bridge. **Van Catwijck** (✉ Langebrug 89a  ☎ 071/566–5244), in the former studio of Jacob Swanenburgh—one of Rembrandt's first tutors—has a wide variety of old-master paintings for sale, in addition to 19th- and 20th-century works. **Van Ruiten & Zn.** (✉ Korte Rapenburg 12  ☎ 071/512–6290) is one of the oldest antiques shops in the city. Manned by three generations of antiquarians, this shop has an extensive collection of antique silver, in addition to gold and silver jewelry. A plaque on the front of the building says that Gerrit Dou (1613–75), one of Leiden's great painters, once lived here.

# Delft

**Fodor'sChoice**  24 km (15 mi) southwest of Leiden, 14 km (9 mi) southeast of The Hague,
★  *71 km (44 mi) southwest of Amsterdam.*

With time-burnished canals and streets, Delft possesses a peaceful calm that recalls the quieter pace of the Golden Age of the 17th century. Back then the town counted among its citizens the artist Johannes Vermeer, who decided one spring day to paint the city gates and landscape across the Kolk harbor from a house's window on the Schieweg (now the Hooikade). The result was the 1660 *View of Delft* (now the star of the Mauritshuis Museum in The Hague), famously called by Marcel Proust "the most beautiful painting in the world." Spending a few hours in certain parts of Delft, in fact, puts you in the company of Vermeer. Imagine a tiny Amsterdam, canals reduced to dollhouse proportions, narrower bridges, merchants' houses less grand, and you have the essence of Old Delft. But even though the city has one foot firmly planted in the past, another is firmly planted in the present: Delft teems with hip cafés, jazz festivals, and revelers spilling out of bars.

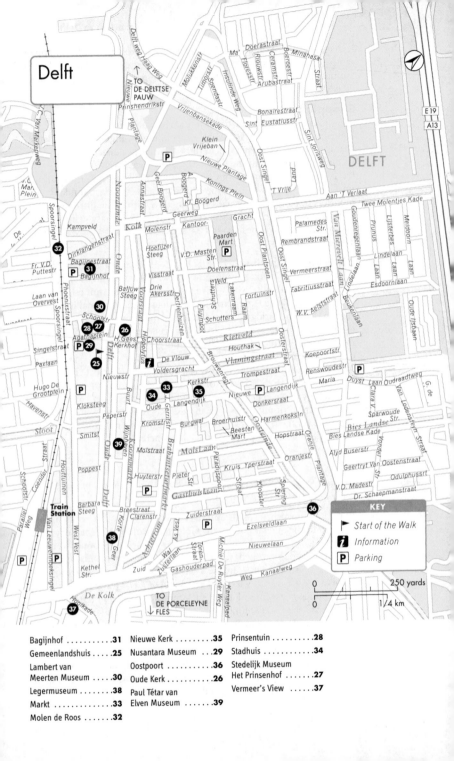

# Delft

TO
DE DELFTSE
PAUW

TO
DE PORCELEYNE
↓ FLES

Train
Station

DELFT

E 19
A13

**KEY**

► *Start of the Walk*

🛈 *Information*

P *Parking*

0          250 yards

0          1/4 km

For many travelers, few spots in Holland are as intimate and attractive as this town, whose famous blue-and-white earthenware has traveled around the world. Compact and easy to traverse, despite its web of canals, Delft is best explored on foot, although water taxis are available in summer to give you an armchair ride through the heart of town. Many streets in Oude Delft are lined with medieval Gothic and Renaissance houses, and tree-shadowed canals still reflect the same blue sky from which the pottery and tile makers of 350 years ago snatched their matchless color. At many corners you see a small humpbacked bridge or facade that looks as lovely as Delftware itself.

Everything you might want to see in this compact city is in the old center, where the best views are also to be found. Just across from the train station, walk up Westvest and turn right onto Binnenwatersloot—into the historic city center—to be greeted by a modern, sculptured interpretation of Vermeer's *Melk Meisje* (Milk Maid), in creamy-white stone. There are further sights to look at as you head down the pretty, tree-lined **Oude Delft** canal, which has numerous historic gabled houses along its banks and takes the honors for being the first canal dug in the city and probably the first city canal to be dug anywhere in the Netherlands. ▶ ㉕ The **Gemeenlandshuis** (⊠ Oude Delft 167) is a spectacular example of 16th-century Gothic and is adorned with brightly painted shields and a coat of arms. A few yards east of here, on the corner of Hippolytus-buurt and Cameretten, are a row of *visbanken* (fish stalls), built along the canal in 1650. Fish has been sold over the counter here pretty much ever since.

**need a break?** **Kleyweg's Stads-Koffyhuis** (⊠ Oude Delft 133 ☎ 015/212–4625) looks out over the oldest and one of the most beautiful canals in Delft. Inside, you'll find a *stamtafel,* a large table laid out with newspapers and magazines, where anyone may sit and chat. There are also smaller individual tables where you can enjoy good coffee, delicious pancakes, and terrific apple pie. In fine weather, the tables on the barge moored on the canal are very popular. The café is closed Sunday.

Following Oude Delft brings you to the very heart of historic Delft, where you'll find the grouping of the Oude Kerk, the Prinsenhof Museum, and ㉖ the Museum Lambert van Meerten. The Gothic **Oude Kerk** (Old Church), with its tower 6 feet off kilter, is the last resting place of Vermeer. The tower seems to lean in all directions at once, but then, this is the oldest church in Delft, having been founded in 1200. Building went on until the 15th century, which accounts for the combination of architectural styles, and much of its austere interior dates from the latter part of the work. The tower, dating to 1350, started leaning in the Middle Ages, and today the tilt to the east is somewhat stabilized by the 3-foot tilt to the north. The tower, whose tilt prevents ascension by visitors, holds the largest carillon bell in the Netherlands; weighing nearly 20,000 pounds, it now is used only on state occasions. ⊠ *Heilige Geestkerkhof* ☎ *015/212–3015* 🖃 *Combined ticket to Oude Kerk and Nieuwe Kerk €2.50* ☉ *Apr.–Oct., Mon.–Sat. 9–6; Nov.–Mar., Mon.–Sat. 11–4.*

★ ㉗ A former dignitary-hosting convent of St. Agatha, **Stedelijk Museum Het Prinsenhof** is directly across the Oude Delft from the Oude Kerk and is celebrated as the residence of Prince William the Silent, beloved as *Vader des Vaderlands* (Father of the Nation) for his role in the Spanish Revolt and a hero whose tragic end here gave this structure the sobriquet "cradle of Dutch liberty." The complex of buildings was taken over by the government of the new Dutch Republic in 1572 and given to William of Orange for his use as a residence. On July 10, 1584, fevered by monies offered by Philip II of Spain, Bathasar Gerard, a Catholic fanatic, gained admittance to the mansion and succeeded in shooting the prince on the staircase hall, since known as Moordhal (Murder Hall). The fatal bullet holes—the *teykenen der koogelen*—are still visible (protected by glass) in the stairwell. Today, the imposing structure is a museum, with a 15th-century chapel, a quaint courtyard, and a bevy of elegantly furnished 17th-century rooms filled with antique pottery, silver, tapestries, and House of Orange portraits, along with exhibits on Dutch history. ⊠ *Sint Agathaplein 1* ☎ *015/260–2358* ⊕ *www.gemeentemusea-delft.nl* ⊠ *€5; combined ticket to Het Prinsenhof, Nusantara, and Lambert van Meerten museums €6* ⊘ *Tues.–Sat. 10–5, Sun. 1–5.*

Between the Prinsenhof and the Nusantara Museum is the Agathaplein, a Late Gothic leafy courtyard, built around 1400, which has huge chestnut trees shading an adjacent green, and a somewhat cultivated square,
㉘ the **Prinsentuin** (Prince's Garden), which, if it's not too busy, is a calming place for a five-minute respite from the city streets.

㉙ The **Nusantara Museum** is in the same courtyard as the Prinsenhof Museum. It has a colorful and fascinating collection of ethnographic costumes and artifacts from the Dutch East Indies—most of it tragically pillaged during the 17th century by members of the Dutch East India Company. A large Javanese *gamelan* (percussion orchestra) takes center stage inside, and is surrounded by Indo-European batik, Hindu statuettes, shields and intricately carved spears, diamond-encrusted daggers, *wayang kulit* (shadow puppets), and a beautifully carved tomb. Other displays chart the history of the spice trade. ⊠ *Sint Agathaplein 4* ☎ *015/260–2358* ⊕ *www.gemeentemusea-delft.nl* ⊠ *€3.50; combined ticket to Het Prinsenhof, Nusantara, and Lambert van Meerten museums €6* ⊘ *Tues.–Sat. 10–5, Sun. 1–5.*

★ ㉚ Within the shadow of the Oude Kerk is the **Lambert van Meerten Museum,** a Renaissance-era, canal-side mansion whose gloriously paneled rooms provides a noble setting for antique tiles, tin-glazed earthenware, paintings, and an extensive collection of ebony-veneer furniture. Although much of the works on display are not the original patrician owner's (who lost a fortune when his distillery burned down and he had to auction off everything), the house and some of his collection was bought back by Van Meerten's friends. Note especially the great collection of tiles, whose subjects range from foodstuffs to warships. The gardens here are alluring, with a spherical sundial, two busts, and a stone gateway leading the eye through to the tangled woods beyond. ⊠ *Oude Delft 199* ☎ *015/260–2358* ⊕ *www.gemeentemusea-delft.nl* ⊠ *€3.50; combined*

# A BRIEF HISTORY OF DELFT

**DELFT HAS MORE THAN PAINTERLY CHARM**— it nearly rivals Leiden for historical import. Great men lived and died here. By the end of the 16th century Prince William of Orange (known as William the Silent) settled in Delft to wage his war against Spanish rule. He never left: in his mansion the founder of the nation was assassinated in 1584 by a spy of the Spanish Duke of Alva and buried with great pomp in the Nieuwe Kerk (New Church). Here, too, is buried Grotius, the great humanist and father of international law. Delft was also home to Anthonie van Leeuwenhoek, who mastered the fledgling invention of the microscope and was born the same year as Vermeer, 1632. Vermeer, many people will be interested to know, was just one of many artists who set up shop in Delft. Delft could support so many artists because it had grown fat with the trade in butter, cloth, beer and, in the 17th century, pottery.

The canal waters of Delft didn't always take a smooth course—literally. In the 17th century, the town's canal water became tainted, leading to a decline from 200 breweries to 20. In 1654 an accidental gunpowder explosion (the "Thunderclap") leveled half the town and killed hundreds, including Carel Fabritius, Rembrandt's most famous student and considered the leading master of the city. But Delft quickly rebounded, thanks to riches the city amassed as the headquarters of the Dutch East India Company. The porcelains brought back by their traders from the Far East proved irresistible, and in 1645, De Porceleyne Fles started making and exporting the blue-and-white earthenware that was to make the town famous. Civil war in China had dried up the source for porcelains, and Delft potters leaped in and created the blue faience that soon became known as Delft Blue.

---

ticket to Het Prinsenhof, Nusantara, and Lambert van Meerten museums €6 ☯ Tues.–Sat. 10–5, Sun. 1–5.

On the Oude Delft, beyond the Lambert van Meerten Museum, is a weather-beaten 13th-century Gothic gate, with ancient-looking stone re-
**31** lief, that leads through to a small courtyard, the **Bagijnhof.** The city sided with the (Protestant) Dutch rebels during the Eighty Years' War, and when the (Catholic) Spanish were driven out in 1572, the city reverted to Protestantism, leaving many Catholic communities in dire straits. One group of women was permitted to stay and practice their religion, but according to a new law, their place of worship had to be very modest: a drab exterior in the Bagijnhof hides their sumptuously Baroque church.

**32** Just to the west of Oude Delft is Phoenixstraat, where you'll find **Molen de Roos** (Rose Windmill), once a flour mill and originally on the town ramparts. The hexagonal base dates back to 1728. The platform encircling the mill about halfway up was restored in 1990. The mill sails get going every Saturday, when you can climb up the vertiginous stairs to get a view from the platform as the sails swoosh by. ✉ Phoenixstraat 111–112 ☏ 015/212–1589 ✆ Free ☯ Sat. 10–4, but only when a blue flag is flying from the sails.

**㉝** From the Oude Kerk area, head south several blocks to find the **Markt** square, bracketed by two town landmarks, the Stadhuis (Town Hall) and the Nieuwe Kerk. Here, too, are cafés, restaurants, and souvenir shops (most selling imitation Delftware) and, on Thursday, a busy general market. Markt 52 is the site of Johannes Vermeer's house, where the 17th-century painter spent much of his youth. Not far away is a statue of Grotius, or Hugo de Groot, born in Delft in 1583, who was one of Holland's most famous humanists and lawyers.

**㉞** At the west end of the Markt is the **Stadhuis** (Town Hall), but only the solid 13th-century tower remains from the medieval building. It rises above the surrounding gray-stone edifice, which has bright red shutters and lavish detailing, designed in 1618 by Hendrick de Keyser, certainly one of the most prolific architects of the Golden Age. Inside is a grand staircase and Council Chamber with a famous old map of Delft. You can view the Town Hall interior only by making arrangements through the Delft tourist office, which can also issue you a ticket to visit the torture chamber in Het Steen, the 13th-century tower. ⊠ *Markt 87* ☉ *Weekdays 10–4.*

**㉟** Presiding over the markt is the Late Gothic **Nieuwe Kerk** (New Church), built between 1483 and 1510. More than a century's worth of Dutch craftsmanship went into its erection, as though its founders knew it would one day be the last resting place of the builder of Holland into a nation, William the Silent, and his descendants of the House of Orange. In 1872 noted architect P. J. H. Cuypers raised the tower to its current height. No fewer than 22 columns surround the ornate black marble and alabaster tomb of William of Orange, designed by Hendrick de Keyser and son. Figures of Justice, Liberty, and Valor surround a carving of the prince, at whose feet is shown his small dog, which starved to death after refusing to eat following his owner's death. Below is the Royal Crypt, where 41 members of the House of Orange–Nassau are buried. Throughout the church are paintings, stained-glass windows, and memorabilia associated with the Dutch royal family. There are other mausoleums, most notably that of lawyer-philosopher Hugo de Groot, or Grotius. In summer it is possible to climb the 380-odd steps of the church tower for an unparalleled view that stretches as far as Scheveningen to the north and Rotterdam to the south. ⊠ *Markt 2* ☏ *015/212–3025* 🎟 *Combined ticket for Oude Kerk and Nieuwe Kerk €2.50, tower €2* ☉ *Apr.–Oct., Mon.–Sat. 9–6; Nov.–Mar., Mon.–Sat. 11–4.*

**㊱** At the eastern end of the Markt, you can take Oosteinde south to the twin turrets of the fairy-tale **Oostpoort** (East Gate), the only remaining city gate, dating back to 1400, with the spires added in 1514. Parts of it are a private residence, but you can still walk over the drawbridge. Although it is a short walk out of the center, the effort of getting there is more than rewarded with the view.

From Oostpoort, head west back toward the train station, taking Zuiderstraat or hewing instead to the canal bank over to the Zuidwal avenue, which leads to the site of Rotterdamse Poort. Here, at the south end of Oude Delft canal, cross the busy road to overlook the harbor; here is

**㊲** "**Vermeer's View**," for it was on the far side of this big canal that Ver-

# VERMEER: SPHINX OF DELFT

**AS ONE OF THE MOST ADORED ARTISTS IN THE WORLD,** Johannes Vermeer (1632–75) has been the subject of blockbuster museum exhibitions, theater pieces (Peter Greenaway's Writing to Vermeer), and best-selling novels (Tracy Chevalier's Girl with a Pearl Earring, transformed in 2003 into a sumptuous movie). He enjoys cultlike popularity, yet his reputation rests on just 35 paintings. Of course, those paintings—ordinary domestic scenes depicting figures caught in an amber light and in fleeting gestures that nearly anticipate cinema—are among the most extraordinary ever created. But Vermeer's glory is of a relatively recent vintage. He died at age 42, worn out by economic woes; at his death, a change in taste for a style of flamboyant art saw his name fall into total obscurity. Only in the mid-19th century did critics rightfully reattribute to him his masterpieces. Yet ever since Proust proclaimed his View of Delft (Mauritshuis, The Hague) "the most beautiful painting in the world," audiences worldwide have been enraptured by Vermeer's spellbinding work.

Like most artists, Vermeer courted fame, as his legendary Artist in His Studio (Kunsthistoriches Museum, Vienna) reveals. This imposing work (which long hung in his atelier to impress prospective patrons) shows Vermeer sitting at his easel painting a model garbed as Clio, the Muse of History. Her crown of laurels and trumpet, art historians have recently announced, prove that she is, instead, a symbol for fickle Fame. The expected Vermeerian icons—swagged tapestry, gleaming brass chandelier, map of Holland on the wall—are in place, but all eyes first fall on the figure of the artist, whom we see from behind. "This artist who keeps his back to us," as Proust put it, doesn't reveal his face, or little else. Indeed, the more books that are devoted to Vermeer, the less we seem to know of him.

How did he paint scenes of such an incomparable quietude, yet live in a house filled with his 11 children? Why are his early works influenced by Caravaggio, but there is no proof he ever visited Italy? His family was Calvinist, but did he convert when he married a Catholic wife? Did he use a camera obscura box to capture his amazing light effects? In an age fraught with drama—Holland was at war with France—why did he bar the outside world from his paintings? Such questions are difficult to answer, for between baptism and betrothal (a span of 20 years), the archives are totally mute about Vermeer. But we do know that his grandfather was arrested for counterfeiting money and that his father ran the heavily mortgaged inn known as the Mechelen, set on the Voldersgracht just a few paces from Delft's Nieuwe Kerk; his father also sidelined as an art dealer, as did Johannes himself. Vermeer's rich mother-in-law didn't want him to marry her daughter, but the artist won her over. He married Catharina Bolnes and enrolled as the youngest syndic of the Guild of St. Luke—Delft's thriving confraternity of painters—in 1654.

In the end, the only "reality" that matters is the one that Vermeer caught within the four walls of his house—but that unique universe is enough. His light captures the most transient of effects—you almost find yourself looking around to see where the sunlight has fallen, half expecting it to be dappling your own face. And then there is the telling way Vermeer captures an entire story in a single moment, as in the Glass of Wine (Staatliche Museum, Berlin). A man stands over a woman as she drains her glass, his hand firmly clasping the silver-lipped jug as though intending to refill it—laying the question of his intentions (is he planning to get her tipsy?) open to interpretation. Here, as always, Vermeer keeps us guessing.

meer stood when painting his famous cityscape. For a profile of the artist, *see* the Close-Up box "Vermeer: Sphinx of Delft," *above.*

A few blocks north of Zuidwal and not far from the main station is Delft's former armory, the **Legermuseum** (Netherlands Army Museum), which makes an appropriate setting for an impressive military museum. Despite the gentle images of Dutch life, the origins of the Dutch Republic were violent. It took nothing less than the Eighty Years' War (1568–1648) to finally achieve independence from the Spanish crown. In addition to the guns, swords, and other implements of warfare, all periods of Dutch military history are explored in detail, from Roman times to the German occupation during World War II. ✉ *Korte Geer 1* ☎ *015/215–0500* ⊕ *www.armymuseum.nl* 🎟 *€5* ☉ *Weekdays 10–5, weekends noon–5.*

Several blocks north of the Legermuseum is an 18th-century canal-side mansion housing the **Paul Tétar van Elven Museum,** created by a 19th-century painter. The interior is charmingly redolent of Ye Olde Delft, complete with painted ceilings, antiques, and even a reproduction of an artist's atelier done up in the Old Dutch style. ✉ *Koornmarkt 67* ☎ *015/212–4206* 🎟 *€2.50* ☉ *Apr.–Oct., Tues.–Sun. 1–5.*

If you want to purchase Delftware, head south of the city center to **De Porceleyne Fles** (The Porcelain Jar). The factory first opened its doors in 1653 and is the only one of the 32 major, 17th-century Dutch pottery works still in operation; tours are given through the facility, but you can also potter around by yourself. In one room is a stunning full-scale recreation of Rembrandt's *Night Watch,* comprising 480 handpainted tiles. Here you can also watch craftsmen as they work, applying black paint containing cobalt oxide, which turns to the fabled blue only when fired. The on-site gift shop is stocked with porcelain ware to tempt all shoppers. When you're all shopped out, you can unwind in the adjacent café, which looks out onto a leafy cloistered courtyard. ✉ *Rotterdamseweg 196* ☎ *015/251–2030* ⊕ *www.royaldelft.com* 🎟 *€4* ☉ *Mon.–Sat. 9–5; Mar.–Oct., also Sun. 9–5. Closed Dec. 25–Jan. 1.*

In addition to De Porceleyne Fles, visitors can also tour **De Delftse Pauw,** which offers tours through the pottery works to watch painting demonstrations. ✉ *Delftweg 133* ☎ *015/212–4920* ⊕ *www.delftsepauw.com* 🎟 *Free* ☉ *Apr.–Oct., Mon.–Sun. 9–4:30; Nov.–Mar., weekdays 9–4:30, weekends 11–1.*

## Where to Stay & Eat

★ $$$–$$$$ ✕ **De Zwethheul.** Delft's classiest restaurant is also its best hidden: set a little outside town, it can easily be reached by cab. In a restored 18th-century building, this award-winner actually began as a humble pancake house. In fine weather, you can eat on a beautiful terrace overlooking the Schie River. Specialties of the house include Bresse chicken ravioli with baked crayfish, and lamb in basil sauce. The sommelier and his wine list are among the best in Holland. ✉ *Rotterdamseweg 480* ☎ *010/470–4166* ♨ *Reservations essential* ▤ *AE, DC, MC, V* ☉ *Closed Mon. No lunch weekends.*

$$–$$$$ ✕ **Le Vieux Jean.** The tiny, family-run restaurant serves tasty meat-and-potatoes fare as well as good fish dishes such as *kabeljauw* (cod with

asparagus sauce). In the adjoining *proeflokaal* (tasting room) you can buy wine and spirits. ✉ *Heilige Geestkerkhof 3* ☎ *015/213–0433* ♨ *Reservations essential* ⊟ *AE, DC, MC, V* ☺ *Closed Sun. and Mon.*

★ **$$$** ✕ **L'Orage.** In cool shades of blue, with pristine white linen, Restaurant L'Orage has a sublime aura; as soon as you walk through the door, you anticipate the sensational dining options on offer. It is owned and run by Denmark-born Jannie Munk—Delft's very own prizewinning lady chef—who is now reaching out to a wider public thanks to the professional classes she offers in her kitchen. Her architect-husband, Pim Hienkans, was the mastermind behind the look of the place, accented by a huge, hinged glass roof to create an indoors-outdoors feeling. Munk creates delicious fish dishes, many based on recipes from her native country. Sometimes if the kitchen is in the mood, you'll be treated with *amuse-bouches*—three or four of the tastiest dishes on the menu in miniature—to accompany your drinks. Best bet for your main course is the roasted Welsh steak with truffle sauce. ✉ *Oude Delft 111b* ☎ *015/212–3629* ♨ *Reservations essential* ⊟ *AE, DC, MC, V* ☺ *Closed Mon. No lunch.*

★ **$–$$** ✕ **Stadscafé de Waag.** The ancient brick-and-stone walls of this cavernous former weigh house are adorned with hulking 17th-century balance scales. Tables on the mezzanine in the rear overlook the Wijnhaven canal, while those on the terrace in front nestle under the magnificent, looming, town clock tower. All the while, tastefully unobtrusive music creates a cool vibe for a mixed clientele. Happily, dishes such as Flemish asparagus with ham and egg, or *parelhoen* (guinea fowl) in a rich dark broth, are equal to the fabulous setting. ✉ *Markt 11* ☎ *015/213–0393* ⊟ *AE, MC, V.*

**¢–$$** ✕ **Café Vlaanderen.** Board games keep you entertained on a rainy day inside the extensive café, but sunny skies will make you head for the tables set under leafy lime trees out front on the Beestenmarkt. Out back is an equally shady garden. The deluxe fish wrap makes a delicious light lunch. ✉ *Beestenmarkt 16* ☎ *015/213–3311* ⊟ *MC, V.*

**¢–$** ✕ **De Wijnhaven.** This Delft staple has loyal regulars, drawn by the many terrace tables overlooking a narrow canal, music-festival-week songsters, and a mean Indonesian satay. There's a smart restaurant on the first floor, but the bar and mezzanine have plenty to offer, with lunch snacks, a reasonable menu for dinner with the latest tracks on the speakers, and great fries and salads. ✉ *Wijnhaven 22* ☎ *015/214–1460* ⊟ *MC, V.*

**¢** ✕ **De Nonnerie.** In the vaulted cellar of the famous Prinsenhof Museum, this luncheon-only tearoom has a sedate, elegant atmosphere. If you can, get a table in the grassy courtyard under an umbrella, and—since you're within the House of Orange—order an Oranjeboom beer to wash down the fine *Delftsche Meesters palet* (three small sandwiches of pâté, salmon, and Dutch cheese) served here. Entry is via the archway from Oude Delft into the Prinsenhof Museum, down a signposted path beside the gardens. ✉ *Sint Agathaplein* ☎ *015/212–1860* ⊟ *No credit cards* ☺ *Closed Mon. No dinner.*

**$$–$$$** ▦ **Best Western Delft Museumhotel & Residence.** Spread through a complex of 11 buildings and a warren of corridors, this sprawling hotel is opposite the Oude Kerk and adjacent to the Prinsenhof Museum. Unfortunately, the historic charm of the rooms was lost in an anonymous chain-hotel makeover—only the canal views compensate. As if to make amends, the management has cut loose with an over-the-top display of antiques in the public areas. ✉ *Oude Delft 189, 2611 HD* ☎ *015/215–3070* 🖶 *015/215–3079* ⊕ *www.museumhotel.nl* ⇨ *49 rooms, 2 suites* ⚲ *In-room safes, minibars, cable TV, in-room data ports; no a/c in some rooms* ⊟ *AE, DC, MC, V.*

**$–$$$** 🏨 **Bridges House.** The history of this hotel goes back to Jan Steen—one of the great painters of The Hague School—who lived and painted here. His contemporaries didn't recognize his talent, so he opened an inn and operated a brewery to supplement his income. The current owner has re-created a patrician's house in a tasteful refurbishment. Antiques grace each spacious room, all adorned with extra-long beds with bespoke Pullman mattresses. The bathrooms are fitted with enormous showerheads for a wake-up blast, and all have tubs. The breakfast room overlooks the canal. For longer stays, consider one of the apartments. ✉ *Oude Delft 74, 2611 CD* ☎ *015/212–4036* 🖶 *015/213–3600* ⊕ *www.bridgeshouse.com* ⇨ *10 rooms, 2 studio apartments* ⚲ *Cable TV, in-room data ports; no a/c* ⊟ *MC, V* ⧈ *BP.*

**★ $$** 🏨 **Johannes Vermeer.** It's surprising that no one else thought of it before, but this is the first Delft hotel to pay homage to the town's most famous local son. The buildings of this former cigar factory were completely modernized and turned into a sumptuous hotel in 2000. You'll be spoiled for choice of old-master views: rooms at the front overlook a canal, while rooms at the back have a sweeping city view that takes in three churches. In tasteful greens and yellows, the decor is unobtrusive, and the staff are pleasantly friendly. The garden behind the hotel is a mellow place to have a drink. The restaurant is open only for groups (advance arrangements essential). It's too bad, because the walls of the restaurant are adorned with painted copies of the entire works of Vermeer, with his *Girl with a Pearl Earring* inevitably taking center stage. ✉ *Molslaan 18-22, 2611 RM* ☎ *015/212–6466* 🖶 *015/213–4835* ⊕ *www.hotelvermeer.nl* ⇨ *24 rooms, 1 suite* ⚲ *Cable TV, in-room data ports* ⊟ *AE, DC, MC, V* ⧈ *BP.*

**★ $–$$** 🏨 **Leeuwenbrug.** Facing one of Delft's quieter waterways, this traditional and well-maintained hotel has an Old Dutch–style canal-side lounge, an ideal spot to sip a drink and rest up aching feet after a hard day's touring and shopping. The rooms are large, airy, and tastefully contemporary in decor; those in the annex are particularly appealing. Rooms at the front have canal views. The staff are very friendly and helpful, and often go out of their way to make guests feel welcome. ✉ *Koornmarkt 16, 2611 EE* ☎ *015/214–7741* 🖶 *015/215–9759* ⊕ *www.leeuwenbrug.nl* ⇨ *36 rooms* ⚲ *Cable TV, in-room data ports, bar; no a/c* ⊟ *AE, MC, V* ⧈ *BP.*

**¢** 🏨 **B&B Oosteinde.** This small yet friendly bed-and-breakfast is the only one of its kind in the city. Located behind the Beestenmarkt, near the fairy-tale twin towers of the city gate at Oostpoort, this welcoming house makes you feel like one of the family. Larger rooms can sleep three or four. A minimum stay of two nights is required. There are sinks in the

# BUYING DELFTWARE

**NO VISIT TO DELFT** *is complete without stopping off at the Royal Porcelain Factory to see plates and tulip vases being painted by hand and perhaps picking up a souvenir or two. These wares bear the worthy name of De Porceleyne Fles. On the bottom of each object is a triple signature: a plump vase topped by a straight line, the stylized letter "F" below it, and the word "Delft." Blue is no longer the only official color. In 1948, a rich red cracked glaze was premiered depicting profuse flowers, graceful birds, and leaping gazelles. There is New Delft, a range of green, gold, and black hues, whose exquisite minuscule figures are drawn to resemble an old Persian tapestry; the Pynacker Delft, borrowing Japanese motifs in rich oranges and golds; and the brighter Polychrome Delft, which can strike a brilliant sunflower-yellow effect.*

rooms, but bathroom facilities are shared. ✉ *Oosteinde 156, 2611 SR* ☎☎ *015/213–4238* ⊕ *www.bb-oosteinde.nl* ⌂ *3 rooms without bath* ⌂ *Cable TV, some pets allowed; no a/c* ▭ *No credit cards* ⦿ *BP.*

## Festivals

From February until December, there are annual festivals celebrating music, theater, and comedy. Highlights include the De Koninck Blues Festival in mid-February, held in 20 bars and cafés across the city; Queen's Birthday celebrations in April; canal-side concerts from the end of June through July and August; a week of chamber music during the last week in August at the Prinsenhof; the African Festival in early August; the Delft Jazz and Blues Festival at the end of August; a waiters' race in the Beestenmarkt in early September; and the City of Lights in mid-December. For more details, log on to (⊕ www.delft.com) or contact the **Delft Tourist Information Point** (✉ Hippolytusbuurt 4 ☎ 0900/515–1555).

## Nightlife

The most humming nightspot—in fact, the only club (nearly all others are students-only)—in Delft is **Speakers** (✉ Burgwal 45–49 ☎ 015/ 212–4446 ⊕ www.speakers.nl). Each night there is something different going on. Stand-up comedy, in English as well as Dutch, is usually on Wednesday, with concerts on Thursday; Friday night sees theme night (1970s, for instance); Saturday hosts the techno-beat crowd; and Sunday offers salsa parties. Open regular hours are a restaurant, bar, and sidewalk café.

## The Outdoors

BICYCLING   Bike rentals are available at the **railway station** (☎ 015/214–3033), open weekdays 5:45 AM–midnight, weekends 6:30 AM–midnight. Fees run €6.50–€7.50 per day, with ID and a security deposit of €50. For biking routes through Delft, Delfshaven, and Schiedam, get maps from the Delft Tourist Information Point.

### Shopping

In Delft, Friday until 9 PM is designated*koopavond* (evening shopping). A large weekly market is held every Thursday from 9 to 5 at Marktplein, with a flower market along the Hippolytusbuurt also on Thursday from 9 to 5. Every Saturday, there is a general market at the Brabanttse Turfmarkt/Burgwal. Saturday in summer, there is a flea market on the canals in the town center and an art market at Heilige Geestkerkhof.

DELFTWARE  **De Porceleyne Fles** (⊠ Royal Delftware Factory, Rotterdamseweg 196 ☏ 015/251–2030) is home to the popular blue-and-white Delft pottery. Regular demonstrations of molding and painting pottery are given by the artisans. The pottery factories of **De Delftse Pauw** (⊠ Delftweg 133 ☏ 015/212–4920), although not as famous as De Porceleyne Fles, produce work of equally high quality. **Atelier de Candelaer** (⊠ Kerkstraat 14 ☏ 015/213–1848) makes a convenient stop-off for comparisons of Delftware with other pottery.

# ROTTERDAM

As a city with few remnants of its fabled past, Rotterdam enjoys a future that is perhaps the brightest of all cities in Holland despite the terrible destruction that occurred on May 14, 1940, when Nazi bombs swept away some 30,000 homes, shops, churches, and schools in the course of a few brief hours. To the surprise of those who didn't know the vigor and hard-headedness of the Rotterdam Dutch, a new city of concrete, steel, and glass arose in the 1950s and '60s, phoenixlike, from the ashes of its destruction. And today—with some of the most architecturally important buildings of the beginning of the 21st century continuing to rise—a few pundits believe that were it not for the devastation of World War II, Rotterdam might never have become the dynamic and influential world port it is today.

Thanks to its location on the delta of two great river systems, the Rijn (Rhine) and the Maas (Meuse), and the enormous Europoort and North Sea projects, Rotterdam has become the largest seaport in the world. Through its harbors—and there are many—pass more tons of shipping each year than through all of France combined. New industry settled in (which the Rotterdammers greatly welcomed: "The question is not how large a tanker the channel will allow," one executive was quoted, "but rather how deep you want us to dredge it so your ship can get through"), followed by new populations. After the repair of the harbors in 1952, there was an increasing demand for labor, so recruits arrived from Italy, Spain, Greece, Turkey, and Morocco, followed in the 1970s by Cape Verdeans and Netherlands Antilleans.

The city divides itself into four main sectors but doesn't really have a central district. The **Kop van Zuid** and **Entrepot** districts are on the south side of the bridge. Here, famous architects such as Sir Norman Foster and Renzo Piano are designing housing, theaters, and public buildings to complete the area's transformation into a modern and luxurious commercial and residential district. **Delfshaven, Oude Haven,** and **Leuvehaven** are old harbors, but that's just where the comparison stops. In particularly charming Delfshaven you'll find a harbor so narrow it looks like a canal, lined with gabled houses dating back centuries and creating a classic Dutch scene. The Oude Haven, on the other hand, is surrounded by buildings not more than 20 years old, some of which, like the Blaak Rail station and Kijk-Kubus, are among Rotterdam's most-photographed buildings. **Museumpark** is known as the cultural heart of the city, because it is home to four museums and bordered by a Sculpture Terrace; you can museum-hop from collections of giant animal skeletons to city history to Golden Age art. (Incidentally, if you plan to visit a lot of museums, it is always worth buying a Museum Jaarkaart [Museum Year Card], or MJK for short; this pass gives you free entry to more than 440 museums throughout the country for a year and free entry to 15 in Rotterdam, and is available on showing ID at VVV offices and participating museums for €25.)

Like Amsterdam's, Rotterdam's name is taken from a river—in this case the Rotte, which empties into the Maas at this point. The city's birth extends back to the 10th century, when, despite the constant threat from the sea, a small group of early Rotterdammers settled on the Rotte banks along a small stream running through the boggy, peaty area. The settlement flourished, but it was not until the Golden Age (1550–1650), when Holland was a world power, that the city became a center of trade, home to both the United East India Company and the West India Company. The city's really spectacular growth dates from 1870 when the Nieuwe Waterweg was completed, a 17-km-long (11-mi-long) artificial channel leading directly to the sea.

## Along the Waterstad: From the Eastern Docklands to Delfshaven

Men like Erasmus, Grotius, Vermeer, Van Leeuwenhoek, and William the Silent walked the quays of Rotterdam in centuries past, but they would scarcely believe what has become of their harbor town today. They would be thoroughly lost wandering through 21st-century Rotterdam—and so would you: unlike most other cities, it doesn't have a historical city center. If you go to what is called the center of Rotterdam, you'll find yourself in the middle of a very big, rather bland shopping area. Rather, this tour wanders through the harbor-front areas of the city, covering a good amount of ground. Many "sights" on the tour are visual in themselves (you can't enter the buildings), but most buildings and artworks on this route show Rotterdam off in its best designer-cool mode. Many of the city's museums are included in our second Rotterdam walk.

The Nieuwe Maas River has flowed through Rotterdam for 700 years, dividing the city in two, and acting as the city's lifeline. A continual procession of some 30,000 oceangoing ships and some 130,000 river barges passes through Rotterdam to and from the North Sea. A top option for visitors to the city is boat tours around the harbor, ranging from a hydrofoil called the *Flying Dutchman* to the very popular **Spido boat tours** (✉ Willemsplein 85 ☎ 010/275–9988); a variety of water taxis and water buses also operate in the Waterstad (the docks and harbors along the banks of the river). There is also a water-bus link between Rotterdam and Dordrecht, which stops at several places along the way, including Alblasserdam, home of the famous Kinderdijk windmills.

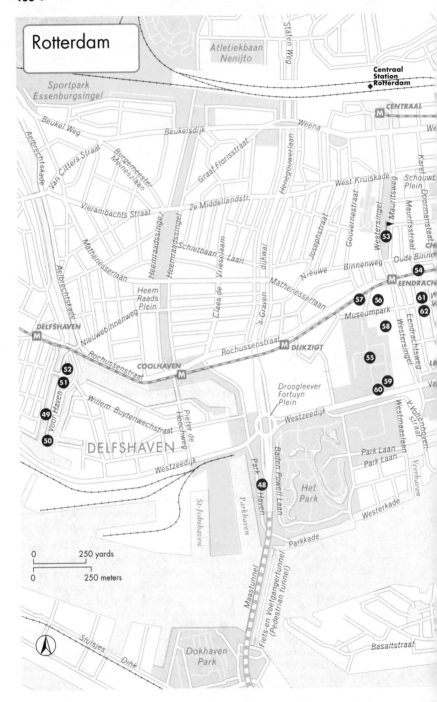

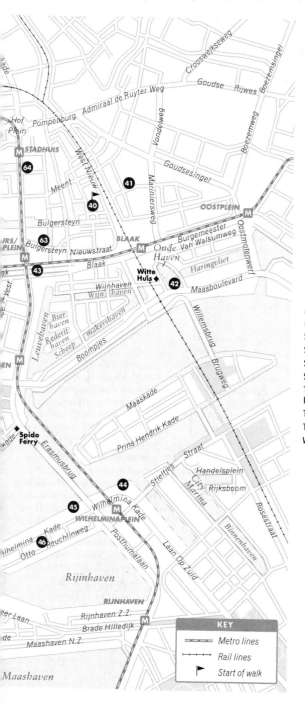

a good
walk

Begin at "The Kettle"—the train, tram, and metro station, **Blaak.** The simplest way to get here is take Tram No. 1 from the front of Centraal Station, which leaves every 10 minutes, getting off at tram stop Blaak. The Blaak station gained its nickname from its attention-getting roof, which has steel arches looping overhead. As you leave the station, heading toward the church at the far end of Binnenrotte square, you'll see, to your right, one of Rotterdam's most-photographed buildings, the precarious-looking **Blaakse Bos** (Blocks Forest), whose architect, Piet Blom, intended to create a "forest" with cubic shapes back in 1984.

Head first for the enormous church, the **Sint Laurenskerk** ⓭ ▶, which houses one of the biggest organs in Europe. If you're lucky, your visit may coincide with a rehearsing organist blasting out a tune.

Then walk around to the Grotekerkplein, the square on the far side of the Binnenrotte, where Hendrick de Keyser's statue of Erasmus stands. De Keyser is most famed as an architect, with Delft's ornate Town Hall his main showpiece. Turn and walk back the way you came, toward the gray-and-yellow cube houses to the left. If you fancy a trip to yesteryear, the **Nationaal Schoolmuseum** ⓮ is almost opposite Sint Laurenskerk, across the Binnenrotte square (walk down Librijesteeg to the Nieuwe Markt); here you can sit in a 1920s classroom and try your hand at writing with chalk on slate.

Back on the market square, head back to Blaak station, but bear left before reaching the tram stop, making for the direction of the spectacular, if somewhat kitschy, Blaakse Bos. On your left is a flight of nondescript concrete stairs; at their top, follow the enclosed avenue, marveling at these extraordinarily positioned houses as you walk. This route conveniently acts as a pedestrian bridge over the divided highway below, so when you leave No. 70, turn left and keep walking through this so-called "forest." Another flight of steps leads you down this side to the **Oude Haven** (Old Harbor). Walk left as you leave the cube houses, and you come to the cafés on the waterfront, perfect for a quick break. This area is called the **Openlucht Binnenvaart Museum** ⓯, or Open-Air Maritime Museum. Take your time walking around the harbor side—there are plenty of interesting old boats to look at—to reach the **Witte Huis**, or White House, which dates back to 1898, when it was Europe's first "skyscraper" (you can also take a time-out at the building's ground-floor café, 't Bolwerk, at Geldersekade 1c, which has a great view of the Oude Haven and Blaak station).

Take the cobbled road running alongside the Witte Huis, the **Wijnhaven.** You never know what might be moored alongside you here—expect tugs and yachts, even a navy warship. You have a short walk, not longer than five minutes along the Wijnhaven, walking past three bridges to your left. This is a real working harbor, where you are likely to see masts being re-varnished, and seagulls cawing overhead remind you of how near the sea you are. Walk up the length of the Wijnhaven. At the end of the pier turn right, following the water, toward the enormous statue ahead of you: the tragic figure of Ossip Zadkine's *De Verwoeste Stad* (Destroyed City), a metaphor of the Rotterdam that was shattered by bombs in 1940.

The big building to your left, across the small dockyard, is the **Maritiem Museum Rotterdam** ㊸, complete with small lighthouse and four boats, including the prize exhibit, the much-visited *De Buffel* warship. Walk around the front of the museum and cross the harbor via the pontoon bridge by *De Buffel*, returning along Wijnhaven to the last bridge you passed: the historic **Regentessbrug**, adorned with bronze lions mounted gracefully on pillars. Cross the bridge, and you're on Glashaven. You can either walk straight up this small street to Boompjes, the main road running alongside the Nieuwe Maas ahead, or, if you enjoy wandering along romantic old harbors, you can loop around three little harbors, with a path leading off to your right, along Wijnkade, where old ships are moored, taking you around the waterfront of Bierhaven, Rederijhaven, and Scheepmakershaven. The old boats stand in marked contrast to the modern cityscape around you. At any point you can make your way back to Glashaven and continue on. If you are walking around all three harbors, you can walk around only one side of the third, Scheepmakershaven. As you rejoin Glashaven again, turning to your right, walk up to Boompjes ("little trees"). Cross this busy road at the pedestrian crossing and walk to the Nieuwe Maas's waterfront to fully appreciate the vista spread out before you.

To your left stretches the red **Willems Bridge**, linking the north bank with the man-made island, and beyond it, connecting the island to the south bank, the vast green structure of De Hef, an ancient railway bridge. To your right is the enormous pylon of the Erasmus Bridge, which acts as an extension of the Coolsingel road, bringing the heart of Rotterdam straight down onto the Kop van Zuid district, shrouded in new buildings, many laden with interpretations as modernist statements. This is where you are headed next.

Turn now toward the **Erasmus Bridge**, and allow it to draw you nearer. The large pleasure boats docked on either side of the locally called Swan Bridge offer waterfront tours. One, the *Spido*, tours the new harbor area and the flood barrier toward the North Sea, and the other, bound for the opposite direction, is a tour that heads out to the giant windmills at Kinderdijk. You'll cross a small bridge to get to the Erasmus Brug bridge-ramp, but as it is incorporated into the road, you may not notice it. Built in 1996 at a cost of €160 million, Ben van Berkel's Erasmus Bridge is 2,600 feet long, with a 450-foot-high tower and an angled arm holding the suspension cables that has given it the nickname "The Swan." Once over the bridge take the pedestrian path off to the left-hand side, so you can get the best view of the Kop van Zuid developments.

As you begin to descend the far side, keep your eyes peeled for the curiosities all along the bank. Nearest the riverbank you can see what looks like a group of massive flattened mushrooms: the **Dynamic Rocks**, actually seats for pedestrians. Farther right is the **Tower of Numbers** ㊹ building, which, along with the nearby Garden of Lost Numbers, comments on past and future Rotterdam.

There is an enormous amount of upscale development on the Kop van Zuid, on the Wilhelminapier, and in the rejuvenated district (former warehouses) of the Entrepot—the latest in residential planning, which projects south of the marina. Inevitably, the commercial buildings are the most flamboyant and attract the most attention, but this tour also passes some strikingly designed housing developments. As you walk down the ramp onto the Kop van Zuid, turn left onto **Wilhelminakade Walk** down to the river, where you can sit on the Dynamic Rocks. Walk up to the Bridgemaster's House by climbing the raised walkway that looks down over the Garden of Lost Numbers. At the far end, return to street level. Cross the paving area to your right, and follow Wilhelminakade, turning left onto Stieltjesstraat to cross over the bridge. Continue on until you see an old segment of wall on your left, all that remains of the Gemeentelijke Handelsinrichtingen, one of Lodewijk Pincoffs' buildings. Pincoffs, a true pioneer of urban planning, initiated the development of this neighborhood in the 19th century.

Walk down Levie Vorstkade, the road immediately on your right, running alongside the Spoorweghaven (Railway Harbor), for about 100 yards until you reach the **Loods 24** installation. This is a memorial consisting of what appear to be five enormous swords protruding from the ground, with the hilts shielding large lamps. These towering lamps are far more than streetlights. Built in 1999 they symbolically refer to 50 years of Jewish liberation, memorializing lives lost in concentration camps. The name Loods 24 (Warehouse 24) refers to the former warehouse on Kop van Zuid where 12,000 Jewish Rotterdammers were made to gather before their deportation between 1942 and 1945.

From Levie Vorstkade, turn left onto Helmersstraat, following the walkway between two exclusive and modernist residential buildings. Ahead of you, you have a good view of the Vijf Werelddelen—a terrace of restored warehouses, now home to chic apartments with sumptuous balconies, and designer shops that cater to the residents. You'll also see the **City Marina**. Overlooking the marina is a small, old crane on four stilts with a flag hanging off it, a reminder of the working history of the area.

At the end of Helmersstraat, turn left on Louis Pregerkade, and head straight for the **Poortgebouw**, the old building directly ahead of you. Built in 1879, the former offices of harbor planner Lodewijk Pincoffs was supposed to have become a legal brothel in the late 1980s but is now home to a commune (which hosts vegetarian meals every Wednesday and Sunday).

From the Poortgebouw, head west, back along the Maas River in the direction of the Erasmus Bridge. As you recross the first small bridge on Stieltjesstraat, instead of heading toward the Erasmus Bridge to the right, go straight across Wilhelminakade and through the big glass doors into the Galleria, to **Wilhelminaplein**. The metro station is open normal hours, but the Galleria—the link between the station and the new buildings—is open weekdays from early morning to 7 at night only. A glass building with a soaring ceiling, the Galleria is worth a stroll. If you come on a weekend, when the Galleria is closed, turn right after crossing Wilhelminakade, and walk around the building, making sure to peek in the glass doors to see the massive square beyond.

Cross Posthumalaan. Ahead of you is the deep-red **Nieuw Luxor Theater,** another of Peter Wilson's projects. It is known for the technical wizardry of the interior. The building even has its own jetty. Opposite the Luxor Theater is Italian architect Renzo Piano's famous **Toren op Zuid** ㊺ office complex. Continue up the Wilhelminakade, passing a converted warehouse, 't Leidsche Veem, on your left. On your right, at Wilhelminapier 699, is Café Rotterdam, in the former departure hall of the Holland-Amerika Lijn; enormous cruise liners moor alongside the café these days. Almost opposite on your left is the **Las Palmas** ㊻ workshop, built in 1953, due to be the 2007 home of the Nederlands Fotomuseum. Just up on your right is Sir Norman Foster's Center for Maritime Simulation Training.

A little farther up the pier from the Maritime Simulation Center, ahead to your right, is the **World Port Center,** taken as the major work of Sir Norman's on the pier and completed in 2000. This 32-story building has a curvaceous facade, looking almost like a sail, swelling as it fills with wind. Sir Norman received the Pritzker Architecture Prize in 1999, an award also made to Renzo Piano and Rem Koolhaas. Rotterdam-born Rem Koolhaas's project **De Rotterdam** is planned for a spot between Piano's Toren op Zuid and Café Rotterdam. The complex is to be enormous, incorporating a massive multiscreen cinema, a hotel, a health center, a swimming pool, shops, and offices on the middle floors and housing on the upper floors. It will be one building but will give the impression of being three separate towers, 8 feet taller than Piano's Toren, and just 3 feet shorter than Sir Norman's World Port Center. The newest kid on the block, on the south side of the pier, is the striking 500-foot-high **Montevideo** apartment building; its slightly off-center sides make it look like a stack of giant boxes. Completed in 2005, it has become the highest residential tower in the Netherlands.

In the shadow of the Montevideo tower, the last building currently on the pier offers a stark contrast with the futuristic designs all around it. The Hotel New York, formerly the Holland-America Line (HAL) headquarters, was built in 1901 and renovated and opened as a stylish hotel in 1993. After stopping for a welcome drink in Hotel New York's bar, or on the terrace outside, walk toward the Rijhaven, a harbor on the far side of the pier from the Erasmus Bridge. On the dockside, take a ramp down to a water taxi, denoted by a small sign. Boats ferry passengers across the river regularly every 10 minutes (€2.50 one-way); most have an open top at the back, where you can get the best view. As you cross over the river to the opposite bank, look to your right for a view of the Erasmus Bridge. To your left is the Euromast, in the middle of Het Park. The boat docks in the pretty **Veerhaven,** an old yacht-filled harbor between two tree-lined quays. Turn to your right as you leave your water taxi, and walk along Willemskade, a renovated riverside street, now amply furnished with benches and trees in pots, making a very pleasant spot for a break. The enormous **Wereld Museum** ㊼ is on your left, four floors and with impressive exhibitions focusing on non-Western cultures, with excellent audio and video coverage, in addition to exhibits. After visiting the museum, walk back to the Veerhaven, keeping it to your left as you walk right around it. On the corner of Westerstraat is Loos, another top spot for a time-out if you didn't stop at Hotel New York.

Walk the whole way around this small harbor, taking in the picturesque moored yachts. On the opposite side of the harbor entrance is the Westerkade, so walk along this waterfront looking out across the river on your left. You pass several restaurants, the umbrella-shaded tables outside Zee Zout, and, farther up, the noted Dewi Sri restaurant. On your right is a park, the biggest in the city center, and simply called **Het Park**— it's where Rotterdammers head when the weather turns warm. When you reach the park, there is a path parallel with the river to your left, but you need to take one of the smaller paths cutting diagonally into the park, keeping the banks of the landscaped canal to your right. This takes you in the direction of the Euromast, but make sure you cross in front of the small gardens of De Heuvel, a gorgeous old private house. Cut left in front of the house, over a bridge taking you through a deep green and heavily foliaged grotto. If you're concerned about directions, look up, because you can't miss the **Euromast** ❽. As soon as you reach a bank, strike left to the footpath bridge over the divided highway ahead. Walking over the bridge takes you directly to the Euromast. You can go up it, for a fantastic panoramic view, and many added attractions; walk around it to the right, and walk up the green park ahead, keeping a harbor, Parkhaven, to your left. If you hear a high-pitched zipping noise, look overhead as a rappeler crazy enough to jump off the main viewing area of the tower plummets over the top.

You could end your walk at the Euromast, but if you have the time and energy to spare, it's worthwhile continuing on to the historic Delfshaven area. At the top of Parkhaven, the park-side harbor, take a left onto Westzeedijk. Wait at the first tram stop you come to for a No. 8 tram, traveling in the direction of **Delfshaven** ❾ to avoid a long and rather dull walk. On the tram don't get out at Delfshaven but at Schiemond. This drops you at the bottom of Voorhaven, a harbor so small it resembles a canal, and if you look back and to your right, you see the windmill that marks the beginning of the last stage of this walk. Although the housing in the area seems modern, it is just a shield, and the old merchant houses still stand here and about. To get to the mill, walk five minutes around the canal to your right, heading initially in the direction in which the tram departed. Take the first right, a path leading down a flight of steps, and follow the short path as it leads to a road ahead, Middenkous. Branch right, so the windmill is straight ahead of you, across the small harbor. As you round the corner, you are greeted with old historic facades similar to those of other city centers.

In this protected historical landscape, walk along the Voorhaven and marvel at the many old buildings that form an open-air museum. Take time to look at the flat-bow, shallow-bottom Dutch barges in the harbor. If you want to look inside a working mill, the **Korenmolen de Distilleerketel** ❺⓪ is open on Wednesday and Saturday. Nearby, a fascinating account of Rotterdam's history is found in **Museum de Dubbelde Palmboom** ❺①, or Museum of Double Palm Trees, which looks at the city's history as a "junction," with a special emphasis on Delfshaven itself.

From the museum, head up the harbor and take the first street on your right, Piet Heynstraat, named for the 17th-century Delfshaven-born sea hero. He is commemorated with a plaque on the door of the house where he was born, No. 6, and with a statue, found if you walk to the end of this street and go up the two flights of steps opposite: here on Piet Heyn-plein a raised belvedere with benches has him poised over the Achter Haven (literally, "the harbor behind"). You can see the windmill to your right, behind the houses, and there are yachts moored below. Go back to the harbor and turn right. As you continue up Voorhaven, look up to see a big sundial on the facade of the **Oudekerk/Pilgrimvaders Kerk** ☺ (Old Church/Pilgrim Fathers' Church); otherwise you might miss it, as its brickwork front totally melds into the terraces on either side. Next door to the church is the De Pelgrim café, the perfect place to take a well-earned rest at the end of this long walk. As the day draws to a close, you could have dinner at any of the charming cafés and restaurants here in Delfshaven. To get back to the center of town, head to the end of Ael-brechtskolk and turn left. The tram you need is just down the main road, the Schiedamse Weg—the stop is helpfully called Delfshaven. Tram No. 4 heading in the direction of Centraal Station picks you up here, taking you from this seedy end of Nieuwe Binnenweg to the Westersingel, renowned for its diverse restaurants and bars. The tram turns up the Westersingel to Centraal Station.

TIMING  Not including the time spent in museums, galleries, and vertically commuting up the Euromast, this walk takes approximately four hours—so, in effect, this tour can take an entire day, especially if you allow more time to look at galleries and antiques shops and plan on browsing. Note that most museums in the city are closed Monday.

## What to See

★ ⓯ **Delfshaven.** The last remaining nook of old Rotterdam, an open-air museum with rows of gabled houses lining the historic waterfront, Delfshaven is now an area of trendy galleries, cafés, and restaurants. Walk along the Voorhaven and marvel at the many historic buildings; most of the port area has been reconstructed, with many of its 110 buildings now appearing just as they were when originally built. There are several time-stained streets here, notably Piet Heynstraat. Piet Heijn was a Delfshaven-born sea hero (1577–1629), who captured a Spanish treasure fleet in 1628. His honor as Fleet Admiral was short-lived, as he was killed in a sea battle the following year. He is commemorated with a plaque on the door of the house where he was born, No. 6, and with a statue, found at the end of the street by the water, on Piet Heynplein, where a raised lookout point furnished with benches has him straining eternally toward this harbor, the Achter Haven, which was Delfshaven's first claim to fame.

To compete with the monopoly that Rotterdam had with its harbors, the authorities in Delft requested that the Earl of Aelbrecht (who ruled the area) allow them to have a private connection to the Maas River. The earl granted them permission, and the canal was dug by hand, between 1389 and 1404. This, as its very name attests, was the harbor of Delft, before the surrounding countryside made the entire area an urban settlement. The city made a living out of fishing; then, in the 17th century, riches arrived with the ships that the East India Company was bringing into the country. Here, too, traders of the malt whisky and *jenever* (Dutch gin) distilleries did a roaring business. Rotterdam annexed the harbor in 1886, but after the harbor mouth silted up, it was decided in 1972 to make Delfshaven over into a protected historic district.

For historic sights in Delfshaven's environs, check out the working mill of **Korenmolen de Distilleerketel** (open Wednesday and Saturday only), the fascinating **Museum de Dubbelde Palmboom** on Rotterdam city history, and the **Oudekerk/Pilgrimvaders Kerk.** In addition to housing these sights, the district is home to many bars, cafés, galleries, and antiques shops. Note that the affluent quays of pretty, ultraclean Delfshaven are juxtaposed with a vastly different surrounding area, a transition most marked at the top of Aelbrechtskolk, the lane leading off Voorhaven to the main road at the top, the Schiedamse Weg. Here, the litter-strewn, scruffy streets form a depressing sight, as it seems the city council doesn't care about its own residents, seemingly preferring to invest solely in the visitor area. As for locating Delfshaven, the street running alongside the Voorhaven starts off simply as Voorhaven to the south, from the windmill up, and becomes Aelbrechtskolk to the north, near the main road and tram line; Tram No. 4 connects Delfshaven with the rest of the city, as does the nearby Delfshaven metro station. ⊠ *Achterhaven and Voorhaven, Delfshaven.*

48 **Euromast.** For a great overview of the contrast between Delfshaven and the majority of the city, the Euromast provides a spectacular view of the city and harbor, if you can handle the 600-foot-high vista. Designed by Maaskant in 1960, it was for many years Holland's highest building; when a new medical facility was built for the Erasmus University, an additional 25 feet were added to the tower in six days, restoring it to its premier position. On a clear day, you can just about see the coast from the top. The tower not only affords panoramic views of Rotterdam Harbor, but also packs in a number of other attractions. The **Euroscoop** is a rotating panoramic elevator that carries you another 300 feet from the observation deck up to the top of the mast. Alternatively, take part in a rappel down (make reservations by calling the number below). The park at the base of the Euromast is where many Rotterdammers spend time when the weather is good. ⊠ *Parkhaven 20, Delfshaven* ☎ *010/436–4811* ⊕ *www.euromast.com or www.abseilen.nl* ⊡ *€8, rappel €39.50* ⊙ *Apr.–Sept., daily 9:30 AM–11 PM; Oct.–Mar., daily 10 AM–11 PM.*

50 **Korenmolen de Distilleerketel.** Set in the historic district of Delfshaven, this mill is the only working flour mill in the city. Formerly employed to grind malt to make jenever, the dusty-hair miller now mills grain for specific bakeries in the city, which means it is closed most of the week. ⊠ *Voorhaven 210, Delfshaven* ☎ *010/477–9181* ⊡ *€2* ⊙ *Wed. 11–5 and Sat. 10–4.*

46 **Las Palmas.** Built in 1953, this former workshop center is scheduled to be renovated into a major museum housing the Nederlands Fotomuseum in 2007. International photographs, films, and new media will compose

the collections. Check their Web site for the latest updates. ⊕ *www. nederlandsfotomuseum.nl.*

★ ✋ ❹ **Maritiem Museum Rotterdam.** A sea lover's delight, the Maritime Museum is Rotterdam's noted nautical collection. Appropriately perched at the head of the Leuvehaven harbor, it was founded by Prince Hendrik in 1874. Set against the background of modern and historical maritime objects, the seafaring ways of old Rotterdammers make more sense. The first floor is occupied with shipbuilding; on the second floor there are models, steam engines, cranes, and nautical instruments. Of note is the replica of the wooden figurehead of Erasmus from the ship *De Liefde* (Love), which was originally named *Erasmus. De Liefde* was part of a fleet of five merchant ships that attempted to find a new route to India and the Far East in 1598. The others were all lost, but *De Liefde* was the first European ship to reach Japan.

Children have half a floor dedicated to them, called, no less, "Professor Plons" (Professor Plunge), where museum staff are on hand to help with looking through a real periscope, donning a hard hat and taking to the driving seat of a scaled-down crane, and engaging in many other activities dealing with the themes of water and ships. Kids will also be gaga over the museum's prize exhibit, the warship *De Buffel,* moored in the harbor outside, dating back to 1868. The ship has been perfectly restored and is fitted out sumptuously, as can be seen in the mahogany-deck captain's cabin. ✉ *Leuvehaven 1, Witte de With* ☎ *010/413–2680* ⊕ *www.maritiemmuseum.nl* ☜ *€5* ⊗ *July and Aug., Mon.–Sat. 10–5, Sun. 11–5; Sept.–June, Tues.–Sat. 10–5, Sun. 11–5.*

❺ **Museum de Dubbelde Palmboom.** Devoted to the history of Rotterdam and its role as an international nexus, this museum traces the city's history from prehistoric times to the current day. The special and very fascinating focus is on how exotic wares imported by the East India Company affected the city. The building itself is literally redolent of history: not only do its heavy beams and brick floors waft you back to yesteryear, but there even seems to be a faint smell of grains, recalling its many years spent as a warehouse.

Ask for the very informative guide in English, as all the labeling is in Dutch. The first floor has some fascinating archaeological finds: one of the spouted ancient jugs, eye-catchingly red striped, has been traced to a town near Cologne, providing proof of trading contacts with the region, as traveling merchants were apparently very active in trading ceramics. One of the prettiest marine tile depictions shows the Maas River with a ship (named the *Rotterdam*), dating to 1697. There is a 1945 replica of a shipping agent's office, which would have been used by a representative of the merchants who used the route regularly to organize customs and the loading and unloading of goods. ✉ *Voorhaven 12, Delfshaven* ☎ *010/476–1533* ⊕ *www.dedubbeldepalmboom.nl* ☜ *€3* ⊗ *Tues.–Fri. 10–5, weekends 11–5.*

❹ **Nationaal Schoolmuseum** (National School Museum). In a 1920s classroom you can take a seat at an old desk and try your hand at writing with an ink-dip pen or using chalk on a slate, making for a charming journey back to the good old days. ✉ *Nieuwemarkt 1a, Meent* ☎ *010/404–5425* ⊕ *www.schoolmuseum.nl* 🎫 *€4* ⊙ *Tues.–Sat. 10–5, Sun. 1–5.*

**㊷ Openlucht Binnenvaart Museum.** This open-air maritime museum is a dreamy place to wander, looking at all the old Dutch barges moored up in a harbor that used to be reserved for seagoing vessels. Unfortunately, the modern architecture surrounding the pier makes for a rude contrast. This is a harbor that you walk around on your own—there is no guide, no gate, and no admission. ✉ *Oude Haven, Delfshaven.*

**㊿ Oudekerk/Pilgrimvaders Kerk** (Pilgrim Fathers' Church). On July 22, 1620, 16 men, 11 women, and 19 children sailed from Delfshaven on the *Speedwell.* Their final destination was America, where they helped found the Plymouth Colony in Massachusetts, New England. Puritan Protestants fleeing England for religious freedom usually went to Amsterdam, but this group, which arrived in 1608, decided to live in Leiden, then 10 years later opted to travel on to the New World by leaving from Rotterdam. On July 20, 1620, they left Leiden by boat, and via Delft they reached Delfshaven, where they spent their last night in Holland. After a sermon from their vicar, John Robinson, in what has since become this church, they boarded the *Speedwell,* sailing to Southampton, England, then left on the *Mayflower* on September 5, reaching Cape Cod 60 days later.

This church was built in 1417 as the Chapel of Sint Anthonius, then extended and restyled in the Late Gothic period. However, in 1761 the ceilings were raised, and the current style dates back to this Regency revamp, when an ornate wooden clock tower was also added. Next to the choir is a vestry from 1819, where you can find a memorial plaque to the Pilgrim Fathers on the wall. The bell tower has a tiny balcony. The church is now owned by the Trust for Old Dutch Churches. ✉ *Aelbrechtskolk 16, Delfshaven* ☎ *010/482–3041* ⊙ *Sat. 1–4.*

▶ **㊵ Sint Laurenskerk.** Built between 1449 and 1525, this church is juxtaposed against its modern surroundings. Of the three organs contained inside, the main organ ranks as one of Europe's largest. Hendrick de Keyser's statue of Erasmus in the square was buried in the gardens of the Museum Boijmans van Beuningen during the war and miraculously survived. ✉ *Grotekerkplein, Sint Laurenskwartier* ☎ *010/477–4156* ⊙ *Tues.–Sat. 10–4.*

**㊺ Toren op Zuid.** An office complex by celebrated modern architect Renzo Piano, this structure houses the head offices of KPN Telecom. Its eye-catching billboard facade glitters with 1,000-odd green lamps flashing on and off, creating images provided by the city of Rotterdam, in addition to images provided by KPN and an art academy. The facade fronting the Erasmus Bridge leans forward by 6 degrees, which is the same as the angle of the bridge's pylon. It is also said that Piano could have been making a humorous reference to his homeland, as the Tower of Pisa leans at the same angle. ✉ *Wilhelminakade 123, Kop van Zuid.*

**㊹ Tower of Numbers.** Near Piano's Toren op Zuid structure is this creation of Australian architect Peter Wilson. The tower is topped by five LED (light-emitting diodes) boxes, hung from a mast, with digital figures showing, among other things, the time and the world population. This "fluxus" is in contrast to the fixity of the **Garden of Lost Numbers,** found below the yellow bridge-watcher's house designed as a series of numbers set into the pavement. These numbers refer to the city's decommissioned harbor, all of which once were identified by numbers. As Rotterdam has such a heightened awareness of lost identity, these stainless-steel figures serve as a remembrance of things past. ⊠ *Wilhelminakade, Kop van Zuid.*

🖐 ④⑦ **Wereld Museum.** On a corner of rustic Veerhaven, surrounded by old sailing boats moored along modern yachts, this museum is devoted to non-Western cultures, many of which have had a sizable influence on Rotterdam. One of the permanent exhibitions is "Rotterdammers," which explores how the city developed in the 20th century with the arrival of immigrants from around the world. But another attraction is wonderful for children: the **Hotel "Het Reispaleis"** ("The Travel Palace" Hotel), a collection of "hotel" rooms of travelers from different countries that kids can explore either with museum staff or with parents, learning about other cultures as they visit the room of a "guest" in the "hotel" (who is supposedly out in town): knickknacks spell out the occupant's culture, job, and religion (one, for instance, is for a Moroccan photographer), and children are encouraged to try on clothes, shoes, and hats, and look in bedside tables to see what journals the guest has been reading. Video displays allow the guest to talk about his or her job, home, and friends (in pictures around the room). Result: children explore someone else's culture, seeing what is important to that person, in a "real" context. ⊠ *Willemskade 25, Scheepvaartkwartier* ☎ *010/270–7172* ⊕ *www.wereldmuseum.rotterdam.nl* ⊠ €6 ☉ *Tues.–Sun. 10–5.*

## The City Center & the Museum Quarter

Sightseeing in Rotterdam automatically divides itself into twin tours: the waterfronts (outlined in the above section) and the city center. Rotterdam's central nexus includes many impressive museums, but you'll also find art in unexpected places, such as the Sculpture Terrace near Centraal Station. Here, too, two popular parks face each other across the Westersingel: the Skate Park, Europe's largest—a reminder that Rotterdam is the only city in Holland where the youth population is on the rise—and the cultural heart of Rotterdam, the Museumpark. Architectural wizard Rem Koolhaas designed the Museumpark, an urban garden where you find four of Rotterdam's most dazzling museums. Juxtapose old masters, modern art, and industrial design at the Museum Boijmans van Beuningen; make sense of the city as a development in modern architecture at the Netherlands Architecture Center; explore a spectacular exhibition space that you spiral through in the Kunsthal; and marvel at giant animal skeletons in the Natural History Museum. The park itself is laden with modern and classical sculptures, providing a wealth of opportunities to chill out if an attack of museum feet or gallery gout strikes.

Other delights on tap are the galleries and cafés of Witte de Withstraat and the Center for Contemporary Art and the Netherlands Photography Museum, two outposts for the increasingly hip and hot Dutch avant-garde art scene. A dramatic change of pace awaits at the gorgeous 17th-century mansion, the Schielandshuis, now part of Rotterdam's historical museum. Beyond the Lijnbaan shopping district—radical in its day, it was the progenitor of the American shopping mall—the walk winds up with a visit to Rotterdam city's mayoral offices in the sumptuous 1920s City Hall.

**a good walk**

Start in front of Centraal Station, with your back to the station. Ahead of you across Stations Plein—the main square in front of the station—is an elegant building, the Millennium Tower. Walk toward it, being careful of the trams, bikes, and taxis. When you reach the tower, go around it, to the right, onto Kruisplein. Continue down the street, which, once separated by a canal, becomes Mauritsweg on the left-hand side and Westersingel on the right. After crossing West Kruiskade, about halfway down the road is a long brick terrace along a grassy-banked canal: the **Sculpture Terrace** ⑬ ▶, one of Rotterdam's city council's most celebrated recent projects. Take a seat on a nearby bench and make your own interpretation of masterworks by such sculptors as Rodin and Henri Laurens.

Continue up the Westersingel, crossing to the left-hand side, to turn left onto Westblaak to head to the Skate Park. If you plan to omit this leg, don't take the turn, but continue straight (the walk catches up later on the Westersingel). The **Skate Park** ⑭ is on the central traffic island, so massive screens are in place to prevent motorists from watching daredevil kids jumping off high-sided half-pipes. After you've watched (or participated) to your fill, double back to the Westersingel. Turn left and walk up the right-hand side, taking the next road on the right, called Museumpark, which leads to the city's famous **Museum Quarter,** with its four major museums and the **Museumpark** ⑮. Two minutes up the road on the left is the celebrated Museum Boijmans van Beuningen. You have a chance to visit this colossal gallery shortly, but first continue on to the white house on your right, the **Chabot Museum** ⑯, with works on view by the leading Dutch expressionist painter and sculptor Henk Chabot. When you come out of the Chabot Museum, turn right for one more stop-off before the Boijmans: take the ramp over the fountain to the **Nederlands Architectuurinstituut** ⑰ (or NAI; Netherlands Architecture Institute), paying close attention to the extraordinary sculpture on your left, Auke de Vries's installation, essentially a frame built out of the water, accented with metal spirals. The NAi hosts temporary displays on architecture and interior design in seven exhibition spaces.

Turn to your left, and walk across the open square to the **Museum Boijmans van Beuningen** ⑱, the greatest of all Rotterdam's museums, with a celebrated array of old-master paintings. In the gardens in the back of the museum, there are a number of old and new artworks; Claes Oldenburg's modern *Screw Arch* occupies center position in front of the museum's glass-front café, which is set among eerily black pools. Leaving the museum's gardens, turn right and walk back to the square and head left via the main path through the central gardens of the Museumpark, a project masterminded by design great Rem Koolhaas and his Office for Metropolitan Architecture (OMA). Walking over the bridge lands you neatly on a small square in front of the Kunsthal (on your left) and the Natuurmuseum (on your right).

The **Kunsthal** 59 is a huge, warehouse-looking building, which breaks the mold for traditional galleries with its nonsequential spiraling route through rooms. The Kunsthal's café is the perfect spot for a break, set under trees and opposite the **Natuurmuseum** 60, or Natural History Museum, in a pretty villa with an enormous modern extension. From the Natuurmuseum, walk up the central ramp of the Kunsthal to get up onto the top of the dike and to the Westzeedijk road. Turn left on the dike and walk up to the junction ahead where a left takes you to the bottom end of Westersingel and what is now Eendrachtsweg. Walk back toward the center of town along this tree-lined street. At the first main junction, the road to the left is Museumpark (which you took earlier), so take the road on the right, Witte de Withstraat, a street renowned for its galleries and fabulous cafés. Stop off at any point along the way, but don't miss the **Nederlands Fotomuseum** 61, Holland's Photography Museum. Although it doesn't have any permanent exhibitions, the temporary shows focus on serious talent, crossing the spectrum in styles and themes.

Almost opposite is **TENT Centrum Beeldende Kunst** (Rotterdam Center for Visual Arts) 62, which showcases both established artists and new talent. Again, exhibitions are on a temporary basis, so you never know which artists you'll encounter. This place doubles as a massive dispenser of information about cultural events, and you can easily find out what's on view in city galleries. The building here is a work of art in itself, with massive crater shapes sculpting the facade. On leaving TENT, turn right and keep walking up the street, which becomes Schilderstraat, just before meeting the larger Schiedamse Dijk. Take a right down this street to have a look at the **Walk of Fame,** where various celebs have made handprints or, more unusually, footprints, framed in the sidewalk.

Next stop is the **Maritiem Museum,** so when you get to the end of the Walk of Fame, turn and double back, walking right up the Schiedamse Dijk to the junction, where the museum is on your right. If you missed the Maritiem Museum on our first walk of the waterfront, or haven't done that walk yet, take this opportunity to get in the picture by finding out more about Rotterdam's great history of shipbuilding—kids will love the "Professor Plunge" floor, with scaled-down, hands-on periscopes, boats, and tubs of water. Just behind the museum is Ossip Zadkine's *Destroyed City* statue, from which you can head to Het Schielandshuis. If you look across Blaak, you can see this 17th-century house, but you need to walk back to the junction of Blaak and Schiedamse Dijk, to the pedestrian crossing by the Maritiem Museum. Cross over, and bear right onto Korte Hoogstraat, to reach **Het Schielandshuis** 63, almost engulfed by the skyscrapers towering over it. This brave mansion manages to hold its own; as the only remaining building of the Golden Age in the city, it is appropriate that it now houses Rotterdam's history museum. Among its remarkable exhibits are vintage clothes dating back to the 18th century and the famous Atlas von Stolk collection of old maps.

After visiting the museum, turn left on Korte Hoogstraat, away from the Maritiem Museum. Take your next left when you reach Beursplein, and go down the steps into the shopping mall, officially called Beurstraverse but nicknamed "Koopgoot" (the "Shopping Gutter"). Walk under the road and through to the other side: this not only gives you a chance to window-shop but is also an opportunity to decide whether you admire this Pieter de Bruijn–designed, multiuse complex.

Walk up the steps of the far side, turn right, and walk around the square back to Coolsingel. The biggest department store in the city is now on your left: the Bijenkorf, or "beehive," a name referring to the patterning of the exterior. Opposite, across Coolsingel, is the **World Trade Center**. From the Bijenkorf, turn left up Coolsingel. Look to your right as you walk, where you see the post office and the City Hall, or **Stadhuis** ⑭, the only buildings dating from the 1920s in this area. You can look around part of the interior on weekdays. Cross the road from the Stadhuis to the Stadhuisplein, looking to your right at the fountain at the top of Coolsingel. There are several bars on your right as you cross Stadhuisplein, a popular hangout for the late-teen crowd. Beyond Stadhuisplein, turn left onto Lijnbaan. Following the need to re-create the city center post-1940, town planners decided to go for a completely new approach in their urban design, opening the area to projects such as Lijnbaan, which in 1953 heralded the launch of dedicated shopping precincts, separated from housing. It's aesthetically dull but historically important if you're interested in where the mall concept originated. Ahead on Lijnbaan, turn right onto Van Oldenbarneveldtstraat, one of the best places to look for designer wear.

Back on Westersingel/Mauritsweg at the end of Van Oldenbarneveldtstraat, turn right (the station will be ahead of you), then next right, onto Aert van Nesstraat to take you to the **Schouwburgplein.** This whole square was restyled by landscape designer Adriaan Geuze and has quirky features such as street lamps that double as sculptures. The Pathé cinema on the square is a postmodern statement, for it really is an architectural space more than anything else, with its upper cinemas perched on poles, enclosed by transparent walls, a fittingly futuristic touch to conclude this walk through modern Rotterdam. Finish with a well-deserved time-out at Café Floor, on the south side of the square.

TIMING    You can cover this walk in four hours with a few museum visits, and some much-needed breaks in museum cafés along the route. If you can't rush gallery viewing, however, you may need a full day to take everything in.

## What to See

⑤⑥ **Chabot Museum.** This museum displays the private art collection of leading Dutch expressionist painter and sculptor Henk Chabot, who was active between the two world wars, depicting peasants, market gardeners, and, later, refugees and prisoners. ✉ *Museumpark 11, Museumpark* ☎ *010/436–3713* ⊕ *www.chabotmuseum.nl* ✆ *€5* ⊙ *Tues.–Fri. 11–4:30, Sat. 11–5, Sun. noon–5.*

★ ⑥③ **Het Schielandshuis.** Staunchly defending its position against the high-rise Robeco Tower and the giant Hollandse Banke Unie surrounding it, this palatial 17th-century mansion is almost engulfed by the modern city. Happily, it holds its own as a part of Rotterdam's historical museum (the other half is the Dubbelde Palmboom in Delfshaven). Built between 1662 and 1665 in Dutch Neoclassical by the Schieland family, it burned down in 1864, but the facade survived, and the interior was carefully restored. Inside are Baroque- and Rococo-style rooms reconstructed from houses in the area, clothing from the 18th century to the present day, and the famous collection of maps, the Atlas van Stolk. Because of the frailty of the paper, only a tiny selection of vintage maps is on display at any one time, usually under a specific theme. The museum's café is in a lovely garden. ⊠ *Korte Hoogstraat 31, Centrum* 🕾 *010/217–6767* ⊕ *www.hmr.rotterdam.nl* ▢ *€3* ⊗ *Tues.–Fri. 10–5, weekends 11–5.*

**59** **Kunsthal.** The corrugated exterior of this "art house" sits at one end of the visitor-friendly museum quarter and hosts major temporary exhibitions: "Charlie Chaplin in Pictures" and "Parisian Painters—Renoir to Picasso" are two typical examples. There is no permanent collection, other than the massive, multistory boxlike center itself, for it was designed by architect-prophet Rem Koolhaas. Some say the design bridging the gap between the Museumpark and the dike is a clever spatial creation; others consider it ugly, pointing to the mix of facades in half glass, half brick, and half corrugated iron, which has led to rusted iron, stained concrete, and long cracks in the central walkway. The steep concrete ramp through the middle of the building, leading pedestrians up, mirrors the route through the galleries, which direct you up and around the exhibition spaces in a spiral. Critics point out elements that are not thought out, such as reaching the top of the gallery to find that the only way down is the route by which you came up. Others decry the glass upper floor, which makes for embarrassment or titillated viewing, depending on which side of the floor/ceiling you are on. The biggest complaint is the lack of elevator, compounded by the hazards of the central ramp, whose steep angle makes this a potential ski slope for wheelchair users. If you just want to look from the outside, the gallery's café, on the more-pleasing-to-the-eye side, is a lovely, tree-shaded spot for a coffee, but face your chair toward the park, not the busy avenue at the top of the dike. As with the Pathé cinema on the Schouwburgplein, this postmodern facade is not representative of the function behind it; rooms here can be adapted to provide any function, from exhibition space to theaters. Such is the way of the future.

A tiny history of Rotterdam-born Rem Koolhaas: after opening his renowned firm, the Office for Metropolitan Architecture (OMA), in 1975, he studied in London and at Cornell University before becoming visiting Fellow at the Institute for Architecture and Urban Studies in New York. While in the city, he wrote his landmark *Delirious New York, a Retroactive Manifesto for Manhattan,* published in 1978. He has been a professor of architecture and urban design at Harvard University since 1995, the same year in which the work of his office was the subject of a retrospective exhibition held in the Museum of Modern Art in New York. Many critics have dubbed him the architectural messiah of the 21st century; whether their prophecy is fulfilled remains to be seen. ⊠ *Westzeedijk 341, Museumpark* 🕾 *010/440–0301* ⊕ *www.kunsthal. nl* ▢ *€8.50* ⊗ *Tues.–Sat. 10–5, Sun. 11–5.*

**⑤⑧ Museum Boijmans van Beuningen.** Rotterdam's finest shrine to art, with
FodorsChoice treasures ranging from Pieter Bruegel the Elder's 16th-century *Tower*
★ *of Babel* to Mondriaan's extraordinary *Composition in Yellow and Blue*, this museum ranks as one of the greatest painting collections in Europe. If it's not quite in the same class as Amsterdam's Rijksmuseum or The Hague's Mauritshuis, it ranks a very respectable third. Created more than 150 years ago—when Otto Boijmans unloaded a motley collection of objects on the city, then greatly enhanced by the bequest of Daniel van Beuningen in 1955—it is housed in a stunning building ideally designed to hold the collections of painting, sculpture, ceramics, prints, and furnishings.

The greatest attraction here is the collection of old masters, housed in the first floor of the west wing (pick up a museum map at the front desk, as it is easy to get lost here). This survey of West European art extends from the 14th century to the middle of the 19th century. In particular 15th- and 16th-century art from the northern and southern Netherlands, and 17th-century Dutch painting are well represented, including painters such as Van Eyck, Rubens, and Rembrandt. Highlights include Bruegel's famous *Tower of Babel* (1563), a fascinating depiction of the Genesis 11:1–9 account of how the people of the land of Shinar used brick and lime to construct a city with a tower that would reach up to heaven. The Lord thought otherwise, preventing the builders from completing their task and scattering the peoples of Shinar abroad so that humankind, previously united by a single, common language, became divided into nations no longer able to communicate with each other. Bruegel had visited Rome, and his Tower of Babel is said to have been based on the Colosseum. He has painted the tower as an immense structure occupying almost the entire picture space, although spotted with microscopic figures.

Other notable works include Peter Paul Rubens's *Nereid and Triton* (1636), originally designed for the Torre de la Parada, a hall owned by King Philip IV of Spain. Carel Fabritius's great *Self Portrait* dates from 1650; Fabritius was Rembrandt's most gifted pupil, and this is one of the finest portraits in Dutch art. Jan van Eyck's *Three Marys at the Open Sepulchre* (1425–35) is the only panel by this father of the Early Netherlandish school still in Holland. Another classic on view is the Dutch master Hieronymous Bosch's *Prodigal Son.* The modern art section runs the gamut from Monet to Warhol and beyond, covering the period from 1850 up to the present, with famous works of Monet, Kandinsky, Magritte, and Dalí. German and American art and contemporary sculpture have been recently acquired, and the museum's holdings in contemporary art have become one of the major collections in Holland. In the Decorative Art and Design collection, both precious ornamental objects and everyday utensils dating from medieval times are displayed. The collection includes majolica, tinware, silver, glass, preindustrial utensils, and modern decorative art. The museum has extended this collection to emphasize the importance of industrial design.

In addition to an extensive collection of graphics, the Prints Room displays one of the world's largest collections of drawings. Numerous schools from the Middle Ages to the present day are represented. The collection contains work by such masters as Pisanello, Dürer, Rembrandt, Watteau, and Cézanne.

In the museum café, note the fantastic collection of chairs, each by a different designer. Nearby, more artworks embellish the museum gardens. ⊠ *Museumpark 18–20, Museumpark* ☎ *010/441–9475* ⊕ *www. boijmans.nl* ✉ *€7* ☉ *Tues.–Sat. 10–5, Sun. 11–5.*

**⑤⑤ Museumpark.** A project masterminded by Rem Koolhaas's Office for Metropolitan Architecture (OMA) in collaboration with French architect Yves Brunier, this modern urban garden is made up of different zones, extending from the Museum Boijmans van Beuningen to the Kunsthal. The idea is that each section is screened off from the last and creates a different impression—but each block of the garden isn't as radically different as this theory builds it up to be. The one part you should linger over is just before the bridge, where there is a memorial to city engineer G. J. de Jongh. Various artists had a hand in this, with Chabot responsible for the inscription on the wall and Jaap Gidding designing the beautiful mosaic at the base of the monument, which represents Rotterdam and its surroundings at the end of the 1920s. Sculptor R. Bolle designed the bronze railings, with harbor and street scenes from the period when De Jongh was working in Rotterdam. ⊠ *Museumpark to the north, Westersingel to the east, Westzeedijk to the south, and bounded by a canal on the west side, Museumpark.*

**☝ ⑥⓪ Natuurmuseum** (Natural History Museum). Located in a historic villalike structure together with an enormous glass wing (echoing the hip Kunsthal next door), the Natural History Museum lures in its visitors with glass views of exhibits within, including skeletons of creatures you'll be hard put to identify. As soon as you enter the foyer, you are face-to-face with a mounted scary-hairy gorilla. It doesn't stop there: in one room the skeleton of a giraffe stretches as far up as you can crane your own neck. Continue on to be met by a tiger and arching elephant tusks. There is an "ironic" re-creation of a trophy hunter's display, with turtles mounted on a wall, arranged according to size. In another area, a dinner table is set, with the skulls of a human, a cow, an anteater, a lion, a zebra, and a pig as guests. Before each of them is a plate laden with their respective dining preferences. Children, meanwhile, are especially interested in the 40-foot-long skeleton of a sperm whale. ⊠ *Westzeedijk 345, Museumpark* ☎ *010/436–4222* ⊕ *www.nmr.nl* ✉ *€4* ☉ *Tues.–Sat. 10–5, Sun. 11–5.*

**⑤⑦ Nederlands Architectuurinstituut.** Fittingly, for a city of exciting modern architecture, Rotterdam is the home of the **NAi**, or the Netherlands Architecture Institute. The striking glass-and-metal building—designed by Rotterdam local Joe Conen in 1993—hosts temporary displays on architecture and interior design in seven exhibition spaces, giving a holistic interpretation of the history and development of architecture, especially the urban design and spatial planning of Rotterdam. Outside, the gallery under the archive section is illuminated at night. ⊠ *Museumpark 25, Museumpark* ☎ *010/440–1200* ⊕ *www.nai.nl* ✉ *€6.50* ☉ *Tues.–Sat. 10–5, Sun. 11–5.*

**⑥ Nederlands Fotomuseum.** Although Holland's Photography Museum doesn't have any permanent exhibits, the changing exhibitions are well worth looking at, and there is an extensive library open during the week for reference. The museum is scheduled to move in 2007 to the Las Palmas building in the Kop van Zuid neighborhood. Check the Web site for information. ⊠ *Witte de Withstraat 63, Witte de With* ☎ *010/213–2011* ⊕ *www.nederlandsfotomuseum.nl* 🗺 *€3.50; combined entry with TENT Center for Visual Arts €5* ⊙ *Tues.–Sun. 11–5.*

▶ **㊾ Sculpture Terrace.** Set along the Westersingel, this outdoor venue exhibits sculptures of the past 100 years, dotting the grassy bank of the canal and creating a sculpture garden. Highlights here include Rodin's headless *L'homme qui marche* (Walking Man), Henri Laurens's *La Grande Musicienne* (The Great Musician), and Umberto Mastroianni's *Gli Amanti* (The Lovers), a fascinating jumble of triangular-shape points. *Westersingel.* ⊠ *Museumpark.*

**㊿ Skate Park.** If you plan on trying out the largest outdoor skate park in the country, it's best to head here in the morning, when it's not too busy. Rent in-line skates or roller skates for €10 for the day (you need to show ID and leave a deposit) from nearby Rotterdam Sport Import. ⊠ *Witte de Withstraat 57, Witte de With* ☎ *010/461–0066.*

**㊽ Stadhuis** (City Hall). At the top of the Coolsingel, this elegant 1920s building is the hallowed seat of the mayor of Rotterdam and is open for guided tours on weekdays. A bronze bust of the architect, Henri Evans, is in the central hall. With the neighboring post-office building, the two early-1920s buildings are the sole survivors of their era. ⊠ *Coolsingel 40, Centrum* ☎ *0800/1545 (toll-free).*

**㊷ TENT Centrum Beeldende Kunst.** The Rotterdam Center for Visual Arts is usually simply called TENT, an apt acronym for showcasing modern art by local artists of the last decade. Shows range from edgy, happening-now issues (such as squatting) to tranquil designs for city gardens. The ground floor is devoted to up-and-coming artists, and the upper floor exhibits established artists' work. Artists also have a workplace to experiment with new projects. All exhibitions are temporary, lasting a maximum of three months, so call ahead to find out about the current show. Every first and third Thursday of the month there is an exciting free evening program. ⊠ *Witte de Withstraat 50, Witte de With* ☎ *010/413–5498* ⊕ *www.tentplaza.nl* 🗺 *€2.30; combined entry with Nederlands Fotomuseum €5* ⊙ *Tues.–Sun. 11–6.*

**VVV Archicenter.** Rotterdam's main information center is also a gallery containing many of the architectural projects that have graced Rotterdam in recent years. Architectural tour maps and leaflets are available here, along with all sorts of information, including background on the many residential housing projects on the outskirts of the city. For lots more information on the city's dynamic and daring future architectural plans, also check out the Infracentrum Rotterdam, at Weena 705. Both these centers nicely supplement the role of the city's tourist office. ⊠ *c/o NAi, Museumpark 25, Museumpark* ☎ *010/436–9909.*

## Where to Eat

★ $$$$ ✕ **Parkheuvel.** Overlooking the Maas, this posh restaurant, run by chef-owner Cees Helder, is said to be popular among the harbor barons, who can oversee their dockside territory from the bay windows of this tastefully modern, semicircular building. Table are covered with cream-color linens and wood-frame chairs are elegantly upholstered. The service here is as effortlessly attentive as you would expect from an establishment that lays claim to the title of Holland's best restaurant. Luxuries such as truffles are added to the freshest ingredients, with the day's menu dictated by the availability of the best produce at that morning's markets. Kudos and salaams are offered up by diners to many of the chef's specialties, including the grilled turbot with an anchovy mousse and crispy potatoes. ⊠ *Heuvellaan 21, Centrum* ☎ *010/436–0530* ◬ *Reservations essential* ▤ *AE, DC, MC, V* ☾ *Closed Sun. No lunch Sat.*

$$$–$$$$ ✕ **Brancatelli.** Around the windblown environs of the Erasmus Bridge you can find several eateries specializing in Mediterranean cuisine, Brancatelli being the best. "Kitsch" is the word that springs to mind when you spot the large glass animals on every table; add a pre-programmed player piano, and you are going to either laugh or cringe. If you feel a smile tickling, then the (very) pink table settings won't be too much, either. The friendly staff really play on being Italian, making, as they say, "a nice evening" of it, especially for groups. A typical four- or five-course menu is usually fish-based. Even if the price pushes up your expectations, the presentation and sheer quality of the dishes justify the cost. ⊠ *Boompjes 264, Centrum* ☎ *010/411–4151* ◬ *Reservations essential* ▤ *AE, DC, MC, V* ☾ *No lunch weekends.*

$$$–$$$$ ✕ **De Engel.** The international kitchen of this former town house has created a loyal following, who flock here for excellent food, a sash-window view over the Westersingel, and intimate setting (tables are very close together). The very friendly staff are more than helpful with their recommendations, as are your next-table neighbors. For a special taste treat, try the truffle soup, or the skate wing with garlic sauce. Note that this is not the same establishment as Grand Café Engels, on the Stationsplein, which is much more mainstream. ⊠ *Eendrachtsweg 19, Centrum* ☎ *010/413–8256* ◬ *Reservations essential* ▤ *AE, MC, V* ☾ *Closed Sun. No lunch.*

★ $$$ ✕ **Kip.** Dark wooden floors, unobtrusive lighting, and a big fireplace make Kip's traditional interior warm and cozy. As befits the restaurant's name, the chicken breast (from a special Dutch breed called *Hollandse blauwhoender*) with truffles is the most popular dish, but the kitchen offers a whole lot more. There's always a daily-changing fish option, such as cod with saffron and fennel sauce, and plenty of meatier fare, such as veal in wild mushroom sauce. The menu must work, because this spot is always packed. In summer, a leafy garden at the back provides welcome respite from the bustle of the big city. ⊠ *Van Vollenhovenstraat 25, Scheepvaartkwartier* ☎ *010/436–9923* ◬ *Reservations essential* ▤ *AE, DC, MC, V* ☾ *No lunch.*

$$–$$$ ✕ **Loos.** In the grand style of Rotterdam's cafés, Loos has a range of international magazines and newspapers on its reading racks, and in a fun

gesture, six clocks with different time zones decorate one wall. You enter and see what looks like a forest of tables, but this trompe l'oeil effect is largely caused by a wall-size mirror. Palms create privacy between tables, and add to a feeling of outdoor dining. As for the food, some dishes are excellent, including such delights as roasted-pepper-and-smoked-apple soup with aniseed cream; monkfish with truffle-butter sauce; and steak with Armagnac-soaked raisins and a duck-liver-and-truffle sauce. If you want to eat less luxuriously, try the bar menu—but you will miss out. ⊠ *Westplein 1, Scheepvaartkwartier* ☎ *010/411–7723* ⊟ *AE, MC, V* ⊗ *No lunch weekends.*

$$–$$$ ✕ **Zee Zout.** On the corner of an elegant, riverfront terrace, around the corner from the old Veerhaven moored with old sailing ships, the charming "Sea Salt" restaurant mirrors the freshness of its sea-based menu in crisp linen tablecloths and its spotlessly clean open kitchen, where watching the staff work whets your appetite. A large fish mosaic on the wall looks out across the river to the floodlighted Erasmus Bridge; a window awning adds to the romance of the view. Try the turbot accompanied by thyme-and-rosemary-flavored polenta and snow peas. ⊠ *Westerkade 11b, Scheepvaartkwartier* ☎ *010/436–5049* ⚱ *Reservations essential* ⊟ *AE, DC, MC, V* ⊗ *Closed Sun. and Mon. No lunch Sat.*

$–$$$ ✕ **Asian Glories.** Reputed to be the city's best Cantonese restaurant, Asian Glories serves lunches, dinners, and Sunday brunches in a tasteful modern Asian interior or outdoors on its terrace. It's hard to choose what is most delicious; their dim sum, fresh oysters, mussels in black bean sauce, and Peking Duck consistently get raves from fussy eaters. Leave room for an exotic dessert such as ice cream with rice and red bean sauce. ⊠ *Leeuwenstraat 15, Centrum* ☎ *010/411–7107* ⊟ *AE, DC, MC, V* ⊗ *Closed Wed.*

$$ ✕ **Bla Bla.** Just around the corner from the historic heart of Delfshaven, this restaurant is always lively and frequently crowded. There is always a choice of four main vegetarian dishes, inspired by cuisines from around the world, and the menu changes often. Make sure you're having dinner on the early side to get the freshest ingredients—and a seat. ⊠ *Piet Heynsplein 35, Delfshaven* ☎ *010/477–4448* ⊟ *V* ⊗ *Closed Mon. and Tues. No lunch.*

$$ ✕ **Café Floor.** Adjacent to the Stadsschouwburg (Municipal Theater), Café Floor doesn't look too inviting from the outside, but the interior is modern, light, and airy; the staff are friendly; and the kitchen produces excellent food. Try the lamb brochette so tender the meat practically dissolves on your tongue. The delicious passion-fruit cheesecake comes from Café Dudok's kitchen. The beautiful garden at the back, and accompanying birdsong from the local fauna, make this a restful stop. This place is very popular with local and international regulars, so be prepared to be patient if you go late-ish on a Saturday. ⊠ *Schouwburg-plein 28, Centrum* ☎ *010/404–5288* ⊟ *AE, MC, V.*

$$ ✕ **Zinc.** This restaurant is wildly popular, and usually so packed that conversation must be carried on at sonic-boom levels. The staff's attention can't be faulted as they chirpily refill and replenish water, bread, and butter without being asked. The food, however, can be a disappointment, with dishes sometimes overcooked and poorly presented. Critics cluck over the open kitchen, where standards seem worrisomely

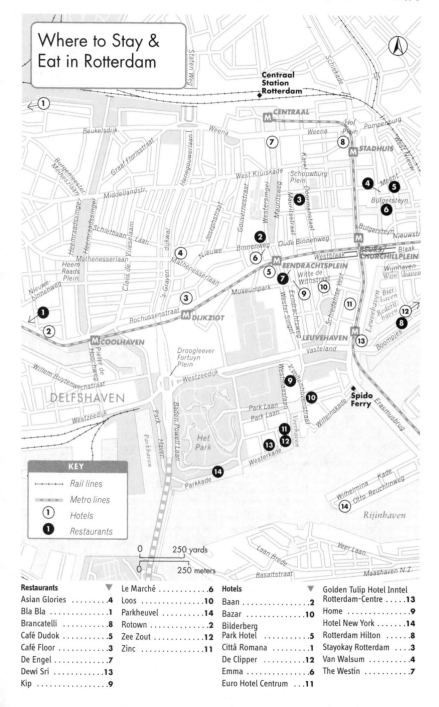

# Where to Stay & Eat in Rotterdam

**KEY**

| | |
|---|---|
| +−−−+−−− | Rail lines |
| ▭▭▭▭ | Metro lines |
| ① | Hotels |
| ❶ | Restaurants |

0     250 yards

0     250 meters

**Restaurants** ▼

| | |
|---|---|
| Asian Glories | .........**4** |
| Bla Bla | ...............**1** |
| Brancatelli | ............**8** |
| Café Dudok | ...........**5** |
| Café Floor | ............**3** |
| De Engel | ...............**7** |
| Dewi Sri | ..............**13** |
| Kip | ....................**9** |
| Le Marché | ............**6** |
| Loos | .................**10** |
| Parkheuvel | ...........**14** |
| Rotown | ................**2** |
| Zee Zout | .............**12** |
| Zinc | .................**11** |

**Hotels** ▼

| | |
|---|---|
| Baan | .................**2** |
| Bazar | ................**10** |
| Bilderberg Park Hotel | ....**5** |
| Città Romana | ..........**1** |
| De Clipper | ............**12** |
| Emma | ................**6** |
| Euro Hotel Centrum | ...**11** |
| Golden Tulip Hotel Inntel Rotterdam-Centre | .....**13** |
| Home | .................**9** |
| Hotel New York | .......**14** |
| Rotterdam Hilton | .....**8** |
| Stayokay Rotterdam | ...**3** |
| Van Walsum | ..........**4** |
| The Westin | ...........**7** |

low. That said, this is a leading Rotterdam-scene arena and hipsters will really enjoy the party. ⊠ *Calandstraat 12a, Scheepvaartkwartier* ☎ *010/ 436–6579* ⌂ *Reservations essential* ▭ *No credit cards* ☉ *Closed Mon. No lunch.*

$–$$   ✕ **Dewi Sri.** This restaurant has rijsttafel to dream about, with creative takes on traditional Indonesian dishes. Choose from a multitude of tantalizing options from Indonesian, Javanese, and Sumatran menus. Some diners may find the mock wood carvings a little heavy, given the subtle flavors of the food being served. The large restaurant upstairs could feel quite empty midweek, but the staff are incredibly polite, appearing discreetly at your table just as soon as you feel the need to ask for something. All in all, this probably has the best Indonesian food in Rotterdam, so don't let the decor faze you. If you can't find space in the Dewi Sri, it shares its premises with the adjacent Warisan restaurant, which serves similarly priced and equally mouthwatering Thai food. ⊠ *Westerkade 20–21, Scheepvaartkwartier* ☎ *010/436–0263* ▭ *AE, DC, MC, V* ☉ *No lunch July and Aug or weekends Sept.–June.*

★ ¢–$$   ✕ **Café Dudok.** Lofty ceilings, a cavernous former warehouse, long reading tables stacked with international magazines and papers—little wonder this place attracts an artsy crowd. At its most mellow, this spot is perfect for a lazy afternoon treat of delicious homemade pastries, but you can come here for breakfast, lunch, high tea, dinner, or even a snack after midnight. They also offer a small selection for vegetarians. The brasserie, on a mezzanine above the open kitchen at the back, looks out over the Rotte River. Since it's terribly crowded at times, you should get here unfashionably early to avoid disappointment—there's nowhere else like it in Rotterdam. ⊠ *Meent 88, Centrum* ☎ *010/433–3102* ▭ *AE, DC, MC, V.*

$   ✕ **Rotown.** This arts center venue is more celebrated for its funky bar than for its restaurant proper. A buzz fills the dining area, a spillover from the crowd up front. The menu is quite extensive, but the staff doesn't write down your order, so expect an informal, slapdash approach (if you're very unlucky, courses could even come in the wrong order, and a main course, brought out too early, will be reheated and returned later). But if you like a stylish, party-hearty atmosphere (bands often play at the bar), this could be worth it. ⊠ *Nieuwe Binnenweg 17-19, Centrum* ☎ *010/436–2669* ▭ *AE, DC, MC, V for dinner only.*

¢   ✕ **Le Marché.** A market stall in the V&D department store, Le Marche has a nice luncheon option: a tempting variety of reasonably priced sandwiches. On the top floor the self-serve café La Place transforms the roof into a sunny terrace in summer. ⊠ *Hoogstraat 185, Centrum* ☎ *0900/ 235–8363* ▭ *No credit cards* ☉ *Closed Sun.*

## Where to Stay

★ $$$$   ▥ **The Westin.** The only five-star hotel in the city is on the first 14 floors of the Millennium tower, smack opposite Centraal Station. Although this is primarily a business hotel, the slick-yet-friendly service of this landmark draws celebrity guests, such as pop and rock stars who perform at Rotterdam's celebrated Ahoy' concert theater, Robbie Williams and Kylie Minogue among the more prominent. With regal purple corridors, lined with copies of masterpieces from Vermeer to Van Gogh, and bright spacious rooms—each fitted out with a luxuriously huge bed, topped with a 10-layer mattress and sumptuous snowy-white linen—it's hard not to feel like a member of the glitterati yourself. All the lavish bathrooms have tubs. The panorama across town makes the extra rates for rooms from the fourth floor up more than worthwhile, with many looking out over the Erasmus Bridge and the skyline (both dramatically floodlighted after dark). In the Lighthouse restaurant, chef Fred Smits serves superb nouvelle cuisine. Try the Irish Black Angus beefsteak served with tiger prawns or the fried brill fish fillet with anchovy risotto and smoked emperor salmon, accompanied by crispy ham and salsify. In keeping with the spirit of Rotterdam, the decor has a maritime theme; even the bar is in the form of a ship's prow. Fans adore the four-course afternoon high tea. There's a glass-covered skywalk to De Doelen concert and business center on the Stadsschouwburgplein, so on concert nights make the most of the Lighthouse's special dining offers to see just how good the chef really is. ⊠ *Weena 686, 3012 CN, Centrum* ☎ *010/ 430–2000, 00800/325–95959 (toll-free within Holland)* 🖷 *010/430– 2001* ⊕ *www.westin.nl* 🗊 *224 rooms, 7 suites* ⚓ *Restaurant, in-room safes, minibars, cable TV, in-room data ports, Wi-Fi, health club, bar, laundry service, some pets allowed* ▤ *AE, DC, MC, V.*

**$$–$$$$** 🏨 **Bilderberg Parkhotel.** Although this hotel welcomes you with a townhouse facade dramatically yoked to a metallic skyscraper, its interior is fairly unexciting, both in terms of style and appearance. Rooms are decorated in traditional English style; higher-priced rooms are more modern looking. However, it does offer a wide spectrum of top-brass services. The Restaurant 70 serves a fusion of new style–global–traditional cuisine in the classical surroundings of the old wing of the hotel. Just a few minutes' walk from the Museum Boijmans van Beuningen, this spot is centrally located. Another plus is the staff, which offers the sort of apparently effortless, unobtrusive attention to your every need that makes a stay here very pleasant. ⊠ *Westersingel 70, 3015 LB, Centrum* ☎ *010/ 436–3611, 0800/024–5245 within Holland), 800/641–0300 (from the U.S.* 🖷 *010/436–4212* ⊕ *www.parkhotelrotterdam.nl* 🗊 *187 rooms, 2 suites* ⚓ *Restaurant, minibars, cable TV, in-room data ports, health club, sauna, bar, laundry service, some pets allowed; no a/c in some rooms* ▤ *AE, DC, MC, V.*

**$$–$$$$** 🏨 **Rotterdam Hilton.** During the International Film Festival at the end of January, this hotel often hosts some of the notable participants, thanks in part to its top facilities, a number of suites, meeting rooms, and luxury appointments and amenities. A major plus is its location, right in the middle of downtown. Since it tends to appeal to visitors who want a name they can rely on, it can get filled with tour groups. ⊠ *Weena 10, 3012 CM, Centrum* ☎ *010/710–8000* 🖷 *010/710–8080* ⊕ *www. rotterdam.hilton.com* 🗊 *246 rooms, 8 suites* ⚓ *Minibars, cable TV, in-room data ports, health club, hair salon, bar, lounge, laundry service, some pets allowed* ▤ *AE, DC, MC, V.*

**$$–$$$** 🏨 **Città Romana.** You generally don't think of resorts when you think of Rotterdam, but this vast place is considered a pleasant retreat set a half hour from the city center. More than 200 charming thatch-roof, gable-window cottages are stylishly furnished (although we could do without those mock-orange columns in the public areas). Located 10 minutes' drive from the North Sea and 5 minutes' walk from a local lake, Haringvliet, its villas come fully furnished and even have chairs and sun beds for the gardens. The living room is complete with open kitchen, and most villas have two bathrooms. ⊠ *Parkweg 1, 3220 AB Hellevoetsluis* 🕾 *0181/ 334455* 🖷 *0181/334433* ⊕ *www.cittaromana.com* 💬 *263 villas* ⧖ *Restaurant, café, cable TV, pool, gym, parking (fee); no a/c* ⊟ *MC, V.*

★ **$–$$$** 🖼 **Hotel New York.** Rotterdam is very much a commercial harbor city, with hotels aimed primarily at the business trade; the Hotel New York, a converted shipping office from the first part of the 20th century, is a particularly atmospheric exception. The twin towers rising over the water of the Nieuwe Maas, across from the city center, were known to Rotterdammers for decades as the headquarters of the Holland-America Line, before being renovated and opened as a hotel. Rooms are individually decorated, with high ceilings contrasting with the modern decor, so it's not just the view that boosts the price. The enormous restaurant (which seats 400) somehow maintains an intimate café atmosphere, although those in the know delight in the afternoon tea served here but don't stay for dinner. Other amenities include an oyster bar, tea salon, and water taxi connecting the Kop van Zuid with the city center. ⊠ *Koninginnenhoofd 1, 3072 AD, Kop van Zuid* 🕾 *010/439–0500* 🖷 *010/484–2701* ⊕ *www.hotelnewyork.nl* 💬 *71 rooms, 1 penthouse apartment* ⧖ *Restaurant, room service, cable TV, in-room data ports; no a/c* ⊟ *AE, DC, MC, V.*

**$$** 🖼 **Euro Hotel Centrum.** Despite the business-like, anonymous name, this is a welcoming and comfortable modern hotel with lots of flowers and plants, so the overall feeling is spruce and well cared for. They have family rooms, in case you're traveling with children. This place is particularly handy for Museumpark and strolls along the Westersingel. Enjoy the buffet breakfast before setting out. ⊠ *Baan 14–20, 3011 CB, Centrum* 🕾 *010/214–1922* 🖷 *010/214–0187* ⊕ *www.eurohotelcentrum. nl* 💬 *53 rooms, 2 suites* ⧖ *Cable TV, in-room data ports, bar; no a/c* ⊟ *AE, MC, V* ⫶Ⓞ⫶ *CP.*

**$–$$** 🖼 **Golden Tulip Hotel Inntel Rotterdam-Centre.** The majority of the rooms in this modern high-rise, built at the opening to the Leuvehaven inner harbor, have water views. All 150 guest rooms are simply but tastefully decorated, wearing a designer-look edge. The conservatory-style breakfast room overlooks a terrace for true relaxation. Hotel guests can use two neighboring restaurants, then add dinner to the hotel bill. The staff are incredibly friendly and make all effort to make your stay pleasant. The top-floor restaurant, Le Papillon, has long-reaching views across the Maas, as do the rooftop health club and swimming pool. ⊠ *Leuvehaven 80, 3011 EA, Centrum* 🕾 *010/413–4139* 🖷 *010/413–3222* ⊕ *www.hotelinntel.com* 💬 *263 rooms* ⧖ *Restaurant, café, minibars, cable TV, in-room data ports, pool, health club; no a/c* ⊟ *AE, DC, MC, V.*

**$–$$** 🖼 **Van Walsum.** On a residential boulevard within walking distance of the Museum Boijmans van Beuningen and major attractions, the Van Walsum is near the Euromast. The gregarious owner proudly restores and reequips his rooms, floor by floor, on a continuously rotating basis, with the always-modern decor of each floor determined by that year's best buys in furniture, carpeting, and bathroom tiles. There is a bar-lounge and a small restaurant that has a summer garden extension. ⊠ *Mathenesserlaan 199–201, 3014 HC, Centrum* ☎ *010/436–3275* 🖷 *010/436–4410* ⊕ *www.hotelvanwalsum.nl* 🛏 *29 rooms* ⚐ *Restaurant, cable TV, bar, Internet room, parking (fee); no a/c* ⊟ *AE, DC, MC, V* ⏍ *CP.*

★ $ 🖭 **Bazar.** The well-traveled owner has created havens from his wanderings, with hot, deep colors evoking Turkey and Morocco throughout the individually styled rooms on the second floor, and motifs conjuring up Africa and South America on the third and fourth floors respectively. Although there is an elevator, it goes only to the third floor. The restaurant of the same name on the ground floor has, needless to say, a very international menu. The location on the young, busy Witte de Withstraat draws a nicely "in" crowd to both hotel and restaurant. ⊠ *Witte de Withstraat 16, 3012 BP, Witte de With* ☎ *010/206–5151* 🖷 *010/206–5159* ⊕ *www.hotelbazar.nl* 🛏 *27 rooms* ⚐ *Restaurant, minibars, cable TV, in-room data ports, some pets allowed; no a/c* ⊟ *AE, DC, MC, V* ⏍ *CP.*

$ 🖭 **Emma.** At this hotel on social, busy Nieuwe Binnenweg, plenty of shops and nightspots are conveniently close; the nearest sidewalk café is right opposite the hotel. This is the third generation of the Orsini family seeing to the comfort of the hotel's guests. Furnishings are modern, and there is an elevator. Staffed by a friendly and approachable team, this place offers special rates for groups and those staying longer. ⊠ *Nieuwe Binnenweg 6, 3015 BA, Centrum* ☎ *010/436–5533* 🖷 *010/436–7658* ⊕ *www.hotelemma.nl* 🛏 *24 rooms* ⚐ *Minibars, cable TV, in-room data ports, lounge, some pets allowed; no a/c* ⊟ *AE, DC, MC, V* ⏍ *CP.*

¢–$ 🖭 **Baan.** This is a comfortable family-run hotel overlooking the Coolhaven harbor, and only five minutes from the waterside at Delfshaven. After a renovation in 2004, the bright rooms have tasteful furnishings and accessories in blue and yellow pastel shades. ⊠ *Rochussenstraat 345, 3023 DH, Centrum* ☎ *010/477–0555* 🖷 *010/476–9450* ⊕ *www.hotelbaan.nl* 🛏 *14 rooms* ⚐ *Cable TV; no a/c* ⊟ *AE, MC, V* ⏍ *CP.*

¢ 🖭 **De Clipper.** Perhaps the most unusual way to spend a night in Rotterdam is on a boat moored in one of the harbors in the heart of the city. Because the skipper here can also take you off on sailing trips (book way in advance for this), you'll find that sometimes this hotel is literally missing. This is really a floating hostel: the somewhat cramped rooms (bunk beds only) are shared in twos and fours—the cost is per person—so come in a group if you don't fancy mixing it up. Because of the limited space and the boat's popularity among the backpacking crowd, reserve well ahead if you want to stay on a weekend. ⊠ *Scheepmakershaven (opposite No. 26), Centrum* ☎ *06/3835–3943* ⊕ *www.hostelboat.nl* 🛏 *8 rooms with 28 beds and shared baths* ⚐ *Wi-Fi; no a/c, no TV* ⊟ *MC, V* ⏍ *CP.*

¢ 🖭 **Home.** On the liveliest street in town, five minutes from the Museumpark, this hotel is right in the middle of Rotterdam's best dining, shopping, and nightlife. When you're back at the hotel, incredibly helpful staff are on hand for recommendations and assistance, making this a pad you really want to come back to. The rate drops the longer you stay, by as much as 50% if you stay more than 30 days—and plenty of people do, as en-suite kitchenettes and sitting areas in each room make this a popular choice for longer stays. ⊠ *Witte de Withstraat 81a, 3012 BN, Witte de With* ☎ *010/411–2121* 🖷 *010/414–1690* 🖃 *80 rooms* ⚲ *Kitchenettes, cable TV; no a/c, no room phones* ☰ *AE, MC, V.*

¢ 🏨 **Stayokay Rotterdam.** If you're running on a budget, this modern hostel right in the middle of the city, between Delfshaven and the Museumpark, is just the ticket. Dorms are shared with three, five, or seven others, and you can use a fully equipped kitchen. If you book way in advance, you might be lucky and get one of the double rooms, best for extra privacy, where you have your own en-suite facilities. ⊠ *Rochussenstraat 107–109, 3015 EH, Centrum* ☎ *010/436–5763* 🖷 *010/436–5569* ⊕ *www.stayokay.com* 🖃 *2 rooms for 2 people, 20 dorm rooms with shared baths* ⚲ *Kitchen, bar, laundry facilities; no a/c, no TV* ☰ *MC, V* 🍽 *CP.*

# Nightlife & the Arts

## The Arts

Rotterdam's arts calendar extends throughout the year. You can book tickets and find out what's on around town through the local tourist information office, the VVV. **VVV Rotterdam** (⊠ Coolsingel 67, 3012 AC, Centrum ☎ 0900/403–4065).

DANCE   Rotterdam's resident modern dance company, **Scapino Ballet,** has the reputation of being one of the most formidably talented troupes in the country. It performs at **Rotterdamse Schouwburg** (⊠ Schouwburgplein 25, Centrum ☎ 010/404–4111 ⊕ www.scapinoballet.nl).

FILM   Partly because of the annual avant-garde **International Film Festival Rotterdam,** held in late January–early February, there is a lot of general interest in film in this city—as a result, you have many screens to choose from. The **Pathé** (⊠ Schouwburgplein 101, Centrum ☎ 0900/1458) is the place to head for blockbusters. A film theater with a special program is the **Theater Lantaren/Venster** (⊠ Gouvernestraat 133, Centrum ☎ 010/277–2277), which shows art films in addition to hosting small-scale dance and theater performances. There's an open-air cinema at the Museumpark in September.

MUSIC   Rotterdam's renowned concert orchestra is the excellent **Rotterdam Philharmonic Orchestra,** which performs at the large concert hall **De Doelen** (⊠ Schouwburgplein 50, Centrum ☎ 010/217–1717 ⊕ www.dedoelen. nl). Attracting 400,000 visitors a year, the orchestra is known for its adventurous range of music—this troupe plays not just Beethoven but has also tackled the score from the film *Jurassic Park.*

## Nightlife

To get your bearings and find your way around the party scene, look out for glossy party fliers in cafés, record stores, and clothes shops selling clubbing gear. The best nights tend to be Thursday to Saturday, 11 PM to 5 AM. Most venues have a clubbing floor, with DJs working the crowd and more ambient rooms for smoking or just plain relaxing. From hard-core techno—whose birthplace was right here in Rotterdam—to early-hour chill-out cafés, there is a wide gamut of nighttime entertainment. Innovation is the name of the game—just take a look at the city's 1980s elektro band Kiem, famed for using a drum kit created from used parts of an abandoned ship in the harbor. West Kruiskade (also known as China Town) is the place to go if you want lively bars and music from around the world. Nieuwe Binnenweg and Witte de Withstraat have many busy late-night cafés and clubs. Oude Haven is particularly popular with students, and the Schouwburgplein is favored by visitors to the nearby theaters and cinemas. Stadshuisplein has a number of tacky discos and bars. The Kop van Zuid district is still developing, but there are one or two bars worth visiting.

CAFÉS **Breakaway** (✉ Karel Doormanstraat 1, near Centraal Station, Centrum ☎ 010/233–0922) is busy, with a young international crowd, and the nearest you'll get to a Dutch take on an American bar. **Café Rotterdam** (✉ Wilhelminakade 699, Kop van Zuid ☎ 010/290–8442) is on the Wilhelminakade in the up-and-coming Kop van Zuid district, between the architectural designs of Sir Norman Foster and Renzo Piano. This former shipping terminal is now a massive meeting center, with a large café and fantastic view of the white Erasmus Bridge. **Cambrinus** (✉ Blaak 4, Blaak ☎ 010/414–6702) is a cozy café opposite Blaak station, with a terrace on the Oude Haven. This is a popular mecca for beer lovers, with a dizzying 150 to choose from.

**De Consul** (✉ Westersingel 28, Museumpark ☎ 010/436–3323) offers movies, as well as new age and pop music. With two floors, music drifts through the place from the bar upstairs. **De Schouw** (✉ Witte de Withstraat 80, Witte de With ☎ 010/412–4253), an erstwhile brown café and former journalists' haunt, is now a trendy brown bar with a mix of artists and students. **Temptation Swing Café** (✉ Stadhuisplein 41, Meent ☎ 010/414–6400) attracts a late-night crowd with an intimate dance floor and music, including salsa, merengue, and rhumba, that gets everyone's feet moving. Temptation is closed Monday and Tuesday.

CLUBS In a former pedestrian tunnel, the **Blauwe Vis** (✉ Weena-Zuid 33, Centrum ☎ 010/213–4243), or Blue Fish, is a seafood restaurant until the late hours, when the mood changes and the music really kicks in with soul, jazz, and funk. The long, narrow **Club Vibes** (✉ Westersingel 50a, Museumpark ☎ 010/436–6389) has a friendly staff who chat at the bar to early punters—this is another place you shouldn't arrive at before 1:30 AM. Music is mostly 1970s and 1980s, with some more mainstream 1990s nights. Three floors and one of the best live music lineups make **Nighttown** (✉ West Kruiskade 26–28, Centrum ☎ 010/436–1210 ⊕ www.nighttown.nl ✉ €12–€20, €1.80 membership fee required) *the* place to be in Rotterdam. If you can't get tickets for the big-band nights, make sure you catch the after-event party, definitely not to be missed. Music ranges from hip-hop to drum and bass, funk, techno, and pop. The adjoining café Fresh Up has very mellow music Thursday night, with R&B till late. **Now & Wow** (✉ Graansilo, Maashaven ZZ 2, Rotterdam Zuid/Maashaven ☎ 010/477–1074 ⊕ www.now-wow.com ✉ €15) is the wildest addition to the clubbing scene in Rotterdam. It's in a warehouse by metro station Maashaven. On Saturday night, a weekly MTC Party (Music Takes Control) pushes the envelope for excess. **Rotown** (✉ Nieuwe Binnenweg 19, Museumpark ☎ 010/436–

2669), a high-style restaurant, has new-talent bands playing on Saturday night.

GAY & LESBIAN BARS **Club Vibes** (⊠ Westersingel 50a, Museumpark ☎ 010/436–6389) hosts gay-only nights on Sunday. Very much part of the late-night scene, **Gay Palace** (⊠ Schiedamsesingel 139, Centrum ☎ 010/414–1486) attracts crowds of young gay and lesbian Rotterdammers to its large dance floor.

JAZZ In August the **Heineken Jazz Festival** (☎ 010/413–3972) fills Rotterdam's streets and cafés with music and bopping youth. **Dizzy** (⊠ 's-Gravendijkwal 127, 's-Gravendijkwal ☎ 010/477–3014 ⊕ www.dizzy. nl) is *the* jazz café if you appreciate live performances. A big terrace out back hosts both Dutch and international musicians every Tuesday and Sunday. The café also serves good, reasonably priced food. Come early if you want a seat. Concerts and jamming sessions are free.

POP & ROCK For mega-events, choose between the **Ahoy'**, which holds pop concerts and large-scale operas, and **De Kuip**, Rotterdam's major football stadium, which boasts of its Bob Dylan, Rolling Stones, and U2 concerts. Tickets for both venues often sell out quickly, but De Kuip has a better sound system. **Ahoy'** (⊠ Ahoy'-weg 10, Zuidplein ☎ 010/293–3300) hosts major pop concerts for big names such as Kylie Minogue, Green Day, and Jamiroquai, but also hosts classical philharmonic orchestras, top jazz musicians, and top performance companies like Cirque du Soleil. Despite being able to seat more than 51,000 people, concerts at **De Kuip/Feyenoord Stadion** (⊠ Van Zandvlietplein 1, Kop van Zuid ☎ 010/492–9444 or 010/482–4843) usually sell out.

# Shopping

Rotterdam is the number one shopping city in the south of Holland. Its famous Lijnbaan and Beurstraverse shopping centers, as well as the surrounding areas, offer a dazzling variety of shops and department stores. Rotterdam is where the shopping mall was born: the opening of the Lijnbaan—which dissects the pedestrianized area between the Stadhuisplein and the Schouwburgplein in the city center—in 1953 heralded the launch of dedicated shopping precincts (that is, separated from housing). It continues to be a commercial success, although you'll find the buildings very dull aesthetically. Here you'll find many of the biggest chains in Holland, such as Mango, MEXX, Morgan, Invito, and Sacha.

The archways and fountains of the Beurstraverse—at the bottom of the Coolsingel, near the Stadhuis—make this newer, pedestrianized area more pleasing to walk around. It is now one of the most expensive places to rent shop space, and like most other unusual buildings in Rotterdam has a nickname: Koopgoot, which can mean "shopping channel" (if you like it) or "shopping gutter" (if you don't). The majority of the stores are chains, with branches of Benetton, Sting, Zara, Dockers, the Body Shop, and Esprit. The two main department stores have entrances on the lower-street level: Hema and the more luxurious Bijenkorf. Van Oldenbarneveldtstraat and Nieuwe Binnenweg are the places to be if you want something different. There is a huge variety of alternative fashion to be found here.

## Department Stores

**De Bijenkorf** (✉ Coolsingel 105, Centrum ☎ 0900/0919) is a favorite department store, designed by Marcel Breuer (the great Bauhaus architect) with an exterior that looks like its name, a beehive. The best department store in Rotterdam, it covers four floors. There's a good range of clothing and shoes from both designers and the store's own label, plus a selection of cosmetics and perfume on the ground floor, with a Chill Out department on the same floor geared toward street- and club-wear; here, on some Saturdays a DJ keeps it mellow, and you can even get a haircut at in-store Kinki Kappers. De Bijenkorf is well known for its excellent household-goods line, ranging from lights and furniture to sumptuous fabrics and rugs. Check out the second-floor restaurant with its view out over the Coolsingel and Naum Gabo's sculpture *Constructie*. For less-expensive wares, head to **Hema** (✉ Beursplein 2, Centrum ☎ 010/282–9900), popular with the ever-practical Dutch, who appreciate quality goods at low prices. Tools, cosmetics, and undergarments are the best buys here. Slightly more upmarket than Hema is **V&D** (✉ Hoogstraat 185, Centrum ☎ 0900/235–8363), great for household goods, stationery, and other everyday necessities. Rest your tired tootsies and admire the city view from the rooftop café, La Place, where you can indulge in a wide selection of snacks and full meals.

## Shopping Districts & Streets

Exclusive shops and boutiques can be found in the Entrepotgebied, Delfshaven, Witte de Withstraat, Nieuwe and Oude Binnenweg, and Van Oldenbarneveldtstraat. West Kruiskade and its vicinity offer a wide assortment of multicultural products in the many Chinese, Suriname, Mediterranean, and Arabic shops. The shops in the city center are open every Sunday afternoon, and there is late-night shopping—until 9—every Friday.

## Specialty Stores

There are numerous specialty stores across town, and depending on what you are looking for, you should be able to find it somewhere.

ANTIQUES Look along the **Voorhaven** and its continuation **Aelbrechtskolk**, in Delfshaven, for the best antiques. On Sunday head to the **Schiedamsdijk**, where you can expect to find a market that specializes in antiques and old books, open noon–5.

ART GALLERIES Many galleries provide the opportunity both to look at art and buy it. These can be found along the Westersingel and in the Museumpark area, but the top galleries are on Witte de Withstraat, also lined with numerous cafés, making it an ideal street to spend some time window-shopping.

**Mama Showroom for Media and Moving Art** (✉ Witte de Withstraat 29–31, Witte de With ☎ 010/433–0695 or 010/233–1313 ⊕ www.mamamedia.nl) encourages the collaboration of emerging, experimental artists. If you're looking for new, exciting, and innovative art with high standards, you'll find it here. Some of the work may shock; some might make you laugh out loud in delight; but all of it is art-critic-worthy. Consider film- and video-based art by the Dutch Galleon of Mayhem or the inflatable sculptures by a group of "artoonists," including a giant rabbit by Florentijn Hofman. The gallery is open Wednesday–Sunday 1–6.

BOOKS **Donner Boeken** (✉ Lijnbaan 150, Centrum ☎ 010/413–2070) is the biggest bookstore in Rotterdam. Its 10 floors include an excellent range of English-language books, which are distributed throughout the shop under specific headings.

DESIGN Serious collectors go mad at **Beljon** (✉ Oude Binnenweg 102, Centrum ☎ 010/282–7539 ⊕ www.beljon.com), which stocks new and second-hand retro-style furniture. The self-styled "mini-department store" carries avant-garde jewelry and footwear as well as clothing for men and women from Danish design label Bruuns Bazaar. **Dille & Kamille** (✉ Korte Hoogstraat 22, Centrum ☎ 010/411–3338) is a fantastic store for anyone interested in cooking. From herbs to sturdy wooden spoons to recipe books, this is a browser's heaven. It is one of the few shops in the Netherlands that still carries traditional Dutch household items, such as a huge water kettle to make tea for 25, a nutmeg mill, or a *zeepklopper,* a device that holds a bar of soap and can whip up bubbles—a forerunner to liquid dish-washing detergent. You should also walk through the **Entrepot Harbor design district,** alongside the city marina at Kop van Zuid, where there are several interior-design stores. More like a museum of modern art and home furnishings than a mere gallery, the **Galerie ECCE** (✉ Witte de Withstraat 17a–19a, Witte de With ☎ 010/413–9770 ⊕ www.galerie-ecce.nl) has an exclusive collection of ultramodern furniture, lamps, and glassware from Dutch and European designers and offers a custom-design service. You'll find a variety of smaller unique design items, suitable for gifts, such as coasters and wall sconces. The gallery has a new exhibition of paintings and sculpture every two months, and also specializes in the production of trompe l'oeil wall paintings. **Regalo** (✉ Beurstraverse 115, Centrum ☎ 010/213–0871) sells quirky products and fun things from Alessi and other great design signatures. The owner builds her collection around her regular customers' tastes.

FASHION **Rigter** (✉ Oude Binnenweg 129, Centrum ☎ 010/413–3282) has fabulous men's shoes, from its own brand to Dutch shoe king Van Bommel, making this a must-stop for a pair of funky, original street wear. For fashion suggestions, start with **Sister Moon** (✉ Nieuwe Binnenweg 89b, Centrum ☎ 010/436–1508), which has a small collection of exclusive hip clothing for men and women in the party scene; part of the boutique is devoted to trendy secondhand togs. Graffiti artists favor **Urban Unit** (✉ Nieuwe Binnenweg 53, Centrum ☎ 010/436–3825), loving the look of the men's sneakers and street wear on sale (while stocking up on spray cans and other graffiti supplies). On Van Oldenbarneveldtstraat the prices rise as the stores get more label based. **Van Dijk** (✉ Van Oldenbarneveldtstraat 105, Centrum ☎ 010/411–2644) stocks Costume National and Helmut Lang, and the owner, Wendela, has two of her own design labels. You can find trendy shoes, bags, and accessories here and have plenty of room to try on clothes in the *paskamers* (fitting rooms).

Where there's fashion, there's music: keep in mind that Holland's largest concentration of international record stores can be found on the Nieuwe Binnenweg, ranging from techno to ambient, rock to Latin and African.

### Street Markets

The expansive **Binnenrotteplein,** between Sint Laurenskerk and Blaak railway station, is home to one of the largest street markets in the country, every Tuesday and Saturday from 9 to 5 and Friday from noon to 5. Among the 520 stalls you can find a flea market, book market, household items, used goods, food, fish, clothes, and flowers. From April to December, a fun shopping market with 200 stands is held on Sunday from noon to 5. There are often special attractions for children, and you can chill out on the terrace.

## Brielle

⑥⑤   *22 km (14 mi) west of Rotterdam.*

A popular side trip from Rotterdam, the town of Brielle, past Rotterdam's industrial harbors, is famous as the redoubt of the legendary Sea Beggars and, as such, remains a historic haven worth reaching. Look for the wind turbines that herald your approach to the coast. Upon arrival, you'll find that the narrow lanes weaving through Brielle are relatively traffic free, meaning it is a town made for exploring on foot; its restored fortress girdle makes a walk around the ramparts equally possible. By car from Rotterdam head west, following signs for the Hoek van Holland on the A15, then the N15, until Brielle is signposted. By public transport from Rotterdam Centraal, take the metro to Spijkenisse Centrum, then take Bus No. 103.

Brielle prospered throughout the Middle Ages, owing to its location on the Goote River, near the mouth of the Maas River, which provided direct access to the sea. When the Goote silted up, Brielle lost the source of its wealth; the town was on the brink of drifting into obscurity when the provinces of the Netherlands revolted against Spanish rule. Protestant rebels (called *Geuzen*—beggars—by the Spanish) led the 1568 uprising, launching pirate attacks and seizing Spanish galleons. On April 1, 1572, the Sea Beggars unexpectedly converged outside Brielle with 5,000 men in 36 boats. They broke into the Spanish garrison, overwhelming them so totally that their victory inspired the Dutch people to renew their efforts to oust the Spanish.

The annual **Liberation Day** (Bevrijdingsdag in Dutch) festivities commemorating Brielle's release are not to be missed. Every year on April 1, the locals turn back the clock to 1572 to commemorate the liberation from the Spanish, filling the streets with straw and selling traditional crafts from stalls across town. Locals dress as Spaniards and Sea Beggars to reenact Brielle's liberation, battering down the town gates complete with cannon and musket fire and hand-to-hand fighting. Inevitably, the Spanish lose and their leaders are paraded through the streets in wooden cages. The day ends in a celebration worthy of the Middle Ages, with the mass consumption of spit-roasted meat and goblets of wine.

Today, Brielle is an idyllic small town, with narrow streets, grassy-banked fortifications surrounded by a moat, and numerous historic monuments. The imposing 15th-century **Sint Catharijnekerk** (St. Catherine's church) has witnessed a substantial part of Dutch royal history. In

1688, Mary Stuart waved good-bye from the church tower to her departing husband, William III, who was soon to become king of England. From the top, 318 steps up, you can see the Maas River and Rotterdam harbor. Local heroes from the Liberation Day battles are immortalized in stained-glass windows. ⊠ *Sint Catharijneplein* ☎ *0181/475475* ⊕ *www.catharijnekerk.nl* 🖾 *€1* ⊙ *June–Sept., Mon.–Sat. 10:30–4:30, Sun. services only.*

The **Historisch Museum Den Briel** (Brielle Historical Museum) is in a 17th-century former town jail on the second floor; the voice of an "18th-century prisoner" addresses you (in Dutch) via a loudspeaker. Among historical retellings of Brielle's liberation are paintings by local artists and a re-created medieval marketplace on the ground floor. ⊠ *Markt 1* ☎ *0181/475475* ⊕ *www.historischmuseumdenbriel.nl* 🖾 *€2* ⊙ *Apr.–Oct., Tues.–Fri. 10–5, Sat. 10–4, Sun. noon–4; Nov.–Mar., Tues.–Sat. 10–4.*

Halfway up Voorstraat, a small road on the left leads to the centuries-old **Asylplein Hofjes** (almshouses). The grassy square is ornamented with a sculpted sea nymph that, surrounded by roses and ornamental trees, looks eternally in the direction from which the rebels came to liberate the town from the Spanish in the 16th century.

In fine weather, tables from **De Hoofdwacht** (⊠ Markt 7), the largest bar on the central markt, spill across the square. Don't miss the ornate bell tower on top of the former Town Hall opposite, which now houses the Brielle VVV and the Historical Museum. The tightly packed buildings provide shelter from winds whipping off the nearby Brielse Meer (Brielle Lake), making the café an ideal break stop.

## Where to Stay & Eat

¢–$$ ✕ **Coccinelle.** On a traffic-free shopping street, this quiet, mustard-yellow brasserie offers satisfying meals in a tranquil setting, including a pretty garden terrace. The menu changes to reflect the season, but you might find tuna on ratatouille with a caramelized garlic sauce or a simple but elegant club sandwich at lunch. There's always at least one good vegetarian option. ⊠ *Voorstraat 41* ☎ *0181/415230* ▭ *V* ⊙ *Closed Mon. and Tues.*

$ ✕ **Pablo.** At this Indonesian restaurant the menu changes regularly, with the *Pablo'tjes* (house specials) always well worth trying. ⊠ *Voorstraat 87–91* ☎ *0181/412960* ▭ *AE, MC, V* ⊙ *Closed Mon.*

$–$$ ✕▥ **Hotel de Zalm.** A very popular town-house hotel, the De Zalm caters equally to business travelers, leisure travelers, and cyclists following the long-distance North Sea route. Special rates are available on weekends. Rooms are light and airy, and have comfortable leather armchairs for maximum relaxation. The inspired restaurant (closed Sunday) makes the absolute most of Brielle's location, with an extensive range of North Sea fish. Savor *zeetong* (sole) with chunky Belgian chips and salad for lunch, or opt for a lightly baked monkfish in leek sauce for dinner. ⊠ *Voorstraat 6, 3132 BJ* ☎ *0181/413388* 🖷 *0181/417712* ⊕ *www.dezalm.be* ⟿ *37 rooms* ⚪ *Cable TV, Wi-Fi; no a/c in some rooms* ▭ *AE, DC, MC, V* ⊙⬤ *BP.*

## Festivals

On the second Saturday in June, **Street Theater** takes over Brielle when miming mummers prance about the streets. The last Sunday in July sees the **Brielle Blues**, a popular open-air event that brings floods of music lovers to town.

# Kinderdijk

★ ⑥⑥ *55 km (34 mi) southwest of Amsterdam.*

Once you leave the urban center of Rotterdam behind, you quickly find yourself in rural surroundings, with meadows, greenhouses, and farmhouses. In one such area, in the Alblasserwaard—a polder enclosed by the Rivers Noord and Lek—you come across the Kinderdijk Windmills, arguably the most famous tourist sight in Holland. Its description so often gets mutated to sound saccharine sweet that many visitors discount a visit, mistakenly thinking it must be faux. The name (which means "child's dike") comes from a legend that probably has a lot to do with its chocolate-boxy aura: a baby was washed up here in a cradle after the great floods of 1421, with a cat sitting on its tummy to keep them both from tumbling out. Nevertheless, the sight of 19 mills under sail is magnificently, romantically impressive. The mills loom large, even in the distance—partly because they are: eight of the mills are among the largest in the world. They line Het Nieuwe Waterschap in pairs, each facing another on opposite banks.

The windmills date back to the 18th century, and the site is on the UNESCO World Heritage list. The mills enable the Dutch to live on reclaimed riverbeds. Water had to be drained from the land, and 150 years ago 10,000 windmills were in operation across the country. In 1740, 19 mills were built in the meadows of Kinderdijk, to drain the excess water from the Alblasserwaard polders, which lie below sea level. The mill sails harnessed the energy of the wind to scoop up the water. Electrical pumping stations have now taken over water management, but the majority of mills operate at certain times for the delight of tourists. The mills are open in rotation, so there is always one interior to visit during opening hours. Looking around the inside of a mill provides a fascinating insight into how the millers and their families lived. Tours can be taken of the mechanical workings if you want to get a closer look.

The mills are under sail from 2 to 5 on the first Saturday in May and June, then every Saturday in July and August. Throughout the second week in September the mills are illuminated at night, really pulling out the tourist stops. You can walk around the mills whenever you like; the opening times given below refer to visiting the interior of the mill. There is an unremarkable hotel nearby if you want to stay over, but most people opt to visit on a day trip. The mills are 55 km (34 mi) southwest of Amsterdam, just to the northeast of the town. By public transport, head first to Rotterdam Centraal Station. From there, take the metro to Rotterdam Zuidplein, then Bus No. 154 (end destination Utrecht). There are very few restaurants in Kinderdijk, so consider bringing along a picnic if the weather is good. ✉ *Molenkade, Kinderdijk* ☎ *078/691–5179* 🖾 *Interior of mill €1.50* ☉ *Interior Apr.–Sept., daily 9:30–5:30.*

## The Outdoors

From May to October you can join a guided tour and take a half-hour boat trip out to see the mills using the tour company, **Rederij JC Vos en Zn. lines** (☎ 0180/512174), based off Molenkade in Kinderdijk. Tours are offered daily from 10 to 5 for €2.50.

From mid-April to late September, **Rebus** (✉ Boompjeskade, Rotterdam ☎ 010/218–3131 ⊕ www.rebus-info.nl) operates three-hour cruises twice daily to Kinderdijk from the center of Rotterdam, leaving at 10:45 and 2:15. Trips cost €12.50.

# DORDRECHT TO MUIDEN

Continuing the circuit starting from Amsterdam and extending from Haarlem to Delft and on to Rotterdam, any grand tour of central Holland should head back northwest past the famous town of Gouda to the province of Utrecht. Although this is the smallest province in the country, it has such a variety of geographical features for the visitor that it has often been called "Holland in a nutshell." It is in this area that the late Queen Juliana chose to live, so that she could bring up her four daughters in peaceful and unspoiled home life. True, they lived in a palace, but Soestdijk Palace is also a home, just as Holland's ruler was both queen and mother. Utrecht is now a bustling modern town, but it is studded with some impressive relics of history, including the Dom Tower of the "church that isn't there." Northward lies the garden district of Gooiland, a tranquil overture to the nearby bustle of Amsterdam and such sumptuous treasures as the Kasteel de Haar, home to the Barons van Zuylen.

## Dordrecht

**❻❼** *23 km (14 mi) southeast of Rotterdam.*

Claiming to be the oldest town in the province of Zuid Holland, Dordrecht lies just east of the main road leading south to Antwerp and Brussels. Thanks to its location in the midst of a tangle of Rhine and Maas waterways, it was once among the most important towns in Holland. Fortified in 1271, it was badly damaged by the St. Elisabeth flood of 1421, an event recalled by a stained-glass window in the town's Grote Kerk.

Today the city is a mix of old and new. Much of it is given over to shipbuilding and yachting facilities, but the old sector is worth visiting along the riverfront (indeed, the best view of the city is from the opposite, north bank) and in the streets leading back to the Voorstraat. Houses lean in every which direction, some at unfeasible angles as if they've been dropped from a great height, and you begin to wonder how they don't topple over. Dominating the scene is the imposing mass of the 15th-century **Grote Kerk/Onze Lieve Vrouwekerk** (Great Church/Our Lady Church), whose tower is a good 6 feet off the vertical and whose chancel bends left to symbolize the head of Christ inclining toward his left shoulder. A window pictures the 1421 disaster, and the huge 2,600-pipe organ has a 10-second echo. The white interior is accented by a mahogany sounding board and a bronze screen (which used to be kept brilliantly polished by the local schoolchildren). It was in this church that the Protestant synod met in 1618 to settle the controversy between Arminius and Gomaurus, two professors of theology at Leiden. The outcome was Prince Maurits's choosing for Gomaurus, who believed in a less-strict Calvinism. From the church, follow the Voorstraat (on the far side of the canal), with old houses at every turn, to the Groenmarkt, where at No. 107 you'll find *Huis de Sleutel* (Key House), the city's oldest surviving house (1550). ✉ *Lange Geldersekade 2* ☎ *078/614–4660* 💶 *€1 contribution requested, tower €1* ☉ *Apr.–Oct., Tues.–Sat. 10:30–4:30, Sun. noon–4; Nov. and Dec., Tues., Thurs., and 1st and 3rd Sat. of the month 2–4.*

★ To the east of the Grote Kerk, on the quay of the Nieuwe Haven (New Harbor) is the **Museum Simon van Gijn.** This lavish 18th-century house was occupied from 1864 to 1922 by art collector Simon van Gijn, who left his home and collection to the city. There are magnificent period rooms on view, along with—up the stairs in the attic—the childless banker's extensive antique toy collection. ✉ *Nieuwe Haven 29–30* ☎ *078/639–8200* ⊕ *www.simonvangijn.nl* 💶 *€5.50* ☉ *Tues.–Sun. 11–5.*

Stroll up the tree-lined Steegoversloot in the town center (which runs from the Spuihaven harbor-canal to the Wijnhaven harbor-canal) to have a surreptitious peek into the working artists' and potters' studios, many of which are open to the public. Keep your eyes peeled for a narrow lane leading off in the direction of **Het Hof** (The Court), originally a 13th-century Augustian monastery, but rebuilt in the 16th century after a fire. In the Statenzaal, a video presentation takes you back to the meeting of the First Assembly of the Seven Provinces. Cloister gardens offer an island of calm. Leave the Hof via the west entrance; here on Hofstraat, take time to look at the extraordinary terrace, probably the closest thing you'll see to gingerbread-biscuit houses, each with individual decoration that, in a pinch, could be colored icing. ✉ *Het Hof* ☎ *078/613–4626* 💶 *Free* ☉ *Tues.–Sat. 1–5.*

The leading sight on Museumstraat is the **Dordrechts Museum,** stuffed with many paintings, drawings, and prints by Netherlandish artists, especially native son and fabled landscape artist Albert Cuyp and, to boot, works by his father, Jacob. Star names here include Ferdinand Bol and Nicolaes Maes—famed as pupils of Rembrandt. The collection extends to the 20th century, and there are some important works on view by Karel Appel. ✉ *Museumstraat 40* ☎ *078/648–2148* ⊕ *www. dordrechtsmuseum.nl* 💶 *€5* ☉ *Tues.–Sun. 11–5.*

Just past the Dordrechts Museum, a gateway leads into the **Arend Maartenshof** (Arend Maarten's Court), a beautiful old former almshouse dating from 1625 and consisting of several wings that surround a flower-filled courtyard. The building is now a home for the elderly. If the door is open (opening times appear to fluctuate according to the whims of the caretaker), have a look inside the first building to the right as you enter. The interior of this tiny room has been restored and is decorated to appear as it would have looked in 1701, with a heavy wooden table and original portraits of the almshouse patrons. ✉ *Museumstraat 56* ☉ *Hrs vary.*

On the Maas side of the Maartensgaat harbor is the statuesque **Cathar- ijnepoort** (Catherine's Gate), one of two medieval town gates, which takes you through the city walls to a wharf and dates from 1652. At the far end of the Wolwevershaven you come to the **Groothoofdspoort,** the much larger and extensively decorated city gate. This one leads out onto a vast jetty. It was originally built between 1440 and 1450, but what you see now is a Renaissance fill-in around the medieval archway, dating from 1618. Nonetheless, the colorful display of shields and balconied tower certainly make it worth the walk. Through the gate you stand overlooking the exact confluence of the Oude Maas, the Noord, and the Merwede rivers—often touted as one of the best river prospects in all the land.

### Where to Stay & Eat

¢–$$   ✕ **Café Merz.** Low, blackened, wood-beam ceilings, and a host of sofas so inviting you may never want to leave, greet you as you walk into this cozy restaurant-bar. At the back, the dining room is painted in lighter shades, with simple modern furnishings conducive to relaxed dining. The menu covers all the usual Dutch café standards, from chicken satay to steak with an array of sauces, but the presentation has a touch of panache that sets it apart from the rest, and the flavors never disappoint. The weekly specials are a particularly good value Out in front, the summer terrace has great harborside views. ⊠ *Korte Kalkhaven 3* ☎ *078/ 613–2582* ▤ *AE, MC, V* ⊘ *Closed Mon. No lunch weekends.*

¢–$   ✕ **Petit Restaurant Jongepier.** There are several restaurants around Groothoofdspoort, all with fabulous river- and harborside settings, make it a relaxing place to hang out, especially on a summer's evening. However, prices in most establishments reflect the quality of the view, rather than of the food and service. This restaurant is the best of the bunch, with a friendly staff and simple yet tasty fare. The menu does- n't stretch itself far beyond good, solid steaks and salads, but with a back- drop such as this, you won't care. ⊠ *Groothoofd 8* ☎ *078/639–0855* ▤ *AE, DC, MC, V.*

$–$$   ▦ **Hotel Dordrecht.** Opposite one of Dordrecht's many historic harbors, this large town-house hotel provides comfortable rooms with tasteful interiors and slick service that is hard to beat, especially given the price range of the four-poster beds with hot tub en suite. An in-house chef serves dinner, with daily specialties. ⊠ *Achterhakkers 72, 3311 JA* ☎ *078/613–6011* 🖷 *078/613–7470* ⊕ *www.hoteldordrecht.nl* ⬐ *21 rooms* ⚐ *Restaurant, minibars, cable TV, in-room data ports, bar, some pets allowed* ▤ *AE, DC, MC, V* ⧉ *BP.*

### Festivals & Markets

Dordrecht's historic setting lends itself to cultural events. The Italian opera **Belcanto Festival** is held in Het Hof in late summer, and **Jazz Days** floods the city with more music lovers. **Dordt in Stoom** is a biannual, three-day event that attracts steam-power enthusiasts. The annual **Antiquarian Book Market** is held in early July, and a **Christmas Market** in December (check with VVV for time, location, and ticket details for individual events).

### Sports & the Outdoors

Take a **Waterrondje Dordt** (☎ 078/613–0094) or a canal tour, of Dor- drecht on board a launch through the harbors. Tours start on the hour from the Wijnbrug and last an hour. Buy tickets from the booth at the door of the restaurant De Stroper, next to the tour boat's docking area; tours are offered April to the end of May, September, and October, daily 2–5; June to August, daily 11–5, with tickets costing €5. About 5 km (3 mi) outside the city center is the **Biesbosch National Park,** an enormous marshlands area with meadows and reed lands, intersected by rivers and streams. Swim in one of the natural pools, or bike on cycle tracks that rollerbladers can also use; between the mountain-bike tracks there's even a golf course. Hire canoes or join a boat trip along one of the naviga- ble rivers, from the Biesbosch Visitor Center. There is no adequate pub- lic transport to the Biesbosch from Dordrecht, though Bus No. 5 can take you to within 45 minutes' walk of the **Biesboschcentrum Dordrecht.** ⊠ *Baanhoekweg 53, 3313 LP* ☎ *078/630–5353* ⊕ *www.dordt.nl/ biesboschcentrum* ☉ *Visitor center Nov.–Feb., Tues.–Sun. 9:30–4; Mar., Apr., Sept., and Oct., Tues.–Sun. 9:30–5; May–Aug., daily 9:30–6.*

You can rent bikes right next to the station, from the **Rijwiel Shop** (⊠ Sta- tionsplein 6 ☎ 078/635–6830). Rental costs are €6.50 per day, with ID and €50 deposit.

## Shopping
Dordrecht is known for its antiques shops, many of them situated along the Voorstraat (where, in 1877, Vincent van Gogh is said to have worked for a few months in a bookshop). As you walk up toward the Groothoofd area, prices tend to drop as shops have a more secondhand, rummage- sale appearance. Late-night shopping is on Thursday, and shops are open on the last Sunday of the month.

# Gouda

🄖 *53 km (33 mi) southwest of Amsterdam, 13 km (8 mi) southeast of Rot- terdam.*

There is more to Gouda than the rich cheese that made it famous (pro- nounced *howdah,* not *goo*-da). A walk through the town is a lesson in Dutch history: a clock on the east side of the Gothic Town Hall tells the story of its founding in July 1272. When the clock strikes, every half hour, figures representing spectators and standard-bearers emerge from the clock's castle door. After the chimes ring out, a miniature Count Floris appears and hands a charter to a town official. The city's most famous son was the medieval philosopher Erasmus, the offspring of a local priest— so they say; some historians say Erasmus may have been conceived in Gouda, but he was actually born in Rotterdam. Gouda took full advantage of its commercial rights, prospering on its trade in beer, then diversify- ing into pipe making and ceramics—by about 1750, half the popula- tion worked in the pottery industry.

According to popular myth, in winter Rotterdammers would undertake a challenge to skate up to Gouda on frozen canals, buy a pipe, and skate home without breaking the fragile stem. Gouda's candles are another city classic: the industry didn't become dominant until the mid-19th cen- tury, but it's honored in the 20,000-plus candles used to illuminate the square during the annual Christmas tree ceremony, **Gouda bij Kerstlicht,**

(Gouda by Candlelight). This lovely event is held in mid-December—it's memorable to see all the electric lights in the town turned off, with flickering candles the only illumination. Over the centuries, periods of prosperity were followed by economic collapse, particularly under French occupation in the 1790s. By the early 19th century, once-rich Gouda had become synonymous with "beggar," but the industrial revolution restored its fortunes. One of the world's largest multinationals, Unilever, started off making candles and soap here.

One of the most quaint of all town halls in Holland is Gouda's hyper-Gothic **Stadhuis**, built in 1450 and still the focal point of the market square. With its icicle-like spires, pretty shutters, and melodious carillon, it's the ultimate photo-op: no wonder couples flock here for weddings. Inside are ornately carved marble fireplaces and 17th-century tapestries in the **Trouwzaal** (Marriage Room); and in the exhibition space on the second floor, the history of the city is traced through drawings, photographs, and maps. As you walk around to the main entrance on the southwest side, don't miss the northeast facade. Notice how locals in the know walk up the left-hand side of the double staircase at the entrance—because convicted criminals once used the right-hand one on their way to the gallows. ⊠ *Markt 1* ☎ *0182/588475* ⊙ *Weekdays 10–4, Sat. 11–3.*

The **De Waag** (Weigh House) is behind the Stadhuis in a building built in 1668. In case you can't guess what it was used for, the enormous gable stone shows cheeses being weighed. Today this is a **Kaasexposeum** (Cheese Museum), with interactive presentations about dairy products and cheeses. Downstairs, on one of the original scales, an attendant weighs young visitors and quotes their weight in an equivalent number of cheeses. ⊠ *Markt 35–36* ☎ *0182/529996* ⊞ €2 ⊙ *Tues.–Sun. 1–5, Thurs. 10–5.*

★ **Sint Janskerk** (St. John's Church), called the Grote Kerk (Great Church), is the longest in Holland and has memorable stained-glass windows, which some connoisseurs rank right up there with those of Chartres for delicacy of color and boldness of design. Most of the building dates from the late 15th century; very little has changed since the tower was finished in 1600. The stained glass dates mostly from the 16th century. Miraculously, the windows survived the Protestant iconoclasts, the French revolutionaries, and World War II. Altogether, the church contains 70 stained-glass windows, some as high as 60 feet. In addition to depicting John the Baptist and Christ, they portray Philip II, the King of Spain, and Mary Tudor, the Queen of England. The most recent window was created in 1947 as an expression of joy at the liberation of the Netherlands from German occupation. The magnificent organ dates from the early 18th century and is still played every week between April and September. On Sunday, the church is open only to worshippers. ⊠ *Achter de Kerk 16* ☎ *0182/512684* ⊞ €2 ⊙ *Mar.–Oct., Mon.–Sat. 9–5; Nov.–Feb., Mon.–Sat. 10–4.*

The **Museum Het Catharina Gasthuis** (Catharina Hospital Museum) is housed in the Catharina Hospital, which was founded in 1302. In the

17th century the front was replaced with a classical facade, most probably the work of Pieter Post, who also built the Weigh House. The museum's collections cover nearly every aspect of life in Gouda: 16th-century altarpieces from the church, antique toys, a reconstructed 17th-century pharmacy, kitchen, and classroom; paintings by artists of the Barbizon and Hague schools; a fine work by Jan Steen, *The Quack*; and applied arts from the 16th to the 20th century. ⊠ *Achter de Kerk 14* ☎ *0182/588440* ⌨ *Combined ticket with De Moriaan €4* ☉ *Tues.–Sun. 11–5.*

The **Stedelijk Museum de Moriaan** (Blackamoor Municipal Museum) houses collections of pottery and clay pipes in a Late Gothic building that was originally a sugar refinery and later belonged to a company selling spices and tobacco. Gouda's pipe industry was started 300 years ago by British soldiers stationed in Holland as mercenaries in the pay of Prince Maurits. In their spare time they fashioned clay pipes of various shapes and styles, and soon the locals began copying them, leading to Gouda becoming the country's leading pipe and ceramic producer. The figure above the door with the pipe in its mouth is a "Moriaan" (Blackamoor), which was also the company name. Gouda pottery was famous in the 19th century, and the floral earthenware on display represents some of the finest work by Gouda craftsmen, manufactured by companies such as the Royal Earthenware Factory, Goedewaagen, and Zenith. Ultimately, cheaper imitations took over the market. As for pipes, look for the so-called "mystery" pipes: new, they are pure white, but as they turn brown through use, a pattern appears on the bowl. If you buy an example today, just what the design will be the buyer never knows in advance. ⊠ *Westhaven 29* ☎ *0182/588444* ⌨ *Combined ticket with St. Catharina Gasthuis €4* ☉ *Tues.–Sun. 11–5.*

## Where to Stay & Eat

**$$$** ✕ **Rôtisserie L'Etoile.** Despite the French name, this restaurant is a blend of all things Mediterranean. The interior has warm, natural tints, and intimate corners for tête-à-tête dinners. Specialties of the house include sea bass with a curry paste in a classic butter sauce. Lunchtime dishes are simpler and include good salads and baguette sandwiches. The flower-bedecked roof garden has a good view over the adjacent canal. ⊠ *Blekerssingel 1* ☎ *0182/512253* ▭ *AE, MC, V* ☉ *Closed Sun. and Mon. No lunch Sat.*

**$$** ✕ **Buiten Eten & Drinken.** The name means "eat and drink outdoors" and refers to the large garden at the back of the restaurant, where you can enjoy dining under the stars when the weather permits. There's lots of room indoors, too, where a local artist has painted the four seasons on the walls. Enjoy the apple-syrup glazed duck breast with a Szechuan pepper sauce, or let the English chef spoil you with a bread-and-butter pudding. There's a good selection of wines from all over the world. ⊠ *Oosthaven 23* ☎ *0182/524884* ▭ *AE, MC, V* ☉ *Closed Mon. No lunch.*

**$–$$** ✕ **Tapas.** Spanish tapas bars are springing up all over Holland. This one scores high on quality and hospitality. The interior is unpretentious, with cozy tables and candlelight. Friendly staff serve the tapas, those delectable small appetizers that hail from Spain, in two rounds: first, warm ones, then a cold selection. You can also opt for a main dish. On weekends, you're treated to live music from flamenco guitarists and Gypsy King wannabes. ⊠ *Lange Groenendaal 57* ☎ *0182/523035* ⊟ *AE, DC, MC, V* ☺ *Closed Mon. No lunch.*

¢ 🏨 **De Utrechtse Dom.** In a quiet residential area east of Sint Jans, this friendly family-run hotel is a homey option. The building was originally a coach house—and thereby hangs a tale: traders from Utrecht would stable their horses here while doing business in the town, but what money they made was invariably spent on beer. That meant no money left for bed, so they came to sleep with their horses on the floor. Over time, the "stables" became a hotel. The quiet courtyard at the back is a good place to sit and admire your new candle and clay pipe purchases. ⊠ *Geuzenstraat 6, 2801 XV* ☎ *0182/528833* 🖷 *0182/549534* ⊕ *www.hotelgouda.nl* ⊃ *14 rooms* ⚲ *Minibars, cable TV, some pets allowed; no a/c, no room phones* ⊟ *AE, DC, MC, V* ⵔⵔ *CP.*

### Festivals & Concerts

**Gouda by Candlelight** is a Christmas staple, held in mid-December. All the electric lights in the market are switched off, and the windows in the Stadhuis and surrounding houses are decorated with candles and with an enormous Christmas tree taking center stage. Not as faux as it sounds, you get really carried away on the Christmas spirit of the event. The Catharina Gasthuis and Sint Janskerk host monthly **chamber music concerts,** which alternate between the two venues. Buy tickets up to an hour before the classical recitals start.

### The Outdoors

BICYCLING Gouda is compact enough to explore on foot, but a bicycle makes it easy to tour the rich dairy region that surrounds it. **Rijwiel Shop Gouda** (⊠ Stationsplein 10 ☎ 0182/519751), next to the train station, rents bikes for €6.50 or €7.50, with ID and a deposit of €50. Unusual for a station outlet, it is closed weekends.

### Shopping

Although the first thing you think of buying in Gouda is cheese, the town also has a thriving trade in crafts. It's also well known for its candles and claims to produce a large percentage of Holland's "Delft" blue. Gouda also has its own ceramic style, which incorporates richer colors. In its heyday, Gouda also supplied much of the country with soap and *stroopwafels* (syrup waffles).

CANDLES With a prime location, directly opposite the front of Sint Janskerk, **'t Keldertje** (⊠ Achter de Kerk 9H ☎ 0182/523912), or "Little Cellar," is a tiny, inviting, alcove shop that somehow manages to cram hundreds of colorful candles into its displays. You'll find every conceivable size here, from compact tea lights that will look great on your dinner table, to great towers of wax you can barely lift and that might endanger your baggage allowance.

CHEESE MARKETS Every Thursday morning from June through August, farmers and *porters* (cheese carriers) dress in traditional costume to go through the ritual of a **Goudse Kaasmarkt** (Gouda Cheese Market) beside the Waag, for the benefit of tourists, since Gouda is the best-known type of Dutch cheese. Expect Goudse "locals" to play on their heritage: outside De Waag a porter, dressed in yellow clogs, with a yoke across his shoulders, greets visitors as they approach. This is probably the best place to buy cheese if you want to shop in open-air style; it is usually sold as *Jonge kaas* (mild cheese), *Oude kaas* (extra mature cheese), or *Belegen* (medium mature). There are many thatched-roof *kaasboerderijen* (cheese farms) near Gouda, several of which are on the picturesque River Vlist. If you're driving through, look out for signs reading *kaas te koop* (cheese for sale), since this indicates a farm shop where you may be able to look behind the scenes as well as buy freshly made Gouda. If you are using public transport, the VVV organizes excursions and short bicycle rides to nearby dairy farms where you can follow the whole process from cow to cheese counter.

PIPES & CERAMICS

At Peperstraat 76 you can see the enormously mustached Adrie Moerings making pipes in the traditional way. Just wander into his open studio, **Adrie Moerings Pottenbakkerij en Pijpenmakerij** or Adrie Moerings Pottery Kiln and Pipe Maker (✉ Peperstraat 76 ☎ 0182/512842), and watch him throw a pot or demonstrate pipe making. He is perhaps the last man in Holland who still makes clay pipes professionally. His pottery is on sale at the back of the shop.

## Utrecht

*58 km (36 mi) northeast of Rotterdam, 40 km (25 mi) southeast of Amsterdam.*

Birthplace of the 16th-century pope Adrian VI, the only Dutch pope, Utrecht has been a powerful bishopric since the 7th century and is still a major religious center and home to Holland's largest university. It was here that the Dutch Republic was established in 1579 with the signing of the Union of Utrecht. Today, Utrecht has so many curiosities, high-gabled houses, fascinating water gates, hip shops, artsy cafés, and winding canals that the traveler can almost forgive the city for being one of the busiest and most modern in Holland. Happily, the central core of Utrecht remains redolent with history, particularly along the Oudegracht (Old Canal), which winds through the central shopping district (to the east of the station shopping complex). Utrecht's storybook cityscape was long dominated by its famous 367-foot-high tower of the cathedral, known as the Domtoren. But the tall Holiday Inn and the modern Hoog Catharijne complex have joined the Dom in the skies, and this combination of two differing worlds at close quarters sums up the contrasts seen everywhere these days in Holland. If you arrive by train, you might be forgiven for thinking Utrecht is one enormous covered shopping mall, since the station is incorporated into the warren of 200-plus shops that is the Hoog Catharijne. You could get lost in the mall maze for a day, but if you follow signs for *Centrum* (town center) through the shopping precinct and keep walking with determination, you will eventually come out on Achter Clarenburg in the historic center.

First settled by Romans, Utrecht achieved its first glory in the 16th century, when the religious power of the town was made manifest in the building of four churches at points of an enormous imaginary cross, with

Utrecht's **Dom** (cathedral) in the center. The soaring tower of "the cathedral that is missing" on the skyline directs you to the center of the action. Once, before the Union of Utrecht was signed and the Protestants took the reins of power, the city skyline was punctured by more than 40 church spires.

**69** The **Oudegracht,** the long central canal—which suffers a confusing name change at several points en route through the city—is unique in Holland, for its esplanade has upper and lower levels, with shops and galleries opening onto street level, and restaurants and cafés on the walkway just above the water level of the city's unique sunken canals (sinking water levels centuries ago led to the excavation of a lower story).

Make your way to the central Domplein, where you'll find the **RonDom,** a one-stop cultural and historical information center for the historic quarter, where you can buy tickets for almost everything as well as book a guided tour or barge trip. There is an excellent range and display of free leaflets, to which you should help yourself (they usually prove more informative than the VVV). ☒ *Domplein 9* ☎ *030/233–3036* 🖷 *030/230–0108* ⊕ *www.domtoren.nl* ☉ *Weekdays 10–5, weekends noon–5.*

Two or three blocks to the east of the Domplein is the supercharming **Nationaal Museum van Speelklok tot Pierement,** or National Musical Box and Street Organ Museum, housed in an old church. The Music Factory occupies budding musicians, and a large collection of automated musical instruments from the 15th to the 19th century absorbs adults. Soundproofing ensures no conflict of interests. Wander by yourself, or wait for a tour (also in English), for only on these are the dazzling automata put into play, and you can marvel at an ancient furry rabbit popping up out of a cabbage and beating time with its ears to the music, along with many other delights. Fittingly for Holland, the development of the barrel organ—still the bane of shoppers on many busy streets—is charted from the Renaissance onward in a gleaming white interior. In the center of the church, the children's Music Factory has displays of historical instruments hardy enough for three-year-olds to try—they can go at it on percussion instruments, bicycle bells, and harps. There are also interactive stands where children can shout into voice distorters, or watch themselves on a TV screen as they sing. ⊠ *Steenweg 6* ☏ *030/231-2789* ⊕ *www.museumspeelklok.nl* ⊠ *€6* ⊗ *Tues.–Sat. 10–5, Sun. noon–5; guided tours every hr.*

Soaring lancet windows add to the impression of majestic height of the famous tower of "the cathedral that is missing," the 14th-century **❼ Domtoren** (Cathedral tower). The sole remnant of an enormous house of worship that was destroyed by a storm late in the 17th century (the outline of its nave can still be seen in the paving squares of the Domplein), it is more than 367 feet high. Not only is it the highest tower in the country, but its more than 50 bells make it the largest musical instrument in Holland. The tower is so big that city buses drive through an arch in its base. You can climb the tower, but make sure you feel up to the 465 steps. The panoramic view is worth the blisters, though, for it stretches 40 km (25 mi) to Amsterdam on a clear day. ⊠ *Domplein* ☏ *030/233-3036* ⊠ *€7.50* ⊗ *Apr.–Sept., Mon.–Sat. 10–5, Sun. noon–5; Oct.–Mar., Sun.–Fri. noon–5, Sat. 10–5; view by tour only; last tour at 4.*

Holding its own against the imposing Domtoren across the square, the **❼ grand Gothic Domkerk** (Cathedral) was built during the 13th and 14th centuries and designed in the style of Tournai Cathedral in Belgium. It has five chapels radiating around the ambulatory of the chancel, as well as a number of funerary monuments, including that of a 14th-century bishop. The entire space between the tower and the Domkerk was originally occupied by the nave of the huge cathedral, which was destroyed in a freak tornado in 1674 and not rebuilt. Many other buildings were damaged, and the exhibition inside Domkerk shows interesting before-and-after sketches. Today only the chancel and tower remain, separated by an open space, now a sunny square edged by a road. Behind the chancel is the **Pandhof**, a 15th-century cloister with a formal herb garden with medicinal herbs, replanted in the 1960s. If you're lucky you'll come upon classical musicians, making the most of the wondrous acoustics. A free concert is held every Saturday at 3:30. ⊠ *Achter de Dom 1* ☏ *030/231-0403* ⊠ *Free; guided tours €1.50 suggested donation* ⊗ *May–Sept., weekdays 10–5, Sat. 10–3:30, Sun. 2–4; Oct.–Apr., weekdays 11–4, Sat. 10–3:30, Sun. 2–4.*

**73** Just a few blocks south of the Domplein brings you to the **Museum Cathar-ijneconvent** (Convent of St. Catherine Museum), a vast and comprehensive collection of religious history and sacred art that occupies a former convent near the Nieuwe Gracht (New Canal). There are magnificent altarpieces, ecclesiastical vestments, beautifully illustrated manuscripts, sculptures, and paintings—including works by Rembrandt and Frans Hals. Note the painting of a silvery-bearded God, by Pieter de Grebber (1640), holding what appears to be a crystal ball, inviting Jesus to sit at his right hand, in a cherub-bedecked chair. Temporary exhibitions here are first-rate. Cross the first-story walkway to get a great view of the cloister gardens. Unfortunately, the labeling of exhibits is all in Dutch, so if you don't know your religious history, you'll be in the dark. ✉ *Lange Nieuwestraat 38* ☎ *030/231-7296* ⊕ *www.catharijneconvent. nl* 🖃 *€7* 🕑 *Tues.–Fri. 10–5, weekends 11–5.*

**74** South by several blocks of the Het Catharijneconvent is the **Centraal Museum,** which brought in a number of hot Dutch designers to work on its renovation. "Central" is the word to describe this place's collection, since it ranges from a 10th-century boat to a Viktor and Rolf A-Bomb coat, from Golden Age paintings to minimalist home furnishings. Karijn de Kooning's work on the spatial layout and wall colors cannily encourages you to view these collections from different angles. From a multitude of options you choose your own path through the museum, up spiral staircases, along underpasses, and in glass elevators.

What you see depends on the theme of the current temporary exhibitions, but of the permanent displays, don't miss the **Utrecht Boat,** the complete 1,000-year-old wooden hull of a ship, excavated from a nearby riverbed in 1930, which has survived remarkably intact. The museum also has a collection of Golden Age art, including Abraham Bloemaert's sublime *Adoration of the Magi* (1624), and artists from the Utrecht school such as Van Bronkhorst, as well as later Dutch painters, with particularly good pieces by Ad Dekkers and modern-day artist Marlene Dumas. Across the square, modern-art lovers will make a beeline for the **Gerrit Rietveld Wing,** focused on the most famous of all De Stijl architects and designers. There is a reconstruction of his studio and lots of original Rietveld furniture.

Visitors have access to the garden, where paths cut through long grass create a meadow-like feel; when you sit outside you are transported back to the days of Napoléon, when the complex's stables held his cavalry. The museum's depot service offers artwork not exhibited to the public for a private viewing for €20. Put in your request an hour before viewing during the week, and on weekends, request before 3 on the preceding Friday. ✉ *Nicolaaskerkhof 10* ☎ *030/236-2362* ⊕ *www. centraalmuseum.nl* 🖃 *€8* 🕑 *Tues.–Sun. 11–5.*

**75** The **Universiteits Museum** (University Museum), on the same street as the Convent of St. Catherine, deals with both the history of Utrecht University and the fields of science. The first thing to grab your attention is the building itself: architects visit specially to look at Koen van Velsen's square building and his garden "boxes." A glassed-in corridor runs the length of the building, giving an immense feeling of space.

One collection, bought by William I and donated to the museum, verges on the ghoulish: skulls, anatomical models, and preserved "things" in jars; medical ethics would prevent these exhibits from being preserved now, most notably the embryos, which only increases their fascination for youngsters. On the third floor kids can have a field day as the museum turns up its hands-on approach to the max. In the Youth Lab children put on mini–lab coats to do experiments and play with optical illusions (with assistants patrolling the floor to provide guidance and assistance on Wednesday, Saturday, and Sunday afternoons). A former orangery is now a garden-fronted café. You are strongly encouraged to ask for a guided tour, not just because labeling is mainly in Dutch but also because the guides are particularly proficient in illuminating the history of each collection. ✉ *Lange Nieuwestraat 106* ☎ *030/253–8008* 🌐 *www.museum.uu.nl* 🎫 *€5* 🕓 *Tues.–Sun. 11–5.*

★ 76 The **Rietveld-Schröderhuis** (Rietveld-Schröder House) exemplifies several key principles of the De Stijl movement that affected not only art but also modern architecture, furniture design, and even typography in the early part of the 20th century. The house was designed for the Schröder family by Gerrit Rietveld, one of the leading architects of De Stijl, who has many objects on view in Utrecht's Centraal Museum. The open plan, the direct communion with nature from every room, and the use of neutral white or gray on large surfaces, with primary colors to identify linear details, are typical De Stijl characteristics. Rietveld is best known outside Holland for his "Red-Blue-Yellow" chair design. The house is about a mile east of the city center. From Utrecht's central train station, take Bus No. 4 to the Hoogstraat area. Tours must be reserved in advance. ✉ *Prins Hendriklaan 50; tours start from visitor center, Erasmuslaan 5* ☎ *030/236–2310* 🌐 *www.centraalmuseum.nl* 🎫 *€16 (includes guided tour)* 🕓 *By appointment only Tues.–Sat. 11–5.*

★ 77 A massive makeover and expansion program, completed in 2005, has transformed the **Spoorwegmuseum** (Railway Museum) into one of Holland's finest museums. Entrance is via a converted 19th-century train station just past the city wall. Beyond this is a huge new exhibition space, built in the style of a 19th-century rail yard. In addition to dozens of locomotives, trams, and carriages from the earliest days of steam to sleek electric trains, the workshop encloses three large sheds, called "werelden," or "worlds," through which you are invited to take a tour of railway history.

In World 1, you follow an audio tour (available in English) through a recreation of an early-19th-century English mine. The tour is led by a fictional 1839 train conductor named John Middlemis, who explains how carts used for transporting coal along rails in mines were the inspiration behind the first passenger railway. World 2 houses a theater, in which you watch a stage production based on a trip aboard the Orient Express in the late 19th century. In World 3, you sit in carriages that seat four at a time and ride on tracks between, toward, and under hulking locomotives. The bright lights, sounds, and billowing steam bring the Golden Age of the early 20th century to life.

Above this, in a room accessible via the mezzanine, is the museum's sizable collection of model trains. And outside is a children's area where kids get to ride the *Jumbo Express,* an adventure trip that takes them past lakes, through tunnels, and past water jets. The museum is an easy walk from the city center. Alternatively, trains run between here and Utrecht Centraal Station seven times daily for €2. ⊠ *Maliebaanstation* ☎ *030/230–6206* ⊕ *www.spoorwegmuseum.nl* ⊠ *€12.50* ⊙ *Tues.–Sun. 10–5; daily 10–5 during school vacations.*

Utrecht is a day-tripper's paradise, as it is in the very center of a superabundant region of castles, moated great houses, forests, and arboretums. To the northwest of the city are the estates of the Van Zuylen family—Slot Zuylen and Kasteel de Haar. Although those palaces remain at the top of the list, also check out the gorgeous gardens, concerts, and art exhibitions at **Kasteel Groeneveld** (Groeneveld Castle; ⊠ Groeneveld 2, Baarn ☎ 035/542–0446 ⊠ €2), just northeast of Utrecht. To the south of the city is Doorn, which has several delightful sights. Stroll in the beautiful **Arboretum von Gimborn** (⊠ Vossensteinsesteeg 8, Doorn ☎ 030/253–5177). Doorn's most fabled attraction is the **Kasteel Huis Doorn** (⊠ Doorn Castle, Langbroekerweg 10, Doorn ☎ 0343/421020 ⊠ €5.50), where you can see how royalty lived at the turn of the 20th century. This was also somewhat notoriously the last home of the deposed German kaiser William II from 1920 to 1941; Hitler ordered the kaiser's state funeral to be held here.

## Where to Stay & Eat

Utrecht hotel rooms are much in demand, since the city is a business and college center. Always book as far in advance as you can. The **Utrecht VVV** (☎ 0900/128–8732) can help with bookings.

$$–$$$ ✕ **Het Grachtenhuys.** There is the feeling of being in a gracious home at this canal-house restaurant overlooking the fashionable New Canal. The owners offer a choice of French-influenced Dutch cuisine classics. The menu changes regularly, but tempting selections might include lamb with a green olive sauce, or scallops with asparagus in oyster sauce. ⊠ *Nieuwegracht 33* ☎ *030/231–7494* ⚲ *Reservations essential* ▤ *AE, DC, MC, V* ⊙ *No lunch.*

$$–$$$ ✕ **Polman's Huis.** This grand café of the old school is a Utrecht institution. Its spacious Jugendstil–art deco interior is authentic. Other reasons to find your way here are the relaxing atmosphere and range of meal choices, from a simple quiche to a steamed fish dinner, from a kitchen that uses Mediterranean influences. ⊠ *Keistraat 2* ☎ *030/231–3368* ▤ *MC, V* ⊙ *Closed Sun.*

$–$$ ✕ **Café le Journal.** This spot has the widest terrace and so catches the most sun (when there is sun to be had) of the cafés along Winkenburgstraat and Neude. Large trees soften the view across the square, so this is a prime place for lazy weekend afternoons. Inside, floor-to-ceiling framed pictures make you feel like you're in Italy. The menu is excellent and wide-ranging. Although the café is relatively big, there is no feeling of being processed when you come here, thanks to the charming staff. Even when it is busy, you can linger over a *koffie verkerd* (café au lait) as long as you want. ⊠ *Neude 32* ☎ *030/236–4839* ▤ *No credit cards.*

★ $–$$  ✕ **De Zakkendrager.** As you walk down the narrow alleyway to this gem, it's easy to be misled by its unassuming exterior. Students, concertgoers from the nearby Vredenburg Music Center, and fashionable young locals come here for generous portions of grilled meats, excellent salads, and an unusually large vegetarian range. The atmosphere is even better—the restaurant is cozy, friendly, and informal. The rear half opens out into a breezy conservatory with panoramic views through glass walls and ceiling panels. In the walled garden at the back, a 180-year-old beech tree towers over everything. The green decor inside echoes the foliage, creating an oasis of calm away from the bustle of the city. ✉ *Zakkendragerssteeg 22–26* ☎ *030/231–7578* ▭ *AE, DC, MC, V.*

★ $–$$  ✕ **Winkel van Sinkel.** This Neoclassical *paleis* (palace) started out in the 18th century as Holland's first department store, before becoming Utrecht's foremost social hot spot. Fronted with columns and cast-iron statues of women, it conjures up images of Grecian luxe and abundance. The enormous statues were produced in England in the mid-19th century and shipped over, but they were too heavy for the crane that unloaded them, which collapsed, thereby earning the ladies the nickname "the fallen women." You can dine either on the terrace overlooking the canal or in the high-ceilinged Grote Zaal. The menu is designed to satisfy all tastes, with tempting selections such paella, rib-eye steaks, or, for vegetarians, a delicious spring vegetable ravioli. If you fancy eating after-hours, the Nachtrestaurant serves tapas until late, and a nightclub kicks in late every weekend. Monthly events include salsa and Latino nights. Check out the Web site for more details. ✉ *Oudegracht 158; Nachtrestaurant entry via Aan de Werf* ☎ *030/230–3036* ⊕ *www. dewinkelvansinkel.nl* ▭ *No credit cards.*

$  ✕ **Eetcafé de Poort.** This place is on Ledig Erf, one of Utrecht's small squares, which become hives of energy and filled with huge shade umbrellas when the sun comes out. This café's tables spill over the bridge, so you can sit overlooking canal-side gardens. On the far side of the plaza, black-and-white squares are painted onto the pavement, carrying out a popular chess theme from the surrounding cafés. ✉ *Tolsteegbarriere 2* ☎ *030/231–4572* ▭ *No credit cards.*

★ $$$$  ✕▣ **Grand Hotel Karel V.** This former military hospital and restored 11th-century convent has been transformed into Utrecht's most luxurious hotel. The Garden Wing is a separate building surrounded by extensive gardens but lacks the historic aura of the main building, where Napoléon's brother Louis once resided. Canopied guest bedrooms are comfortably large, if the terra-cotta and gold furnishings are a bit overdone. Accent pieces are very new and yet not modern, and enormously heavy curtains are roped back to reveal almost floor-to-ceiling sash windows. The sumptuous dining room glitters with opulent metallic murals, and designer-oversize vases—a regal setting for the excellent fare. A lighter-eating alternative is the Brasserie Goeie Louisa, where you can be served in the gardens or courtyard, if the weather is fine; note the afternoon tea and garden barbecue menus. ✉ *Geertebolwerk 1, 3511 XA* ☎ *030/ 233–7555* 🖶 *030/233–7500* ⊕ *www.karelv.nl* �']️ *70 rooms, 21 suites* ⌂ *Restaurant, café, minibars, cable TV, in-room data ports, health club, bar, some pets allowed* ▭ *AE, DC, MC, V.*

**$$** 🏨 **Malie Hotel.** Located on a tree-lined avenue behind a stylish 19th-century facade, this classically designed hotel is both modern and attractive. Guest rooms are brightly decorated, though simply furnished. The breakfast room overlooks a pretty garden, which guests have access to, and the bar-lounge doubles as a small art gallery. ⊠ *Maliestraat 2, 3581 SL* 🕾 *030/231–6424* 🖷 *030/234–0661* ⊕ *www.maliehotel.nl* ↩ *45 rooms* ♿ *Cable TV, bar, Internet room* 🖃 *AE, MC, V* 🍴 *CP.*

**$$** 🏨 **NH Centre Utrecht Hotel.** In the shadow of Sint Janskerk and opposite a leafy square, this friendly, modern hotel in a 19th-century jacket offers pretty and well-kept rooms at excellent prices. The attractive exterior of the 1870 building has art nouveau leanings, while the interior is very 21st century. Rooms are airy and stylishly understated, with floral-theme paintings on the walls. Some bathrooms have tubs. In the center of town, the hotel is within walking distance of the canals, and well as plenty of shopping and dining. ⊠ *Janskerkhof 10, 3512 BL* 🕾 *030/231–3169* 🖷 *030/231–0148* ⊕ *www.nh-hotel.nl* ↩ *45 rooms* ♿ *Restaurant, cable TV, Wi-Fi, bar; no a/c* 🖃 *AE, MC, V.*

**$** 🏨 **Hotel Ouwi.** A convivial family hotel, this is just off one of the main transit routes to the city center. The rooms are tight and simple in furnishings and decor, but they're very clean and tidy. ⊠ *F. C. Dondersstraat 12, 3572 JH* 🕾 *030/271–6303* 🖷 *030/271–4619* ⊕ *www.hotel-ouwi. nl* ↩ *30 rooms* ♿ *Cable TV, in-room data ports, some pets allowed; no a/c, no room phones* 🖃 *AE, DC, MC, V* 🍴 *CP.*

**¢** 🏨 **Stayokay Hostel Bunnik.** Backpackers and travelers on a budget can find a bargain bunk in shared dorms just outside Utrecht, only 10 minutes from town by bus. ⊠ *Rhijnauwenselaan 14, 3981 HH Bunnik* 🕾 *030/656–1277* 🖷 *030/657–1065* ⊕ *www.stayokay.com* ↩ *23 dorm rooms of 2, 3, 4, 5, 6, 7, 8, or 12 beds* ♿ *Restaurant, bar, Internet room; no a/c, no room phones, no TV* 🖃 *AE, V* 🍴 *CP.*

## Nightlife & the Arts

THE ARTS   In Utrecht you can find dance on the programs of **Stadsschouwburg** (⊠ Lucas Bolwerk 24 🕾 030/232–4125), which has a major performance hall as well as the Blauwe Zaal (Blue Room) for small productions. The annual **Spring Dance** festival brings international performers to town in June, with the biggest events usually on the big squares in the center of town, the Neude.

The **Vredenburg Muziek Centrum** (⊠ Vredenburgpassage 77 🕾 030/231–4544 box office, 030/286–2286 information ⊕ www.vredenburg.nl) is the biggest venue in Utrecht for classical and pop concerts. Utrecht's **Festival Oude Muziek** (🕾 030/232–9010 ⊕ www.oudemuziek.nl), or Festival of Early Music, in late summer each year is immensely popular, selling out rapidly. Note the full programs of concerts in Utrecht's many fine churches, including the **Dom** (🕾 030/231–0403), **St. Peter's Church** (🕾 030/231–1485), and **St. Catherine's Church** (🕾 030/231–4030 or 030/231–8526).

The annual mid- to late-September **Film Festival** is a seriously taken review of the past year of Dutch productions held in Winkel van Sinkel café and cinemas around town.

NIGHTLIFE  Utrecht's students strike a lively note at cafés around the center, more during the week than over weekends. Larger cafés such as the **Winkel van Sinkel** and **Oudaen** are gathering spots for all ages. **De Roze Wolk** (⊠ Oudegracht 43-werf ☎ 030/232–2066) is a mellow gay and lesbian bar with a friendly atmosphere and a canal-side dance space in the cellar. **Nachtwinkel** (⊠ Oudegracht 158 ☎ 030/230–3030) hosts Winkel van Sinkel's weekend serious fun nights, packing both floors with frenetic clubbers. **Polman's Huis** attracts a lively crowd of students and thirtysomethings. **Trianon** (⊠ Oudegracht 252 ☎ 030/231–6939) is a fast-growing salsa club that organizes great dance events—on some nights there are salsa classes earlier in the evening before the party starts. There are also demonstrations, dance lessons, and workshops on offer at the center, as well as Spanish- and Portuguese-language lessons.

Every March heralds the start of the blues season, with a weekend in the Vredenburg Center, and the annual **Blues Festival** takes place in early June, in venues across town. Late April sees the start of the jazz season, with a weekend session in the Vredenburg.

### Sports & the Outdoors

BICYCLING  Rent bikes from the **Rijwiel Shop** (⊠ Centraal Station Utrecht ☎ 030/231–1159). Costs are €6.50–€7.50 with ID and a €50 deposit. The shop is below the far north end of tracks 18 and 19. Water ski–bikes can be found at **Canal Bike** (⊠ Oudegracht, opposite City Hall ☎ 020/626–5574 [head office in Amsterdam]).

## Kasteel de Haar

**78**  *10 km (6 mi) northwest of Utrecht.*

Fodor'sChoice
  ★

The spectacular **Kasteel de Haar** (Haar Castle) is not only the largest castle in the Netherlands, but also the most sumptuously furnished. Thanks to the fortuitous way the Barons van Zuylen had of marrying Rothschilds, their family home grew into an Neo-Gothic extravaganza replete with moat, fairy-tale spires, and machicolated towers. The castle was founded back in 1165, but several renovations and many millions later, the family expanded the house under the eye of P. J. H. Cuypers, designer of Amsterdam's Centraal Station and Rijksmuseum in 1892. Inside the castle are acres of tapestries, medieval iron chandeliers, and the requisite ancestral portraits snootily studying you as you wander through chivalric halls so opulent and vast they could be opera sets. One portrait is of Belle van Zuylen, one of Holland's most noted 18th-century writers; you can visit her home, **Slot Zuylen** (⊠ Zuylen Castle, Tournooiveld 1, Oud Zuilen ☎ 030/244–0255 ⊕ www.slotzuylen.com ⊠ €6) on the outskirts of Utrecht on your way to Kasteel de Haar. Slot Zuylen can be seen only via hourly guided tours from mid-May to mid-September, Tuesday through Thursday, 11 to 4, on Saturday from 2 to 4, and on Sunday from 1 to 4. From mid-March to mid-May and mid-September to mid-November, tours are led on Saturday from 2 to 4, and on Sunday from 1 to 4.

At de Haar, be sure to explore the magnificent gardens and park, dotted with romantic paths, fanciful statues, and little bridges. As was the wont of aristo owners in the 19th century, entire villages were relocated to expand their estate parks, and in this case, Haarzuilens was reconstructed a mile from the castle. Designed in 1898 around a village square, all its cottages have red-and-white doors and shutters, reflecting the armorial colors of the Van Zuylen family. Every year in September, the village fun-fair is kicked off by the current baron to the accompaniment of a fire-works display. As for the castle itself, you can view its grand interiors only via one of the guided tours (no kids under five), which leave on the hour and are led only in Dutch. No matter, the objects of beauty on display can be understood in any language. Once you explore this enchanted do-main, you'll easily understand why Marie-Hélène van Zuylen, who grew up here, went on to become Baroness Guy de Rothschild, the late-20th-century's "Queen of Paris," famous for her grand houses and costume balls. Directions for car travelers are given on the castle Web site. For pub-lic transport, take Bus No. 127 from Utrecht Centraal Station, direction Breukelen/Kockengen, until the Brink stop in Haarzuilens, a 15-minute walk from the castle. You can also train it to Vleuten and then take a taxi. ⊠*Kasteellaan 1, near Haarzuilens* ☎*030/677–8515* ⊕*www.kasteeldehaar. nl* ☜*€7.50, parking €2.50* ⊙*Grounds daily 10–5; castle Tues.–Fri. noon–3, weekends 1–4. Hrs may vary; call to confirm.*

# Muiden

**㉙** *8 km (5 mi) northeast of Naarden, 12 km (7½ mi) southeast of Am-sterdam.*

The route into this petite village takes you to a narrow tree-lined av-enue where you think you have entered a miniature regality—an excel-lent preparation for a visit to **Rijksmuseum Muiderslot,** or Muiden Castle, another contender for that honorific, the largest castle in Holland.

★ ☺

One of Holland's most history-soaked abodes, several notable Dutch events took place in this medieval fortress. In 1280, Floris V, Count of Holland, had a stone fortress built strategically here at the mouth of the River Vecht, then the main route to Utrecht, the principal center of commerce in northern Holland. Unfortunately, greed got the better of him and he in-stituted a toll to be paid by all vessels passing through his stretch of the estuary. His scheme irked the locals, and in short order, Floris was cap-tured while out hunting in 1296, imprisoned in his own castle, then bru-tally murdered. In a further act of vengeance the castle and surrounding buildings were destroyed by a warring bishop from Mechelen.

A vision out of a fairy tale, the castle you see today was rebuilt on the remains of Floris's original, almost a century later in 1370. The 17th-century furnishings you see as you tour the castle originate from its most famous occupant, poet Pieter Corneliszoon Hooft (1581–1647), who was Muiden's *drost* (bailiff) and summered here from 1609 to 1647, filling it with Baroque-era treasures to amuse his *Muiderkring* (literary circle)—the country's most famous gathering of Dutch intellectuals. Most notable is the desk where Hooft wrote his poems, standing up. The rooms have other curiosities, such as an enclosed family box bed, where children slept underneath in drawers and adults slept sitting up (the cord pulled open a vent when it all got a bit too close).

The castle is also an ideal place for a stroll, with an herb garden, plum orchard, and paths running right around the moat. There are guided tours of the gardens, scheduled on the first Saturday of each month, starting at 11. There are also falconry demonstration days at the castle, which take you back in time to the days of Count Floris. It's not surprising that 35,000 of its 120,000 annual visitors are children, and guides provide animated group tours with activities specifically geared toward them. If your kids are interested, ask about joining an international school tour, where the guide takes the children through in English. Visitors must be accompanied by a guide. Tours leave several times each hour. Call ahead to confirm times for tours in English. By public transport, take Bus No. 136 (two an hour) from Amstel Station in Amsterdam. ⊠ *Herengracht 1* ☎ *0294/261325* ⊕ *www.muiderslot.nl* ☒ *€7* ⊙ *Apr.–Oct., weekdays 10–5, weekends 1–5; Nov.–Mar., weekends 1–4; last tours leave 1 hr before closing.*

---

**need a break?**

Take a beer outside at the **Café Ome Ko** (⊠ Herengracht 71 ☎ 0294/261330) to sit at one of the many tables on the River Vecht with the calming—and unusual, in Holland—sound of whooshing water, thanks to the adjacent lock gates. Only beverages are served, but dessert is your vista of Muiden Castle in the distance as you look up the river.

### Where to Eat

**$$–$$$** ✕ **De Doelen.** To fully appreciate the setting of this restaurant, come for lunch, not dinner, so you can sit under lime trees and eat overlooking the rural canal lock and small harbor, filled with yachts. With the entire menu stuffed with temptations such as crispy, baked sole, you'll be hard-pressed to stop yourself from coming back for dinner, too. ⊠ *Sluis 1* ☎ *0294/263200* ▤ *AE, DC, MC, V.*

# METROPOLITAN HOLLAND ESSENTIALS

## Transportation

In combination with trains, the efficient system of buses and trams in the metropolitan area will easily take care of most of your transportation needs. Bus service is available in all cities in this region, and trams operate within The Hague, Rotterdam, and Utrecht. Trams also run between Delft and The Hague; buses offer services across the Randstad to certain smaller towns served only by secondary rail connections. Bus lanes are shared only with taxis, meaning they remain uncongested, ensuring that you travel more swiftly than the rest of the traffic in rush hour.

Rotterdam also has a subway, referred to as the metro, with only two lines (east to west and north to south) that extend into the suburbs and cross in the city center for easy transfers. All three options are excellent for transport within the city.

The same ticket can be used in buses, trams, and metros Holland-wide. Called a *strippenkaart* (strip ticket), a 2- or 3-strip ticket can be bought directly from the bus driver. If you buy a ticket in advance, this works out much cheaper per journey: a 15-strip ticket is €6.50 and a 45-strip ticket costs €19.20. You can buy these at railway stations, from post offices, and from many bookshops and cigarette kiosks, and they remain valid until there are no further strips left, or for one year from the first stamp. *See* Tickets, *in* Bus Travel *in* Smart Travel Tips for how to use the strippenkaart.

🛈 **Public Transportation Information** ☎ 0900/9292.

### BY AIR

Amsterdam Schiphol Airport is 50 km (30 mi) north of Rotterdam and has efficient road and rail links. Its comprehensive Web site provides real-time information about flight arrivals and departures, as well as all transport and parking facilities. **Rotterdam Airport,** 17 km (11 mi) northwest of Rotterdam, is the biggest of the regional airports, providing daily service to a number of European cities. However, to reach the airport from Rotterdam you need to take Bus No. 33 from Centraal Station, or a taxi, as there are no rail links. If you take a taxi, expect to pay around €25.

🛈 **Airport Information Amsterdam Schiphol Airport** ☎ 0900/0141 ⊕ www.schiphol. nl. **Rotterdam Airport** ☎ 010/446-3444.

### BY BIKE

In this flat land, a bicycle is an ideal means of getting around, and cities have safe cycle lanes on busy roads. Bikes are best rented at outlets near most railway stations, called **Rijwiel** shops. These shops are generally open long hours every day, and the bikes are invariably new and well maintained. Rates are €6.50–€8.40, and you must show ID and pay a deposit of €50. Cheaper bikes have back-pedal brakes and no gears. Other local rental centers can be found in the regional *Gouden Gids* (Yellow Pages), under *Fietsen en Bromfietsen*.

### BY BOAT

TOURS  The best way to see Rotterdam's waterfront is by boat; **Spido Harbor Tours** offers excursions lasting from just over an hour to a full day. In Delft, Dordrecht, Kinderdijk, Leiden, Rotterdam, and Utrecht guided sightseeing boat tours allow you to explore the cities. Ask at the local VVV office in the towns you would like to tour for the latest departure information and routes. In summer, **Rebus** runs three-hour cruises to the Kinderdijk windmills, leaving from the center of Rotterdam, for €12.50.

In July and August in Leiden, **Groene Hart Cruises** runs three-hour boat trips, including a windmill cruise for €11 on Wednesday, or across the Braassemermeer and Kager lakes on Tuesday and Thursday for €12, departing from the *haven* (harbor) at 1 PM. In Utrecht, opt for one of the many guided tours operated by the **RonDom,** a one-stop cultural and historical information center for the museum quarter, where you can buy tickets for almost everything as well as book a guided tour or a barge trip.

🛈 **Groene Hart Cruises** ☎ 071/541-3183. **Rebus** ✉ Boompjeskade, Rotterdam ☎ 010/218-3131 ⊕ www.rebus-info.nl. **RonDom** ✉ Domplein 9, Utrecht ☎ 030/233-3036. **Rondvaart Delft** ✉ Koornmarkt 113 ☎ 015/212-6385. **Spido Harbor Tours** ✉ Willemsplein 85add city? ☎ 010/275-9988 ⊕ www.spido.nl. **Utrecht Tourist Office** ✉ Vredenburg 90 ☎ 06/3403-4805.

If you are traveling to the United Kingdom, there are two daily Stena line crossings between the Hoek van Holland—the main port for ferries and boats heading to England—to Harwich, on the fast car ferry, taking approximately 3 hours. The overnight crossing takes about 7 hours. These ferry crossings can be booked at the international travel window in large railway stations. The PO North Sea Ferries run an overnight crossing between the Europoort in Rotterdam and Hull, England, which takes about 14 hours. 🖪 **PO North Sea Ferries** ⊠ Beneluxhaven, Havennummer 5805, Rotterdam/Europoort ☎ 020/201-3333 ⊕ www.poferries.nl **Stena** ⊠ Hoek van Holland Terminal, Stationsweg 10, Hoek van Holland ☎ 0174/315800, 0900/8123 reservations [10¢ per min] 🖷 0174/389389 ⊕ www.stenaline.nl.

### BY CAR

Using a car in the Randstad, with the complexity of one-way streets in city centers, makes driving a real headache, let alone the added burdens of parking and expense. In addition, there is also the consideration of traffic, especially around rush hour, when driving between Haarlem and Delft can take up to three times longer than traveling by train. If you decide to travel by car, you can reach Rotterdam directly from Amsterdam by taking E19 via Amsterdam Schiphol Airport. The city is bounded by the A20 on the northern outskirts, the A16 on the east, the A15 on the south, and the A4 on the west. N200 or A9 goes to Haarlem from Amsterdam (from there N208 leads through the bulb district to Leiden); to reach Leiden and Delft directly from Amsterdam, take E19 via Amsterdam Schiphol Airport; to continue to Dordrecht and Utrecht from Rotterdam, take A15 and then the A27, or to reach Utrecht directly from Rotterdam (or via Gouda), take E25. Take E30/A12 from The Hague to Utrecht to bypass the congestion of Rotterdam.

🖪 **Car-Rental Agencies Avis** ⊠ Marconistraat 1a, Rotterdam ☎ 010/433-2233 🖾 Rotterdam Airport ☎ 010/298-2424. **Budget** ⊠ Rotterdam Airport ☎ 010/437-8622 🖾 Abraham van Stolkweg 96, Rotterdam ☎ 010/415-1833. **Europcar** ⊠ Walenburghof 17, Rotterdam ☎ 010/465-6400 🖾 Rotterdam Airport ☎ 0900/1576.

### BY TAXI

Taxis are available at railway stations, at major hotels, and, in larger cities, at taxi stands in key locations. You can also order a taxi by using the telephone numbers below. Expect to pay at least €30 for a 30-minute journey between Rotterdam and Delft.

When you buy your train ticket from a station office, you can buy a *treintaxi* (a taxi that operates out of train stations) ticket from some smaller stations for a standard €4.10 per person, per ride. It doesn't matter where you're going, so long as it's within the city limits. The fare is so cheap because it's shared—but with waiting time at a guaranteed maximum of 10 minutes following your call, you won't be hanging around long. Treintaxis are ideal for getting to sights on the outskirts of smaller towns. Call one of the numbers below to order a taxi in metropolitan Holland, but for treintaxis, simply go to the ticket window at the smaller train station; note that not all small towns have this service.

🖪 Taxi Companies **Delft** ☎ 015/361-3030. **Haarlem** ☎ 023/540-0600. **Leiden** ☎ 071/521-2144. **Rotterdam** ☎ 010/462-6060 or 010/425-7000. **Utrecht** ☎ 030/230-0400.

**BY TRAIN**

Getting about by rail is the ideal means of intercity transport in the metropolitan area. Trains are fast, frequent, clean, and reliable, and stations in all towns are centrally located, usually within walking distance of major sights. All international and intercity trains from Brussels and Paris stop in Rotterdam Centraal. From here connections can be taken to travel directly to Delft (15 minutes northwest), Leiden (35 minutes northwest), and Haarlem (55 minutes northwest), on a twice-hourly *sneltrain* (express train) in the direction of Amsterdam. Intercity trains to Amsterdam traveling via Schiphol also stop in Leiden, but not Delft or Haarlem. For Gouda (20–25 minutes northeast) take a *snel-* or *stoptrein* (local train) in the direction of Arnhem, Nijmegen, or Utrecht. Intercities heading to Arnhem, Nijmegen, and Enschede also stop in Utrecht, where the faster trains shorten the journey time (35–50 minutes northwest). Seat reservations aren't permitted.

When traveling around the metropolitan area, a sneltrain leaves Amsterdam twice an hour for Haarlem, which also stops in Leiden, Delft, Rotterdam, and Dordrecht. From Rotterdam, a sneltrain leaves twice an hour for Gouda and Utrecht. For Muiden and Naarden, take a train to Amsterdam Amstel (in the city suburbs), then Bus No. 136, which stops in Muiden and Naarden. For Naarden, you can also take a train from Amsterdam Centraal to Naarden-Bussum, then walk 20 minutes to Naarden. Returning to Amsterdam, take Bus No. 136.

🚆**Intercity** ☎0900/9292. **Rotterdam Centraal** ☎0900/9292. **Treintaxi** ☎0900/873–4682.

## Contacts & Resources

**EMERGENCIES**

Pharmacies stay open late on a rotating basis. Call one of the numbers listed below for addresses on a given night.

🚆 Emergency Services **National Emergency Alarm Number** ☎112 for police, fire, and ambulance.

🚆 Hospitals **Delft** ⊠ Reinier de Graaf Gasthuis, Reinier De Graafweg 3–11 ☎015/260-3060. **Haarlem** ⊠ Spaarne Ziekenhuis, Van Heythuijzenweg 1 ☎023/514-1516. **Leiden** ⊠ Academisch Ziekenhuis Leiden, Rijnsburgerweg 10 ☎071/526-9111. **Rotterdam** ⊠ Erasmus MC, Dr. Molewaterplein 40–50 ☎010/463-9222. **Utrecht** ⊠ Universitair Medisch Centrum Utrecht, Heidelberglaan 100 ☎030/250-9111.

**VISITOR INFORMATION**

Each VVV (tourist board) across the country has information principally on its own town and region. Contact the VVV of the area you plan to travel to, and ask directly for information, as there is no one central office; information lines cost €.70 per minute.

🚆 Tourist Information **VVV Brielle** ⊠ Markt 1 ☎0181/475475. **Toeristen Informatie Punt Delft (Delft Tourist Information Point)** ⊠ Hippolytusbuurt 4, 2611 HN ☎0900/515-1555. **VVV Dordrecht** ⊠ Stationsweg 1, 3311 JW ☎0900/463-6888. **VVV Gouda** ⊠ Markt 27, 2801 JJ ☎0900/468-3288. **VVV Haarlem** ⊠ Stationsplein 1, 2011 LR ☎0900/616-1600. **VVV Kinderdijk (c/o Alblasserdam)** ⊠ Cortgene 2 [inside City Hall] ☎078/692-1355. **VVV Leiden** ⊠ Stationsweg 2d, 2312 AV ☎0900/222-2333. **VVV Muiden** ( ⇨ VVV Naarden). **VVV Naarden** ⊠ Adriaan Dortsmanplein 1b, 1411 RC ☎035/694-2836. **VVV Rotterdam** ⊠ Coolsingel 67, 3012 AC ☎0900/403-4065. **VVV Utrecht** ⊠ Vinkenburgstraat 19, 3512 AA ☎0900/128-8732.

# The Hague

## WORD OF MOUTH

"While in The Hague, don't forget to visit the new Escher Museum. The collection is very extensive and includes family photo albums. On the top floor there is a virtual reality exhibit that fits right in with his work."

—wen47

"The Mauritshuis and the beautiful old parliament buildings right next door to it are a must."

—Rockknocker

**IT'S ALL TOO EASY TO SEE THE HAGUE** as nothing more than Amsterdam's prissy maiden aunt. Its status as Holland's seat of government, its role as a diplomatic capital, and its worldwide reputation as a center of legislative excellence (the town is home to the International Court of Justice) doesn't do much to contradict its staid image. Those who experience Den Haag—to use the Dutch name—up close and personal, however, will be won over by its elegance and unexpected quirkiness. Here you'll find the latest in contemporary architecture sitting comfortably beside 17th-century mansions resplendent with ornate frescoes and glittering chandeliers. You'll walk down narrow winding streets and through wide-open places; indeed, The Hague has more than 25 parks. In the city's galleries and museums, you'll have the chance to see old masters from the Dutch 17th-century Golden Age as well as later works by Holland's leading modern artists.

As befits such a multifaceted city, The Hague has more than one name. Its official Dutch name is 's-Gravenhage, literally, "the Count's Hedge," harking back to the early 13th century, when the Count of Holland's hunting lodge was based in a small woodland village called Die Haghe— and Den Haag is the locution still favored by the Dutch in conversation today. In 1248, Count Willem II built a larger house; the noted Knights' Hall, or Ridderzaal, was added in 1280; and gradually Den Haag became the focus of government functions. Throughout the 17th and 18th centuries, the city was the seat of government for the United Provinces, but only with the Napoleonic occupation (the French entered the city in 1795) did the town receive a full civic charter, bestowed upon it by Bonaparte's brother, Louis. Between 1814 and 1831, The Hague shared political-capital status with Brussels—a less-than-happy power split, with parliaments meeting alternately in the two cities. By 1814, both government and court had returned to The Hague, although the title of capital city stayed with Amsterdam. In 1899 the first international conference for the suppression of war was held at The Hague, leading to the Permanent Court of Arbitration and the building of the Peace Palace (1913). Today, The Hague is home to the reigning monarch, Queen Beatrix, and visitors can enjoy the many buildings that are a testament to her family's history. Royal residences include the beautiful cream-color Noordeinde Palace (closed to the public), Lange Voorhout Palace (currently a museum), and Huis ten Bosch, the private home of the queen herself.

Should you by any chance find The Hague's pace a little too refined, a little too gracious, there's always the fishing port and seaside casino town of Scheveningen just up the road, which couldn't offer a greater contrast. Almost seamlessly connected to The Hague and nicknamed "our national bathing place," the town boasts all the bright lights, glitz, and tackiness that you'd expect of a traditional vacation mecca. If you fancy a flutter at the casino tables or a spot of fishing or a dip in the stupendously icy North Sea (now that really *is* something to write home about), this is the place to visit.

Other than side trips out of town to Scheveningen, The Hague is custom-built for the eager army of bipeds who discover it every year. A walk through the town—since it isn't too large, it's never an overly aerobic one—exercises the spirit as well as the limbs.

*Numbers in the text correspond to numbers in the margin and on The Hague map.*

**3**

**If you have 1 day**

Begin with a gentle tour of the **Binnenhof** ❷—the time-burnished, governmental complex that remains the heart of town. Arrive as soon as it opens (10 AM), and even if the weather's not great, a palpable mistiness might be hanging over these 13th-century courtyards, halls, and palace buildings. From here, move around the corner to the exquisite **Mauritshuis** ❸—home of such wonders as Vermeer's *View of Delft* and his even more magical *Girl with a Pearl Earring*; if you feel pushed for time, ask for the free brochure "The Highlights of the Mauritshuis in 45 Minutes." Ready for lunch? Walk through dignified Lange Voorhout and head for one of the cafés on Denneweg, where a sandwich stuffed with tarragon chicken or grilled steak, washed down with a cold beer, should keep you going for an hour or two. Take time to explore Denneweg's delightful boutiques, and then head for the **Gemeentemuseum Den Haag** ⓬, repository of fine modern art, including the world's largest collection of Mondriaans. If you can drag yourself away before 4 PM, it's worth diving into the next-door science-oriented **Museon** ⓾, a model of Dutch modernity. State-of-the-art interactive exhibits make for a fascinating, if whirlwind, visit. If you want to continue wandering through the 17th-century Golden Age, forget the Museon and set your sights on the treasure troves of the **Museum Mesdag** ❾, the **Museum Bredius** ❻, and the **Schilderijengalerij Prins Willem V** ⓱ (Prince William V Painting Gallery), three magnificent art collections housed in stately interiors worthy of king and connoisseur. In the evening, treat yourself to a cocktail at the gilded Des Indes hotel, and then head for supper at one of the restaurants on quiet Molenstraat.

**If you have 3 days**

With more time at your disposal, you can afford to do things at a less-frenetic pace. On Day 1, concentrate on the **Binnenhof** ❷ and the **Mauritshuis** ❸; then send yourself dizzy in M. C. Escher's bizarre world of optical illusions found within the **Escher in Het Paleis Museum** ❼. Once your eyes have recovered, head for the intimate **Schilderijengalerij Prins Willem V** ⓱, whose walls are almost literally wallpapered with paintings collected by the Stadholder Prince in the late 18th century. For something totally different, the **Gevangenpoort Museum** ⓰ next door has a collection of instruments of torture that will make you appreciate living in the 21st century. Then do a little leisurely shopping—window or otherwise—in the nearby Noordeinde area, or head off in the opposite direction for Denneweg. On your second day, lose yourself among the Mondriaans at the **Gemeentemuseum Den Haag** ⓬ before enjoying lunch in the light-filled restaurant there; then spend plenty of time at the science **Museon** ⓾ next door. Finally, round off your day with an awe-inspiring film experience at the **Omniversum** ⓫. Here, thanks to the place's vast semi-domed screen, you'll feel not so much that you're watching a wildlife movie as actually *in* it. Shift down a cultural gear or two on Day 3 with a trip to the seaside resort of **Scheveningen** ⓲. Dabble your toes in the water, walk around the old village, and enjoy either a soothing visit to the Sculptures by the Sea exhibit or, as an antidote to artistic overload, a massage at the Vitalizee spa. For lunch, try herring from a stall, or indulge in afternoon tea in the splendidly painted hall of the Kurhaus hotel. Head back to The Hague in the evening and catch a performance by either the Nederlands Dans Theater at the Lucent, or the city's resident orchestra at Dr. Anton Philipszaal next door.

## Exploring The Hague

For a city that sees so much political, legal, and diplomatic action, The Hague can seem surprisingly quiet, thus a delight to those who want to escape the crowds. It may be home to around 450,000 people and see a steady influx of visitors, but even on a Saturday you're unlikely to find yourself joined cheek-by-jowl with an infinitude of other people. Because it's a compact city, you can easily cover most of the key sights—the medieval complex of the Binnenhof, the masterpiece-filled Mauritshuis, and the nearby lovely streets of Lange Voorhout, Denneweg, and Noordeinde—on foot from Centraal Station. Most of the modern venues—the wide-ranging municipal Gemeentemuseum, the miniature version of Holland that is the Madurodam, the science-orientated Museon and Omniversum—are to the north of town. The Hague's predictably efficient bus and tram network can take you there, and on to Scheveningen, with frequent departures from either station; a tram from the center of town will do likewise. The transport lines you need to look for are as follows: for the Gemeentemuseum, Omniversum, Museon, and GEM/Museum of Photography, Tram No. 17 or Bus No. 4 from Centraal Station, or Tram No. 10 from Hollands Spoor Station; for Madurodam, Tram No. 9 from either station.

### About the Restaurants & Hotels

For a good selection of a restaurant's fare, opt for a set, prix-fixe menu. This will give you three, four, or even five courses, sometimes including appropriate wine servings, for a bargain price. As in other towns in Holland, you won't have to dress up to chow down. Local diners usually start their evening meal around 7 PM, not the 5:30–6 start experienced elsewhere in Holland. In general, it's always wise to reserve in advance, although if you arrive early without a prior booking, you may nevertheless be seated.

With more than 20 million visitors a year, The Hague needs plenty of spare beds. The daily round of international business, though, means that hotels quickly fill up with conference delegates, diplomats, and visiting lawyers, so rooms at the better places need to be booked well in advance of a planned visit. When it comes to sleeping in style, The Hague boasts one of the grandest traditional hotels in the country, the Des Indes hotel—dripping with crystal chandeliers and stuffed with both antiques and a history of famous guests, including everyone from glamorous Dutch spy Mata Hari to crooner Bing Crosby. Elsewhere, hotel accommodations can be a little on the bland side; The Hague's smaller, family-run bed-and-breakfast facilities will offer homey, more individual surroundings. Assume all rooms have air-conditioning, TV, telephones, and private bath, unless otherwise noted.

If you arrive in The Hague without a room, the reservations department of **The Hague Visitors and Convention Bureau** (☎ 070/338–5815 ⊕ www. denhaag.com) should be able to help you. It's open weekdays 8:30–5. Alternatively, head for the VVV Babylon by Centraal Station.

| WHAT IT COSTS In euros | | | | | |
|---|---|---|---|---|---|
| | **$$$$** | **$$$** | **$$** | **$** | **¢** |
| RESTAURANTS | over €30 | €22–€30 | €15–€22 | €10–€15 | under €10 |
| HOTELS | over €230 | €165–€230 | €120–€165 | €75–€120 | under €75 |

Restaurant prices are per person for a main course only, excluding tax (6% for food and 19% for alcoholic beverages) and service; note that if a restaurant offers only prix-fixe meals, it has been given the price category that reflects the full prix-fixe price. Hotel prices are for a standard double room in high season, including the 6% VAT.

## Timing

Done at a pace that will allow you to soak up The Hague's historical atmosphere, a minimal tour around the city center should take you about three or four hours. If you take time to visit all the sights en route, you're looking at a very full day. At the very least, allow 30 minutes for each site you choose to visit (some people would spend their lives at the Mauritshuis).

Before you start out, bear a couple of things in mind. First, as in all other Dutch cities, both walking surfaces and the weather can change at short notice; if you're going to be on your feet all day, make sure you're equipped with both an umbrella and sturdy walking shoes. Second, despite The Hague's international status, museums and galleries usually close by 5 PM, so don't plan any early-evening art visitations without careful checking. Many sites are also closed Monday, so plan accordingly.

# THE CENTRUM: HEART OF THE HAGUE

The Hague's center is crammed with the best the city has to offer in terms of art, history, and architecture. An exploration of a relatively small area will take you through busy thoroughfares and quiet backstreets, into the famed Mauritshuis Museum and past the bourgeois homes of the 17th century. If you want to explore the political hub of the Netherlands, you can do so at the Binnenhof, home to the famous Ridderzaal (Knights' Hall) and the Houses of Parliament. Or, if you want a little peace and quiet, turn onto the leafy Lange Voorhout and stroll through what in the 19th century was the place to see and be seen. (This is the street Queen Beatrix takes to get to services in the Kloosterkerk at the corner.) Just off the Lange Voorhout is the Denneweg, whose book- and antiques shops and fashion boutiques combine the quaint and the cutting-edge in just a few blocks. Wandering streets like these, you'll understand immediately how The Hague earned its reputation for elegance, restraint, and charm.

a good
walk

Heading out the west exit of the Centraal train station (by track No. 1), cross the tram tracks and proceed into the pedestrian street, which turns out to be a covered plaza that is actually the inside of an office complex (a good introduction to the Dutch obsession with efficient use of space). Continue straight down a long block to a prime example of The Hague's innovative municipal architecture: the gleaming white **Stadhuis Atrium** ① ▶, completed in 1995, which combines town hall and library. Locals refer to it as either the White Swan or, less affectionately, the Ice Palace. At the far end of the Stadhuis, bear right, crossing straight over Kalvermarkt and into little Bagijnestraat. Follow the pedestrianized alley to the left and then right, past some restaurants and into Lange Poten. Again, follow the road around to the left, then bear right into noisy Hofweg until you reach the government complex of the **Binnenhof** ②, home of the legendary Knights' Hall, or Ridderzaal. Once you've headed right to take a look at the Knights' Hall, exit via the arched, cream-color gatehouse. This will bring you to the front of the perfectly proportioned **Mauritshuis** ③, where you can feast your eyes on no fewer than 15 Rembrandts and 3 Vermeers, among many other treasures.

For a perfect time-out, head to the restful lake, the **Hofvijver** ④, behind the museum. From here, walk along Korte Vijverberg with its horse-chestnut trees and to the **Haags Historisch Museum** ⑤, where you can explore seven centuries of the city's history. Walk on a little way until you reach busy Tournooiveld; if you cross over and turn left here, you'll come to the **Museum Bredius** ⑥ on Lange Vijverberg; bearing right on Tournooiveld will bring you to elegant, tree-lined Lange Voorhout, dominated by the stately Des Indes hotel. Adjacent to this is **Escher in Het Paleis** ⑦, an 18th-century former palace that now is a museum housing the eye-crossing works of artist M. C. Escher. Take the road between the two—Vos in Tuinstraat—leading into Denneweg. Head all the way up this lovely street, pausing to be diverted by the gorgeous art and antiques shops. When the street ends, turn left and walk along Mauritskade. Soon, you'll arrive at busy Parkstraat and, as you look to your right on crossing it, you'll notice Plein 1813, with its monument commemorating the end of Napoleonic occupation.

Should you want to make a lengthy detour, the **Vredespaleis** ⑧, or Peace Palace, and the lushly beautiful 19th-century **Museum Mesdag** ⑨ are situated in the direction behind the Plein, and beyond them is the Statenkwartier district, which harbors four of the city's museums: the science-oriented **Museon** ⑩; the **Omniversum** ⑪, home of the IMAX theater; the famous modern art collection of the **Gemeentemuseum Den Haag** ⑫; and the **GEM Museum of Contemporary Art/Museum of Photography** ⑬. It's a good hike to the Statenkwartier museums, but if you choose to walk, you can either view many of the stately embassies en route along the Tobias Asserlaan and Johan de Wittlaan, or take a slightly longer walk along the Scheveningseweg through the Scheveningse Bosjes (the woods between The Hague and Scheveningen), turning left on the Adriaan Goekooplaan. If, on the other hand, you want to save your feet, catch a tram (No. 10) at the Vredespaleis and get off at Statenplein. If none of this detour appeals to you, just continue down Mauritskade for some time until you reach Noordeinde. Directly on the opposite side of Mauritskade is Zeestraat, where both the **Museum voor Communicatie** ⓮, or Communication Museum, and the evocative **Panorama Mesdag** ⓯ are situated. If you don't fancy a detour to check these two out, keep on heading down into Noordeinde, where you can't miss the elegant Royal Palace on your right (the statue in front of it is of Prince William of Orange). Keep on for several more side streets; then turn left onto the pleasant Plaats, where you've earned a cold beer at Café Juliana. Finally, from Plaats, turn right into Buitenhof, and you'll see both the **Gevangenpoort Museum** ⓰, notorious for its torture collection, and the charming painting collection of the **Schilderijengalerij Prins Willem V** ⓱, giving you a choice of either the barbaric or the sublime as a final stop.

## What to See

❷ **Binnenhof and the Ridderzaal** (Inner Court and the Knights' Hall). The governmental heart of the Netherlands, the complex of the Binnenhof (or Inner Court) is in the very center of town yet tranquilly set apart from it, thanks to the charming Hofvijver (court lake). Although much of the day-to-day governing of the country goes on here in its legislative halls, the setting of the Binnenhof is anything but prosaic. All its pomp and decorum come into full play every third Tuesday of September, when you will see Queen Beatrix driven in a golden coach to the 13th-century Ridderzaal, or Knights' Hall, to open the new session of Parliament. Her cortege passes through much of the city, coming and going, in a display of color and ceremony that has few equals in Holland. The Binnenhof makes a suitable backdrop. For many centuries the court of the Counts of Holland, it is now a complex of buildings from a spectrum of different eras.

FodorśChoice
★

As you enter, the former castle of the Earls of Holland, complete with twin turrets, dominates. This was originally built by Count Floris V and became a meeting hall for the Knights of the Order of the Golden Fleece, one of the most regal societies of the Middle Ages. Its medieval towers recall an era when architects were as much concerned with defense as shelter, its shape suggesting more of a church than a castle. Inside, the Great Hall has seen several transformations. Today, it is adorned with vast beams spanning a width of 59 feet, flags of the 12 Dutch provinces, a vast rose window bearing the coats of arms of the major Dutch cities, and a sense of history. Note the carved heads positioned near the beams; when the hall served as a court, judges would tell the accused to fess up, otherwise these "eavesdroppers" would have words with the heavenly powers. In 1900 the hall was restored to its original 13th-century glory, and it now looks much as it would have when built for the counts as a venue for their feasts and revelries. In 1904 Queen Wilhelmina opened Parliament here for the first time; since that time the hall has been referred to as the Knights' Hall. It continues to play a key role in Dutch legislative life.

The Binnenhof also incorporates the halls used by the First and Second Chambers of the States General (equivalent to the U.S. Senate and House of Representatives). You can wander freely around the open outer courtyard, but entrance to the Knights' Hall and either the First or Second Chamber is by guided tour only. In the atmospheric reception area below the Knights' Hall there's a free exhibition detailing the political history of the Low Countries. ⊠ *Binnenhof 8a* ☎ *070/364–6144* 🎫 *€6* ⊘ *Mon.–Sat. 10–4 (some areas, including Knights' Hall, may be closed when government meetings are taking place).*

🖐 ❼ **Escher in Het Paleis Museum** (Escher Museum). First known as the Lange
Fodor'sChoice ⭐ Voorhout Palace, this lovely building was originally the residence of Caroline of Nassau, daughter of Prince Willem IV. In 1765 Mozart gave a concert for her here. Later, the intimately scaled house became Queen Emma's winter residence, then the official Hague reception chamber for the queens Wilhelmina, Juliana, and Beatrix. But in 2001 it was transformed into a museum devoted to the Dutch graphic artist M. C. Escher (1892–1972), whose prints and engravings of unforgettable images—roofs becoming floors, water flowing upward, fish transforming into birds—became world famous in the 1960s and '70s. Replete with ever-repeating Baroque pillars, Palladian portals, and parallel horizons, the perspectival tricks of Maurits Cornelis Escher presage the "virtual reality" games and worlds of today. Fittingly, the museum now features an Escher Experience where you don a helmet and join 30 other passengers through a 360-degree trip into his unique world. Concave and convex, radical metamorphoses, and dazzling optical illusions are on view in the impressive selection of his prints (including the famed *Day and Night* and *Ascending and Descending*); distorted rooms and video cameras make children big and adults small; and there are rooms that are Escher prints blown up to the nth power. Don't forget to look up as you walk around—the latest addition to the museum is a series of custom-designed chandeliers in each room, designed by Dutch sculptor Hans van Bentem and inspired by Escher's work. These delightfully playful creations include umbrellas, sea horses, birds, bottles, and even a giant skull and crossbones. A family ticket for €20 makes this an even more attractive museum for kids. ⊠ *Lange Voorhout 74* ☎ *070/427–7730* ⊕ *www.escherinhetpaleis.nl* 🎫 *€7.50* ⊘ *Tues.–Sun. 11–5.*

> **need a break?** Down a quiet side street, off Vos in Tuinstraat and very near the Escher in Het Paleis Museum, the friendly **Le Café Hathor** (⊠ Maliestraat 22 ☎ 070/346–4081) is a great spot for a snack, a full lunch, or just a quiet drink. Wood-paneled walls and flickering candles on each table create an intimately cozy atmosphere inside, while in good weather, tables on a raft outside overlook a gently flowing canal.

⓭ **GEM Museum of Contemporary Art/Museum of Photography.** These small museums occupy an elegant 1962 annex, first constructed as part of the Haags Gemeentemuseum. About six temporary exhibitions are mounted every year, highlighting international trends in contemporary video, painting, sculpture, performance art, film, and digital art. Additional pluses are evening open hours and the eye-catching Gember café (open until m.. night), which is replete with dazzling "moderne" lighting fixtures. The café is perched over the water-lily-covered Gemeentemuseum pond—if you're lucky, you'll enjoy gazing at one of The Hague's ubiquitous herons (the city's emblem) posing on the pond as you sip your cappuccino. ⊠ *Stadhouderslaan 43* ☎ *070/338–1133 GEM, 070/338–1144 Museum of Photography* ⊕ *www.gem-online.nl or www.fotomuseumdenhaag.nl* ⊠ *€5 (good for both museums)* ☉ *Tues.–Sun. noon–8.*

**⑫** **Gemeentemuseum Den Haag** (Hague Municipal Museum). Designed by

Fodor'sChoice H. P. Berlage (the grand old master of modern Dutch architecture),

★ completed in 1935, and restored in the late 1990s, the Gemeentemuseum is considered one of the finest examples of 20th-century museum architecture. Although its collection ranges from A to Z—sumptuous period rooms highlighting Golden Age silver, Greek and Chinese pottery, a celebrated group of historic musical instruments, and paintings by Johann Jongkind, Claude Monet, and Vincent van Gogh—it is best known as the home of the world's largest collection of works by Piet Mondriaan (1872–1944), the greatest artist of the Dutch De Stijl movement. The collection is particularly strong in his early works, those breathlessly beautiful watercolors of chrysanthemums, and bleak Holland landscapes. The crowning masterpiece, however, and widely considered one of the landmarks of modern art, is Mondriaan's *Victory Boogie Woogie*—an iconic work, begun in 1942 but left unfinished at the artist's death. The painting's signature black-and-white grid interspersed with blocks of primary color arrived only in 1998, when the Netherlands Institute for Cultural Heritage controversially paid 80 million guilders for the work (until then American-owned).

In addition to more than 150 works by Mondriaan, there are around 50 drawings by Karel Appel, one of the founders of the revolutionary CoBrA group (its name is a combination of the first letters of Danish, Belgian, and Dutch capital cities). "I paint like a barbarian in a barbarous age," Appel once said; see if you think the same sentiments apply to his drawings. Elsewhere in the museum are paintings by artists of The Hague School. Elsewhere, be sure to see the dollhouse with real doll-size Delft Blue chinaware. The museum's Costume Gallery contains no fewer than 55,000 items (although not all are on display at one time!), providing endless inspiration for dedicated students of fashion. ⊠ *Stadhouderslaan 41* ☎ *070/338–1111* ⊕ *www.gemeentemuseum.nl* ⊠ *€8* ☉ *Tues.–Sun. 11–5.*

**⑯** **Gevangenpoort Museum** (Prison's Gate Museum). Now a museum showcasing enough instruments of inhumanity to satisfy any criminologist, the Gevangenpoort, or Prison's Gate, was originally a gatehouse to the local duke's castle, then converted to a prison around 1420. In 1882, it opened in its current incarnation as both a monument to its own past and a national museum displaying apparatuses of punishment. After a slide presentation, the guided tour will take you through the torture chamber, the women's section, and the area where the rich were once imprisoned. For those who are interested in seeing such things as a branding iron with The Hague's coat of arms, the Gevangenpoort Museum offers a fascinating, if chilling, experience. Don't be surprised if your ʒuide pulls a few stunts on you. ✉ *Buitenhof 33* ☎ *070/346–0861* ⊕ *www.gevangenpoort.nl* ✉ *€4* ☼ *Tues.–Fri. 10–5, weekends noon–5. Guided tours only, every hr on the hr.*

★ ❺ **Haags Historisch Museum** (Hague Historical Museum). One of the series of museums that encircle the Hofvijver lake, The Hague Historical Museum is housed in the Sebastiaansdoelen, a magnificent Classical-Baroque mansion dating from 1636, built to house the Civic Guard of St. Sebastian. Worthy of a visit in itself, this mansion holds collections that offer an in-depth look at The Hague's past. Treasures here include Jan van Goyen's enormous 17th-century panoramic painting of the city, a collection of medieval church silver, a dollhouse from 1910, and the dreamy views out the windows over the Hofvijver lake and the greensward of the Lange Voorhout. ✉ *Korte Vijverberg 7* ☎ *070/364–6940* ⊕ *www. haagshistorischmuseum.nl* ✉ *€4* ☼ *Tues.–Fri. 10–5, weekends noon–5.*

❹ **Hofvijver** (Court Lake). Beside the Binnenhof, this long, rectangular reflecting pool—the venerable remains of a medieval moat—comes complete with tall fountains and a row of pink-blossomed horse-chestnut trees. Today, the lake is spectacularly surrounded by some of The Hague's most elegant historic buildings and museums.

❸ **Mauritshuis.** Home to the enigmatic gaze of the Dutch "Mona Lisa"— Vermeer's *Girl with a Pearl Earring*—and several other of the most reproduced paintings in the world, the Mauritshuis is one of the greatest art museums in Europe. Here, in only a dozen rooms, is one of the richest feasts of Dutch art anywhere: 14 Rembrandts (including the *Anatomy Lesson*), 10 Jan Steens, and 3 Vermeers, with his incomparable *View of Delft* taking pride of place. As an added treat, the building itself is worthy of a 17th-century master's brush: a cream-color mansion tucked into a corner behind the Parliament complex and overlooking the Hofvijver court lake. It was built to a strictly classical design around 1640 for one Johan Maurits, Count of Nassau-Siegen and governor-general of Dutch Brazil, and the pair behind its creation, Jacob van Campen and Pieter Post, were the two most important Dutch architects of their era.

**Fodor's**Choice ★

Don't miss local boy Paulus Potter's vast canvas *The Bull*, complete with steaming cow dung; the 7-foot-by-11-foot painting leaves nothing to be said on the subject of beef on the hoof, and the artist (1625–54) never surpassed it during his brief 29 years of life. The rediscovery of Johannes Vermeer's (1632–75) *View of Delft* in the late 19th century all but assured the artist's refound fame; note the disturbing shadows Vermeer casts across the waterside buildings in his painting, which serve to emphasize the golden accents falling on the church spire of Delft's Nieuwe Kerk. In the same room is Vermeer's most haunting work, *Girl with a Pearl Earring,* which inspired Tracy Chevalier's 1999 best-selling novel as well as the 2003 filmed version. A novel may be the only way to understand this sphinxlike lady, as historians have never determined who she is. Some think it is Maria, the eldest of Vermeer's 11 children; the novel sets out that it is Vermeer's maid. Considering the complete lack of ostentatious dress and iconographic symbols, the latter could be a real possibility. No matter who it is, the picture has a glowing light and an immediacy that make it one of the loveliest portraits ever painted.

For something completely different, look to the works of Jan Steen (1626–79), who portrayed the daily life of ordinary people in the Netherlands of the 17th century. His painting *The Way You Hear It Is the Way You Sing It* is particularly telling. Even comparatively minor paintings are real jewels. Case in point: Hendrick Avercamp's charming *Winter Scene* of 1610, where you can search out, among the tiny figures, a bared buttock or two, a drowning couple, and, in the foreground, a dandy. ⊠ *Korte Vijverberg 8* ☎ *070/302–3435* ⊕ *www.mauritshuis.nl* 🎟 *€7.50* ⊙ *Tues.–Sat. 10–5, Sun. 11–5.*

⟳ ❿ **Museon.** With lots of hands-on, interactive displays, this bills itself as "the most fun-packed popular science museum in the Netherlands." Permanent exhibitions center on the origins of the universe and evolution, with three themes: Earth, Our Home; Between Man and the Stars; and Ecos, an environmental show. The frequent special exhibitions here are always engagingly presented, with archaeological and intercultural subjects the common themes, plus there are children's workshops on Wednesday and Sunday afternoons (book in advance). The Museon is conveniently next door to the Gemeentemuseum, so you can easily combine a visit to both. ⊠ *Stadhouderslaan 37* ☎ *070/338–1338* ⊕ *www.museon.nl* 🎟 *€6* ⊙ *Tues.–Sun. 11–5.*

❻ **Museum Bredius.** Housed in an 18th-century patrician mansion, the collection of traveler and art connoisseur Abraham Bredius (1855–1946) supports the argument that private collections are often the most delightful. It includes works by the likes of Cuyp and Jan Steen, as well as nearly 200 paintings by Dutch "little masters"—whose art Bredius trumpeted—of the period, all held together by the thread of a personal vision. Once curator of the Mauritshuis, Bredius was the first art historian who began to question the authenticity of Rembrandt canvases (there were zillions of them in the 19th century), setting into motion the enormous seismic quake of connoisseurship that, today, has reduced the master's oeuvre to fewer than 1,000 works. The house itself, overlooking the north side of the Hofvijver (court lake), makes a quaint setting for the paintings. Salons are fitted out with Neoclassical moldings and armoires stuffed with Delft porcelains and important silverware. ⊠ *Lange Vijverberg 14* ☎ *070/362–0729* ⊕ *www.museumbredius.nl* 🎟 *€4.50* ⊙ *Tues.–Sun. noon–5.*

*FodorsChoice ★*

❾ **Museum Mesdag.** Enter the beauteous world of a 19th-century Dutch connoisseur, aesthetic, and art collector with one step into this oft-overlooked treasure-house, nearly wallpapered with grand paintings, glittering frames, and exquisite period fabrics and tapestries. The former town house of noted 19th-century Dutch painter H. W. Mesdag, famed for his vast *Panorama Mesdag,* was left by the artist as a repository for his collection of works from The Hague School. Mesdag was best known for painting seascapes and the life of fisherfolk in the nearby village of Scheveningen, and served as a relentless ambassador for The Hague School, traveling around the world and bringing back some impressive objets d'art from

*FodorsChoice ★*

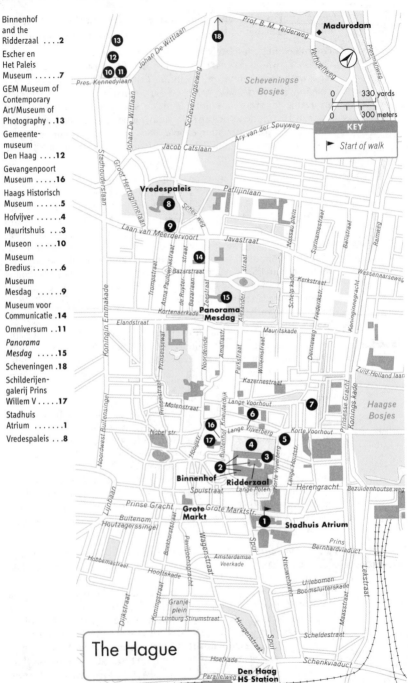

The Hague

Japan. Stay a while in these silk-lined rooms—note the collection of 19th-century Dutch ceramics—and you can easily visualize the sumptuous gatherings the artist and his wife, Sientje (also a painter), hosted for the leading Netherlandish art society of its day, Pulchri. ☒ *Laan van Meerdervoort 7f* ☎ *070/364–6940* ⊕ *www.museummesdag.nl* 🖼 *€5* ☉ *Tues.–Sun. noon–5.*

🕑 ⑭ **Museum voor Communicatie** (Communication Museum). Ultramodern and with lots of space, light, and activities, the Communication Museum looks at the ways in which people have gotten in touch with one another over the years, from carrier pigeon to e-mail. There's a Eureka exhibit designed for children 8–12 that allows them to experiment with faxes and computers. Much of the signage is in Dutch, although English-speaking audio guides are available. ☒ *Zeestraat 82* ☎ *070/330–7500* ⊕ *www.muscom.nl* 🖼 *€6* ☉ *Weekdays 10–5, weekends noon–5.*

⑪ **Omniversum.** The IMAX theater shows a rotating program of film spectaculars, including several with nature-based and futuristic themes, on a screen six stories high. Like the GEM/Museum of Photography around the corner, it's one of the few Hague museums open in the evenings. ☒*Pres. Kennedylaan 5* ☎*0900/666–4837* ⊕*www.omniversum.nl* 🖼€9 ☉*Showings hourly Mon. 10–3, Tues. and Wed. 10–5, Thurs.–Sun. 10–10.*

★ ⑮ ***Panorama Mesdag.*** Long before TV was capable of reproducing reality, painted panoramas gave viewers the chance to immerse themselves in another world. The *Panorama Mesdag*, painted in 1880 by the renowned marine artist Hendrik Willem Mesdag and a team that included his wife, Sientje Mesdag-van Houtenback, is one of the largest and finest surviving examples of the genre. A truly spectacular, nearly Cineramic vision, it offers a sweeping view of the kind of scene so beloved by The Hague School's artists: the sea, the dunes of Holland, and the picturesque fishing village of Scheveningen. To enhance the effect of the painting, you are first led through a narrow, dark passage, then up a spiral staircase, and finally onto a "sand dune" viewing platform. That's when the painting first hits you. To the west is The Hague, detailed so perfectly that old-time residents can identify particular houses. So lifelike is the 45-foot-high panorama that encompasses you in its 400-foot circumference that it's hard to resist the temptation to step across the guardrail onto the dune and stride down to the water's edge. Elsewhere, the rooms that lead to the *Panorama* house a good collection of oil paintings and watercolors by Mr. and Mrs. Mesdag, as well as temporary exhibitions. A few blocks away is the painter's house, now the Mesdag Museum. ☒*Zeestraat 65* ☎*070/364–4544* ⊕*www.panorama-mesdag. nl* 🖼*€5* ☉*Mon.–Sat. 10–5, Sun. noon–5.*

★ ⑰ **Schilderijengalerij Prins Willem V** (Prince William V Painting Gallery). One of the last remaining Dutch art *kabinets,* this princely gallery is lined with tier upon tier of old-master paintings, inimitably hung in 18th-century *touche-touche* fashion (there's nary an inch between each painting). In 1773 Willem V created this new gallery in his palace, to which the citizenry were invited three days each week, thus earning it a reputation as the Netherlands' first public museum (until then, most collections were seen only by special appointment). Although the cream of the collection was moved eventually to the Mauritshuis across the Hofvijver lake, many fetching works remain here. The long, narrow room has fine Louis XVI stucco ceilings embellished with motifs from the world of art and architecture, but it nevertheless exudes an intimate, homey atmosphere, as if a friend who just happened to own a collection that included works by Jan Steen, Paulus Potter, and Rembrandt had asked you over to see them. The museum is scheduled to be closed until 2007 for a major renovation. Check the Web site for the latest information. ⊠ *Buitenhof 35* ☎ *070/362–4444* ⊕ *www.mauritshuis.nl* 💳 *€1.50 (free with entry to Mauritshuis)* ◷ *Tues.–Sun. 11–4.*

▶ ❶ **Stadhuis Atrium** (Town Hall). Completed in 1995, Richard Meier's Neo-Modernist complex, comprising the Town Hall, Central Library, and Municipal Record Office, is an awe-inspiring creation in aluminum, glass, and white epoxy resin. Inside, you can take the elevator to the 11th floor (weekdays only) to get the full effect of the Atrium's vastness. What also makes the place so mesmerizing is the American architect's attention to mathematical relationships; every aspect of the design, including, apparently, the pointing between the tiles, is based on measurements that are multiples of 17.73 inches. Meier has endeavored to show the building, both literally and metaphorically, in its best light. "The clouds in The Hague are incredible," he says. "When the sun breaks through, it's often like a beautiful painting. The natural light in the Town Hall is a reflection of that light, and this is what you experience when you walk through the building." ⊠ *Spui 70* ☎ *070/353–3099* 💳 *Free* ◷ *Mon.–Wed. and Fri. 7 AM–7 PM, Thurs. 7 AM–9:30 PM, Sat. 9:30–5.*

★ ❽ **Vredespaleis** (Peace Palace). Facing the world across a broad lawn, this building houses the International Court of Justice plus a 500,000-volume law library. The court was initiated in 1899 by Czar Nicolas II of Russia, who invited 26 nations to meet in The Hague to set up a permanent world court of arbitration. The current building was constructed in 1903 with a $1.5 million gift from the Scottish-American industrialist Andrew Carnegie. Built in Flemish style, its red-and-gray granite-and-brick pile has become a local landmark. Gifts from each of the participating nations embellish the interior, with examples of their national craftsmanship in the form of statuary, stained-glass windows, gates, doors, and clocks. Cases can be heard here only with the consent of both parties; comparatively few litigations are heard here these days, although some still make headlines, such as the famous trial of Slobodan Milosevic. ⊠ *Carnegieplein 2* ☎ *070/302–4242* ⊕ *www.vredespaleis.nl* 💳 *€5* ◷ *Weekdays, guided tours only, at 10, 11, 2, 3, and 4 when court is not in session.*

# WHERE TO STAY & EAT

★ **$$$–$$$$** ✕ **Marc Smeets.** Hotel restaurants may not have the bona fides of a eatery with its own address but that is an academic question here at one of The Hague's top culinary temples. The decor is luxe and stylish, thanks to shimmering chandeliers, creamy white walls, mirrors, and gigantic

# ON THE MENU IN THE HAGUE

**YOU CAN FIND** all the hearty Dutch classics in The Hague. Enjoy herring from a roadside stall, remembering that there is an art to eating this: pick your fish up by its tail (it'll be surrounded by half-moons of aromatic onions), dangle the morsel into your mouth, then knock it back with a good slug of the jenever (Dutch gin) that you'll have decanted into your hip flask at the start of the day. Should your blood-sugar level feel like it's sinking, pavement pounders can turn to another local delicacy: Haagse hopjes, the coffee-flavor hard candies created at the end of the 18th century to assuage the cravings of a Baron Hop and still sucked today throughout the Netherlands. But Eurocrats, diplomats, and lawyers tend to demand more substantial culinary fare, and The Hague can satisfy the most exacting of palates. From French haute cuisine to Tex-Mex, you'll be able to sample it here, and as you'd expect of a town that is only a stone's throw from the seaside, the fruits de mer seafood platters are of the very freshest variety. Meanwhile, The Hague's Indonesian restaurants are second to none, which is understandable considering it's considered the hometown of the Netherlands' Indonesian population. By all means, have a rijsttafel (rice table) blowout.

red-orange banquettes. The fireworks happen in this peaceful cocoon when the food arrives. Thanks to owner and chef Marc Smeets' winning ways, his more-than-nouvelle combinations often dazzle the tongue, as you'll find savoring his roast leg of venison with mashed potatoes and turnip tops, flavored with lemon and rosemary; or his panfried sea bream with risotto and rhubarb cream. It is all as dee-scrumptious as it sounds. ⊠ *Buitenhof 39–42* ☎ *070/363–7930* ⊕ *www.marcsmeets. nl* ▤ *AE, DC, MC, V* ☉ *Closed Sun.*

**$$$–$$$$** ✕ **Restaurant Julien.** A glamorous belle epoque interior, lush with Tiffany-style chandeliers and ornate mirrors, echoes an equally decadent menu. Try the fresh and succulent *fruits-de-mer* (seafood) platter or the less-traditional spring chicken with lobster, chanterelle mushrooms, and curry sauce. Finish off with a Dutch cheese plate or one of the delicious house desserts, such as the bourbon crème brûlée. Julien prides itself on an extensive wine list. ⊠ *Vos in Tuinstraat 2a* ☎ *070/365–8602* ⊕ *www. julien.nl* ▤ *V* ☉ *Closed Sun.*

★ **$$$–$$$$** ✕ **Zo uit de Zee.** The name means "fresh from the sea," and the emphasis in the kitchen is just that. There are plenty of oysters and scallops to start off with, followed by, say, a wonderful grilled sea bream in a lemongrass sauce. Set on a quiet canal parallel to the Denneweg, Zo uit de Zee's decor balances white stucco with brickwork and Delftware tiles. Touches of stained glass in the windows and fish artwork on the walls adds color. The atmosphere is convivial without being boisterous. Desserts highlight the seasonal; a typical fall lineup relies on lots of pears and nuts. ⊠ *Hooikade 14* ☎ *070/346–2603* ▭ *AE, MC, V.*

★ **$$–$$$$** ✕ **It Rains Fishes.** Crown Prince Willem Alexander has been known to pop in here, so you know it must be good. A gleaming eggshell, ivory, and mirrored jewel box, It Rains Fishes is run by a team of five international chefs, whose predominantly aquatic specialties combine Thai, Malaysian, Indonesian, and French flavors. Its name, taken from a Thai folktale of fishes jumping from the river after a heavy rainfall, finds a few echoes in the restaurant's decor, with the occasional painted fish leaping around on the ceiling and walls. Specialties include sea bass with lemon and tarragon oil, or king crab in the shell with Malay black pepper sauce. For an unorthodox but totally winning dessert, choose the Thai basil and chocolate sorbet. Outdoor dining is available in good weather. ⊠ *Noordeinde 123* ☎ *070/365–2598* ⊕ *www.itrainsfishes.nl* ▭ *AE, DC, MC, V* ☉ *No lunch Sat.*

★ **$–$$$** ✕ **Le Haricot Vert.** In a 17th-century building that once housed the staff of the nearby Noordeinde palace, Le Haricot Vert is a popular haunt for locals who come to enjoy good food in an intimate, candlelit atmosphere. Every possible wall surface is hung with china, sections of stained glass, pictures, and mirrors, and the overall effect is one of beguiling, romantic clutter. Dishes such as grilled sardines with ratatouille, and lamb fillet served with rosemary and sweet peppers, combine Dutch classics with French flair. The menu changes seasonally, so you can expect irresistible asparagus in spring and game in winter. ⊠ *Molenstraat 9a–11* ☎ *070/365–2278* ▭ *AE, MC, V* ☉ *Closed Sun. No lunch Mon.–Wed.*

★ **$$** ✕ **Garoeda.** Named after a golden eagle in Indonesian mythology, a symbol of happiness and friendship, Garoeda is something of an institution among Hagenaars, many of whom consider it the best Indonesian spot in town. Established in 1949 and spread over five floors, the restaurant is decorated with Eastern art, and filled with wicker chairs and lush plants to give it a unique "colonial" atmosphere. Waiters are dressed in traditional costume and are more than happy to advise patrons new to the Indonesian dining experience. In addition to a choice of no less than seven different rijsttafels (Indonesian lunch dishes made with rice, vegetables, and sometimes meat), there is also an extensive à la carte menu, featuring some more unusual finds, such as spicy mussels and crispy roasted chicken in soy sauce. ⊠ *Kneuterdijk 18a* ☎ *070/346–5319* ▭ *AE, DC, MC, V.*

**$$** ✕ **Sapphire Tower Restaurant.** Recommended by no less an expert than the concierge from the magisterial Des Indes hotel, the Sapphire is behind Centraal Station, set above an apartment tower, and thus can claim to be The Hague's highest restaurant. The spectacular views it offers over the city are equaled by the great Chinese food (though some say the portions could be bigger); live music on Saturday and a sophisticated cocktail bar also make the place worth visiting. ⊠ *Jan van Riebeekstraat 571* ☎ *070/383–6767* ⊕ *www.sapphire.nl* ▭ *AE, MC, V* ☉ *No lunch weekends.*

★ **$–$$** ✕ **Dudok Brasserie.** These days, Dudok is *the* in place in The Hague, because it's ideal for people-of-every-stripe-watching, from politicians debating over a beer, to the jeunesse d'orée toying with their salads, to pensioners tucking into an afternoon tea of cream cakes and salmon sandwiches. The vast granite-and-metal interior looks like a cross between a 1930s railway station and an ultracontemporary factory, and besides the countless small tables and roomy bar area, there's a communal central table and a packed magazine rack to keep solo diners busy. The menu combines international dishes—carpaccio of beef, steaks, and grilled chicken—with traditional Dutch fare such as mustard soup (surprisingly mild and flavorsome) and sausage with cabbage. Additional pluses include a terrace for outdoor dining and a 1:30 AM closing on Saturday. ⊠ *Hofweg 1a* ☎ *070/890–0100* ⊕ *www.dudok.nl* ⊟ *AE, DC, MC, V.*

**$–$$** ✕ **Fouquet.** For a taste of Provence and the warm south, Fouquet fits the bill, with its mix of French and Mediterranean-style cuisine. Its interior, warmed by terra-cotta frescoed walls, may be more reminiscent of Italy than France, but that's merely hair-splitting. Imaginative, well-priced dishes include guinea fowl with red pepper sauce, and lamb with honey and thyme. If the weather is nice, make the most of the pretty, parasol-bedecked terrace for an alfresco meal. ⊠ *Javastraat 31a* ☎ *070/360–6273* ⊕ *www.fouquet.nl* ⊟ *AE, DC, MC, V* ⊙ *No lunch.*

**$–$$** ✕ **Juliana's.** Sit outside on the bustling square and watch the world go by, or opt for the interior, which combines French-Victorian-style wooden banquettes and mirrors, with a very Dutch fresco featuring a map of old Den Haag. Food here is of the substantial, international variety—everything from steak to baked scampi to tapas. ⊠ *Plaats 11* ☎ *070/365–0235* ⊕ *www.julianas.nl* ⊟ *AE, DC, MC, V.*

★ **$–$$** ✕ **Plato.** Festooned with gilded mirrors, candles, and flowers, this informal restaurant attracts a hip, laid-back crowd. Try to get a table in the beautiful covered atrium at the back. The menu reaches all over the globe: from Italian tortellini to Sumatran beef in coconut sauce. High tea at Plato is an exceptional experience: besides delicious scones with clotted cream and elegantly trimmed cucumber sandwiches, you get small portions of delightful cheese fondue, shepherd's pie, and stir-fried noodles—all washed down with a glass of sparkling wine, of course. ⊠ *Frederikstraat 32* ☎ *070/363–6744* ⊕ *www.restaurant-plato.nl* ⊟ *AE, DC, MC, V.*

**$–$$** ✕ **'T Goude Hooft.** Magnificently dating from 1423 but rebuilt in 1660, the oldest restaurant in The Hague has a well-preserved interior, with plenty of wooden beams, brass chandeliers, and "antique" furniture all richly redolent of the Dutch Golden Age. In warm weather, the large terrace overlooking the market square makes a pleasant spot in which to enjoy a drink and a platter of *bitterballen.* (What are these croquettes made of? No one will tell you, but they are basically stuffed with finely ground meat, then deep-fried.) For something more substantial, try the wine-enriched beef stew. ⊠ *Dagelijkse Groenmarkt 13* ☎ *070/346–9713* ⊟ *MC, V.*

★ **¢–$** ✕ **Eetlokaal Lokanta.** A well-priced menu and funky, colorful decorations, like floral oilcloths on the tables and gilded tissue holders, make this eatery popular with trendy young locals, who flock in to enjoy a delicious combination of Greek, Turkish, and Moroccan dishes. Try the *imam* *beyildi* (Turkish for "the imam fainted"), the name for a dish of eggplant stuffed with a spicy meat mixture. Because Lokanta is less expensive than some other places on this central street, it fills up fast, so get there early or reserve ahead. ✉ *Buitenhof 4* ☎ *070/392–0870* ▭ *MC, V* ⊘ *No lunch Sun.*

¢–$ ✕ **Greve.** Take your place at one of many wooden tables spread out between the giant cacti and huge earthenware pots in this airy and trendy café. Opt for the mouthwatering delight of grilled swordfish with guacamole or the hearty chicken soup thick with fresh vegetables. You'll need to make your mind up fairly quickly, as service in this chatty, communal, and informal eatery is surprisingly speedy. Greve also has a formal dining room, which offers the same menu in slightly more formal surrounds. ✉ *Torenstraat 138* ☎ *070/360–3919* ▭ *AE, DC, MC, V (restaurant only)* ⊘ *Restaurant closed Sun. and Mon.*

★ $$$$ ✕▥ **Le Méridien Hotel Des Indes.** A stately grande dame of the hotel world and once a 19th-century mansion built principally for grand balls and entertainment, the Des Indes has a graciousness that makes it one of the world's premier hotels. Stay here and you'll be following in the footsteps of Empress Josephine of France, Theodore Roosevelt, and the legendary ballerina Anna Pavlova (who, sorry to note, died here after contracting pneumonia on her travels). The Des Indes sits on one of the city's most prestigious squares, in the heart of The Hague, surrounded by all the important buildings: the Parliament, embassies, ministries, and the best shops. The interior is a harmonious blend of belle epoque elements: marble fluted columns, brocaded walls, a good deal of gilding. Luxurious and ample bedrooms have all the best facilities—there are even Jacuzzis in some of them (although not the belle epoque ones). The former inner courtyard is now a towering reception area leading to the superb formal dining room—all crystal and linen—called Le Restaurant. On offer here is ambitious French-Mediterranean cuisine. Chef VanBeusekom changes the Menu Royal every week, so the ingredients are always in season; and there is always a dish that bring Holland's East Indies past to mind. After all, this hotel isn't called Des Indes for nothing. ✉ *Lange Voorhout 54–56, 2514 EG* ☎ *070/361–2345* 🖷 *070/361–2350* ⊕ *www.desindes.com* ⮑ *79 rooms, 13 suites* ⌂ *Restaurant, minibars, cable TV, in-room data ports, pool, health club, massage, parking (fee), no-smoking rooms* ▭ *AE, DC, MC, V.*

★ $$–$$$$ ✕▥ **Savelberg.** In the ancient village of Voorburg—just to the southeast of the city in a leafy suburb—and surrounded by woods, Savelberg offers restful accommodation and exceptional dining in a prizewinning restaurant. The hotel is country-house style: a lovingly restored 18th-century mansion with 14 bedrooms, plenty of antique mahogany furniture, and beautiful paintings. Here, honeymooners and pleasure seekers can rub shoulders with visitors from the international political scene. At dinnertime (the restaurant is closed Sunday and Monday) if you enjoy being at the heart of the action, choose to sit at the special chef's table in a corner of the vast kitchen, which gives a bird's-eye view of chef Henk Savelberg and his team at work. Everything from the bread to the after-dinner chocolates is lovingly handmade in-house. Specialties include Salade Van Kreeft "Savelberg," where the lobster is cracked and shelled, then combined with haricot beans, truffles, artichokes, and goose side. Or try grilled turbot with broad beans and chanterelle ⊠ *Oosteinde 14, 2271 EH Voorburg* ☎ *070/387–2081* 🖷 *070/. 7715* ⊕ *www.restauranthotelsavelberg.nl* 🗗 *14 rooms* 👌 *Restaurant, cable TV, bar, free parking; no a/c* ⊟ *AE, DC, MC, V.*

**$–$$$** ✕🖻 **Corona.** Created from what were once three 17th-century homes, the Hotel Corona is conveniently located across from the historic Binnenhof complex, near the Mauritshuis and Museum Bredius, and at the edge of the shopping district. Relatively few rooms, decorated in warm pastels and with chintz curtains, help to create a cozy feel. If you don't have the energy to venture beyond its confines after a day of sightseeing, you can eat very well at its award-winning Corona restaurant, Marc Smeets. Though its interior style is a little on the corporate side, the atmosphere is elegant and relaxed, and you can dine by the light of candles and crystal chandeliers. French-style dishes include Dutch shrimps served with a compote of tomatoes, sirloin steak with eggplant and wild mushrooms, and dark-chocolate pie. If you don't want to go whole hog, settle for simple salads, hearty soups, and sandwiches at the hotel's Brasserie Buitenhof. ⊠ *Buitenhof 39–42, 2513 AH* ☎ *070/363–7930* 🖷 *070/361–5785* ⊕ *www.corona.nl* 🗗 *36 rooms, 17 with bath* 👌 *2 restaurants, minibars, cable TV, bar, parking (fee), some pets allowed; no a/c* ⊟ *AE, DC, MC, V.*

**★ $$$–$$$$** 🖻 **Parkhotel Den Haag.** Situated in lovely Molenstraat, a boutique- and café-busy street with a bohemian feel, the Parkhotel has been sheltering visitors since 1912. The building still exults in plenty of art nouveau detailing; architecture buffs won't want to miss its fabulous five-story brick-and-stone stairway, for example. Today, friendly staff plus light, airy rooms complete with all the modern conveniences (including snazzy bathrooms) add to its charms. ⊠ *Molenstraat 53, 2513 BJ* ☎ *070/362–4371* 🖷 *070/361–4525* ⊕ *www.parkhoteldenhaag.nl* 🗗 *120 rooms* 👌 *Restaurant, cable TV, in-room data ports, bar, parking (fee); no a/c* ⊟ *AE, DC, MC, V* ⍟ *BP.*

**$$–$$$$** 🖻 **Sofitel.** From the outside, it looks like a black-and-white Rubik's Cube, but inside the emphasis is firmly on luxury and comfort. Rooms are decorated in creams and terra-cotta, and the in-house restaurant relies on Dutch old masters for its artistic theme. The location, adjacent to Centraal Station and only a few minutes' walk from the city center, can't be faulted. And if you don't want to go out, the bartender in the colorful bar, with checkerboard flooring, can mix you a mean tequila sunrise. ⊠ *Koningin Julianaplein 35, 2595 AA* ☎ *070/381–4901* 🖷 *070/382–5927* ⊕ *www.sofitel.nl* 🗗 *143 rooms* 👌 *Restaurant, cable TV, in-room data ports, bar, parking (fee)* ⊟ *AE, DC, MC, V.*

**$$–$$$** 🖻 **Novotel.** It's a case of "Lights, camera, action!" in this Novotel, housed as it is in what was once a cinema. Its interior designers have cleverly capitalized on this former life, with the entrance foyer and lounge atmospherically decorated with movie posters, cameras, and directors' chairs. It all helps to create a sense of individuality in what might otherwise be just another bland chain hotel. The guest rooms, safely decorated in shades of peach and blue, aren't quite as interesting, but what they lack in imagination they more than make up for in cleanliness and modern conveniences. And the Novotel's location is ideal for shopping and sightseeing. ✉ *Hofweg 5–7, 2511 AA* ☎ *070/364–8846* 📠 *070/356–2889* ⊕ *www.accorhotels.nl* 🛏 *104 rooms, 2 suites* ⚐ *Restaurant, cable TV, in-room data ports, bar, parking (fee)* 🚌 *AE, DC, MC, V.*

$ ⬚ **Delta.** With its light interior, pale woods, and frosted-glass-and-metal detailing, the Delta is the closest The Hague gets to a boutique-style hotel. The light-filled breakfast area has fresh flowers on each table; bedrooms are small and white, with contemporary furniture and walk-in-style shower rooms. A spiral staircase and no elevator means this isn't a place for the infirm, but its location—north of the center yet within walking distance of Denneweg—is still pretty appealing. ✉ *Anna Paulownastraat 8, 2518 BE* ☎ *070/362–4999* 📠 *070/345–4440* 🛏 *11 rooms* ⚐ *Minibars; no a/c* 🚌 *AE, DC, MC, V* ⏀ *BP.*

$ ⬚ **Petit.** This quiet, family-style hotel, operated by a young couple and fronted by a pretty little garden, is on a residential boulevard between the Peace Palace and The Hague Municipal Museum. Occupying two large houses that date from 1895, Petit is simply and tastefully furnished in warm shades of red and gold, with the occasional period stained-glass accent. The pleasant, wood-paneled bar-lounge is a nice place to relax. ✉ *Groothertoginnelaan 42, 2517 EH* ☎ *070/346–5500* 📠 *070/346–3257* ⊕ *www.hotelpetit.nl* 🛏 *20 rooms* ⚐ *Minibars, cable TV, Wi-Fi, bar, parking (fee); no a/c* 🚌 *AE, DC, MC, V* ⏀ *BP.*

$ ⬚ **Sebel.** The friendly owners of this hotel have expanded into two buildings between the city center and the Peace Palace. Tidy and comfortable, the rooms are large but sparsely furnished, and have high ceilings and tall windows for lots of light and air. ✉ *Zoutmanstraat 40, 2518 GR* ☎ *070/345–9200* 📠 *070/345–5855* ⊕ *www.hotelsebel.nl* 🛏 *27 rooms* ⚐ *Cable TV, in-room data ports, bar, parking (fee); no a/c* 🚌 *AE, DC, MC, V* ⏀ *BP.*

¢–$ ⬚ **Staten.** Away from the bustling town center, the small and quiet Staten is conveniently close to the Gemeentemuseum/Museon complex and set on a high-end shopping street in the chic Statenkwartier district. The rooms feel somewhat old-fashioned, but you can't argue with the price. You can have your breakfast on a pleasant geranium-festooned balcony if weather permits. ✉ *Frederik Hendriklaan 299, 2582 CE* ☎ *070/354–3943* 📠 *070/331–7042* ⊕ *www.statenhotel.nl* 🛏 *10 rooms, 8 with bath* ⚐ *No a/c* 🚌 *MC, V* ⏀ *BP.*

¢ ⬚ **Aristo.** The Aristo's owners take pride in having run a clean if simple establishment for more than 40 years. Just a half block from the bustling Hollands Spoor Station, they manage to maintain an old-fashioned family-hotel atmosphere. There are only a few rooms on each floor, so it never gets too noisy. All rooms here share assorted bathrooms. ✉ *Stationsweg 164–166, 2515 BS* ☎ *070/389–0847* 📠 *070/389–0847* 🛏 *11 rooms without bath* ⚐ *Bar, parking (fee); no a/c, no room phones, no room TVs* 🚌 *No credit cards* ⏀ *BP.*

¢ ⬚ **Stayokay.** Stayokay is one of the leading hostel chains in Holland, and this one enjoys a location close to Hollands Spoor train station. Besides the 10 double rooms, there are rooms for three to eight. Rooms here are fitted out with two to eight beds (all twins—even some bunk beds!). Clean, modern, and light, the hostel is in a renovated former warehouse and has a deck on the water plus a library, Internet stations, and a pool

# FESTIVALS & ALL THAT JAZZ

**WHAT IS IT ABOUT HAGENAARS AND FESTIVALS?** *Any excuse, and they'll arrange one. Every year, visitors and locals alike can share in a variety of unusual events that—in some cases quite literally—provide The Hague with more than a little color. Centered on Scheveningen, there are two great summer festivals, the first of which is the International Sand Sculpture Competition. Forget bucket-and-spade-constructed castles; the entries are on a giant scale, and of the highest order of art. Teams from around the world compete to create fantastic beasts, vast palaces, and mythological gods; at night the sculptures are romantically floodlighted. In August there's also the Scheveningen International Fireworks Festival—four consecutive nights of glorious Catherine wheels and diadems bursting skyward from the shore. Join the throng along the pier, boulevard, and beach, or, for the best vantage point, book passage on a boat and do your oohing and aahing from the sea. Ever since its inauguration in 1976, the immensely popular North Sea Jazz festival, held each July at the Netherlands Congress Centre in The Hague, has attracted top global names from the world of jazz, including Count Basie, Dizzy Gillespie, and more recently, Jamie Cullum and Al Green. At this writing, however, the event's future is uncertain. The 2005 festival was announced as being the last ever, but rumors abound that it may survive in another form, and possibly shift location to the Ahoy' arena in Rotterdam. Keep an eye on the official Web site (www.northseajazz.nl) for up-to-date news. For more details on all festivals, contact the VVV ☎ 015/215-7756.*

table for when you just can't sightsee any more. ⊠ *Scheepmakersstraat 27, 2515 VA* ☎ *070/315-7888* 🖶 *070/315-7877* ⊕ *www.stayokay.com* ⇨ *38 rooms each with 2–8 beds and shared baths* ♢ *Restaurant, bar, parking (fee); no a/c, no room phones, no room TVs* ▭ *No credit cards* ⅋⦵ *BP.*

## NIGHTLIFE & THE ARTS

### The Arts

The Hague has a thriving cultural life—you only have to look at the gleaming Spui arts complex of theaters for proof. The resident orchestra and ballet company are so popular throughout the Netherlands that it is nearly essential that you make your reservations before you arrive in town if you want to be sure of a ticket. And if you do catch a show, you'll note an unusual phenomenon from the otherwise normally reserved Dutch: the standing ovation. For some mysterious reason, this response seems to be given with far greater frequency than in other countries. For information on cultural events, call the **Uit information** (⊠ Uitpost Den Haag ☎ 070/363-3833 weekdays 9–5) in The Hague. In addition, you can pick up the monthly *Den Haag Agenda,* published by the VVV tourist office, which will keep you up to date on every worthwhile event that's happening in town during your stay.

### Dance

The **Nederlands Danstheater** (✉ Spuiplein 152 ☎ 070/880–0333 ⊕ www. ldt.nl) is the national modern dance company and makes its home at the Lucent Dance Theatre, the world's only theater built exclusively for dance performances. It has an international reputation for ground-breaking productions, which might cause a run on tickets.

### Music

The Hague's **Residentie Orkest** has an excellent worldwide reputation and performs at **Dr. Anton Philipszaal** (✉ Spuiplein 150 ☎ 070/880–0333 ⊕ www.residentieorkest.nl).

### Theater

**De Appel** company has a lively, experimental approach to theater and performs at its own **Appeltheater** (✉ Duinstraat 6 ☎ 070/350–2200 ⊕ www.toneelgroepdeappel.nl). Mainstream Dutch theater is presented by the national theater company **Het Nationale Toneel,** which performs at the **Royal Schouwburg** (✉ Korte Voorhout 3 ☎ 0900/345–6789 ⊕ www.ks.nl).

For an outing with children, visit **Kooman's Poppentheater** (✉ Franken-straat 66 ☎ 070/355–9305 ⊕ www. kooman-poppentheater.nl), which performs musical shows with puppets every Wednesday and Saturday. Advance booking is recommended.

## Nightlife

Though The Hague seems fairly quiet at night, don't be fooled. Behind the reserved facade are plenty of clubs and bars tucked away, often in the city's tiny backstreets. If you like your nightlife of the pumpingly loud variety, you'd best hop on a tram out to Scheveningen.

The latest local and international bands can be heard at **Het Paard** (✉ Prinsengracht 12 ☎ 070/360–1838), where you can also dance and watch movies and multimedia shows. The huge **Marathon** (✉ Wijn-daelerweg 3 ☎ 070/368–0324) offers a wide variety of music and at-tracts a young, energetic crowd.

**Tapperij Le Duc** (✉ Noordeinde 137 ☎ 070/364–2394) has a delightful old-world ambience, with lots of wood, tiles, and a magnificent fireplace. **De Paap** (✉ Papestraat 32 ☎ 070/365–2002) has live music most nights and a cozy, welcoming atmosphere. The beer's cheap, too. **Boterwaag** (✉ Grote Markt 8a ☎ 070/365–9686 ⊕ www.september.nl) is located in a 17th-century weigh house. Its high, vaulted brick ceilings make the bar feel open and airy even when packed, and draws in a trendy young crowd.

**Paas** (✉ Dunne Bierkade 16a ☎ 070/360–0019) sits beside a picturesque canal between Hollands Spoor Station and the city center. A haven for beer connoisseurs, it offers 150 brews, by far the best selection in town. Dunne Bierkade is home to many other bars and restaurants, and has been dubbed the city's "Avenue Culinaire." **Schlemmer** (✉ Lange Houtstraat 17 ☎ 070/360–9000) is Den Haag's place to see and be seen. Its location in the city center around the corner from the Parliament building means you could rub shoulders with Dutch politicians or movie stars. If you hear awed chattering when someone you don't recognize walks in, they're probably big in Holland.

To enjoy an aperitif in an upmarket setting and surrounded by the great and the good of The Hague, a trip to **Bodega de Posthoorn** (⊠ Lange Voorhout 39a ☎ 070/360–4906) is a must. You can have light meals, here, too. **Frenz** (⊠ Kazernestraat 106 ☎ 070/363–6657) is a lively gay outpost for both sexes. **Stairs** (⊠ Nieuwe Schoolstraat 11 ☎ 070/364–8191), gay-oriented (but women are welcome), is friendly and relaxed.

# SHOPPING

There is a plethora of intimate, idiosyncratic specialty boutiques to explore in The Hague, and in the larger department stores you can kid yourself that you're there only to admire the architecture—several are housed in period gems. With its historic and artistic connections, the city's art and antiques trade has naturally developed a strong reputation, and you can certainly find treasure here. Despite the Dutch reputation for thrift, haggling for antiques isn't "done." That said, you can almost always secure some kind of discount if you offer to pay in cash. Late-night shopping in The Hague is on Thursday until 9. Increasingly in the center of town, you'll find larger stores open on Sunday. Many shops take a half day or don't open at all on Monday.

## Department Stores

**De Bijenkorf** (⊠ Wagenstraat 32 [entrance on Grote Markstraat] ☎ 070/426–2700) is Holland's premier department-store chain. It has a reputation for combining class with accessibility and is excellent for cutting-edge housewares, fashion accessories, and clothing basics. Do look, too, at the building's period detailing: the stained-glass windows, carvings, and original flooring that adorn the sweeping stairway on the left of the store.

**Hema** (⊠ Grote Markstraat 57 ☎ 070/365–9844) is next door to its big sister De Bijenkorf (the stores are owned by the same group). If you've forgotten to pack something vital, from pajamas to sunscreen, this is where you'll find a replacement. Goods are well made and well priced.

The **Maison de Bonneterie** (⊠ Gravenstraat 2 ☎ 070/330–5300) is The Hague's most exclusive department store—and it's got the "By Royal Appointment" labels to prove it. Built in 1913 and with an enormous central atrium, it's a glittering mixture of glass and light. On Maison de Bonneterie's four floors you'll find everything from Ralph Lauren shirts to wax candles.

## Shopping Streets

Denneweg, Frederikstraat, and Noordeinde are the main areas for antiques shops, galleries, and home-ware boutiques. For other quirky, one-of-a-kind gift shops, try Molenstraat and Papestraat, two of The

Hague's most atmospheric streets. You'll find small chain stores in the pretty, light-filled Hague Passage (Spuistraat 26), dating from 1882–85, the Netherlands' last remaining period shopping mall. In the maze of little streets behind the Passage there are more fashion and home-ware boutiques, and on Saturday you can shop to the accompaniment of a barrel organ. Between the Venestraat and Nieuwstraat is the charmingly named Haagsche Bluf (the name is akin to the "hot air" coming out of Washington, D.C.) pedestrian mall, featuring mainly clothing chain stores. For department stores, head for Grote Markstraat.

## Specialty Stores

### Antiques & Fine Art

There are so many reputable antiques and art specialists on Noordeinde and Denneweg that a trip down either street is sure to prove fruitful. **Smelik Stokking** (⊠ Noordeinde 101 and 150 ☎ 070/364–0767) specializes in contemporary art, welcomes browsers, and has a pretty sculpture garden full of unusual pieces. **Voorhuis Kunst en Antiek** (⊠ Noordeinde 88 ☎ 070/392–4138) has a suit of armor positioned outside its door that seems to demand that shoppers enter. Inside, various rooms are filled with seemingly every style of furniture, dating from the 17th century onward. **Fred Spoor** (⊠ Denneweg 68 ☎ 070/346–0149) has a wide selection of pewter ware, plus elegant brass candle sconces, tables, and chairs—family heirlooms just crying out for a new home.

### Books & Prints

**M. Heeneman** (⊠ Prinsestraat 47 ☎ 070/364–4748) is a respected dealer who specializes in Dutch antiquarian prints, maps, and architectural renderings. Staff in this small shop are happy to advise customers, and purchases are wrapped in beautiful paper that depicts a fantasy old Dutch town. You'll always be able to buy English-language newspapers at the city's train stations, but otherwise the centrally located **Verwijs** (⊠ Passage 39 ☎ 070/311–4848), one of a chain of bookstores, sells a good range of English-language magazines and books. **A. Houtschild** (⊠ Papestraat 13 ☎ 070/346–7949) has a broad selection of books, including great coffee-table art titles.

### Clothing

Both men and women can find classics with a twist in natural linens, cottons, and wools at **Hoogeweegen Rouwers** (⊠ Noordeinde 23 ☎ 070/365–7473). The service is as timeless as the clothes—it's the sort of place where purchases are carefully wrapped in tissue paper. For handmade men's shirts, visit the diplomats' favorite supplier, **FG Van den Heuvel** (⊠ Hoge Nieuwstraat 36 ☎ 070/350–3468), in business since 1882.

### Crystal, China & Housewares

**Ninaber van Eyben** (⊠ Hoogstraat 5 ☎ 070/365–5321) sells the classic Dutch lifestyle look—antique-finish globes, silverware, and traditional blue-and-white china. There's plenty of room to look around without fear of breaking anything. To see the cutting-edge side of contemporary Dutch housewares, visit **Steitner & Bloos** (⊠ Molenstraat 39 ☎ 070/360–5170). You'll find steel bathroom accessories, geometrically shaped lights, and sofas, tables, and chairs designed along clean, graphic lines.

## Foodstuffs

For tea, coffee, and jam try the charming **Betjeman and Barton**
erikstraat 3 ☏ 070/362–3435). You'll also find elegant tea caddies and
spongeware teapots from Amsterdam here.

### Gifts, Souvenirs & Jewelry

Tucked away from the crowds is **Emma** (✉ Molenstraat 22 ☏ 070/345–
7027), a tiny, very feminine store complete with whitewashed walls and
a wooden floor. The owner specializes in silver plate and costume jewelry, much imported from Paris and Berlin. She also stocks a small range
of fabulous chandeliers, sometimes in unusual colors such as purple. The
tiny, family-run store **Loose** (✉ Papestraat 3 ☏ 070/346–0404) is a toy
shop for grown-ups. Glass cabinets are filled with rolling pins, pots, and
pans no bigger than a fingernail just perfect for dollhouse enthusiasts.
Meanwhile there are also larger wooden toys, a wonderful selection of
old Dutch books and albums, and, in the rear of the store, a wide range
of old prints. If you want to make your own gifts or kill some time with
older kids, a good place to visit is the funky DIY-jewelry store **Bija**
(✉ Prinsestraat 60 ☏ 070/362–8186). You can choose delicate beads—
candylike glass ones, metallic baubles, or fake pearls—then join the
others at the big table and string them into pretty necklaces and earrings.
Customers at **Backers & Zoon** (✉ Noordeinde 58 ☏ 070/346–6422) receive the sort of personal, attentive service one would expect from an
old-fashioned family jeweler. There's a sophisticated stock of pieces, including signet rings, diamond rings, and Fabergé-style accessories. Prices
are not for the fainthearted. For contemporary jewelry with a young-at-
heart feel, pay a visit to **Goudsmid Trudith** (✉ Spekstraat 4 ☏ 070/427–
1622), which sells chunky, tactile pieces studded with semiprecious
stones. **Papier Damen** (✉ 186 Noordeinde ☏ 070/360–0166) sells exquisite
handmade papers and gift wrap, as well as covered notebooks.

## Street Markets

The main traditional street market (an organic farmer's market at that)
in The Hague is generally held outside the **Grote Kerk** on Wednesday from
11 to 6. From the beginning of May until the end of October on Thursday and Sunday, there's an antiques market on **Lange Voorhout**. Wandering through the stalls on a fine day, perhaps to the accompaniment
of a nearby street musician, makes for a lovely experience, plus there's
a seasonal alfresco café where you can order coffee and apple cake. From
January to April and October through December, on Thursday there's
an antiques market on the **Plein**; check with the VVV for details.

# SIDE TRIP: SCHEVENINGEN

**❶⑧**

FodorśChoice
★

The Dutch have been building seaside homes at **Scheveningen** since the
17th century, but it wasn't until Jacob Pronk opened the first bathing
resort in 1818 that the town really took off as a vacation resort. Today,
many visitors come here for more racy pleasures: the casino and the clubs,
the music that pumps out from the seafront restaurants, and the general sense that Scheveningen is where the action is. But of course there

are less-hectic pastimes to pursue: a walk on the promenade, a potter down the pier, a selection of health and beauty treatments, or maybe a deep-sea fishing trip. If you visit the town on a Sunday, don't miss the opportunity to walk to the old village near the harbors (there are three inner harbors, added in succession as Scheveningen's fishing industry grew)—you might still see some of the older local women wearing traditional dress, complete with shawls and distinctive white caps. And the town's famous and grand old lady, the **Kurhaus hotel,** is certainly well worth a visit, if only to enjoy a cup of tea while marveling at the magnificent dome and painted ceilings of its Kurzaal restaurant.

When Scheveningen's frenetic pace becomes too demanding, step into the **Beelden aan Zee Museum** (Sculptures by the Sea Museum). Situated both next to and under the pretty Pavilion von Weid, it's an oasis of calm where you can explore the unique Scholten-Miltenburg sculpture collection, whose highlights include a 230-foot-long etched-glass wall. ⊠ *Harteveltstraat 1* ☎ *070/358–5857* ⊕ *www.beeldenaanzee.nl* ☒ *€6* ⊙ *Tues.–Sun. 11–5.*

Feeling lucky? Blackjack, poker, and the roulette wheel await at the **Holland Casino;** afterward, you can blow winnings at the in-house bar, brasserie, and restaurant. You have to be over 18 to attend. ⊠ *Kurhausweg 1* ☎ *070/306–7777* ⊕ *www.hollandcasino.nl* ☒ *€3.50* ⊙ *Daily 10 AM–3 AM.*

☙ Statistically, the Dutch are the tallest people in Europe, and never must
**Fodor'sChoice** they be more aware of their size than when they visit **Madurodam.** Set
★ in a sprawling "village" with pathways, tram tracks, and railway station, every important building of the Netherlands is reproduced here, on a scale of 1:25. Many aspects of Dutch life ancient and modern can be found here: medieval knights joust in the courtyard of Gouda's magnificent Town Hall; windmills turn; the famous cheese-weighing rite is carried out in Alkmaar; a fire in the harbor is extinguished; the awe-inspiring Delta Works storm surge barrier (constructed after the disastrous flooding of 1953) holds the ocean at bay; and planes land on the newest runway at Schiphol Airport, which requires them to taxi over a highway. The world's longest miniature railway is here, too. There are also two restaurants, a picnic area, and a playground, and the entire exhibit is surrounded by gardens. The sunset hour provides a fairy-tale experience as some 50,000 lights are turned on in the houses. In July and August there is also an after-dark sound-and-light presentation, free to park visitors. ⊠ *George Maduroplein 1* ☎ *070/416–2400* ⊕ *www.madurodam.nl* ☒ *€12* ⊙ *Sept.–Mar., daily 9–6; Apr.–June, daily 9–8; July and Aug., daily 9 AM–10 PM.*

**The Pier** at Scheveningen dates from 1901, but was extensively restored in 2000. Today, you can simply enjoy the view under cover of glass, or take part in more energetic activities, including bungee jumping from the tower at the far end. The 984-foot-long promenade deck is on two levels: a top deck that's exposed to the sun and wind, and a glass-protected inside deck. The transparency of the entire structure offers marvelous views of sun, sea, and sandy beaches. ⊠ *Strandweg.*

Take a step back in time at the **Scheveningen Museum.** Located in a former school, and extensively renovated in 2005, it tells the fascinating story of Scheveningen's role both as fishing village and seaside resort. ⊠ *Nepunusstraat 92* ☎ *070/350–0830* ⊕ *www.museumscheveningen. nl* 🎫 *€3.40* ⊙ *Tues.–Sat. 11–5, Sun. 1–5.*

☾ In the **Scheveningen Sea Life Centre** you will encounter hundreds of exotic sea creatures, from starfish to stingrays. The imaginative design of this aquarium includes a transparent tunnel, 30 feet long, where sharks swim above your head. There's also a ray petting pool. ⊠ *Strandweg 13* ☎ *070/354–2100* ⊕ *www.sealife.nl* 🎫 *€10* ⊙ *Daily 10–6.*

The **Vitalizee Spa Baths** offer an opportunity for nonstop pampering. Besides the sun beds, saunas, and baths here, you can splurge for a facial or massage. Pop in for just a day, or arrange a longer program. Tuesday from 10 to 6 is reserved for women only. ⊠ *Strandweg 13f* ☎ *070/ 416–6500* ⊕ *www.vitalizee.nl* 🎫 *Varies with treatment* ⊙ *Daily 10 AM–11:30 PM.*

off the beaten path

**DUINRELL THEME PARK –** Set in the woods and dunes of nearby Wassenaar, the Duinrell theme park has rides, slides, and a fairyland for kids, as well as the tropical Tikibad indoor pool center, featuring Europe's biggest waterslides. You can also rent a bungalow. To get ☾ there via public transport, take Bus No. 43 or No. 90 from The Hague. ⊠ *Duinrell 1, Wassenaar* ☎ *070/515–5255* ⊕ *www. duinrell.nl* 🎫 *€17* ⊙ *Theme park Apr.–June, Sept., and Oct., daily 10–5; July and Aug., daily 10–6. Tikibad daily 10–10.*

## Where to Stay & Eat

Stretching out beside the pier for hundreds of yards in either direction are dozens of beachside restaurants and cafés. All have reasonably priced and virtually identical menus featuring steak and fish. Just take a stroll and decide which one's decor most appeals to you. They all tend to get crowded on warmer summer days when beachcombers flock in to take a break and sip a chilled beer.

★ $$$$ ✕ **Restaurant Seinpost.** The perfect place to eat seafood is, of course, overlooking the sea—something you can do in magnificent style at this much-acclaimed restaurant. In a nautical atmosphere (think glass, pale wood, rattan chairs, and seashell accessories), begin your fishy feast with smoked eel served on a blin and accompanied by a tangle of cucumber spaghetti. Then take your pick from one of seven different types of oyster (yes, there really are that many), or perhaps you'd prefer turbot served with morels gathered from the sand dunes of Scheveningen. Dutch specialties include new herring, and the cheeses that have ripened in the restaurant's own cellar. ⊠ *Zeekant 60* ☎ *070/355–5250* ⊕ *www. seinpost.nl* ⊟ *AE, DC, MC, V* ⊙ *Closed Sun. No lunch Sat.*

★ $$$$ ✕▨ **Kurhaus.** Holding the prime position at the center of the beach at Scheveningen, this vast hotel first opened its doors in 1885. Since then, it has enjoyed a rich history. Just 14 months after its initial opening, it was almost completely destroyed by fire (allegedly started by a maid accompanying the Heineken brewing family on their vacation). The Kurhaus was restored, and phoenixlike, was up and running again by June 1887. Since then, guests have included Winston Churchill, Marlene Dietrich, and Luciano Pavarotti. Today it is fully modernized. Now engulfed on the street side by shops and apartments, it still has its famous turn-of-the-20th-century profile from the amusement pier, and you can dine on a buffet supper (with dancing on Friday) in the magnificent Kurzaal with its fancifully painted, coffered ceiling high overhead. The guest rooms are grand and opulently decorated in a variety of modern and traditional styles. In addition, guests can make use of the adjoining *Kuur Thermen Vitalizee* center with its saunas, plunge rooms, and herbal baths. ⊠ *Gevers Deynootplein 30, 2586 CK* ☎ *070/416–2636* 🖶 *070/416–2646* 🌐 *www.kurhaus.nl* 🛏 *245 rooms, 10 suites* ⌂ *2 restaurants, minibars, cable TV, in-room data ports, gym, bar, parking (fee), some pets allowed, no-smoking rooms* ▭ *AE, DC, MC, V.*

$ 🏨 **City Hotel.** Just off the beach in Scheveningen, this small, spanking-clean, brightly decorated, and very friendly family hotel spreads through several houses. It's on a main street leading to the waterfront. ⊠ *Renbaanstraat 1–3 and 17–23, 2586 EW* ☎ *070/355–7966* 🖶 *070/354–0503* 🛏 *28 rooms, 14 with bath* ⌂ *Restaurant, bar, parking (fee); no a/c* ▭ *AE, DC, MC, V* ⏐◎⏐ *BP.*

# THE HAGUE ESSENTIALS

## Transportation

More than 30 buses and tram lines in The Hague whisk travelers all over the city. Most of the sights in the town center are within a 15-minute walk from either of the city's train stations, but Tram lines Nos. 3 and 17 cover many of the sights, and Tram No. 10 will get you to the Statenkwartier museums. For information on specific lines, ask at the HTM offices in The Hague's stations, or at offices listed below. For information on public transport (trains, buses, trams, and ferries), call the national information line.

🚩 HTM ⊠ Wagenstraat 35 ☎ 070/390-7722 ⊠ Venestraat 9 ☎ 070/390-7722. **Public Transportation Information** ☎ 0900/9292 🌐 www.9292ov.nl.

### BY AIR
Amsterdam Schiphol Airport is half an hour by train from The Hague. Its comprehensive telephone service, charged at €0.10 per minute, provides information about flight arrivals and departures, as well as all transport and parking facilities (press No. 2 for English).

🚩 **Amsterdam Schiphol Airport** ☎ 0900/0141.

### BY BIKE
Bicycles can be rented at railway stations or by contacting local rental facilities. With plenty of cycle lanes, The Hague is as safe for cyclists as anywhere else in the Netherlands. Be wary of bikes with back-pedal brakes, which can be alarming if you're not used to them. Most rail-

way station shops will rent you a model with handlebar brakes for a slightly higher rate.

### BY CAR

To reach The Hague directly from Amsterdam, take E19 via Amsterdam Schiphol Airport. To reach the city from Utrecht, take the A12. Once you're approaching the city, follow the signs for the central parking route. This is an extremely helpful ring road that covers the many inexpensive parking lots within the city center.

🚗 Car Rentals **Avis** ✉ Theresiastraat 216 ☎ 070/385-0698. **Europcar** ✉ De Savornin Lohmanplein 5 ☎ 070/361-9191.

### BY TAXI

Taxis are available at the railway stations. Alternatively, to get one to collect you from your location, try one of the taxi firms recommended by the VVV: HTMC, ATC Taxi, or Baantax. You can't hail cabs in the street.

🚕 **ATC Taxi** ☎ 070/317-8877. **Baantax** ☎ 070/350-4924. **HTMC** ☎ 070/390-7722.

### BY TRAIN

There are two railway stations in The Hague: one is in the central business district, the **Station Hollands Spoor** (✉ Stationsweg). The other station, **Centraal Station** (✉ Koningin Julianaplein), is in the residential area. Trains from Amsterdam run directly to both the Centraal and Hollands Spoor stations, but the Centraal stop is an end stop, whereas Hollands Spoor is a through destination and is used as a stop for trains to and from Amsterdam, Delft, and Rotterdam. Travel from Hollands Spoor to these cities is more often by Intercity (express) train and will not involve a transfer.

🚆 **Intercity Express Trains** ☎ 0900/9292.

## Contacts & Resources

### EMERGENCIES

Pharmacies stay open late on a rotating basis; call for addresses on a given night. Tourist Assistance Service is an organization serving foreign tourists who've fallen victim to crime or been involved in an accident; it's open seven days a week.

🚨 Emergency Services **National Emergency Alarm Number** ☎ 112 for police, fire, and ambulance.

🏥 Hospital **The Hague** ✉ Bronovolaan 5 ☎ 070/312-4141.

📞 Hot Line **Tourist Assistance Service** ☎ 070/424-4000.

💊 Late-Night Pharmacies **Late-Night Pharmacy Information** ☎ 070/345-1000.

### TOURS

A Royal Tour that takes in the palaces and administrative buildings associated with Queen Beatrix operates April–September; the cost is €26.50 per person. The VVV also arranges a variety of tours covering everything from royalty to architecture. Or you can purchase booklets that will allow you to follow a walking tour at your own pace. The VVV does tours and has brochures for them, as well as tickets, at the VVV offices.

De Ooievaart runs boat tours around The Hague's canals. The boats depart from Bierkade and offer a peaceful and relaxing way to see the city. Trips last 1½ hours, cost €8.75, and can be bought from the VVV. 🚩 **Day Trips Department, Den Haag Marketing** ☎ 070/338-5816. **De Ooievaart** ☎ 070/338-5815.

## VISITOR INFORMATION

VVV Babylon (The Hague Information Office) is open January–May and September–December, Monday–Saturday 10–5; June–August, Monday–Saturday 10–5, Sunday, 11–5. VVV City Mondial on Wagenstraat is open Tuesday–Saturday 10–5. VVV Scheveningen is open Monday–Sunday; hours vary.

🚩 Tourist Information **VVV Babylon** ⊠ Koningin Julianaplein 30, Babylon shopping center ☎ 0900/340-3505. **VVV City Mondial** ⊠ Wagenstraat 193 ☎ 070/402-3336. **VVV Scheveningen** ⊠ Gevers Deynootweg 1134 ☎ 0900/340-3505.

# The Border Provinces & Maastricht

**4**

By Anna
Lambert
Revised by Tim
Skelton

**THE REGION BORDERING BELGIUM AND GERMANY** south of the heavily urbanized Randstad region is considered by many Dutch to be like "another country." Northern Calvinists find their Catholic southern cousins (with their softly accented singsong speech and ebullient mannerisms) almost a breed apart. The Catholic Dutch are more gregarious and outspoken than their northern counterparts; they also pursue the good life of food, drink, and conviviality with more gusto, and less guilt, than their Calvinist-influenced countrymen who live "above the Great Rivers."

Little wonder, then, that a trip "down south" means a change of gear, a chance to relax and indulge in life's finer pleasures. In fact, when Amsterdammers want to spend a weekend eating well and being pampered in elegant hotels, they think first of the southern provinces of their own country, where some of the most delectable culinary delights await. You can take your pick from fresh Zeeland shellfish or the gastronomically assured kitchens of Maastricht—for throughout the region there are restaurants of exceptional quality. Meanwhile, Limburg's castles often harbor luxurious hotels, which are far more special than many found in the big Randstad cities.

## Exploring the Border Provinces & Maastricht

Study the map and you'll see that the three southern provinces zigzag their way along the long border between the Netherlands and Belgium from the North Sea coast to the German frontier. In most Dutch provinces the sea presses in to the land, constantly striving to win a foothold, but Zeeland (Sea Land), to the contrary, pushes out into the water, invading the invader's territory and looking for trouble—a collection of flat, open, and windswept islands and peninsulas, known for their agriculture and shellfish. Noord Brabant, also known simply as Brabant, is a wooded and water-laced industrial area bordered on both east and north by the Maas River. Limburg is a region of hills and half-timbered farmhouses that extends along the Maas River deep into the south. The capital city, Maastricht, remains a mecca of sophistication, its antiques shops and famous fine-art fair drawing merchants and millionaires from around the world. With its excellent museums, glorious treasure-filled churches, and the sheer quality of life that it offers, it is a must-do destination.

Dotted throughout the entire southern region are other historic and picturesque towns, such as Veere, and Thorn, with their museums and 17th-century architecture—all perfect for a memorable day or two of escape and exploration.

The border provinces are spread out, so allow time to get a real feel for the area. If you're not keen on byways and side trips, concentrate on the eastern and western extremes of the region—Zeeland and Maastricht.

### About the Restaurants & Hotels

You'll enjoy your food in the border provinces—the locals certainly do. With its proximity to the coast, Zeeland is a great place to try seafood, including oysters, mussels, and lobsters. But the real culinary hub of the

4

The Netherlands' southern region is a beguiling mix of sounds, sights, and tastes that often prove the exception to the Dutch rule. Because the southern provinces cover a particularly extensive area, this is one part of the country where it may well pay to rent a car. But if you prefer not to drive, you can happily reach all the major sites by train or bus. By supplementing these modes of transportation with a rented bike, or your feet when going off the beaten track, you'll have both town and country well covered—especially if you follow these suggested tours.

*Numbers in the text correspond to numbers in the margin and on the Border Provinces and Maastricht maps.*

If you have
3 days

If you have three days, sticking closely to ⊞ **Maastricht** ⑮–㉜ means you can fully explore both the city and the glorious Limburg scenery. It is possible to cover a lot of ground in three days provided you do a good deal of driving and are willing to treat some sites as whistle-stops. At this pace, you'll be exhausted by the end of your tour, but it'll be worth it. So—presuming you've come down south from Amsterdam way—begin with tiny **Heusden** ⑩ in North Brabant, an ancient fortified town that's the epitome of picture-postcard prettiness. In the afternoon, head for the province's capital, **'s-Hertogenbosch** ⑨, whose magical cathedral, 17th-century houses, and excellent museum will give you an in-depth impression of the past, and particularly of the historic Dutch Golden Age. Take time to sample a fabled pastry, the chocolate-drenched *Bossche bol,* whose sugar content should be enough to fuel you onward. Leave in the early evening for the drive toward the North Sea coast, perhaps stopping over in ⊞ **Bergen Op Zoom** ⑥. On Day 2, head for Neeltje Jans Island and the Waterland Neeltje Jans Delta Expo—the massive dam and flood barrier that, together with its accompanying exhibition, eloquently conveys the Netherlands' long, hard struggle with the sea. Spend the morning here, and then head south for ⊞ **Veere** ②, once an important seaport and still rightfully considered one of the Netherlands' prettiest towns.

If you're planning on spending the night in Maastricht, be warned that, depending on road conditions, the drive from Veere could take up to three hours, so allow time for the journey (heading via Belgium is the quickest). For a truly relaxing night in Limburg's capital, book yourself into the spectacular blend of ancient and modern that is the Kruisherenhotel, or, if a little pampering is in order, in the Château St. Gerlach with its superlative French restaurant, just outside town in Valkenburg. Spend the next day marveling at Maastricht's many treasures and soaking up the café-society atmosphere. Eat early in town (the grilled meat and fish specialties at Sagittarius are particularly tasty); then, in the cool of the evening, work off the after-effects with a walk or bike ride through the surrounding countryside, with its fields and wildflowers, which should ensure a deep, fresh-air-induced sleep on your final night.

If you have
5 days

Five days will allow you to take things at a more leisurely pace. After visiting **Veere** ②, travel on to spend the second night in ⊞ **Eindhoven** ⑪, home of the first Philips lightbulb factory and still Holland's high-tech headquarters. Here you'll find the Van Abbemuseum, one of Europe's most remarkable collections of contemporary art. Alternatively, travel farther south to **Thorn** ⑫, an ancient "white village" whose impressive abbey church allows for great photo opportunities. Spend your last two days exploring the cobbled streets and churches of 🚉 **Maastricht** ⑮–㉜, being sure to carve out visits to the Bonnefanten museum and the chilly but fascinating marl caves of Sint Pietersberg; the guided, lamp-lighted tour through its mysterious passages could leave you feeling like something of a pioneer.

region is Limburg, where the influence of neighboring cuisines is apparent in the frying pans of the local chefs. You may pay slightly more to fill your belly in Limburg, but you won't regret it. Anyplace in the border provinces worth its salt will be busy Thursday through Sunday, and without a reservation you'll often find yourself with your nose pressed forlornly against the wrong side of a restaurant window.

Hotel standards are consistently high, and it is repeatedly said that you'll be more comfortable (and in more stylish surroundings) here than in any other region in Holland. Behind a 17th-century facade, rooms may come equipped with all modern conveniences. And because the Dutch are so interested in interior design and home comforts, even many smaller hotels and family-owned inns are lovingly decorated. Assume all rooms have air-conditioning, TV, telephones, and private bath, unless otherwise noted.

| WHAT IT COSTS In euros | | | | | |
|---|---|---|---|---|---|
| | **$$$$** | **$$$** | **$$** | **$** | **¢** |
| RESTAURANTS | over €30 | €22–€30 | €15–€22 | €10–€15 | under €10 |
| HOTELS | over €230 | €165–€230 | €120–€165 | €75–€120 | under €75 |

Restaurant prices are per person for a main course only, excluding tax (6% for food and 19% for alcoholic beverages) and service; note that if a restaurant offers only prix-fixe meals, it has been given the price category that reflects the full prix-fixe price. Hotel prices are for a standard double room in high season, including the 6% VAT.

## Timing

So far as timing your visit is concerned, late spring and fall are the ideal seasons. You can never count on the weather, though; even in high summer, a single day can bring not just sunshine but also hail and rain. If you can't stand crowds, it's best to avoid the Easter holiday and July and August. In late spring, the days get longer and more golden and the weather can be balmy. Fall days can be particularly glorious, when the bronze-leaf Limburg woods really come into their own. That said, there are some busy times that you won't want to avoid: the region is at its liveliest at Carnival time (usually mid to late February), and gourmets visit in spring to make the most of the asparagus season (early May–June 24). The mussel season (mid-October–April) usually starts off with parties in village squares around Zeeland, where you'll find steaming cauldrons full of as many of these tasty shellfish critters as you can eat.

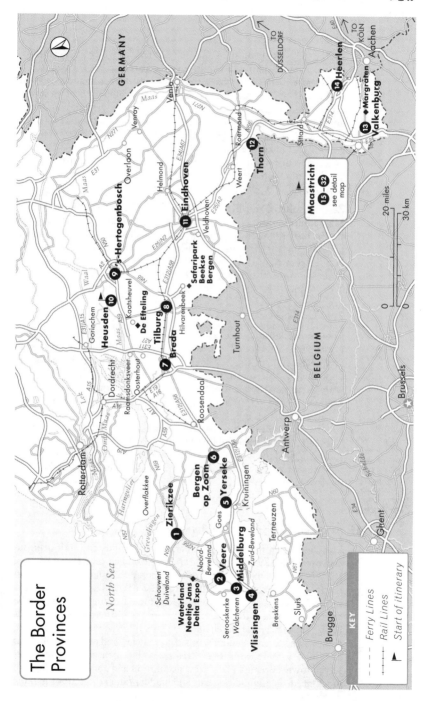

# The Border Provinces

GERMANY

TO
DÜSSELDORF

TO
KÖLN

Aachen

**14** Heerlen

**13** ◆ Margraten
Valkenburg

Maas

Venray

Venlo

L2N

E34/A67

Roermond

Sittard

E25

**12**
Thorn

N271

Overloon

Helmond

E25/A2

Weert

**Maastricht**
**15 – 32**
see detail
map

Maas

N31

E31

Maas

E34/A67

Veldhoven

20 miles

30 km

's-Hertogenbosch
**9**

A2

E261/N2

**11** Eindhoven

0

Waal

N90

Kaatsheuvel

◆ Safaripark
Beekse
Bergen

Gorinchem

**Heusden**
**10**

▲ De Efteling

Hilvarenbeek

A15

E311/A15

E37

**Tilburg**
**8**

E312/A58

Turnhout

E34

BELGIUM

Dordrecht

Raamsdonksveer

Oosterhout

E19
A16

A27

**Breda**
**7**

E311

E312/A58

Brussels

Lek

Oud Maas

A16

A59

Roosendaal

Antwerp

Schelde

Rotterdam

A29

N59

Overflakkee

**6**
Bergen
op Zoom

E312/A4

Kruiningen

E34/A58

Ghent

Grevelingen

N57

**5** Yerseke

Goes

N60

Zierikzee
**1**

Noord-
Beveland

N256

Zuid-Beveland

Terneuzen

N61

Schouwen
Duiveland

**Waterland**
**Neeltje Jans**
◆ **Delta Expo**

Serooskerke

Walcheren

**2** Veere

**3** Middelburg

**4**

Breskens

Sluis

Brugge

North Sea

**Vissingen**

KEY

- - - Ferry Lines
–┼– Rail Lines
▲ Start of itinerary

# ZEELAND

On the fingerlike peninsulas and islands of the province of Zeeland you are never more than a few miles from a major body of water. You're never more than a few inches above sea level, either, if above it at all: floods have put this province almost completely under water on several occasions, most recently in 1953. Once one of the wealthiest and most important of the Dutch provinces, the entire area was known for its seafaring and trading skills. The provincial capital of Middelburg boasted its own East India Company, and the Scottish wool trade was centered on Veere. The province's coat of arms shows a lion rising from the sea, and its Latin motto means "I struggle and I survive," words that were to prove all too apposite in the 20th century.

Zeeland suffered terribly during World War II. The Germans bombed Middelburg, and nearly destroyed its Town Hall and 12th-century abbey. Toward the end of the war, the Allies demolished the Walcheren dikes as a means of flooding the island, in the hope of flushing out the Nazis. Repaired in 1944, the dikes sadly weren't strong enough to withstand the force of the famous 1953 storm. Today, new and stronger dikes, dams, and bridges connect Zeeland's four chief islands and peninsulas (Schouwen Duiveland, Noord-Beveland, Walcheren, and Zuid-Beveland).

There's a delightful sense of the past in this area of the Netherlands—historic towns such as Zierikzee, Veere, and Middelburg boast Gothic architecture, 17th-century merchants' houses, and town halls bedecked with towers, turrets, and carillons. Old traditions are honored, with some local women in Walcheren still wearing lace caps, old-fashioned buttoned-up shirtwaists, and black-and-white skirts, many of them appearing in force on a Middelburg market day. But no one could say that Zeeland is frozen in a time warp: it can't afford to be. The Delta Works dam and flood barrier provides state-of-the-art protection against the elements (and the Delta Expo lets you discover how this was accomplished), and Vlissingen is a model of the bustling modern ferry terminal.

## Zierikzee

**❶** *65 km (40 mi) southwest of Rotterdam.*

Traveling south from Rotterdam across the islands and frail peninsulas, along the A29 and N59, you come to the chief center of Schouwen Duiveland: the small, old city of Zierikzee. A yachting port with an attractive old harbor where 17th- and 18th-century houses line the quaysides, Zierikzee has cobblestone streets, three historic gateways, and a canal connecting it to the open waters of the Oosterschelde. It stands in the midst of typical Dutch imagery: busy tillers of the soil, black-and-white cattle, distant windmills, broad green fields, and neat rows of plants and flowers. Founded in 849, Zierikzee is among the nation's best-preserved towns. Because of its strategic location and ability to supply two much-needed commodities, salt and madder (an herb used for making red dye), the town enjoyed considerable prosperity from the Middle Ages onward. Zierikzee's most spectacular attraction is the great clock tower of the cathedral, **Sint Lievens Monstertoren,** begun in 1454 but never completed (when it reached a height of 184 feet, the townspeople ran out of money). The rest of the cathedral was destroyed by fire in 1872. Nearby, look out for the unusual onion-shape dome topping the wooden tower of the **Stadhuis** (Town Hall), dating from 1550. At its peak is a statue of every seaman's favorite, the sea god Neptune. Inside the building is a small municipal museum, the **Gemeentemuseum,** whose treasures include ship models, silver, local costumes, and a room decorated with traditional tiles made in the area. The intricately constructed ceiling in the Harquebusiers' Hall is worth careful examination. ⊠ *Meelstraat 6* ☎ *0111/454409 or 0111/454464* 🖃 *€2* ⊙ *Mon.–Sat. 10–5, Sun. noon–5.*

★ ☽ **Waterland Neeltje Jans** offers a firsthand tour of the most important achievement of Dutch hydraulic engineering. The Delta Works, a massive dam and flood barrier that closed up the sea arms in response to the flood disaster of 1953, is most impressive, plus there are exhibits documenting the 2,000-year history of the Dutch people's struggle with the sea. Films and slide shows, working scale models, and displays of materials give a comprehensive overview of dikes, dams, and underwater supports. The visit includes a boat trip in good weather. There is also a water playground with all kinds of interesting aquatic-based contraptions, a storm surge barrier one can stand on, a new futuristic-style whale pavilion, and even a hurricane simulator. Some attractions are closed in winter. ⊠ *Eiland Neeltje Jans, Burgh-Haamstede, (6 km [4 mi] south of Burgh-Haamstede on the N57)* ☎ *0111/652702* ⊕ *www.neeltjejans. nl* 🖃 *Apr.–Oct. €15, Nov.–mid-Mar. €9.50* ⊙ *Apr.–Oct., daily 10–5:30; Nov.–Mar., Wed.–Sun. 10–5.*

## Veere

**❷** *15 km (9 mi) east of Domburg, 7 km (4 mi) northeast of Middelburg,* Fodor'sChoice *100 km (62 mi) southwest of Rotterdam.*
★

One of the prettiest towns in the Netherlands, Veere is well worth a stop to explore its quiet streets and admire its elegant architecture. A village of 2,000 (compared with 20,000 in the 16th century) and the principal sailing port of the Veerse Meer (Veerse Lake, created when they closed off the estuary with a dike), the town was an important seaport during the 16th century, with a busy trade in wool, linen, and salt.

Veere's Gothic **Stadhuis** (Town Hall), built of sandstone and begun in 1474, has a fairy-tale facade that harks back to the town's glory days. It is decorated with statues commemorating Veere's former lords and ladies, notably members of the Van Borselen family. The extraordinary building, among the Netherlands' most impressive, also has a minaret-style Renaissance tower, added in 1599, that contains a 48-bell carillon. The whole thing seems unexpectedly grand for the sleepy village of today. Inside is one of the country's oldest formal audience chambers, resplendent with portraits and Gobelin tapestries and displaying a silver goblet given to Count Maximilian of Burgundy in 1546 by Emperor Charles V. Maximilian, who left it as a gift when he came to inspect the town cistern. ⊠ *Markt 5* ☎ *0118/506064* ⛉ *€2* ☾ *May–Oct., Mon.–Sat. 1–5.*

The **Museum de Schotse Huizen** (The Scots' Houses Museum) stands beside 16th-century buildings, which face the town's small inner harbor, that were once the offices and warehouses of Scottish wool merchants. Highly ornate, the buildings are named Het Lammetje (The Little Lamb) and De Struys (The Ostrich); you'll know which is which by studying the facade stones. Inside is a collection of local costumes, porcelain, furniture (don't miss the Zeeland "star cabinet" inlaid with star shapes in ivory and wood), household items, and paintings. It's all delightfully old-world Dutch: the blue-and-white tiled fireplace, high ceilings, and exposed brickwork may make you feel like you've stepped into a Vermeer painting. ⊠ *Kaai 25–27* ☎ *0118/501744* ⊕ *www.deschotsehuizen.nl* ⛉ *€3* ☾ *Daily 1–5.*

The massive **Grote Kerk** (Great Church) dates from the 15th century and has had a turbulent history. In 1686 its interior was destroyed by fire, and in the 19th century Napoléon requisitioned it as a barracks and hospital, which also didn't help. Its lofty, though incomplete, tower offers great views. Just next to the church is the pretty **municipal well,** another Gothic structure, built by order of Maximilian of Burgundy, in 1551, to collect rainwater falling from the church roof, which was needed by the wool merchants to conduct their flourishing trade. ⊠ *Oudestraat 26* ☎ *0118/501829* ⛉ *€1.50, tower €1.50* ☾ *Apr.–Sept., Mon.–Sat. 11–4:30, Sun. noon–4:30.*

When the dam between Walcheren and Noord-Beveland was finished in 1961, Veere was no longer a seaport, and instead found itself separated from the sea. So Veere is now on the shore of the saltwater Veerse Meer, 26 km (16 mi) long and one of the largest lakes in Holland. In the past two decades it has developed into a major water-sports center in which every form of aquatic activity is practiced.

### Where to Stay & Eat

★ **$-$$** ✕⊡ **De Campveerse Toren Hotel & Restaurant.** Down on the quay, this fabled redoubt is landmarked by its spectacular 15th-century tower, a former gunpowder magazine and part of what were once Veere's city wall fortifications. Overlooking the water and a tiny jetty, replete with bobbing boats, the brick tower—now home to the hotel restaurant—has lovely stepped gables and enjoys a great history: William of Orange and his bride Charlotte of Bourbon celebrated their wedding feast here in 1575. Today you can enjoy servings of fresh local oysters, smoked eel, or grilled lamb. Whereas the public salons are accented with antiques, most guest rooms are simple but comfortable; several are in the massive 17th-century stone hall adjacent to the Campveerse Toren tower, two are in the tower themselves, and others are in quaint two-story houses, one of which, the Sterntje, has two luxurious deluxe apartments that offer fabulous views over the harbor and Veerse Meer. ⊠ *Kaai 2, 4351 AA* ☎ *0118/501291* 🖷 *0118/501695* ⊕ *www.campveersetoren.nl*

⚐ *Reservations essential* ⇨ *12 rooms, 2 apartments* ⚑ *Restaurant, cable TV, some pets allowed; no a/c* ☰ *AE, DC, MC, V* ⦿| *BP.*

¢–$ ✕⊞ **'t Waepen van Veere.** The family-run hotel-restaurant a couple of doors from the towering City Hall often blows its trumpet about its fine restaurant, which offers a full-blast Menu Gourmand, serves fine renditions of Zeeland-style fish soup, grilled sole, and asparagus in season, and comes replete with the usual nouvelle trimmings, such as a scallop *"cappuccino" de coquilles St-Jacques* and lobster with chanterelles and truffles. Good-value rooms are simply decorated with dark-wood contemporary furniture, white walls, and cream curtains. A special gastronomic three-day weekend food-and-board plan is offered. ⊠ *Markt 23–27, 4351 AG* ☎ *0118/501231* 🖷 *0118/506009* ⊕ *www.waepen. nl* ⚐ *Reservations essential* ⇨ *11 rooms* ⚑ *Restaurant, cable TV, some pets allowed; no a/c* ☰ *AE, MC, V* ⦿| *MAP* ⊘ *Closed Jan.–mid-Feb. and Mon. and Tues. in late Feb., Mar., Nov., and Dec.*

## Middelburg

❸ *7 km (4 mi) southwest of Veere, 97 km (60 mi) west of Breda.*

Fodor'sChoice
★

Middelburg, the ancient capital of the province of Zeeland, has one great advantage that has helped ensure its safety in this water-dominated area: it is on the rise of a slight incline. The town was an important trading post in early times, beginning with cloth and French wine imports, followed by the presence of the Dutch East and West India companies during the 17th century. Today it is a bustling, friendly town that—despite severe bombing during World War II—preserves many impressive monuments. Thanks to its excellent Abdij complex, visitors can enjoy all kinds of exhibitions, from displays on local history and a fossilized mammoth to a costume hall and a collection of contemporary art. All in all, Middelburg is a particularly fascinating Dutch city. The only way to enjoy it is to walk around, for hidden away in the old stronghold called the **Binnenhof**, or Inner Town, are many splendid examples of old architecture—note the Blauwpoort (Blue Gateway), the Kuiperspoort (Cooper's Gate), the Koepoort (Cow Gate), and Vismarkt (Fish Market) in a picturesque square—plus placid canals reflecting former glory.

A testimony to Middelburg's past grandeur, the elaborately decorated **Stadhuis** (Town Hall) stands resplendent on the market square. Begun in 1452, and said to have been inspired by the Stadhuis in Brussels, it is one of the great showpieces of southern-Dutch Gothic architecture. The building was designed as a grand home for the town's prestigious cloth guild. It is adorned with statues of past counts and countesses of Zeeland; much of the facade, however, is not authentic, having been added as part of an overenthusiastic 19th-century restoration. Inside, the most impressive room is the austere Vleeshal (Meat Market), which is now used for exhibitions. To see the rest of the building's 17th-century furniture and tapestries, you will need to join a guided tour. These are normally in Dutch and German, but if you ask nicely, most guides will offer some commentary in English. ⊠ *Markt* ☎ *0118/652200* 🖃 *Vleeshal free, tours €3.95* ⊘ *Tues.–Sun. 1–5 (Vleeshal); tours Apr.–Sept., Sat.–Thurs. 11:30 and 3:15.*

The heart of Middelburg is the 12th-century **Abdij** (Abbey Complex), which incorporates three churches, countless provincial government offices (Zeeland's local government meets here on a monthly basis), the Roosevelt Studiecentrum (a major research library), the provincial cultural and historical museum, and a tall tower that overlooks the city and surrounding countryside. Although badly damaged in World War II, the entire complex has been faithfully reconstructed. **Onze Lieve Vrouwe Abdij** (Our Beloved Lady Abbey) was founded in 1150 as a Premonstratensian abbey and served as a monastery until 1574. There's a sweet-smelling herb garden in the courtyard and a 100,000-year-old Zeeland mammoth to admire. You can also visit the cloisters, regional government halls, and crypt. ⊠ *Abdij* ☎ *0118/616616* ⚏ *Free* ☉ *Apr.–Nov., Mon.–Sat. 10–6, Sun. noon–6.*

Although the main building and permanent collection of the **Zeeuws Museum** (Zeeland Museum) are off-limits until a renovation is complete in 2007, the museum association continues to host temporary exhibitions in locations around town. Once the permanent collection is back on display, you can see tapestries illustrating major sea battles of the 16th century fought between Holland and Spain; an ornately decorated wood "curiosity cabinet"; historical clothes and costumes; display boards on life in Zeeland since the Middle Ages; and canvases by Mondriaan and Toorop. ⊠ *Abdij 3* ☎ *0118/653000* ⊕ *www.zeeuwsmuseum.nl.*

Of particular interest to American visitors is the **Roosevelt Studiecentrum** (Roosevelt Study Center), whose exhibition hall has a permanent display on the life and times of the Roosevelts. Theodore and Franklin Delano Roosevelt were descendants of a Zeeland family; the purpose of this center is to make known the historical links between the United States and the Netherlands and particularly to publicize the role of the United States in Europe during the 20th century. ⊠ *Abdij 9* ☎ *0118/631590* ⊕ *www.roosevelt.nl* ⚏ *Free* ☉ *Apr.–Oct., weekdays 11–12:30 and 1:30–4:30.*

You can climb the 207 steps to the top of the octagonal **"Lange Jan" Abdijtoren** ("Long John" Abbey Tower), which is attached to the Choral Church of the Abbey Complex. The stone tower, 280 feet high, was constructed in the 14th century and is topped with an 18th-century onion-shape dome. This is a landmark that's visible not only throughout the town but throughout most of Walcheren. There are carillon concerts on Thursday for an hour beginning midday, and more often in July and August. ⊠ *Abdij* ☎ *0118/612525* ⚏ *€3.50* ☉ *Apr.–Oct., Mon.–Sat. 11–4.*

☺ Buildings and landmarks typical of the Middelburg region have been duplicated in one-twentieth actual size in **Miniatuur Walcheren** (Miniature Walcheren), a miniature city within a garden that is home to 1,400 bonsai trees and approximately 300 different types of plants. The skillfully made models include houses, churches, and windmills, and a reconstruction of Veerse Lake replete with motorized boats. Trees and plants are executed on a tiny scale, along with traveling buses, trains, and barges. ⊠ *Molenwater 1* ☎ *0118/612525* ⚏ *€8* ☉ *Apr.–June, Sept., and Oct., daily 10–6; July and Aug., daily 10–7.*

# ON THE MENU IN THE BORDER PROVINCES

**D**UTCH FOODIES know that "south of the rivers" they'll find some of the best food in the country—from the fat, succulent oysters and mussels of Zeeland to the French- and German-influenced cuisine of Limburg (around Maastricht), such as Limburgse vlaai, a delicious custard-and-fruit tart. The region's white asparagus (Limburg produces 80% of the crop that's devoured by a grateful Dutch nation) and its earthy cave mushrooms are superb and serve as both ingredients and inspiration for those master chefs in their hillside château-restaurants. Just like the landscape, dishes in this area differ considerably from those elsewhere. Because of the Franco-Germanic influence, you'll find that people generally eat later here; expect to dine around 8 PM, though you would also be welcomed from 6:30 PM on.

## Where to Stay & Eat

**$$$–$$$$** ✕ **Het Groot Paradys.** Facing the Damplein market square in a 16th-century house, this renowned and intimate restaurant retains a traditional town-house decor, crowned by shining chandeliers. Head chef Ferdie Dolk serves up predominantly French cuisine with an emphasis on local ingredients. Seafood lovers are in for a treat, and oyster aficionados should consider taking up residence. The wine list sees renowned French labels nestle side-by-side with an impressive selection from Australia and New Zealand. Fresh-baked breads are the pride of the kitchen. ⊠ *Damplein 13* ☎ *0118/651200* ⌂ *Reservations essential* ▤ *AE, DC, MC, V* ☾ *Closed Sun. and Mon. No lunch Sat.*

**$$** ✕ **Nummer 7.** Under the same ownership as the more famous Het Groot Paradys, this restaurant has a finesse all its own, in a relaxed setting of pale-yellow walls and marble tables. It is not every day you can eat a three-course meal, with generous portions of such delights as North Sea crab salad, pork with truffle sauce, and white chocolate mousse, and still pay less than €25. ⊠ *Rotterdamsekaai 7* ☎ *0118/627077* ▤ *AE, DC, MC, V* ☾ *Closed Mon. No lunch.*

**★ $–$$** ✕ **De Mug.** The building housing this cozy restaurant and bar dates from 1500, and some of the wood-paneled walls and tiled floors in the warren of rooms look like they've been there since day one. The syrup-lacquered pork steak with abbey beer sauce, and the baked halibut with lobster bisque jus, are both excellent, while the spareribs come highly recommended by the locals. Vegetarians are so well served, they get their own menu. If you order the house wine by the bottle, you are only charged for what you drink. ⊠ *Vlasmarkt 54–56* ☎ *0118/614851* ⌂ *Reservations essential* ▤ *MC, V* ☾ *Closed Sun. and Mon. No lunch.*

**$–$$** ✕ **De Vriendschap.** The split-level interior successfully blends dark-brown girders with soft orange lighting and organic elements such as bamboo screens and lobster pots, while out on the terrace in summer you dine with a grand view of the soaring 15th-century Town Hall. Starters include Japanese-influenced raw fish, and there is a good choice of seafood-based main courses, often prepared with a Mediterranean touch. The plump, locally harvested mussels are particularly good. ⊠ *Markt 75* ☎ *0118/612257* ▤ *AE, MC, V.*

**$–$$** ▣ **Le Beau Rivage.** This attractive hotel occupies a gabled turn-of-the-20th-century canal-side brick building near the city center. The rooms are comfortable and decorated in pale colors with modern prints on the walls; the management is efficient and friendly. ⊠ *Loskade 19, 4331 HW* ☎ *0118/638060* ▤ *0118/629673* ♚ *9 rooms, 1 suite* ♨ *Cable TV, in-room data ports; no a/c* ▤ *AE, DC, MC, V* ❙⊙❙ *BP.*

### Nightlife

The bar at the front of the restaurant **De Mug** (⊠ Vlasmarkt 56) is warm and inviting, and there's a wide selection of beer, including the restaurant's own Mug Bitter, brewed since 1988. There's live jazz on the last Tuesday of each month. **Rockdesert** (⊠ Damplein 20) attracts a young and very lively clientele; it's great if you like your music loud and throbbing.

### Sports & the Outdoors

BEACHES In the vicinity of Middelburg, you will find the best beaches at **Domburg, Kouderkerke, Oostkapelle, Vrouwenpolder/Serooskerke, Westkapelle,** and **Zoutelande;** all have beach houses to rent, and all but Vrouwenpolder/Serooskerke have beach pavilions.

BICYCLING You can rent bicycles from **Stationsrijwielstalling** (⊠ Kanaalweg 22 ☎ 0118/612178). ID and a deposit of €50 is required.

BOATING In central Middelburg you can take an open-top boat to explore the town's canals. These leave from **Lange Viele bridge** (⊠ Achter de Houttuinen 39 ☎ 0118/643272 ⊕ www.rondvaartmiddelburg.nl) April–October, Monday–Saturday 11–5, Sunday noon–5. The ticket price is €5.50

TOURNAMENT In Molenwater in Middelburg, there's a **tilting at the ring,** or *rigrijderij,* event, in which competitors reenact the medieval knights game, mounting horses and trying to spear small rings with lances. The event takes place every July and August. Times vary, so check with the VVV.

### Shopping

Middelburg's **fruit market** is held on Saturday. The **summer antiques and curiosities market** is at the Vismarkt mid-June–August, Thursday 9–4. Late shopping is on Thursday until 9.

## Vlissingen

❹ *7 km (4 mi) south of Middelburg.*

Known in English as Flushing, this major port and ferry terminal at the mouth of the Schelde has long played a key role in Dutch naval history: it was from here that Philip II finally embarked for Spain back in 1559. Between 1585 and 1616, the town was "lent" to the English, as insurance against costs incurred by the Earl of Leicester when preserving the United Provinces after William the Silent's murder. Heavily damaged by bombing in World War II, Vlissingen also suffered badly during the dis-

# SEA SURGE: THE FLOOD OF 1953

**ON THE NIGHT OF JANUARY 31, 1953,** *a storm blew up that was to prove a disaster for the Netherlands and see its landscape altered forever. Dangerously high tides were forecast for Rotterdam, Willemstad, and Bergen op Zoom and they arrived with dire consequences: by morning, 1,855 Dutch people had drowned and hundreds more were left homeless. Proving woefully inadequate, 48 km (32 mi) of dikes burst, with another 139 km (92 mi) suffering extensive damage, resulting in widespread flooding. The Dutch Red Cross Organization began a collection of clothing, food, and blankets, and by Monday, February 2, a fund of Fl 2 million (€ 900,000) had been established. Meanwhile, planes, helicopters, and land forces continued to evacuate victims and mounted an intense program of air-dropping food and life rafts onto villages and visible islands of dry ground.*

*The vast scale of the disaster and the sense of tragedy that followed led, in 1958, to the creation of the Delta Act, a plan allowing the construction of a network of barriers that would close off the estuaries toward the southwest of the region. Today, only the New Waterway and the Westerschelde remain open to facilitate ships' access to Rotterdam and Antwerp. The Oosterschelde (Eastern Scheldt) basin can be closed off by an enormous storm-surge barrier consisting of 62 steel gates. On October 4, 1986, Queen Beatrix led a ceremony opening the storm-surge barrier, thereby marking the official completion of the Delta Expo.*

astrous flood of 1953. Today, the town is known as an industrial center with important naval shipyards and a college. The compact center, however, remains an attractive place to wander, with many fine old buildings surrounding the inner yacht harbor. Facing the Schelde River and high above the water is Vlissingen's great boulevard, successively called De Ruyter, Bankert, and Evertsen, after famous Dutch sea captains; at the south end is a wide terrace called the Rotonde, and nearby is tranquil Bellamy Park.

☾  At the 1823 **Arsenaal,** visitors learn about life at sea in a theme park–like environment. Imaginative, hands-on displays include a parrot island, a ray petting pool, and an underwater world. All the while, animatronic marauding pirates scale the building's outer walls on ropes. Climb up the watchtower to see panoramic views across Zeeland, Belgium, and the Westerschelde. ✉ *Arsenaalplein 1* ☎ *0118/415400* 🖃 *€ 11* ☉ *Feb.–June, Sept., and Oct., daily 10–7; July and Aug., daily 10–8; Nov.–Jan., Wed. and Fri.–Sun. 10–7.*

☾  Opened in 2002, the **Zeeuws maritiem muZEEum** (Mu-Sea-Um) charts the rich maritime history of Zeeland. Housed in several buildings overlooking the picturesque inner harbor, some dating from the 16th and 18th centuries yet interconnected by wholly appropriate modern architecture, it has at its heart an expertly restored Golden Age mansion dating from 1641. The museum lets you get acquainted with the fascinating struggle between the locals and the sea through themes such as Adventure, Water, Work, and Glory. Locals will point with pride to the exhibits on Michael de Ruyter (1607–76), Vlissingen's most famous son. As a Dutch admiral he distinguished himself during the third war against the English in the early 1670s. There are also exhibits detailing the town's involvement with the Dutch East India Company. For children there are informative games, computer presentations, and even a treasure hunt. ⊠ *Nieuwendijk 11* ☎ *0118/412498* ⊕ *www.muzeeum.nl* ☑ *€6* ☉ *Weekdays 10–5, weekends 1–5.*

In quieter days of yore, Vlissingen was known as a particularly pleasant place; newcomers, the story went, "woke up unconscious," for the air is heavy and soft and the sea air most conducive to slumber. The many ships that pass here en route to Antwerp are not asleep, however, since it is here that the sea pilots hand over control to river pilots. You can watch this happening from the Boulevard de Ruyter, named after the 17th-century admiral whose statue is here.

### Where to Stay

**$–$$$** 🏨 **Best Western Grand Hotel Arion.** For an excellent view over the sea, this hotel, built in 1995, has clean rooms furnished in a palette of soft colors and with modern furniture. Rooms facing the sea are considerably higher priced than those at the back, but the difference in vistas more than compensates. There's also a lively bar area. ⊠ *266 Blvd. Bankert, 4382 AC* ☎ *0118/410502* 🖷 *0118/416362* ⊕ *www.hotelarion. nl* 🛏 *68 rooms* ♿ *Restaurant, cable TV, in-room data ports, some minibars, bar, some pets allowed; no a/c* 🖃 *AE, DC, MC, V.*

## Yerseke

**❺** *40 km (25 mi) east of Vlissingen, 35 km (22 mi) east of Middelburg.*

The small fishing port of Yerseke is the oyster nursery of Europe. Lobster boats dock at the piers along the waterfront; the beds that nurture some of the finest, sweetest, and most flavorful oysters and mussels in the world lie in pits below the seawalls. In the small buildings on the docks shellfish are sorted and packed for shipment. On the third Saturday of August, Yerseke celebrates with a **Mosseldag** (mussel festival). There are special tours around the oyster beds during the season (mid-September–April) and regular tours of the Oosterschelde (the eastern area of seawater around the Yerseke region) departing from Julianahaven.

If you're really mad about bivalves, the tiny **Oosterschelde Museum,** next door to the VVV (the sign on the door just says "Yerseke Museum"), charts the history of the mussel and oyster business in the region in quaintly dusty exhibit cases. The explanations are all in Dutch, but the enthusiastic, English-speaking curator will probably be around to give you a personalized tour. ⊠ *Kerkplein 1* ☎ *0113/571864* ☑ *1.50* ☉ *Mid-May–mid-Sept., daily 10–noon and 1–4; mid-Sept.–mid-May, Mon.–Sat. 10–noon and 1–4.*

## Where to Stay & Eat

Zeeland-style cooking often pairs delicately poached fish with a generous bath of rich, wine-based sauce. One particularly delicious way in which mussels are prepared is by baking them with *Zeeuws spek* (Zeeland grilled bacon) and caramelized onions. The fresh oysters are usually consumed raw.

★ **$$$$** ✕ **Nolet's Restaurant Het Reymerswale.** Yerseke's best and most expensive restaurant is run by the Nolet family. The restaurant interior doubles as a museum on Reymerswaele, with many excavated exhibits from the village that gave the world the Flemish painter Marinus van Reymerswaele but was overrun by the sea some 500 years ago. The beamed second-floor dining room overlooking the water is spacious and graciously decorated. It has a comfortable lounge area with a fireplace and a summer porch in back. There is also an impressive aquarium, whose inhabitants are apparently not destined for the end of your fork. The menu's focus is, naturally, on seafood, classically prepared with the finest standards—grilled turbot, and sea bass in basil sauce with sun-dried tomatoes, are the house specialties. From April to July you can also satisfy your lobster cravings. ⊠ *Burgemeester Sinkelaan 5* ☎ *0113/571642* △ *Reservations essential* ⊟ *AE, DC, MC, V* ⊘ *Closed Jan., 2 wks in May, and Tues. and Wed.*

**$$–$$$$** ✕ **Nolet's Vistro.** The name of this bistro-style annex next to Nolet's Restaurant (they share the same kitchen) alludes to the emphasis on seafood; *vis* is Dutch for fish. This spot has a marginally less-formal setting, and less emphasis on creativity and presentation, but the lobsters, crabs, oysters, mussels, and fish are just as fresh. ⊠ *Burgemeester Sinkelaan 6* ☎ *0113/572101* △ *Reservations essential* ⊟ *AE, DC, MC, V* ⊘ *Closed Jan., 2 wks in May, and Mon.*

**$–$$$** ✕ **Nolet.** This simple and traditional restaurant is run by another branch of the Nolet family and offers crustaceans, bivalves, and fish prepared Zeeland style, poached, baked, or grilled. ⊠ *Lepelstraat 7* ☎ *0113/571309* ⊟ *AE, MC* ⊘ *Closed Mon.*

★ **$$$–$$$$** ✕▥ **Manoir Inter Scaldes.** Seven kilometers (4 mi) south of Yerseke is the simple farm town of Kruiningen, a firm fixture on the culinary map for many years. Master chef and local boy Jannis Brevet has picked up a string of awards and accolades for his luxurious concoctions at previous restaurants. People come from far and wide—some even by helicopter—to feast on delights such as local oysters served with cardamom potato cream, followed by scallops with truffles and smooth cauliflower mousseline, and rounded off with curd cheese soufflé accompanied by lemon and bourbon vanilla. The bright conservatory restaurant looks out onto lush English-style gardens with hedgerows and impressive floral arrangements. For lucky diners who want to stay overnight, there is a luxuriously appointed, Relais & Châteaux 12-room *manoir* on the premises, in a beautiful building on the far side of the restaurant's garden—a long, two-story house brimming with sash windows and "thatched" coves. Two of the "deluxe" rooms have balconies and hot tubs. For dining (the restaurant is closed Monday and Tuesday), reservations are essential, as are jacket and tie. ⊠ *Zandweg 2, 4416 NA Kru-*

*iningen* ☎ *0113/381753* 🖷 *0113/381763* ⊕ *www.interscaldes.nl* 🠒 *12 rooms* ⚹ *Restaurant, minibars, cable TV, helipad, some pets allowed* ▭ *AE, DC, MC, V* 🍽 *FAP.*

# NOORD BRABANT

Once upon a time—1190 to 1430, to be precise—Brabant was an independent duchy; in fact, the area didn't officially join the Netherlands until the Treaty of Münster in 1648. Perhaps this historic separateness goes some way toward explaining the region's markedly individual feel. Despite the intimate appeal of many of its towns, it's one of the largest provinces in the country and has the delightful old city of 's-Hertogenbosch as its capital, home to a magnificent cathedral, an excellent museum, and plenty of well-preserved 17th-century houses. Other interesting towns include photogenic Breda and Bergen op Zoom. Bustling Eindhoven, meanwhile, testifies to the success of 20th-century Dutch industry, linked as it is to the Philips lightbulb. Aesthetic purists be warned: with all that industry, Eindhoven cannot be described as pretty. But in the North Brabant region as a whole, you can enjoy plenty of lighthearted pleasures: in particular, De Efteling, a fairy-tale theme park planned with typically Dutch efficiency and imagination, that is packed at all times with visitors young and old.

## Bergen op Zoom

❻ *36 km (22 mi) east of Yerseke, 40 km (25 mi) west of Breda.*

Bergen op Zoom enjoyed its heyday in the Middle Ages, when it was the site of two large annual fairs. With an old port that was once connected to the Oosterschelde, the town had a solid reputation for hardiness: twice it withstood Spanish sieges, first in 1588, then again in 1622. On the bustling **Grote Markt** (market square), and in the surrounding streets, many old buildings still stand as testament to the Golden Age. The town comes fully into its own at Carnival time, with the festivities regarded as among the liveliest in the region—for some people, the party unofficially kicks off about four weeks early. Locals dress up in lace curtains and old clothing during the official celebrations in order to show their equality.

★ If you appreciate truly splendid interiors and striking medieval architecture, you won't be disappointed by the **Markiezenhof,** one of the Netherlands' grandest houses. Markiezenhof was built in the 15th and 16th centuries by the Keldermans, a notable Mechelen-based family firm of architects, for the marquesses of Bergen, who owned and tended the house until 1795. The outside courtyards and facades are dazzling examples of Late Gothic architectural exuberance. Inside, the Louis XIV, Louis XV, and Louis XVI rooms are lavishly decorated with crystal chandeliers, plasterwork ceilings, parquet flooring, and fine oil paintings. In the great hall, it's hard not to notice the vast carved chimneypiece with its representation of St. Christopher. Rooms on the upper floors host temporary exhibits, and the third floor is home to an incongruous yet interesting exhibition about the history of *kermis*: the Dutch funfair.

⊠ *Steenbergsestraat 8* ☎ *0164/277077* ⊕ *www.markiezenhof.nl* 🎫 *€5*
⊙ *Tues.–Sun. 11–5.*

## Where to Stay & Eat

¢–$$ ✕ **Bolke Beer.** Nestled in the corner of a leafy square in the shadow of the imposing Markiezenhof, this lively café with a dark-wood interior is a popular dining spot and gets busy most nights. Specialties to look out for include charcoal-grilled steaks and great spareribs. ⊠ *Beursplein 2-4* ☎ *0164/245670* ⊟ *MC, V.*

★ $–$$$$ 🏨 **Hotel de Draak.** Simply bursting with history, magnificent halls, and stylish guest rooms, the De Draak began life as an inn way back in 1397, and is the Netherlands' oldest hotel. In that very year, a fire destroyed the entire town except for this structure, which, in the 19th century, was taken over by the church fathers and expanded into a presbytery for the successive deans of Bergen op Zoom (the town church is just beyond the hotel courtyard). Today, Het Wapen van Henegouwen and three other historic buildings—St. Joris, De Draak, and De Borse—make up the hotel complex, which is headlined by its Great Hall and Markiezen Hall, spectacular set-pieces that still look ready to welcome the 17th-century burgomasters of Rembrandt (and, today, often host corporate conferences). Guest quarters have been ravishingly updated, with a mix of old and new—beamed ceilings, bright white walls, Swedish woods, fine antique Dutch cupboards, and strikingly modern prints and photographs. Most rooms are large, and some have air-conditioning. The friendly De Draak is *the* place to stay during Carnival, so if you're looking for a bed for that time, book well in advance. ⊠ *Grote Markt 36, 4611 NT* ☎ *0164/ 252050* 🖷 *0164/257001* ⊕ *www.hoteldedraak.com* 🛏 *44 rooms, 22 suites* ⚐ *Restaurant, minibars, cable TV, in-room data ports, Wi-Fi, bar, meeting rooms, some pets allowed; no a/c in some rooms* ⊟ *AE, DC, MC, V* ⦿ *BP* ⊙ *Closed Christmas wk.*

★ ¢–$ 🏨 **Landgoed de Hertgang.** For car-trippers, this is a delightful place to stay just outside Bergen op Zoom. It's a private family home with five large, tastefully converted rooms, featuring luxuries such as TVs, toiletries, some double washbasins, and deep baths. The house may be large, but the place is cozy even in winter. Excellent breakfasts include pastries and ham and cheese, but it's the garden that's a particular delight; enormous, and perfect for exploring, it contains sculptures by various Dutch artists as well as peacocks ambling about the lawn. ⊠ *Klaverblokken 18, 4661 HJ Halsteren* ☎ *0164/683801* ⊕ *www. hertgang.nl* 🛏 *4 rooms* ⚐ *Some pets allowed; no a/c in some rooms, no TV in some rooms* ⊟ *No credit cards* ⦿ *CP.*

# Breda

❼ *96 km (60 mi) east of Middelburg, 165 km (103 mi) northwest of*
**Fodor'sChoice** *Maastricht.*
★

Historically known as "the Baronie," Breda—a name familiar to art aficionados because of *The Surrender of Breda,* the masterpiece painted by the great 17th-century Spanish painter Velázquez—lies on the main road between Rotterdam and Antwerp and at the junction of several railway lines. Dwarfed by its Gothic-Brabantine Grote Kerk and threaded by pedestrian streets lined with pleasant houses, the city had its first glory days during the 16th and 17th centuries, when it was the seat of the powerful Counts of Nassau, ancestors of the current Dutch royal family. It was also the site of several large breweries, so much so that it was believed local average daily consumption was among the highest in Holland. However, as the VVV is keen to assure visitors, the people in those times could hold far more of their liquor (thanks to less alcoholic content) without ill effect than we can today—so we shouldn't have visions about an entire city ambling about intoxicated. Today, this small city (with a population of 126,000), dotted with parks, maintains a quiet, medieval charm that belies its modern role as a major manufacturing center.

The heart of the city, the imposing 15th- and 16th-century **Grote Kerk** (Great Church), built in the French-influenced Brabant Gothic style in brick and sandstone, was the family church of the House of Orange–Nassau. William of Orange's first wife and child are buried here, as are several of his ancestors. After a restoration, the splendor of its architecture is once again evident, as is the magnificence of the blue-and-gold-painted 18th-century organ and the triptych painted by the noted 16th-century master Jan van Scorel. In the choir stalls, note several remarkable carvings, one featuring a motorcycle, that depict aspects of the town's experience during the Second World War. The beautiful church tower, visible from all over town, is 318 feet high and was originally home to watchmen, whose job it was to toll the bells if they spotted fire, and to sound a horn to mark each new hour; you can climb the tower's 275 steps. ✉ *Kerkplein* ☎ *076/521–8267* 🎫 *€2.50* ☉ *Mon.–Sat. 10–5, Sun. 1–5.*

Just behind the Grote Kerk is the Grote Markt; pride of place on this central market square is Breda's **Stadhuis** (Town Hall), built in 1767. It counts among its treasures a copy of the celebrated Velázquez painting of the surrender of Breda to the Spanish commander Spinola in 1625, today one of the greatest paintings in Madrid's Prado, where it is known as *Las Lanzas,* in reference to the multitude of bristling lances in this stirring canvas. ✉ *Grote Markt 38* ☎ *076/529–3000* ☉ *Wed.–Sat. 10:30–5, Sun. and Tues. 1–5.*

need a break? Restaurants and cafés surround the Grote Markt. **Grand Café Danté** (✉ Grote Markt 19 ☎ 076/530–9585), occupies the former *vleeshal* (meat market), a cavernous high-ceilinged hall reached through a stone arch doorway guarded by two fearsome lions. The salads here are garnished to please everyone, from carnivores to vegans.

Alternatively, if you need cooling down, the **Ijssalon Toetie Froetie** (✉ Grote Markt 21 ☎ 076/521–1436), or Tootie-Fruitie Ice Cream Salon, has an appealing '50s-diner interior, with mirrors, glass, and marble everywhere. Sit down for a sundae, or take a delicious vanilla or chocolate cone away with you.

The entrance to the **Begijnhof** (Beguine Court) is several blocks from the Grote Markt, along Catherinastraat, marked by the austere **Waalse Kerk** (Walloon Church). Begijnhofs are homes named after their resident beguines, unmarried or widowed laywomen who dedicate their lives to prayer and charitable works. Beguines in turn are named for their beige-color robes. This particular Begijnhof was occupied until 1990. Its peaceful and attractive courtyard is one of only two remaining cloisters of this type in the Netherlands (the other is in Amsterdam). A formally laid-out fragrant herb garden occupies the center of the court. ⊠ *Catherinastraat 83.*

Just beyond the Begijnhof, between the main railway station and the city center, is the **Stadspark Valkenburg** (Valkenburg Park), dating from 1350 and named after the falconry house in the forest, part of the castle grounds, where the birds were trained for hawking. The area was redesigned in the 17th century as an elaborate French-style garden by the Counts of Nassau. The Renaissance-inspired **Kasteel van Breda** (Breda Castle) was built by Count Hendrik III of Nassau around 1536, on the former site of a castle dating from the 12th century. One of its most famous occupants was Charles II, who promulgated his Declaration of Breda (1660) from here to announce his terms for ascending the throne of England. In 1667, the Treaty of Breda was signed here; one of its results was that the Dutch colony of Nieuw Amsterdam was given to the English. The castle sits majestically beyond the moat and now houses the KMA (Royal Military Academy). It can only be visited on city walks organized by the VVV in summer. It is also the memorable site for the annual August National Tattoo festival of military bands. ⊠ *Kasteelplein* ☎ *076/522–8800 local VVV office.*

To the west of the Kasteel van Breda, beyond the west end of Cingelstraat, is the **Spanjaardsgat** (Spaniards' Gate), built by order of Henrik III around 1530 in an effort to improve the drainage of the castle moats. Legend has it the liberation of Breda from Spain took place on this very spot, though historians consider this far-fetched. On Shrove Tuesday in 1590, the story goes, as the Spaniards were partying, one Adriaan van Bergen steered his rickety old peat barge into the city. Stashed away under the peat were a band of soldiers who emerged and overwhelmed the tipsy Spanish.

## Where to Stay & Eat

★ **$$$–$$$$** ✕ **Wolfslaar.** In a beautiful, 17th-century manorhouse whose grand windows flood it with light, chef Maarten Camps offers a French-inspired seasonal menu. Imaginative combinations include grilled halibut with asparagus, and dessert puddings are tops—try the white-chocolate mousse served with seasonal fruit that somehow manages to be both decadent and light at the same time. For weekday lunches you can enjoy lighter fare—salads and pastries—out on the spacious terrace, a lovely setting when the weather is fine. Often host to corporate events, Wolfslaar also offers cooking classes (check their Web site). ⊠ *Wolfslaardreef 100–102* ☎ *076/560–8008* ⊕ *www.wolfslaar.com* ☐ *AE, DC, MC, V* ☺ *Closed Sun. and Mon. No lunch Sat.*

**$–$$** ✕ **Restaurant Charelli.** Run by a young, enthusiastic chef and decorated in a low-key manner with simple wooden tables and mosaics, Charelli serves particularly good salads, some with goat cheese or chicken. Fish choices are also excellent; try the monkfish wrapped in Serrano ham with a Noilly Prat sauce. Outside, there's a pretty plant-filled garden where you can enjoy your choice when the weather is fine. ⊠ *Coothplein 35* ☎ *076/522–4039* ⊕ *www.charelli.nl* ▭ *AE, MC, V* ⊗ *Closed Mon.*

**$–$$** ⊡ **Mercure.** Next to the railway station in a building that formerly housed the offices of the telephone company, this member of the French hotel chain is a straightforward business hotel with a no-nonsense approach to decorating. Still, rooms are spacious, and the staff exhibit a certain Gallic charm. ⊠ *Stationsplein 14, 4811 BB* ☎ *076/522–0200* 🖨 *076/521–4967* ⊕ *www.accorhotels.com* ⇦ *36 rooms, 4 suites* ♨ *Restaurant, minibars, cable TV, in-room DVD, in-room data ports, bar, meeting rooms, some pets allowed* ▭ *AE, DC, MC, V.*

**$** ⊡ **De Klok.** This small hotel is a busy and friendly part of the lively market square of Breda. There is a terrace out front, and a bar and restaurant occupy the lobby. Double rooms are generously sized and brightly furnished. Baths may have shower or tub; some quads are available. ⊠ *Grote Markt 26–28, 4811 XR* ☎ *076/521–4082* 🖨 *076/514–3463* ⊕ *www.hotel-de-klok.nl* ⇦ *21 rooms* ♨ *Restaurant, cable TV, Wi-Fi, bar, some pets allowed; no a/c* ▭ *DC, MC, V* ⦿ *BP.*

### Nightlife & the Arts

The **Holland Casino Breda** (⊠ Kloosterplein 20 ☎ 076/525–1100 ⊕ www.hollandcasino.nl), the largest casino in Europe, is housed in a former monastery: the previous occupants must be spinning in their tombs. You can play blackjack, roulette, and other favorites.

For a week in late August every year, the air in Breda fills with the sounds of the National Tattoo—a great festival with military and civilian marching bands from around Europe. Complete with spectacular lighting effects and the theatrical setting of Breda Castle's forecourt, the **Nationale Taptoe** (⊠ Postbus 90002, 4800 PA ☎ 076/522–0519) is truly a drum-thumping, baton-twirling occasion to remember.

### Shopping

Breda has a general market open Tuesday–Friday, as well as a market for secondhand goods on Wednesday, at Grote Markt. Late shopping is on Thursday.

## Tilburg

**8** *24 km (15 mi) east of Breda, 125 km (79 mi) east of Middelburg.*

In terms of population (183,000), Tilburg is one of Holland's largest towns. It has a rich industrial heritage, having made its fortune through textiles. In the 1870s, 125 woolen mills in the area employed more than 4,500 people. Today, the main industries are technological (photographic equipment and high-tech printing). The town is not photogenic, but there are some good museums worth seeking out.

Just past Wilheminapark, 20 minutes' walk from the city center, is the **Nederlands Textielmuseum.** Housed—appropriately enough—in a converted textile factory, it tells visitors the complete story of the Dutch textile industry. A functioning 1906 steam engine is just one of a number of machines on view that totally revolutionized the industry. In addition, there are experts on hand to display skills such as weaving and spinning, and you can see fabrics from around the world, as well as an interesting collection of Dutch household textiles. Before leaving, pick up a silk scarf or linen tea towel as a souvenir from the museum's gift shop. ☒ *Goirkestraat 96* ☎ *013/536–7475* ⊕ *www.textielmuseum.nl* ☒ *€5.50* ☉ *Tues.–Fri. 10–5, weekends noon–5.*

Northwest of the railway station you'll find the pride and joy of Tilburg's citizens: **De Pont** is a magnificent gallery set up in the name of local businessman Jan de Pont, who left a legacy upon his death in 1987 to fund a foundation for the promotion of contemporary art. A former woolen mill was converted into a vast, light-filled exhibition space, with an impressive central hall. Artists on display often include such contemporary, cutting-edge masters as Anish Kapoor, Jan Dibbets, and Guido Geelen. Smaller wool-processing sheds are used for temporary exhibitions and, every two years, De Pont's large walled garden is offered as "a room without a roof" to a different artist. De Pont also has a well-stocked bookshop and a very relaxing café. ☒ *Wilheminapark 1* ☎ *013/ 543–8300* ⊕ *www.depont.nl* ☒ *€6* ☉ *Tues.–Sun. 11–5.*

☺ Even sober adults are turned into wide-eyed, joy-filled children by **De** FodorsChoice **Efteling,** once crowned "best amusement park in the world." Located ★ just north of Tilburg, this enormous fairy-tale park offers a wealth of rides and amusements, but to call some of these treats just that misses the mark. Yes, you'll find all manner of mechanical thrill-inducing contraptions, from imitation bobsled runs to a giant swinging pirate ship, but the real jewels here are to be found in the "Enchanted Forest"—a bona fide domain of trees and plants adorned with fanciful and witty dioramas by Dutch artist Anton Pieck that depict classic fairy tales. Here, you'll see Sleeping Beauty's chest heave as she breathes and be surprised by elves and goblins galore. Attractions are pitched at all levels: the adventure maze with its wobbly bridges and hidden water spouts thrills kids barely old enough to demand "Again! Again!" The Vogel Rok roller coaster, on the other hand, is enclosed in a darkened dome and has the potential to embarrass even the sturdiest adults when, on leaving, they recognize the look of blank terror on their faces, as caught on photos snapped at a particularly g-force-inducing corner. The charm of De Efteling is compounded by its laid-back feel. From the air it looks more like a forest than a theme park, and it certainly isn't overcommercialized; you can even take in your own food and drink. The Netherlands' most popular attraction, it lures large crowds most of the time and especially in July and August, so plan to arrive as early as possible. Luckily, entertainers are on hand to keep you amused as you line up for the various rides. ☒ *Europalaan 1, Kaatsheuvel* ☎ *0416/288111* ⊕ *www. efteling.nl* ☒ *Mid-July–Aug. €26, other times €24; parking €6* ☉ *Apr.–mid-July, Sept., and Oct., daily 10–6; mid-July–Aug., Sun.–Fri. 10–9, Sat. 10–midnight.*

The Netherlands gets immeasurably more exotic just southeast of ☺ Tilburg, where the **Safaripark Beekse Bergen** is home to hundreds of animals from Africa, Asia, South America, Australia, and Europe. There are lions, cheetahs, giraffes, zebras, kangaroos, and much more. Ride a safari bus or take your own car, although going on foot (perfectly safe!)

gets you much closer, particularly to the elephants and monkeys. There is also a safari boat that lets you see the animals from the water. **Speelland** (Playland), strategically located next to the main entrance, is ideal for children who didn't use up all their energy on safari. A broad assortment of slides, swings, climbing frames, water attractions, and adventure possibilities should have them snoring soundly on the journey back to your lodgings. ⊠ *Beekse Bergen 1, Hilvarenbeek* ☎ *013/549–1200* ⊕ *www.beeksebergen.nl* ✉ *€14.75; €15.95 combined with Speelland* ☉ *Dec. and Jan., daily 10–4; Nov. and Feb., daily 10–4:30; Mar.–June, Sept., and Oct., daily 10–5; July and Aug., daily 10–6.*

### Where to Stay

★ $–$$$$   🏨 **Golden Tulip Efteling Hotel.** If you plan to stay late at the storybook realms of De Efteling, there is an on-site hotel whose fairy-tale-castle design, spacious rooms, and modern conveniences echo those of the theme park. In fact, there are even theme rooms, so you can opt, for example, to sleep in canopy beds under a briar roof in the Sleeping Beauty suite (don't prick your hand on the spinning wheel!); get crowned when you book the Royal Suite, replete with thrones and enchanting wood-timbered sloping roofs; or, for 1950s-style diehards, find yourself sleeping in a vintage Chevrolet that's been converted into a bed. As you would expect, the place is extremely child-friendly, with lots of play areas and reduced portions available at mealtimes. The Hoffelijke Heraut (Happy Messenger) restaurant is gracious and pretty and offers a floor show where a countess arrives to audition members of the audience in a talent-show hunt. ⊠ *Horst 31, 5171 RA Kaatsheuvel* ☎ *0416/287111* 🖷 *0416/281515* ⊕ *www.efteling.nl* ⬦ *120 rooms, 16 suites* ⚷ *Restaurant, some minibars, cable TV, bar, shops, babysitting, some pets allowed, free parking; no a/c in some rooms* ▤ *AE, DC, MC, V* ❢❢ *MAP.*

### The Arts

Tilburg's main theater complex, the **Stadsschouwburg** (⊠ Louis Bouwmeesterplein 1 ☎ 013/543–2220), is an important venue for theater, opera, and dance troupes. The Schouwburg en Concertzaal (playhouse and concert hall) has an experimental program that embraces everything from classical opera to Dutch modern dance, plus there are occasional visits from overseas troupes. The arts complex also includes a film house and a relaxed café.

## 's-Hertogenbosch (Den Bosch)

❾   *23 km (14 mi) northeast of Tilburg, 45 km (28 mi) east of Breda, 130*
*km (83 mi) northwest of Maastricht.*
★

The hometown of celebrated painter Hieronymus Bosch, 's-Hertogenbosch has considerable charms (although few reminders of its native son, other than his statue in the Markt square), a particularly lively Carnival, and a cathedral crawling with appropriately devilish gargoyles. The name 's-Hertogenbosch means "The Duke's Woods" in Old Dutch, and although that is the official name of this medieval city, the name you will hear more commonly is Den Bosch (pronounced "den boss"), "The Woods." Not much remains of the woods for which it was named, the forests having long since been replaced by marshes and residential and industrial development. Start by crossing straight over the road opposite the station entrance and over the bridge (this city is picturesquely threaded by canals), and head down and right into Vismarkt. Around Molenstraat, you'll find yourself in the old Uilenberg district, filled with elegant backstreets graced by well-preserved 17th-century mansions that now house shops and restaurants. Take a left onto Korenbrugstraat, then a right onto Kruisstraat (which becomes Snellestraat), and another left onto Miderbroederstraat, which will bring you to the Markt square. On your right is the imposing gray sandstone facade of the Town Hall, built around 1670, and ahead of you is the statue of Hieronymus Bosch. Tucked around the corner to the left is the main tourist office in **De Moriaan,** the city's oldest house, where you can get information about lesser-known sights in the city. These include the Het Provinciehuis, with a modern art collection; the Museum Slager, with a group of 19th-century paintings; and Het Zwanenbroedershuis, the headquarters of the Illustrious Brotherhood of Our Dear Lady, a philanthropic group whose members included Hieronymus Bosch and whose historic house still contains some impressive antiques, many of which relate to church music, a society specialty.

**need a break?** There is a very special treat in store for you in 's-Hertogenbosch: a *Bossche bol* is a ball-shape cream-puff pastry, filled with whipped cream, dipped in dark chocolate, and served chilled. **Patisserie Jan de Groot** (✉ Stationsweg 24), on the road leading from the railway station, makes the best in town and serves light lunches, too.

★ From the Markt it's a short stroll to the only cathedral in the Netherlands. With spidery Late Gothic windows and a noble Romanesque tower, the magnificent **Sint-Janskathedraal** (St. John's Cathedral) stands out as Den Bosch's principal attraction. Built between 1380 and 1520 in the Brabant Gothic style and abundantly decorated with statuary, grotesques, and sculptural detail, it is a cruciform, five-aisle basilica with numerous side chapels around the apse. Its nave is supported by double flying buttresses unique in the region. But the most famous feature is the army of little stone figures swarming over the flying buttresses and up the steep copings in a frantic effort either to escape the grasps of the demon-gargoyles or to reach heaven as quickly as possible. We don't know what Hieronymus Bosch (1450–1516)—whose 15th-century canvases filled with devils, pitchforks, roasting bodies, and grotesque semi-human monsters marked him as a surrealist before the word was invented—thought of them, but visiting German artist Albrecht Dürer was enamored with their exuberant charm. Inside are several treasures, including a fine carved 16th-century Altar of the Passion, but head for the chapel on the northeast side of the church built by the Illustrious Brotherhood of Our Dear Lady. Bosch was once a member of this confraternity, and the grisaille murals in situ have sometimes been attributed to him (more likely, his students). Bosch came from a family of artists, and his ribald paintings, giant altarpieces, and anecdotal genre scenes (his pictures of daily life, such as cripples and card-conjurers, were among the first ever painted) all made him a celebrated figure throughout Europe; in the following two centuries, every great king or court had to have their Bosch, whether it was simply a tapestry knockoff of a picture or an actual, and extremely rare, painting (it is now thought there are only 30 of his paintings in the world). The large square on the south flank of the church is called Parade. ⊠ *Parade* ☎ *073/613–9740* 🖱 *Free* 🕑 *Mon.–Sat. 10–5, Sun. 1–5.*

From the cathedral and the Parade square head southwest via Lange Putstraat and Waterstraat to the **Noordbrabants Museum** (North Brabant Museum), one of the Netherlands' foremost provincial museums. You'll recognize it by the enormous bronze dog, just waiting to be patted, that sits in the museum's driveway. The exhibits are housed in the imposing former residence of the provincial governor. Inside, in the light, bright, and imaginatively converted interior, you'll find historical, archaeological, and cultural exhibits related to the history of Brabant, as well as an outstanding art collection. This includes many particularly fine examples of Dutch floral painting, with most of the 17th- and 18th-century floral masters on view, plus works by Brabant artists of various periods. ⊠ *Verwersstraat 41, from Parade, follow Lange Putstraat* ☎ *073/687–7877* ⊕ *www.noordbrabantsmuseum.nl* 🖱 *€7* 🕑 *Weekdays 10–5, weekends noon–5.*

One of the nicest places to spend time in 's-Hertogenbosch is on the water, with a **boat trip along the city canals** (☎ 0900/202–0178 ⊕ www.binnendieze.nl), passing under low bridges and overhanging trees. You can buy tickets at Molenstraat 15a, and boats depart at regular intervals from the pier opposite. For trips along the Dommel, or all the way to Heusden, contact Rederij Wolthuis (☎ 073/631–2048 ⊕ www.rederijwolthuis.nl). Fares start at €5 per person.

Ⓒ Approximately 12 km (8 mi) west of s'Hertogenbosch, **Het Land van Ooit** (Ever Land) is an intimate theme park set in woodland where children are deemed to be in charge. A whole army of wandering minstrels, entertainers, and costumed lackeys ceremoniously greet all little half-pints to emphasize the point. A knight's tournament, shows in numerous theaters, assorted "giants," a haunted mansion, a pretty-in-pink mansion, plus plenty of small-scale attractions should keep the kids—particularly younger ones—delighted all day. ⊠ *Parklaan 40, Drunen* ☎ *0416/ 377775* ⊕*www.ooit.nl* 🖱 *€17* 🕑 *Apr. 30–mid-Sept. and mid-Oct.–Oct. 31, daily 10–5; mid-Sept.–mid-Oct., weekends 10–5.*

## Where to Stay & Eat
There are plenty of good, ambience-rich restaurants in Den Bosch, though hotels are a little more on the bland side.

★ **$$$$** ✕ **Chalet Royal.** For a mouthwatering definition of French cuisine this spacious, refined restaurant is hard to beat—as devotees from miles around will tell you. Set in a charming, turn-of-the-20th-century Brabant villa— with an open fire to warm winter evenings—the restaurant is noted for its lobster with truffle sauce, roast wild duck, and a trio of desserts including the imaginative rhubarb-and-star-anise sorbet. There's an enormous wine list, an appropriate calling card for the extensive wine cellar below your feet. Opting for a food-and-wine arrangement could see you starting off with duck salad complemented by a light, fruity 1994 Nederburg Prelude, with your main course of pheasant and wild mushrooms accentuated by an aromatic California cabernet sauvignon. You can round off your meal with a selection of fine French cheeses and don't forget to enjoy the delicious Brabant Gothic decor touches. ⊠ *Wilhelminaplein 1* ☎*073/613–5771* ⊕*www.chaletroyal.nl* ▤ *AE, DC, MC, V* ⊗ *Closed Sun. and Mon. No lunch Sat.*

¢–$$ ✕ **Pilkington's.** In the shadow of the St. Jans tower, this informal restaurant has a British touch, with such old-fashioned favorites as shepherd's pie on the menu. But there's also grilled veal, fresh fish, and all manner of other delights. In good weather the walled garden, covered with climbing roses, is a must. You can also stop off here just for afternoon tea with coffee and cake, and on Sunday mornings for a full English breakfast. ⊠ *Torenstraat 5* ☎*073/612–2923* ⊕*www.pilkingtons. nl* ▤ *AE, DC, MC, V.*

$$ ✕ 🏨 **Golden Tulip Hotel Central.** More than just a typical full-service business hotel, the Hotel Central has a family-run atmosphere, especially reflected in the warmth of the service. The rooms have a modern, tailored look. The restaurant, De Leeuwenborgh, with a separate entrance on the square, is intimate and graciously appointed. Its mirrors are etched with images of the city's important buildings, and the menu is French-influenced. ⊠ *Burgermeester Loeffplein 98, 5211 RX* ☎*073/ 692–6926* 🖨 *073/614–5699* ⊕ *www.hotel-central.nl* ➫ *121 rooms, 3 suites* ⬧ *Restaurant, minibars, cable TV, Wi-Fi, bar, meeting rooms, some pets allowed; no a/c in some rooms* ▤ *AE, DC, MC, V.*

¢ 🏨 **Het Tuynhuys.** If you've got a car, delightfully unorthodox accommodations await in Den Dungen, just 7 km (4 mi) southeast of Den Bosch: a rustic-style self-contained little cottage, set in the garden of a private house, with a spacious sitting-dining area, two beds, a shower, and a kitchenette. Het Tuynhuys (The Garden House) is decorated in restful blue, with some antique furniture, plus pictures and ornaments picked up by the owners on their travels abroad. It's not luxurious, but it is charming—and in the morning, breakfast is brought to your door. ⊠ *Brinkhoeve, Grinsel 74, 5721 TL Den Dungen* ☎*073/644–3732* ⊕ *www.sbkbb.nl* ➫ *1 cottage* ⬧ *Microwave, refrigerator; no a/c* ▤ *No credit cards* ⦿❘ *BP.*

## Nightlife & the Arts

Once a week, 's-Hertogenbosch offers back-to-back **carillon recitals** from two sets of bells. The Town Hall bells play every Wednesday morning from 10 to 11, followed by another carillon concert at the cathedral from 11:30 to 12:30.

Sporty types and young businesspeople frequent **Silva Ducis** (⊠ Parade 6–7 ☎ 073/613–0405), an elegant grand café that looks out onto the most attractive square in town. There is a wide range of beer to choose from and jazz or classical music in the background.

## The Outdoors

**Stationsfietsstalling Van Deursen** (⊠ Stationsplein 22 ☎ 073/613–4737), beneath the station forecourt, rents solid and reliable Dutch town bikes for €6.50 per day. You'll need ID and a deposit of €50. Some bikes may have back-pedal brakes, which can take some getting used to if you've not encountered them before.

## Shopping

There is a large general market every Wednesday and Saturday on the market square. Equestrian lovers may be interested in the sale of horses that takes place every Thursday from 7:30 to noon in the Braban-thallen. Late shopping is on Thursday.

The shop of the **North Brabant Museum** (⊠ Verwersstraat 41 ☎ 073/687–7877) offers an exceptional collection of art books covering many periods and styles of Dutch and international art.

For quirky gifts, **Farfallino** (⊠ Lange Putstraat 10 ☎ 073/614–0481) sells everything from drink coasters to mugs and pepper pots, all in zingy colors. Next door to Favfallino is **Wolvers Porselein** (⊠ Lange Putstraat 6 ☎ 073/613–2444), which specializes in wafer-thin art pottery. You'll want to buy it, but the question is, will you be able to get it home in one piece? There are no fixed opening hours, so call ahead to make an appointment.

## Heusden

▶ ⑩ *14 km (9 mi) northwest of s'-Hertogenbosch.*

Fodor'sChoice
★

Fronting the Maas River, the little town of Heusden is a must-visit stop. The entire town radiates a very special atmosphere, composed as it is of windmills, harbors, little cobbled streets, perfectly restored buildings, and history—no less than 11 centuries of it. Best of all, Heusden is a perfect place to explore on foot; in fact, visitors are asked to leave their cars in designated lots outside the town center.

The Heusden story is a stirring one. Its strategic importance and heavy fortifications led the counts of Holland and Gelderland to battle the Dukes of Brabant over its possession; it later became a major defense post against the Spaniards in the Dutch war of independence (1568–1648). Between 1794 and 1813, the town was occupied by the French, after which it fell into a long economic decline. Heusden suffered greatly in the Second World War: before the Nazi forces retreated from the advancing Allies in November 1944, they blew up the medieval tower of Sint Catharijne Kerk together with the City Hall, killing the 134 townspeople hiding in its cellar. With postwar modernization looming, it was proposed that Heusden's remaining buildings be razed and replaced with high-rise apartments. The local population put up a fierce resistance, and in the 1960s the Dutch government decreed that the place should become a national historic monument, not as a museum but as a living town. Since 1968, the equivalent of $75 million has been spent on restoration, and the result—full of character and charm without being faux—is a hit with both the 1,500 residents and Heusden's 300,000 annual visitors.

A stroll around town makes for a fascinating and extremely pleasant afternoon. Outside the center, the **Kasteel** and its ramparts are on the former site of a 12th-century stone fortress. Though its original purpose was defensive, its downfall came with a later incarnation as a powder magazine (when lightning struck the fortress tower in 1680, it blew up—together with about a quarter of Heusden's other buildings). The ramparts were modified in 1581 by Jacob Kempt, one of Europe's leading defense experts, on the orders of William of Orange. The result—completed in 1613—was a system admired throughout Europe: to protect the city from attack, eight bulwarks and ramparts were erected in conjunction with a series of brick tunnels through which defending militia could enter and exit the inner city; these were once protected by the small triangular islands known as *ravelijnen,* which are still visible. Kempt's system succeeded in protecting Heusden until the French occupation of 1794. ⊠ *Hertogin Johanna van Brabantstraat.*

The **Vismarkt** (fish market, facing the Stadshaven, inner town) operated until 1900; salmon and sturgeon were the specialties. At the far end of the marketplace, look out for the columned **Visbank,** or "Fish Bank," where fish were laid out, built in 1796 during the French occupation, to connect the marketplace with the pretty inner harbor. To the right of the Visbank is a reproduction of the old customhouse (currently home to a wine wholesaler), where duty was collected on goods that had arrived via the harbor.

Built over a range of periods, the **Gouverneurshuis** (Governor's House) and the **Sint Catharijne Kerk** (Catherine Church) became the center for Protestant worship when Heusden pledged its loyalty to William of Orange in 1578. The Governor's House was built originally as part of the church complex, to be a home for its pastor, around 1592; later in the mid-17th century it was taken over by the military governor. Sint Catharijne Kerk dates from around 1210, and its treasures include a glorious rib-vaulted roof, an ancient clock dating from the mid-14th century, and the ornate tomb of Johan Baron von Friesheim, a commander-governor of Heusden who died in 1733. ⊠ *Putterstraat 14-16* ☎ *0416/662295* 🖃 *Gouverneurshuis €1.50* ⊗ *Mid-Apr–Sept., Wed.–Sun. 2–5; Oct.–mid-Apr., Sun. 2–5.*

**need a break?** If you can't get enough of Heusden's charm, even when it's time to put your feet up, **Eetcafé Havenzicht** (⊠ Vismarkt 2 ☎ 0416/662723) offers the quintessential Dutch view through its windows as you tuck into your hard-earned coffee and apple tart. In the foreground is the picturesque duck-filled harbor, while behind it is a classic white drawbridge and two black wooden windmills.

### Where to Stay & Eat

★ $–$$$ ✕🖬 **In Den Verdwaalde Koogel.** This elegant hotel-restaurant's name translates as the "In the Stray Bullet," a reference to a leftover from World War II that's still visible in the hotel's exterior. Beside the bullet hole, the 17th-century step-gabled facade is beautiful, with French doors and flower-strewn window boxes. Inside are 12 individually decorated guest rooms with original architectural features like exposed brickwork. The restaurant is regarded as the best in town; try the delicious local game paired with an excellent wine. In winter you can dine beside a large fireplace under exposed ceiling beams, and in summer, you can sit outside on the terrace, near the very heart of Heusden. ⊠ *Vismarkt 1, 5256 BC* ☎ *0416/661933* 🖨 *0416/661295* ⊕ *www.indenverdwaaldekoogel.nl* 🛏 *12 rooms* ⚘ *Restaurant, minibars, some pets allowed; no a/c* ▤ *MC,* *V* 🍴 *BP.*

## Eindhoven

**⑪** *38 km (24 mi) southeast of Heusden, 32 km (20 mi) south of 's-Hertogenbosch, 100 km (62 mi) north of Maastricht.*

Called "the town that Anton built," Eindhoven was put on the map by Dutch industrialist and visionary Anton Philips. A century ago, it was a small town of 6,500 souls, surrounded by a handful of tiny villages. Today, all those villages have been swallowed up in one of the more remarkable cities in Holland, with more than 200,000 inhabitants, and an industry that has literally illuminated the world since Eindhoven's first lightbulb factory opened in 1891. Philips may have moved its head office to Amsterdam, but the Eindhoven region is still home to Europe's third-largest concentration of high-tech companies, after Paris and Munich. Since the bombings of World War II, there is no longer any traditional, historic center to explore, but new and interesting examples of contemporary architecture are constantly springing up. Instead of the usual dose of aesthetic beauty, expect to find a technically innovative center with an exceptional museum of modern art, the unusual DAF Museum, and an open-air historical museum where you can really get your hands dirty.

West of Eindhoven's central square, there's an interesting example of early-20th-century industrial architecture. Known to locals as the "White Lady," this complex of buildings, originally constructed for the Philips company, includes the **Philips Lichttoren** (Philips Light Tower), built in 1921 as the factory where the longevity of the bulbs' filaments could be tested. It was once Eindhoven's most prominent building, and is still one of its best-known landmarks. Outside the tower, there's a statue known as "the little lightbulb maker" commemorating the women who made the first lightbulbs. ⊠ *Emmasingel 12* ☎ *040/296–2937.*

If you're keen to learn more about Eindhoven's Philips connection, you can visit the lovingly restored **Philips Gloeilampenfabriekje** (Philips Lightbulb Factory). This small brick building, which originally opened for business in 1891, helped turn the page to a new chapter in the book of Europe's industrial heritage. A renovation shows the way it would have looked in the days when the first incandescent bulbs were produced here. The factory was also restocked with authentic tools. Expert guides explain the history of the plant, and demonstrate how the equipment worked. ⊠ *Emmasingel 31* ☎ *040/297–9106* ⊕ *www.philipsfabriek1891. nl* 🎟 *€4* ⊙ *Guided tours Wed.–Fri. at 2, Sat. at 1 and 2.*

**Centrum Kunstlicht in de Kunst** (Artificial Light in Art Center). Sharing a building with Philips Lightbulb Factory, this fascinating art gallery carries on the light theme of its neighbor. Simple artworks, most created post 1970, feature electric lighting in one prominent way or other. Some of the animated light sculptures made with neon, spotlights, and mirrors will make you dizzy if you stare at them for too long. ⊠ *Emmasingel 31* ☎ *040/ 275–5183* ⊕ *www.kunstlichtkunst.nl* ⊠ *€4* ☉ *Tues.–Sun. noon–4.*

Fodor'sChoice ★ On the southern fringe of the city center, the **Stedelijk van Abbemuseum** (Municipal Van Abbe Museum) houses an extraordinary collection of modern and contemporary art. The collection began in 1936 as the simple wish of a local cigar maker, Henri van Abbe, to be able to visit a museum in his own town. The museum's extension, opened in 2003, is striking even from the outside; its angled walls, with their gray mosaic-style finish, offer a refreshing counterpoint to the ordered red brickwork of the original building. Inside, depending on which tenth of the museum's own collection is on display, you can see examples of every major trend of the last hundred years.

The small but first-rate Cubist collection includes pieces by Picasso, Mondriaan, and Chagall, and chances are you won't find a richer offering of Russian avant-garde art outside Russia. There are also plenty of three-dimensional works on display, from a disorienting balloon-headed gossiping couple to Moholy Nagy's mechanical Light-Room-Modulator, to the latest names being dropped in New York City, including Lawrence Weiner and Matt Mulican. The building itself is an integral part of the exhibition. Standing on the top floor looking down at the intriguing way in which balconies, walkways, and walls bisect, you could almost be gazing into a real-life M. C. Escher drawing. The 80-foot-high tower also serves as a canvas, and is refreshed by guest artists on a regular basis. Inside, Marten van Severen, a noted Belgian designer, has graced the interiors with high-style minimalist accents. The Van Abbemuseum also boasts one of the most comprehensive art libraries in the country. ⊠ *Bilderdijklaan 10* ☎ *040/238–1000* ⊕ *www.vanabbemuseum.nl* ⊠ *€8.50* ☉ *Tues.–Sun. 11–5.*

☺ The **Historisch Openluchtmuseum** (Historical Open-Air Museum), just past Eindhoven's central ring road in a leafy waterside area of Genneper Park, is one of those educational but entertaining experiences that the Dutch do so well. Find out what it was like to live in a village, here called "Eversham," during the Iron Age (the period between 750 and 50 BC) or in medieval times (AD 500–1600) in a city called "Endehoven" as volunteers in appropriate costume busy themselves in and around their dwellings, happy to answer any questions you might have about ancient life. You can join in, too, if the idea grabs you—there is bread to be baked (and sampled), wool to be spun, animals to look after, and old bones to be shaped into tools, toys, and weapons. ⊠ *Boutenslaan 161b* ☎ *040/ 252–2281* ⊕ *www.historisch-openluchtmuseum-eindhoven.nl* ⊠ *€6.50* ☉ *Apr.–Oct., daily 10–5; Nov.–Mar., daily noon–5.*

☺ East of the center, the **DAF Museum**, a tribute to Holland's best-known and best-loved vehicle, will delight car buffs. The museum is housed in the restored brewery where, in 1928, Hub van Doorne started his car factory. His workshop has been preserved, and in one corner of the museum you'll find a recreation of an Eindhoven square from the 1930s. The DAF car has acquired something of a cult status throughout Europe. In February 1958, Hub's dream to produce a luxury-quality car everyone could afford became reality when the first DAF car was launched at the Amsterdam motor show. It was small, economical to run, could carry four people, and—most revolutionary of all—was ultraeasy to drive, thanks to Van Doorne's innovative "Variomatic" gear-change system. Many thousands were produced, but DAF eventually fell from favor; the last DAF-stamped car was produced in 1975, after which Volvo took over the company. Today, DAF revivalists have ensured a newfound status for the boxy little numbers, with collectors competing to possess their easy-driving power and chunky design. Cars fill the mezzanine of the massive exhibition hall, while down below are an array of trucks and buses—the mainstay of the company's current output. Meanwhile, kids and parents alike will enjoy trying their hand at mastering the controls in one of the truck simulators. ⊠ *Tongelresestraat 27* ☏ *040/244–4364* ⊕ *www.dafmuseum.nl* ⊡ *€6* ۩ *Tues.–Sun. 10–5.*

## Where to Stay & Eat

$$$$  ✕ **De Karpendonkse Hoeve.** In this light-filled, classy restaurant—it's found its way to more than one list of Holland's finest—chef Peter Koehn produces classic dishes with a twist. Terrine de foie gras in a Sauternes jelly, panfried sole, and lobster soup are some signature dishes. The finesse and care to details is ever apparent, as you'll note when you see the restaurant initials stamped on every pat of butter. ⊠ *Sumatralaan 3* ☏ *040/281–3663* ☖ *Reservations essential* ▭ *AE, DC, MC, V* ۩ *Closed Sun. No lunch Sat.*

$$$  ✕ **Restaurant Sala Thai.** In a residential area just west of the center, the Sala Thai manages the perfect blend of tranquil dining room, friendly service, and high-quality Thai food. The platter of house starters, which includes chicken or beef satay, battered shrimp, and vegetable spring rolls, is to die for, as is the spicy coconut soup. While you're waiting, check out the bric-a-brac flown in from Thailand to decorate the walls. ⊠ *Staringstraat 31* ☏ *040/243–4101* ☖ *Reservations essential* ▭ *AE, DC, MC, V* ۩ *No lunch.*

$–$$  ✕ **Grand Café Berlage.** This spacious art deco brasserie has a large, attractive garden replete with plenty of trees and parasols for cooling down after all your exertions. The lunch menu is particularly extensive; take your pick from well-filled baguettes, inventive salads, and sturdier fare like pasta with oyster mushrooms or chunky hamburgers dressed in bacon. ⊠ *Kleine Berge 16* ☏ *040/245–7481* ▭ *AE, MC, V.*

$  ✕ **Plaza Futura.** On the ground floor of the cultural center of the same name, this restaurant serves an eclectic range of inexpensive dishes. The culinary world tour covers every continent, from West African lamb stew to Oriental beef, and includes a weekly offerings themed to the films being shown at the art cinema upstairs. Vegetarians will feel particularly welcome here. Have a drink at the bar, with its arty, semi-refurbished factory feel, or on the large street-side sitting area lined by boulders and fake telegraph poles. On Tuesday and Friday evenings in July and August, films are projected on a large screen outside. ⊠ *Leenderweg 65* ☏ *040/294–6840* ⊕ *www.plazafutura.nl* ▭ *AE, MC, V* ۩ *No lunch.*

$–$$$  ▥ **Mandarin Park Plaza Hotel.** The Mandarin is unique in that it was designed to meet East Asian standards of service. Its decor includes small bridges spanning water gardens, used as footpaths through the lobby. Its several restaurants are all Asian in theme and cuisine: one serves fine Chinese specialties, another offers a range of Indonesian and Asian dishes, and the third is a Japanese steak house. The French influence is felt via a Parisian coffee shop. ⊠ *Geldropseweg 17, 5611 SC* ☎ *040/ 212–5055* 📠 *040/212–1555* ⊕ *www.parkplazaeurope.com* ⤳ *88 rooms, 14 suites ☆ 3 restaurants, minibars, cable TV, in-room data ports, Wi-Fi, indoor pool, 2 saunas, meeting rooms, parking (fee), no-smoking rooms* ▤ *AE, DC, MC, V.*

### Bicycling

Good-quality bikes can be rented from the **Rijwiel Shop** (⊠ Stationsplein ☎ 040/243–6617), outside the railway station, with ID and a deposit of €50.

# LIMBURG

If you want to feel you're really getting away from it all, Limburg, the Netherlands' most southerly province, is the place to go—one of the few areas where you can take a walk without hearing a background hum of traffic or stumbling across a group of modern homes. This is *echt landschap*—real countryside.

Not only does the gently hilly countryside with its woods and rivers mean that outdoor types can pursue a whole range of activities, from cycling to kayaking, but urbanites can make the most of Maastricht's historical and culinary offerings. In between there are pretty villages, more Roman ruins, and, in Valkenburg, some 21st-century pleasures (theme parks, a spa, and a casino)—in short, something to keep everyone happy. There are plenty of places to stay, from campsites to first-class hotels, but don't underestimate Limburg's popularity; it's such a convenient destination, not just for the Dutch but for the Belgians and the Germans, too, that at times its best-known towns become even busier than Amsterdam. To be sure of a bed or a table, book well in advance.

## Thorn

**⑫** *44 km (28 mi) southeast of Eindhoven.*

Fodor'sChoice
★

As you travel south toward the bustling metropolis of Maastricht, this village is worth a quick stop. Thorn may have been named by a pre-Christian sect whose god was named Thor. Today, it's also known as a "white village" because of its abundance of white-painted 18th-century houses. A less-familiar term is "the musical village" because of the number of musical societies here (on a fine day, you may even be able to hear a local group practicing as you tour the backstreets). The 10th-century **abbey church** was built by Count Ansfried, whose uncle was the Archbishop of Trier. He himself later entered the church, becoming Bishop of Utrecht, and was given land grants and the right to create his own principality as a reward for his faithful service to Otto I. Ansfried and his wife, Hilsondis, founded two religious orders in Thorn, one for men and one for women, installing their daughter as the first abbess.

Inside Thorn's beautiful **Stifskerk** (abbey church) all is light and space. The church has been remodeled throughout the centuries following the architectural fads of the day. In the 12th century it was Romanesque in style; toward the end of the 13th century it was rebuilt in Gothic style, and in the 16th century, Baroque elements such as the priests' and noblewomens' choirs were added. The church also possesses an outstanding Baroque-era altar.

## Valkenburg

**⑬** *56 km (35 mi) south of Thorn, 16 km (10 mi) east of Maastricht*

**Fodor'sChoice**
★ Those who think Holland is monstrously flat should visit Valkenburg, whose district is known as the Dutch Alps. Even though a leap of imagination is needed to agree, its steep, 1,000-foot-high hills are at least some justification. You won't have to tax your imagination, however, when confronted with the city's marvels, which include natural wonders and a storybook amusement park. As Limburg's chief tourist center, Valkenburg attracts Dutch, Belgian, and German visitors throughout the year, and much of the time it is crowded to excess. Crowds aside, though, it's worth a visit for its caves and its castle (walking shoes and sweaters recommended), and the spa and the casino provide a welcome respite for those who've had their fill of high culture and Mother Earth. Younger visitors, too, will appreciate the town, with the thrills and spills of bobsled rides and the amusement park known as the **Sprookjesbos** (Fairytale Woods) on offer.

The ruins of the **Kasteelvalkenburg** make for a fascinating walk that offers wonderful views over the Geul Valley. The castle was destroyed in 1672 on the orders of William III after he had vanquished its French occupiers. It remains under restoration, and you can combine a visit here with a guided tour of the **Fluweelengrot** cave, a by-product of the region's marlstone-quarrying industry. Its dank atmosphere is enhanced with wall paintings, sculptures, and even bats. A secret passageway leads to the castle. You can also see signatures of American soldiers who hid here during World War II. From mid-November to mid-December each year, a Christmas market is held inside the caves. No guided tours take place during this time, but you can wander freely, and browse among stalls selling everything you never conceived of needing for the festive season. ⊠ *Daalhemerweg 27* ☎ *043/609–0110* ⊕ *www. kasteelvalkenburg.nl* ☒ *€6.20 (castle and cave), €3.50 (Christmas market)* ☉ *Oct.–Mar., daily 10–4:30; Apr.–June, daily 10–5:30; July–Sept., daily 10–6.*

If you're not completely caved in by your visit to the Fluwelengrot, your next stop might be the **Gemeentegrot** (town caves), which you can explore courtesy of a minitrain. Some of the fossils on view are more than 100 million years old. There's also a rather magical underground lake, which, with its ghostly, greenish light, looks almost phosphorescent. ⊠ *Cauberg 4* ☎ *043/601–2271* ⊕ *www.gemeentegrot.nl* ☒ *€4* ☉ *Easter–Oct., Mon.–Sat. 9–5, Sun. 10–5; Nov.–Easter, weekdays guided tour at 2 only, weekends at 10 and 4.*

🕙 At the **Sprookjesbos** (Fairy-tale Woods) theme park, the young—and the young at heart—can enjoy an encounter with some 17 fairy-tale stars, including Snow White and the Seven Dwarfs and Little Red Riding Hood. There's a cheap and cheerful family restaurant, but the bad and the ugly might prefer to eat at the Wild West Saloon. Afterward, listen to the sounds of the water organ while majestic fountains play, or explore a couple of playgrounds packed with enough slides and swings to exhaust even the most energetic of toddlers. You might even embark on the special swinging Pirate Ship—just make sure everyone has digested lunch before you set sail. ⊠ *Oud-Valkenburgerweg* ☎ *043/601–2985* ⊕ *www. sprookjesbos.nl* ⌑ *€7* ⊙ *Apr.–mid-Sept., daily 10–5.*

One of the special treats to be had in Valkenburg is at **Thermae 2000,** a decadently luxurious hill spa that offers a complete range of services, including indoor and outdoor spring-fed pools, a sauna, a steam bath, yoga/ meditation, hydro-gymnastics, aerobics, sports massage, herbal and mud baths, and more. ⊠ *Kuurpark Cauberg 27* ☎ *043/609–2000* ⊕ *www. thermae.nl* ⌑ *€16.50 (2 hrs) to €28 (full day)* ⊙ *Daily 9 AM–11 PM.*

## Where to Stay & Eat

★ **$$$$** ✕🏠 **Hotel Château St. Gerlach.** Located in an old tenant farm on the Château St. Gerlach estate, this gorgeous hotel offers accommodations that range from plush, Provençal-style rooms with swagged drapes, antique furniture, and fine paintings, to simpler but still-luxurious rooms that make a feature of the building's rustic past, with exposed beams and open brickwork. Guests can tackle a variety of activities if they wish, from painting to music, plus there's a Roman-style swimming pool and sauna where you can try a Kneipp herbal treatment. The St. Gerlach is the sort of unstuffy place where they'll lend you a pair of rubber boots if you want to go walking in the nearby countryside, and yet the staff is comfortable playing host to world leaders—George W. Bush stayed here during a 2005 visit to the Netherlands. Children are welcome, and the hotel will arrange for a babysitter for you if necessary. But that's not all. The in-house restaurant attracts gourmands who come to feast on dishes such as asparagus salad, lobster, guinea fowl with truffle jus, and lemongrass-scented crème brulée. Be warned: with such tempting largess at hand, your only problem may be finding the will to venture beyond the hotel gates. ⊠ *Joseph Corneli Allée 1, 6301 KK* ☎ *043/608– 8888* 🖶 *043/604–2883* ⊕ *www.stgerlach.com* ⤴ *56 rooms, 2 suites* ⌓ *Restaurant, minibars, cable TV, pool, sauna, babysitting, some pets allowed; no a/c in some rooms* ▭ *AE, DC, MC, V* ⎆ *MAP.*

★ **$$–$$$** ✕🏠 **Prinses Juliana.** The classic French haute cuisine served here has been recognized internationally for years. Members of the Dutch royal family and many foreign dignitaries have tended their appetites here. The decor is elegant in an unadorned way so you can pay attention to the food, which might be a rack of lamb or panfried turbot. For less-formal dining in warm weather, there is a relaxing terrace. If you want to stay overnight, the suite-style rooms are bright, spacious, and as elegant as the hotel. ⊠ *Broekhem 11, 6301 HD* ☎ *043/601–2244* 🖶 *043/ 601–4405* ⊕ *www.juliana.nl* ⤴ *15 rooms* ⌓ *Restaurant, minibars; no a/c* ▭ *AE, DC, MC, V* ⎆ *MAP* ⊙ *Restaurant closed Mon.*

★ $$–$$$  ✕▥ **Kasteel Geulzicht.** Amid gentle hills near the village of Houthem-St. Gerlach, this 19th-century fantasia of a Renaissance castle is a Disney-esque vision complete with crenellations, stepped gables, and a looming tower. The dramatic appeal continues inside with halls and rooms decked with rich wainscotting, Gobelin tapestries, chandeliers, and period furniture. In the main salon, enormous leather chairs and sofas add a *gezelligheid* (congenial and welcoming) appeal to this vast and sometimes daunting fortress. Here you can sit back and admire the magnificent mural on the ceiling. Despite the castle's grand architecture and sumptuous entrance hall, the hotel actually has a cozy, family-run atmosphere, and the guest rooms (some occupying the castle turrets and tower) are made for mortals, not legendary knights. A few antiques adorn these rooms, but they are mostly modern and pleasant. Some bathrooms have sunken Roman-style baths or hot tubs. Because the entire estate is open only to hotel guests, you can often enjoy the flagstone garden terrace all to yourself. ⊠ *Vogelzangweg 2, 6325 PN Berg en Terblijt, 6 km (4 mi) east of Maastricht, 3 km (2 mi) from Thermae 2000 Spa* ☎ *043/604–0432* 🖶 *043/604–2011* ⊕ *www.kasteelgeulzicht.nl* ⇆ *9 rooms, 1 suite* ⌂ *Restaurant, minibars, bar, some pets allowed; no a/c* ▤ *AE, DC, MC, V* ❘◎❘ *MAP.*

### Nightlife
The **Holland Casino Valkenburg** (⊠ Kuurpark Cauberg 28 ☎ 043/609–9600 ⊕ www.hollandcasino.nl) offers blackjack, roulette, and Punto Banco in chic surroundings.

## Heerlen

🄮 *14 km (9 mi) northeast of Valkenburg, 26 km (16 mi) northeast of Maastricht.*

Although it shares an ancient Roman past with Maastricht, Heerlen—the second-largest city of the province—has an appeal at first glance less distinctly felt. In the absence of obvious monuments, it comes across as simply a hardworking, average Limburg town, whose recent wealth was founded on coal. But the discovery in 1940 of the ancient foundations of a large, elaborate bathhouse established the historic importance of Coriovallum (as Heerlen was once known) as a meeting place for the Roman troops stationed in this northern outpost and placed Heerlen on the tourist radar. After extensive excavations in the 1960s and '70s, the entire area is now on display for history-loving visitors.

Now enclosed in a large, glass-encircled building, the **Thermenmuseum** (Baths Museum) has catwalks over a perfectly preserved Roman bath complex. Built around the beginning of the 2nd century AD, the *thermae* (baths) incorporated open-air sports fields, a large swimming pool, shops, restaurants, and the enclosed bathhouse complex, which included a large dressing room, the hot-air sweating room, and a series of baths (warm, lukewarm, cold, and immersion). The museum's sound-and-light show documents one Lucius the Potter's first visit to the baths. In the museum hall, a series of lively models and reconstructions give the visitor an idea of what it was like to live and work in the Roman trading center of Coriovallum. ✉ *Coriovallumstraat 9* ☎ *045/560–5100* 🌐 *www.thermenmuseum.nl* 🎫 *€3.75* ⏲ *Tues.–Fri. 10–5, weekends noon–5.*

From the 14th to the 20th century, **Kasteel Hoensbroek** (Hoensbroek Castle) belonged to the same family, who added on bits here and there as the years went by. Nowadays, it is open to the public as the largest and best preserved of the castles in South Limburg. You can see sections dating from the 13th century and products of various architectural styles, including Baroque and Maasland-Renaissance. There are several sparsely but appropriately furnished rooms and various small galleries that show temporary exhibitions. ✉ *Klinkertstraat 118, Hoensbroek, 5 km (3 mi) northwest of Heerlen* ☎ *045/522–7272* 🌐 *www.kasteelhoensbroek.nl* 🎫 *€5* ⏲ *Daily 10–5:30.*

4

### Where to Stay & Eat

**$$** ✕ **Het Vervolg.** In its first year of operation, this stylish new restaurant was already turning heads and receiving awards and accolades. Tempting dishes to look out for include shrimp tempura, and duck breast and fennel salad with curried mayonnaise. Three- and four-course fixed-price menus are a good value if you come hungry. ✉ *Laanderstraat 27* ☎ *045/571–4241* ✍ *Reservations essential* 💳 *AE, DC, MC, V* ⏲ *Closed Mon. No lunch weekends.*

★ **$$–$$$$** ✕🏨 **Kasteel Erenstein.** An elegant 14th-century moated château set in a sprawling park, this spot is rightly known for its restaurant, whose menu and wine cellar are French. The dining area is adorned with voluminous chandeliers and a couple of very regal-looking portraits, but the atmosphere is anything but stuffy and exclusive: the staff pride themselves on the easy-going bistro-style atmosphere, so leave your bow tie and cummerbund in your suitcase. Across the road, a traditional whitewashed Limburg farmstead houses the luxury hotel. Many rooms have beamed ceilings, and some are bi-level and skylighted; others have rooftop balconies. As with the restaurant, there is a completely unpretentious vibe about the place despite its inherent grandeur. ✉ *Oud Erensteinerweg 6, 6468 PC Kerkrade, 8 km (5 mi) east of Heerlen* ☎ *045/546–1333* 📠 *045/546–0748* 🌐 *www.chateauhotels.nl* 🛏 *30 rooms, 14 suites* 👍 *Restaurant, minibars, bar, some pets allowed; no a/c* 💳 *AE, DC, MC, V* 🍽 *MAP* ⏲ *Restaurant closed Sun.*

★ **$$$–$$$$** ✕🏨 **Kasteel Wittem.** This fairy-tale castle-hotel, with its duck-filled moat, spindle-roof tower, and series of peekaboo dormers dotting the roof, is human in scale. Since AD 1100 it has been a citadel, an abbey, the home to the Knights Scavandrie, a barony created by Emperor Charles V, and a base once used by William the Silent to defeat the Spaniards in the 16th century. The family that has owned it for more than 35 years welcomes you to a comfortable environment furnished in vintage Dutch. The intimate dining room (closed Monday), offering French cuisine, has towering windows open to views of gardens and fields. There is a summer terrace beside the moat. ✉ *Wittemer Allée 3, 6286 AA Wittem, 15 km (9 mi) east of Maastricht, 14 km (9 mi) south of Heerlen* ☎ *043/450–1208* 📠 *043/450–1260* 🌐 *www.kasteelwittem.nl* 🛏 *12 rooms* 👍 *Restaurant; no a/c* 💳 *AE, DC, MC, V* 🍽 *MAP.*

# MAASTRICHT

The Dutch have an ongoing love affair with Maastricht—22 km (15 mi) southeast of Heerlen, 207 km (130 mi) southeast of Amsterdam, and 25 km (16 mi) west of Aachen (Germany)—and once you've been there, it's easy to understand why it regularly tops polls as the best holiday spot in the country. Yet the Dutch will be the first to tell you, perhaps paradoxically, that the city is just so . . . un-Dutch. Randstad dwellers farther north point enviously to the legacy of Maastricht's years of Burgundian rule, resulting in the Burgundian *levensstijl* (lifestyle). This is best defined as a capacity for seizing the moment, enjoying life to the fullest, and indulging all the senses—witness the local diet. Not for Maastricht's residents a bowl of *erwtensoep* (pea soup) and a *broodje* (sandwich); more likely, you'll find them tucking into guinea fowl and a good bottle of wine, followed by a generous piece of patisserie.

It's little wonder that, in their ebullient lifestyle, Maastricht dwellers seem to have more in common with southern Europeans than their cool, northern cousins. One major fact may explain why: as the nation's oldest city, Maastricht enjoys a history that began with the Romans, who founded the city more than 2,000 years ago. Maastricht takes its name from the Latin *Mosae Trajectum*—the point where the Maas River could be crossed. The initial walled Roman settlement was abandoned at the end of the 4th century. From then until 722, the place became a bishop's see, with St. Servatius (whose cyclopean church still graces the city) and St. Hubert the first and last bishops, respectively. By 1204, Maastricht was being ruled jointly by the Duke of Brabant and the Prince-Bishop of Liège, an arrangement that prevailed until 1795.

As the river's crossing point, Maastricht has always been strategically significant, and both the Spanish and French have laid siege to it in their time. When the city fell to the French in 1673, among the casualties was D'Artagnan, the inspiration behind the character of the same name in Alexandre Dumas's novel *The Three Musketeers,* who was fatally wounded while rescuing John Churchill (later Duke of Marlborough and an ancestor of Winston Churchill). For his deeds, Dumas is remembered with a statue in Maastricht's Waldeckpark. Later, during the occupation of 1795, the French forces made Maastricht the capital of a French province, the Department of the Lower Meuse. After Napoléon was routed at Waterloo, and the subsequent unification between Belgium and the Netherlands came to an end, Maastricht miraculously remained in Dutch hands.

With its reputation as a crossroads between Germanic and Latin cultures, Maastricht was an appropriate venue for the signing of the famous treaty of 1992, which regulated the affairs of the European Union and heralded the birth of the euro. Today, wedged somewhat hesitantly between Belgium and Germany, Maastricht retains an intriguing mixture of three languages (Dutch, French, and German) and a variety of traditions.

# CARNIVAL IN HOLLAND

**THERE IS NO WAY AROUND IT:** *to understand Carnaval (to use the Dutch spelling) you must experience it. In a last fling of pre-Lenten indulgence, the Catholics of the south set their controls to full blast. In the four days before the onset of Lent, business in the south comes to a virtual halt as residents concentrate on the one thing on everyone's mind: partying. Visitors are made especially welcome, whirled up into the action in no time at all. Preparations for the festivities begin months in advance, including, in November, the election of a "Prince of Carnival." He is given the arduous task of leading the revels throughout the four days before Ash Wednesday.*

*Then there are the costumes: when the parade passes by, expect to see a plethora of fairy-tale characters, local heroes, orange-painted faces, and psychedelic-color wigs. Costumes often take the form of humanlike bananas,*

*potatoes, and hams that somehow manage to elbow their way down tiny local sidewalks along with the flowing crowd, to reappear later cavorting at the all-night parties. Maastricht's Carnival is generally held to be the most lively of the region, with a main parade, a special children's parade, plus a contest to select the best brass bands. A fair number of Carnival aficionados consider Bergen op Zoom and Den Bosch's festivities better versions; these towns are smaller and, being farther from the borders, seem to offer a more authentically Dutch experience. You may not get much sleep if you're visiting during Carnival time, but you are sure to eat well if you join the revelers on the street putting away hotcakes and nonnevotten (deep-fried dough balls) to ward off the cold. And intrepid travelers will certainly make plenty of friends.*

## Exploring Maastricht

Maastricht's charm, coupled with its border location, makes one thing inevitable: an influx of visitors in the thousands. On high church days and holidays you may find yourself unable to move freely in the streets, let alone find a seat at a café. At off-peak times, however (early spring, fall, and winter), tourists with a sense of adventure can escape the worst of the crowds by scampering down tiny side streets and mazelike alleyways, to emerge once more into the hustle and bustle of the town's major squares. It's a relatively small city, but should your sense of direction by any chance fail, you can always rely on the soaring red tower of Sint Janskerk to reestablish your bearings. Restaurants are spread far and wide, although there is a higher-than-average concentration around the Vrijthof, Onze Lieve Vrouwplein, and the restored inner harbor, 't Bassin.

For a unique view of the city, not to mention a cooling alternative to sidewalks teeming with humanity, a cruise down the Maas River should prove both edifying and soothing to the soul.

Begin on the east side of town at the **Bonnefantenmuseum** ⑮ ⌐, a striking building designed by the architect Aldo Rossi, featuring an end tower shaped like an old-fashioned space rocket. Inside, a jewel-like collection of religious sculptures, Renaissance oil paintings, and genre paintings by the likes of Brueghel are complemented by large-scale contemporary artworks. When you've had your fill, head out with the museum behind you and the river to your left. It will be clear from the river traffic that the Maas is still one of Maastricht's major arteries: you'll see sand-laden barges, houseboats complete with clothes-strewn washing lines, and pleasure cruisers full of tourists, all gently making their way up and down the river.

As you head north, stop to marvel at the graceful, sweeping, 540-foot steel arch of the Hoge Brug (High Bridge), opened in 2003 to pedestrians and cyclists as a handy shortcut between the Bonnefantenmuseum and Onze Lieve Vrouweplein. Farther on, cross over **Sint Servaasbrug** ⑯, built between 1280 and 1298 and one of the oldest bridges in the Netherlands, pausing to admire the view of the town center's skyline. Head straight on down Maastrichter Brugstraat, and turn right into Kleine Straat. Here, you'll find the VVV (tourist office), housed in the impressively ancient **Dinghuis** ⑰, originally a courthouse dating from the turn of the 15th century. Just around the corner on Jodenstraat is **De Historische Drukkerij** ⑱, a venerable printing shop, and a few blocks to the northwest is the enchanting **Poppen Museum** ⑲, or Doll Museum. Several blocks north is the **Stadhuis** ⑳, on the Markt square, adorned with the noted statue of '**t Mooswief** ㉑. The walk from the VVV along shop-lined Grote Staat shortly brings you onto the **Vrijthof** ㉒ square, and Maastricht at its liveliest. On the square, look out for the colonnaded Military Guard House (Militaire Hoofdwacht), an elegant 18th-century building of gray Namur stone from which the city's borders were once controlled. To the left you'll also see the russet-color **Museum Spaans Gouvernement** ㉓ (Spanish Government Museum), with its period interiors and Renaissance-style arcade in the courtyard. Keep an eye out for the gable stones adorning the buildings around the square; often elaborately decorated, they show the name of the house and the year it was built. A particularly fine example is at No. 15, "In den Ouden Vogelstruys" ("In the Old Ostrich").

On the square, head to the far left up Henric van Veldekeplein, and at this point you'll almost certainly want to make a couple of stops. First, take the trip up the lofty tower of **Sint Janskerk** ㉔ and admire the breathtaking views; then immerse yourself in the Gothic splendors on offer next door, courtesy of **Sint Servaasbasiliek** ㉕, and its glittering St. Servatius' Treasury. Then it's back down Veldekeplein (don't miss the magnificent residential 17th-century mansion on your right) and across Vrijthof onto Bredestraat. Head on past Hondstraat on your right, and take the next right onto **Onze Lieve Vrouweplein** ㉖. If you've wondered before what the Dutch mean when they talk about Maastricht's "French feel," you'll understand now: this leafy square, filled with tables and strung with fairy lights, retains an intimate, Provençal atmosphere even when packed, and those who come here to relax over a bottle of wine with friends certainly seem full of joie de vivre. Just to the northeast are two notable sites that bear witness to the ancient Roman history of the town: **Op de Thermen** ㉗ and **Derlon Cellar** ㉘.

But providing a compelling backdrop to all the action is the magnificent, twin-towered **Onze Lieve Vrouwebasiliek** ㉙, or Basilica of Our Beloved Lady. Dating to before the year 1000, it is the oldest church in Maastricht and formed the hub of the Liège governership before the city's walls were constructed in 1229. Savor the stillness of its incense-scented interior before taking the side road bearing to the right as you look at the church, and heading past street cafés and the right-hand turn onto Sint Benardusstraat, taking you up to the city wall. With the river in front of you, walk up the steps onto Onze Lieve Vrouwewal, constructed some time after 1229 as part of the first medieval city wall. Today it's crowned with balconied period residences, jaunty in spring with red geraniums, and some with interesting gated entrances worth noting. End your walk with a visit to the **Helpoort** ㉚, the gatehouse at the bottom of the wall's steps, formerly part of the wall itself, which houses a little museum full of Maastricht lore. If you feel the need to fortify yourself, now would be a good time to head back toward Onze Lieve Vrouweplein for a glass of Limburg wine or a local beer. But if you have energy left for more exploring, head southwest to the **Natuurhistorisch Museum** ㉛, with its lovely botanical gardens, then continue southward to tunnel back to the ancient past in the evocative **Grotten Sint Pietersberg** ㉜.

TIMING For the walk only, allow about 1¾ hours, but if you take in all the sights and detours and use it as the springboard for tangential explorations, it could easily take the full day. Bear in mind that many museums and shops are closed Monday.

## What to See

★ ▶ ❶ **Bonnefantenmuseum** (Bonnefanten Museum). Set on the east bank of the Maas, this E-shape building with its lofty tower was designed by the famed Italian architect Aldo Rossi. Its spacious, light-filled interior makes this a worthy home for Limburg's excellent provincial museum. Here, diversity is the order of the day: not only are there displays on the archaeological history of the province, but there is an art collection with gems from 13th- to 15th-century Romanesque and Gothic Mosan sculpture of the Maas region; 14th- to 16th-century Italian paintings; and 16th- to 18th-century paintings of the South Netherlands, including works by Jan Brueghel and Pieter Brueghel the Younger. An intriguing and intelligently selected exhibition of contemporary art includes work by many important Dutch painters of the late 20th century, several of them from Limburg. Artists represented include LeWitt, Signer, Kounellis, and Mangold. Don't miss the Sol LeWitt–designed upper chamber of the tower, where an overwhelming and dizzying white-on-black spiral gradually scales the walls from floor to ceiling. A changing array of temporary exhibitions and installation pieces means there is always something to suit every taste. ✉ *Ave. Céramique 250* ☏ *043/329–0190* ⊕ *www.bonnefanten.nl* ✇ *€7* ☺ *Tues.–Sun. 11–5.*

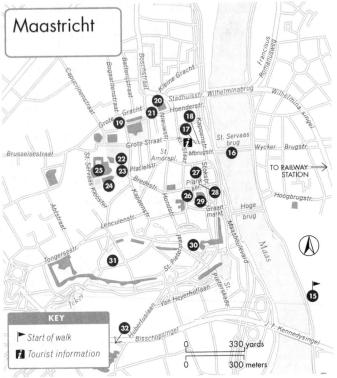

Maastricht

KEY

▶ *Start of walk*

🛈 *Tourist information*

0 ————— 330 yards
0 ————— 300 meters

**❶⑧ De Historische Drukkerij.** You may end up with inky fingers at this period printing shop, a stone's throw from the tourist office and still in use today. The shop dates from around 1900 and has changed very little. A self-guided tour reveals much about traditional typesetting skills and shows ancient presses in action, plus there's a display detailing the history of printing. It all makes for a lively, quirky excursion. ✉ *Jodenstraat 22* ☎ *043/321–6376* ⊕ *www.drukmuseum.nl* 🎫 *€2.50* 🕐 *Mar.–July and Sept.–Nov., Fri. and Sat. 1–5.*

**❷⑧ Derlon Cellar.** Before builders began work on the Derlon hotel, city archaeologists made an extensive survey of its site. The earth yielded fascinating artifacts and examples of architecture from the 2nd through the 4th century, including a 3rd-century well and a section from a pre-Roman cobblestone road, all of which have been preserved beneath the building. Display cabinets and panels contain additional information and finds. ✉ *Plankstraat 21* 🎫 *Free* 🕐 *Sun. noon–4.*

**❶⑦ Dinghuis.** The city's VVV tourist board couldn't have found a more interesting home than this edifice, built around 1470 as the seat of the former Lord Chief Justice of Maastricht and once used as a prison by Napoléon. It's been restored several times. Note the building's beautiful stone gable and timbered side wall toward its Jodenstraat side. Venture inside if you want to have a look at its dark, cozy interior—just be prepared to face plenty of other tourists, who will be busy picking up leaflets and booking their hotel rooms. ⊠ *Kleine Straat 1* ☎ *043/325–2121* 🖅 *Free* ☉ *May–Oct., Mon.–Sat. 9–6, Sun. 11–3; Nov.–Apr., weekdays 9–6, Sat. 9–5.*

㉜ **Grotten Sint Pietersberg** (Caves of Mount St. Peter). A warm sweater and sturdy shoes are essential as you head for an experience to mark you as an intrepid explorer. These man-made corridors, approximately 200 km (124 mi) of chambers and passageways, carved deep into the limestone hills, have yielded building stone since Roman times. In some areas the mining was so extensive the ceiling is nearly 40 feet high; this means that graffiti left by the Romans are now far above your head, though the signatures of such visitors as Napoléon can still be seen. There are almost as many anecdotes regarding the caves' history as there are chambers; the tale of how Rembrandt's *Night Watch* was hidden here during World War II is just one example, or ask to hear the creepy story of the four 17th-century monks who lost their way when the thread they were using as a guideline failed. Because the caves are complex, dark, and chilly you can visit them only with a guide, and you may be asked to carry a gas lamp—your only light source. Be aware that your guide will speak only the dominant language of the group he or she is accompanying. Check when buying your tickets—if you're in a predominantly Dutch group, for example, it would be best to pick up an English-language guidebook, or plan your visit around the early-afternoon English-language tours. ⊠ *Grotten Noord (Northern System), Luikerweg 71, Zonneberg Caves, Slavante 1 (near Enci Cement Works)* ☎ *043/325–2121* 🖅 *€3.75* ☉ *Apr.–June, Sept., and Oct., English-language tours at 2 daily (Northern System); July and Aug., English-language tours at 2 daily (Zonneberg Caves).*

㉚ **Helpoort** (City Gate). The Netherlands' oldest remaining city gate lies at the end of the first medieval rampart wall, dating from 1229. The small museum inside gives the lowdown on its history, and as you leave you'll go through a gate, which would originally have been fitted with a portcullis. The projecting parapet above the gateway had a special use in times of battle: its floor had special openings through which the enemy could be bombarded. ⊠ *Bottom of steps at end of Onze Lieve Vrouwewal* ☎ *043/325–7833* 🖅 *Donation appreciated* ☉ *Easter–Oct., daily 1:30-4:30.*

㉑ **'t Mooswief** (Greengrocer's Wife). The jolly statue of a roly-poly woman carrying a basket of vegetables stands on one side of the **Grote Markt** (market square). Keep your eyes open, too, for the flame-carrying bronze statue of Jan Pieter Minckelers (by Bart van Hove), who, appropriately enough, invented the gaslight. Wednesday and Friday are market days in Maastricht, and the square is chockablock with stalls and stands offering fruit, vegetables, meats, household items, and fish (Friday).

㉓ **Museum Spaans Gouvernement** (Spanish Government Museum). Housed in a lovely red-front mansion dating from the 16th century (it was originally built as a chapter house), this was the home of the Duke of Brabant from the end of the 14th century. Today, the museum is a feast of opulent detailing: crystal chandeliers, fine period furniture, and ornate wall frescos are all to be found here. In the Renaissance-style courtyard, carved medallions depict Charles V, Isabelle of Portugal, and Philip II, all of whom stayed in the house at one time or another. Interior-design fans can admire rooms decorated in the authentic Liège style of the mid-18th-century, as well as silver, porcelain, and paintings from the large Wagner–de Wit collection. ⊠ *Vrijthof 18* ☎ *043/321–1327* ⊕ *www. museumspaansgouvernement.nl* ✉ *€2.50* ⊗ *Wed.–Sun. 1–5.*

☾ ❸ **Natuurhistorisch Museum** (Natural History Museum). With some 550,000 natural objects covering 11,000 species of life, the Natural History Museum is one of the largest of its kind in the Netherlands. Plenty of interactive displays, audiovisual explanations, and computers to tinker with mean that no one could charge the museum with a dated outlook. Marvel at the museum's collection of gemstones, or—if the weather's fine—enjoy the sights and smells of its lush **botanical gardens.** Here, laid out in a variety of beds and terraces, is a collection of rare and common plants native to the Limburg region. The peace and quiet of the lush grounds make it hard to believe you're in the heart of the city. ⊠ *De Bosquetplein 6–7* ☎ *043/350–5490* ⊕ *www.nhmmaastricht.nl* ✉ *€3.50* ⊗ *Weekdays 10–5, weekends 2–5.*

❷❾ **Onze Lieve Vrouwebasiliek** (Our Beloved Lady Basilica). Maastricht's oldest monument was erected atop an ancient Roman temple. The Westwork, a massive flat facade in Romanesque style that is topped with two round turrets, is the oldest part of the structure, dating from the 11th and 12th centuries. Inside is a two-story apse with a double row of columns and a half-dome roof. You'll also find two crypts, both dating from the Romanesque period, and restful 16th-century cloisters. Though the treasure house here isn't as spectacular as the one at St. Servatius, there's still plenty to relish, including capes, copes, and tapestries rich with detail (look out for the Levite tapestry of St. Lambertus, Maastricht's last bishop), ivories, statues, silver, and other ecclesiastical relics. ⊠ *Onze Lieve Vrouweplein* ☎ *043/325–1851* ✉ *Church free, treasure chamber €1.75* ⊗ *Easter–Oct., Mon.–Sat. 11–5, Sun. 1–5.*

❷❻ **Onze Lieve Vrouweplein** (Our Beloved Lady Square). The basilica of the same name opens out onto this tree-shaded, intimate square—one of Maastricht's prettiest and most atmospheric spots.

❷❼ **Op de Thermen.** This small residential square, discovered in 1840, was once the site of a Roman villa and baths. It hints at the Roman heritage that lies deep beneath the surface of Maastricht. Paving stones indicate the outline of the ancient buildings—red for a 1st-century house with under-floor heating, gray for a 2nd-century bathhouse, and white for a 4th-century bathhouse. ⊠ *Between Luikerweg and Stokstraat.*

☾ ❶❾ **Poppen Museum** (Doll Museum). Children and adults alike will love this exhibition of all kinds of toys, dating from 1780 to 1950. As well as teddy bears, windup monkeys, and china dolls, also on view are all the appropriate accessories to make their little lives complete—umbrellas, handbags, and outfits, plus tiny furniture and the grandest of miniature dinner services. And should the unsilenceable cry "I want one of those!" go up from any tykes, rest assured there's also a store selling toys and replicas, proceeds from which are donated to worthy causes. Note that the museum is only open on request, so call ahead, or arrange a visit via the tourist office. ⊠ *Grote Gracht 41* ☎ *043/326–0123* ⌑ *€3.50.*

**㉔ Sint Janskerk** (St. John's Church). Beautiful in its simplicity, this 14th-century Gothic church has been in the possession of the Dutch Reformed Church since 1633. In its stark, bare, sandstone interior you'll find murals and fine sculpted corbels depicting the 12 disciples, a carved pulpit by Coenrad Pierkens dating from 1780, plus a wonderfully mellow-sounding organ. The tall, red tower of the church offers panoramic views of the city; your voluntary donation goes toward its upkeep. ⊠ *Vrijthof (enter on Henric van Veldekeplein)* ☎ *043/347–8880* ⌑ *Church free, donation appreciated; tower €1.25* ☉ *Easter–Oct., Mon.–Sat. 11–4.*

**★ ㉕ Sint Servaasbasiliek** (St. Servatius Basilica). Beneath the magnificent and historic 7th-century church lie the bones of its namesake, the 4th-century saint whose choice of Maastricht as the location for his see stimulated the development of the city after the departure of the Romans in 402. Restoration work on the basilica used the same bright paint colors as the original interior design. The focal points of the church are the richly carved 13th-century **Berg Portal** and the **Schatkamer van Sint Servaas** (Treasure Chamber of St. Servatius) in the 12th-century chapel. This extraordinary collection of treasures dates from 827 and contains religious relics (some of them donated by Charlemagne) and exquisitely wrought liturgical objects. The most important item in the collection is the 12th-century Noodkist, an elaborately decorated, gold-plated oak chest, adorned with gold and silver figures and containing the bones and relics of St. Servatius and other local bishops. For a simpler strain of beauty, investigate the musty lower crypt, where ancient excavations create a strong sense of the past. ⊠ *Vrijthof* ☎ *043/325–7878* ⊕ *www.sintservaas.nl* ⌑ *€3.50* ☉ *Nov.–Apr., daily 10–5; May–Oct., daily 10–6.*

**㉑ Sint Servaasbrug** (St. Servatius Bridge). The span crosses the Maas between the old and new parts of town and offers the best views of the old city. Built solidly of gray Namur stone in the late 13th century to replace an earlier, nine-arched wooden version, it is one of the oldest bridges in the Netherlands. ⊠ *Maasboulevard, Wycker Brugstraat.*

**㉒ Stadhuis** (Town Hall). Maastricht's civic building stands imposingly at one end of the large market square. Designed in 1662 by the architect Pieter Post—he of Mauritshuis (The Hague) fame—it's a proud testament to burgher prosperity, filled with fine tapestries, stucco, and paintings. The sumptuous entrance hall with its moldings and painted ceiling is open to the public. The tower dates from 1684 and houses a carillon of 49 bells—listen for them between 3:30 and 4:15 PM if you're in the neighborhood on a Saturday. ⊠ *Markt 78* ☎ *043/350–5050* ⌑ *Free* ☉ *Weekdays 8:30–12:30 and 2–5:30.*

**Stokstraat.** Now a fashionable street lined with galleries and boutiques, Stokstraat was the heart of the original Roman settlement of Maastricht.

**㉒ Vrijthof.** Each February, this enormous square explodes with the festivities of Carnival. It is also the location for the taste-bud-tantalizing Preuvenemint, which takes place toward the end of August). Ringed with restaurants, grand cafés, dance clubs, and traditional pubs, it is the major public gathering place of Maastricht, year-round.

> **need a break?**
>
> A cheerful place to stop any time of day is the plant-, candle-, and chandelier-filled **Brasserie Britannique** (⊠ Vrijthof 6 ☎ 043/321–8691). It serves breakfast (with champagne if you like) as well as simple light meals throughout the day, and drinks, including a house beer, until midnight.

## Where to Stay & Eat

With more award-winning restaurants than anywhere else in the Netherlands, Maastricht offers the very highest pinnacles of Dutch cuisine, and you'll notice the difference both in taste and finesse. Quality sometimes comes at a price, but you may not mind paying an extra few euros for delicacies such as earthy, rich, cave-grown mushrooms; seasonal asparagus (white and sweet, not green and acidic); and creamy but whiffy Rommedoe cheese. Diners are sometimes surprised to discover they can also quaff a selection of quality local white wines while they enjoy the French-style cuisine and delicious patisseries for which the city is famed. The Apostelhoeve vineyard is the oldest wine-growing estate in the country, and produces four dry, fruity whites made from Müller Thurgau, Auxerrois, Riesling, and Pinot Gris grapes, each of which are worth sampling.

When it comes to finding a bed for the night, many Dutch claim you'll find the country's best and best-value hotels in Maastricht, especially in its range of boutique hotels. Although you won't see Zen-like minimalist design (with the Hotel Bergère a notable exception), what you will find are plenty of intimate, unusual places, some with as few as six rooms, lovingly furnished in classic style.

★ $$$$ ✕ **Château Neercanne.** Built in 1698 as a pleasure dome for one of Maastricht's military governors, this spot—comfortably distant from the crowds of central Maastricht—is extremely special. No wonder Queen Beatrix chose it as the venue for her state banquet with Europe's leaders during the Maastricht summit of 1991 (you can still see the guests' signatures on the ceiling of the château's caves). Still the only terraced kasteel in the Netherlands, the château was built in 1698 by Baron Daniël de Dopff. Both château and grounds were extensively restored from the 1950s to the 1980s. There are a variety of dining spaces here—some exclusively available for group bookings—but anyone can enjoy the pretty restaurant known as L' Auberge, with its glorious views over the terraces. Outstanding dishes include creamy spinach soup with smoked eel, and chocolate *delice* with vanilla cream and a Cointreau sauce. The finest of wines are stored in the château's caves. You can walk off any excess calories in the magnificent Baroque-style garden (landmarked by UNESCO), created in the Louis XIV style by De Dorff and overlooking the Jekervallei valley, which is home to the area's finest vineyards, including· that of Neercanne itself. ✉ *Cannerweg 800* ☎ *043/325–1359* ⊕ *www.neercanne.com* ♺ *Reservations essential* ▭ *AE, DC, MC, V.*

★ $$$$ ✕ **Toine Hermsen.** Despite receiving significant culinary honors, Toine is not a pretentious place. It is, however, unashamedly elegant: think crystal, crisp white napery, and gleaming silverware. But it's the food that dominates. A menu might begin with carpaccio of salmon with lemon-dill sauce and move on to Bresse duck with tomato confit, bell peppers, and potatoes in Provençale sauce; for dessert perhaps almond phyllo pastry with cherry filling and vanilla ice cream topped with champagne sauce. There are fixed-price menus for three, four, and five courses. ✉ *Sint Bernardusstraat 2–4* ☎ *043/325–8400* ♺ *Reservations essential* 🏛*Jacket and tie* ▭ *AE, DC, MC, V* ⊘ *Closed Sun. No lunch Sat. and Mon.*

$$$–$$$$ ✕ **Mediterraneo.** Given Maastricht's plethora of fine French restaurants, a visit to Mediterraneo—an Italian spot that enjoys an excellent reputation throughout the Netherlands—makes a refreshing change. Decor is rustic and warm, with tiles, mirrors, and plenty of plants. Deceptively simple-sounding dishes packed full of Tuscan flavors include homemade ravioli with potato-and-truffle filling; a salad of mushroom, artichoke, and shrimp; and turbot cooked with capers and lemon. Naturally, a bottle of vintage Barolo should help you appreciate the experience even more. ✉ *Rechtstraat 73* ☎ *043/325–5037* ♺ *Reservations essential* ▭ *AE, DC, MC, V* ⊘ *Closed Sun. No lunch.*

$$$–$$$$ ✕ **'t Pakhoes.** Clever use has been made of an old brick warehouse (which began life as an ammunition magazine centuries ago) to create this four-story restaurant, each floor having a different atmosphere. Begin your "tour" with an aperitif on the ground floor, and then work your way up through the building for successive courses. In summer, simply settle down to dine in the shade of an umbrella with a view across the Maas. The food of chef's Guidy Wolfs has a French-Belgian slant; try the quails in honey sauce with onion marmalade, or blow the diet in style with the fresh lobster salad, nicely rejuvenated with a creamy mango-and-curry sauce. ✉ *Waterpoort 4–6* ☎ *043/325–7000* ♺ *Reservations essential* ▭ *AE, DC, MC, V* ⊘ *Closed Sun. Lunch by prior arrangement only.*

$$$ ✕ **Roxy's.** Wicker chairs, a wood-beamed ceiling, and wooden tables add a laid-back atmosphere to Roxy's, located just a stone's throw from the Vrijthof. This is a reliable outpost for meat and fish lovers, who can tuck into grilled beefsteak, lobster, or monkfish stir-fried with coriander, Kaffir lime, and glass noodles. ✉ *Kruiserengang 4* ☎ *043/321–1219* ♺ *Reservations essential* ▭ *AE, DC, MC, V* ⊘ *Closed Tues. Lunch by prior arrangement only.*

$$–$$$ ✕ **'t Hegske.** This romantic spot is near Sint Amorsplein off Vrijthof. A forest of climbing plants completely obscures the outer wall on the street side, and there is a bubbling fountain in the interior courtyard. The warmth of half-timbered walls, hanging baskets, and antique collectibles here and there adds to the intimacy. The kitchen is open, the cuisine classic French. ✉ *Heggenstraat 3a* ☎ *043/325–1762* ♺ *Reservations essential* ▭ *AE, DC, MC, V* ⊘ *No lunch.*

$$–$$$ ✕ **Sagittarius Seafood & Grillades.** You'll find it hard to resist the aroma of garlic butter and freshly grilled seafood that invariably wafts from

this narrow little restaurant. The young staff manage to be both friendly and solicitous without being overbearing. Food flavors here are rich, robust, and redolent of southern France. Close your eyes in the warmth of the rear conservatory, overhung with leafy branches, and you may be instantly whisked to the shores of the Mediterranean. Start with grilled sardines or a Roquefort, date, and walnut salad, then pamper your taste buds with lobster served with a champagne sabayon. ⊠ *Bredestraat 7* ☎ *043/321–1492* ⌕ *Reservations essential* ▭ *AE, DC, MC, V* ☉ *Closed Sun.–Tues.*

¢–$$$ ⨯ **Gio's Cucina Casalinga.** White linen tablecloths, candles, a dark-oak floor, and an overabundance of deep-red roses create an intimate and elegant backdrop for some excellent yet unpretentious Italian cuisine (the restaurant's name means Gio's "Homey Kitchen"). You can fill yourself up adequately with pizza or pasta for less than €10, but you'd be selling yourself short. Choose a set menu and watch your table fill up with enormous homemade ravioli, king prawn dishes, anchovies on toast overlaid with long rasps of Parmesan, and exquisitely crunchy vegetables prepared with enough garlic to destroy the entire vampire population of Europe. Gio himself ambles amiably around, chatting with the clientele, while a battalion of Italians in the kitchen below help prepare the food. ⊠ *Vrijthof 29* ☎ *043/325–6275* ▭ *AE, DC, MC, V* ☉ *Closed Mon.*

★ $$ ⨯ **Petit Bonheur.** In its original incarnation around 1700, the Petit Bonheur was a farm located just inside the city walls. Today it is like a little sliver of Provence transported into the heart of Maastricht. Try to get a table in the secluded cobbled courtyard to dine below a canopy of grapevines in summer or underneath a retractable roof once winter sets in. You might even be able to sample an aperitif in the hemispherical cellar, where dusty wine bottles abound and a filled-in well bears testimony to many occupations of the city; locals used to hide their valuables here. The food is heavily influenced by modern French and Belgian cuisines and includes such delights as rack of lamb with rosemary and chili peppers. The Petit Bonheur also has hotel rooms upstairs if the Burgundian lifestyle begins to take its toll. ⊠ *Achter de Molens 2* ☎ *043/325–8088* ⊕ *www.petitbonheur.nl* ⌕ *Reservations essential* ▭ *AE, MC, V* ☉ *No lunch.*

$–$$ ⨯ **La Ville.** During the day you can take your pick of delicious salads and light meals. In the evening the friendly and enthusiastic staff serve hearty, French-influenced cuisine, such as filet mignon with shallots and red-wine sauce. The restaurant is on Maastricht's prettiest square and has tables outside in good weather. ⊠ *Onze Lieve Vrouweplein 28* ☎ *043/321–9889* ⌕ *Reservations essential* ▭ *AE, DC, MC, V.*

¢–$ ⨯ **Café Charlemagne.** A perfect place for those who want hearty fare in the center of town, Café Charlemagne is opposite the Onze Lieve Vrouwe Basilica. The darkish interior nods at the traditional, brightened with candles and a gargantuan chandelier. In summer, when tables spill out onto the leafy outside square, the place comes alive. Choose from steak, the simply fried cod, or even an Indonesian saté. In the warm months, the goat-cheese salad is a good option. ⊠ *Onze Lieve Vrouweplein 24* ☎ *043/321–9373* ▭ *DC, MC, V.*

¢–$ ✕ **De Blindgenger.** Just off Onze Lieve Vrouweplein, De Blindgenger is a particularly warm and cheerful pub with large windows looking onto the street. The tables are plain and unadorned, the service is relaxed, and the menu has a good selection of fish dishes, including mussels when in season. ✉ *Koestraat 3* ☎ *043/325–0619* ⚓ *Reservations not accepted* ▭ *MC, V.*

$–$$ ✕▦ **Kasteel Elsloo.** This grand 17th-century manorhouse, with its own park and botanical garden, was once the property of one of Limburg's leading families and the scene of many a glittering occasion, including the 19th-century wedding of a daughter of the family to the Prince of Monaco. Guest rooms are spacious and restfully decorated in creams and pastels. Adjacent to the mustard-yellow bar, topped off by country-style chandeliers, the restaurant has a palatial manor-house feel to it, thanks to its soaring, spectacular stone vaults; the kitchen is traditional French, serving such dishes as beef with onion confit and port sauce. ✉ *Maasberg 1, 6181 GV Elsloo, 10 km (6 mi) northeast of Maastricht* ☎ *046/437–7666* 📠 *046/437–7570* ⊕ *www.kasteelelsloo. nl* ➷ *23 rooms, 1 suite* ♢ *Restaurant, bar, some pets allowed; no a/c* ▭ *AE, DC, MC, V* ⦿ *MAP.*

¢–$ ✕▦ **Maison du Chene.** Located close to the action, this long-established hotel (almost 150 years old) allows you to step right out the front door on to the Markt market square. The interior is simple, with cream-color walls, tile floors, and a long antique wooden table at the front. The adjoining restaurant serves a variety of dishes, including a fish choice that varies according to whatever caught the chef's eye at the market that day. ✉ *Boschstraat 104, 6211 AZ* ☎ *043/321–3523* 📠 *043/325–8082* ⊕ *www.maastrichthotel.com* ➷ *24 rooms, 18 with bath* ♢ *Restaurant; no a/c* ▭ *AE, DC, MC, V.*

$$$$ ▦ **Derlon Maastricht.** The relaxed and quiet elegance of Onze Lieve Vrouweplein is perfectly reflected in this small luxury hotel. Guest rooms are graciously sized and decorated in relaxing white and blue tones, and each has a distinct contemporary work of art. Rooms at the front face the tree-filled square, and eight suites were added in 2005. A unique feature of this hotel is a private museum in the cellar, with exhibits ranging from the 1st century BC to the 15th century AD. There is a gratifying personal quality to the service, especially in the elegant restaurant. ✉ *Onze Lieve Vrouweplein 6, 6211 HD* ☎ *043/321–6770* 📠 *043/ 325–1933* ⊕ *www.derlon.com* ➷ *41 rooms, 8 suites* ♢ *Restaurant, minibars, cable TV, Wi-Fi, shops, meeting room, some pets allowed* ▭ *AE, DC, MC, V* ⦿ *MAP.*

★ $$$$ ▦ **Kruisherenhotel Maastricht.** As soon as the Kruisherenhotel opened its doors in mid-2005, it was instantly recognized as a classic among design hotels. Even before you reach the lobby, channeled in though a shiny copper funnel, it's clear that something special is happening here. Housed in a former abbey, dating from 1438, the building has been lovingly restored and decked with eye-catching furnishings created by interior designer Henk Vos, and lighting by artist Ingo Maurer. The cavernous but bright lobby and bar area—in the abbey's old church—is simply breathtaking, as Gothic architecture blends seamlessly with cutting-edge 21st-century design. At one end, a cozy bar has seating lined with plush red velvet upholstery. Next to the bar, a meeting room replete with a lime-green glass table backs onto a glass-walled champagne cellar. Above all this, an open breakfast area is perched on a mezzanine running the length of the nave. From there your eye will be drawn to the magnificent arched windows and high vaulted ceiling. Reached via medieval corridors that stretch around the central sculpture-filled courtyard, the individually designed luxury bedrooms are as modern as they come, filled with clean lines, light colors, state-of-the-art bathrooms, and flat-screen TVs. All things combined, this is the wow factor cranked up to the nth degree. ⊠ *Kruisherengang 19-23, 6211 NW* ☎ *043/329–2020* 🖷 *043/ 323–3030* ⊕ *www.chateauhotels.nl* 🛏 *60 rooms* ⌂ *Restaurant, bar, mini-bars, cable TV, in-room data ports* ▤ *AE, DC, MC, V.*

**$$$** 🖻 **Hotel Bergère.** As part of the Design Hotels group, the emphasis here is not only on service but on aesthetics—if cutting-edge modernism is your thing, you'll appreciate its combination of clean lines and cool woods. Features include "La Byb" (an in-house library where you'll find international books, magazines, and newspapers), a state-of the-art fitness center offering great views of Maastricht's skyline, a designer florist and gift shop, and water beds in some rooms. ⊠ *Stationsstraat 40, 6221 BR* ☎ *043/328–2525* 🖷 *043/328–2526* ⊕ *www.la-bergere.com* 🛏 *74 rooms* ⌂ *Cable TV, Wi-Fi, gym, shop, parking (fee); no a/c* ▤ *AE, DC, MC, V.*

★ **$–$$$** 🖻 **Hotel Botticelli.** Billing its philosophy as "the simple art of living," the Hotel Botticelli doesn't disappoint. Two buildings dating from the 18th century and originally built for a local wine merchant have been lovingly converted into a quiet and spacious hotel. Decor-wise, the place takes its inspiration from Italy, with warm colors and a number of Renaissance-style sculptures scattered here and there. Each room has been individually decorated using paint effects such as stippling, sponging, and trompe l'oeil—but, like the furnishings, the overall effect is classily understated. And wherever possible, the hotel's original features have been retained, so you may stay in a room with a beamed ceiling or an antique chimney breast. The central courtyard separating the two buildings is the perfect place to relax with a drink after a day spent sightseeing. ⊠ *Papenstraat 11, 6211 LG* ☎ *043/352–6300* 🖷 *043/352–6336* ⊕ *www.botticellihotel.nl* 🛏 *18 rooms* ⌂ *Minibars, cable TV, in-room DVD, bar* ▤ *AE, DC, MC, V.*

**$–$$** 🖻 **Best Western Hotel Du Casque.** Smack-dab in the center of old Maastricht, this hotel has a tradition that dates back to a 15th-century inn, although today's building is a modern postwar structure. Some rooms overlook the Vrijthof square, and there's direct access to a steak house with a terrace fronting the square. ⊠ *Helmstraat 14, 6211 TA* ☎ *043/ 321–4343* 🖷 *043/325–5155* ⊕ *www.hotelducasque.nl* 🛏 *41 rooms* ⌂ *Minibars, cable TV, Wi-Fi, parking (fee), some pets allowed; no a/c* ▤ *AE, DC, MC, V.*

**$** 🖻 **Dis.** This tiny hotel has an unusual location: a historic building above an art gallery that bears the same name. Guest rooms are clean, spacious, and bright with white cotton bed linen, some antique furniture, and wooden beams. Contemporary art from the gallery lends splashes of color to the walls. Downstairs, enjoy breakfast among the paintings and plants while admiring the ceiling and the ancient archways. ⊠ *Tafel-straat 28, 6211 JD* ☎ *043/321–5479* 🖷 *043/325–7026* ⊕ *www.hoteldis. nl* 🖙 *6 rooms* 🛆 *Minibars, cable TV; no a/c* ▭ *AE, MC, V.*

$ 🏨 **Hotel de Traverse.** If you're looking for country solitude, this historic B&B only 10 minutes from Maastricht is your place. Spacious rooms are in the barn of an 18th-century former tiendschuur, a tithing way station where local farmers came to pay their 10% property tax. Meandering roads through Limburg hills, and Pluto, the resident pooch, welcome you to a very hospitable rural retreat. Breakfast, served with homemade jam, is complimentary. ⊠ *Franse Steeg 1, 6268 NW Gasthuis* ☎ *043/407–3980* 🖷 *043/407–3301* ⊕ *www.detraverse.nl* 🖙 *5 rooms* 🛆 *Dining room, cable TV, Wi-Fi, tennis court, parking (free), some pets allowed; no a/c* ▭ *AE, DC, MC, V* ◎| *CP.*

$ 🏨 **Hotel d'Orangerie.** In a building built in 1752, this is a delightful, intimate little hotel with just 22 rooms, 9 of which have views over the river. The English-style decor combines country-house coziness with contemporary touches, translating to period-style lamps and desks, plus comfortable beds with padded headboards and modern, marble-clad bathrooms. The breakfast room boasts a marble fireplace, chandeliers, and pretty frescoed walls, and on sunny days, you can enjoy your croissant on the tiny grottolike terrace behind the breakfast room. Renovation work is planned for 2006, though disruption for guests should be kept to a minimum. ⊠ *Kleine Gracht 4, 6211 CB* ☎ *043/326–1111* 🖷 *043/326–1287* ⊕ *www.hotel-orangerie.nl* 🖙 *22 rooms* 🛆 *Minibars, cable TV, bar, parking (fee); no a/c* ▭ *AE, DC, MC.*

¢ 🏨 **De Poshoorn.** Conveniently situated between the railway station and the Old Town, the De Poshoorn has smallish rooms, but they are spotlessly clean and brightly decorated in light shades. The hotel is above an ambience-rich café with a friendly clientele and good beer, and service is attentive and efficient. ⊠ *Stationsstraat 47, 6211 BN* ☎ *043/321–7334* 🖷 *043/321–0747* ⊕ *www.poshoorn.nl* 🖙 *11 rooms* 🛆 *No a/c* ▭ *AE, DC, MC, V.*

## Nightlife & the Arts

Maastricht enjoys a thriving multicultural arts scene, which attracts world-class performers from all over Europe. Its status as a student town ensures a particularly lively nightlife, so you'll always be able to find some sort of evening entertainment here. For information on what is going on during your visit, check *Week In Week Uit*, a weekly culture agenda you will find around town.

### The Arts

CARILLON CONCERTS In summer the air rings with a series of evening concerts played by carillonneurs on various church bells of the city, and throughout the year there are midday concerts every Saturday from 3:30 to 4:15 from the cheerful 43-bell carillon atop the Town Hall in the market square.

CLASSICAL MUSIC In Maastricht, the **Limburgse Symfonie Orkest** (⊕ www.lso.nl) (Limburg Symphony Orchestra) is the leading regional orchestra. It performs at the **Theater aan Het Vrijthof** (⊠ Vrijthof 47 ☎ 043/350–5555); the box office is open Monday–Saturday 11–4. Maastricht has a thriving and talented student and amateur music scene. Performances can be caught at the **Theater Kumulus** (⊠ Herbenusstraat 89 ☎ 043/350–5656 ⊕ www. kumulus.nl).

In July and August, Maastricht's great churches make magnificent settings for organ recitals, which usually take place on Tuesday evenings and Sunday afternoons. Contact **Pro Organo Maastricht** (⊠ Jekerschans 75 ☎ 043/321–0890) for more details.

THEATER  The main theater of Maastricht, the **Theater aan Het Vrijthof** (Theater at Vrijthof; ⊠ Vrijthof 47 ☎ 043/350–5555 ⊕ www.theateraanhetvrijthof. nl) has a reputation for exciting programming that extends beyond the city limits. Top-quality national and international companies perform here. The **Het Vervolg Theater** (⊠ Plein 1992–15 ☎ 043/350–3050 ⊕ www.hetvervolg.nl) stages experimental and esoteric work.

## Nightlife

CAFÉS  In the heart of the city, with a terrace that hums with life on summer evenings, **De Lanteern** (⊠ Onze Lieve Vrouweplein 26 ☎ 043/744–0272) attracts everyone from tourists to the corner shopkeeper. A special pub to visit is the very old **In den Ouden Vogelstruys** (⊠ Vrijthof 15 ☎ 043/ 321–4888), first mentioned in town records of the 13th century. It has remained virtually unchanged since 1730 (except, of course, for the modern conveniences of electricity and beer on tap). Named for a type of potbellied gin bottle, **Sjinkerij de Bóbbel** (⊠ Wolfstraat 32 ☎ 043/321– 7413) is a traditional Maastricht pub with an atmosphere to match— well worth visiting if you've time. Informal yet understatedly elegant, it's the sort of place that produces the buzz of good conversation. It has sand on the floor, simple wooden chairs, and marble-top tables.

On the opposite side of the Maas River from the city center, **Cafe Zondag** (⊠ Wijcker Brugstraat 43 ☎ 043/321–9300) is a bright, airy place with large windows and an easy-on-the-eye gray/yellow interior. It is a relaxing place for snacks during the day and very popular in the evenings. Near the St Servaas Bridge, **Take One** (⊠ Rechtstraat 28 ☎ 043/321– 6423) is a temple where beer lovers gather to worship. At the last count, around 130 different offerings were available.

A five-minute walk north from the Grote Markt, 't Bassin is a restored old harbor that is now used as a yachting marina. On the wharf are several arched warehouse cellars that have been converted into chic bars and restaurants. In the early evening the area attracts a well-heeled mature crowd in search of an aperitif and a quick bite before the theater. Later on, the young, hip, and trendy arrive as a first stop on their tour of Maastricht's happening nightspots. In the heart of the action, **Ramblassin** (⊠ Bassinkade 6 ☎ 043/326–5474) has trendy sofas, tapas, and a waterside terrace.

DANCE CLUBS  The somewhat utilitarian interior of **De Kadans** (⊠ Kesselskade 62 ☎ 043/321–1937) regularly comes alive during midweek salsa nights and on weekends. It is generally open until 2 AM Sunday–Tuesday, and to 5 AM Wednesday–Saturday. **Night Live** (⊠ Kesselskade 43 ☎ 0900/

202–0158) is extremely popular with those with plenty of energy to burn and attracts performances from top DJs. It is open Wednesday–Saturday, and you can bop 'til you drop from 10 PM to 5 in the morning.

GAY BARS  **La Ferme** (⊠ Rechtstraat 29 ☎ 043/321–8928), with a light show and the latest music, is a vortex of South Netherlands gay life. Near the railway station, and decorated with Dutch Rail flotsam and jetsam, **La Gare** (⊠ Spoorweglaan 6 ☎ 043/325–9090) has a long bar, a tiny dance floor, and chatty customers.

## The Outdoors

### Ballooning

On a late spring or summer evening, you'll often see colorful hot-air balloons floating gently over Maastricht. Providing the ultimate high, they allow a bird's-eye view of the Limburg countryside, including the point where Holland, Germany, and Belgium meet. The **VVV** can arrange trips for you—contact one of its offices for details.

### Beaches

For a spot of beach living away from the sea, you could visit the **Dagstrand Oost-Maarland** (⊠ Oosterweg 5, between Maastricht and Eijsden ☎ 043/409–4441 ⊕ www.dagstrand.nl), on the east bank of a lake just south of Maastricht. You can swim, surf, and canoe, plus there's miniature golf and a beach pavilion with cafés.

### Bicycling

Rent bicycles at **Fietspecialist Aon de Stasie** (⊠ Stationsplein ☎ 043/321–1100), outside the railway station to the right. Town bikes cost €7 per day plus a €50 deposit, while a 21-gear hybrid goes for €9 per day with a deposit of €100. If you plan to do any biking in the surrounding hills, €14.75 per day and €100 deposit will get you a mountain bike—this is a rare occasion in the Netherlands where you might actually need one. You must show ID to rent.

## Shopping

If you're after luxury goods, high-quality gifts, or antiques, Maastricht is the place where you'll find them. Shopping here is a delight, with plenty of distinctive small boutiques to satisfy both window-shoppers and those with money to burn. The larger chain stores are concentrated in the pedestrian cross streets that connect and surround the three main squares of the city. **Maastrichter Brugstraat** takes you into the network of intriguing shopping streets from the Sint Servaasbrug. **Maastrichter Smedenstraat** and **Plankstraat** are lined with exclusive shops, with Wolfstraat and the exceptionally fashionable Stokstraat intersecting both of them. In the other direction, Kleine Staat and Grote Staat lead to **Vrijthof,** with a mixed bag of shopping opportunities. Off Grote Staat is a trio of small shopping streets—Spilstraat, Nieuwestraat, and Muntstraat—that end at the Markt. Off Helmstraat is a shopping square, **W. C. Entre Deux,** which is closed for extensive redevelopment until fall 2006. Late-night shopping is on Thursday.

Maastricht has a tri-country general market in front of the Town Hall on Wednesday and Friday mornings, and there's a flea market opposite the railway station on Saturday. Thursday sees the farmers' market arrive—also on Stationsstraat—where the range of cheese, jams, and honeys are worth exploring.

## Antiques, Prints & Paintings

Each year in March, Maastricht hosts the **European Fine Art Fair** (⌂ European Fine Art Foundation, Broekwal 64, 5268 HD Helvoirt ☎ 0411/645090 ⊕ www.tefaf.com) for 10 days beginning in mid-March. Major dealers and the most famous collectors around for antiques and fine arts from all over Europe have made this *the* international show for top-quality, big-ticket (we're talking $35 million Rembrandts), drop-dead name paintings, and objets d'art. Billionaires and art lovers flock here to see the special treasures saved up for this show in old-master paintings, drawings, and prints; furniture and objects; and textiles, tapestries, and rugs. There are also music programs and lectures.

The fair transforms the city from an easygoing, fine-living, understated kind of place to a magnet for the world's wealthiest, most glamorous art and antiques lovers. It takes place in the unprepossessing **Maastricht Exhibition and Congress Centre (MECC)** (⌂ Forum 100 ☎ 043/383–8383) and has been running annually since 1987. Tickets to the event cost around €45 for two, though the price includes an appropriately glossy catalog. Despite its size (around 200 dealers take part, with visitor numbers passing 66,000), it's an event that has always maintained exceptional standards. This is due to the vetting procedure each antique must undergo before it can be approved for exhibition. For two days before the fair opens, a team of experts examines items to weed out pieces of dubious authenticity.

Of those items that pass the test, the best known and most sought after are probably the old-master paintings of the Renaissance to Baroque eras. Approximately 60% of important 17th-century Dutch and Flemish art on the market at any one time can be found at this event. In recent years, the Maastricht Art Fair has also worked hard to increase its reputation as a hunting ground for 19th- and 20th-century art, with Picassos, Cézannes, and Modiglianis heating up the action. Annual sales are measured in hundreds of millions of dollars, not surprising when you realize that the show draws from the ranks of museum curators to dedicated connoisseurs to moneyed collectors. They know that if it's an early Rembrandt they're after, or perhaps a diamond-and-emerald Cartier necklace, or an 18th-century French drawing room, complete with furniture and walls, this is the place to look. For exact dates, times, and prices of the next event, contact the European Fine Art Fair Foundation.

**Maaslands Antiquariat** (⌂ Stokstraat 20 ☎ 043/325–0510 ⊕ www.maaslands.nl) is a very smart shop with an excellent reputation—and prices to match. It specializes in prints, maps, and books relating to the 17th-century provinces of the Low Countries and also stocks a range of engravings and lithographs dating from later periods. Staff will help you track down exactly what you're looking for.

**Robert Noortman** (⊠ Vrijthof 49  ☎ 043/321–6745  ⊕ www.noortman.
com) is famed as the man who offered a $35.6 million Rembrandt por-
trait of an elderly lady for sale at the Maastricht Art Fair, and his firm has
provided works of art to such venerable institutions as the Rijksmuseum,
the Metropolitan Museum of Art in New York City, and the Tel Aviv Museum. His glorious Vrijthof gallery is in an old mansion whose walls are
bejeweled with great 17th-century Dutch paintings. Who knows what you
might find on a visit here—another Rembrandt, perhaps? (In fact, yes;
Noortman was also the purchaser of a $9 million Rembrandt portrait of
a man—let's hope one of them sells soon for Noortman's sake.) One thing's
for sure, though—anything on sale here certainly won't be going for a song.

## Children

**De Winkel van Nijntje** (⊠ Maastrichter Smedenstraat 2  ☎ 043/326–
0326) delights toddlers of all ages who are fans of Dick Bruna's cheeky
rabbit Miffy (or Nijntje—a diminutive of *konijn*, Dutch for "rabbit"),
who has been making fans the world over since 1955. Here you can find
every kind of Miffy item, from the original Dutch storybooks plus English-language translations to Miffy bubble bath, rucksacks, toys, and
crockery—all emblazoned with images of Bruna's simple, colorful character and her friends.

## Clothes & Fashion Accessories

**Clio** (⊠ Sint Amorsplein 11  ☎ 043/325–0802) seems a world away
from Maastricht's crowds, thanks to its cool, shady interior. On display
are Swiss watches, bold modern jewelry, unisex scents, and leather
handbags in every imaginable shape and color.

**Elle & Lune** (⊠ Sint Amorsplein 8  ☎ 043/321–4969), in a small center-
city square, sells exquisite, elegant lace-trimmed lingerie; La Perla neg-
ligees and nightgowns; and classic swimsuits. Colors range from timeless
black and white to ice-cream pastels.

**Galerie Amarna** (⊠ Stokstraat 9  ☎ 043/326–2429) features one-of-a-kind
women's wear in floaty chiffons, plus quirky hats. The use of color and
pattern is sure to be a talking point back home, and with such lightweight
fabrics, whatever you buy won't take up much room in your suitcase.

## Food & Provisions

**Adriaan** (⊠ Sint Pieterstraat 36  ☎ 043/325–8865) has shelves stacked
with delicious concoctions: ocher-color mustards, ruby-red jams and jel-
lies, mayonnaise, marmalades, and chutneys. You can even see them being
concocted in the back kitchen—irresistible.

**Finbec** (⊠ Stationsstraat 42  ☎ 043/321–2596) is a French/Italian-
influenced deli with a mouthwatering range of cooked meats and homemade salads. You'll also find local Limburg specialties here, including
rabbit with prunes.

**Joosten** (⊠ Wycker Brugstraat 43  ☎ 043/321–4464) is the source where
you can stock up on local white wines and cheeses (and sample the latter before you buy). The waxy white goat cheese is a fine choice, as of
course is the Rommedoe—a richly pungent cheese not often found outside the province of Limburg—and both make perfect picnic fare.

## Gifts & Housewares

**Boutique Elizabeth** (⊠ Sporenstraat 18 ☎ 043/325–5869) allures shoppers with a checkerboard floor, plenty of space, and a fountain gently playing at the back of the store, all of which add character to Elizabeth's furniture and furnishings. The mix here features everything from period cupboards and antique school satchels to modern bridge sets, cushions, and wrought-iron clothes hooks. It's a great place for browsing.

**Frissen Pieters** (⊠ Stokstraat 49 ☎ 043/321–2277) is a gorgeous, light-filled florist where the blooms are of the old-world variety: think languidly drooping roses and sweet-scented stock in chintz colors. Elegant home accessories here include silver wine coolers with leather handles, creamy china, chandeliers, and crystal.

**Gaia** (⊠ Bredestraat 22 ☎ 043/350–0478) offers very chic and very "now" goodies. East meets West in this colorful but cool housewares shop where you'll find crackle-glazed plates, woven throws in jewel tones, candles, and incense holders; the staff is welcoming and enthusiastic, whether you buy or not.

**Gay Jongen** (⊠ Rechtstraat 59 ☎ 043/321–6824) is the place to head for state-of-the-art, exotic accessories and furniture, especially for the bathroom and kitchen. You'll find pared-down china, cutting-edge cutlery, and intriguing accoutrements.

# THE BORDER PROVINCES & MAASTRICHT ESSENTIALS

## Transportation

### BY AIR

There is absolutely no need to take internal flights; the country is simply too small to warrant it. Instead, travel from north to south via train, bus, or car.

CARRIERS  KLM City Hopper operates a service direct from London Heathrow to Eindhoven. An additional service to Eindhoven from the United Kingdom is scheduled by Ryanair from London Stanstead.
**Airlines & Contacts KLM City Hopper** ☎ 020/474-7747 ⊕ www.klm.com. **Ryanair** ⊕ www.ryanair.com.

AIRPORTS  There are airports in Eindhoven and Maastricht. In addition to regular flights to Maastricht from Amsterdam, **KLM City Hopper** (☎ 020/474–7747) operates a service direct from London Heathrow to Eindhoven. **Ryanair** (⊕ www.ryanair.com) connects Eindhoven to London Stanstead, and also to a number of other European destinations. From the Maastricht railway station, Buses 61 (Monday–Saturday) and 51 (Sunday) pass Maastricht Airport. Eindhoven Airport can be reached by Bus No. 401 from the main railway station.
**Eindhoven Airport** ⊠ Luchthavenweg 25, 5657 EA ☎ 040/291-9818 ⊕ www.eindhovenairport.nl. **Maastricht Aachen Airport** ⊠ Vliegveldweg 90, 6199 AD Beek ☎ 043/358-9898 ⊕ www.maa.nl.

## BY BIKE

In this flat land, a bicycle is an ideal means of getting around, and cities have safe cycle lanes on busy roads. Bikes are best rented at outlets near most railway stations, called **Rijwiel** shops. The shops maintain long hours and the bikes are invariably new and well maintained. Rates are €6.50–€8.40, and an ID and deposit of €50 are usually required. Cheaper bikes have back-pedal brakes and no gears, which can unnerve the inexperienced. It's worth paying a little extra for gears and handle-bar brakes. Other local rental centers can be found in the regional *Gouden Gids* (Yellow Pages), under *Fietsen en Bromfietsen* (Bicycles and Mopeds).

## BY BUS

Local and regional buses leave from and return to the Dutch railway stations. The public transportation number and Web site for the entire country is listed below. Operators can also give you information about local bus routes.

**Public transportation number** ☎ 0900/9292 ⊕ www.9292ov.nl.

## BY CAR

To reach Zeeland take E19 from Amsterdam to Rotterdam and pick up A29 south; connect with N59 west to Zierikzee and N256 across the Zeelandbrug bridge to Goes, where you can pick up E312/A58 west to Middelburg, capital of Zeeland province.

To reach the provinces of Brabant and Limburg, take E25/A2 from Amsterdam south through Utrecht. Pick up A27 south to Breda, or stay on E25 through 's-Hertogenbosch to reach Eindhoven and other points south. To travel from Zeeland across to Maastricht, it is far quicker to travel via Antwerp (in Belgium), taking the A4, then the E313 and E314.

**Car Rentals Europcar** ⊠ Maastricht Aachen Airport ☎ 043/361-23100 ⊕ www.europcar.com. **Sixt Autoverhuur** ⊠ Spoorweglaan 18, 6221 BS Maastricht ☎ 043/310-1737 ⊕ www.e-sixt.nl ⊠ Eindhoven Airport ☎ 040/251-1163.

## BY TAXI

If you are not traveling under your own steam, you may want to hire a taxi to get to some of the more distant castles. To summon a taxi, call the number listed below for each respective city.

**Taxi Companies Breda** ☎ 076/561-0504. **Eindhoven** ☎ 040/244-3333. **'s-Hertogenbosch** ☎ 073/631-2900. **Maastricht** ☎ 043/363-3333. **Middelburg** ☎ 0118/612600.

## BY TRAIN

There are frequent Intercity express trains from Amsterdam direct to 's-Hertogenbosch, Eindhoven, Middelburg, or Maastricht. To reach Breda, connect either in Dordrecht or 's-Hertogenbosch. Intercity trains also cross the country, west to east within the border provinces. To get all the way from Middelburg to Maastricht, it is necessary to connect in Roosendaal, Breda, and Eindhoven. Traveling by train between cities is generally fast and efficient.

**Intercity** ☎ 0900/9292 ⊕ www.ns.nl.

## Contacts & Resources

### EMERGENCIES

🔳 **National Emergency Alarm Number** ☎ 112 for police, fire, and ambulance.
🔳 Hospitals **Breda** ☎ 076/595-1000. **Eindhoven** ☎ 040/239-9111. **'s-Hertogenbosch** ☎ 073/699-2000. **Maastricht** ☎ 043/387-6543. **Middelburg** ☎ 0118/425000.

### TOURS

The Maastricht Tourist Office offers a 1- to 1½-hour guided tour of the city for €3.75. Tours of Zeeland are available through Touringcarbedrijf Van Fraassen.

🔳 Fees & Schedules **Maastricht Tourist Office** ✉ Kleine Staat 1 ☎ 043/325-2121. **Touringcarbedrijf Van Fraassen** ✉ President Rooseveltlaan 768, Vlissingen ☎ 0118/419220.

BOAT TOURS For cruises on the Maas River, contact Rederij Stiphout. Fares start at €5.75.

🔳 Fees & Schedules **Rederij Stiphout** ✉ Maaspromenade 58, 6211 JW Maastricht ☎ 043/351-5300 ⊕ www.stiphout.nl.

WALKING TOURS The Middelburg Tourist Office offers guided walking tours (1½ hours, April–September, Saturday–Thursday) for €4.50 per person.

🔳 Fees & Schedules **Middelburg Tourist Office** ✉ Markt 65a ☎ 0118/659900.

### VISITOR INFORMATION

🔳 Tourist Information To access the Web sites for each town and city listed below, log on to www.vvv(town name).nl, except where stated below.

**VVV Breda** ✉ Willemstraat 17-19 ✉ Grote Markt 38 ☎ 0900/522-2444. **VVV Eindhoven** ✉ Stationsplein 17 ☎ 0900/112-2363. **VVV Heerlen** ✉ Oranje Nassaustraat 16 ☎ 0900/9798 ⊕ www.vvvzuidlimburg.nl. **VVV 's-Hertogenbosch** ✉ Markt 77 ☎ 0900/112-2334 ⊕ www.vvvs-hertogenbosch.nl. **VVV Heusden** ✉ Hoogstraat 4 ☎ 0416/662100. **VVV Maastricht** ✉ Kleine Staat 1 ☎ 043/325-2121 🖷 043/321-3746. **Tourist Shop Middelburg** ✉ Markt 65c ☎ 0118/674300 ⊕ www.touristshop.nl. **VVV Tilburg** ✉ Spoorlaan 364 ☎ 0900/202-0815. **VVV Veere** ✉ Oudestraat 28 ☎ 0118/501365 ⊕ www.zeeland.nl. **VVV Vlissingen** ✉ Oude Markt 3 ☎ 0118/422190 ⊕ www.zeeland.nl. **VVV Yerseke** ✉ Kerkplein 1 ☎ 0113/574374 ⊕ www.zeeland.nl. **VVV Zierikzee** ✉ Nieuw Haven 7 ☎ 0900/202-0233 ⊕ www.zeeland.nl.

# The Green Heart

5

## WORD OF MOUTH

"The Kröller-Müller museum is mind-blowing. You cannot believe how many Van Goghs there are, right next to Picassos, Monets, etc., and all in a beautiful nature park. Bicycles [are free] on site."
—Peter

"Oh, you must visit Giethoorn! It's a lovely little village with canals instead of streets. Take the train to Meppel and a taxi the 5 or so miles to Giethoorn."

—valerie russo

By Shirley J. S.
Agudo

**LIKE A MYSTERY PACKAGE THAT REVEALS A SERIES** of ever-smaller, ever-more-intriguing boxes, the wooded heart of the Netherlands is an unfolding treasure, its great national park acting as the wrappings. The provinces of Overijssel and Gelderland, and the Green Heart's adopted daughter, Amersfoort—too green and medieval not to include here—are a minestrone of spices in this garden soup of a region. Start with the woodlands, dunes, and heath of the Veluwe core with its national parks and palaces, plus a priceless art museum buried deep in the forest. Blend in towns steeped in a strong brew of history, ranging from Staphorst with its customs reminiscent of the Amish, to the Hanseatic cluster of former market towns. Garnish with the punter's paradise of Giethoorn, complete with its Venetian playground of canals providing the only means of transport through a village of thatch-roof cottages; Zutphen's famous medieval library (where the books are still chained to their ancient lecterns); the "Operation Market Garden" spot where the famous World War II Battle of Arnhem took place; and the seemingly misplaced Charles Dickens museum in teeny-tiny Bronkhorst—the smallest official town in the Netherlands, a mere whisper of cobbled streets in a china-cup brim.

To better understand this area's recipe for success, remember that 700 years before the advent of the European Common Market or the European Union, there was an association of northern European trading cities called the Hanseatic League. It began as a pact among itinerant merchants to travel together for mutual safety, but in time it became an alliance of more than 150 towns and cities scattered over the Continent. Among the important members of that league were the Dutch cities of Zwolle, Kampen, Deventer, and Zutphen along the River IJssel. Their beat lives on in the well-endowed mansions, churches, and monuments from that period, historic reminders of a bygone period of wealth and prosperity.

## Exploring the Green Heart

Although the Ranstad may be the pulse of Holland, the Green Heart, in all its throbbing glory, is the impulsive, natural beauty. Only a deep breath away, it lures you with open spaces and open arms. Heathland, forests, wetland farms, a sprawling national park, and a royal garden akin to that of Versailles make this a perfect area in which to let your hair down. The Rivers IJssel and Rhine wend their way through towns where castles and medieval market squares mark time in a slower beat than in the more heavily populated west, the rhythm of life here being hushed, undulating, and restorative.

Gelderland, the largest province and central core of Holland, lies southwest of its fraternal twin, the province of Overijssel, and is home to the combined splendor of the Hoge Veluwe National Park and the Royal Forest, a dazzling oasis of peace carved by a regal preference for this area. Although biking and hiking are popular all over the Green Heart, the Hoge Veluwe is particularly suited for such excursions and appeals to the outdoorsman in everyone. Farther east, arranged in an arc that stretches from north to south, is Overijssel and its historic Hanseatic towns and Arnhem, scene of the famous World War II battle of September 1944.

**5**

Poised center stage, the Green Heart, with its distinctive topography, beats to an altogether different drummer from the rest of the motherland. Here one finds a visible concerto of forests primeval, heaths and moors with a Roman bearing, a medieval second act, and a contemporary cadence. Harmoniously, it blends Hanseatic strains, war-torn turbulence, and princely pursuits into a melody where the past is made accessible. With leading lures such as Holland's greatest park reserve, De Hoge Veluwe—home to the Kröller-Müller Museum's Van Goghs—Apeldoorn's magisterial Het Loo Palace, and the medieval enclave of Amersfoort, it's little wonder you'll fall in love with this region, heart and soul.

Roughly an hour or so from Amsterdam, the provinces of Gelderland and Overijssel lend themselves perfectly to exploration starting out from that city. If quieter surroundings suit you better, consider making Amersfoort your base. It is central to the entire country. You can combine a Hanseatic tour with a wilderness expedition through the Hoge Veluwe, with stops at various points of interest along the perimeter.

*Numbers in the text correspond to numbers in the margin and on the Amersfoort and The Green Heart maps.*

**If you have 3 days**

Short escapes should include a visit to **Otterlo/De Hoge Veluwe National Park** ⑲ ➤ and its Kröller-Müller Museum—a private ode to Dutch painter Vincent van Gogh and friends in a spectacular setting in the forest—which can easily fill an entire day, especially if you include time for a brief bike excursion on one of their 1,000 white bikes. Allow another day to explore at least one of the Hanseatic towns—such as **Zutphen** ⑳, **Zwolle** ⑬, **Kampen** ⑯, **Deventer** ⑰, or **Nijmegen** ㉓—and another day to visit the palace of Het Loo in **Apeldoorn** ⑱, a royal retreat in the Royal Forest. Or, if war history intrigues you, venture to **Arnhem** ㉒, where one of the most famous battles of World War II took place.

**If you have 5 days**

After hitting the highlights of the three-day itinerary, allow time to visit one or more of the other Hanseatic towns—such as **Kampen** ⑯, **Zwolle** ⑬, **Deventer** ⑰, **Zutphen** ⑳, or **Nijmegen** ㉓—and then choose one of the smaller villages: **Bronkhorst** ㉑, the smallest town in the country and a self-contained national monument piping with local artisans; **Giethoorn** ⑮, the "Venice of the North," where the mode of transport is via canals instead of streets; or **Staphorst** ⑭, a time warp of a village where some locals still wear traditional costume. Alternatively, you may wish to spend time in **Amersfoort** ①– ⑫, a medieval enclave and one of our favorite picks, either en route to or returning from the other destinations, as it is the closest to an Amsterdam base.

## About the Restaurants & Hotels

Fortunately, those traveling to the Green Heart will appreciate the somewhat braver cuisine than is typically to be found throughout the quieter areas of Holland. Whereas Dutch cooking seems to inspire only the Dutch themselves, "the national menu," if you will, whereby each restaurant seems to have the same basic choices, can begin to bore even the most tolerant tourist. The Green Heart, however, seems to offer more gusto with at least a selection of local wild game on the menu. If you do prefer simple fare, the cafés or *eetcafés* ("eating cafés") as they were, offer a step up from the snack bars one finds on many corners, with French-bread (*stokbrood*) sandwiches at lunchtime and reasonably priced, standard but hearty meals in the evenings. Hours are in keeping with general guidelines across Holland that dictate early-evening meals hovering around 6 PM in marked contrast to the significantly later dinner hours of their European neighbors.

From moat-fronted castles to campsites, from city mansions to country inns to woodland cottages, the Green Heart has something to suit every whim and budget. Camping is popular, particularly in and around the Hoge Veluwe National Park, and the local VVV information offices can provide you with an endless list of choices. Rather than staying in a town, you might opt for one of the village hotels—some are simple, others have a country-house atmosphere, but many have a special charm and relaxing sense of isolation. Mostrooms do not have air-conditioning, but you can normally count on TV and telephones unless otherwise noted.

| | **WHAT IT COSTS** In euros | | | | |
|---|---|---|---|---|---|
| | **$$$$** | **$$$** | **$$** | **$** | **¢** |
| RESTAURANTS | over €30 | €22–€30 | €15–€22 | €10–€15 | under €10 |
| HOTELS | over €230 | €165–€230 | €120–€165 | €75–€120 | under €75 |

Restaurant prices are per person for a main course only, excluding tax (6% for food and 19% for alcoholic beverages) and service; note that if a restaurant offers only prix-fixe meals, it has been given the price category that reflects the full prix-fixe price. Hotel prices are for a standard double room in high season, including the 6% VAT.

### Timing

Fall is an ideal time to visit this region, because not only do the restaurants offer all sorts of delicious game dishes, but the scenery of the Hoge Veluwe is spectacular at this time. Stretches of the park were especially planted with trees that make a brilliant mosaic of gold, crimson, and orange in autumn. Summer and spring are equally good times to visit, but Gelderland is an extremely popular vacation area among the Dutch themselves so expect lots of company if you tour during the peak months of July and August. In spring, cherry, apple, and pear trees are at their peak and May is a fine time to visit the Dutch Open Air Museum at Arnhem. Winter can be a bit dreary, but you will at least have all the dreariness to yourself.

# AMERSFOORT: GATEWAY FROM UTRECHT

Fodor'sChoice Get thee to Amersfoort, a medieval town pulsing with Middle Ages blood
★ in the western artery surrounding the Green Heart. Officially part of the province of Utrecht, Amersfoort begs to cross the line, like a knight in shining armor with dual loyalties. Poised for battle with its fortress

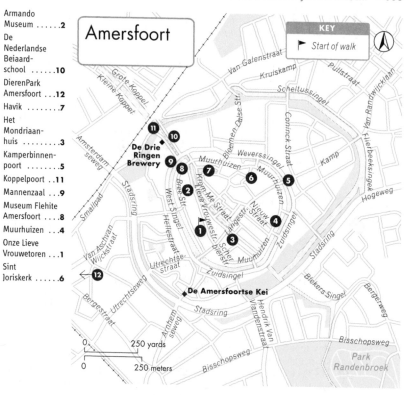

gates and double-ringed canal—the only such vein in all of Europe—it is a highly walkable town with winding, cobblestone streets, parts of which are closed to traffic, where you can almost hear the clack of hooves of jousting horses.

Before you set out to explore the town—about 50 km (32 mi) from Amsterdam—be sure to pick up a copy of the VVV information office's indispensable walking guide "City Walk through Amersfoort" (€2.75) in both Dutch and English, featuring Piet Mondriaan's birthplace; Amersfoort's famous carillon school; unique wallhouses (built into and out of the old city wall); a dashing museum chiseled out of the medieval foundation, with a nearby 14th-century hospice where history literally comes alive each summer; a modern art museum housed in a church where homage is paid to a living artist; and the local brewery.

▶ ❶ Salvaged by someone's grace, the most prominent tower in Amersfoort, **Onze Lieve Vrouwetoren** (Tower of Our Lady), is a 328-foot masterpiece thrusting against the sky; the once-adjoined church blew up in 1787 during its days as an ammunition depot when sparks from a soldier's knife ignited its contents. Seventeen people were killed, but the tower, which marks the exact epicenter of the Netherlands, remained intact. ⊠ *Lieve*

*Vrouwekerkhof ☉ July and Aug., Tues.–Sun. 10–6, weekends noon–5; or by special appointment through the VVV.*

❷ Fast-forward to a living Dutch modern artist who, rare enough, already has a museum in his honor, the **Armando Museum**, which, even rarer, is housed in an early-19th-century Neoclassical church, **De Elleboogkerk.** Known for his diverse talents as a painter, sculptor, writer, film and theater director, and violinist, Armando (born in 1929), as he is simply known, draws upon the war years he spent growing up near the Amersfoort internment camp as the basis for much of his work. There is a free guided tour every third Sunday of each month at 2:30 with entrance ticket. ⊠ *Langegracht 36, 3800 AR* ☎ *033/461–4088* 💶 *€3.50* ☉ *Tues.–Fri. 11–5, weekends noon–5.*

**need a break?**

If the time of day is right (open Thursday–Saturday 1–7) and you're hankering for a beer, why not go to the source—directly across from the De Nederlandse Beiaardschool (Dutch Carilloneur's School) is **De Drie Ringen brewery** (The Three Rings; ⊠ Kleine Spui 18 ☎ 033/465–6575), a little spout of a place where you can freely sample the wares, the most popular of which is the Blond beer, one of six types produced here. At the **Stadscafé** (⊠ Stadhuisplein 7 ☎ 033/469–5718), a well-lighted restaurant-cum-gallery, salads and pastas are tossed up with a sprinkling of jazz, classical, or Motown music. It's open only on weekdays for breakfast and lunch.

❸ Pity that they have no originals (which are mostly in the Gemeentemuseum in The Hague), but the birthplace of Dutch artist Piet Mondriaan (1872–1944), **Het Mondriaanhuis,** now a museum about his life and work with an exact replica of his famed studio in Paris, is worth seeing if you're intrigued by his cubist/Neo-Plasticist work. There is a gift and coffee shop on-site. ⊠ *Kortegracht 11, 3811 KG* ☎ *033/462–0180* 💶 *€3* ☉ *Tues.–Fri. 10–5, weekends 1–5.*

❹ Unique to Amersfoort are the **Muurhuizen** (wallhouses), some of medieval origin, built along the foundation of the original inner-city wall and, indeed, from its very rubble, as the wall itself was demolished in the 15th century for outward expansion of the town. Walk around the entire perimeter until you reach **Tinnenburg** at No. 25, a former merchant's house and cotton-spinning site mentioned in a 1414 document, where you can see in the masonry how the house was attached to the fortress gate. (Take a discreet peek at another old merchant's mansion across the canal at Zuidsingel 38; built around 1780, this "house with the purple windows" once served as the temporary residence of William V and his wife, Wilhelmina, of Prussia and is now, strangely enough, the domain of seven fortunate nuns, who dislike gawkers.)

❺ Heralding you to enter, the **Kamperbinnenpoort,** the last remaining part of the ancient inner-city wall, leads to the 21st-century version of former market stalls—a thoroughfare of modern-day shops sentried along Langestraat and its side street, Krommestraat, and farther on to the Varkensmarkt (Pig Market) and Utrechtsestraat. Late-night shopping is on Thursday evening until 9.

**6** Dating from the 12th century, **Sint Joriskerk** (St. George's Church) and its immediate environs take center stage in the oldest inhabited area of Amersfoort. The chapel was altered and expanded over the centuries until it achieved its current form, a three-hall church, in the 16th century. Besides religious services, there are concerts and living-history enactments here, as well. The hof or courtyard surrounding the church offers its own concerto of sorts as it resonates with the sounds of summer from the outdoor cafés, festival music, street performers, and a market humming with activity on Friday mornings and Saturday year-round. Completing the score, the chimes on the adjacent 16th-century weigh house play on the hour and the wooden doors below eject a mechanized St. George slaying the dragon, a constant reminder of days of yore.

**7** The **Havik,** a charming old merchant-and-artisan area, was Amersfoort's original harbor until the Koppelpoort replaced it. The former **Beer Brewers' Guild** at No. 35 looks strikingly like the redbrick gabled house in Dutch artist Johannes Vermeer's street scene that he painted in Delft. The narrow house at No. 33 was once a passageway to the hof, the administrative center of this crossroads.

**8** Couched canal-side in three splendidly gabled Muurhuizen, or wallhouses (circa 1500), is the **Museum Flehite Amersfoort** of local artifacts and art relating to the history of the region, including a medieval prison door; a beam and post from which people were hanged during the Middle Ages and on up to the end of the 18th century; and the Vanitas painting by Matthias Withoos (1627–1703). ⊠ *Westsingel 50, 3811 BC* ☎ *033/461– 9987* ⊕ *www.museumflehite.nl* 🖾 *€5* ☉ *Tues.–Fri. 11–5, weekends 1–5.*

**9** Part of the **Museum Flehite Amersfoort,** and located across the street, is the men's ward, or **Mannenzaal,** of the **St. Pieters en Bloklandsgasthuis** (Hospice), originally established in the 14th century and in use until the beginning of the 20th century, and containing no fewer than 22 cupboard beds or *bedsteden* where otherwise homeless men slept, two in a bed, until 1838. Adjacent to the chapel, this ward, which appears as it did from the 16th century until 1907, is the scene for a dramatic living-history forum in July and August whereby local volunteers reenact life in the ward as if they were back in the early 1900s. Pose any question and they will respond as if they were in that time frame, making for an ear- and eye-opening experience for young and old. ⊠ *Westsingel 47, 3811 BC* ☎ *033/472–0669* 🖾 *Free with admission to Flehite Museum* ☉ *Tues.–Fri. 11–1 and 2–4:30, weekends 1–4:30.*

If you've been hearing bells, you're not imagining things, as the **Tower of Our Lady** is home to not one but two carillons and seven swinging bells, 100 bells in total, whose glorious tones resound every 15 minutes and *al concerto virtuoso* (Thursday 8 PM–9 PM, Friday 10 AM–11 AM, and Saturday 1–2 and 4–5 PM). Take a seat in an outdoor café and be **10** swept away by concerts of students from the world-famous **De Nederlandse Beiaardschool** (Dutch Carilloneurs' School), one of only two in the world devoted to the art of the carillon. ⊠ *Grote Spui 11, 3811 GA* ☎ *033/475–2638, 0900/112–2364 tours* ⊕ *www.hku.nl* ☉ *Tours by appointment through VVV Amersfoort.*

⓫ The **Koppelpoort** is uniquely both a land and water gate predating 1427. Part of the outer defensive wall, the north side of the port retains its wooden annex where boiling tar and oil were dropped on the heads of would-be intruders. Guards stationed above on precarious platforms would raise a flag to alert the guard on the Onze Lieve Vrouwetoren, who in turn raised a flag to alert the other ports surrounding the city. Amersfoort was thus protected. If you want to see the two tread wheels inside, you can arrange a tour through the VVV.

⓬ Every kid's dream zoo come true, the **DierenPark Amersfoort** (Animal Park) features an ancient village and the chance to come face to face with lions, tigers, and bears. ⊠ *Barchman Wuytierslaan 224, 3819 AC* ☏ *033/422–7100* ⊕ *www.amersfoort-zoo.nl* ▱ *€15.50* ☉ *Apr.–Oct., daily 9–6.*

## Where to Stay & Eat

¢–$$$ ✕ **San Giorgio.** An Italian restaurant in a 14th-century abbey ... that'za San Giorgio, pure heaven on earth. Blend in some arias sung by live singers (Monday only, October–April, reservations essential) and presto, you have their special "Mangia alla Classica," offered at a fixed-price menu (€42.50). ⊠ *Krommestraat 44* ☏ *033/461–5685* ▭ *AE, DC, MC, V* ☉ *No lunch.*

★ $$ ✕ **Eethuis Bij de Stadsmuur.** Aptly named, this "Eatery by the City Wall" is indeed near remnants of the old city wall, in a building dating from 1485. The cuisine may be French, but the Delft chandeliers keep you mindful of where you are. The food is so good, and the creamy yellow dining room so restful that you may be reluctant to go anywhere else the following night. The service is impeccable and personable. ⊠ *Kamp 88* ☏ *033/475–6096* ⊕ *www.eethuisbijdestadsmuur.nl* ▭ *MC, V* ☉ *Closed Mon. and Tues., plus last wk of July, first 2 wks of Aug., and 1 wk in Feb. No lunch.*

$–$$ ✕ **Bistro in den Vollen Pot.** Just follow your nose and the unmissable Tower of Our Lady to this very popular bistro with "a full pot" of Dutch/French food, a truly *gezellig* (cozy) place. ⊠ *Lieve Vrouwekerkhof 8–10* ☏ *033/463–2329* ⊕ *www.bistroindenvollenpot.nl* ▱ *Reservations essential* ▭ *AE, DC, MC, V.*

$–$$ ✕ **Far East.** This spot offers Asian cooking at its best, with a mouthwatering menu spotlighting China's many provinces with dishes that are often a feast for the eyes. ⊠ *Kamp 74* ☏ *033/472–5021* ▭ *AE, DC, MC, V* ☉ *Closed Tues. No lunch.*

$–$$ ✕ **Mama Roux.** In a picture-window-perfect location overlooking the hof marketplace, this is a great place to have lunch during bustling market days. Mama makes a great house salad with cheese and nuts, and the best cappuccino in town, served with *Koffie Kaatje* ("Coffee Kate")— a glass of coffee liqueur with a dollop of cream. ⊠ *Hof 9* ☏ *033/462–0023* ▭ *No credit cards* ☉ *Closed Mon.*

$–$$ ▥ **Golden Tulip Berghotel Amersfoort.** Perched atop Amersfoort's highest point, this hotel—only a 15-minute walk from the station, a 20-minute walk to the center of town, and a 5-minute drive to the local zoo—previously catered to the rich and famous of Holland as a deluxe hotel that not only accommodated VIPs, but came complete with a stable for their horses as well. Today it caters to you with its indoor pool, solarium,

# ON THE MENU IN THE GREEN HEART

**WITH THE ROYAL GAME RESERVE** *in the north and the fruit- and vegetable-growing region to the east, the restaurants of the Green Heart are well supplied with abundant, high-quality ingredients from their own backyard. Although the main game season is fall, clever restaurateurs manage to find something for almost every month; some even go hunting themselves. Braised hare is a specialty, and the local boar and venison are delicious, as is the pheasant. Sampling local game is a must,* *whether prepared as a family-style stew in a simple restaurant or as the culinary creation of one of the area's top chefs. Top it off with the wintertime pleasures of Glüwein, a hot-mulled wine that has made inroads from neighboring Germany, and a thick, hearty bowl of unmistakably Dutch pea soup (erwtensoep), and you'll be ready for your own hunt.*

and free sauna, and all the in-room amenities you expect, even if you show up saddleless. ⊠ *Utrechtseweg 225, 3818 EG* ☎ *033/422–4222* 🖷 *033/465–0505* ⊕ *www.berghotel.nl* 🛏 *85 rooms, 5 suites* ♨ *Restaurant, room service, minibars, cable TV with movies and video games, Wi-Fi, indoor pool, sauna, bicycles, 2 bars, lounge, dry cleaning, laundry service, business services, convention center, meeting rooms, free parking, no-smoking floors* 🚾 *AE, DC, MC, V.*

★ **$–$$** 🏨 **Logies de Tabaksplant.** By far the best value and the best location for exploring Amersfoort is Mieke and Theo's bed-and-breakfast, one of 350 declared monuments in town, built between 1600 and 1650 by a rich tobacco grower (and hence the name, "Tobacco Plant Lodging"). A breath away from the Kamperbinnenpoort gate and the heart of the shopping area, this completely modernized facility offers in-room coffee/tea-making facilities, high-tech refrigerators, and a choice of rooms with or without bathrooms and kitchens. Room No. 21 sports a Jacuzzi and breakfast in bed for the recently married or discriminating duo. Don't hesitate on this one too long; it books up quickly. ⊠ *Coninckstraat 15, 3811 WD* ☎ *033/472–9797* 🖷 *033/470–0756* ⊕ *www.tabaksplant.nl* 🛏 *24 rooms, 21 with bath; 5 apartments* ♨ *Some kitchenettes, minibars, cable TV, in-room data ports, Wi-Fi, bar, business services, meeting rooms, no-smoking rooms, some pets allowed* 🚾 *MC, V* 🍴 *CP.*

¢–$$ 🏨 **Tulip Inn Amersfoort.** In a beautiful wooded area just a 10-minute bike ride from the old city center and a 5-minute drive from the local zoo, this one-level hotel is part of a chain of well-respected inns throughout the country. ⊠ *Stichtse Rotonde 11, 3818 GV* ☎ *033/462–0054* 🖷 *033/461–9281* ⊕ *www.tiamersfoort.nl* 🛏 *93 rooms, 1 suite* ♨ *Restaurant, some in-room safes, cable TV with movies, Wi-Fi, bicycles, bar, lobby lounge, shop, dry cleaning, laundry service, business services, meeting rooms, free parking, some pets allowed, no-smoking rooms; no a/c in some rooms* 🚾 *AE, DC, MC, V* 🍴 *BP.*

**$** ⛉ **Logement de Gaaper.** A fitting remedy for weary travelers, this former pharmacy from the 1860s is now a renovated hotel with original beams and elements from what happens to be the oldest brick house in Amersfoort, dating from 1250. Easy to spot on the main hof marketplace, the hotel is landmarked by its wooden model of De Gaaper's (literally, "the gaper's") Head, a traditional symbol of a pharmacy. ⊠ *Hof 39, 3811 CK* ☎ *033/453–1795* 🖶 *033/453–1796* ⊕ *www.degaaper.nl* 🛏 *18 rooms* ⚘ *Café, minibars, cable TV, in-room broadband, bar, dry cleaning, laundry service; no a/c in some rooms, no smoking* ▤ *MC, V* ⫶⊙⫶ *CP.*

### Nightlife & the Arts

**Het Filmhuis** (The Filmhouse; ⊠ Groenmarkt 8 ☎ 033/465–5550) is a hip, casual place in grand café style, with light music on Sunday in winter and a band outside in the square every Saturday in summer. A popular option is **In den Grooten Slock** (⊠ Zevenhuizen 1 ☎ 033/461–3239), with original fittings and furnishings. The 1930s-style, one and only jazz café in town, **Lazy Louis Jazz Café** (⊠ Arnhemsestraat 1–3 ☎ 033/461–3638) serves lunch and dinner. Have a convivial dram and a game of billiards in one of the oldest bars in Amersfoort, **Onder de Linde** (Under the Linden Tree; ⊠ Appelmarkt 16 ☎ 033/461–4203), a 1530 building with a bar established under that name since 1775.

### The Outdoors

**Eemlijn** (⊕ www.eemlijn.nl) offers boat trips on the Eem River;e you can hop on or off with or without your bike. The boat alights on the Kleine Koppel between Brabantsestraat and Geldersestraat and takes about eight hours for the round-trip. For a shorter experience hop off in Soest, Baarn, Eemdijk, or Spakenburg, and return by bike. There is no service from November to April. Contact the VVV office (☎ 033/463–2804) for details. In July and August, 45-minute canal-boat rides with narration are conducted by **Waterlijn** (⊕ www.amersfoort-rondvaarten.nl) at Krommestraat 5.

# OVERIJSSEL PROVINCE

The garden party of the Netherlands, the province of Overijssel or "the land beyond the IJssel" River is a backyard scene set with a centerpiece of parks, nature reserves, forests, wetlands, and more rolling terrain than its northern and western neighbors. Imposing castles and historic towns hark back to medieval days in this realm, where the ancient tradition of storytelling lives on. From peat to punters, it's home turf to a diverse slice of Dutch culture and hospitality, with everything from Hanseatic towns to a Dutch version of Venice and a microculture that appears frozen in a time warp.

## Zwolle

**⓭** *41 km (26 mi) north of Apeldoorn, 87 km (54 mi) east of Amsterdam, 68 km (43 mi) northeast of Amersfoort.*

Seen from the air, Zwolle, founded in 800 and the provincial capital of the province of Overijssel, is really a star-shape island surrounded

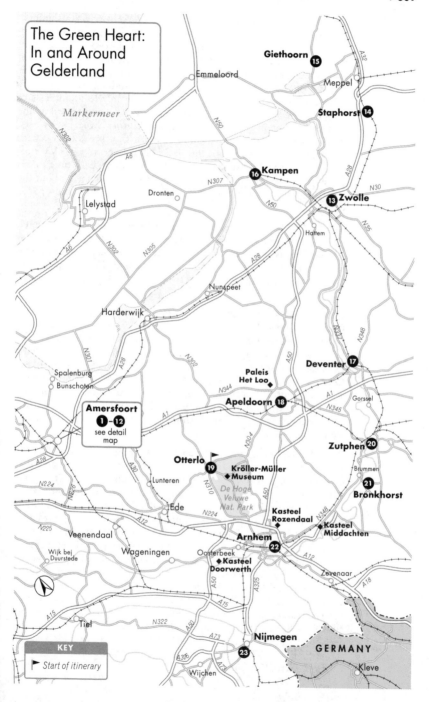

The Green Heart:
In and Around
Gelderland

**KEY**
► *Start of itinerary*

by a ring of canals flanked by the IJssel and Vecht rivers, a shiningly strategic location for an important depot of trade between the Netherlands and Germany during the time of the Hanseatic League. Religious philosopher Thomas à Kempis lived here in the early 1400s when he wrote his influential work *Imitation of Christ*, and Dutch painter Gerard Terborch (1617–81) was born here. Today it is a university town flickering with nightlife, and home not only to an impressive museum housed in a city mansion but to what many regard as the best restaurant in the Netherlands, *De Librije*. Sweet on sweets, Zwolle is also known for its candies and for shortbread fingers with chocolate tips (*blauwvingers*. translated "blue fingers.") The VVV office's "Town Walk" brochure in English, for those with time to explore, provides a great route for seeing Zwolle. Ask them about the wooden shoe (*klompen*) canoes for hire as well—great photo-ops for your album.

Confined within the towers of the castlelike **Sassenpoort** (Saxon gate), for centuries a prison and the only one of the original town gates of 1406 left standing, is an exhibit of Zwolle's deep-rooted history. The cannon in front dates from around 1580, and a chiming clock completes the fantasy. ⊠ *Sassenstraat* ☎ *038/421–6626* 🎫 *€0.45* ⊗ *Fri. 2–5, weekends noon–5.*

The **Grote Kerkplein** is the main square of Zwolle and the site of the Gothic **Stadhuis** (Town Hall). There is also a charming shop, **Zwollse Balletjes Huis** (⊠ Grote Kerkplein 13 ☎ 038/421–8815) that sells the local sweet specialty, *Zwollse balletjes* (fruit-and-spice-flavor hard candies in the shape of little cushions). The Gothic **Sint Michaelskerk** (St. Michael's Church), which dates from 1370 to 1446 and contains a magnificent 18th-century organ with 4,000 pipes, made by the Schnitger brothers from Hamburg, is the final resting place of the 17th-century genre painter Gerard Terborch, Zwolle's native son. ⊠ *Grote Kerkplein.*

Pause before you go inside the **Stedelijk Museum Zwolle** (Zwolle Municipal Museum) to note the imposing 16th-century city mansion next to the contemporary museum entrance, for this is, in fact, the main reason for being here. It *is*, indeed, the crux of the museum, a remarkable period house with a wainscoted living/dining room featuring works of art by Hendrick Avercamp and Zwolle natives Gerard Terborch and Hendrick Ten Oever, and every nostalgic woman's dream kitchen complete with floor-to-ceiling tiles, scullery, linen press—and the imaginary chief cook and bottle washer, all exemplifying the lifestyle of the prosperous family once resident here. Changing exhibits on three floors of the modern side of the museum are accessible by way of a central glass staircase and fire escape–like stairs on the last, rather hidden, stretch. (Hints: Be sure to go all the way up to Rooms 8–11 of the mansion, and later, to step outside via the coffee shop to see the Vermeerian back of the mansion.) ⊠ *Melkmarkt 41, 8001 BC* ☎ *038/421–4650* ⊕ *www.museum.zwolle.nl* 🎫 *€3.50* ⊗ *Tues.–Sat. 10–5, Sun. 1–5.*

**off the beaten path**

**ANTON PIECK MUSEUM** – About 6 km (4 mi) southwest of Zwolle, like a chocolate box begging to be opened, the Pieck Museum is your chance for an intimate glimpse of the work of one of the more famed early-20th-century illustrators of Grimm's fairy tales. A delectable courtyard entrance lets you enter a miniworld of 17th-century houses, adorned with requisite windmill, gift shop, and rooms filled with vintage editions and the artist's creations. From Zwolle, take a train taxi or bus (No. 90) to Hattem-Centrum. ✉ *Achterstraat 46–48, Hattem* ☎ *038/444–2192* ⊕ *www.antonpieckmuseum-hattem.nl* ☒ *€4.75* ☉ *May–Nov., Mon.–Sat. 10–5; July and Aug. also open Sun. 1–5; Dec.–Apr., Tues.–Sat. 10–5.*

## Where to Stay & Eat

**$$$–$$$$**
**Fodor'sChoice**
★

✕ **De Librije.** Housed in the stunning, beamed former library of a 15th-century monastery, owner-chef Jonnie Boer's restaurant is lined with accolades, searing his reputation as one of the country's best chefs, if not Holland's crème de la crème. With creativity extraordinaire, he has mastered what he calls "Cuisine Pure," based on fresh, locally produced ingredients such as nettles, water mint, wild mushrooms, and even cattails (the plant version), and all manner of local fish from in and around his native Giethoorn, about which he's written a delightful cookbook, *Purer.* One signature dish is the sublime *polderduif,* wild pigeon from the surrounding water lands, served with a sauce of local berries. Regular De Librije followers insist on the pike perch with apple syrup and Riesling wine sauce, the scallops with vanilla, Giethoorn lamb, duck liver lollies (yes, duck liver on a stick), and turbot with Jabugo ham, although we'd defy you to find anything blasé on Jonnie's menu, right down to the homemade lavender mayonnaise. Cross your fingers that his crepe soufflé with preserved Gieten blueberries in brandy and sautéed apple—his mother's own recipe— is on the menu. ✉ *Broerenkerkplein 13* ☎ *038/421–2083* ⊕ *www.delibrije. nl* ⌖ *Reservations essential* ☰ *AE, DC, MC, V* ☉ *Closed Sun. and Mon., 3 wks in summer, and 2 wks at Christmas. No lunch Tues. or Sat.*

**$$–$$$**

✕ **Restaurant Poppe.** Any restaurant daring enough to have the kitchen greet you as you enter through former blacksmith stalls and wind up being classy to boot is a spot with confident panache. Sidestepping the atmosphere, the food is a full dressage of everything from duck liver pâté with grapes and figs to ostrich. You'll feel like you're riding high at this showstopper. ✉ *Luttekestraat 66* ☎ *038/421–3050* ⊕ *www.restaurant-poppe.nl* ⌖ *Reservations essential* ☰ *AE, DC, MC, V.*

**★ ¢**

✕ **Tapas Bar La Bodega.** More than a place to drink, this authentically Spanish bar with a chef who hails from San Sebastian is a great place to dabble in those savory treats called tapas. Specialties include *calamares* (squid), *gambas a la plancha* (grilled shrimp), tortilla *española* (potato and egg omelet), *salpicón de mariscos* (seafood salad), paella (the Spanish national dish of rice, chicken, and seafood), Manchego cheese, and chocolate *con churros* (hot chocolate with long sugar doughnuts). Can't decide? Go for the combo plate with eight different hot and cold tapas. The Spanish mainland is further represented by fine sherries, wines, and music. ✉ *Bethlehemskerkplein 36* ☎ *038/422–9139* ⊕ *www. tapasbarlabodega.nl* ☰ *No credit cards* ☉ *No lunch.*

$$-$$$    ☒ **Bilderberg Grand Hotel Wientjes.** The grande dame of Zwolle where every whim is catered to, this stately former mayor's residence is convenient to both the train station and the city center and exudes modern comfort. Among special features are bike rentals with a picnic hamper provided by the chef. Champagne is served with breakfast. ☒ *Stationsweg 7, 8011 CZ* ☎ *038/425–4254* 🖷 *038/425–4260* ⊕ *www.bilderberg. nl* ↰ *57 rooms, 2 suites* ⚭ *Restaurant, café, room service, in-room safes, minibars, cable TV, Wi-Fi, bicycles, bar, lobby lounge, babysitting, dry cleaning, laundry service, business services, meeting rooms, parking (fee), some pets allowed, no-smoking floor* ▭ *AE, DC, MC, V* ⦿| *BP.*

## Nightlife

As a university town, Zwolle offers a variety of heady nightlife. **Café Roots** (☒ Grote Markt 13b ☎ 038/421–6318) is a basement dance venue with American overtones and a surprise theme party every Friday night. A favorite for party animals is **De Bommel Café** (☒ Jufferenwal 19b ☎ 038/421–1759), where dancing has even been spotted on top of the bar. **Eetcafé de Casteleyn** (☒ Kamperstraat 33 ☎ 038/421–8099) powers along with hard-driving music and servers who entertain the crowds. **Grand Café de Harmonie** (☒ Grote Markt 13a ☎ 038/422–0019) is billed as the largest grand café in the Netherlands, with easy-listening music. **Tapperij de Joffer** (☒ Jufferenwal 5–7 ☎ 038/422–5223) is a bulwark of students and housed in a 1738 monument. For beer tasting at its best, **'t Proeflokaal van Zwolle** (☒ Blijmarkt 3 ☎ 038/421–7808) is a top place.

## The Outdoors

CANOEING    In summertime it's not only possible, but highly pleasurable, to canoe on the waterways in and around Zwolle. **Vadesto Kanocentrum** (☒ Veenrand 5, 8051 DW Hattem ☎ 038/444–5428) at the Potgietersingel rents canoes. The VVV sells canoeing maps.

## Shopping

A great shopping route that ends in decadence is to start at the Grote Markt and head down Diezerstraat. Note the crooked gabled building at the corner of this intersection, now a nut shop, and a bit farther down, the scary druggist above the entrance of No. 14, now a women's clothing store retaining some of the old pharmacy interior. At the end of this long street, near the bridge and the old city wall, is your shop-till-you-drop reward: 42 different flavors of artificial-color-free ice cream, three of them without sugar, at the **IJssalon Salute** (☒ Diezerstraat 121 ☎ 038/423–7566). There's usually a run on *croccantino*, ice cream made with almonds in caramelized sugar. Market days in Zwolle are Friday morning and Saturday. Late shopping is on Thursday until 9.

# Staphorst

🄬    *57 km (37 mi) north of Apeldoorn, 25 km (16 mi) north of Zwolle.*

Fodor'sChoice ★    Staphorst and the twin neighboring towns, Rouveen and IJhorst, win the time-warp prize, yet their sternly religious, fiercely independent Calvinist-cum-Dutch-Reformed-Protestants want no accolades. In fact,

they want no attention at all, and will shameles͟
bugs who insist on photographing them in their trac͟
tumes with colorful floral overlays, and matching skullcap͟
to snap their thatched farmhouses trimmed with blue (to
evil), green (youth), and white (purity) accents. Of the 16,000 p͟
in the three villages, approximately 600 women and children still wea͟
the local garb; only about 5 men, the youngest of whom is in his late
70s at this writing, still dress all in black, particularly on Sunday when
families go not once, but twice, to church. You can attend the services,
but be forewarned—they last about two hours each, seemingly made
all the longer by psalms sung in a *very* slow, exaggerated drone. Women
must wear a dress or skirt, stockings, and a head covering of some kind
to be admitted.

Amish they are not. Staphorstians do believe in conveniences such as
electricity, and they do drive cars. They have, however, espoused some
rather strong beliefs until the not-so-distant past, such as prohibiting
childhood immunizations (dismissed only since the 1970s when the
government required certain inoculations) and, perhaps the most para-
doxical of all, the "open bedroom window" policy, by which unmarried daughters' bedrooms were purposely outfitted with easy window
access so male suitors could slip into the room and under the sheets, as
it were, of the shuttered cupboard beds called bedsteden. The rest is history. It wasn't until a local official banned this so-called *"queesten"* (quest)
practice in 1920 and forbade "making love in the window" that bars
were installed on the culprit windows, an example of which can be seen,
along with the inviting bedsteden, at the ★ **Gemeentelijke Museum-
boerderij** (Museum Farm), the real McCoy. Coffee and sweets are available. ⊠ *Gemeenteweg 67, 7951 CE* ☎ *0522/462526* ✉ *€2* ☉ *Apr.–Oct.,
Mon.–Sat. 10–5.*

## Where to Stay & Eat

★ **$$** ✕⊡ **Chateau de Havixhorst.** Both storks and gentry have landed at this
18th-century haven of manorial tranquility, ideal for some regal R&R
with just the right infusion of fuss. Be one with nature while perched,
like the nesting and highly discriminating storks on the roof, in a moated
castle (now a national monument) with king-size designer rooms and
up-to-date bathrooms. Once upon a time, Havixhorst was the most im-
portant residence in the province of Drenthe, just over the border from
Staphorst, and lorded over by the wealthy and powerful Vos van Steen-
wijk family. Only since 1980 has the Wijland family turned it into a ro-
mantic hotel and highly respected restaurant (open for lunch
Tuesday–Friday only by reservation; dinner Tuesday–Saturday). Chil-
dren can roam the woods, catch creepy-crawlies in the moat, and visit
the local stork sanctuary, De Lokkerij, just a five-minute walk through
the forest. Breakfast is served to order, and the homemade jams com-
plete the exquisite experience. Go on, enter this realm . . . you only live
once. ⊠ *Schiphorsterweg 34–36, 7966 AC De Schiphorst* ☎ *0522/
441487* 🖷 *0522/441489* ⊕ *www.dehavixhorst.nl* ❧ *8 suites* ⌂ *Restau-
rant, room service, Wi-Fi, cable TV, bicycles, lounge, meeting rooms,
free parking* ⊟ *AE, DC, MC, V.*

*...shun the shutter. ...nal black cos- ...Be content ...ard off ...pple*

*...north of Zwolle, 111 km (72 mi) east of Amsterdam, 25 ...orthwest of Staphorst.*

...st-place prize for photogenic towns, Giethoorn is a verdant, ...version of Venice—an irresistible punter's paradise where ...esidents and tourists but cows, horses, milk cans, and bridal ...e transported on canals in this roadless matrix of waterways ...ssed by wooden footbridges lighted at night. Flanked by a pro- tus... of thatch-roof cottages, the village makes you wonder whether you're in Hansel and Gretel's garden or Alice in Wonderland's fantasy.

The reality is that Giethoorn was settled around 1230 by a group of flagellants escaping religious persecution, making their living by digging peat (turf that was dried and used for fuel). The village owes its name to the countless number of wild goat horns they found here, presumably from the beasts buried by the floods that frequently plagued the area.

In winter, this unparalleled beauty turns into a skating scene straight out of a 17th-century Avercamp snowscape. Indeed, the "Holland-Venice" ice-skating tour (as it is aptly dubbed because of its Venetian-like backdrop), which begins here in ferociously frigid winters, is a sight to behold. In spring and summer, the narrow transport canals, excavated by manual labor as late as 1924, swell with punts—long flat-bottomed boats propelled with poles—and whisper-quiet motorboats (charging about €5 for an hour's cruise). Do-it-yourselfers can rent watercraft of varying types. On the last Saturday evening of each August, illuminated gondolas bedecked with flowers parade in a **Gondelvaart.** There's also a jazz-and-blues festival every mid- to-late August. (Because it's hidden from the main road and inaccessible to cars, the best way to reach the charming core of Giethoorn is to turn off Beulakerweg at the sign for "Centrum-Dorp" [Center-Village], follow the "P" sign to the parking area, and walk a short distance to the Binnenpad thoroughfare.)

★ ⊙ For a look back in time, the farmhouse museum **'t Olde Maat Uus** (The Old Maat Family House) provides a richly detailed portrait of life and work in 1800s Giethoorn. Among the household treasures are examples of bedsteden (Dutch cupboard beds), a 100-year-old incubator for babies, a posture board for children deemed "less than straight," an early outhouse named Uussie, and a thatching exhibit. At one point a family of 13 lived within these four walls, so have your kids try to figure out where they all slept. ⊠ *Binnenpad 52, 8355 BT* ☎ *0521/362244* ✉ €3 ⊙ *Easter–Oct., Mon.–Sat. 11–5, Sun. noon–5; Nov.–Easter, Sun. noon–5.*

### Where to Stay & Eat

**$$$$** ✕ **De Lindenhof.** Something to write home about is owner-chef/rising star Martin Kruithof's famous fare served in a farmhouse setting just outside the main village—including the Dutch eel he smokes on an open fire in the lovely garden. (Come on, try it . . . you need *something* to write about on that postcard.) ⊠ *Beulakerweg 77* ☎ *0521/361444* ⊕ *www.restaurantdelindenhof.nl* ⌣ *Reservations essential* ⊟ *AE, DC, MC, V* ⊙ *Closed Thurs.*

# ONCE UPON A VILLAGE

FOR THE TRAVELER *seeking a dichotomy of pleasures away from the madding crowd of Amsterdam, the Green Heart wrestles up a yin and yang of poignant and pretty. Pulling your heartstrings in both directions, the dilemma is which to see first—the plethora of memorials, monuments, and museums devoted to the horrors of war and the costs of freedom (for the WWII buff, perhaps the best known of the historic sites are in and around Arnhem, including the Airborne Museum Hartenstein and the Rhine Bridge),* or the panting, prepossessing villages and towns prickling the area. Between Bronkhorst, officially the smallest town in Holland; Giethoorn, a fairy-tale version of Venice; Staphorst, a time warp; Amersfoort with its medieval bodice; and Zutphen chained to its medieval books, who needs fantasy—or the rest of Holland, for that matter?

**$$** ✗ **'t Achterhuus.** For the best lunch or dinner in the main village of Giethoorn, plant yourself at this thatch-roof, converted farmhouse restaurant with an outdoor terrace facing the canal. After dining, a guide will take you on a canal cruise on one of their boats (€3.40 per hour). ⊠ *Ds. T. O. Hylkemaweg 43* ☎ *0521/361674* ⊕ *www.achterhuus.nl* ⚲ *Reservations essential* ⊟ *AE, DC, MC, V* ⊘ *Closed Tues. and Wed. Oct.–Apr.*

**¢** ▦ **Fam. Heida B&B.** In quiet repose, this bed-and-breakfast is canal-side and just off the footpath. Choose between the main house or the separate cottage, which just happens to be the smallest house in Giethoorn. It sleeps three, with a double bed and a single. Surrounding gardens add a bountiful splash of color. Note that bathrooms are shared in the main-house accommodations. ⊠ *Zuiderpad 18, 8355 CA* ☎ *0521/361117* ⊕ *www.fam-heida.nl* ⚲ *4 rooms in main house, 1 with bath; cottage* ⚘ *Boating, bicycles, free parking, no-smoking rooms; no room phones, no room TVs* ⊟ *No credit cards* ❏ *CP.*

**¢** ▦ **Mol/Groenewegen.** Smack-dab in the heart of charm central, this simple but spartan B&B wins hands down for location. Although inaccessible by car, parking is not far away. Bicycles, canoes, kayaks, and punts are available for rent. ⊠ *Binnenpad 28, 8355 BR* ☎ *0521/361359* 🖷 *0521/362567* ⊕ *www.molgroenewegen.nl* ⚲ *6 rooms, 4 with bath* ⚘ *Cable TV in 1 room, bicycles, boating, free parking, no-smoking rooms; no room phones* ⊟ *No credit cards* ❏ *CP* ⊘ *Closed Oct.8–Mar.*

## Shopping

You can lose track of time in **Het Winkeltje** (⊠ *Ds. T. O. Hylkemaweg 32*, on the right as you come from the parking area, before you reach 't Achterhuus restaurant and 't Olde Maat Uus museum ☎ *0521/362269*); "The Little Shop" is a rabbit warren crammed with antiques and small collectibles, including a wide range of kitchenware and linens.

## Kampen

**16**

Fodor'sChoice ★

*14 km (9 mi) northwest of Zwolle, 103 km (64 mi) northeast of Amsterdam.*

Kampen is a schizophrenic puff of smoke along the IJssel River where cigar manufacturing took over in the 1820s after a phlegmatic hiatus following its Hanseatic heyday as a herring hub. Once the viceroy in the pack, Kampen's wealth dried up when the harbor silted up near the end of the Middle Ages. As if preserved in amber, however, the town boasts nearly 500 historic monuments outlined by the remaining 3 of its 21 phantom city gates. Sunday, when Kampen turns into a veritable ghost town, is an ideal time for a city walk to view the rich display of monuments and *gevelstenen* (façade stones). You can pick up a walking-tour brochure map called "Town Walk in the Hanseatic Town of Kampen" (€2.25) at the VVV Kampen or the Stedelijk Museum Kampen in advance (it is not open Sunday). A visit to Kampen, where one of the longest cigars in the world exists, makes for a good day trip that can be combined with a family outing to ☺ **Walibi World** (☎ 032/132-9999 ⊕ www.walibiworld.nl) amusement park in nearby Dronten, billed as the "Roller Coaster Capital of Europe," where you can stay in one of 142 bungalows.

The best view of the ancient skyline is from the **Stadsbrug** (Town Bridge) across the river. From there you can take a medieval circuit past the defensive city gates: stroll down the waterfront to the **Koornmarktspoort** (Grain Market Gate) on IJsselkade, recognizable by its two 14th-century towers. Peek into the **Sint Nikolaskerk** (Church of St. Nicholas) on the Koornmarkt, then cross over to the old moat and Ebbingstraat where **Cellebroederspoort** (Cloister Brothers Gate) still stands; farther north on Ebbingstraat is the **Broederpoort** (Brother Gate).

Rapunzel has reputedly been sighted overlooking the onion-shape tower on the 14th-century **Oude Raadhuis,** where statues on its gabled facade depict Charlemagne, Alexander the Great, and less-martial figures representing Moderation, Fidelity, Justice, and Love. Inside, the **Schepenzaal,** the oak-lined and timber-vaulted Magistrates' Hall with its elaborately carved chimneypiece, is a stunning example of a medieval courtroom. ⊠ *Oudestraat 133, 8261 CL* ☎ *038/331-7361.*

The **Stedelijk Museum Kampen** (Kampen Municipal Museum) occupies a perfectly preserved Gothic merchant's house where, in addition to minting your own Kampen coins from an original mold, you can see exhibits on local history and industry, such as eel fishing and cigar making. ⊠ *Oudestraat 158, 8260 GA* ☎ *038/333-2294* ✉ *€3* ☉ *Mid-Sept.–mid-June, Tues.–Sat. 11–5; mid-June–mid-Sept., Tues.–Sat. 11–5, Sun. 1–5.*

See the 15-foot-long cigar, reputedly one of the longest in the world (the Cubans claim to have the longest) at the **Kampen Tabakmuseum.** ⊠ *Botermarkt 3, 8261 GR* ☎ *038/332-5353* ✉ *€1.20* ☉ *Apr.–Nov., Thurs.–Sat. 11–12:30 and 1:30–5 or by appointment.*

## Where to Stay & Eat

★ **$$** ✕ **Restaurant d'Olde Vismark.** Talk about romance! Chef Ron Wesseler began his international career in a bakery, made five trips around the world as a ship manager with the Holland America line, and disembarked in Kampen after sailing down the Rhine. Come enjoy his fish specialties or vegetarian delights with views of the IJssel River (you were expecting the Mediterranean?) and fantasize about his past, unless yours was more exciting. Desserts served in a cloud of mist and surprise menus are part of the draw, so reservations are highly recommended. ⊠ *IJsselkade 45* ☎ *038/331–3490* ⊕ *www.vismark.nl* ▭ *AE, DC, MC, V.*

¢ ▦ **De Stadsboerderij.** Built in the 17th to 20th century, this former "City Farm" was the real McCoy until the 1980s. Renovations have modernized the structure, but many original features have been retained. If being boxed in, literally, appeals to you, ask for the large bedroom with two original box or cupboard beds built into the wall, Dutch-style. After all, there's something to be said for cozy. Likewise, former stalls have been transformed into a living room. If you can't sleep, count the black and white tiles, not sheep, that date from the early 1600s. It's a five-minute walk or taxi ride from the central train station. ⊠ *Groenestraat 148–150, 8261 VL* ☎ *038/333–0678* ⊕ *www.stadsboerderij.nl* ⇆ *3 rooms without bath* ⚘ *Cable TV in 2 rooms, some free parking, some pets allowed; no room phones, no smoking* ▭ *No credit cards* ¶◎¶ *CP.*

## Deventer

**17** 39 km (24 mi) south of Zwolle, 16 km (10 mi) east of Apeldoorn, 107
Fodor'sChoice *km (67 mi) east of Amsterdam.*
★

Meticulously medieval Deventer, one of the oldest towns in the Netherlands, is paved with holy grails and cornerstones of thought. It was founded late in the 8th century by an English cleric named Lebuinus, whose mission in life was to convert the Saxons to Christianity, and by the 9th century it was a prosperous port and a powerful bishopric. But it was also a center of learning and printing, which was the medium used to disseminate the thoughts of scholars such as Thomas à Kempis, Erasmus, and, in the 17th century, French philosopher René Descartes, as well as Pope Adrian VI, all of whom made their home here at various times. Be sure to pick up two brochures at the local VVV: "Deventer, A Hospitable Hanseatic City" and "Town Walk," both in English, which will guide you past the oldest brick house in the country on Sandrasteeg, dating from 1100. True to its roots, there is an annual medieval fair held here on Ascension Day in May, harking back to Deventer's role as one of the largest marketplaces in the Middle Ages.

Deventer's Late Gothic **Waag** (Weigh House), begun in 1528, is a stately testament to the city's Hanseatic past. Inside, an exhibition on town history, from prehistoric times to the present day, includes the Netherlands' oldest bicycle, the spindly *Vélociède,* built in 1870. ⊠ *Brink 56, 7411 BV* ☎ *0570/693780* ⊠ *€2.30* ⊗ *Mon.–Sat. 10–5, Sun. 1–5.*

☼ Two huge medieval houses barely contain the **Speelgoed-en Blikmuseum** (Toys and Tin Museum), an enchanting collection of toys dating from the Middle Ages to the 20th century. There are dolls, puppets, and tin soldiers galore, and an exceptional collection of mechanical toys and electric trains. In the museum's darkroom you can see a 17th-century magic lantern and a host of other optical playthings. ☒ *Brink 47, 7411 BV* ☎ *0570/693786* 🖳 *€3.30* ☉ *Tues.–Sat. 10–5, Sun. 1–5.*

Cobbled streets and crooked gables lead to the 13th-century Romanesque Gothic **Bergkerk** (Church on the Mountain), with pleasing views down medieval side streets (Bergstraat and Roggestraat are particularly evocative.) ☒ *Bergkerkplein* ☉ *Open for expositions.*

The **Lebuinuskerk** (St. Lebuinus's Church), a huge stone cross-basilica, built in the 10th century on the site of Lebuinus's small wooden church, has some fine 16th-century murals and a 700-year-old floor. Hanging in the 15th-century tower is the oldest extant carillon made by the Hemony brothers, who in the 17th century were the most celebrated bell makers in the world. The tower can be climbed in summer months for a wide view of the town; the carillon is played at least twice a week. ☒ *Grote Kerkhof* 🖳 *Free* ☉ *Mar.–Oct., Mon.–Sat. 11–5; Nov.–Feb., Mon.–Sat. 11–4.*

### Where to Stay

★ $ 🏨 **Huis Nieuw Rande.** On the outskirts of town this country-manor hotel sits on 380 acres of woodland surrounded by Shetland ponies, undulating streams, and a garden landscaped by Jan Zocher, famed for the Vondelpark in Amsterdam. Largely devoid of televisions and the like, it's a writer's paradise, but even those without a poem in their soul will fall for the seclusion and tranquility offered here. Request the Rosendael room in the main house—a princely room with a priceless view of the surrounding countryside, replete with ponies and peace—or for a family or group affair of 8–10 people, rent the Klein (Little) Rande, a private cottage by the woods complete with all the amenities, including two baths, kitchen, and living/dining room, as well as a TV and CD player for the uninspired. ☒ *Schapenzandweg 3, 7431 PZ Diepenveen* ☎ *0570/593666* 🖶 *0570/593667* 🌐 *www.huisnieuwrande.nl* 🛏 *9 rooms in main house, 1 cottage* 🖧 *Wi-Fi, free parking, no-smoking rooms; no room phones, TV in cottage* ☰ *AE, MC, V* ⵏ◻ *CP.*

### Shopping

Friday and Saturday are market days in Deventer, when the Brink, or main square, is crowded with fresh-produce stalls and a few antiques dealers. On the first Sunday in August the largest **book market** in the Netherlands stretches for 3 km (2 mi) along the IJssel River.

# GELDERLAND PROVINCE & DE HOGE VELUWE

The riches of Gelderland, the largest province of the Netherlands, are hugely evident. Even its name—*geld,* meaning "money"—refers to the region's wealthy aristocracy. Royalty recognized its appeal when they chose this wooded province for their palatial residence, Paleis Het Loo, discriminatingly placing it in the very midst of the forest, the perfect ground for their hunting pursuits. And as with the province of Overijssel, the

# WILD LIFE

**THE CORE OF THE GREEN HEART,** *as its name implies, is verdant and lush, thereby lending itself to a unique concentration of wildlife, particularly in the national park area of the Veluwe between Apeldoorn and Arnhem. Countless red and roe deer, mouflons (wild sheep), wild boar, and a variety of small animals are visible in grazing pastures and fields, affording good game observation in the park, with De Hoge Veluwe being the most visitor-friendly area, thanks to its tailor-made*

*lookout towers. According to the visitor center there—which can provide you with suggested game-watching tactics and mapped-out posts—the best time of day to catch the big game is late afternoon or early evening when the animals leave their cover in search of food. With October being mating time for the mouflons, it's a good time to hazard a surreptitious peek as the rams fight over the ewes, slamming their distinctive curled horns against each other in battle.*

Hanseatic League seconded it, so central were the two provinces for trade routes and burgeoning markets.

Central to Gelderland's appeal is the Veluwe, which, despite the unfortunate translation of its name as "badland" (referring to its infertility as farmland), is the largest expanse of natural beauty in northwestern Europe. A true hinterland of heaths, moors, dunes, and untouched forests above sea level and therefore protected from saltwater floods, it offers a wealth of recreational opportunities concentrated around hiking and biking just north of the Rhine River. Inhabited by wild game, a large portion of the Veluwe is a protected national park, De Hoge Veluwe, which fills much of the triangle formed by the three main cities of the Green Heart: Arnhem, known for its World War II battle; Apeldoorn, where Het Loo Palace is located; and Amersfoort, the medieval lady of the pack.

## Apeldoorn

**18** *16 km (10 mi) southwest of Deventer, 44 km (28 mi) east of Amersfoort, 89 km (56 mi) east of Amsterdam.*

Though not much of an attraction in itself except for the old town center situated around the Raadhuisplein, the small city of Apeldoorn is the gateway to the Royal Forest and the Hoge Veluwe National Park, the latter an absolute must on your itinerary. But before you give it up for naught, there's a palatial reason to come to this neck of the woods: the recently occupied royal palace of **Het Loo,** the Dutch version of Versailles.

FodorsChoice ★ Begun in 1685 on the site of a 14th- and 15th-century castle and hunting lodge in the midst of the Royal Forest, **Paleis Het Loo** (Het Loo Palace, i.e., The Woods Palace) served as a country residence for Dutch William III and his wife Mary Stuart (daughter of James II of England). The castle expanded into a full-blown royal palace when the couple, famously known as "William and Mary," became king and queen of England. As was the case in many royal (and many not-so-royal) households, Mary's quarters were in the east wing and William's in the west. Constructed of brick and outfitted with what are said to be the world's first sash windows, the spectacularly beautiful palace—one of the most glorious examples of Dutch Neoclassicism—and its Dutch Baroque gardens exemplify symmetry, order, and unity.

A vaulted avenue of tall beeches leads to the central courtyard, where you enter through a grilled, blue-and-gold gate. Special exhibits fill some of the rooms, and there is a video that documents the building's history and restoration prior to its opening to the public in 1984. Many rooms are furnished as they were for William and Mary, but are also maintained in the manner in which they were used by later Dutch monarchs, including Queen Wilhelmina, grandmother of the current Queen Beatrix. Wilhelmina became queen at the age of 10 and was the last regent to make this her summer home, residing in The Hague and Amsterdam throughout much of the year. She died here in 1962. A peek at her playroom may make you envious, but consider that, besides her English nanny, her tutors were all elderly men and that she had no brothers or sisters with whom to play, only a donkey, a pony, and the doll collection on display. Indeed, her office used in later life has a decidedly manly feel, and she was known to be a very intense, serious woman of large stature.

Certain rooms deserve particular attention, such as Queen Mary's petite and homey kitchen where she made jam; her bedroom with its lavish canopied four-poster bed brought from Kensington Palace in London where she formerly lived; and the hunting trophy room of Prince Henry, husband of Queen Wilhelmina.

Four gardens, meticulously planted in the same fashion as they were in the 17th century after being designed by Daniel Marot, an ancestor of the late actress Audrey Hepburn, are decorated with statues and fountains fed by the waters of the Rhine, including two in the form of globes. The terrestrial one shows the world as it was perceived in the 17th century, and the celestial one corresponds to the sky above the palace at the time of Princess Mary Stuart's birth. Rivaling Versailles, the king's fountain was meant to shoot water higher than that of Louis XIV's. Separate king's and queen's gardens provide respective views from their individual domains; the king's is dominated by plantings in blue and orange, the colors of the Dutch royal family, and the queen's by pastel flowers and fruit trees.

You can feast at one of the two palace restaurants offering short-order fare: the self-service **Theehuis** (Teahouse) near the exit and part of the old stables, a favorite of many with its wicker chairs and an outdoor café complete with strutting, well-bred peacocks, or the **Balzaal** (Ballroom) in the West Wing with the same simple fare in a more lavish setting. Catering to every whim (that *is*, after all, what palace life is all about), there is also an ice-cream stand as you exit. Guided tours in English are available by appointment, and concerts are held the last Friday of every month at 8:15 PM (contact the palace or VVV for tickets). A map of walking routes in the palace park is available at the entrance. If you don't have a car, take Bus No. 102 or 104 from the bus/train station to get to Het Loo. ⊠ *Koninklijk Park, 7315 JA* ☎ *055/577–2448* ⊕ *www. hetloo.nl* ✉ *€9, parking €3* ☉ *Tues.–Sun. 10–5.*

What kid hasn't wondered what it's like to be a policeman or police-woman and wear a bulletproof vest? Now's their chance to do just that at **Het Nederlands Politie Museum,** where they can also be fingerprinted, climb into police cars and helicopters, and get a close-up look at 200 years of Dutch uniforms, weapons, and equipment. May the force be with you. ⊠*Arnhemseweg 346* ☎*055/543–0691* ⊕*www.politiemuseum. nl* ✉ *€3* ☉ *Tues.–Fri. 10–5, weekends 1–5.*

Mingle with your primate relatives at the **Apenheul** park, the only such zoo in the world where more than 350 monkeys, apes, chimpanzees, and gorillas wander freely in the woods and, some of them, all over you. Among bright flocks of tropical birds, your evolutionary cousins will saunter right up to you—in fact, squirrel monkeys, highly adept pick-pockets, will even get in your bags (bags can and should be checked to avoid problems). Situated in **Park Berg & Bos,** a beautiful nature park with walking routes and a large lake, it's the perfect spot for a family outing and picnic—that is, if your hairy friends don't eat it first. On summer nights, a romantic light-and-sound show, **Lumido,** takes place in the park. An awesome playground features a child-friendly wooden observation tower without a single nail in it, perfect for the little monkeys in *your* family. ⊠ *JC Wilslaan 21, 7313 HK* ☎ *055/357–5757* ⊕ *www. apenheul.nl* ✉ *€13, parking €4* ☉ *Apr.–June, Sept.–Nov. 1, daily 9:30–5; July and Aug., daily 9:30–6.*

off the beaten path

**STEAM TRAIN TO DIEREN –** At various times of the year you can ride a nostalgic steam train from Apeldoorn to the town of Dieren. Reservations are not necessary, and the train leaves from the central station. Food and drinks are available on board, and bikes are allowed. ☎ *055/506–1989* ⊕ *www.stoomtrein.org* ✉ *€9.50 round-trip, €6.50 one-way.*

## Where to Stay & Eat

★ **$–$$$** ✕ **Spicebrush.** If you've been traveling too long and your shoes are beginning to feel wooden, Spicebrush will sweep you off your feet and transport you back to the good ol' USA, complete with not one but two copies of the Statue of Liberty, Chicago Bulls horns, a neon Bud Beer sign, and good vibrations on tap. Specializing in steaks, barbecue ribs, seafood, and a bold Tex-Mex menu, Spicebrush's only failing is that it's not open for lunch. The Mexican fajitas are *numero uno,* their quality equaled by the fresh green salad, great garlic bread, and Dutch coffee-flavor chocolates called *koffieboontjes* (coffee beans) served with java. ⊠ *Marktplein 9* ☎*055/522–5064* ⊕*www.spicebrush.nl* ▭*AE, DC, MC, V* ☉*No lunch.*

**¢–$$** ✕ **Grand Café de Notaris.** A cozy place to sit in the old town center and watch the world go by, this outdoor café specializes in *saté,* pork on a skewer with a peanut sauce worth writing home about. ⊠ *Raadhuisplein 1* ☎*055/578–5887* ⊕ *www.grandcafedenotaris.com* ▭*AE, DC, MC, V.*

★ $–$$$   ⊞ **Bilderberg Hotel de Keizerskroon.** Royal service . . . what else would you expect from a savvy hotel within walking distance of Het Loo Palace? It's so close, in fact, that you can almost hear the walls speak of its privileged past. A grand country inn once patronized by Czar Peter the Great, the Keizerskroon was a haunt of visiting royalty and those living vicariously. Princely attention to detail is their forte (wonder if the czar ever had heated towels . . .), with every manner of organized adventure, from bicycle tours and horseback riding through the adjacent forests, to sightseeing flights over castles (or your own flying lessons at a nearby airfield), and game tracking through the Royal Forest. Rooms are everything one would expect, and more. There is a bus stop close to the hotel, for a 10-minute trip to the center. ⊠ *Koningstraat 7, 7315 HR* ☎ *055/521–7744* 🖷 *055/521–4737* ⊕ *www.keizerskroon.nl* 🛏 *86 rooms, 8 suites* ⚭ *Restaurant, room service, in-room safes, minibars, cable TV with movies, Wi-Fi, indoor pool, gym, sauna, steam room, Turkish bath, bicycles, bar, lounge, babysitting, dry cleaning, laundry service, meeting rooms, parking (fee), some pets allowed, no-smoking floors; no a/c in some rooms* ⊟ *AE, DC, MC, V* ⦿| *BP.*

$   ⊞ **Hotel Astra.** On a quiet residential side street within walking distance of the center, Astra is a bed-and-breakfast furnished in the manner of a comfortable Dutch home. Rooms are large for this type of accommodation, and there is a pleasant garden terrace behind the house. ⊠ *Bas Backerlaan 12–14, 7316 DZ* ☎ *055/522–3022* 🖷 *055/522–3021* ⊕ *www.hotelastra.nl* 🛏 *29 rooms* ⚭ *Restaurant, in-room safes, cable TV, Wi-Fi, bicycles, bar, dry cleaning, laundry service, business services, meeting room, free parking, no-smoking rooms* ⊟ *AE, DC, MC, V* ⦿| *BP* ☉ *Closed Dec. 18–Jan. 8.*

## Nightlife & the Arts

Although there are no discos in town at this time, the main hive of nightlife buzzes around **Caterplein** square. Incomparable for atmosphere are the concerts on the last Friday of every month at the beautiful **Paleis Het Loo** (⊠ Koninklijk Park 1 ☎ 055/521–2244).

## The Outdoors

Apeldoorn has several stunning parks—Oranjepark, Prinsenpark, Emmapark, and Wilhelminapark—and is known for its much-loved cycle paths along the Apeldoorn Canal and through the surrounding forest.

## Shopping

Market days in Apeldoorn are Monday and Wednesday mornings and all day Saturday at Marktplein in the city center. An attractive mall, **De Oranjerie** (⊠ Oranjerie 265), with underground parking, is in the center. Late shopping night is Thursday until 9.

**en route**   If you have a car, head out to the village of Hoog Soeren from Apeldoorn, a must-drive through a real enchanted forest. Only a higher power and the Dutch could have such manicured, pristine forests. The dappled light in early spring and summer, starkly contrasted with the Hoge Veluwe turf that you enter just beyond the forest, is like a slice of heaven on Earth.

## Otterlo/De Hoge Veluwe

► ⑲ *78 km (49 mi) southeast of Amsterdam, 20 km (13 mi) south of Apeldoorn, 35 km (22 mi) southeast of Amersfoort.*

When German heiress Hélène Müller married Dutch industrialist Anton Kröller at the turn of the 20th century, their combined wealth and complementary tastes were destined to give pleasure to generations to come. She loved art and could afford to collect it; he bought up land in Gelderland and eventually created a foundation to maintain it as a national park, building a museum to house the fruits of their expensive and discriminating taste. Today you can wander through the vast forests, heath, dunes, and moors of the Hoge Veluwe National Park, Kröller's land, and see the descendants of the wild boar and deer with which he stocked the estate. Or you can visit the world-famous museum in the middle of the park, established by Hélène and containing one of the best collections of Van Goghs in the world, as well as an excellent selection of late-19th-century and modern art. Additionally, you can visit the philanthropists' own house and hunting lodge. Children can caper about the largest sculpture garden in Europe, and the whole family can pick up one of the free bikes that are available in the park and trundle off down wooded lanes. (Note that Otterlo is only one entrance of several to the Hoge Veluwe, but it is widely considered the main gateway to the park.)

**Fodor's**Choice **De Hoge Veluwe,** once the private property of the Kröller-Müller family,
★ is the largest national park in Holland, covering 13,300 acres of forest and rolling grassland, moors, and sand dunes, where it is possible to stroll without limit, apart from a few areas reserved for wildlife. The traditional hunting grounds of the Dutch royal family, it is populated with red deer, boar, roes, mouflons (wild sheep), and many birds; it is also filled with towering pines and hardwood trees (oak, beech, and birch), dotted with small villages (**Hoge Soeren,** near Apeldoorn, is particularly charming), and laced with paths for cars, bicycles, and walkers, more than 42 km (27 mi) of which are specifically designated for bicycling. Indeed, there are more than 1,000 white bicycles at your disposal here, free to use with the price of entrance (available at the entrances to the park, at the visitor center, De Koperen Kop restaurant, and at the Kröller-Müller museum; return them to any bike rack when you are finished).

There is a landlocked, always shifting sand dune to marvel at; the world's first museum of all things that live (or have lived) underground; plus an old hunting lodge beside a pond that provides a nice stopping place. At the heart of the park is the visitor center (**Bezoekers Centrum**), which contains exhibits on the park and an observation point for game-watching. **Jachthuis Sint Hubertus** (St. Hubert Hunting Lodge) was the private home and hunting lodge of the Kröller-Müllers, a monumental house planned in the shape of antlers, built between 1914 and 1920 by Dutch architect H. P. Berlage around the legend of St. Hubert, the patron saint of hunters. Rooms with art deco furniture follow in sequence from dark to light, representing Hubert's spiritual development and path of enlightenment from agnostic to saint. Free guided tours of the lodge, which is still used as a residence for visiting dignitaries, may be arranged at the park entrance only.

**Museonder** is the first underground museum in the world, offering visitors a fascinating look at life below the surface, including a simulated earthquake. A campsite at the Hoenderloo entrance is open from April to the end of October (☎ 055/378–2232), and there are four restaurants in the park: the stylish Rijzenburg, at the Schaarsbergen entrance (☎ 026/443–6733; closed Monday and February); and De Koperen Kop, a self-service restaurant in the center of the park opposite the visitor center (☎ 031/859–1289), another self-service one at the Kröller-Müller Museum, and a kiosk near the Jachthuis (open only in summer). The best opportunity for game-watching is at the end of the afternoon and toward evening, and park officials advise that you stay in your car when you spot any wildlife. Special observation sites are signified by antlers on the maps that are provided at the entrances. To enter the park from the A1, A50, or A12 motorways, follow the signs to "Park Hoge Veluwe." ✉ *Entrances at Hoenderloo, Otterlo, and Schaarsbergen* ☎ *0318/591627, 0900/464–3835 at €0.45 per min* ⊕ *www.hogeveluwe.nl* ☑ *€5, cars €5; half-price entrance after 5 PM, May–Sept.; weekly tickets available* ⊘ *Nov.–Mar., daily 9–5:30; Apr., daily 8–8; May and Aug., daily 8–9; June and July, daily 8–10; Sept., daily 9–8; Oct., daily 9–7.*

Fodor'sChoice ★ The **Kröller-Müller Museum** ranks as the third-most-important museum of art in the Netherlands, after the Rijksmuseum and the Vincent van Gogh Museum in Amsterdam. Opened in 1938, it is the repository of a remarkable private collection of late-19th-century and early-20th-century paintings, the nucleus of which are 278 works by Van Gogh (about 50 of which rotate on display at any given time) that, when combined with the collection in the Amsterdam museum, constitutes nearly four-fifths of his entire oeuvre. Hélène Kröller, née Müller, had a remarkable eye as well as a sixth sense about which painters created art for the ages. Her first purchase was most likely Van Gogh's *Faded Sunflowers*. Among his other well-known paintings in her collection are the *Potato Eaters, Bridge at Arles,* and *L'Arlesienne,* copied from a drawing by Gauguin.

But Hélène Kröller-Müller was not myopic in her appreciation and perception. She augmented her collection of Van Goghs with works by Georges Seurat, Pable Picasso, Odile Redon, Georges Braque, and Piet Mondriaan. The museum also contains 16th- and 17th-century Dutch paintings, ceramics, Chinese and Japanese porcelains, and contemporary sculpture. The building itself, designed by Henry van de Velde, artfully brings nature into the galleries through its broad windows, glass walkways, and patios. The gardens and woods around the museum form a stunning open-air gallery, the largest in Europe with a collection of 20th-century sculptures that include works by Auguste Rodin, Richard Serra, Barbara Hepworth, and Alberto Giacometti. There is a gift shop and self-service restaurant on-site. For more information on the Kröller-Müllers, *see* the Passion and Paint: Hélène Kröller-Müller and Van

# PASSION & PAINT: HÉLÈNE KRÖLLER-MÜLLER & VAN GOGH

**DESCRIBING HIM AS "ONE OF** the great souls of our modern art, on whom the spirit of the times had no grasp . . .," heiress Hélène Kröller-Müller fed on Dutch artist Vincent van Gogh's (1853–90) elusive disparity. As such, he occupied a special place in her thinking and, hence, in her visionary art collection. While her industrialist husband was busy buying up wasteland as his own visionary enterprise (later to become the Hoge Veluwe National Park), Hélène, inspired by art appreciation classes, was fervently buying art, some of it with the brushstrokes still damp.

In 1912 alone, she added 35 Van Gogh paintings to her collection, the first of which was most likely his Faded Sunflowers (1887), the nucleus of a burgeoning collection that now includes 92 paintings, 183 drawings, one etching, and two lithographs by a misunderstood genius.

Reputed to have sold only a single painting in his lifetime, Van Gogh committed suicide at the age of 37, penniless and plagued by deep depression. An individualist, the servant of no school but the unwitting master of many a painter, Van Gogh left Holland to bring his private revolution in art to Paris and southern France.

Because many of those lovely southern vistas have completely changed, you have to go to Amsterdam, to Moscow, or to the museum here to view Van Gogh's great canvases. People continue to make the trek to Arles in southern France, forgetting that it was a completely inhospitable place to the artist—the townsfolk, in fact, formed a petition to ban him from their town, setting into motion his retreat into a mental institution and final despair and death.

His posthumous fame, of course, accelerated to such proportions that in 1990, his portrait of Dr. Gachet, his personal medical and psychological guru of sorts, sold at Christie's auction house in New York for the most money ever paid for one painting—a staggering $82 million. Not bad for a basically untrained artist and former lay preacher—a man who desperately longed to be loved yet repeatedly met with in-your-face rejection.

His greatest lost love was a mousy, plain, Dutch woman named Margot Begemann, next-door neighbor to his parents in Nuenen, where he returned for a brief stint in Holland. Despite their mutual affection and deep love, however, she was, at the "tender" age of fortysomething (10 years older than Vincent), forced by her own parents to deny his existence, so unpromising (oh, ship of fools) they felt poor Vincent was. She attempted suicide; Vincent saved her, but after helping her back to her parents' doorstep, they were forever banned from mutual sight.

Little wonder, then, that Vincent, succumbing to madness, cut off a piece of his ear in a self-deprecating argument with fellow-artist and friend Paul Gauguin. Ultimately, he shot himself in a cornfield outside Paris, dragging his defeated body back to his one-room apartment where a viewless skylight served as his final window on life, a seemingly dire fate for someone whose eyes were the root of his soul.

For Vincent, fame came too late. The Kröller-Müllers, on the other hand, were perceptive enough to recognize his poignant talent, and accumulated the vast holding of his work that makes up the foundation of their now-public collection, the Kröller-Müller Museum at the core of Hoge Veluwe National Park.

Gogh box, *below* ✉ *Houtkampweg 6, in Hoge Veluwe National Park, 6730 AA Otterlo* ☎ *0318/591241* ⊕ *www.kmm.nl* ✆ *Park and museum €10* ✆ *Park and museum Tues.–Sun. 10–5; sculpture garden closes at 4:30.*

See and buy is the game plan at the **Nederlands Tegelmuseum** (Netherlands Tile Museum), where all manner of Dutch tiles, from as far back as the 13th century, including those old Dutch standbys, Makkum and Delft, are displayed in a former summerhouse in the village of Otterlo, not far from the Hoge Veluwe. For those with a decorative eye, the tiles for purchase in the gift shop will be irresistible. ✉ *Eikenzoom 12, 6731 BH Otterlo* ☎ *0318/591519* ✆ *€2.75* ✆ *Tues.–Fri. 10–5, weekends 1–5.*

## Where to Stay & Eat

**$$$** ✕ **Restaurant Rijzenburg.** In an old farmhouse dating from 1860 and brimming with antiques, this popular restaurant is known far and wide for its fine Dutch/French cuisine served at an all-you-can-eat buffet (a concept virtually unheard of in Holland). The restaurant capitalizes on its location at the most southerly entrance to the Hoge Veluwe National Park by offering a special package that includes entrance to the park, bike rental, and the buffet (plus apple pie and coffee) for €29.95. ✉ *Koningsweg 17, at Rijzenburg entrance to Hoge Veluwe near Schaarsbergen* ☎ *026/443–6733* ⊕ *www.rijzenburg.nl* ⚑ *Reservations essential* ▤ *No credit cards* ✆ *Closed first 2 wks of Jan.*

**¢** ✕ **'t Pannenkoekhuis Schaarsbergen.** The Schaarsbergen Pancake House, housed in a Brabant-province-style Dutch farmhouse from the 1800s, is a sweet and savory answer to the "Let's eat something different today" dilemma. Offering up 100 different varieties of pancakes (yes, it is possible), there's something to suit every fancy—except that you can't eat them in the Netherlands at breakfast time. Remember, when in Rome . . . ✉ *Kemperbergweg 673* ☎ *026/443–1434* ⊕ *www.pannenkoekhuis.net* ▤ *MC, V* ✆ *Closed Mon.*

**$** ✕▥ **Engelanderhof.** Known just as much for its restaurant (closed end of October–April) as for the quality of its accommodations, the Engelanderhof is only a few minutes' drive from the Hoge Veluwe National Park, and you can relax around the cozy fire in winter before dining on fresh fish or wild game in season. ✉ *Arnhemseweg 484, 7361 CM* ☎ *055/506–3318* 🖷 *055/506–3220* ⊕ *www.engelanderhof.nl* ⚑ *26 rooms, 2 suites* ⚒ *Restaurant, cable TV, in-room data ports, lounge, dry cleaning, laundry service, convention center, some pets allowed (fee), no-smoking rooms* ▤ *AE, MC, V* ⚎ *CP.*

**¢** ▥ **De Wittehoeve.** Cozy on up to this bed-and-breakfast in a recreation of a 19th-century farmhouse where guests are invited to "bring your own horse." If you'd rather just saddle in for the night than arrive on horseback, just come as you are. This hotel is only a 10-minute walk from the Hoge Veluwe National Park and, with no phones or TVs, you may think you've discovered a little piece of heaven, depending on your perspective. ✉ *Brouwersweg 30, 7351 BS Hoenderloo* ☎ *055/378–2012* 🖷 *055/378–2015* ⊕ *www.de-witte-hoeve.nl* ⚑ *8 rooms* ⚒ *Bicycles (fee), some pets allowed, no-smoking rooms; no room phones, no room TVs* ▤ *No credit cards* ⚎ *CP.*

## The Outdoors

CAMPING  One of the best recommended campsites in the Hoge Veluwe park area is **De Pampel** (⌗ Woeste Hoefweg 35 ☎ 055/378–1760), a large, five-star campsite at €16.50–€22.50, near the Hoenderloo entrance to the park. A popular camping option in the Hoge Veluwe is **Veluws Hof** (⌗ Krimweg 154 ☎ 055/378–1777), a moderate-size campsite at €22.24 per night per site, also near the Hoenderloo entrance to the park.

## Zutphen

**⑳** *17 km (11 mi) southeast of Apeldoorn, 64 km (40 mi) east of Amersfoort, 107 km (67 mi) east of Amsterdam.*

Don't be put off when you spot the hideous green, yellow, and orange bridge as you're coming into town over the IJssel River, or by the matching green Town Hall evident when you arrive, for Zutphen defies any attempt to modernize its very obvious medieval core. Enveloping the visitor with its Middle Age cloak, this "Tower City," known for its many spires, is justifiably prized for its ancient library, the only medieval one in continental western Europe, and for the numerous specialty shops on its three central market squares which evoke images from its former Hanseatic culture. Like an illuminated manuscript balanced on a lectern between the Hoge Veluwe to the west and the Achterhoek and Germany to the east, Zutphen was one of the region's wealthiest towns during the 14th and 15th centuries. Today the once-walled town is a patchwork quilt made up of prized medieval houses and courtyards, churches and towers, and remnants of old city gates. Guided walking tours are conducted by the local VVV office from April to September, and there are boat tours along the canals.

★  A feast for the eyes both inside and out, **Sint Walburgiskerk** (St. Walburga's Church), begun in the 12th century in Romanesque style and enlarged in the 16th century in Gothic style, is ornamented with 14th- to16th-century frescoes on the walls and vaulted ceiling, a 17th-century pulpit with an intricately carved lectern, a stunning Bader organ from 1643, a brass baptismal font cast in Belgium in 1527, and a magnificent Gothic, tiara-shape wrought-iron chandelier depicting the names of the Apostles around its base. The **Librije** (Library), originally constructed for that purpose in a chapel-like room connected to the church, is where you'll find the true treasures of Zutphen (the library must be toured with a guide and times can be somewhat irregular). Dating from 1561, this medieval library, built by a church warden to enable regular citizens, tempted by reform, to read about Catholicism under its starch-white, vaulted ceiling, still houses some 750 rare and beautiful early works (including 85 incunabula, or books printed before 1501), more than 300 of which are chained to the original rows of carved-wood reading stands with adjoining monastic benches.

Highlights of the collection include 20 editions by Erasmus, including a small schoolbook he wrote, works of all the western church fathers (St. Augustine, St. Jerome, St. George, and St. Ambrose), a first edition of the work of Copernicus, one edition of Martin Luther's complete works

(1564–70), as well as the oldest book in the library, a 1469 commentary by Thomas Aquinas. It took almost a full year to complete a book in those days, making them prohibitively expensive and therefore available only to the sinfully rich. Also, *very* few people were able to read, particularly in Latin, so the books were a privilege merely to behold for those educated few, as it is our privilege today to see them in this setting. ⊠ *Kerkhof 3, 7201 DM* ☎ *0575/514178* ⊕ *www.walburgiskerk. nl* ⊠ *€1.20, combined with library €3* ⊗ *June, Tues.–Sat. 1:30–4:30; July and Aug., Mon. 1:30–4:30, Tues.–Sat. 10:30–4:30.*

Shelved behind the Sint Walburgiskerk is the **Grafisch Museum** (Graphics Museum), a two-level, shoplike exhibit of printing presses, typesetting, and bookbinding implements, including one man's amazing collection of some 1,600 seals used to emboss the leather tomes. ⊠ *Kerkhof 16, 7201 DM* ☎ *0575/542329* ⊠ *€2.50* ⊗ *Wed.–Fri. 1–4:30, Sat. 11–3.*

The small **Henriette Polak Museum** offers changing exhibitions from its substantial collection of 20th-century Dutch figurative art and paintings, most notably *Landschap* (Landscape) by Wim Oepts. Climb the stairs to the attic to see the tiny room used in the 17th century as a *schuilkerk*, a secret Roman Catholic church. ⊠ *Zaadmarkt 88, 7200 VB* ☎ *0575/516878* ⊠ *€4.50, includes admission to Stedelijk Museum Zutphen* ⊗ *Tues.–Fri. 11–5, weekends 1:30–5.*

The **Stedelijk Museum Zutphen** houses an eclectic collection of historical art, archaeology of the region, modern house interiors, and vintage toys. ⊠ *Rozengracht 3, 7201 JL* ☎ *0575/516878* ⊠ *€4.50, includes admission to Henriette Polak Museum* ⊗ *Tues.–Fri. 11–5, weekends 1:30–5.*

## Where to Stay & Eat

**$$–$$$** ✕ **Restaurant 't Schulten Hues.** The ground floor is a brasserie in the refurbished premises of a former pharmacy, and downstairs is a 14th-century vaulted cellar. The fare is French with Dutch influence, and specialties include local ingredients such as sweetbreads, frog legs, and smoked eel. Go ahead . . .experiment. ⊠ *Houtmarkt 79* ☎ *0575/510005* ▤ *AE, DC, MC, V* ⊗ *Closed Mon. and Tues.*

**★ $$** ✕▥ **Eden Hotel Zutphen.** Facing the Sint Walburgiskerk and medieval library in a 17th-century building on the oldest square in Zutphen, this high-standard hotel has completely modernized rooms in the main wing and carriage house. The restaurant has something for everyone: fish, veal, rack of lamb, and vegetarian entrées, all with a French accent. ⊠ *'s Gravenhof 6, 7201 DN* ☎ *0575/546111* 🖷 *0575/545999* ⊕ *www. edenhotelzutphen.nl* ⇨ *71 rooms, 3 suites* ⚝ *Restaurant, minibars, cable TV with movies, Wi-Fi, bicycles, bar, lounge, babysitting, dry cleaning, laundry service, business services, meeting rooms, parking (fee), no-smoking floors* ▤ *AE, DC, MC, V.*

**¢–$** ✕▥ **Berkhotel.** Old-world English charm is at the core of this country-style inn with a town heart. A grand restaurant, **De Kloostertuin**, with chandeliers, palms, and candlelight, features an eclectic mix of French, Thai, Indian, Moroccan, Russian, and vegetarian cuisine. ⊠ *Mar-*

*spoortstraat 19, 7201 JA* ☎ *0575/511135* 🖷 *0575/541950* ⊕ *ww berkhotel.nl* ➭ *19 rooms, 10 with bath; 1 suite* ⚒ *Restaurant, cable TV, bar, lounge, shop, parking (fee), some pets allowed (fee)* ⊟ *AE, DC, MC, V* ❖❖ *CP.*

### Nightlife
**Café Camelot** (⊠ Groenmarkt 34 ☎ 0575/511804) is a welcoming "brown café" where the walls are desirably (to the Dutch, anyhow) left stained with years' worth of tobacco smoke. Home, in this instance, to a mixed crowd, it offers rock and golden oldies over the sound system, and a good assortment of specialty beers.

## Bronkhorst

**㉑** *9 km (5 mi) south of Zutphen.*

Fodor'sChoice
★

It's as though Dickens's Tiny Tim has left his thumbprint on Bronkhorst, the tiniest official town in the Netherlands, with a population of just 160. The entire hamlet, established in 1344, has been declared a national monument, and it's easy to see why as you wander along its cobblestone streets paved with nostalgia and punctuated with a dickens of a lot of curiosity shops where local craftsmen ply their traditional trades. Pick up an English copy of "A Town Walk—Bronkhorst" (€1.79, available at local restaurants or the Zutphen VVV). The most curious spot *is*, in fact, the **Charles Dickens Museum,** the passion-turned-museum-shop of Sjef de Jong, a lifelong Dickens fan and devotee, and Scrooge imitator. Among a good collection of memorabilia, you can see Dickens's walking stick and a ticket used by the British royal family for his last performance. Literary fans will swoon over the museum's antiquarian bookshop, The Old Curiosity Shop, where copies of Dickens's works are available for purchase. About a week before Christmas, Mr. De Jong, with the help of the locals, turns Bronkhorst into an animated *Christmas Carol* tableau with street and church performances in a completely illuminated village. (The shop does not take credit cards.) ⊠ *Onderstraat 2, 7226 LD* ☎ *0575/451623* ⊕ *www.dickensmuseum.nl* 🎟 *Free* ☉ *Easter–late Oct., daily 10–5; late Oct.–Easter, weekends 11–5.*

### Where to Stay & Eat

★ $ ╳🖾 **Herberg de Gouden Leeuw.** Experience the best that Dutch hospitality and ambience have to offer in this stunning 16th- and 17th-century farmhouse inn combining country-style Dutch with English decor. In a village so cute and quaint it almost squeaks, this luxurious farmhouse is the next best thing to hearth and home, perhaps even better. Set just across from the town's Dickens Museum and a 14th-century chapel, this romantic inn complete with 17th-century tile tableaux is worth fighting for a reservation, even if it's only for dinner at their excellent restaurant (closed Monday and Tuesday from November through March), which serves local game, asparagus, and lobster in season. Bicycle and walking paths abound along the nearby IJssel River, providing tranquility and repose. For a luxurious but oh-so-homey experience, head here. ⊠ *Bovenstraat 2, 7226 LM* ☎ *0575/451231* 🖷 *0575/450123* ⊕ *www.herbergdegoudenleeuw. com* ➭ *4 rooms, 2 suites* ⚒ *Restaurant, café, bar, cable TV, in-room broad-*

band, bicycles, meeting rooms, free parking, some pets allowed, no-smoking rooms ☰ MC, V ⦿ CP.

## Shopping
**Artgallery Lötters** (✉ Bovenstraat 14 ☎ 0575/452598), a former cheese farm, is a gallery with art from Zimbabwe. **Heren van Bronkhorst** (✉ Onderstraat 1 ☎ 0575/452535) is a well-known antiques shop. Local artisans can be found at **Lötters Edelstenen** (✉ Bovenstraat 1 ☎ 0575/452657), a gem-and-mineral shop.

# Arnhem

**22**

Fodor'sChoice
★

*99 km (62 mi) southeast of Amsterdam, 50 km (31 mi) southeast of Amersfoort, 25 km (16 mi) southwest of Bronkhorst.*

In war log and movie terms, Arnhem may be known as the basis for *A Bridge Too Far,* but this historic city is certainly not out of reach for military buffs who like to combine their field research with great shopping, parks, and castles in the sky, all in close proximity to the great Hoge Veluwe National Park. Central to what was the largest airborne operation of World War II, Arnhem's famous bridge over the Rhine, the Rijnbrug, now called **John Frostbrug,** became the rope of the four-day tug-of-war between the Allies and the German forces intent on trying to further penetrate the area. Left with the short end of the rope, 1,748 Allied troops lost their lives in the fight for the bridge.

Today, trolley buses unique to Arnhem weave their environmentally friendly way around this largely pedestrianized town, the fifth-largest shopping area in the Netherlands. Although much of Arnhem was destroyed during World War II, there are a few bastions that survived the bombing, namely the **Korenmarkt** square of old warehouses, which now throbs nightly with a mix of pubs, cafés, restaurants, and dance clubs. A weekly market is held in the shadows of Arnhem's **Grote Kerk** (Great Church) or **Eusebiuskerk** as it is properly called, a three-aisle cross-basilica that dates back to the 15th century. Accessible by a glass-enclosed elevator that passes one of the largest carillons in Europe, the reconstructed tower offers a panoramic view of the town and its famous bridge. ✉ Kerkplein 1 ☎ 026/443–5068 ⊕ www.eusebius.nl 🖰 €2.50 ☾ Apr.–Oct., Tues.–Sat. 10–5, Sun. noon–5; Nov.–Mar., Tues.–Sat. 11–4, Sun. noon–4.

Lurking around one side of the Grote Kerk is the 16th-century Stadhuis or **Duivelshuis** (Devil's House) at Koningstraat 38, which, strangely enough, suffered no damage whatsoever during World War II. The demonic sculptures on the building's facade were carved by order of General Maarten van Rossum, allegedly as payback for the city fathers' refusal to allow him to pave the front steps of his town hall with gold. (Dutch hellfire-and-brimstone painter Hieronymus Bosch could have had a field day with this one, particularly in light of the fact that it was the city church tower that fell.)

Oosterbeek, now a very posh town just west of Arnhem, where 10,000 of the First British Airborne Division parachuted down on September

17, 1944, is today the setting for the **Airborne Museum Hartenstein,** where all manner of military memorabilia, weapons, and equipment depict the crucial battle that took place. An English-language audiovisual presentation brings it to life. Ask at the desk for a map of other nearby war-related sites or a guided tour. ⊠ *Utrechtseweg 232, Oosterbeek* ☎ *026/333–7710* ⊕ *www.airbornemuseum.com* 🖃 *€4.80* ⊙ *Apr.–Oct., Mon.–Sat. 10–5; Nov.–Mar., Mon.–Sat. 11–5, Sun. noon–5.*

Just to the north of Oosterbeek lies the **Arnhem/Oosterbeek War Cemetery,** also known as the Airborne Cemetery, resting place of those Allies who fell during the Battle of Arnhem.

For a small-dose culture break, the **Historisch Museum Arnhem** (Historic Museum), just on the rim of Arnhem's main shopping area, offers a gratifying range of art, furniture, silver, ceramics, and town history served up in a delightful 18th-century mansion, a former soap factory, and orphanage. Highlights include an 1800 dollhouse in a china cabinet, a wax portrait of a 12-year-old girl (who drowned along with her mother and brother when their ship sank on the Rhine River while en route to a friend's estate in Arnhem), paintings of the town by Bartholomeus Springer and others on the top floor, and old photos taken before and after the World War II siege. ⊠ *Bovenbeekstraat 21, 6811 CV* ☎ *026/442–6900* ⊕ *www.hmarnhem.nl* 🖃 *€3.50* ⊙ *Tues.–Fri. 10–5, weekends 11–5.*

For a look at daily civilian life in wartime Arnhem, go to the **Arnhem Oorlogsmuseum '40–'45.** ⊠ *Kemperbergweg 780, 6816 RX* ☎ *026/442–0958* 🖃 *€3.50* ⊙ *Tues.–Sun. 10–5.*

Captured in Arnhem's **Museum voor Moderne Kunst** (Museum for Modern Art) is the magic realism and contemporary art of modern Dutch masters Charlie Toorop, Dick Ket, and Carel Willink, plus a sculpture garden overlooking the Rhine River. If you dare, take a gander at the statue of a man in the phone booth–like structure outside (warning: he's rated X). ⊠ *Utrechtseweg 87, 6812 AA* ☎ *026/351–2431* ⊕ *www.mmkarnhem.nl* 🖃 *€6* ⊙ *Tues.–Fri. 10–5, weekends 11–5.*

**need a break?** Withdraw to **Coffee Grounds** (⊠ Korenstraat 6–8 ☎ 026/370–5110) for an American blast of bagels, brownies, doughnuts, muffins, cheesecake, and perhaps the only take-out coffee on Dutch soil (excepting McDonald's). If you haven't tried raw herring yet, head for **Gamba's** (⊠ Jansstraat 12 ☎ 026/351–2224), where the freshest seafood delicacies are served. (Go on, smother it in onions and pickles like the Dutch do. You'll be donning wooden shoes before you know it.)

★ ☾ If time doesn't allow you to make it to every province of the Netherlands, why not "cheat" a little by visiting the **Nederlands Openluchtmuseum** (Dutch Open Air Museum), a 109-acre park that re-creates Dutch country life through a colorful cross section of historic buildings and dwellings transported from all over the country, complete with windmills, fully furnished thatch-roof farmhouses, craft shops, and the "klomp" of wooden shoes. Children can participate in farm life, ride old-fashioned toys, play in a 1930s playground, and when they tire, take a tram to the next stop. For those who still don't get the picture, a *HollandRama* mobile time capsule provides a glimpse of life in Holland. (The museum is on the northern outskirts of town.) ⊠ *Schelmseweg 89, 6818 SJ* ☎ *026/357–6111* ⊕ *www.openluchtmuseum.nl* 🖾 *€11.70* ☉ *Apr.–Oct., daily 10–5; Nov.–Mar., Tues.–Sun. 10–4:30.*

Not far from Arnhem's train station lies the verdant, 185-acre **Sonsbeek Park** with its striking 15th-century white mill house, the **Witte Molen,** and a visitor center, **Bezoekerscentrum,** where you can get information about the park, see the inner workings of an old water mill, and buy some homemade "windmill bread," *Molenbrood,* or the flour to mill your own. Take time to wander through the woodlands past lakes and streams, peer out over Arnhem from the **Belvedere** lookout point, and ogle the stately **Huis (House) Sonsbeek,** the massive white villa on the hill, now an art gallery. ⊠ *Zijpendaalseweg 24a* ☎ *026/445–0660* ⊕ *www.dewatermolen.nl* 🖾 *Free* ☉ *Visitor center Tues.–Fri. 10–5, weekends 11–5; water mill Tues.–Thurs. 10–4:30.*

Up the hill from the water mill in **Sonsbeek Park** rises one of four beckoning castles in the Arnhem area, the 1762 **Kasteel (Castle) Zijpendaal** where you can catch a glimpse into another realm. ⊠ *Zijpendaalseweg 44, 6814 CL* ☎ *026/355–2555* ⊕ *www.hgl-vhk.nl* 🖾 *€2.50* ☉ *Guided tours mid-Apr.–Oct., Tues.–Fri. and Sun. at 1, 2, 3, and 4.*

**off the beaten path**

The **CASTLES OF ARNHEM** – A castle tour in surrounding Arnhem should first take you to medieval **Kasteel Doorwerth** (⊠ Fonteinallee 2, Doorwerth ☎ 026/339–7406). Authentically furnished and magnificently decorated, **Kasteel Middachten** (⊠ Landgoed Middachten 3, De Steeg ☎ 026/495–4998) is a fun outing, but mind the trick floor. **Kasteel Rozendaal** (⊠ Rozendaal 1, Rozendaal ☎ 026/364–4645) crowns a town that is on a par with Wassenaar (near The Hague) as the wealthiest in the Netherlands. Contact the local VVV information office for details.

## Where to Stay & Eat

★ **¢–$$** ✕ **La Puerta.** One of the original places in Arnhem where you can eat underground in a 15th-century cellar, this tapas bar–restaurant features 65 different tapas as well as full meals, with live music on Friday and Saturday. ⊠ *Varkensstraat 48a* ☎ *026/351–0106* ⊕ *www.tapaslapuerta. nl* 🍽 *AE, DC, MC, V* ☉ *Closed Tues. June–Aug. No lunch.*

**$$–$$$** 🏨 **Best Western Hotel Haarhuis.** By American standards, this hotel offers all the comforts of home in the center of town, directly across from the train station. ⊠ *Stationsplein 1, 6800 AG* ☎ *026/442–7441* 🖨 *026/ 442–7449* ⊕ *www.hotelhaarhuis.nl* 🛏 *74 rooms, 10 suites* ⚖ *Restaurant, room service, minibars, cable TV with movies, Wi-Fi, gym, bar, lobby lounge, business services, convention center, meeting rooms, parking (fee), some pets allowed (fee), no-smoking floors; no a/c in some rooms* 🍽 *AE, DC, MC, V* ⭢⊙ *BP.*

**$** 🏨 **Hotel Blanc.** This small hotel, directly across from the railway station in central Arnhem, is situated in a turn-of-the-20th-century town house and offers bright, comfortable rooms and a friendly café. ✉ Co-ehoornstraat 4, 6811 LA ☎ 026/442–8072 🖷 026/443–4749 ⊕ *www. hotel-blanc.nl* ➥ *20 rooms* ⚭ *Restaurant, in-room safes, cable TV with movies, in-room broadband, bar, lounge, meeting rooms, some pets allowed, parking (fee)* ▱ *AE, DC, MC, V* ❑ *CP.*

★ $ ▦ **Molendal.** By far our favorite choice for Arnhem, this Jugendstil-style city mansion, on a Boston-row-house-look-alike street close to the town center and station (and bordering the magnificent Sonsbeek Park), is a joy to behold with its imposing staircases, light-filled spacious rooms, and modern bathrooms. Enjoy your buffet breakfast in the cozy sun-room while Fleur, the resident pooch, makes you feel at home. ✉ *Cron-jéstraat 15, 6814 AG* ☎ *026/442–4858* 🖷 *026/443–6614* ⊕ *www. hotel-molendal.nl* ➥ *15 rooms, 2 suites* ⚭ *Café, room service, mini-bars, cable TV, Wi-Fi, bar, lounge, dry cleaning, laundry service, some free parking, some pets allowed, no-smoking floors£* ▱ *AE, DC, MC, V* ❑ *CP.*

$ ▦ **NH Rijnhotel.** If you want to be in the middle of the action and still have a view of the Rhine—since that seems to be the thing to do when you come here—it's only a 10–15 minute walk to the center of town from this serene hotel where all the rooms and the terrace offer magnificent river views. If you'd rather bike than walk or cruise, two-wheelers can be reserved in advance in summer. It's only a short pedal to the nearby Dutch Open Air Museum. ✉ *Onderlangs 10, 6812 CG* ☎ *026/443–4642* 🖷 *026/445–4847* ⊕ *www.nhhotels.com* ➥ *60 rooms, 8 suites* ⚭ *Restaurant, room service, bar, minibars, cable TV with movies, bicycles, lounge, dry cleaning, laundry service, meeting rooms, free parking, some pets allowed, no-smoking floors* ▱ *AE, DC, MC, V.*

## Shopping

You may want to increase your credit-card limit before you travel to Arnhem, because the shops are a booby trap waiting to blast you into debt. Market days are Friday morning and Saturday at Kerkplein, and late shopping is on Thursday until 9. A few of the best picks, in addition to the pocket of antiques shops on Bakkerstraat, are the following: **Alexander van den Hoven** (✉ Bentinckstraat 4 ☎ 026/443–4086), a designer jewelry shop, has pearls to make your pupils dilate. **Black Point** (✉ Nieuwstad 2 ☎ 026/443–0073) is a gasping breath of fresh-air fashion for women who think that black and white are the only respectable colors. **Brassa** (✉ Bakkerstraat 11a ☎ 026/442–7589) is the place for clocks, kitchenware, fun postcards, and funky gifts such as the stuffed-animal heads for that incessantly needy child back home. **De Bijenkorf** (✉ Ketelstraat 45 ☎ 026/371–5700) is the Dutch version of Bloomingdale's, with a superb cafeteria upstairs. **Hendriksen** (✉ Vijzelstraat 11–12 ☎ 026/443–7454) is a men's and women's European fashion house with only good taste for sale. **Noack** (✉ Vijzelstraat 23 ☎ 026/442–4861), an old-world delicatessen and Dutch souvenir/specialty shop, is perfect for Aunt Mary's last-minute gift. **Wim Poll-mann** (✉ Vijzelstraat 18 ☎ 026/442–4103), a tableware emporium extraordinaire, has a bargain basement at medieval prices and shipping to the United States.

# THE GREEN HEART ESSENTIALS

## Transportation

### BY BIKE

Free bicycles are provided for visitors in the Hoge Veluwe National Park. You can also rent bicycles at most railway stations.

🚲 **Bike Rentals Blakborn** ✉ Soerenseweg 3, Apeldoorn ☎ 055/521-5679. **Hotel Restaurant de Harmonie** ✉ Beulakerweg 55, Giethoorn ☎ 0521/361372. **NS Rijwielshop** ✉ Stationsplein, Zutphen ☎ 0575/519327.

**Prinsen** ✉ Beulakerweg 137, Giethoorn ☎ 0521/361261. **Scholten** ✉ Luttekestraat 7, Zwolle ☎ 038/421-7378.

### BY BUS

A comprehensive network of local and regional bus services in the Green Heart provides a useful supplement to the train service.

🚌 **Public transportation** ☎ 0900/9292.

### BY CAR

From Amsterdam, take A1 to Amersfoort, Apeldoorn, and Deventer or Zutphen; A2 and A12 to Arnhem; or A1 and A28 to Zwolle, continuing on, if you like, to Staphorst. Likewise, Giethoorn is in the same neighborhood via the N331 and N334 from Zwolle. Kampen is another good detour en route to Zwolle, with a deviation via the N50. Nijmegen is easily reached from Arnhem by A325. Bronkhorst is accessible either from Arnhem on the A348, or from Zutphen via the N345 or N314.

🚗 **Car Rentals Alamo** ☎ 023/556-3666 in Holland. **Avis** ☎ 0800/235-2847 in Holland. **Budget** ☎ 023/568-8888 in Holland. **Europecar** ☎ 070/381-1812 in Holland. **Hertz** ☎ 0900/235-4378 in Holland.

### BY TAXI

Taxis wait at city railway stations; additional stands may be available in central shopping and hotel districts.

### BY TRAIN

Frequent express Intercity trains link Amsterdam with Amersfoort, Apeldoorn, Deventer, Zwolle, Arnhem, and Nijmegen. To reach Zutphen by train, change in either Arnhem or Zwolle.

🚆 **The Netherlands Railways (NS)** ☎ 0900/9292 ⊕ www.ns.nl.

## Contacts & Resources

### EMERGENCIES

🚨 **Emergency Services National Emergency Alarm Number** ☎ 112 for police, fire, and ambulance.

### TOURS

The tourist offices in most cities in the region organize walking tours in summer months. Inquire for times, minimum group size, and whether or not English translation is offered or can be arranged.

In summer (late June–late August) the VVV Apeldoorn offers a variety of tours through the surrounding nature parks.

🗐 Fees & Schedules **VVV Apeldoorn** ☎ 0900/1681636 or 055/578-8884.

## VISITOR INFORMATION

🗐 Tourist Information **VVV Amersfoort** ⊠ Stationsplein 9–11, 3818 LE ☎ 033/463-2804, 0900/112-2364 in Holland ⊕ www.vvvamersfoort.nl ⊕ www.aantrekkelijkamersfoort.nl. **VVV Apeldoorn** ⊠ Stationstraat 72, 7311 MH ☎ 055/578-8884, 0900/168-1636 in Holland [€0.45 per min] 🖷 055/521-1290 ⊕ www.vvvapeldoorn.nl. **Arnhem Tourist Information** ⊠ Velperbuitensingel 25, 6828 CV ☎ 024/329-7878, 0900/112-2344 in Holland 🖷 024/329-7879 ⊕ www.vvv.web.nl. **VVV Deventer** ⊠ Keizerstraat 22, 7411 HH ☎ 0570/691410, 0900/353-5355 in Holland 🖷 0570/643338 ⊕ www.vvvdeventer.nl. **VVV Giethoorn** ⊠ Beulakerweg 114a, 8355 AL ☎ 0900/567-4637 **VVV Kampen** ⊠ Oudestraat 151, 8261 CL ☎ 038/331-3500 🖷 038/332-8900 ⊕ www.vvvkampen.nl. **VVV Nijmegen** ⊠ Keizer Karelplein 2, 6511 NC ☎ 024/329-7878, 0900/112-2344 in Holland ⊕ www.vvvnijmegen.nl. **VVV Staphorst** ⊠ Gemeenteweg 4, 7951 CN ☎ 0900/112-2375. **VVV Zutphen** ⊠ Stationsplein 39, 7200 BC ☎ 0575/519-355 or 0900/269-2888 🖷 0575/517928 ⊕ www.vvvzutphen.nl. **VVV Zwolle** ⊠ Grote-Kerkplein 14, 8011 PK ☎ 038/421-6798 🖷 038/422-2679 ⊕ www.vvvzwolle.nl.

# The North & the Wadden Sea Islands

6

## WORD OF MOUTH

"If you get a chance, get up to Harlingen, the port where the ferries leave to go to the Frisian islands of Terschelling, Texel, Vlieland, etc. You want to visit West-Terschelling and go to the darling main street with cobblestone and bakery shops galore with lots of sugar bread. Go to the other side of the island on bike [to] have a picnic and see the North Sea."

—Tricia

"If you like small, small towns, I suggest going to Makkum to see the pottery works and Workum for the Jopie Huisman Museum."

—donna

By Shirley J. S. Agudo

**IF THE DUTCH COUNTRYSIDE IS ONE OF THE BEST-KEPT TRAVEL SECRETS,** then Holland's North and its islands are its softest whisper. A fairy-tale land, these northern reaches conjure up images of Hans Christian Andersen, Hans Brinker, and Don Quixote rolled into one—the wooden shoes (*klompen*) worn mostly by the farmers in the province of Drenthe to guard their feet against the dampness of the fields; the ice skates of Friesland's tour de force, the Elfstedentocht 11-city skating tour; and the windmills, those lyrical symbols of mind over matter. As Danish writer Andersen, himself the son of a shoemaker, wrote in 1847, "The housemaids here wear wooden shoes which look like Chinese shoes seen through a magnifying glass." Such is still the case in the North, although it is now mainly the farmer and his wife, rather than the housemaid, who wear them. Fabled images perhaps, but here in never-never land, the fairy tale comes true.

The northern provinces of Friesland, Groningen, and Drenthe—which include four of the five islands canopied across the Wadden Sea coast and linked to the North Sea—were home to Holland's earliest settlers, the Stone Age inhabitants who left mysterious, megalithic boulder configurations here as proof of their presence. These provinces retain much of the past, flavoring today's quintessentially Dutch villages with a spicy blend of prehistoric and medieval tartness unique to this area.

Friesland, the rebel of the pack, with its own language and customs, is mostly a waterway linked by patches of land, offering every conceivable water sport known to mankind, as well as some known only to the Frisians.

Groningen, bordering Germany on the east, is the hopping hub of the North, a pyrotechnic mix of university verve and manorial splendor. Surrounded by *borgen,* the manor houses of the once-rich-and-famous, the port city of Groningen, which is also capital of the province, pulses with the academic vibrancy of its ancient seat of learning and the inherent nightlife. Despite its extra buzz of brain cells, however, this province favors old-fashioned local traditions, such as using richly tapestried rugs as tablecloths. Groninger Museum is worth the trip alone.

Drenthe, "*mooi* (beautiful) Drenthe," as the Dutch automatically respond when you mention this province, is the noble matriarch of the Dutch family and consequently rich in history, her bodice a vestment of idyllic beauty . . . corseted by meandering Drentse Aa streams and an endless procession of poplar-lined country roads interlaced by some 300 km (187 mi) of bicycle paths winding through green fields and moors. Van Gogh himself wanted to live here forever, so intense was the painterly effect the region had on him. A worse fate could have befallen him (and did, unfortunately), and he not only cut off his ear to spite his face but also shot himself in a cornfield in France. If only he had stayed in Drenthe . . .

Clinging to the North Sea, the five Wadden Sea islands of Vlieland, Terschelling, Ameland, Texel, and Schiermonnikoog are havens of nature for beach, bird, and bike lovers alike, as well as for the city-weary. Although similar in many respects, each island has its own character and appeal, the closest being only a 20-minute ferry ride from the coast and the farthest just two hours away. Of Caribbean clime they are not, but they do enjoy about twice as much sunshine as the mainland, albeit with more breezes. Two of the islands are off-limits to visitors' cars, making them particularly captivating refuges of peace and quiet, and the tidal mudflats of the Wadden Sea make for a uniquely curious approach.

Late spring, summer, and early fall are, of course, the best times to tour the North and the islands, especially if you like water sports, camping, biking, and hiking. For ice-skating fans, a good Dutch winter replete with frozen canals and the chance-in-a-lifetime Elfstedentocht is a chilling enticement.

## Exploring the North & the Islands

You can get a good taste of the area by beginning in Leeuwarden, capital of Friesland, then looping through the Frisian countryside and heading either westward to the Elfstedentocht towns and on to one or more of the islands, or eastward to the thriving city of Groningen and the idyllic Drenthe countryside. If you are driving, there is no problem in getting around these relatively off-the-beaten-track provinces. If not, your best bet may be to take the train from Amsterdam to Enkhuizen, from which you can catch the ferry that crosses the IJsselmeer to Stavoren in Friesland, where another train continues to Leeuwarden via Hindeloopen, Workum, and Sneek. From Leeuwarden there are trains and buses that thread out through the northern sector.

### About the Restaurants & Hotels

Although Vincent van Gogh's brooding painting *The Potato Eaters* was based on the province of Noord Brabant, it could just as easily depict this area. When the lakes and canals begin to freeze over and the promise of another 11-city ice tour, the Elfstedentocht, approaches, northerners rely on their most satiating staples to get them by, one of which is the potato. Dishes such as *stamppot,* a wedding of cabbage and the spud, often laced with a vegetable or two, have wedged their way into the comfort zone and stomachs of the North where fields are starched with potato crop. Other marriages of hearty ingredients such as brown beans and bacon (*bruine bonen met spek,*) and lamb (*lamsvlees*) with mustard and honey sauce, all local products, are abundant here. One of the most hearty of Dutch foods, the thick, sausage-studded pea soup known as *erwtensoep,* which typically kicks in as the leaves begin to fall, is a national—and Fodor's—favorite that seems to line the extensive waterways of this region. Spicy mustard soup, with its kick-in-the-pants flavor, is equally popular and a must-try on your culinary byways. Rounding out the menu are cranberries, homegrown on the island of Terschelling; shrimp and mussels crawling in from the North Sea; and *suikerbrood,* literally sugar bread, a Frisian quick energy fix from the northwestern province of Friesland that's punctuated and coated with enough locally processed sugar to set you reeling on your route. Not surprisingly, with all that heavy food and a tad more oppressive climate, life tends to move a bit slower in the North. The 6 PM dinner hour is still sacred, as in the rest of the

Coming into view as the mist rises, like a curtain being raised on a play, are these iconic images of Holland's north. First, the water-locked, seemingly unassuming land. Then the farmers, their clog-shod feet still as entrenched in the fields as Van Gogh's potato eaters. Enter the tranquil cows favored in old-master paintings and, finally, ice-skaters right out of a 17th-century Avercamp painting. In the North, the sky takes center stage, its vastness interrupted only by the sails of windmills and the spires of church towers, standing sentrylike over this land of low horizons. Here, you'll find the provinces of Friesland, Groningen, and Drenthe—three Vermeer-stock lasses adorned with pearl earrings and a strand of island beads—bowing to the audience, clear pigments of your imagination.

In addition to the local **VVV** tourist information offices in almost every town in the North and on every island; you can also search ⊕ www.northofholland.com for more information.

*Numbers in the text correspond to numbers in the margin and on the North/ Islands and the Groningen maps.*

If you have
## 4 days

With only four days, you could fly from Amsterdam into the Eelde airport near Groningen, and rent a car or take the train from there, or you could drive across the Afsluitdijk, the dike running from North Holland province to Friesland. With Eelde as your starting point—incidentally, this town has a fine Museum Voor Figuratieve Kunst de Buitenplaats (De Buitenplaats Country Estate Museum for Figurative Art), which concentrates on figurative art in the Netherlands after 1945, and merits equal attention for its organic architecture and landscape design—make for ⊡ **Groningen** ❽–❽ ▶ for an injection of nightlife, taking in the Groninger Museum and perhaps a canal boat ride around the city before heading for the Grote Markt area and preparing for an all-nighter. Next day, a quiet tour of the Groningen countryside could be in order, either to **Menkemaborg** ❽ or to **Fraeylemaborg** in ⊡ **Slochteren** ❽; to the mustard-vinegar-candle-making complex in Eenrum and the seal sanctuary in nearby Pieterburen if you have children; or to the megalithic *hunebedden* tombs and information center in **Borger** ❽, in Drenthe, and perhaps the WW II transition camp, Kamp Westerbork, near Assen if you're a history or military buff. While you're in the neighborhood, stop at the Royal Goudewaagen Delft factory in Nieuwe Buinen and ship home some hand-painted pottery. Your third day could be spent in Friesland, west of Groningen, in one of the 11 medieval towns on the famous Elfstedentocht ice-skating tour or, if it's summer, on one of the Wadden Sea islands easily accessible by ferry, and then backtrack to Amsterdam if that is your base. Leading sights in Friesland include the museums in ⊡ **Leeuwarden** ❶, that gem of a harbor town, ⊡ **Harlingen** ❸, and **Hindeloopen** ❻, famous for its elaborately painted interiors and furniture. If you decide to drive across the dike, you could do this tour in reverse, as you will be crossing into Friesland first.

**If you have 9 days**

Nine days allows you to explore both Leeuwarden and Groningen, the major cities of Friesland and Groningen provinces. Take advantage of your extra time to do some shopping in both towns. While in 🖼 **Groningen** ❽–❸, rent a canoe or water bike for an afternoon, and allow some time for outdoor café sitting on the Grote Markt. Expand your repertoire in Drenthe to include an afternoon or a full day of bicycling through Van Gogh's favorite countryside, and if you have munchkins along, take them to the Verkeerspark in 🖼 **Assen** ❼ for a half day in this driving-course park for youngsters where they learn and practice the rules of the road in kid-friendly vehicles. As you traverse through Friesland, be sure to catch Mata Hari at the Fries Museum in 🖼 **Leeuwarden** ❶; visit the one-of-a-kind planetarium in **Franeker** ❷; buy some world-famous ceramics at the Royal Tichelaar factory in **Makkum** ❹ and some ornately painted wooden pieces in **Hindeloopen** ❻ (where you can see rooms full of the local art at the Hidde Nijland Stichting Museum, and ice skates galore chronicling the Elfstedentocht tour at Het Eerste Friese Schaatsmuseum). From there, you could spy on Jopie Huisman's unique junk collection, which he turned into art at his one-man museum in **Workum** ❺; and have a Kodak moment in postcard-perfect **Sloten** ❼. Be sure to allow time, weather permitting, to visit one or more of the Wadden Sea islands, such as **Texel** ❶❾–❷⓿, **Terschelling** ❷❷, **Vlieland** ❷❶, or **Ameland** ❷❸, for a leisurely bike outing.

country, and often arrives even a bit earlier given the preponderance of early-rising farmers in the area. Doors also seem to shut a bit earlier in all but the lively city of Groningen.

Manor house or lighthouse tonight? The North and the islands have a particularly varied range of places to prop your pillow, from the decked-out luxury of the romantic lighthouse, the Vuurtoren, in Harlingen, to the oh-so-idyllic but classy bed-and-breakfast lodgings such as Logement 't Olde Hof in Westervelde near Assen, to the gracious old country houses, such as De Klinze in Oudkerk, or Landgoed Lauswolt in Beetsterzwaag. The **Erfgoed Logies group** (☎ 050/535–0202 for color brochure 🖷 050/535–0203 ⊕ www.erfgoedlogies.nl) of historic B&B properties offers a very high standard of accommodation in a wide variety of characteristically Dutch farmhouses and estates. In July and August rates are higher and rooms are at a premium, so be sure to make reservations in advance. Many hotels are closed from November to March, particularly on the islands. Also, most hotels do not have air-conditioning, but stifling heat is not usually a problem.

| WHAT IT COSTS In euros | | | | | |
|---|---|---|---|---|---|
| | **$$$$** | **$$$** | **$$** | **$** | **¢** |
| RESTAURANTS | over €30 | €22–€30 | €15–€22 | €10–€15 | under €10 |
| HOTELS | over €230 | €165–€230 | €120–€165 | €75–€120 | under €75 |

Restaurant prices are per person for a main course only, excluding tax (6% for food and 19% for alcoholic beverages) and service; note that if a restaurant offers only prix-fixe meals, it has been given the price category that reflects the full prix-fixe price. Hotel prices are for a standard double room in high season, including the 6% VAT.

## Timing

Though the fields and pastures of Friesland stay green practically all year around, the drizzles and showers of late fall and early spring have much to do with it. Your best chances of good weather, then, are the months of May through September. The islands are very popular with the vacationing Dutch, so be sure to make reservations.

# FRIESLAND

Throughout eternity, the Dutch have had to keep their heads above water, living as they do on land reclaimed from the sea and surrounded by dikes—the saucer effect. But the Frisian people of the province of Friesland seem to delight in keeping their heads at water's edge in a land stenciled over a fluid background of seemingly endless waterways. Floating, as it were, this outdoor sports haven is second to none, home to every imaginable water sport, including the popular sailing regatta that ignites the Frisian town of Sneek near Bolsward on the first Friday in August, and the infamously grueling Elfstedentocht 11-city ice-skating race and tour, which takes place only when this piece of heaven totally freezes over. At last count there were 14,184 acres of water, including 13 large lakes and 17 smaller ones, not to mention the network of canals and streams. Clean air, a profusion of nature reserves, lush pastureland, 22,487 acres of forest, with scenery dotted by Frisian cows and horses and steeply sloping farmhouse roofs, all primly and properly reflected in the underpinning maze of waterways, make this northwestern province very seductive.

Fiercely independent, the feisty Frisians boast their own language (Frisian), an ancient tongue that has Germanic roots with traces of Dutch, English, and German still apparent; their own flag, bearing the leaves of the water lily—their "national" plant—appearing like red hearts on a white-and-blue ground; their own "national" anthem; their own "national" animal, the swan, whose image adorns the peaks of many rooftops; and, indeed, their own outlook on life. Generally regarded as hospitable, reliable, and straightforward, Frisians are also known to be fiercely stubborn in their individuality. Leeuwarden, capital of the province, is the largest Frisian town, with bustling markets, shopping, and a decent nightlife, and Sloten, a mere dot of a village, is so picturesque that it looks as thought it came straight out of a storybook.

## Leeuwarden

❶ *132 km (83 mi) north of Amsterdam.*

Eclectic and electric Leeuwarden, capital of the province of Friesland, was the official residence of the first king of the Netherlands, William I, and was also the birthplace of two artists of deception: M. C. Escher, master of geometric distortions and tricks of perspective, and Mata Hari, the dancer-turned-spy who flaunted her notorious brand of deceit. Also born here was Saskia, wife of the great Dutch master of art, Rembrandt, whose portrait of her is in Leeuwarden's Fries Museum. When the ice thickens, which happens infrequently, Leeuwarden is also the starting and finishing point for a uniquely Dutch ice-skating race, the Elfst-

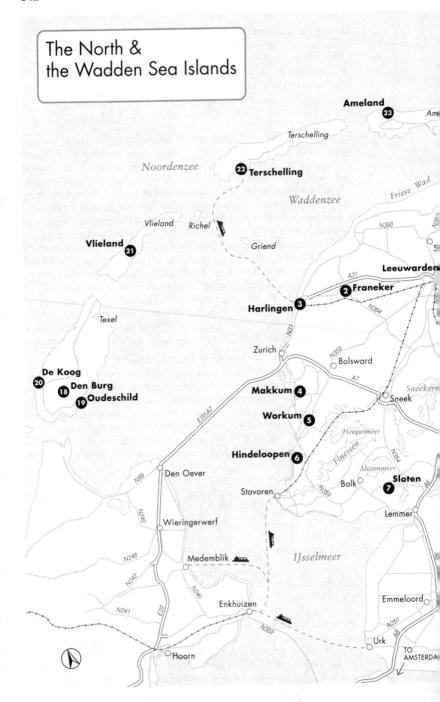

# The North &
# the Wadden Sea Islands

**Ameland**
**23** Am

Terschelling

*Noordenzee*

**22** **Terschelling**

*Waddenzee*

Friese Wad

N393

N365

*Vlieland* *Richel*

**Vlieland**
**21**

*Griend*

**Leeuwarden**

A31

**2** **Franeker**

N384

**Harlingen** **3**

N31

*Texel*

Zurich

N359
Bolsward

**De Koog**
**20**

**18** **Den Burg**

**Makkum** **4**

A7

*Sneeker*

**19** **Oudeschild**

**Workum** **5**

Sneek

*Heegermeer*

E22/A7

*Fluessen*

N354

**Hindeloopen** **6**

*Slotenmeer*

**Sloten**

Balk

**7**

N99
Den Oever

Stavoren

N359

Lemmer

A6

N240

Wieringerwerf

N248

N242

*IJsselmeer*

Medemblik

N240

Emmeloord

N351

N241

E22

Enkhuizen

A6

N302

Urk

**TO**
**AMSTERDAM**

Hoorn

edentocht, which traverses 11 medieval cities across Friesland (see Poetry In Motion–The Elfstedentocht box, *below*). During the thaw of the year, it's the cows that get all the attention here in one of the largest cattle markets in Europe, a weekly event proving Leeuwarden's position as the focal point of the Dutch dairy industry. Just ask "Us Mem," the cow that stands over the town (at the plaza off Harlingersingel) as a proud symbol of Frisian prosperity. Leeuwarden has a strong U.S. connection as well, for it was here in 1782 that the first official recognition of the new American nation was declared, prompting a much-needed loan from the Dutch government. Local ties go back even further than that, however, because Peter Stuyvesant, an early governor of New York, then called Nieuw Amsterdam, hailed from this area. All in all, it's a charming town where the carillon bells peal out over tiled roofs and canals.

Home to one of the world's finest collections of ceramics, the **Nederlands Keramiekmuseum Het Princessehof** (the Netherlands Ceramics Museum—The Princess's Palace) takes pride of place in Leeuwarden's old part of town near the Oldehove tower. The birthplace of artist M. C. Escher in 1898 and the former residence of Marie Louise of Hessen-Kassell, widow of the first prince of Orange, Johan William Friso (whose 1740 dining room has been preserved) is a grand Baroque monument. A treasure trove of international ceramics, both ancient and modern, the museum documents the history of Asian and European pottery, featuring a remarkable collection of Chinese stoneware and porcelain dating from the 3rd millennium BC through the 20th century. By pattern and subject matter, it displays one of the largest tile collections in the world and is especially famous for its Spanish, Portuguese, Italian, and Dutch tiles, the Spanish ones displayed in a vaulted room reminiscent of Spain's Alhambra palace. There is a fine café and also affordable ceramic giftware in the museum shop. ⊠ *Grote Kerkstraat 11, 8911 DZ, from railway station, follow wide street across Nieuwestad canal, then left to next bridge and continue along Kleine Kerkstraat* ☎ *058/294–8958* ⊑ *€6, combination ticket to Fries Museum €9* ☾ *Tues.–Sun. 11–5.*

Tinker, tailor, soldier, spy . . . they're all here at the **Fries Museum en Verzetsmuseum** (Frisian Museum and Museum of the Resistance), where 19th-century Frisian shops and period rooms, costumes, a war-resistance exhibit, and Mata Hari are all featured in this ornate Renaissance-era building, the **Kanselarij**, or the Chancellery (linked on two sides of the street by an underground tunnel), where George of Saxony lived when he governed the region in the 16th century. An unlikely place, then, for Rembrandt's treasured portrait of his wife to end up? Not at all, for she was born in this town as the daughter of a former mayor of Leeuwarden and married in 1634 in the nearby village of Sint Annaparochie.

Mata Hari, the other renowned local daughter, has been accorded an entire room crammed with memorabilia, including her original scrapbook, her perfume bottle, and a monogrammed linen napkin. There's also a multimedia display about her mysterious life. Born Margaretha Zelle (Leeuwarden 1876–Paris 1917), Mata Hari—a Malaysian nickname literally translated as "eye of the day," which she certainly became—

found herself divorced and poor and set her sights on Paris, where she sensationalized the world as one of the highest-paid exotic dancers in Europe. During World War I, she found herself once again in an even more precarious position: suspected double agent for both the Germans (code name "H-21") and the French, a role for which she proved naively unsuitable. In 1917, she was arrested in Paris as a pro-German spy and was ultimately sentenced to death. Twelve French rifle shots put an end to her femme fatale life, but her enigmatic story lives on here. The Fries Museum also houses a world-famous collection of silver, highlighted by the Beerenburg Cup, a 16th-century test of "spirit" whereby the procurer spun the windmill on it while trying to down the liquor inside before the *molen* (windmill) stopped turning; failing that, he became responsible for a round of drinks. Look for the silver *Rinkelbels,* akin to present-day rattles, given to celebrate the birth of a child. Dutch ones had whistles on them, and sometimes a stone or animal tooth to ward off evil spirits. ⊠ *Turfmarkt 11, 8911 KS* ☎ *058/255–5500* ⊕ *www.friesmuseum.nl* 🎟 *€5, free on Wed., combination ticket for Nederlands Ceramics Museum €9* ☉ *Tues.–Sun. 11–5.*

Standing in a blissfully peaceful square in the old part of town and close to the Ceramics Museum, the 13th-century **Grotekerk** (Great Church), a Jacobin church, was reconstructed and restored over a span of centuries. It is the traditional burial place of the Nassau line, ancestors of the royal family, and is well known for its large Müller organ, frescoes, and stained-glass windows. ⊠ *Jacobinerkerkhof* ☎ *058/212–8313* 🎟 *Free* ☉ *June–Aug., Tues.–Thurs. and Sat. 11–4, Fri. 1–4.*

**need a break?** In an old wooden sailing boat, you can enjoy no fewer than 90 kinds of traditional Dutch pancakes, both sweet and savory. The **Pannekoekschip** (Pancake Ship; ⊠ Willemskade 69 ☎ 058/212–0903) is moored midway between the railway station and the center of town and is open Tuesday 5–9 and Wednesday–Sunday noon–9 (note that pancakes are not breakfast fare for the Dutch).

Mata Hari lived in Leeuwarden from 1883 to 1890, and her house is now the **Frysk Letterkundich Museum en Dokumintaasjesintrum/Tresoar** (Frisian Literary Museum and Document Center/Tresoar), which promotes the use of the Frisian language through exhibitions on Frisian literature. (A rather small statue of the famed dancer-spy can be seen at the Korfmakerspijp bridge near her birthplace, now a hair salon, at No. 33 De Kelders.) ⊠ *Boterhoek 1, 8911 BH* ☎ *058/789–0789* ⊕ *www.tresoar.nl* 🎟 *€1* ☉ *Tues.–Fri. 9–5.*

Facing each other across the leafy **Hofplein** are Leeuwarden's **Stadhuis** (Town Hall) and **Hof,** which was the former residence of the Frisian *stadhouders* (governors). In the center of the square is a statue of William Louis, the first stadhouder, locally known as *Us Heit* ("Our Father").

No, you're definitely not in Pisa, but the **Oldehove** tower also leans. Although when building began in 1529 it was designed to be the tallest tower in the Netherlands, the foundation along with its future started to sink, and it was left at a height of merely 130 feet. Fine views are yours if you climb the tower. ✉ *Oldehoosterkerkhof, 8911 DH* 🎫 €2 🕙 *May–Sept., Tues.–Sat. 2–5.*

## Where to Stay & Eat

**$–$$** ✕ **De Grote Wielen.** After a day on your feet, treat yourself to a lakeside dinner where the ripple of the water, reeds swaying in the breeze, serenading waterfowl, and soft light of evening will surely put you at ease. Saucy choices include eel with rémoulade sauce, salmon with white wine sauce, a vegetarian combo, rabbit Stroganoff, pork with creamed mushroom sauce, or veal with calvados sauce. ✉ *Butlan 1* 🕿 *0511/431777* ⊕ *www.restaurantgrotewielen.nl* 🖃 *MC, V* 🕙 *Closed Mon.*

**¢–$$** ✕ **Eetcafé Het Leven.** After 10 years waitressing, Manon Planting up and bought this intimate but lively eatery and has made it into a huge success with a good-value menu full of ethnic surprises and vegetarian dishes. *Gado Gado met Kip* is an exotic mix of rice, chicken, stir-fried vegetables, and peanuts in a peanut sauce worth writing home about (a veggie version is also available). There is a small salad bar (ask to partake from it first, if you like, because Dutch custom is to eat it *with* your meal). And, unusual in Holland, this place offers takeout. "Swingnight," with funk, soul, mellow, R&B, and disco, is Saturday night 10–2 or 3 AM, free admission, in their Café Alfred Silbermann next door. *Kwark*, a yogurt tart with fruit, is the dessert specialty. ✉ *Druifstreek 57 (down the street from Fries Museum)* 🕿 *058/212–1233* ⊕ *www.hetleven-silbermann. nl* 🖃 *AE, V.*

**¢–$$** ✕ **Eetcafé Spinoza.** Three rooms, a 1600s cellar bar, and the shady garden courtyard of an 18th-century city mansion make up this popular, cozy restaurant. It is one of those cavernous spaces that, through the patina of age and subtle lighting, manages also to be intimate. Specialties include a Frisian stew with Beerenburg liqueur, a beef -and-chicken dish in a spicy tomato sauce, and spareribs. Their special menu features ethnic foods and changes every three months. There is also a grill room, a theater-restaurant for live performances, and regular medieval dinners where food served on wooden plates is meant to be eaten with the hands (call for times and reservations). Another section, Jefferson's Wine & Dine Room, caters to students and is less expensive. Friday night, a DJ finds himself in the cellar, and Spinoza really becomes a fun place. ✉ *Eewal 50–52* 🕿 *058/212–9393* ⊕ *www.eetcafespinoza.nl* 🖃 *AE, DC, MC, V* 🕙 *No lunch.*

**$$$** 🏨 **Bilderberg Oranjehotel.** Right in the city center directly across from the train station in this royal capital of Friesland, this hotel offers a very high standard with a king's ransom of amenities to choose from, depending on the level of room, and is part of the Bilderberg group of highly individualized hotels found throughout Holland. Pip's Pub is a popular, English-style meeting place, and the restaurants serve both Frisian (hearty cooking with meat, potatoes, and pea soup) and international cuisine. Bike and boating excursions, typically offered by this chain of hotels, introduce you to the wealth of sites and waterways for which Friesland is famous. A champagne breakfast will set you back €15. ✉ *Stationsweg 4, 8911 AG* 🕿 *058/212–6241* 🖷 *058/212–1441* ⊕ *www. bilderberg.nl* 🛏 *62 rooms, 16 suites* ⚐ *Restaurant, café, room service,* *minibars, cable TV with movies, Wi-Fi, golf privileges, bar, lobby lounge, dry cleaning, laundry service, meeting rooms, parking (fee), some pets allowed, no-smoking rooms* ▭ *AE, DC, MC, V* ⧉ *BP.*

★ **$–$$** ⊞ **Hotel-Paleis Het Stadhouderlijk Hof.** History precedes you at this former royal palace, where the standard rates aren't princely but the room styles and quality of accommodations are fit for any king and his queen. Built in 1550, the palace was originally inhabited by William I, Prince of Orange, Duke of Nassau 1580–84. At one time or another, the current Queen Beatrix's ancestors have reportedly all stayed here, the house having been in their possession until 1971. The red carpet now awaits *you.* Ideally located in the old part of town, just opposite the Town Hall, it's the only place in the Netherlands where you can sleep in a royal palace. For true luxe, the William Ludovicus Suite has a cast-iron, four-poster bed and an enormous bathroom with a Roman tub under a lighted star ceiling supporting three showerheads. So-called "business rooms" are a high-tech indulgence featuring CD players, leather lounge chairs, and showers with six sense-surround massage heads. Depending on the season, breakfast, featuring scrumptious homemade bread, may be taken in the garden. For dinners with a royal touch, head to the hotel's restaurant, replete with haute cuisine, garden views, and grand bouquets. The oldest room of the palace, a 15th-century vaulted cellar called the *hofkelder,* is reserved for special parties. Adding to the allure here, room rates range from the luxe to the very affordable. ✉ *Hofplein 29, 8911 HJ* ☎ *058/216–2180* 🖷 *058/216–3890* ⊕ *www.stadhouderlijkhof.nl* ⬐ *6 rooms, 22 suites* ⬠ *Restaurant, fans, some in-room hot tubs, cable TV, some in-room VCRs, Wi-Fi, dry cleaning, laundry service, meeting rooms, some free parking, some pets allowed, no-smoking rooms* ▭ *AE, DC, MC, V.*

### Nightlife

**Café Mukkes** (✉ Grote Hoogstraat 26 ☎ 058/215–9800) brings a rousing selection of local bands to a crowd of enthusiastic young fans. **Noa** (✉ Nieuwestad 63–65 ☎ 058/213–4792) plays a variety of music. The only Guinness to be found for miles around is served at the **Paddy O'Ryan** (✉ Gouverneursplein 37 ☎ 058/213–7740) along with lilting Irish music (and even an Irish breakfast). **Rumours** (✉ Ruiterskwartier 91 ☎ 058/212–9360) is a popular option.

### Sports & the Outdoors

Leeuwarden is a great base from which to set out to enjoy the area's many water sports and quirky indigenous activities or the islands covered in this chapter. It is from here that the celebrated **Elfstedentocht** 11-city ice-skating tour begins and ends; for more information on this famous event, *see* Poetry in Motion: The Elfstedentocht box, *below.*

CANOEING Friesland offers a wealth of canoeing opportunities along quiet countryside waterways and the connecting canals that course through attractive towns. Printed canoeing routes and special maps are available; check with the respective tourist offices. Five of the largest canoe-renting facilities in Friesland are **De Kievit** (✉ Jousterweg 82, 8465 PL Oudehaske ☎ 0513/677658), **De Ulepanne/Balk** (✉ Tsjamkedijkje 1, 8561 HA Balk ☎ 0514/602982), **Konoverhuur Hollema** (✉ Tsjerkepaed 5, 9264 TG

Earnewald ☎ 0511/539213), **Makkumerstrand** (✉ Suderseewei 19, 5784 GK Makkum ☎ 0515/232285), and **Watersportbedrijf de Drijfveer** (✉ U. Twijnstrawei 31, 8491 CJ Akkrum ☎ 0566/652789).

FIERLJEPPEN     A uniquely Frisian sport is *fierljeppen,* called *polsstokverspringen* in Dutch, which involves pole vaulting over canals (and sometimes in them). It originates, so they say, from farmers having to negotiate the drainage ditches between their fields. For a taste of canal hopping, don't miss the main competition held in Winsum in August—truly for the odd-event seeker. Further information is available from the VVV.

SAILING &     Friesland is bordered by the large and windswept IJsselmeer (Lake IJs-
BOATING     sel) and cut through with a swath of lakes, canals, and small rivers that offer myriad sailing and boating opportunities. Throughout summer you will find weekend racing on the Frisian lakes, including the main event, a two-week series of **Skûtjesilen Races** (late July) using the uniquely Dutch vessels, *skûtjes,* wide-bottom sailing barges built to navigate shallow waters. More than 150 companies throughout Friesland rent boats and sailboats, including **De Blieken** (✉ Garde Jagersweg 4–5, 9001 ZB Grou ☎ 0566/621335), **Top En Twel Zeilcentrum** (✉ It Ges 6, 8606 JK Sneek ☎ 0515/419192), and **Watersportcamping Heeg** (✉ De Burd 25a, 8621 JX Heeg ☎ 0515/442328).

## Shopping

The biggest market in Friesland takes place in Leeuwarden every Friday 8–4 at Wilhelminaplein/Zaailand. Late shopping (until 9 PM) is on Thursday, and the old-time shops on Nieuwesteeg, including the **Museumwinkel** (Museum Shop; ☎ 058/215–3427) at No. 5–7, are nostalgically rewarding.

# Franeker

❷ *17 km (11 mi) west of Leeuwarden, 20 km (13 mi) north of Makkum, 120 km (78 mi) north of Amsterdam.*

In the Middle Ages, Franeker was a leading academic town. Although there is no university here today, there are Renaissance gables aplenty, pretty canals, and a highly unusual museum.

Fodor'sChoice     A late-17th-century, still fully functioning planetarium built, by candlelight, into his living room ceiling by a self-educated, amateur astronomer
★     using 10,000 handmade nails: that's the marvel of the **Eise Eisinga Planetarium,** the creation of math prodigy and wool comber Eise Eisinga, hand-fashioned between 1774 and 1781. His motive? To allay the fears of the local townspeople who were panicked by a local clergyman's prediction that May 8, 1774, would mark the end of the world, when a constellation of the planets Mercury, Venus, Mars, and Jupiter was set to collide with the moon. Eisinga, who had written a brilliant mathematics text at the age of 17 (on display here), set about to prove him wrong with an elaborate reconstruction of the planetary system, including multiple moving moon and sun dials, so ingeniously calibrated that it still precisely indicates the current day, date, and times of sunrise and sunset, not to mention every solar and lunar eclipse. Amazingly, no es-

sential part has ever had to be replaced. Eise's motto? Before you enter the gabled house, look to the right of the main door above a little gate. In Frisian it says: "Voersint eer Ghy begint." (Look before you leap.) ✉ *Eise Eisingastraat 3, 8801 KE* ☎ *0517/393070* ⊕ *www.planetarium-friesland.nl* 💰 *€3.50* ☉ *Tues.–Sat. 10–5, Sun. and Mon. 1–5.*

> **need a break?**
>
> Travel back in time (but right next door) from the Eise Eisinga Planetarium to the cozy Jugendstil/art nouveau tea and coffee shop **De Tuinkamer** (✉ Eise Eisingastraat 2 ☎ 0517/397474). It has, arguably, the best Dutch *appelgebak* (apple pie) in the Netherlands. Afternoon tea with scones is also available, as are soups, sandwiches, and pancakes. A summer-garden room is in back. De Tuinkamer is open Tuesday through Sunday from 9:30 to 6.

## Harlingen

**❸**

**Fodor's**Choice
★

*30 km (19 mi) west of Leeuwarden.*

A pin drop of a seaport, fitted out with gabled merchant houses that wouldn't be out of place in Amsterdam, Harlingen is a place where you may want to linger instead of using it merely as a departure point for the Wadden Sea islands of Terschelling or Vlieland. It's a gem of a harbor town, with none of the seediness of some ports. One of the best reasons to come here, however, is its famous lighthouse hotel, the Vuurtoren. From the main Noorderhaven canal, go one street over to Voorstraat for some of the best local shops. At night, walk along Zoutsloot street to see how the locals live in their prim little lace-curtained houses fronted by gas lanterns. **Gemeentemuseum Het Hannemahuis** (Hannemahuis Municipal Museum), in a lovely old merchant's house, features local Harlingen history, shipping, and tile production. ✉ *Voorstraat 56, 8861 BM* ☎ *0517/413658* ⊕ *www.harlingen.nl* 💰 *€1.55* ☉ *Mid-Mar.–mid-June, Tues.–Sat. 1:30–5; mid-June–Sept., Tues.–Sat. 10–5, Sun. 1:30–5; Oct.–Nov., Tues.–Sat. 1:30–5.*

At Voorstraat 84 in Harlingen, just down the street from the Hannemahuis museum, you can visit the workshop and purchase ceramics at the **Harlinger Aardewerk en Tegelfabriek** (Pottery and Tile Factory), but we recommend saving your money for the considerably more beautiful ceramics only 16 km (10 mi) south in Makkum at Koninklijke (Royal) Tichelaar Makkum.

### Where to Stay & Eat

**$$-$$$** ✕ **Restaurant de Gastronoom.** A *très chic* French overture begins with lobster soup, an aperitif glass of potato cocktail with a smidgen of seafood and succulent brown rolls, then open ravioli with spinach and mussels in a crab sauce . . . and that's just for starters. Dine by candlelight to the sound of the nearby carillon while you contemplate saving enough money for the surrounding shops. Friendly owners Marco and Inez keep it oh so classy. ✉ *Voorstraat 38* ☎ *0517/412172* ⊕ *www.de-gastronoom. nl* ⌂ *Reservations essential* ▭ *AE, DC, V* ☉ *Closed Mon. Oct.–Apr.*

★ **$$$-$$$$** 🏨 **Vuurtoren (Lighthouse) van Harlingen.** Romance is the real reason to come to Harlingen. For once in a lifetime, experience the unparalleled rush that comes from sleeping at the top of a luxurious lighthouse—two people only, please. The romantic dream of Gosse Beerda, a visionary and former journalist, was to do just that, so he bought a lighthouse whose lights had been extinguished, and renovated it to the hilt. The ultimate getaway, the Vuurtoren features a deluxe circular shower with heated tiles and piped-in music; a glamorous, contemporary lounge-bedroom with a kidney-shape bed (with built-in CD player) that doubles as a sofa; and an enclosed hull with dishes and silverware, all encircled by a 360-degree view of the harbor and Harlingen. Take your coffee or tea, champagne or wine, from the minibar—or even the breakfast feast left discreetly inside the door by lighthouse keeper Hilda—up to the top observation deck, from where, on a clear day, you can see the Wadden Sea islands and their respective lighthouses. A VHF radio lets you eavesdrop on the dialogue between sailing vessels and the harbormaster, and there's a wind-force direction meter for those with nothing better to do. Beerda now also offers, canal-side in Harlingen, a two-person luxury lifeboat fitted out with a red-cedar bath. His latest venture is a suite in a renovated crane. You are "beamed up" through a tube-shape elevator to a futuristic-looking suite. In Beerda's inimitable style, you can even choose the color of the water in your shower here and turn the crane by yourself (for the little boy in you). Reserve far in advance for any of these fantasy stays. ⊠ *Lighthouse, Havenweg 1 (information office, Voorstraat 34), 8861 BL* ☎ *0515/540550* 🖷 *0515/543605* ⊕ *www.vuurtoren-harlingen.nl* 🛏 *1 room, 1 boat* ⌂ *Minibar, cable TV, in-room DVD; no room phones, no smoking* ⊟ *No credit cards* ℣❙ *BP.*

**$** 🏠 **Het Heerenlogement.** Once the home of a wealthy family, this imposing, all-white 16th-century building has been converted to a prim and proper hotel and overlooks one of the many rippling harbor canals snaking through Harlingen. Beerenburg, a special Frisian *borrel* or drink made with a secret recipe of spices and herbs, is a specialty served in the hotel pub, and the restaurant food is Dutch with a French accent. Access to the harbor, if you're setting off to one of the islands, is only a 10-minute walk or a cab ride away. ⊠ *Frankereind 23, 8861 AA* ☎ *0517/415846* 🖷 *0517/412762* ⊕ *www.heerenlogement.nl* 🛏 *25 rooms* ⌂ *Restaurant, cable TV, Wi-Fi, bicycles, bar, meeting rooms, parking (fee), some pets allowed* ⊟ *AE, MC, V* ℣❙ *CP.*

# Makkum

**4** *20 km (13 mi) south of Franeker, 37 km (23 mi) southwest of Leeuwarden.*

A shard of a town on the IJsselmeer lake harbor where world-sought-after ceramics are commissioned by the likes of Yoko Ono and the Dutch royal family, Makkum is a real Frisian find. This delightful fishing village can easily be your first stop after crossing the Afsluitdijk (Enclosing Dike) from North Holland province and turning south.

Fodor'sChoice ★ Treasures have been created out of local clay by the same family for more than 400 years, making **Koninklijke (Royal) Tichelaar Makkum** ceramics factory the oldest business in the Netherlands (about 60 years older than the more well-known Delft factory). Metamorphosed into 900 different pieces of hand-painted tiles and decorative earthenware in the popular blue and white, as well as a range of colors in motifs ranging from floral, aviary, country, and humanistic to sleek contemporary lines, the products are of an unsurpassed quality and beauty. After visiting the extensive collection in the factory museum, you'll want to pay a call on the shop. Beware: a visit here may well prove a real lesson in moderation. ⊠ *Turfmarkt 65* ☎ *0515/231341* ⊕ *www.tichelaar.nl* ⊠ *€3.50* ⊙ *Guided factory tours Mon.–Thurs. at 11, 1:30, and 3; Fri. at 11 and 1:30 (reservations suggested). Ongoing video presentation Sat. in lieu of tours. Shop, weekdays 9–5:30, Sat. 10–5.*

## Where to Stay & Eat

¢ ✕⊞ **Hotel-Restaurant de Waag.** If you'd rather spend your extra cash on the pottery for which Makkum is famous than on a five-star hotel, this small but tastefully decorated family hotel, situated in an old weigh house in the center of historic Makkum, just may suit the bill. Located near the IJsselmeerstrand, ideal for swimming or walking along the beach, it provides an entrée to a great area for walking or biking. A cozy restaurant with beamed ceilings prides itself on a chef who creates an imaginative Dutch-French style of cooking—but then it *does* take a fair amount of creativity to combine those cuisines. Why not take them up on the challenge? ⊠ *Markt 13, 8754 CM* ☎ *0515/231447* 🖷 *0515/232737* ⊕ *www.hoteldewaagmakkum.nl* 🛏 *14 rooms* ⚴ *2 restaurants, cable TV, bar, laundry service, some free parking, some pets allowed; no room phones* ☐ *AE, DC, MC, V* ⦿ *CP.*

# Workum

❺ *10 km (6 mi) south of Makkum, 38 km (24 mi) southwest of Leeuwarden.*

This seaside town, one of the oldest in Friesland, harks back to its former trading days as an eel exporter, as witnessed by its elegant 16th- and 17th-century architecture; note the fine gable of Sleeswijckhuys at Noard 5, dating back to 1663. Workum's claim to fame, however, rests with a junk collector–turned–famous artist, a role model for clutter-prone children and adults alike. "One man's junk is another man's treasure." Workum-born Jopie Huisman (1922–2000) could have coined that phrase, but he was more interested in painting it. A junk collector without rival, he saw beauty in banality and transferred it to canvas. Uneducated and uninterested in accumulating wealth, he passionately painted found objects as well as portraits of his cronies. The one-man show at the **Jopie Huisman Museum** features a very clever room where a large portion of his spider-web-laden props, such as rags, worn shoes, and discarded dolls, are displayed. Hauntingly reminiscent of Van Gogh's work in many ways, not many of Huisman's paintings were made available while he lived; indeed, after three of his paintings were stolen from an exhibition, he refused to sell anything again, instead handing it all over to a museum foundation. Today, his work commands five figures. Not bad for a junkyard man. ⊠ *Noard 6* ☎ *0515/543131* ⊕ *www.jopiehuismanmuseum.nl* ⊠ *€3.50* ⊙ *Mar. and Nov., daily 1–5; Apr.–Oct., Mon.–Sat. 10–5, Sun. 1–5.*

## Where to Eat

$$–$$$$   ✕ **Ne Nynke Pleats.** Follow the dike and the signs from Workum to Piaam for lunch or dinner at a typical 18th-century Dutch farmhouse restaurant, run by two young sisters in an achingly bucolic village; find it just past the church, and worth the diversion. There's a free mini–wooden shoe (while supplies last) with cheese appetizer on the Menu of the Day (*Fries Menu*), and outdoor tables overlook a lovely patch of countryside. ⊠ *Buren 25* ☎ *0515/231707* ⊕ *www.nynkepleats.nl* ▤ *MC, V* ⊗ *Closed Jan. and weekdays Sept.–Dec. and Feb.–June. No lunch.*

# Hindeloopen

❻ *6 km (4 mi) south of Workum, 44 km (28 mi) southwest of Leeuwarden.*

FodorsChoice
★

Considered the painted lady of Friesland, Hindeloopen is known for its ornately hand-painted furniture and interiors. In the 18th and 19th centuries, virtually every interior surface was sprayed with elaborate floral, religious, and Renaissance motifs influenced by rich, local sea captains who sailed to Scandinavian and Russian ports. When the town was cut off from the open sea in 1932 with the construction of the Afsluitdijk (Enclosing Dike), its prosperity disappeared along with the fishermen. Today Hindeloopen attracts as many yachters and other water-sports enthusiasts as it does sentimental dreamers. If the ice cooperates in winter, it turns into a Siberian wonderland scene of figure skaters in colorful, traditional costumes, speed skaters (it's one of the towns on the 11-city Elfstedentocht ice-race tour), and horse-drawn-sleigh races. The only word for all of this: enchanting.

★ Wedged under the dike in a building that served as the Town Hall from 1683 to 1919 is the **Museum Hidde Nijland Stichting** (Hidde Nijland Foundation Museum), a vibrant snapshot of 18th- and 19th-century Hindeloopen. Stunning period rooms feature the richly hand-painted, mostly floral-motif furniture and decor for which the village is famous, plus Chinese porcelain and wonderful examples of Dutch *bedsteden,* cupboard beds where families slept sitting up to ward off coughs or the devil and potential death (so they believed). Walls are covered in 18th-century Frisian tiles, and there's a good display of costumes, including traditional red-and-white Hindeloopen bridal dresses whose telltale colors were referred to as "milk and blood." Married women wore a stiff, tall hat and a scarf across the heart to indicate they were "taken." (Wear yours on the right if you're still looking.) ⊠ *Dijkweg 1–3, 8713 KD* ☎ *0514/521420* ⚏ *€3* ⊗ *Apr.–Oct., weekdays 11–5, weekends and holidays 1:30–5.*

The largest collection of skates in the world is to be found at **Het Eerste Friese Schaatsmuseum** (First Frisian Skate Museum), where all manner of memorabilia from the fast and famous Dutch Elfstedentocht ice race is displayed, including a once-frozen toe donated by a die-hard skater who pushed his limits. The wooden-shoe skates conjure up images of Hans Brinker, and the bones carved in the form of skates, dug up by archaeologists, reveal the sport's long history. There is also a restaurant and a shop that sells decorative arts. ⊠ *Kleine Weide 1–3, 8713 KZ* ☎ *0514/521683* ⊕ *www.schaatsmuseum.nl* ☎ *€1.50* ☉ *Mon.–Sat. 10–6, Sun. 1–5.*

## Shopping

For authentic Hindeloopen art, furniture, and decorative pieces, the Nieuwestad and Nieuwe Weide streets house a number of shops. The style can best be described as folk art, using bright colors—mostly reds and greens—with motifs of flowers, biblical themes, and sea imagery all painted on wood. The Zweed family's 18th-century classical-style painting decorates the chairs, cabinets, tables, and seemingly every other object within their reach, a veritable feast for the eyes on view at **Hindelooper Kunst Meine Visser** (⊠ Buren 26 ☎ 0514/521253). **Hindelooper Kunst W. H. Glashouwer** (⊠ Nieuwestad 25 ☎ 0514/521480 ⊕ www. hindeloopen.com) showcases the work of the Glashouwer family, whose stylistic origins date dates from the 17th century and whose techniques were passed from father to son.

## Sloten

**❼** *120 km (78 mi) from Amsterdam, 25 km (16 mi) southeast of Hinde-*
**Fodor'sChoice** *loopen.*
★

Discerning travelers opt to bypass the nearby town of Balk and head instead to Sloten. As the elf of the 11-city Elfstedentocht ice-race towns, Sloten seems to have been frozen in time. Once a fortress at the southwestern gate to Friesland and settled around 1063, it can probably all be seen in about three hours, including museum time and maybe lunch, but there's not a drop in its bucket to be missed. It's one of those park-just-outside-the-village-and-walk-toward-the-church-tower places (only residents' cars allowed within) where time seems to wake up only when the Elfstedentocht connects its fourth dot here. The epitome of charming towns, Sloten has a sleepiness that is to be savored. About as big as a single, priceless postcard image, this walled village comprises in one panoramic view a moat, old sluice gates, a high-water warning cannon, cobbled roads flanked by 17th- and 18th-century gabled facades, and a 1755 windmill for grinding corn. Be sure to see the guillotine in front of the footbridge over the water gate where, according to local legend, a Spanish captain whose crew hid themselves in beer barrels for surprise attacks on Sloten lost his head in 1586, and was cerebrally "hung up to dry" for two weeks as a warning to others. Still shaking in their boots, the current population numbers only 700. Neck- and step-gabled houses, along with lime trees, are reflected in the Diep canal. In summer, yachts skirt the village, a very popular destination for water-sports lovers.

Next to the centrally located Dutch Reformed Church (1647) with its Renaissance, double-stepped gable, the **Stedhus Sleat Museum** is in the old Town Hall (1757). Collections deftly showcase Sloten's history through artifacts, fans, clothes, costumes, jewelry, clocks, and antique cameras. ⊠ *Heerenwal 48, 8556 XW* ☎ *0514/531541* ☎ *€3* ☉ *Apr.–Oct., Tues.–Fri. 11–5, weekends 1–5.*

### Where to Eat

$–$$$  ✕ **Taveerne 't Bolwerk.** In the old center of Sloten you can enjoy canal-side dining in a 17th-century former mayor's house complete with original beams, high ceilings, and tile roof, all of which have been preserved. Every day, from the classic Dutch menu, a surprise concoction from the chef is offered, a welcome overture in an otherwise sleepy, but dreamy, village. ⊠ *Voorstreek 116, 8556 XV* ☎ *0514/531405* ⊕ *www.restauranthetbolwerk.nl* ▤ *MC, V* ☺ *Closed Mon. and Wed. Nov.–Mar.; closed Mon. Apr.–May. No lunch.*

# GRONINGEN: PULSE OF THE NORTH

**Fodor'sChoice**
★

Groningen rocks. As the largest city in the province of the same name, with 180,000 people, half of whom are under 35 years old, it is the throbbing pulse of the North. Historically mentioned by name in 1040 but believed to have been inhabited as early as the 1st century, it was a walled city and member of the Hanseatic League in medieval times that enjoyed six centuries of prosperity as a grain market. Today the city—62 km (39 mi) east of Leeuwarden and 181 km (113 mi) northeast of Amsterdam—is a hotbed of 40,000 university students from two schools and a major commercial center of the northern provinces. In addition to being the sugar capital of Western Europe, it is also heralded as the IT town of Western Europe, and home to the sixth-largest computer in the world, the Blue Gene, at the University of Groningen. Groningen is also a primary ship-building hub and an area rich in natural gas. The nightlife scene is particularly lively, as the town is the only place in Holland where bars and clubs can stay open all night. Culture, punctuated by the daring Groninger Museum, and spectacular countryside drives past manor houses of former silver-spoon merchants round out its rip-roaring repertoire.

## Exploring Groningen

Groningen was once dubbed the "the world's best cycling city" by American magazine *Bicycle,* and it goes without saying that the best way to get around in this town of less than a square mile is on two wheels, or by foot (if you don't get run over by the bicyclists first, that is). Bikes have the run of the road here, as they do in all of the Netherlands—if you hit a bicyclist with your car, it may be deemed your fault regardless of the circumstances. More than half of the city's residents go to work or school by pedaling. Get in the act by renting bikes at the train station (note its art nouveau architecture) or in the center at Oude Boteringestraat 14. There's even a bike taxi and tour service, **TrapTaxi** (☎ 050/577–0782), which hauls passengers around the center via wagon-type carts hitched behind bikes (pick-up point is at the ABN-Amro bank across from the VVV) TrapTaxi operates April through September, daily from 11 AM to 8 PM.

If you come by car, there are several parking garages around town, marked by blue-and-white "P" signs, or you can leave your car just outside the center at either Sontweg on the southeast side or Zaanstraat behind the train station and take the **P & R City Bus** into the center (a bargain at €2

per car). Much of the center is closed off to cars, but be extra cautious around the bike paths when walking. For a relaxing way to see the city, take the hour-long canal-boat cruise **Rondvaartbedrijf Kool Groningen** (✉ Stationsweg 1012 ☎ 050/312–8379), which docks just in front of the Groninger Museum across from the train station and departs year-round at various times throughout the day. Candlelight cruises run from mid-November to the end of December, and there are charters to several local villages from April to September.

**a good walk**

Groningen is a classic walking city. The following route, which will take you approximately two hours to dust the perimeter, begins at the VVV information office at Grote Markt 25, where a friendly staff will help you assemble a package of materials detailing the city highlights you choose to explore in further depth. Be sure to ask for a city map, as well as the walking tour booklet and complete guide to Groningen in English.

For a caffeine boost from a great cappuccino or a rich hot chocolate with whipped cream before you set off, the **De Kosterij** (Martinikerkhof 2), directly across from the VVV, is a perfect spot. Weather permitting, you can sit outside and contemplate your day, or perhaps life's big questions . . . like how you're going to finagle moving to Europe.

Whether you're sitting at the café or heading out the door from the VVV, you're facing the **Grote Markt**, the main square in Groningen where it all happens, from one of the biggest markets—selling everything from vegetables to vintage clothing (daily except for Monday and Sunday, unless it happens to be *Koopzondag*, or Shopping Sunday)—to the throbbing hub of nightlife that it is, particularly with the large population of university students in the vicinity. The columned Town Hall, built in Neoclassical style and dating from 1810, is also situated on this central square.

If the caffeine hasn't kicked in yet and you haven't noticed the Gothic tower above your head, it's time to look up at the **Martinikerk and Martinitoren ⑧ ►** (St. Martin's Church and Tower). Go right, down St. Jansstraat, to the **Provinciehuis** (Provincial Government Building). Although the front facade dates from 1916, the left facade is quite a bit older, going back to 1599. Head up the narrow street to the left of the building, the Kleine Snor, which means "little mustache"; it's the smallest street in Groningen. You'll come directly to the **Prinsenhof** (Princes' Court), originally a cloister-cum-friary, governor's palace, military hospital, and boarding school. Just around the corner on Turfsingel is the entrance to an ancient rose-and-herb garden, an oasis in the middle of a bustling city, the **Prinsenhoftuin ⑨** (Princes' Court Gardens), which has been there since 1625. A canopy of beech hedge creates a covered walkway, and there's a dreamlike alfresco garden "tearoom."

From the garden, make your way down Hofstraat and cross over the Noorderhaven canal to the **Spilsluizen North Side**, an area of landing wharves in earlier days. Proceed down Spilsluizen to the **Ossenmarkt**, in use as a cattle market until 1892, with a square surrounded by houses with striking facades, past the **Gerechtsgebouw** (Court of Justice) and back across the canal to the **Corps de Garde**, a former watch post dating from 1634. Continue down Oude Boteringestraat, where there's a large number of monumental buildings, including No. 44, the former residence of the Queen's Commissioner to Groningen (now a university building) and No. 24, the **Calmerhuis**, one of the oldest stone houses in the city of Groningen. Turn right on Broerstraat to Academieplein and the **Academiegebouw** (University Seat), the main building of the **Rijksuniversiteit Groningen (RUG) ⑩**, the University of Groningen (founded in 1614), a fine example of the Neo-Renaissance style.

Continue on to the Oude Kijk in 't Jatstraat and turn left; go all the way until you hit another square called the **Vismarkt** (Fish Market). To the right side of the plaza is the **Korenbeurs** (Corn Exchange), where grains used to be traded; today it appropriately houses a local supermarket chain. Proceed down the A-Kerkhof NZ to the right of the Korenbeurs, past the **A-Kerk** (A-Church), a Romanesque structure dating from the 15th century, with origins from 1247, and on to the **Noordelijk Scheepvaart en Niemeyer Tabaksmuseum ⑪** (Northern Shipping and Niemeyer Tobacco Museum), in two stone houses considered to be among the oldest in the city. If you have the urge, take a quick detour down Brugstraat, left at Kleine Der A before the bridge, and over to one of the strangest sites in the city—the **Urinoir**. Is it art or is it . . . well, you guessed it, a public toilet? Actually, it's both, the creation of superstar Dutch designer Rem Koolhaas with opaque glass and decorated with human figures by Erwin Olaf.

Whiz along now down Reitemakersryge and turn right on Museumstraat to the **Natuurmuseum** ⑫ (Museum of Natural History) for a glimpse of regional flora, fauna, and geology. Resist the temptation (or not) to shop along Folkingestraat, an eclectic concentration of ethnic shops in the former Jewish Quarter, which just so happens to cut through the Red Light District on Nieuwestad where scantily clad ladies of the night legally display themselves in picture windows and doorways; then continue down Ubbo Emmiusstraat. Just before you reach the canal is a very special shop worth a 10-minute investment: the Minimuseum Shop, at No. 34A, has the largest selection of art postcards anywhere. Inspired by the collection, forge on over across the grassy Ubbo Emmiussingel to the unmissable, floating modern structure begging for attention, the much-talked-about **Groninger Museum** ⑬. This houses a permanent collection of art and objects from the province, Chinese porcelain, and both old and modern works of art, in addition to an ever-changing array of exhibits. If you're hankering by this time to take in some shopping, backtrack to the main thoroughfare of town, the Gedempte Zuiderdiep, and go right until you hit Herestraat to the left, the main shopping, pedestrians-only street. Halfway up the street on the left is a great place for another cappuccino and a sandwich made to order, the Croissanterie Paris at No. 41. If you proceed up this street, you'll end up back at the **Waagplein,** the square modernized by Italian architect Natalini, and to the **Goudkantoor** (Gold Office), perhaps the most beautiful building in Groningen, a 17th-century gabled and red-shuttered former office for weighing gold and silver that is now a restaurant. Facing the front of the Goudkantoor is the Grote Markt, where you began your walk.

## What to See

★ ⑬ **Groninger Museum.** "The most startling museum in the Netherlands," as it has been often called, rises majestically like a ship from the canal directly opposite the train station. A zany architectonic work of art, the Groninger comprises a splash of four brightly colored pavilions connected by below-water walkways. This flashily mosaicked, trapezoidal structure was conceived by Italian designer and architect Alessandro Mendini and made even more capricious by additions from several guest architects. Once across the museum drawbridge, which, when raised to let sailing vessels pass through, reveals a tongue-in-cheek Delft tile motif worth viewing, you'll find exhibits on Groningen history, arts and crafts, and visual art from the 16th century to the present, in addition to some always-exciting temporary exhibits. Pride of place is given over to the fabulous Geldermalsen Porcelain treasure, salvaged only in 1985 from a sunken Dutch trading vessel in the South China Sea—lovers of Asian porcelain will be in heaven. Opened in 1994, the museum is full of surprises, such as the Coop Himmelblau Pavilion, an example of deconstructivism, a new stream of architecture incorporating fallout from fields of tension, the latest movement rejecting tradition and embracing emotion. "Unity in diversity" was Mendini's intent. Seeing is believing. The museum has an audio guide and offers guided English-language tours by reservation for groups of 10 or more. A museum shop and popular Italian café round out the many attractions here. ✉ *Museumeiland 1* ☎ *050/366–6555* ⊕ *www.groninger-museum.nl* 🖃 *€8* 🕐 *Tues.–Sun. 10–5; also Mon. 1–5 in July and Aug.*

▶ ❽ **Martinikerk and Martinitoren** (St. Martin's Church and Tower). Dominating the central Grote Markt square, this church dates from 1230 and was begun as a Romanesque-Gothic cruciform basilica. Finished in the 15th century, it has a Baroque organ, first installed in 1470, as well as splendid murals, the oldest fresco dating from the 13th century; the stained-glass windows date from the late 18th century. The 315-foot-high tower dubbed *d'Olle Grieze* (The Old Gray) by locals is only a little less tall than the mighty Dom Tower of Utrecht, the highest in the country. Groningen's five-story spire has been struck and felled by lightning no fewer than four times since original construction began in 1215; it caught fire in the 1500s from a bonfire set on top to commemorate the retreat of Spanish and Walloon troops; later, it was damaged by grenade fire during the fight for liberation in 1945. Concerts are given with the 52-bell carillon made by the Hemony brothers every Tuesday noon to 1, Saturday 11 to noon, and in summer also on Thursday evening 7:30 to 8:30. (Find a seat at an outdoor café in the square and enjoy.) The foundation of the tower, replaced during World War II with concrete, used to consist entirely of cowhides, perhaps not so strange considering the industry of the region. You can climb the tower up to the third level (323 steps) for a magnificent view of Groningen. St. Martin *is* the patron saint of tourists, but check first to be sure a storm is not impending. ✉ *Martinikerkhof 3* ☎ *050/311–1277* 🖃 *Church €1, tower €3* 🕐 *Church Easter–May and mid-Sept.–mid-Nov., Sat. noon–5; June–mid-Sept., Tues.–Sat. noon–5. Tower daily 11–5.*

🕐 ⓬ **Natuurmuseum.** Woolly mammoths, creepy-crawlies, the Ice Age, geology, wildlife, and land reclamation all feature in this kid-friendly natural history museum. ✉ *Praediniussingel 59* ☎ *050/367–6170* ⊕ *www. natuurmuseum.org* 🖃 *€3* 🕐 *Tues.–Sun. 1–5, weekends 1–5.*

| need a break? | Groningen has a lot of great places for a break, such as the Italian deli **Basarz** (✉ Vismarkt 34 ☎ 050/318–5319), where you can get fresh bread, a wide assortment of olives, cheeses, salads, sandwiches, some delicious prepared dishes, and wines, and, voilà—it's a picnic. Another great place to pack a picnic is at **Kaashandel F. van der Ley** (✉ Oosterstraat 61–63 ☎ 050/312–9331), a cheese shop with a delectable array of 400 cheeses from all over Europe. A selection of olives, crackers, sun-dried tomatoes, and the requisite wines top off your wicker basket, which is also available here. The shop is closed Sunday and Monday. For a quick fish pick-me-up *à la Dutch*, head to the Vismarkt on market days where **Bert Zwier Zeevishandel** sets up his temporary stand selling herring, fish sandwiches, fish-and-chips, and, a great favorite, *kibbeling* (fried cod) pieces with a tartar-type sauce. At **Croissanterie Paris** (✉ Herestraat 41 ☎ 050/314–8143), conveniently located on a pedestrian shopping street, you can design your own sandwich (the grilled *provencette* and the *Italianse* |

*Bol,* or "Italian Roll," are particularly good, as are the huge cappuccinos).

**⑪ Noordelijk Scheepvaart en Niemeyer Tabaksmuseum** (Northern Shipping and Niemeyer Tobacco Museum). This combination museum is housed in the oldest building in Groningen, which dates from the 13th and 14th centuries. Today, still immersed in the shipbuilding and shipping industry, Groningen has amassed a large collection of memorabilia from a diverse range of merchants, from the Hanseatic days to the peat-barge skippers of Granny's days. The maritime section of the museum weaves the story of the ships, the crews, and the voyages they made, right down to the typical skipper's home and the contents of his sea chest. The famous tobacco collection of Royal Theodorus Niemeyer B. V. traces the history of the weed from thousands of years of Native American culture, including objects and folklore touting the healing properties of tobacco, to present-day usage and antismoking campaigns. ⊠ *Brugstraat 24–26* ☎ *050/312–2202* ⊠ *€3* ☉ *Tues.–Sun. 10–5,.*

**★ ⑨ Prinsenhoftuin** (Prinsenhof Garden). Fancy a cup of tea in a priceless 17th-century rose-and-herb garden? A haven of peace and quiet in a bustling city, and the result of more than 250 years of topiary cultivation and hedge growing, the Prinsenhoftuin is one of the purest examples of Renaissance garden style in the Netherlands, and the best part is that you can feast on dainties in its glorious outdoor "tearoom." A wonderful sundial above the entrance gate welcomes you with a Latin saying: "The past is nothing, the future uncertain, the present unstable; ensure that you do not lose this time, which is yours alone." Noted for its promenade walk with hedges cut in the shapes of the letters *A* and *W* (after the first names of former governors of Friesland and Groningen provinces), the garden is neatly tucked away behind the Martinikerk. ⊠ *Turfsingel* ⊠ *Free* ☉ *Apr.–mid-Oct., daily 10–sunset; tearoom during good weather only.*

**⑩ Rijksuniversiteit Groningen (RUG)** (University of Groningen). Founded in 1614, this celebrated university was chosen by Descartes in 1645 to arbitrate his conflicts with Dutch theologians. It is the second oldest, and today one of the largest, in the Netherlands. The main university building, the **Academiegebouw** (University Seat) was built in 1909 in florid Neo-Renaissance style; allegorical figures of Science, History, Prudence, and Mathematics adorn its gable. Some students still don the signature caps of the university: pink for chemistry, blue for theology, red for medicine, white for law, and yellow for math. In the surrounding streets are a number of fashionable houses built by prominent 18th-century citizens. ⊠ *Oude Boteringestraat.*

## Where to Stay & Eat

As a university town and commercial hub of the North, Groningen has something for everyone, from the cheapest to the chicest eateries and lodgings. There are some great ethnic restaurants catering to a more diverse palate, but the penchant for Dutch standbys is still evident, from the raw-herring stands at the markets to the hearty winter menus of thick stews and soups. There are also overnight accommodations to suit everyone,

# ON THE MENU IN THE NORTH

**S**AVORY WINTER SOUPS such as erwtensoep (thick pea soup with bacon or sausage) and mosterdsoep (mustard soup) are comfort foods that slide down really well when the ice takes over outside. Top it off with a Hooghoudt jenever (gin) from Groningen, or a Beerenburg liqueur from Bolsward, touted as Friesland's national drink, traditionally sipped from fûgeltsjes, special stemless glasses, and you'll be ready for the Elfstedentocht. Fill up those extra corners with a slice of karnemelkbrood (buttermilk bread) and wash it down with anijsmelk (warm milk flavored with aniseed), or a mug of Frisian tea served extra sweet. Lekker! (Delicious!) The Frisians also have their own Frysk Menu, a three-course menu, which often includes the local delicacy known as Flielânske fiskskûtel, a fish stew with potatoes and onions that originally hails from the island of Vlieland. Throughout the North, there are always the advertised Dagschotels, the daily special menus or "tourist menus," which are a good three-course value. Eet Smakelijk! ("Enjoy!" indeed).

from the understated classiness of the Hotel de Ville and Hotel Schimmelpenninck Huys to the **Erfgoed Logies group** (☎ 050/535–0202 for color brochures ⊕ www.erfgoedlogies.nl) of historic manor- and farmhouses catering to those wanting a unique experience away from the hubbub of the city. In fact, be mindful of double-pane windows and courtyard versus street-side rooms; in case you've forgotten, university students are known to be nocturnal, especially in a town where there are no closing hours imposed on bars and clubs, and in a country where the legal drinking age is 16 for beer and wine and 18 for hard liquor.

★ $$$–$$$$ ✕ **Muller.** A great place for a romantic rendezvous if one of you has the euro wherewithal, this classic restaurant has a softly lighted and sumptuous interior with cozy, cushy corners. The six-course menu is a culinary delight, especially the imaginative vegetarian option. The wine list and service are excellent. ⊠ Grote Kromme Elleboog 13 ☎ 050/318–3208 ⚑ Reservations essential ▤ AE, DC, MC, V ☾ Closed Sun. and Mon. plus late Dec.–1st wk in Jan., and last wk in July–1st 2 wks of Aug. No lunch.

★ $$$ ✕ **De Parelvisser.** A unique pricing concept and superb food make "the Pearlfisher" a real gem. All main courses are €24 so that, as Chef Ko Rustige says, "People can choose a meal based on what they like and not on price." The specialty is seafood: Dutch shrimp with turnips and a dry sherry sabayon; Scottish scallops with black truffles; Zeeland oysters au gratin with lime and Spanish pepper oil; and, well, you get the picture. For those who get seasick, there's always deer and quail. Save room for the elderberry pie with pistachio ice cream or the "moccaparfait" with chocolate mousse and a coulis of mango. Multicourse meals, whereby a different wine is selected for each course, are popular here, too, as well as "surprise menus" where you're served whatever is cooking in the kitchen. Garden dining is possible in good weather. ⊠ Gelkingestraat 58–60 ☎ 050/368–6044 ⊕ www.schimmelpenninckhuys.nl/parelvisser ▤ AE, DC, MC, V ☾ Closed Sun. and Mon.

**$$$** ✕ **De Pauw.** This chic, highly styled restaurant, done in cream and soft yellows, has a sophisticated and imaginative menu influenced by the cuisines of Provence, Italy, Asia, and the rest of Europe. Dishes include delicate white asparagus shoots (in season), lobster with pesto, and a royal selection of desserts from the trolley. ⊠ *Gelkingestraat 52* ☎ *050/318–1332* ⊕ *www.depauw.nl* ⌂ *Reservations essential* ▭ *AE, DC, MC, V* ⊘ *Closed Aug. and Mon. and Tues. in last 2 wks of July. No lunch.*

**$–$$** ✕ **'t feithhuis.** A hip place for lunch or dinner close to the Martini Church (of which it used to be part in the 16th century), this spot has a trendy reading room–café just off the entrance, along with two levels for dining. Specialties include mustard soup and warm breads topped with mozzarella, tomato, and pesto, as well as salads and pastas. Try the champagne brunch (€21) every Sunday 11–4:30 (with reservations), or the English-style afternoon tea served daily replete with scones. ⊠ *Martinikerkhof 10* ☎ *050/313–5335* ⊕ *www.feithhuis.nl* ▭ *V.*

**¢–$$** ✕ **Da Carlo.** This Italian trattoria on the main street offers 87 different kinds of pizza and almost as many pastas and meat dishes. If you can't decide, order the *Sorpresa della Casa,* the "surprise of the house" with three different pastas. The owner promises "you'll fall in love directly." It's a perfect late-night stop after a movie (the Pathé cinema is just down the street). ⊠ *Gedempte Zuiderdiep 36* ☎ *050/313–5796* ⊕ *www. da-carlo.nl* ▭ *AE, MC, V* ⊘ *No lunch.*

★ **¢–$$** ✕ **Four Roses.** Olé to manager Ton Alferin: this place has the best Mexican-American food this side of Texas, with huge portions, small but mighty margaritas, great guacamole dip, and to-die-for burritos with chicken or beef, black beans, and rice (they'll leave out the black beans if you ask, but why would you?). A rare find (for Holland) is an entire room allotted to nonsmokers. Go before 7 PM on weekends if you don't want a long wait; reservations are taken only for parties of eight or more. ⊠ *Oosterstraat 71* ☎ *050/314–3887* ⊕ *www.4roses.nl* ▭ *V.*

★ **¢–$$** ✕ **Goudkantoor Café Restaurant.** Situated in the most striking building in Groningen—a 17th-century red-shuttered and gabled former tax office–cum–gold-and-silver exchange (19th century), this is a particularly atmospheric place to have a typical but slightly more inventive Dutch lunch or dinner, complete with spicy *mosterdsoep* (mustard soup). ⊠ *Waagplein 1* ☎ *050/589–1888* ⊕ *www.goudkantoor.nl* ▭ *AE, DC, MC, V* ⊘ *Closed Sun.*

**¢–$** ✕ **'t Pannekoekschip.** Kids adore the more than 100 kinds of pancakes at this popular pancake ship—yes, it's literally a ship—just down the street from the casino. Adults, of course, will love these sizzling delights, too, but be aware that pancakes are not breakfast fare in Holland. They're a lunch and dinner specialty, thin and crepe-like, that may be stuffed with any combination of savory ingredients, such as ham, sausage, cheese, fried eggs, pineapple, onion, asparagus, and more. Alright, we admit there's also syrup and other sweet toppings, like chocolate sauce, available. ⊠ *Schuitendiep* ☎ *050/312–0045* ⊕ *www. pannekoekschip.nl* ▭ *No credit cards.*

**¢** ✕ **Cervantes.** A delectable selection of tapas are on tap here, as well as Spanish music and wines. A casual outpost across the street from the casino, Cervantes is one of three associated joints grouped together on a small alleyway called Via Vecchia (look for the wrought-iron gate). Why not go for tapas here first, then slip on over to Hemingway's for a Cuban interlude, and then to adjacent Boccaccio's at the far-end of the passageway for an Italian meal or dessert? After all, gambling can wait. ☒ *Gedempte Kattendiep 23* ☎ *050/311–1875* ⊕ *www.viavecchia. nl* ⊟ *MC, V* ☯ *No lunch.*

★ $$$ ✕⊞ **Landgoed Lauswolt.** Get out the camera and your wallet, Scarlet, and be gone with the wind at this classic and historic country estate–turned–spa resort. The sprawling manor house stands behind a sweeping lawn, all in a quiet wooded village about 30 minutes from Groningen. Splendor and spoils are the keys to indulgence here. The rooms are large and beautifully decorated, and the suites all have separate living rooms. Restaurant de Heeren van Harinxma prides itself on its mix of ingenuity, purity, and contrast in the French-country style and is a member of the Alliance Gourmandise Néerlandaise. Along with highly creative use of internal organs, the award-winning menu here features regular departures from the norm, such as roast barnyard pigeon with a quiche made from the bird's own liver, braised oxtail, and eel from a nearby lake. (Come on, brave it. Travel is meant to be a departure.) Special golf, spa, and gastronomic packages are available. From Groningen, head toward Heerenveen-Drachten via A7, exit Beetsterzwaag, and go through the village; the estate is on the right. ☒ *Van Harinxmaweg 10, 9244 CJ Beetsterzwaag, 40 km (25 mi) southwest of Groningen* ☎ *0512/381245* 🖶 *0512/381496* ⊕ *www.bilderberg.nl* ⇥ *37 rooms, 28 suites* ⚭ *Restaurant, picnic area, in-room safes, some kitchenettes, minibars, cable TV with movies, in-room DVD, tennis court, driving range, 18-hole golf course, 2 pools (1 indoor), lake, hair salon, sauna, spa, steam room, Turkish bath, bicycles, boccie, bar, lobby lounge, shop, babysitting, dry cleaning, laundry service, concierge, business services, convention center, meeting rooms, free parking, some pets allowed, no-smoking rooms* ⊟ *AE, DC, MC, V.*

★ $$ ✕⊞ **Hotel de Ville.** This central, classy hotel with contemporary accents occupies a group of gracious houses once used by the university. Soft lighting, chandeliers, bold antique mirrors, and the warmth of a fire lure you to an inner sanctum of tranquillity. Favored by the likes of Bono of U2, it's the *in* place to stay. Rave reviews are accorded to its Bistro 't Gerecht restaurant. Breakfast is served in the conservatory or on the garden terrace. A thoughtful welcome list of local "musts," in English, adds a ribbon to the package. ☒ *Oude Boteringestraat 43, 9712 GD* ☎ *050/318–1222* 🖶 *050/318–1777* ⊕ *www.deville.nl* ⇥ *62 rooms, 3 suites* ⚭ *Restaurant, room service, in-room safes, minibars, cable TV with movies, Wi-Fi, bicycles, bar, lobby lounge, dry cleaning, meeting rooms, parking (fee), some pets allowed, no-smoking rooms* ⊟ *AE, DC, MC, V.*

★ $$ ✕⊞ **Hotel Schimmelpenninck Huys.** Reeking with history all the way back to the 11th century, this grand old patrician mansion with a Dutch *klok* (bell) gable from the 1600s, once a warren of streets and courtyards, has been cleverly melded into 50 pristine, modern boudoirs and apartments. The scene of revolutionary plotting in the 18th century, it was requisitioned as an officers' barracks during the Eighty Years' War.

In 1988 the building was rescued from occupation by squatters and lovingly restored. Reflecting its checkered history, there's a vaulted 14th-century wine cellar–bar set against the foundation walls of the old city, Baroque- and Empire-style dining rooms, and a Jugendstil Grand Café called Classique, the last very popular with the locals for fine French cuisine. Sweetly enough, they even have their own chocolate shop, La Bonbonnière, a Greek restaurant called Akropolis, and the seafood restaurant De Parelvisser. Be sure to ask for a room either in the newer wing or facing the courtyard, as street-side rooms can be incredibly noisy from university fallout. ⊠ *Oosterstraat 53, 9711 NR* ☎ *050/318–9502* 🖷 *050/318–3164* ⊕ *www.schimmelpenninckhuys.nl* 📲 *43 rooms, 8 suites* ⚸ *3 restaurants, café, some in-room safes, some in-room hot tubs, some kitchenettes, minibars, cable TV, spa, bicycles, bar, lobby lounge, dry cleaning, laundry service, meeting rooms, parking (fee), some pets allowed, no-smoking rooms* ⊟ *AE, DC, MC, V.*

**$–$$** 🏨 **Best Western Cityhotel Groningen.** If you're casino-bound, this trendy, central Best Western hotel is the place to consider, as it is directly across from the gambling mecca and offers special entrance and dinner arrangements. Amenities include a sleek breakfast room and bar adjoining the free 24-hour Internet corner, a coffee- and tea-making cubby on every floor, and a free "relaxation room" with a sauna and Turkish steam bath. Rooms with water beds and Jacuzzis are available. (Ask for a room with an unobstructed view, as the architect has annoyingly blocked out the windows with a "creative" design in some rooms.) ⊠ *Gedempte Kattendiep 25, 9711 PM* ☎ *050/588–6565* 🖷 *050/311–5100* ⊕ *www.edenhotelgroup.com* 📲 *93 rooms* ⚸ *In-room safes, some in-room hot tubs, cable TV with movies, in-room data ports, exercise equipment, sauna, Turkish bath, bicycles, bar, dry cleaning, laundry service, parking (fee), no smoking* ⊟ *AE, DC, MC, V.*

**¢–$** 🏨 **Martini Hotel.** A fantastic location, an ever-so-soothing, teal-green, paneled lobby lounge, and a grand café–bar, not to mention squeaky-clean rooms, await you in the heart of Groningen, inches away from the main pedestrian shopping route and just across the street from the fantastic Mexican restaurant, Four Roses. With all this at a very moderate price, you can't go wrong (that is, unless you have a bad day at the nearby Holland Casino). Apartments are also available for €325–€500 per week. ⊠ *Gedempte Zuiderdiep 8, 9711 HG* ☎ *050/312–9919* 🖷 *050/312–7904* ⊕ *www.martinihotel.nl* 📲 *74 rooms* ⚸ *Café, Wi-Fi, cable TV, bicycles, piano bar, dry cleaning, laundry service, parking (fee), no-smoking floor* ⊟ *AE, MC, V.*

**$** 🏨 **Hotel Corps de Garde.** Near the ancient fortification wall and facing the city center's encircling canal, this small family-owned hotel is in a gracious 17th-century barracks house where the elite sector of the Dutch military was once housed. Partially furnished with antiques, it is a congenial place with spacious, modernized rooms. ⊠ *Oude Boteringestraat 74, 9712 GN* ☎ *050/314–5437* 🖷 *050/313–6320* ⊕ *www.corpsdegarde.nl* 📲 *14 rooms, 3 suites, 4 apartments* ⚸ *Restaurant, room service, some kitchenettes, cable TV, bar, lobby lounge, dry cleaning, laundry service, some free parking, some pets allowed, no-smoking rooms* ⊟ *AE, DC, MC, V.*

# Nightlife

Groningen will knock your socks off with its party-all-night panache. With a prescription to howl, university students turn academia into urban mania in a town with no imposed closing hours on bars, clubs, or discos (such as exist even in Amsterdam) and virtually no cover charges. The hostess-with-the-mostest, Groningen has the most pubs per square mile, after its sister rivals Amsterdam and Maastricht. To top it off, catering to a student population keeps prices low, so you can have a good time for less money here. Curiosity seekers may want to check out the so-called "coffee shops" (as opposed to "koffie shops" or "cafés")— these are places where soft drugs, not legal but tolerated, grace the menu, or the Red Light District on Nieuwestad, a now-legal haven of prostitution where ladies display themselves all day and night in picture windows and doorsteps illuminated by red lights. A former corner café called **Eureka** on the corner seems to say it all. On the other side of the spectrum, classic opera, theater, and cabaret are featured at the **Stadsschouwburg** (⊠ Turfsingel 86). Pop music, as well as cabaret and classical music, are on tap at the **Oosterpoort** (⊠ Trompsingel 27). Ask the VVV office for performance schedules.

### Bars & Pubs

The high concentration of university students here is proportionate to the high density and variety of bars and pubs found in Groningen. Perhaps the largest of them, **De Drie Gezusters** (The Three Sisters; ⊠ Grote Markt 39 ☏ 050/313–4101) is an absolute warren of 19 intimate and innovative bars, 4 of them rotating, 3 of which feature an elevator-like shaft where the DJ shifts from one level to another. Among the theme rooms are a sports bar, a library room with a fireplace, and a ski hut with a chalet motif. There is even a hotel (De Doelen) and café-restaurant spread throughout the barrooms. Needless to say, this is an experience in itself. Of the 19 bars, the Scottish Lady is a student favorite.

For an archetypal Dutch, time-stained "brown café," try **De Pintelier** (⊠ Kleine Kromme Elleboog 9 ☏ 050/318–5100). **Mulder** (⊠ Grote Kromme Elleboog 22 ☏ 050/314–1469) is a happening place for jazz. Particularly popular, **O'Ceallaigh's Irish Pub** (⊠ Gedempte Kattendiep 13 ☏ 050/314–7694 ⊕ www.oceallaighs.nl) is a low-profile home-away-from-home offering traditional Irish music. **Sally O' Brien's Irish Pub** (⊠ Oosterstraat 33 ☏ 050/311–8039) has beef, booze, Irish breakfasts, and a big-screen TV. **Wolthoorn & Co.** (⊠ Turftorenstraat 6 ☏ 050/312–0282) draws in jazz and soft-rock aficionados.

### Casino

The Las Vegas–like **Holland Casino** (⊠ Gedempte Kattendiep 150, 9711 PV ☏ 050/317–2317 ⊕ www.hollandcasino.nl), the only casino in the northern half of the Netherlands, is open daily from 1:30 PM until 3 AM. You must be 18 years of age with a valid ID to be admitted.

### Dancing & Live Music

The most vibrant discos and music venues in Groningen are peppered on or around **Peperstraat**, near the Grote Markt. Best known for being an all-nighter that doesn't get started until midnight is **Benzine Bar** (Gasoline Bar; ✉ Hoekstraat 44 ☎ 050/312–8390), where the music pumps until 10 or 11 in the morning. Up-to-the-minute DJs and a long happy hour attract hordes of students and other young Groningers to **De Blauwe Engel** (✉ Grote Markt 39 ☎ 050/313–7679). For alternative rock, try **De Kar** (✉ Peperstraat 15 ☎ 050/312–6215) **Jazz Café de Spieghel** (✉ Peperstraat 11 ☎ 050/312–6300) swings nightly to mainstream jazz, with live bands over the weekends. The posher, tamer crowd heads to the **News Café** (✉ Waagplein 5 ☎ 050/311–1844). If your taste is for salsa and other Latin rhythms, head for the lively **Troubadour** (✉ Peperstraat 19 ☎ 050/313–2690).

## Gay Bars

A complete listing of gay bars and clubs is available on the **Web** (⊕ www.homogroningen.nl). Groningen's largest and most popular gay disco, **De Golden Arm** (✉ Hardewickerstraat 7 ☎ 050/313–1676), has two dance floors and three bars and is popular with students during the week. With a terrace on a busy shopping street, **El Rubio** (✉ Zwanestraat 26 ☎ 050/314–0039) is a camp way to start an evening among a mixed crowd of gay men and lesbians.

## The Outdoors

Canoeing through the waterways of the province of Groningen can be great fun. Maps with special canoeing routes are available from the VVVs. To rent canoes, contact **Kano 't Peddeltje Groningen** (✉ Herebrug ☎ 050/318–0330), at the bridge to the right of the Groninger Museum and across from the train station. **Hinrichs Watersport** (✉ Damsterweg 32, Schild-meer ☎ 0596/629137), 30 km (19 mi) from Groningen, is a popular starting point for boat rentals.

## Shopping

With a large pedestrian-only area and university students to cater to, Groningen is a great place to shop. Markets are held on the Grote Markt, Tuesday–Saturday. Late-shopping night is Thursday until 9. There's an eclectic range of international shops on **Folkingestraat,** just off the Vismarkt. The best general shopping, including many well-known fashion houses, can be found on **Herestraat, Zwanestraat,** and **Waagstraat.**

The Dutch answer to Bloomingdales, albeit a great deal smaller, is **De Bijenkorf** (✉ Herestraat 57 ☎ 0900/0919), just across from McDonalds. For the teens in tow, the **Chill Out for Rebels** department on the second floor (level three) offers an eclectic collection of hip accessories and fashion with the latest beat playing in the background. For refueling, check out **Café B** on the bottom floor or the treats and truffles just inside the front entrance to the store. For a typical Dutch snack, try the café's warm *saucijzenbroodjes* (sausage rolls). If you're in the market for a pair of wooden clogs, check out the small but good selection at **Blokker** (✉ Herestraat 59 ☎ 050/311–3871), a chain store specializing in housewares.

Antiques lovers will find a web of shops on **Gedempte Zuiderdiep.** For imported table and giftware, **Tafelgoud** (✉ Oude Boteringestraat 7 ☎ 050/311–2707) has a stunning selection, tops being the hand-painted German glass plates. Shipping to the United States is available, and you can pay by credit card. For the largest selection of art postcards and prints anywhere, visit the **Minimuseum** (✉ Ubbo Emmiusstraat 34A ☎ 050/314–6365), where you can also visit Mr. Oegemas's private museum of World War II mementos and photos, particularly pertaining to the Jewish community.

# SIDE TRIPS FROM GRONINGEN

Although there's much to do in the bustling city of Groningen, a day trip through its provincial countryside may be in order. Replete with 16 manor houses, or borgen (⊕ www.borgen.nl) that are open to the public (ask the VVV for the brochure), you're sure to encounter a fantasy en route. To jolt you back to reality before returning to Groningen, sample some of Abraham's spicy mustard at his factory-museum-café in Eenrum, where you can also see or stay at the smallest hotel in the world and visit the nearby seal sanctuary. The more intrepid traveler may want to walk the Pieterpad, a 488-km (305-mi) walking trail beginning in Pieterburen and ending in Maastricht.

## Menkemaborg

**14** *In Uithuizen, 25 km (16 mi) north of Groningen.*

FodorśChoice
★

To the manor born . . . is how you'll wish you'd been when you visit Menkemaborg, a glorious, double-moated, fortified manor house, or *borg,* considered to be one of the finest in the province of Groningen and oozing with exquisite Vermeerian settings down to the finest detail. The furniture, including a showpiece 1777 pipe organ disguised as a phantom secretary, represents the 17th and 18th centuries, all housed in a 14th-century structure. King William III of the Netherlands rested his weary head in the huge 18th-century four-poster bed. Manorial magic pervades the house as a medley of clocks banter at the same time.

As if the master and his lady's digs were not enough to behold, saunter on down to the basement servants' quarters, a remnant of the original house destroyed in 1400, and you'll find the most *gezellig,* or cozy, kitchen and bedroom, complete with Dutch bedsteden, cupboard beds where the servants slept sitting up with mouths closed to prevent devils or the smoke from open hearths from entering their bodies (as they believed in those days). Hygiene consisted of hand washing at the fountain in the main upper corridor, which was fed by a reservoir, and although they look like sentry boxes at the outside entrance, the two little "houses" are really the former privies. The table is always set in the dining room, and the rooms have been furnished as though the manor is still occupied. (If only you didn't have to go home . . .) Reconstructed according to an 18th-century plan found at the house, the garden comes complete with a teahouse and a maze, both fancies of the last inhabitant, the nobleman Gerhard Alberda van Menkema en Dijksterhuis, a bachelor who died in 1902 amid this Dutch splendor. Red-check tablecloths bring you back down to Earth at the 1686 carriage house–turned–café adjacent to the manor house. Elevate your deflated status with a typical English high tea featuring scones and sweet delights, or remain a commoner with Dutch *pannekoeken* (pancakes). Go quickly, fair maidens. You can at least *pretend* that Gerhard has never left. ☒ *Menkemaweg 2, Uithuizen* ☏ *0595/431970* ⊕ *www.menkemaborg.nl* ☝ *House and garden € 4.50, garden only €3* ☉ *Mar.–Apr. 29, Tues.–Sun. 10–noon and 1–4; Apr. 30–Oct. 2, daily 10–5; Oct. 3–Dec., Tues.–Sun. 10–noon and 1–4.*

## Slochteren

★ ⓯ *z20 km (13 mi) east of Groningen.*

A well-preserved, 17th-century moated manor house with 16th-century wings, **Fraeylemaborg** boasts many portraits and mementos of the Dutch royal family and an equally manorial dollhouse with pink brocade walls and matching carpet. Both Johan de Witt and William III graced Fraeylemaborg's premises at one time—and so can you, if you opt to book a room in the old steward's house, now a classy B&B. Other enticements at the manor include a restaurant, an art gallery, a park, and a February antiques fair. ☒ *Hoofdweg 30* ☏ *0598/421568* ⊕ *www.borgen.nl/fraeylemaborg* ☝ *€4.50* ☉ *Mar.–Dec., Tues.–Fri. 10–5, weekends 1–5.*

☬ A perfect day out for kids only 20 km (13 mi) from Groningen can be had in the village of Eenrum at **Abraham's Mosterdmakerij,** a factory museum–restaurant where the congenial manager invites you into the mustard factory to see how mustard (a local specialty) and vinegar are made, and then welcomes you to his charming café serving, what else, mustard soup and other luncheon fare. It's right next to the village windmill, which you can go inside on Wednesday and Saturday from 11 to 5. Then head on over to the resident candle maker where children (yes, you too) can make their own candles in about 20 minutes. As an added attraction, "the smallest hotel in the world," **De Kromme Raake** is also on-site. From Groningen, head north taking the N361 past Winsum and go right on the N984 to Eenrum. ☒ *Molenstraat 5, Eenrum, 20 km (13 mi) north of Groningen* ☏ *0595/491600* ☝ *Mustard factory tour €1.50, museum free, windmill €1.25* ☉ *June–Sept., Tues.–Sun. 11–8; Oct.–May, Wed.–Sun. 11–6.*

☬ An amazing research facility and rehabilitation sanctuary for ill or injured seals rescued in or near the Wadden Sea, the **Zeehondencrèche** (Seal Creche) is a marvelous place to take children. Since the start of the center in 1971, almost 2,000 seals have been rehabilitated and released back into their natural habitat. ☒ *Hoofdstraat 94a, Pieterburen, Groningen ring road, exit Winsum, toward Baflo to Pieterburen* ☏ *0595/526526* ⊕ *www.zeehondencreche.nl* ☝ *€1* ☉ *Daily 9–6.*

The longest walking route in the Netherlands, the **Pieterpad** (⊕ www. wandelnet.nl) passes through towns, fields, marshes, woods, and areas rich in nature. It begins in Pieterburen—28 km (17 mi) northwest of

Groningen (take the N361 north through Winsum, direction Baflo to Pieterburen)—and ends 488 km (305 mi) later in Sint-Pietersberg near Maastricht (hence the name Pieterpad). It can be walked in small segments, and a handbook with routes, cafés, and accommodations is available at VVVs or bookstores.

### Where to Stay

★ $$$–$$$$　🏨 **Grand Hotel "De Kromme Raake."** Listed in the *Guinness Book of Records* as the Smallest Hotel in the World (and part of Abraham's Mosterdmakerij, the mustard museum), this 1920s-style villa-cottage has just one bed—an old-fashioned Dutch bedstede, or "cupboard bed" (albeit double the size of a normal bedstede), contained in a wall and accessorized with a time-warp radio, dressing gowns with nightcaps, and TV. The "Winding Stream," as the hotel's name translates in English, comes complete with a full-scale check-in concierge area and is lyrically back-dropped by the requisite windmill. The flashy black-and-white-tile bath has a luxury tub-shower and a hidden entrance to the cupboard bed behind a mirror. Breakfast arrives surreptitiously at your door in the morning. The hotel sleeps only two for €175 with the champagne breakfast or €275 with afternoon coffee and dessert, a four-course dinner with wine, and, again, the champagne breakfast). If you're looking for an experience and not just a place to stay, this is the place. ⊠ *Molenstraat 5, 9967 SL Eenrum, 23 km (14 mi) northwest of Groningen* 🕾 *0595/491600* 🖷 *0595/491400* ⊕ *www.eenrum.com* 🛏 *1 room* ⚖ *Restaurant, minibar, cable TV, bar, free parking, some pets allowed* ☰ *AE, MC, V* ⑩ *BP.*

# DRENTHE: A STORYBOOK LAND

The oldest, and considered by many to be the most traditional and most beautiful, province of the Netherlands, Drenthe is a storybook land of farmers in wooden shoes (klompen), meandering streams called the Drentse Aa, vast heather fields, fens and forests fairy-dusted with lakes, steeply sloping thatch-roof farmhouses, 500 km (325 mi) of cycling paths, and more horses, cows, and sheep, it seems, than people—all accentuated with quixotic windmills on a seemingly endless horizon. Life *is* but a dream here.

Van Gogh himself was captivated by Drenthe, the quintessential Dutch landscape, so much so that, while painting its alluring scenes, he wrote to his brother Theo, ". . . Drenthe is fantastic. It would give me great peace of mind if I could come and live here forever . . . It is so entirely everything that I think is beautiful here. I mean, it is peaceful here."

## Borger

🔟 *40 km (25 mi) south of Groningen, 200 km (130 mi) east of Amsterdam.*

Eat your heart out, Fred Flintstone. Those Stone Age boulder formations, of which 54 still exist throughout the Hondsrug ridge running between Groningen and Emmen, are the real thing, and Borger is home to the largest one, an 82-foot-long, 44-stone dolmen, or *hunebed* as the Dutch call them, adjacent to what is now the **Nationaal Hunebedden In-**

**formatiecentrum** (National Dolmen Information Center). Its largest capstone weighs an incredible 20 tons. Almost 4,000 years older than Stonehenge, these most ancient of all monuments in the Netherlands are believed to be the megalithic skeletons of burial tombs used by the first farmers in this area, although local legend purports them to have been built by giants referred to as *huynen,* thus the name *hunebed.* Previously covered with a mound of earth, these partially excavated funerary sites have revealed some of the finest known prehistoric implements and pottery, characteristically in the form of funnel-shape beakers, hence the name "Beaker Culture." Strangely, almost all hunebedden (plural for hunebed) lie in a southwest direction, with the entrance to the south. They are believed to have been initially transported from Scandinavia by glacier movement during the Ice Age more than 100,000 years ago, a theory explored in a well-presented exhibition at the museum. You, too, can traverse the Flintenroute, as they call it ("flint" means "hard stone"), a 42-km (27-mi) biking, walking, or driving route past the area's dolmens. Children visiting the Hunebedden Information Center are invited to dress up as Stone Age characters, build their own mini-hunebed, and crawl inside a scaled-down thatch-roof house thought to be typical of that era. (The Drents Museum in Assen further explores the archaeology of this area.) ⊠ *Bronnegerstraat 12* ☎ *0599/236374* 💳 *€4.75* 🕑 *Weekdays 10–5, weekends 11–5.*

A stone's throw away from Borger in Nieuwe Buinen is a blue-and-white fancier's paradise at **Royal Goudewaagen,** a ceramics factory with a museum as well as one of the best places in the Netherlands to overdose on Delftware shopping. Rock-bottom prices can be had in the seconds shop, where errors, barely detectable, mean bliss—less than half the cost of items in the adjacent first-quality room. It is a little-known fact that Royal Goudewaagen produces pottery for Colonial Williamsburg in Virginia. ⊠ *Glaslaan 29a, Nieuwe Buinen* ☎ *0599/616090* 🕑 *Weekdays 10–4.*

## Assen

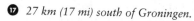 *27 km (17 mi) south of Groningen.*

The provincial capital of Drenthe, Assen used to be a center of contemplation for Cistercian nuns beginning in the 13th century; the convent and former abbey church now house the local museum, which is worth a visit, especially to see its display of bog bodies (preserved in wet, spongy ground composed of decomposing vegetation).

By contrast, Assen is most famous today for its annual Grand Prix qualifying motorcycle races, the **Rizla & Dutch TT** (Tourist Trophy; ☎ 0900/388–2488 ⊕ www.tt-assen.com), which take place in June. True introspection on a more serious note, however, takes place at the WW II transit camp just outside town.

A large part of the center has been pedestrianized for shopping, but keep an eye out for those two-wheelers who do own the bike paths. Wednesday and Saturday are market days, and late-night shopping is on Friday until 9.

If you're traveling by train or bus, it's an easy five-minute walk from the Assen station to the **Drents Museum,** where you will find the Pesse Canoe (from the village of Pesse south of Assen), the oldest water vessel ever found, dating from about 6800 BC, as well as the extremely well-preserved body of a 16-year-old girl, dubbed "Yde" for the nearby village in which she was found in a peat bog by two Drenthe farmers in 1897 (peat was used as fuel to heat homes). Remains of other bodies, clothing, and artifacts at the museum are those of the prehistoric, megalithic tomb builders (such as those found at Borger). Authentic period rooms of the Drenthe area are also worth seeing, as well as a collection of Dutch art from around 1900 (including Van Gogh's *De Turfboot* (The Turfboat), a fine decorative arts and costume collection, and a jewelry collection from AD 400 excavated from the neighboring area of Beilen. For children, there's a Geo Explorer room where they can experience the thrill of the birth of Mother Earth. There is also a 1900s-era café. ⊠ *Brink 1* ☎ *0592/377773* ⊕ *www.drentsmuseum.nl* ⊠ *€6* ☉ *Tues.–Sun. 11–5.*

Nine kilometers (5½ mi) south of Assen in **Hooghalen** is the World War II transit camp **Herinneringscentrum Kamp Westerbork,** where heroine Anne Frank and her family were brought upon their arrest in Amsterdam after having hidden from the Nazis for two years in her now-famous house in Amsterdam. Although all the camp buildings, except for the commander's house and watchtower, have been destroyed, you can walk through the area where the sites of the buildings are marked off and see a remaining section of the train track on which more than 105,000 Jews and Gypsies were transported, most to their deaths, to concentration camps throughout Europe. (The Frank family was on the very last train out of Camp Westerbork; destination: Auschwitz, Poland. Anne was later transferred to the Bergen-Belsen camp in Germany, where she died of typhus.) An excellent museum depicts life in the camp, with actual memorabilia, photos, videos, and even a makeshift barracks room. On-site is a bookshop and café; a bus takes visitors from the museum to the camp site, a healthful 3-km (2-mi) walk or bike ride for those so inclined, through beautiful woods. English tours are available on request. Adjacent to the camp is the largest radio telescope in Western Europe. ⊠ *Oosthalen 8, Hooghalen* ☎ *0593/592600* ⊕ *www.kampwesterbork. nl* ⊠ *€4.50* ☉ *July and Aug., weekdays 10–5, weekends 11–5; Sept.–June, weekdays 10–5, weekends 1–5.*

For a unique experience, visit the **Draaiorgelmuseum** (Street Organ Museum) in Assen, where you can hear concerts on a fine collection of barrel street organs on the second and fourth Sunday of each month 1–5:30 (in December, the second and third Sunday). ⊠ *Rode Heklaan 3* ☎ *0592/ 356718* ⊠ *€3* ☉ *Tours only, weekdays; open on selected Sun. for concerts.*

## Where to Stay & Eat

★ **$–$$$$** ✕ **Ribhouse Texas.** You'll think you're on American soil when you arrive at this rip-roaring steak house, although it's in beautiful Drenthe countryside only 11 km (7 mi) from Assen. Dutch owner Jim Hogevorst and his "pardner," Monica, love the States and have transformed their restaurant into a hoot'n'holler of a place complete with servers in chaps, line dancing, and peanut shells on the floor. Steaks are as good as the place is fun, with the Fred Flintstone rib eye weighing in at 26.5 ounces and a smaller, very tender Lady's Steak, plus ribs and a mixed grill, and good ol' corn on the cob. There's even lobster, if you insist. ⊠ *Hoofdweg 42, Zeegse* ☎ *0592/541360* ⊕ *www.ribhousetexas.nl* ⊟ *AE, MC, V* ⊘ *Closed Mon. and Tues. Sept.–June. No lunch.*

**$-$$** ✕ **De Passage.** For the best in local Dutch fare in the center of Assen, try Alyce Dijkstra's home cooking. Particularly good are *Oma's mosterdsoep* (Grandma's mustard soup) and, in winter, the heartiest pea soup (erwtensoep) this side of the Atlantic. All entrées come with generous portions of refillable vegetable and potato side dishes. Children up to 12 years eat for half price. ⊠ *Gedempte Singel 1* ☎ *0592/300020* ⊟ *MC* ⊘ *Closed Sun.*

**$-$$** 🏠 **Logement 't Olde Hof.** Pure, unadulterated heaven may be experi-
**Fodor'sChoice**  enced here in your own luxury cottage at a very reasonable price. Dirkje
★  Heida has turned her Drenthe-style 1860 farmhouse into a classy, completely restored B&B with several unique options for spending the night (or a lifetime). Our favorite is the Achterhuis ("the house behind"), a haven that sleeps six but is a dream escape for two. Every whim is catered to, from candles to coffee in your own kitchen and Andrea Bocelli on CD. But the tour de force is your own private sauna entered through a very modern bathroom. Luxurious thick bathrobes await. In your free time, you can play a match at the adjacent tennis court, take a dip in the pool, or linger on your own garden patio. Another cottage, called the Venhuis, is a one-room suite with a fireplace and, in a separate bathhouse, a hot tub. But be aware that the bathroom for this honeymoon cottage is a stone's throw away. For some, it might just kill the romance, but if you're game, it's a heavenly retreat complete with your own private deck jutting out into a pond. Besides the cottages, there are three guest rooms in the main house, or Voorhuis ("front house"). Breakfast is brought to you on a tray at a time you designate. ⊠ *Olde Hofweg 5–7, 9337 TD Westervelde, 10 km (6 mi) northwest of Assen* ☎ *0592/ 612733* 🖷 *0592/612016* ⊕ *www.oldehof.nl* ⇖ *3 rooms, 2 guesthouses* ⚱ *Some kitchenettes, minibars, cable TV, tennis court, pool, pond, hot tub, sauna, boating, fishing, bicycles, babysitting, free parking, some pets allowed; no room phones* ⊟ *No credit cards.*

# THE WADDEN SEA ISLANDS

Faced with the choice of visiting one or more of the five islands sandwiched between the North Sea and the Wadden Sea along the northern coastline, you should be aware of the subtle differences that characterize each bead of sand and surf, all rich in shifting dunes, marvelous stretches of beach, particularly varied flora and fauna, and quiet, open spaces stenciled with miles of intricate cycle paths and a proportionate number of bike rental shops. Strung together by island-hopping ferries in summer, the archipelago is also, curiously, accessible by foot. If you're a real stick-in-the-mud for taking life one step at a time, you may enjoy wallowing in knee- to neck-deep water and mud to get there by *Wad-*

# CloseUp

# MUDWALKING & MORE

**THE NORTH IS ACTION COUNTRY,** despite its reputation as a sleepy, somewhat backward region (what isn't, in all fairness, compared to Amsterdam?). If you can't find a sport or outdoor activity in the North, you haven't yet crossed the threshold into Friesland, Groningen, and Drenthe. The entire area, comprising some of the most splendid scenery found in Europe, is nearly overrun with miles and miles of cycling and rambling paths and is home to annual biking races and walking tours. And if you want to kick up a bit more dust, try horseback riding, all manner of water sports (particularly in Friesland), and, in winter, ice-skating on the innumerable canals and lakes gracing the lowlands. Those with a penchant for the obscure will certainly want to try a local version of pole vaulting called fierljeppen, which takes place across canals and ditches, and "horizontal mountain climbing" called Wadlopen ("mudwalking")—wading thigh-deep across the mudflats to the Wadden Sea island of Schiermonnikoog. If you sign up with a tour operator for a mudwalking experience, definitely remember to wear boots that tie or buckle snugly—you need something that won't get yanked off your feet by the mud. And wear boots and clothes that you don't care about too much because they will get muddy.

If luck is with you, you'll hit an Elfstedentocht winter and can watch or participate in the 11-city ice-skating race and tour through Friesland's most picturesque medieval towns. Throughout the year, you can also imitate the famous tour by bike, canoe, horseback, boat, motorbike, car, or even foot. Route information and imitation stamp cards to support your claim that you've traversed each town in the legendary manner are available at local VVV information offices.

lopen, literally "mudflat walking," or simply "mudwalking," whereby you traipse, trample, and trudge alongside an experienced guide (people have drowned attempting this alone) from various departure points on the coast across the shallow Wadden Sea, at low tide, of course, to Schiermonnikoog, and return by boat. Wadlopen takes place between mid-March and early October and can be arranged through various tour operators. In Groningen, call **Stichting Wadloopcentrum Pieterburen** (☎ 0595/528300). You can also try **Wadloopcentrum Dijkstra** (☎ 059/552–8345 ⊕ www.wadloop-dijkstra.nl). In Friesland, call **Wadloopcentrum Fryslan** (☎ 0519/561656).

Enjoying more sunshine than the Dutch mainland, the islands just may turn out to be the pearled oyster in your movable feast. For a superb review of all the islands in English, including hotel information and precise ferry schedules, ask for the "Dutch Frisian Islands" booklet, available at the VVV office or online at ⊕ www.dutch-frisian-islands.com. You can also search ⊕ www.vvv-wadden.nl. These Web sites suggest operators that can take you on Wadden island-hopping trips. For a weather report before you set out, check ⊕ www.weeronline.com/feature/wadden.htm.

# Texel

*85 km (53 mi) north of Amsterdam.*

Fodor'sChoice
★
Texel (pronounced "Tessel") is the most westerly of the Dutch islands and has long been considered a key getaway for Amsterdam's citizenry—masses travel north from Amsterdam to the port of Den Helder, which is the mainland jumping-off port for Texel. By ferry, it's a 20-minute ride to the island. Uniquely belonging to the province of North Holland, Texel is the largest, and some think most touristy, of the Wadden island group. Nicknamed "Holland in miniature" because of its highly varied landscape featuring woodlands, open meadows, saltwater marshes, dunes, and broad beaches, it lends itself to the widest variety of sporting and cultural activities and is, therefore, a firecracker of activity in July and August—not a good time to visit if you dislike crowds. Sheep (which outnumber people), a large variety of birds, 30 km (19 mi) of wide, sandy beaches, and 135 km (88 mi) of cycle paths are characteristic of Texel, as are activities for the more adventuresome, such as surf kayaking, catamaran sailing, island flights, and parachute jumping. A famous 100-km (60-mi) catamaran race, the Ronde om Texel, takes place around the island in mid-June and is preceded by a week of other maritime events. Of the seven villages, Den Burg is the main one with the most shops, not surprisingly heavy on fleece products; De Waal and Oosterend are the more silent partners; and Oudeschild is a fishing haven. De Koog is the night owl in a neon frock. For the ultimate back-to-nature experience, there are nudist beaches at Den Hoorn and south of De Cocksdorp. The **Telekom Taxi** (☎ 322211 locally) takes you from the ferry terminal to your lodgings on the island and picks you up for the return journey if you call an hour ahead. Buy your ferry tickets at the terminal in Den Helder.

One of Texel's remarkable natural features is **De Hoge Berg** (the High Mountain), the 50-foot-high (okay, so it's a mountain to the Dutch) pinnacle of a ridge formed by glacier movement during the last Ice Age and declared a natural monument in 1968. Climbing its grass-covered pathways is hardly a problem, and it offers a stunning overview of the whole island. Throughout the island you can spot the unusual *schapeboet,* sheep shelters that look like truncated barns, some thatched with local reed, with their sloping rumps turned to the westerly winds.

⑱ **Den Burg,** in the island's center, offers the best choice of places to eat and shop. The step-gabled house occupied by the **Oudheidskamer** (Museum of Antiquities) dates from 1599 and gives a sense of local life in times gone by, with exquisitely tiled fireplaces and antique furniture in a homey setting, in addition to a display of local costumes and the smallest herb garden in the country. ⊠ *Kogerstraat 1* ☎ *0222/313135* 💰 *€2.50* ⊙ *Apr.–Oct., weekdays 11–5.*

⑲ **Oudeschild,** the island's historic harbor town, is still used as a port by Texel's modern fishing fleet. During the 17th century, VOC (Dutch East India Company) ships would anchor here, awaiting favorable winds to take them off on their adventurous journeys, and smaller boats would bring them provisions. Sportfishing trips and shrimping fleets now set out from here. The **Maritiem & Jutters Museum** (Maritime and Beachcomber's Museum) contains a bemusing collection of beachcombers' finds and is just next door to the landmark **Molen de Traanroier** (Tear Rower Windmill), which was used for hulling grain. This harbor museum also has exhibitions about the local fishing industry, lifeboats, furnished fishermen's cottages, and marine archaeology, including the finds from a VOC ship that sank in the Wadden Sea in 1640. ⊠ *Barentszstraat 21, Oudeschild* ☎ *0222/314956* ⊕ *www.texelsmaritiem.nl* 🖾 *€4.10* ⊙ *Tues.–Sat. 10–5; July and Aug., Mon.–Sat. 10–5.*

**㉔ De Koog,** a modern seaside town, is a practical base for exploring the North Sea coastline and its nature reserves. In high season it is subject to hordes of sun-seeking tourists. Much of northwestern Texel is new, the result of dikes built early in the 17th century. Sand was deposited on the seaward side of these dikes, forming a second row of dunes that protected the land behind. However, if the sea breaks through the dunes or man-made dikes during a storm, the valleys behind them can become tidal salt marshes. This is how the **De Slufter** and **De Muy** nature reserves were formed, ideal feeding and breeding grounds for birds such as the spoonbill, sandpipers, and even the rare avocet.

☾ Plenty of live animals are on tap at the **EcoMare** nature center for the Wadden tidal flats and the North Sea, a good starting point for discovering the natural wonders of these abundant habitats. There is a seal rehabilitation center, a bird sanctuary, a dogfish shark breeding tank (replete with some mean-machine babies), a natural history museum, and a visitor information center about the Wadden tidal flats, the North Sea, and the island's nature areas. Interactive games for children are available in English, and you can book excursions through the nature areas. ⊠ *Ruijslaan 92, De Koog* ☎ *0222/317741* ⊕ *www.ecomare.nl* 🖾 *€7.50* ⊙ *Daily 9–5.*

## Where to Stay & Eat

While you're out counting Texel's sheep, count on the culinary delights that go hand and hoof with them. These include sheep's-milk cheese and succulent *pré-salé* lamb (with a natural saltiness acquired from grazing in meadows sprayed by the salt-laden sea winds). Organic dairy products and vegetables are also prevalent on the island, the salt marshes making it possible to farm unusual vegetables such as sea aster, a leaf that makes a tasty addition to salads. Holiday accommodations are abundant on Texel, from campsites in the dunes to private villas hidden in woodlands. Contact the VVV for further information, including a variety of packages that can reduce your hotel costs considerably.

**$$–$$$** ✕ **Het Vierspan.** This intimate but sophisticated restaurant serves carefully prepared Continental cuisine emphasizing local products, such as a starter of carpaccio of duck's breast followed by saddle of Texel lamb, or the freshest catch of the day. Popular with the locals—always a good sign—Vierspan is perhaps the finest restaurant on Texel. ⊠ *Gravenstraat 3, Den Burg* ☎ *0222/313176* ⌔ *Reservations essential* ▭ *MC, V* ⊙ *Closed Mon. and Tues.*

**$$$–$$$$** ⌑ **Hotel and Villa Opduin.** Get your dune buggy out . . . this establishment, which aims to uphold the values of the family hotel from which it has developed, is in the middle of the island dunes and the national park of Texel, De Duinen. Though the building is architecturally nothing short of a modern, blocklike monstrosity, the rooms are spacious and filled with light. For a panoramic sea view, opt for one of the luxury top-floor suites. The hotel's original section, Villa Opduin, has simple, cheaper rooms with shared bathrooms. ⊠ *Ruijslaan 22, 1796 AD De Koog* ☎ *0222/317445* 🖷 *0222/317777* ⊕ *www.opduin.nl* ◁ *48 rooms, 42 suites, 6 apartments* ⌂ *3 restaurants, room service, in-room safes, some in-room hot tubs, minibars, cable TV, in-room VCRs, in-room data ports, tennis court, indoor pool, gym, sauna, spa, bicycles, bar, lobby lounge, babysitting, children's programs, dry cleaning, laundry service, business services, convention center, meeting rooms, some pets allowed, no-smoking floors* ▤ *AE, DC, MC, V* ⊙| *BP.*

**$–$$** 🏨 **Hotel de Lindeboom.** This gentleman's house, built in 1897, offers spacious, light, air-conditioned rooms with modern furnishings. Above a popular café-restaurant with a sunny terrace, it overlooks an open square in the peaceful center of town. For even more luxury, go for the suite (with Jacuzzi and Turkish bath) or the room with a sauna. ⊠ *Groeneplaats 14, 1791 CC Den Burg* ☎ *0222/312041* 🖷 *0222/ 310517* ⊕ *www.lindeboomtexel.nl* ◁ *24 rooms, 1 suite* ⌂ *Restaurant, café, a/c, cable TV, in-room data ports, bicycles, bar, lobby lounge, business services, meeting rooms, parking (fee), some pets allowed, no-smoking rooms* ▤ *MC, V* ⊙| *BP.*

**¢** 🏨 **Hotel-Restaurant de Zeven Provinciën.** This old-fashioned tavern, paradoxically with no bar, has simple rooms and nestles safely behind the sea dike on the eastern side of the island. The restaurant, which indeed serves traditional Dutch food, is open throughout the day. ⊠ *De Ruijterstraat 60, 1792 AK Oudeschild* ☎ *0222/312652* 🖷 *0222/313149* ⊕ *www.dezevenprovincientexel.nl* ◁ *14 rooms, 8 with bath* ⌂ *Restaurant, fans, cable TV, bar, free parking, some pets allowed, no-smoking rooms; no room phones* ▤ *AE, MC, V* ⊗ *Closed Oct.–Easter* ⊙| *BP.*

### Sports & the Outdoors

**Bicycling:** Bicycles can be rented from the ferry terminal and all over the island. **Catamaran Sailing: Westerslag** (⊠ Paal 15, Den Burg ☎ 0222/314847 or 0222/312013) offers courses in catamaran sailing. Training courses and rentals are available at **Zeilschool de Eilander** (⊠ Paal 33, De Cocksdorp ☎ 06/2063–4413 cell). **Kayaking: SeaMount Tracks** (⊠ Rommelpot 19, Den Hoorn ☎ 0222/319393) offers weeklong certificate courses. Sea and surf excursions as well as courses are offered by **Zeekanocentrum Texel** (⊠ Abbewaal 7, Den Burg ☎ 0222/316699). **Parachuting: Paracentrum Texel** (⊠ Vliegveld Texel ☎ 0222/311464) offers training and supervised jumps.

# Vlieland

**㉑** *Harlingen is 115 km (71 mi) north of Amsterdam.*

To the east of the popular vacation island Texel lies Vlieland, the Gilligan's island to escape to if you're seeking peace and quiet. Farthest flung from the coast, it is the smallest (in some places little more than half a mile wide) and quietest of the Wadden islands, and no nonresident cars are allowed.

The 90-minute ferry ride from Harlingen rewards you with the sight of sailboats gliding past. In terms of lodging, you can choose to stay on the main street where the action centers around shopping or outdoor-café sitting, or in the peacefulness of the dunes where the ebb and flow of the tides and the light from the lighthouse is your only distraction. Besides taking in the natural beauty of the island and the well-preserved old houses, be sure to take a walk along the prettiest tree-lined street in the village: from the Dorpsstraat thoroughfare, enter the Kerkglop to the Kerkplein square. Walk up the hill between the old church and Het Armhuis Restaurant.

## Terschelling

🢒 *35 km (18 mi) northwest of Texel, 28 km (17 mi) west of Leeuwarden, 115 km (71 mi) north of Amsterdam.*

East of Vlieland is Terschelling, the largest of the Frisian pearls (second only to North Holland's Texel), with just more than 5,000 permanent residents. This 27,180-acre member of the Wadden island chain experiences a population explosion during high season, as it is a favorite Dutch vacation spot with 30 km (19 mi) of beautiful dunes and endless beaches and 70 km (44 mi) of bike trails, about two hours by passenger and car ferry from Harlingen. The island was settled around AD 900, its main industries originally fishing and whaling. Today, 80% of the island is nature reserve. The **Oerol Festival** (for information, contact the VVV) was started in 1986 as the brainchild of a local landlord. Held during the second and third weeks of June, and using the whole island as the set for theatrical productions, it appropriately ends on Midsummer Night and has grown into an international event attracting thousands of visitors. June is also the time when fields of orchids are in bloom, and in August and September the heather and sea lavender burst open. Cranberries grown on the island are used for local jams, liqueurs, and wine.

**West-Terschelling** is the island's main port, surrounding the only natural coastal bay in the whole of Holland. **De Brandaris** lighthouse has kept sailors safe for the last 400 years and towers 150 feet high. The island retains its natural beauty and interest partly because most of the eastern end is a world-class nature reserve, the **Boschplaat Vogelreservaat** (Boschplaat Bird Sanctuary)—off-limits to wingless visitors from mid-March to mid-August. **Museum 't Behouden Huys** (Keeper's House Museum) explains the cultural-historical background of the island and its people. It occupies the former homes of two naval captains dating from 1668; the rooms are richly decorated with tiles and ornate wooden furniture. Also on display are local traditional costumes and tools. ⊠ *Commandeurstraat 30–32, West Terschelling* ☎ *0562/442389* ⊕ *www.behouden-huys.nl* 🎫 *€3* ⊙ *Weekdays 10–5, Sat. 1–5, Sun. (July and Aug. only) 1–5.*

☁ The **Centrum voor Natuur en Landschap** (Center for Nature and Countryside) incorporates an enormous aquarium for marine life from the North Sea and Wadden Sea. During off-season, it opens for the Christmas holiday and one week at the end of February. ⊠ *Burgemeester Reedekerstraat 11, West Terschelling* ☎ *0562/442390* 🎫 *€4* ⊙ *Apr.–Oct., weekdays 9–5, weekends 2–5.*

## Where to Stay & Eat

★ **$$$** ✕ **De Grië.** Situated in a typical Terschelling farmhouse, this top-flight restaurant has a reputation as being the best on all of the islands. Specialties include mouthwatering local lamb and duck in season and pastries with locally grown cranberries. Call, as the opening hours and days vary considerably. ✉ *Oosterend 43, Oosterend* ☎ *0562/448499* ⊕ *www. terschelling.net* ✍ *Reservations essential* ▭ *AE, MC, V* ⊘ *Closed Tues. mid-July–Aug., Tues. and Wed. Sept. and Oct., weekdays in Nov., and first 2½ wks of Dec. No lunch.*

**$** ▥ **Golden Tulip Hotel Schylge.** This super-value modern hotel overlooking the harbor has all the conveniences you might ever need if the weather turns inclement. The rooms are standard but practical for a beach vacation. Ask about weekend and midweek rates. ✉ *Burg. Van Heusdenweg 37, 8881 ED West Terschelling* ☎ *0562/442111* 🖷 *0562/ 442800* ⊕ *www.terschelling.net* ⇌ *88 rooms, 10 suites* ⚮ *2 restaurants, room service, minibars, cable TV, in-room data ports, indoor pool, hair salon, sauna, spa, bicycles, bowling, 2 bars, babysitting, meeting rooms, free parking, no-smoking rooms* ▭ *AE, DC, MC, V* ☉| *CP.*

**$** ▥ **Hotel Oepkes.** This family hotel on the quiet outskirts of town is only two minutes from the ferry terminal. The rooms are simple and clean, and there is no smoking anywhere on the property. ✉ *De Ruyterstraat 3, 8881 AM West Terschelling* ☎ *0562/442005* 🖷 *0562/443345* ⊕ *www. oepkes.nl* ⇌ *20 rooms* ⚮ *Restaurant, in-room safes, cable TV, Wi-Fi, bicycles, bar, lounge, free parking, some pets allowed* ▭ *AE, DC, MC, V* ☉| *CP* ⊘ *Closed Jan.*

# Ameland

㉓ *159 km (99 mi) north of Amsterdam*

The "Wadden Diamond," as the island is known, sparkles to the east of Terschelling with a brilliant carat all its own. Rare flora and fauna give this gemstone a glow that is reflected in its friendly residents and four curious villages. Beautifully restored captains' houses hark back to Ameland's days of whaling infamy. Once a month locals gather at the shore to watch as 10 horses pull an old lifeboat down to the sea, and 8 of them launch it, in an event called the *paardereddingboot* (horse lifeboat). Check with the **VVV Ameland** (✉ Bureweg 2, 9163 KE Nes ☎ 0519/546546 ⊕ www.vvvameland.nl) for the schedule. Specialties of the island include *Nobeltje*, a liqueur born and bred at the **Hotel Nobel** (✉ Gerrit Kosterweg 16, Ballum ☎ 0519/554157), Ameland cheese, and salt-grazed lamb. Cars are permitted on Ameland if you suffer from separation anxiety, but bikes are clearly the way to get around. Port of sail is Holwerd, with a 45-minute travel time.

## Where to Stay & Eat

★ **$–$$** ✕ **Restaurant de Klimop.** Just down the street from the Best Western Hotel Zeewinde is a real find, though it may not look that way from the outside. But go inside and be amazed at the Makkum-tiled fireplace, Dutch glass hanging lamps, and circular wooden floor formerly used for dancing. And the food? Well, we'll bet you'll want to return. You may be on an island, but this chef knows how to serve it up in style.

Try the local salt-grazed lamb in generous proportions, after, that is, your *voorgerecht*, or first course, of shelled mussels with garlic. You'll be hoping that they close down the ferry transport back to the mainland. ✉ *Reeweg, Nes* ☎ *051/954–2296* ▤ *AE, DC, MC, V* ✆ *Closed Tues.*

$ ▤ **Best Western Hotel Zeewinde.** In the heart of the most charming village on the island, this high-standard chain hotel with an un-chain feel is tucked away ever so cozily within walking distance to everything that matters here—outdoor cafés and restaurants, peanut-size shops and enough cute and quaint houses to fill a digital memory card. Every room in the Zeewinde has a small kitchenette with Senseo coffeemaker, but don't linger too long because there's a whole island out there to bike around (the must-do activity) and, as the hotel name "Sea Wind" implies, serene beaches nearby to comb. Breakfast in the homey dining room or out on the terrace, then book the hotel's Island Safari tour with chauffeur (€10 per person; minimum of three people). ✉ *Torenstraat 22, 9163 HE Nes* ☎ *051/954–6500* ▤ *051/954–6509* ⊕ *www.zeewinde.nl* ⤳ *34 rooms △ Dining room, microwaves, refrigerators, cable TV, Wi-Fi, bicycles, bar, lounge, no-smoking rooms* ▤ *AE, MC, V.*

# THE NORTH & THE WADDEN SEA ISLANDS ESSENTIALS

## Transportation

### BY AIR

The quickest way to reach the northern provinces from Amsterdam is to fly from Schiphol airport to the Eelde airport near Groningen. There are five flights per day, and the flight takes only 30 minutes.

### BY BOAT & FERRY

Ferries transport people and bicycles across the IJsselmeer between Enkhuizen and Urk and Enkhuizen and Stavoren May–September. To reach Texel, take the ferry from Den Helder. A return trip costs about €3 round-trip and takes 20 minutes each way. The ferry to Terschelling departs from Harlingen and costs €22.95 round-trip and takes 90 minutes one-way. You can take an express boat instead, which takes 45 minutes, for €3.85 extra. The ferry from Lauwersoog takes you to Schiermonnikoog in 45 minutes and costs €11.42. To get to Ameland, take the ferry from Holwerd (45 minutes one-way and €10.95 round-trip). To get to Vlieland, take the ferry from Harlingen (about 90 minutes one-way and €20.40 round-trip) or the fast boat (45 minutes and €3.90 extra). You can take your car (but not on the express boats) to Ameland and Terschelling, but it will cost you about €100. Unless you have several passengers and are staying for several days, our advice is to leave your car on the mainland and rely on bikes to get you around the islands. That is, after all, what the Wadden island experience is all about.

🛈 Contact the VVV Enkhuizen (☎ 022/831–3164) for the ferry schedule to and from Urk and Stavoren. For information on the ferry schedules to the Wadden islands, log onto the Den Helder ferry web site (www.teso.nl.) and contact the VVV offices in Den Helder

(☎ 022/362-5544), Leeuwarden (☎ 0900/202406), or Groningen (☎ 0900/202-3050) or (www.vvv-wadden.nl). For information on Schiermonnikoog, call ☎ 0900/455-4455 and press 3 for English, or visit www.wpd.nl.

### BY BUS

A comprehensive network of local and regional bus services provides a useful supplement to the train service.
🚹 **Public transportation** ☎ 0900/9292.

### BY CAR

In less than two hours, you can drive to the north via E22 through Noord Holland province, crossing the 32-km (21-mi) Afsluitdijk (Enclosing Dike) that divides the IJsselmeer from the North Sea; from the end of the Enclosing Dike, continue on E22 to Groningen or take A31 to Leeuwarden. You can also take A31 if you are heading to the Wadden islands, but stop at Harlingen, where there are ferries to Terschelling. The ferry for Schiermonnikoog leaves from Lauwersoog: take N361 from Groningen or N355, then N361 from Leeuwarden. Alternatively, if you are heading straight for Groningen or Leeuwarden, you can follow A6 across the province of Flevoland to Joure and then take the E22 for Groningen or turn north on A32 for Leeuwarden. A third option is to drive to Enkhuizen and take the car ferry to Urk. From Urk, take N351 to A6 and continue as above.

To reach the island of Texel, travel north from Amsterdam on N203, N8, A9, N9, and N250 to the port of Den Helder.

EMERGENCIES  **Wegenwacht** (☎ 0800-0888 ⊕ www.routemobil.nl) is a national breakdown and towing service.

RULES OF THE ROAD  In Friesland signs are in two languages, with the town names shown in Frisian as well as in Dutch. As in the rest of the country, you must know which main city or town you are traveling toward, as there are no directional signs of east, west, etc., in the Netherlands. Good planning is key.
🚹 **Car Rentals Alamo** ☎ 023/556-3666 in Holland. **Avis** ☎ 0800/235-2847 in Holland. **Budget** ☎ 023/568-8888 in Holland. **Europcar** ☎ 070/381-1812 in Holland. **Hertz** ☎ 0900/235-4378.

### BY TRAIN

Intercity express trains operate once an hour direct from Amsterdam to both Leeuwarden and Groningen. Be sure you are in the right car; trains often split en route (either at Amersfoort or Zwolle), so there are separate cars for each final destination in both classes of service. In addition to the national rail lines connecting Leeuwarden and Groningen with the south, local trains link up Leeuwarden with the Enkhuizen–Stavoren ferry service; another line connects Leeuwarden with Harlingen (departure point for ferry and hydrofoil services to the Wadden islands) every half hour; and another links Leeuwarden with Groningen and continues to the German border. A small local train in Groningen province connects Groningen with Winsum (a canoeing center), Uithuizen (departure for guided walks to the Wadden islands at low tide), and the port of Eemshaven. Connections to Assen run regularly every hour as well.

For Texel, Intercity trains run direct to Den Helder every hour, with a connecting bus (Connexxion Bus No. 3) to the ferry terminal. The Waddenbiljet all-inclusive return ticket, the easiest and most economical method for getting to Texel, includes bus service on the island itself. Take the train to Harlingen Havens (Harlingen Harbor) for the ferry to Terschelling and Vlieland. Take the train to Groningen and then a bus to Lauwersoog (ARRIVA Bus No. 63) to get to the ferry terminal for Schiermonnikoog; or take the train to Leeuwarden and then Noordned Bus No. 50 to the Lauwersoog ferry. For Ameland, take the train to Leeuwarden, and then change to Noorrdned Bus No. 66 to Holwerd; you can also go to Groningen first, and then get ARRIVA Bus No. 34 to Holwerd. Since the best way to get around the Netherlands is by train, you can search (www.ns.nl) for all train schedules and the amenities provided at each station. An English version is also provided.

CUTTING COSTS If you intend to tour the region by train and you will be including a visit to one of the Wadden islands, it is worth considering a *Waddenbiljet,* an all-inclusive return ticket (€6–€22.50 extra) including all connecting services and ferries. Ask for this arrangement at the train station.
🚆 **Train/public transportation** ☎ 0900/9292 ⊕ www.ns.nl.

# Contacts & Resources

### CAMPING
With more than 100 campgrounds in the province of Friesland alone, the North offers plenty of opportunity for camping. Unfortunately, there is no national or central reservation service for campsites, so you have to contact sites individually. For camping in Leeuwarden, De Kleine Wielen, open April–October, has sites for 350 tents and RVs, as well as places for hikers. In Groningen, Camping Stadspark, open March–October, has 200 sites; it also has accommodation for hikers. In the Assen (Drenthe) area, try Witterzomer in Witten (5 km [3 mi] from Assen), which is open all year. The ANWB office (akin to AAA in the United States) has a wide range of information on campsites throughout Holland.
🚩 **ANWB** ⊠ Kloekhorstraat 12, 9401 BD Assen ☎ 0592/314100. **Camping Stadspark** ⊠ Campinglaan 6, 9727 KH ☎ 050/525-1624. **De Kleine Wielen** ⊠ De Groene Ster 14, 8926 XE ☎ 0511/431660. **Witterzomer** ☎ 0592/393535 ⊕ www.witterzomer.nl.

### EMERGENCIES
🚩 **National Emergency Alarm Number** ☎ 112 for police, fire, and ambulance.

### TOURS
BOAT TOURS Canal cruise trips are available in summer; in Leeuwarden, contact Party Cruise Prinsenhof; in Groningen, Kool Groningen.
🚩 **Fees & Schedules Kool Groningen** ⊠ Stationsweg 1012 ☎ 050/312-8379. **Party Cruise Prinsenhof** ⊠ P. Midamaweg 19 ☎ 0511/539334.

WALKING TOURS *Wadlopen,* or "mudwalking," excursions are permissible *only* with a guide who knows well the timing of the tidal waters on the Wadden Sea (between mid-March and early October). The VVV tourist offices can give you information and recommend qualified guides, or you can contact **De Stichting Wadloopcentrum Pieterburen** (✉ Postbus 1, Pieterburen ☎ 0595/528300 🖷 0595/528318 ⊕ www.wadlopen.com or www. wadlopen.net). For Wadlopen guides from Groningen, call **Stichting Wadloopcentrum Pieterburen** (☎ 0595/528300).

## VISITOR INFORMATION

🚹 **VVV Ameland** ✉ Bureweg 2, 9163 KE Nes ☎ 0519/546546 ⊕ www.vvvameland.nl. **VVV Assen-Drenthe** ✉ Marktstraat 8–10, 9401 JH ☎ 0592/314324 🖷 0592/317306. **VVV Bolsward** ✉ Marktplein 1, 8701 KG ☎ 0900/123–4888. **VVV Den Helder** ✉ Bernhardplein 18, 1781 HH ☎ 022/362–5544 🖷 022/361–4888 **VVV Groningen** ✉ Grote Markt 25, 9712 HS ☎ 0900/202–3050 or 0503/139741 🖷 050/311–0258 ⊕ www.vvvgroningen. nl. **VVV Leeuwarden** ✉ Sophialaan 4, 8911 ☎ 0900/202406 ⊕ www.vvvleeuwarden. nl. **VVV Schiermonnikoog** ✉ Reeweg 5, 9166 PW ☎ 0519/531233 🖷 0529/531325 ⊕ www.vvvschiermonnikoog.nl. **VVV Terschelling** ✉ Willem Barentszkade 19a, 8881 BC ☎ 0562/443000 🖷 0562/442875 ⊕ www.vvv-terschelling.nl. **VVV Texel** ✉ Emmalaan 66, 1791 AV Den Burg ☎ 0222/314741 🖷 0222/314129 ⊕ www.texel.net. **VVV Vlieland** ✉ Havenweg 10, 8899 BB ☎ 0562/451111 ⊕ www.vlieland.net. **VVV Wadden Islands** ⊕ www. wadden.nl.

# UNDERSTANDING HOLLAND

# HOLLAND AT A GLANCE

## Fast Facts

**Name in local language:** Koninkrijk der Nederlanden (Kingdom of the Netherlands)

**Capital:** Amsterdam is the constitutional capital, and The Hague is the administrative and governmental capital.

**National anthem:** Het Wilhelmus

**National motto:** *Je Maintiendrai* (I Will Maintain)

**Type of government:** Constitutional monarchy

**Administrative divisions:** 12 provinces: Drenthe, Flevoland, Friesland, Gelderland, Groningen, Limburg, Noord-Brabant, Noord-Holland, Overijssel, Utrecht, Zeeland, and Zuid-Holland

**Independence:** January 23, 1579—The northern provinces of the Low Countries, under the control of Spain, sign the Union of Utrecht and claim independence. The Netherlands was not recognized internationally until 1648.

**Constitution:** Adopted 1815; amended many times, last time in 2002

**Legal system:** Civil law system incorporating French penal theory; constitution does not permit judicial review of acts of the States General; accepts compulsory International Court of Justice (ICJ) jurisdiction, with reservations

**Suffrage:** 18 years of age

**Legislature:** Bicameral States General consists of the First Chamber (75 seats; members indirectly elected by the country's 12 provincial councils for four-year terms) and the Second Chamber (150 seats; members directly elected by popular vote to serve four-year terms)

**Population:** 16,407,491 (July 2005)

**Population density:** 395 people per square kilometer

**Median age:** 39 years

**Life expectancy:** 78.81 years

**Literacy:** 99% of people over age 15 can read and write

**Languages:** Dutch and Frisian

**Ethnic groups:** Dutch 83%; other 17% (of which 9% are of non-Western origin, mainly Turks, Moroccans, Antilleans, Surinamese, and Indonesians)

**Religion:** Roman Catholic 31%, Dutch Reformed 13%, Calvinist 7%, Muslim 5.5%, other 2.5%, none 41%

**Discoveries & inventions:** In 1683, Antony Leeuwenhoek (1632–1723), a Dutch student of natural history and maker of microscopes, gave the first complete descriptions of the bacteria, protozoans, and spermatozoa.
Dutch mathematician and physicist Christiaan Huygens (1629–95) was the first to use the pendulum in clocks. He also improved telescopes, and in 1655 he discovered a satellite of Saturn. Huygens's principle, opposing the corpuscular theory of Newton, holds that every point on a light-wave front is itself a source of new waves.
In 1957, Dutch-born physician Willem Kolff led a team of scientists in the United States to test an early form of the temporary artificial heart.

*Words are dwarfs, deeds are giants.*
Dutch proverb

*If you keep thinking about what you want to do or what you hope will happen, you don't do it, and it won't happen.*

Desiderius Erasmus

# GOING DUTCH

**IF YOU COME TO HOLLAND EXPECTING** to find all its residents shod in wooden shoes, you're years too late; if you're looking for windmills at every turn, you're looking in the wrong place. Although the wings of windmills do still turn on government subsidy and the wooden shoe recently has been recognized by the European Union (EU) as acceptable safety footwear, the bucolic images that brought tourism here in the decades after World War II have little to do with the Netherlands of the 21st century. *Ja,* this may be a country where you can find the Old World in spades, but this is very, very far from a senile land. Walk through the Red Light District of Amsterdam—gorgeously adorned with some of the most historic structures in town—and be startled by scarlet women sitting immobile behind scarlet-neon framed windows, their pose suggesting that of Whistler's Mother (the resemblance ends there, however). Or marvel at today's Vermeers and Mondriaans now globally championed as being on the very cutting edge of both Web design and urban planning. Holland is bustling, busy, and clangorous, filled with noise and hullabaloo, festivals and floodlights.

But for visitors, it is also a land where you can happily and effortlessly trade in sophisticated modernity for medieval mellowness or the featherbed finesse of the 17th-century Golden Age. A walk down a time-stained alley in Amsterdam or a horseback ride up a dune path along the North Sea often lets you lose five or six centuries in six or seven minutes. And rest assured: there also remains a wealth of villages that have changed little since the time of Hobbema, interiors seemingly plucked from the paintings of Terborch and Rembrandt, and landscapes that suggest the work of Van Ruysdael and—on particularly windy days—even Van Gogh. Holland, in fact, is one big throbbing canvas.

The Netherlands has always had great press agents in its Golden Age painters, who portrayed a shimmering and geo-metric landscape of fields and orchards sporadically dotted with stretches of color-coded tulips, windmills keeping the sea at bay, cozy villages burnished with age and history, and bustling cities bursting with culture and merchant spirit—all forming a grand tapestry by the lacework of canals. The local saying "God made the world but the Dutch made the Netherlands" would sound cocky if it were not true. But one can certainly call the Dutch stubborn: half of this democratic monarchy's 41,526 square km (16,029 square mi) has been reclaimed from the sea, and to this day, it remains a full-time job of many to stop this land from slipping back whence it came. As the primary element, water does much to define this country's landscape, history, people, and politics, and the predominance of water and the relative lack of terra firma have also helped create the image of the Dutch for visitors of days long past. To wit, Sir F. B. Head called the Hollanders a "heavy, barge-built, web-footed race," and that 18th-century English snob William Beckford said, "A certain oysterishness of eye, and flabbiness of complexion, are almost proofs sufficient of their aquatic descent." Although these observers were obviously victims of propagandists of the various Dutch-Anglo Wars, it cannot be denied that the nation's long-ingrained respect for how water derives its power through its flexibility accounts for the Dutch being more renowned for their pragmatism than their stubbornness. And perhaps it was as compensation that the Dutch developed a humor best described as "earthy."

But a certain visionary pragmatism has seen Holland evolve beyond the bucolic images with which it's long been associated to embrace the future and its accompanying flurry of mostly happy contradictions. Certainly its greatest enigma is the fact that although it is one of Europe's smallest countries, the modern and sophisticated Netherlands has an economic strength and cultural wealth that far surpass its size and population. It may be small enough to drive through in a few hours, but with more art treasures per square mile than any other country on Earth and with an international clout that has led it to become one of the largest investors in the U.S. economy, you will need more than a few weeks to unlock all its secrets.

Besides striving to make things as *gezellig*—an endemic word that describes a feeling of comfort and coziness in a social situation—as possible, you should also come equipped with the maximum respect for the concept of the *individual*. After all, it was the painters of the Low Countries who realized that the 17th-century variations of our present-day Mr. Smiths, Mr. Browns, and Mr. Johnsons were just as worthy subjects for the artist's brush as were the St. Marks, St. Matthews, St. Jeromes, St. Sebastians, and the rest. It was these painters who dared to paint simple subjects for the little, though usually extremely well-off, patrons. It was the painters of the Dutch School who first came to the conclusion that the minimum acceptable size for a picture was not 30-by-25 feet. Frescoes and paintings executed to the order of the church and intended to be displayed in cathedrals must be large; but it took the Dutch masters to realize that the private dwellings of the well-to-do bourgeoisie were also suitable places for their works.

And it was the Dutch who first thought of building houses—that is to say, dwellings where these pictures might suitably be hung. Until then, "architecture" meant the building of churches, cathedrals, royal and ducal palaces, or huge municipal buildings. It was the Dutch who were not ashamed to start building pretty, charming, and often beautiful houses—just for ordinary people to live in. That a private house might be or should be tasteful and lovely was practically a revolutionary idea in the 17th century, and it is the upper-middle-class burghers and merchants of Holland to whom we owe so much of our present-day delight in our domestic surroundings. The Dutch were the first people to enshrine the concepts of coziness, intimacy, and privacy in everyday life.

Their pride in home and hearth is one reason why nearly every square inch of the country looks as though it were scrubbed with Dutch cleanser. If the state of a Dutch cottage or apartment is today best explained as a coping mechanism of living in a densely populated land that now numbers more than 16 million souls, that is because, in spite of constant elbow-rubbing in this crowded country, Hollanders retain a strong sense of personal privacy. They also respect your privacy—on first meeting, the Amsterdammer can occasionally be reserved to the point of seeming brusque, but this is not because he is cold or hostile; rather, he regards over-friendliness as an imposition on you. Still, in Holland folks are comfortable with living without curtains and having their lives and possessions open to viewing by passersby. When summer comes, many pack their curtainless trailers and head south, only to cluster together again in crowded trailer parks. Although these actions may help you understand why the Netherlands was the birthplace of TV's *Big Brother* concept—a show that bloomed with the turn-of-the-21st-century's infatuation with "reality TV"—do not conclude that the Dutch are an exhibitionist people. They are merely the "live and let live" philosophy personified.

Centuries of international trade and the welcoming of endless streams of immigrants have also played their role in creating a form of conflict resolution that requires long meetings that strive to make everyone happy; the Dutch have long loved to organize themselves and form societies (as witnessed by the famous group portraits of the 17th century, such as Rembrandt's *Syndics of the Cloth Guild*) for every conceivable purpose. On the opposite side of the coin, the country's brand of liberalism ironically runs on encyclopedias filled with laws, both strict and elastic but always based on libraries full of reports and studies, that seek to give the greatest possible freedoms to the individual. It is, therefore, understandable why the Netherlands is a tangle of inner conflicts—Catholic versus Protestant (it leans 60–40 toward the latter, that 60% still functioning as one of Europe's Reformation strongholds); puritanical versus prurient (you can't buy liquor on Sunday in some areas, and in others prostitutes sit, whalebone-stayed, in display windows).

It is, in fact, a luxury that the Netherlands can afford to take the time and effort to experiment with alternative—and, dare one say, more pragmatic—ways of dealing with the realities of sex and drugs. Its economic power, rooted in the 17th century when it was *the* great colonial power, also accounts for its cultural wealth. In days of seafaring yore, money raised through its colonial outposts overseas was used to buy or commission portraits and paintings by young artists such as Rembrandt, Hals, Vermeer, and Van Ruysdael. But it was not only the arts that were encouraged: the Netherlands was home to the philosophers Descartes, Spinoza, and Comenius; the jurist Grotius; the naturalist Van Leeuwenhoek, inventor of the microscope; and other prominent people of science and letters, who flourished in the country's enlightened tolerance. This tradition continues today with the Netherlands still subsidizing its artists and performers and supporting an educational system in which creativity in every field is respected, revered, and given room to express itself.

Contemporary Dutch design and architecture, in particular, are enjoying a new golden age of sorts. In a tiny land where space has always been maximized and where much is essentially artificial, these arts have long been dealing with issues that the rest of the rapidly shrinking world is only now beginning to recognize. The influence of such homegrown luminaries as Rem Koolhaas, whose architecture springs from a reaction to realities instead of historical legacies, and Viktor & Rolf, whose fashions showcase the country's more flamboyant side, have filtered across the globe. So please enjoy Amsterdam's historical legacy but also keep yourself open to the new. You will then have a well-rounded trip indeed. Now if only the Dutch could do something about their impeccable English—you are abroad, after all . . .

—Steve Korver

# DUTCH VOCABULARY

| | English | Dutch | Pronunciation |
|---|---|---|---|
| **Basics** | | | |
| | Yes/no | Ja, nee | yah, nay |
| | Please | Alstublieft | **ahls**-too-bleeft |
| | Thank you | Dank u | **dahnk** oo |
| | You're welcome | Niets te danken | neets teh **dahn**-ken |
| | Excuse me, sorry | Pardon | pahr-**don** |
| | Good morning | Goede morgen | **hoh**-deh **mor**-ghen |
| | Good evening | Goede avond | **hoh**-deh **ahv**-unt |
| | Goodbye | Dag! | dah |
| **Numbers** | | | |
| | one | een | ehn |
| | two | twee | tveh |
| | three | drie | dree |
| | four | vier | veer |
| | five | vijf | vehf |
| | six | zes | zehss |
| | seven | zeven | **zeh**-vehn |
| | eight | acht | ahkht |
| | nine | negen | **neh**-ghen |
| | ten | tien | teen |
| **Days of the Week** | | | |
| | Sunday | zondag | **zohn**-dagh |
| | Monday | maandag | **mahn**-dagh |
| | Tuesday | dinsdag | **dinns**-dagh |
| | Wednesday | woensdag | **voons**-dagh |
| | Thursday | donderdag | **don**-der-dagh |
| | Friday | vrijdag | **vreh**-dagh |
| | Saturday | zaterdag | **zah**-ter-dagh |
| **Useful Phrases** | | | |
| | Do you speak English? | Spreekt U Engels? | sprehkt oo **ehn**-gls |
| | I don't speak Dutch | Ik spreek geen Nederlands | ihk sprehk **ghen** **Ned**-er-lahnds |
| | I don't understand | Ik begrijp het niet | ihk be-**ghrehp** het neet |

| I don't know | Ik weet niet | ihk **veht** ut neet |
| I'm American/English | Ik ben Amerikaans/Engels | ihk ben Am-er-ee-**kahns**/Ehn-gls |
| Where is . . . | Waar is . . . | vahr iss |
| the train station? | het station? | heht stah-**syohn** |
| the post office? | het postkantoor? | het **pohst**-kahn-tohr |
| the hospital? | het ziekenhuis? | het **zeek**-uhn-haus |
| Where are the restrooms? | waar is de WC? | **vahr** iss de **veh**-seh |
| Left/right | links/rechts | leenks/rehts |
| How much is this? | Hoeveel kost dit? | hoo-**vehl** kohst deet |
| It's expensive/cheap | Het is te duur/goedkoop | het ees teh **dour**/**hood**-kohp |
| I am ill/sick | Ik ben ziek | ihk behn zeek |
| I want to call a doctor | Ik wil een docter bellen | ihk veel ehn **dohk**-ter **behl**-len |
| Help! | Help! | help |
| Stop! | Stoppen! | **stop**-pen |

## Dining Out

| Bill/check | de rekening | de **rehk**-en-eeng |
| Bread | brood | brohd |
| Butter | boter | **boh**-ter |
| Fork | vork | fork |
| I'd like to order | Ik wil graag bestellen | Ihk veel khrah behs-**tell**-en |
| Knife | een mes | ehn mehs |
| Menu | menu/kaart | men-**oo**/kahrt |
| Napkin | en servet | ehn ser-**veht** |
| Pepper | peper | **peh**-per |
| Please give me . . . | mag ik [een] . . . | mahkh ihk [ehn] . . . |
| Salt | zout | zoot |
| Spoon | een lepel | ehn **leh**-pehl |
| Sugar | suiker | **sigh**-kur |

# INDEX

# ABOUT OUR WRITERS

A true Netherlandphile who has lived in Holland for seven years, with a five-year interval in Paris, Shirley Agudo openly admits that she prefers the backroads of the rural Dutch province of Drenthe and the never-dull haven of Amsterdam to the brazen City of Lights. An American expatriate, Shirley runs her own PR business in Holland, where she writes and edits for various publishers and organizations. Her published works include *The Holland Handbook* and *Holland Events Diary*. After traversing five Dutch provinces and five islands to research the chapters on the Green Heart and the North and Wadden Sea Islands, Shirley reports that she's even more passionately in love with this lyrical country below sea level. Only a mega-hole in a dike, she says, could ever sweep her away.

Our Smart Travel Tips updater Becky Baker, born in Glen Falls, New York, followed her Dutch fiancé to the Netherlands in 1995 and has enjoyed living there ever since. An avid traveler all her life, she has been a "guest" of the KGB in a Russian border town, shared ouzo with monks at an island monastery in Turkey, and ridden across Jordan and the West Bank as the sole female on a bus full of Middle Eastern men. In the Netherlands, she works as an English-language copywriter and travel writer, while on weekends she and her husband explore Holland. Becky's favorite Dutch cities are Delft and Maastricht, and one of her favorite activities is bicycling through the breathtaking hills of Limburg.

It was only a matter of time before Nicole Chabot, who grew up in Scotland, London, and Hong Kong, crossed continents and arrived in Amsterdam. Nicole is thoroughly at ease astride her bicycle—according to her it really is the best way to savor the Dutch capital—and running rings around Vondelpark. Nicole has written articles on food and travel for publications that include: *Business Traveller,* the *Holland Herald,* the *South China Morning Post,* and *Wine & Dine* magazine. For this edition, Nicole revised and updated the hotel and shopping sections of the Amsterdam chapter.

After graduating from culinary arts school and cooking her way across Europe and Asia for several years, Margaret Kelly decided to get serious about culture. She settled in the Netherlands, studied Dutch, and received her MA in Cultural Anthropology from the University of Amsterdam. She ran her own translation company for a several years before she decided to hop back across the big pond. Margaret now lives in New York City, and when she's not traveling, eating, drinking, or puttering about in the kitchen, she is the editor of an anthropology journal and a freelance writer. Margaret worked on the Amsterdam chapter.

After years of travel subsidized by carpentry, set design, and B-movie acting, Steve Korver came to Amsterdam to reverse the journey his Dutch parents had made as immigrants to Canada. A decade later, he is established as a lover of raw herring and an obsessive expert on all things Amsterdam. He has written articles on film, books, art, food, and media for such publications as *Time Out, Globe & Mail,* and *Condé Nast Traveler.* For this edition, Steve wrote the sections on sights, restaurants, and nightlife in the Amsterdam chapter.

Kim Renfrew was born in one of the hilliest countries of the world, Wales. In 2000, she moved to Amsterdam, in one of the flattest countries in the world, to fulfill her teen ambition to be a writer. She has written about everything from hip-hop to graveyards, but her passion is finding out everything about her adoptive city and passing it on. She updated the Side Trips from Amsterdam section for this book.

Returning from a round-the-world journey in 1989, Tim Skelton arrived in his native Britain to discover his girlfriend had just moved to the Netherlands, so naturally he followed. Almost 12 years later, and thoroughly addicted to the incomparable Dutch *pannekoeken* (pancakes), he has become a true Eindhovenaar, seduced by the relaxed terrace-café lifestyle. Before revising the Metropolitan Holland, The Hague, and the Border Provinces & Maastricht chapters for this book, Tim considered his proudest achievement as a freelance writer to be having his photograph published in the Russian edition of Playboy magazine. Since then he was short-listed in the 2005 Bradt Travel Guides/ *Independent on Sunday* travel-writing competition. Today, when not updating guidebooks and penning magazine features on travel, science, food, and wildlife, he divides his spare time between writing novels that just need to land on the right publisher's desk; cycling through the canals, fields, and woods of Brabant and Limburg; and continuing on a dedicated personal mission to sample every one of Benelux's 900 different beers.